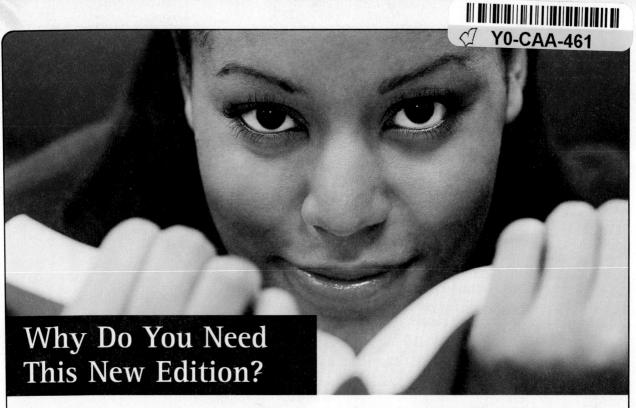

Why Do You Need This New Edition?

If you're wondering why you should buy this edition of *The Master Reader*, **here are 6 good reasons!**

1 Review each chapter on-the-go with our new *Chapter Review Cards.* Easy to tear out and take with you wherever you need to study—on the bus, at your job, in the library—*Chapter Review Cards* boil each chapter down to the fundamentals, making them the perfect tool to check your comprehension or prepare for an exam.

2 Understand what you need to learn with *Learning Outcomes* at the beginning of each chapter. New Learning Outcomes begin each chapter to help you focus on the key skills you need to learn to understand and apply to become a master reader.

3 Write about what you read with new *What Do You Think?* writing prompts. How should bullying be handled in schools? What is the solution to the obesity epidemic? In short, what do *you* think about today's issues? Throughout the book, new *What Do You Think?* questions challenge you to respond to today's issues as explored in our new, longer reading selections at the end of each chapter and in Part Two: Additional Readings.

4 Explore new topics in our many new readings. New topics include building good communication skills, developing good study skills, participating in your community, managing your finances, and many more! With over 25 percent of the readings and accompanying activities new to this edition, you will find topics that help you build new skills to master not only reading, but your life.

5 Master finding the main idea and its supporting details. The table of contents has been rearranged to teach these related topics in order—making it easier for you to learn these fundamental skills.

6 Take your reading online with our new *Connect to MyReadingLab* features. New *Connect to MyReadingLab* sections provide directions for accessing activities for additional practice on Pearson's MyReadingLab program.

PEARSON

More than 4 million students are now using Pearson MyLab products!

MyReadingLab is a dynamic website that provides a wealth of resources geared to meet the diverse teaching and learning needs of today's instructors and students. **MyReadingLab**'s many accessible tools will encourage students to read their text and help them improve their grade in their course.

Here are some of the features that will help you and your students save time and improve results:

Multimedia Tutorials

Students can watch videos and listen to audio clips to learn about key topics.

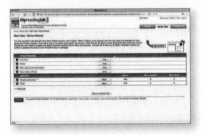

Exercises and Feedback

With thousands of exercises, students will be able to practice their reading skills and increase their reading level. Students will get immediate feedback on their answers so they can understand why they got something wrong or right. Both students and instructors can check the Gradebook to see all scores in one place and monitor improvement over the semester.

A Study Plan for Each Student

After taking a diagnostic test, each student will receive a personalized study plan, so he or she can focus on the topics where the most help is needed—saving time and helping to get a better grade!

Save Time. Improve Results. **www.myreadinglab.com**

Third Edition

The Master Reader

ANNOTATED INSTRUCTOR'S EDITION

D. J. Henry

Daytona State College

Longman

Boston   Columbus   Indianapolis   New York   San Francisco   Upper Saddle River
Amsterdam   Cape Town   Dubai   London   Madrid   Milan   Munich   Paris   Montreal   Toronto
Delhi   Mexico City   Sao Paulo   Sydney   Hong Kong   Seoul   Singapore   Taipei   Tokyo

Editor in Chief: Eric Stano
Senior Acquisitions Editor: Kate Edwards
Editorial Assistant: Lindsey Allen
Associate Development Editor: Erin Reilly
Senior Supplements Editor: Donna Campion
Senior Media Producer: Stefanie Liebman
Marketing Manager: Tom DeMarco
Production Manager: Ellen MacElree
Project Coordination, Text Design, and Electronic Page Makeup: Nesbitt Graphics, Inc.
Cover Designer/Manager: Wendy Ann Fredericks
Cover Photo: Masterfile Corporation. All rights reserved.
Photo Researcher: Rona Tuccillo
Senior Manufacturing Buyer: Dennis J. Para
Printer and Binder: Quad/Graphics—Taunton
Cover Printer: Lehigh-Phoenix Color/Hagerstown

For permission to use copyrighted material, grateful acknowledgment is made to the copyright holders on pp. 715–719, which are hereby made part of this copyright page.

Library of Congress Cataloging-in-Publication Data

Henry, D. J. (Dorothy Jean)
  The master reader / D.J. Henry. -- 3rd ed.
     p. cm.
  Includes bibliographical references and index.
  ISBN 978-0-205-78086-0 (alk. paper)
  1. Reading (Higher education) 2. Reading comprehension. 3. Critical thinking. I. Title.
  LB2395.3.H49 2010
  428.4071'1--dc22

                                                              2010043078

Copyright © 2011, 2009, 2005 by Pearson Education, Inc.

1 2 3 4 5 6 7 8 9 10—QGT—14 13 12 11 10

ISBN-10: 0-205-78086-5 (student ed.)

ISBN-13: 978-0-205-78086-0 (student ed.)

ISBN-10: 0-205-83519-8 (instructor's ed.)

ISBN-13: 978-0-205-83519-5 (instructor's ed.)

Longman
is an imprint of

www.pearsonhighered.com

Brief Contents

Detailed Contents

PART 2

Additional Readings   593

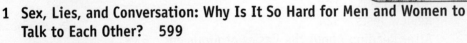

PART 3

Preface

Dear Colleagues:

One of my personal heroes is Oprah Winfrey. She embodies so much of what is wonderful about the human spirit—with her tenacity, generosity, awe-inspiring work ethic, and wisdom, she has influenced our world for the good in profound ways. She is one of our premier teachers. I shall always be grateful for her devotion to reading and for her active work to inspire others to love the printed word. Her devotion to literacy underscores two ideals in our profession: reading empowers an individual life, and our work as instructors is of great and urgent importance. Many of our students come to us needing to reinforce the basic skills that make effective reading and clear thinking possible. Too often they struggle with text structure and feel uncertain about their comprehension. However, with solid instruction and guided practice, these students can discover the power and pleasure of reading. *The Master Reader,* Third Edition, has been designed to address these challenges.

New to This Edition

The following changes have been made to *The Master Reader,* Third Edition, to help students become master readers and critical thinkers.

- **New order for the Main Ideas and Supporting Details Coverage.** Based on extensive feedback from instructors across the country, the order of presentation has been rearranged to bring the main ideas and supporting details coverage together, closer to the beginning of the book. The table of contents now progresses from Main ideas to Implied Main Ideas, to Supporting Details—more in line with the way instructors nationwide present these topics. Of course, each chapter is still self-contained, allowing instructors to easily teach these important topics in any order they choose.

- **New Chapter Review Cards.** New chapter review cards will make studying more accessible and efficient by distilling chapter content down to the fundamentals, helping students to quickly master the basics, to review their understanding on the go, or to prepare for upcoming exams. Because they are made of durable cardstock, students can keep these Review Cards for years to come and pull them out whenever they need a quick review.

- **New Learning Outcomes.** Each chapter now opens with learning outcomes keyed to Bloom's taxonomy. Learning outcomes help students to understand why they are learning the material and help them to set goals for their learning.

- **New "Connect to MyReadingLab" features.** New *Connect to MyReadingLab* sections offer specific activities tied to chapter content for use as lab activities or additional out-of-class practice. Never search for an appropriate online activity again; *Connect to MyReadingLab* provides easy-to-follow click paths and descriptions of specific MyReadingLab activities and how they fit with chapter content.

- **More attention to the connection between reading and writing.** Part Two now opens with a 6-Step Reading/Writing Action Plan that encourages students to see reading as a chance to enter a conversation with the writer and helps students to see how the reading process and the writing process work together to help them participate in this conversation.

- **New "What Do You Think?" writing prompts.** Found at the end of longer reading selections throughout the book, our new "What Do You Think?" writing prompts challenge students to respond to the issues explored.

- **New Reading Level Indications in the Annotated Instructor's Edition.** The reading level of all selections within our Review and Mastery Tests, Additional Readings, and Combined Skills Tests are now indicated in the Annotated Instructor's Edition (levels are not indicated in the student edition).

- **New Longer Reading Selections.** In addition to seven new longer readings in Part Two, over 25 percent of the reading selections and accompanying pedagogy throughout the text have been revised, giving students new reading material that is lively, up to date, and thought-provoking.

- **New Design.** In addition to appearing more modern and mature, the new design visually clarifies the text's different features to help students navigate and find the content they are looking for with greater ease.

Guiding Principles

The Master Reader, Third Edition, was written to develop in students the essential abilities that will enable them to become master readers and critical thinkers.

Practice and Feedback

Aristotle said, "What we have to learn to do, we learn by doing." We all know that the best way *to learn* is *to do*. Thus one of the primary aims of this text is to give students opportunity after opportunity to practice, practice, practice!

Every concept introduced in the book is accompanied by an **explanation** of the concept, an **example** with an explanation of the example, and one or more **practice** exercises. Each chapter also contains **brief skill applications**, **four review tests**, and **four mastery tests**. Furthermore, a durable, removable chapter review card is included for each chapter.

High-Interest Reading Selections

According to French poet, dramatist, and novelist, Victor Hugo, "To learn to read is to light a fire; every syllable that is spelled out is a spark." For developmental students we can fan the sparks by encouraging an enthusiasm for reading. For many, this enthusiasm can be stimulated by reading material that offers high-interest topics written in a fast-paced style. Every effort has been made to create reading passages in examples, reviews, and tests that students will find lively and engaging. Topics are taken from issues arising in popular culture and in current textbooks; some examples are gangs, movies, weight loss, sports figures, depression, interpersonal relationships, drug use, nutrition, inspirational and success stories, role models, stress management, and exercise—all written in active language using a variety of sentence patterns.

Integration of the Reading Process and Reading Skills

Master readers blend individual reading skills into a reading process such as SQ3R. Before reading, master readers skim for new or key vocabulary or main ideas. They create study questions and make connections to their prior knowledge. During reading, they check their comprehension. For example, they annotate the text. They notice thought patterns and the relationship between ideas. They read for the answers to the questions they created before reading. After reading, master readers use outlines, concept maps, and summaries to review what they have read and deepen their understanding. Students are taught to integrate each skill into a reading process in Part One.

In Chapter 1, "A Reading System for Master Readers," students are introduced to SQ3R. In every other Part One chapter students actively apply SQ3R reading strategies in "Before Reading About" and "After Reading About" activities. "Before Reading About" activities are pre-reading exercises that appear at the beginning of each chapter. These activities guide the student to review important concepts studied in earlier chapters, build on prior knowledge, and preview upcoming material. "After Reading About" activities are review activities that appear after the review tests in each chapter. These activities guide students to reflect on their achievements and assume responsibility for learning.

Comprehensive Approach

An ancient Chinese proverb states, "Skill comes from practice." *The Master Reader,* Third Edition, invites skill building by offering several levels of learning. First, students are given an abundance of practice. They are able to focus on individual reading skills through a chapter-by-chapter workbook approach. In each chapter of Part One, Review Tests 3 and 4 offer a multiparagraph passage with items on all the skills taught up to that point. In addition, Chapter 1, "A Reading System for Master Readers," teaches students how to apply their reading skills to the reading process before, during, and after reading by using SQ3R. Students also learn to apply all the skills in combination in Part Two, "Additional Readings," and Part Three, "Combined-Skills Tests."

Textbook Structure

To help students become master readers and critical thinkers, *The Master Reader,* Third Edition, introduces the most important basic reading skills in Part One and then provides sections of additional readings in Part Two, and combined-skills tests in Part Three.

Part One, Becoming a Master Reader

Essential reading skills are introduced sequentially in Part One. Each chapter focuses the student's attention on a particular skill.

- Chapter 1, "A Reading System for Master Readers," guides students through the reading process. Stages of the SQ3R process are explained thoroughly, with ample opportunities for practice, review, and mastery. The aim is to show students how to apply the skills they acquire in each of the chapters before, during, and after reading.

- Chapter 2, "Vocabulary Skills," fosters vocabulary acquisition during reading by using a mnemonic technique: SAGE stands for **S**ynonyms, **A**ntonyms, **G**eneral context, and **E**xample. The chapter also develops language skills by demonstrating how to determine word meanings from prefixes, roots, and suffixes.

- Chapter 3, "Stated Main Ideas," offers both verbal and visual strategies to enable students to see the building-block relationship among topics, main ideas, and supporting details and explains strategies to identify main ideas along with extensive practice in doing so. In addition, this chapter teaches students to identify the central idea of multiparagraph passages.

- Chapter 4, "Implied Main Ideas and Implied Central Ideas," furthers students' understanding about the central idea of longer passages and the main idea by explaining unstated main ideas and unstated central ideas. The chapter offers extensive practice.

- Chapter 5, "Supporting Details," identifies the differences between major and minor details.

- Chapter 6, "Outlines and Concept Maps," reinforces the skills of locating main ideas and identifying major and minor supporting details. The chapter teaches students the structure of a text by offering instruction and practice in the applications of outlines and concept maps.

- Chapter 7, "Transitions and Thought Patterns," introduces the fundamental thought patterns and the words that signal those patterns. Students are given numerous opportunities to practice identifying the signal words and their relationships to the thought patterns they establish. The chapter includes the time order, space order, listing, and classification patterns.

- Chapter 8, "More Thought Patterns," introduces more complex thought patterns and the words that signal those patterns. Just as in Chapter 7, students are given extensive practice opportunities. Chapter 8 introduces the comparison-and-contrast, cause-and-effect, generalization-and-example, and definition patterns.

- Chapter 9, "Fact and Opinion," explains the differences between fact and opinion and develops the higher-level thinking skills that enable students to separate fact from opinion through extensive practice.

- Chapter 10, "Tone and Purpose," continues the students' study of the importance of word choice and the author's purpose. Detailed instruction and extensive practice develop the students' ability to determine whether the author's purpose is to entertain, to inform, or to persuade.

- Chapter 11, "Inferences," carefully addresses the advanced skill of making inferences by dividing the necessary mental processes into units of activity. Students are taught the basic skills necessary to evaluate an author's purpose and choice of words.

- Chapter 12, "The Basics of Argument," teaches the fundamental logical thought process used to examine the author's claim and supports.

Students learn to recognize the author's claim and to evaluate supports as adequate and relevant.

- Chapter 13, "Advanced Argument: Persuasive Techniques," offers extensive explanations and practice of several common biased arguments that use logical fallacies and propaganda techniques. The logical fallacies include personal attack, straw man, begging the question, either-or, false comparison, and false cause. The propaganda techniques covered are name-calling, testimonials, bandwagon, plain folks, card stacking, transfer, and glittering generalities.

Part Two, Additional Readings

Part Two is a collection of ten reading selections followed by skills questions designed to give students real reading opportunities and the ability to gauge their growth. This part begins with a key discussion about the relationship between reading and writing and includes a few pointers on basic writing skills. The readings, which range from magazine articles to book excerpts, were chosen based on each selection's likelihood to engage, encourage, and motivate readers. Each selection is followed by skills questions so that students can practice again all the skills taught in Part One. The skills questions are followed by discussion and writing topics that encourage students to practice making connections among listening, speaking, reading, and writing.

Part Three, Combined-Skills Tests

Part Three is a set of ten reading passages and combined-skills tests. The purpose of this section is to offer the student more opportunities to apply reading skills and strategies comprehensively and to become more familiar with a standardized testing format. Increasing familiarity will help prepare them for the exit exams, standardized reading tests, and future course content quizzes, tests, and exams.

Chapter Features

Each chapter in Part One has several important features that help students become master readers.

Learning Outcomes: New to this edition, each chapter opens with learning outcomes to help students preview and assess their progress as they master chapter content.

"Before Reading About . . .": "Before Reading About . . ." activities appear at the beginning of Chapters 2–13 in Part One. These activities are pre-reading exercises based on SQ3R: they review important concepts studied in earlier chapters, build on prior knowledge, and preview the chapter. The purpose of "Before Reading About . . ." is to actively teach students to develop a reading process that applies individual reading skills as they study.

"After Reading About . . .": "After Reading About . . ." activities appear after Review Test 4 in Chapters 2–13 of Part One. Based on SQ3R, "After Reading About . . ." activities teach students to reflect on their achievements and assume responsibility for their own learning. These activities check students' comprehension of the skill taught in the chapter.

Instruction, example, explanation, and practice. The chapter skill is broken down into components, and each component is introduced and explained. Instruction is followed by an example, an explanation of the example, and a practice. Each of these components has its own instruction, example and explanation, and practice exercises.

Textbook Skills

Textbook Skills. In the last section in each chapter, students are shown various ways in which the skills they are learning apply to reading textbooks. These activities, signaled by the icon to the left, present material selected from a textbook and direct the student to apply the chapter's skill or skills to the passage or visual. In a concerted effort to prepare students to be master readers in their course work, activities that foster textbook skills across the curriculum are also carefully woven throughout the entire text. The Textbook Skills icon signals these activities.

Visual Vocabulary. The influence of technology and the media on reading is evident in the widespread use of graphics in newspapers, magazines, and textbooks. Throughout *The Master Reader*, Third Edition, visual vocabulary is presented as part of the reading process, and students interact with these visuals by completing captions or answering skill-based questions. The aim is to teach students to value photos, graphs, illustrations, and maps as important sources of information.

Applications. Brief application exercises give students a chance to apply each component of the reading skill as a strategy.

Review Tests. Each chapter has four Review Tests. Review Tests 1 and 2 are designed to give ample opportunity for practice on the specific skill taught in the chapter; Review Tests 3 and 4 offer a multiparagraph passage with combined-skills questions based on all the skills taught up to and including that particular chapter. Review Tests 3 and 4 also give "What Do You Think?" writing prompts so that teachers have the opportunity to guide students as they develop critical thinking skills.

Mastery Tests. Each chapter includes four Mastery Tests. Most of the Mastery Tests are based on excerpts from science, history, psychology, social science, and literature textbooks.

Chapter Review Cards. New to this edition, a chapter review card is included for each chapter. The Chapter Review serves as a comprehension check for the reading concepts being taught.

The Longman Teaching and Learning Package

The Master Reader is supported by a series of innovative supplements. Ask your Pearson sales representative for a copy, or download the content at **www.pearsonhighered.com/irc**. Your sales representative will provide you with the username and password to access these materials.

The **Annotated Instructor's Edition (AIE)** is a replica of the student text, with all answers included. Ask your Longman sales representative for ISBN 0-205-83519-8.

The **Instructor's Manual,** prepared by Mary Dubbé of Thomas Nelson Community College, features teaching strategies for each textbook chapter, plus additional readings that engage students and encourage active learning. Each chapter includes an introduction, reproducible handouts, study-strategy cards, and a ten-item quiz. A supplemental section provides a sample syllabus, readability calculations for each reading in *The Master Reader*, Third Edition, nine book quizzes to encourage independent reading and the creation of book groups, sample THEA and Florida State Exit Exams, and a scaffolded book review form. ISBN 0-205-83518-X.

The **Lab Manual,** prepared by Mary Dubbé of Thomas Nelson Community College, is available as a separate student workbook and provides a collection of 65 activities that give additional practice, enrichment, and an assessment for the skills presented in *The Master Reader*, Third Edition. The activities for each chapter include practice exercises, one review test, and two mastery tests that mirror the design of *The Master Reader,* Third Edition. The lab manual is available packaged with *The Master Reader,* Third Edition, for an additional cost. ISBN 0-205-83520-1.

MyReadingLab is a website specifically created for developmental students that provides diagnostics, practice tests, and reporting on student reading skills and reading levels.

Acknowledgments

As I worked on the third edition of this reading series, I felt an overwhelming sense of gratitude and humility for the opportunity to serve the learning community as a textbook author. I would like to thank the entire Longman team for their dedication to providing the best possible materials to foster literacy. To every person, from the editorial team to the representatives in the field, all demonstrate a passion for students, teachers, and learning. It is a joy to be part of such a team. Special thanks are due to the following: Kate Edwards, Acquisitions Editor, and Erin Reilly, Development Editor, for their guidance and support; Kathy Smith with Nesbitt Graphics, Inc. for her tireless devotion to excellence; and Ellen MacElree and the entire production team for their work ethic and gracious attitudes. I would also like to thank Mary Dubbé for authoring the Lab Manual and the Instructor's Manual that supplement this reading series.

For nearly twenty-five years, I worked with the most amazing group of faculty from across the state of Florida as an item-writer, reviewer, or scorer of state-wide assessment exams for student learning and professional certification. The work that we accomplished together continues to inform me as a teacher, writer, and consultant. I owe a debt of gratitude to this group who sacrificed much for the good of our students.

I would also like to acknowledge two of my colleagues at Daytona State College: Dustin Weeks, Librarian, and Sandra Offiah-Hawkins, reading professor. As Tennyson extols in "Ulysses," these are the "souls that have toiled, and wrought, and thought with me." Their influence and support have made me a better person, teacher, and writer.

Finally, I would like to gratefully recognize the invaluable insights provided by the following colleagues and reviewers. I deeply appreciate their investment of time and energy: Tomekia Cooper, Albany Technical College; Jan Eveler, El Paso Community College; Annie Gonzalez, Laredo Community College; Yolanda Nieves, Wilbur Wright College; Margarita Sanchez, McLennan Community College; Michael Vensel, Miami Dade College; and Shari Waldrop, Navarro College.

D. J. Henry
Daytona Beach, Florida

PART ONE

Becoming a Master Reader

A Reading System for Master Readers

1

LEARNING OUTCOMES

After studying this chapter, you should be able to do the following:

1. Define prior knowledge. [Knowledge]
2. Discuss the three phases of the reading process. [Comprehension]
3. Illustrate SQ3R. [Application]
4. Describe your reading process. [Comprehension]
5. Assess your comprehension of prior knowledge and the reading process. [Analysis]
6. Evaluate the importance of prior knowledge and SQ3R. [Analysis]
7. Activate prior knowledge and apply SQ3R to your reading process. [Application]
8. Develop textbook skills: Use SQ3R to master textbook reading. [Evaluate]

Many people think that reading involves simply passing our eyes over the words in the order that they appear on the page. However, reading is an active process during which you draw information from the text to create meaning. When you understand what you've read, you've achieved **comprehension** of the material.

> **Comprehension** is an understanding of what has been read.

Once we understand the **reading process**, we can follow specific steps and apply strategies that will make us master readers. The most important aspect of being a master reader is being an *active reader*.

Active reading means that you ask questions, find answers, and react to the author's ideas. For example, an active reader often marks, or annotates, key ideas by underlining the text or writing notes in the margin. (For more information about annotating a text, see page 594.) In addition, an active reader often checks comprehension by summarizing, or briefly restating the author's major points. (For more information about summarizing, see pages 595–597.) The activities in this chapter are designed to give you the skills you need to become an active reader.

Prior Knowledge

We all have learned a large body of information throughout a lifetime of experience. This body of information is called **prior knowledge**.

Knowledge is gained from experience and stored in memory. For example, a small child hears her father repeat the word *no* frequently as he takes away dangerous objects, removes her from unsafe situations, or wants her to stop certain behaviors. The child quickly learns and will remember the meaning of *no*.

> **Prior knowledge** is the large body of information that is learned throughout a lifetime of experience.

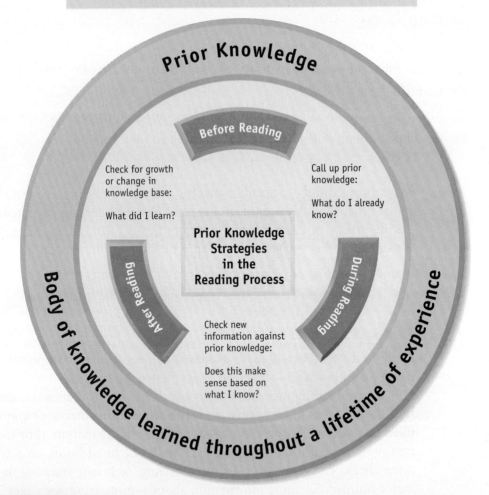

EXAMPLE Read the following passage taken from a college science textbook. In the space provided, list any topics from the passage about which you already have prior knowledge.

The Lunar Surface

Textbook
Skills

[1]When Galileo first pointed his telescope toward the Moon, he saw two different types of terrains—dark lowlands and brighter, highly cratered highlands. [2]Because the dark regions resembled seas on Earth, they were called maria (*mar* = sea, singular, mare). [3]Today, we know that the maria are not oceans but, instead, are flat plains that resulted from immense outpourings of fluid basaltic lavas. [4]By contrast, the light-colored areas resemble Earth's continents, so the first observers dubbed them terrae (Latin for "land"). [5]These areas are now generally referred to as lunar highlands, because they are elevated several kilometers above the maria. [6]Together, the arrangement of terrae and maria result in the well-known "face of the moon."

—From *Foundations of Earth Science*, 5th Edition, p. 409 by Frederick K. Lutgens, Edward J. Tarbuck, and Dennis Tasa. Copyright © 2008 by Pearson Education, Inc. Printed and Electronically reproduced by permission of Pearson Education, Inc., Upper Saddle River, NJ.

Answers may vary.

_____

_____

_____

EXPLANATION If you know something about the terrain of the moon, basaltic lava, or the actual length of a kilometer, then this passage makes more sense to you than it does to someone who does not possess such prior knowledge. However, even if you do not know much about those topics, you may have helpful prior knowledge about some of the other ideas in the passage. For example, most of us have seen and perhaps wondered about the "face of the moon." Our prior knowledge that comes from observing the moon with our own eyes connects with new information in the passage.

The more prior knowledge we have about a topic, the more likely we are to understand that topic. This is why master readers build their knowledge base by reading often!

PRACTICE 1

Read the passage from a college health textbook. Then, answer the questions that follow it.

Textbook
Skills

From Everyday Problems to Emotionally Crippling Behavior

[1]Neuroses are the most common type of mental problem. [2]Although neuroses can cause emotional suffering, neurotic individuals usually can carry out day-to-day activities. [3]Anxiety and phobia are examples of

neuroses; they are generally viewed as cognitive distortions or unsatisfactory ways of reacting to life situations.

[4]Anxiety is often brought on by an imagined fear of impending danger. [5]Americans experience anxiety more than any other mental health problem. [6]Most anxiety is normal and may play an important role in anticipating situations. [7]For example, the fear of being attacked on a deserted street at night may cause a person to take appropriate actions to avoid such a possibility. [8]You have probably experienced anxiety before taking a final exam. [9]Some of the symptoms you may have had are sweating, dry mouth, heavy breathing, and insomnia. [10]This type of anxiety is in response to a realistic situation.

[11]However, some people suffer anxiety over a long period of time and without any apparent cause. [12]A person who has a phobia, for example, has an unreasonable fear of some object or situation. [13]Simple phobias include fear of heights or fear of bees and usually do not interfere with daily activities. [14]Some phobias, however, are more severe and can cause people to lead constricted lives. [15]Because of their irrational fears, some people do not leave the house. [16]Anxiety becomes a serious mental health problem when individuals suffering from it are so emotionally crippled that they cannot continue at school, hold a job, or otherwise lead a satisfying and productive life.

—From *Healthstyles: Decisions for Living* Well, 2nd ed., pp. 58–59 by B. E. Pruitt and Jane J. Stein. Copyright © 1999 by Pearson Education, Inc. Printed and Electronically reproduced by permission of Pearson Education, Inc., Upper Saddle River, NJ.

1. What did you already know about neuroses such as anxiety and phobias? That is, what was your prior knowledge? <u>Answers may vary.</u>

_____

2. When you think of anxiety and phobias, what do you think of? Describe ideas and experiences that come to mind. <u>Answers may vary.</u>

3. Was this an easy passage to understand? How does your prior knowledge affect your understanding of this passage? <u>Answers may vary.</u>

4. List any parts of the passage you had no prior knowledge of: <u>Answers may vary.</u>

 ## The Reading Process

Triggering prior knowledge is a reading skill that you as an active reader can turn into a reading strategy by using it in your reading process. In each of the remaining chapters in Part One, you will be encouraged to begin thinking about how you can connect the reading skills that you are learning to the reading process. Master readers use reading skills as comprehension strategies throughout the reading process.

Master readers break reading into a three-step process. Each step uses its own thinking activities.

1. Before reading, look over, or *preview*, the material. (Previewing brings up prior knowledge.) Ask questions about the material you are about to read.

2. During reading, *test* your understanding of the material.

3. After reading, *review and react* to what you have learned.

One well-known way to apply this reading process is called SQ3R.

SQ3R stands for Survey, Question, Read, Recite, and Review.

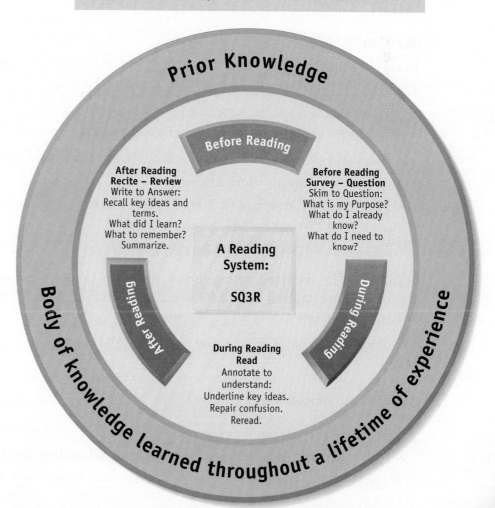

Prior Knowledge

Before Reading

After Reading
Recite – Review
Write to Answer:
Recall key ideas and terms.
What did I learn?
What to remember?
Summarize.

Before Reading
Survey – Question
Skim to Question:
What is my Purpose?
What do I already know?
What do I need to know?

A Reading System:

SQ3R

After Reading

During Reading

During Reading
Read
Annotate to understand:
Underline key ideas.
Repair confusion.
Reread.

Body of knowledge learned throughout a lifetime of experience

SQ3R activates prior knowledge and offers strategies for each phase of the reading process. The following graphic illustrates the phases of the reading process through SQ3R. Master readers repeat or move among phases as needed to repair comprehension.

 Before Reading: Survey and Question

A. Survey

Quickly look over, or **skim**, the reading passage for clues about how it is organized and what it is going to present or teach you.

To skim effectively, look at *italic* and **bold** type and take note of titles, the introduction, and headings. Also look at pictures and graphs. Finally, read the first paragraph, summaries, and questions. Each of these clues provides important information.

B. Question

To aid in comprehension, ask questions before you read. The list of prereading questions that follows can be used in most reading situations.

- What is the topic or subject of the passage? (See Chapter 3.)
- How is the material organized? (See Chapters 6 and 7.)
- What do I already know about this idea? (What is my prior knowledge?)
- What is my purpose for reading?
- What is my reading plan? Do I need to read everything, or can I just skim for the information I need?
- What are the most important parts to remember?

EXAMPLE   The excerpted passage below is from a college communications textbook. Before you read it word for word, skim the passage and fill in the following information:

1. What is the topic of this passage? <u>"the marketplace of ideas"</u>

   _____

2. What do I already know about this topic? <u>Answers may vary.</u>

   _____

3. What is my purpose for reading? That is, why am I reading this? What do I

   need to remember? <u>Answers may vary. Sample answer: to define the term</u>

   <u>"marketplace of ideas"</u>

4. What ideas in the passage are in *italic* and/or **bold** type? marketplace of

ideas, public forum, social discourse, policy formation, supply, all sources of

information, and the title "Supply in the Marketplace of Ideas"

Textbook
Skills

Supply in the Marketplace of Ideas

[1]The *marketplace of ideas* assumes that all ideas should be discussed in the open. [2]The more ideas, the better. [3]Only when ideas (even those thought radical) gain access to the *public forum* can social change occur. [4]Women fought for almost a century before gaining the right to vote through a constitutional amendment adopted in 1920. [5]Their ideas were considered radical by many men—and women.

[6]The marketplace of ideas involves social discourse, and *social discourse* can lead to *policy formation*. [7]For example, the state of Oregon adopted strict recycling standards for its population by the early 1970s, ten to twenty years before most other states did the same. [8]Oregon's marketplace of ideas considered the recycling issue important, and the discussion in that marketplace led to policy changes that other states eventually adopted.

[9]The *supply* for the marketplace of ideas comes from *all sources of information*, including individuals, newspapers, movies, television, recordings, and radio. [10]Consumers, journalists, lobbyists, public-relations personnel, and government officials determine, both as individuals and as groups, what content has use in the marketplace of ideas.

—Folkerts & Lacy, *The Media in Your Life*, 2nd ed., pp. 43–44.

EXPLANATION

1. The title of the passage, "Supply in the Marketplace of Ideas," gives us a clue to the topic of the passage. By quickly looking at the terms in *italic* and **bold** type, you can see that this passage is about the marketplace of ideas.

2. The answer to this question on prior knowledge will vary for each of you. Some of you may be excellent shoppers and thus already have some experience and understanding about the marketplace and the complexity of supply and demand. If so, then you have prior knowledge that can be transferred to the "marketplace of ideas."

3. Wording of your purpose for reading will vary. A sample answer: I need to know what the "marketplace of ideas" means and about its source or supply.

4. The words in *italic* and **bold** type are *marketplace of ideas, public forum, social discourse, policy formation, supply, all sources of information,* and the title.

During Reading: Read and Annotate

After you have surveyed and asked questions about the text, it's time to read the entire passage. Use the following helpful practices while reading.

Read

As you read, think about the importance of the information by continuing to ask questions. For example:

- Does this new information agree with what I already knew?
- Do I need to change my mind about what I thought I knew?
- What is the significance of this information? Do I need to remember this?

In addition to asking questions while you read, acknowledge and resolve any confusion as it occurs.

- Create questions based on the headings, subheadings, and words in *italics* and **bold** type.
- Reread the parts you don't understand.
- Reread whenever your mind drifts during reading.
- Read ahead to see if an idea becomes clearer.
- Determine the meaning of words from their context.
- Look up new or difficult words.
- Think about ideas even when they differ from your own.

Annotate

Make the material your own. Make sure you understand it by repeating the information.

- Create a picture in your mind or on paper.
- Restate the ideas in your own words.
- Mark your text by underlining, circling, or highlighting topics, key terms, and main ideas. (See pages 595–597 for more about how to annotate.)

- Write out answers to the questions you created based on the headings, subheadings, and highlighted words.
- Write a summary of the passage or section.

EXAMPLE

A. Before you read the following excerpt from a college science textbook, survey the passage and answer the following questions.

   1. What is the topic of the passage? "biological rhythms"

   2. What do I already know about the topic of this passage? What is my prior knowledge? Answers may vary.

   3. What is important about this passage? What do I need to remember?
   Answers may vary. Sample answer: the two types of biological rhythms and
   examples of each type

Textbook
Skills

   4. What are the words in **bold** type (which will help me remember what I need to know? circadian rhythms, circannual rhythm, and biological rhythms

B. Once you have surveyed the information, read the passage. During reading, check your understanding by writing answers to the questions based on the ideas in **bold** type.

5. What new or difficult words do I need to look up?
Answers will vary.

6. What are circadian rhythms?
patterns of activity that approximate the length of a day

7. What is an example of circadian rhythms?
Fruit flies (*Dacus tryoni*) always
mate about the same time in
the evening.

Biological Rhythms

[1]Many different types of animals show **circadian rhythms**—patterns of activity that approximate the length of a day. [2]For example, fruit flies (*Dacus tryoni*) always mate at about the same time in the evening; they continue to show this cyclical pattern of mating even when external cues indicating the time of day are not available. [3]This pattern enables the flies to mate under cover of darkness, when the danger of predation is reduced.

[4]Another common cycle in the animal world is a **circannual rhythm**, a cycle lasting approximately one year. [5]A circannual pattern makes it possible for an animal to engage in a behavior during the appropriate season. [6]For example, the golden-mantled ground squirrel (*Citellus lateralis*) enters into hibernation

8. What is a circannual rhythm?

a cycle of behavior lasting approx-

imately one year that allows an

animal to engage in a behavior

during the appropriate season

9. What is an example of a circannual rhythm?

The golden-mantled ground

squirrel hibernates every year

in the late fall.

10. What do you need to reread to understand?

Answers will vary.

approximately the same time every year, during the late fall. [7]Like the fruit flies, the ground squirrel maintains its rhythm when kept in a laboratory, isolated from external factors that could indicate the season. [8]For example, ground squirrels kept in rooms with constant temperature and unchanging light-dark cycles showed a consistent hibernation schedule over a 4-year period.

—Maier, *Comparative Animal Behavior*, p. 431.

EXPLANATION Compare your answers to the ones below. Keep in mind that your wording and examples may be different.

A. Before Reading: Survey and Question

1. The topic of the passage is biological rhythms.

2. Answers to this question will vary.

3. Answers to this question will vary. A possible answer is: The two types of biological rhythms and examples of each type.

4. The terms in **bold** type are: circadian rhythms and circannual rhythm.

B. During Reading: Read and Annotate

5. Answers to this question will vary.

6. Circadian rhythms are patterns of activity that approximate the length of a day.

7. Fruit flies (*Dacus tryoni*) always mate about the same time in the evening.

8. A circannual rhythm is a cycle of behavior lasting approximately one year that allows an animal to engage in a behavior during the appropriate season.

9. The golden-mantled ground squirrel hibernates every year in the late fall.

10. Answers to this question will vary.

 ## After Reading: Recite and Review

Recite

As part of your review, take time to think and write about what you have read.

- Connect new information to your prior knowledge about the topic.
- Form opinions about the material and the author.
- Notice changes in your opinions based on the new information.
- Write about what you have read.

Review

Once you have read the entire selection, go back over the material to review it.

- Summarize the most important parts (for more information about how to summarize, see pages 595–597).
- Return to and answer the questions raised by headings and subheadings.
- Review new words and their meanings based on the way they were used in the passage.

PRACTICE 2

Now that you have learned about each of the three phases of the reading process, practice putting all three together. Think before, during, and after reading. Apply SQ3R to the following passage. Remember the steps:

- **Survey**: Look over the whole passage.
- **Question**: Ask questions about the content. Predict how the new information fits together with or differs from what you already know about the topic.
- **Read**: Continue to question, look up new words, reread, and create pictures in your mind.
- **Recite**: Take notes; write out questions and answers, definitions of words, and new information.
- **Review**: Think about what you have read and written. Use journals to capture your opinions and feelings about what you have read.

A. **Before Reading: Survey and Question.** Skim the passage taken from a college history textbook, and then answer the following questions.

1. What is the topic of this passage? <u>the separation of powers and checks and</u>

   <u>balances in the federal government of the United States</u>

   _____

   _____

2. What do I already know about this information? <u>Answers may vary.</u>

   _____

   _____

   _____

3. What do I need to remember? <u>Sample answer: the meanings and</u>

   <u>importance of the terms *separation of powers* and *checks and balances*</u>

   _____

   _____

4. What ideas are in **bold** type? <u>separation of powers, checks and balances</u>

   _____

   _____

   _____

5–6. *Before you go on:* Use the terms you listed in item 2 to create questions. Write the questions in the blank boxes labeled 5 and 6. Write your answers to these questions in the boxes during reading.

B. **During Reading: Read and Recite.** As you read, answer the questions you created from the ideas in **bold** type.

5. <u>What is the separation</u>
<u>of powers?</u>
<u>Articles I, II, and III of the</u>
<u>Constitution created three</u>
<u>separate branches of govern-</u>
<u>ment: legislative, executive, and</u>
<u>judicial.</u>

Separation of Powers and Checks and Balances

[1]The Founders believed that unlimited power was corrupting and that the concentration of power was dangerous. [2]James Madison wrote, "Ambition must be made to counteract ambition." [3]Articles I, II, and III of the Constitution created three separate branches within the national government: legislative, executive, and judicial. [4]This **separation of powers**

6. What are checks and balances? They are the powers of each branch to check over the actions of other branches.

was designed to place internal controls on governmental power. [5]Power is not only apportioned among three branches of government, but, perhaps, more important, each branch is given important **checks and balances** over the actions of others. [6]According to Madison, "The constant aim is to divide and arrange the several offices in such a manner as that each may be a check on the other." [7]No bill can become a law without the approval of both the House and the Senate. [8]The president shares legislative power through the power to sign or to veto laws of Congress, although Congress may override a presidential veto with a two-thirds vote in each house. [9]The president may also suggest legislation, "give to the Congress Information of the State of the Union, and recommend to their Consideration such Measures as he shall judge necessary and expedient." [10]The president may also convene special sessions of Congress.

[11]However, the president's power of appointment is shared by the Senate, which confirms cabinet and ambassadorial appointments. [12]The president must also secure the advice and consent of the Senate for any treaty. [13]The president must execute the laws, but it is Congress that provides the money to do so. [14]The president and the rest of the executive branch may not spend money that has not been appropriated by Congress. [15]Congress must also authorize the creation of executive departments and agencies. [16]Finally, Congress may impeach and remove the president from office for "Treason, Bribery, or other High Crimes and Misdemeanors."

—Adapted from *Politics in America*, 7th edition, pp. 72–73 by Thomas R. Dye. Copyright © 2007 by Pearson Education, Inc. Reprinted by permission of Pearson Education, Inc., Glenview, IL.

C. After Reading: Review

7. Why is the separation of power important? Answers may vary. Possible answer: Unlimited power corrupts, and any one group or person with too much power can be dangerous.

8. Identify a time when the system of checks and balances has been noticeable. Answers may vary. Possible answers: President Nixon left the office of president to avoid impeachment by Congress. President Clinton was impeached by the House but not by the Senate; thus he remained in office.

Reading a Textbook: Using SQ3R to Master Textbook Reading

Textbook
Skills

You can use the SQ3R reading system to increase your comprehension and retention of information from all types of reading materials, from newspapers to novels. As a college student, you will find SQ3R to be a particularly helpful study method when trying to master information in your textbooks. Most textbooks are designed with special features to help readers understand and learn the vast amount of information within them. Master readers actively use these features as they preview, read, and review textbook material. The following chart lists and explains several features common to most textbooks.

Textbook Features

BOOK FEATURES

Table of Contents	The table of contents, located in the front of the book, is a list of the chapters in the order in which they appear, along with their corresponding page numbers.
Index	The index, located in the back of the book, is an alphabetical list of all the specific topics discussed in the textbook, along with the precise page numbers that deal with each topic.
Glossary	A glossary is an alphabetical list of specialized words and their meanings. Glossaries can be located in a number of places in a textbook, including at the back of the book, in the chapter's preview material, in the margins of the pages where the words are first used, or at the end of the chapter as review material.
Preface	The preface is a type of introduction that discusses the textbook's overall purpose, format, and special features.
Appendices	Appendices are sections of additional material designed to supplement or support your learning; they appear at the back of many textbooks.

CHAPTER FEATURES

Introductions and Previews	Each chapter usually begins with a brief overview of the chapter's contents. Sometimes, this section also includes key questions or objectives to keep in mind as you read.
Headings and Subheadings	Textbook authors divide complex information into smaller sections to organize the ideas. Each section is labeled with a heading. Some sections are divided into subgroups and are given subheadings.
Information Boxes	Information boxes are used to highlight important information; they frequently contain key concepts, definitions, activities, real-life connections, or summaries.

Summaries	A summary is a brief section at the end of a chapter that restates the chapter's main idea and major supporting details.
Review Questions	At the end of a section, the author may supply a set of questions designed to test your comprehension.
Typographical Features	Authors frequently use **bold** and *italic* type to draw attention to important ideas and terms.
Graphics	Graphs, tables, diagrams, maps, photographs, and other graphic aids support the information explained in the paragraphs. Graphics make the information more visually interesting and accessible to visual learners.

Master readers actively use textbook features throughout the process of reading an assignment. For example, a master reader sets up a reading session or a series of sessions to complete a reading assignment. Each reading session is broken into the three reading phases. The time spent in each phase of the process varies based on the reading assignment.

Before Reading: A master reader may begin a reading session with five to ten minutes of before-reading activities such as skimming, noting new or special terms, creating questions, and setting a purpose for the reading session.

During Reading: Then, the master reader reads for a set amount of time, such as thirty minutes. The duration of a reading session depends on many factors such as length or difficulty of the material, time-management issues, and reader interest. For example, the difficulty of the text may require several shorter sessions of reading smaller chunks of the assignment. Master readers avoid marathon sessions that lead to fatigue and loss of concentration. During reading, the master reader stays focused by highlighting the text, taking notes, and repairing any confusion when it occurs.

After Reading: The master reader spends five to fifteen minutes completing notes or writing a summary with information that fulfills the purpose for reading (which was established before reading).

EXAMPLE The following study plan outlines how one student plans to apply SQ3R to the process of reading textbooks. Test your understanding of the steps you can take to use SQ3R to understand textbook material. Fill in the blanks with information that best completes each idea. Answer the question that follows the chart.

Before Reading [5–10 minutes]— **(1)** Survey and **(2)** Question

- Preview textbook: Skim preface, table of contents, and locate index.
- Preview a chapter: Read chapter **(3)** introduction. Preview material, including information boxes, graphics, and end-of-chapter questions.

- Turn chapter **(4)** <u>headings</u>, **(5)** <u>subheadings</u>, and terms in **bold** or *italic* type into questions.
- Preview **(6)** <u>end-of-chapter review</u> questions.

During Reading [around 30 minutes]— (7) <u>Read</u>

- Annotate to understand; underline **(8)** <u>key ideas</u>.
- Note definitions/examples of terms in **(9)** <u>bold</u> or **(10)** <u>italic</u> type.
- Repair **(11)** <u>confusion</u>; check glossaries and indexes for more information.
- Reread or read ahead for clarification. Study graphics to understand key concepts.

After Reading [5–15 minutes]—(12) <u>Review</u> **and (13)** <u>Recite</u>

- Use notes to test recall. Use two-column notes. Consider the following headings: Topics and Details, Terms and Definitions, or Questions and Answers. Create flashcards for important terms.
- Answer **(14)** <u>review questions</u> at the end of the chapter.
- Write a **(15)** <u>summary</u> that paraphrases the chapter.

    How can SQ3R help me read a textbook? <u>Answers may vary.</u>

    _____

    _____

EXPLANATION Compare your answers to the ones given here.

Before Reading (1) *Survey* and (2) *Question*. Several ways to preview the textbook include the following: read the chapter (3) *introduction*, turn chapter (4) *headings* and (5) *subheadings* into questions, and preview (6) *end-of-chapter review* questions.

During Reading (7) *Read*; underline (8) *key ideas* and note the definitions and examples of terms in (9) *bold* or (10) *italic* type. Also repair (11) *confusion*.

After Reading (12) *Review* and (13) *Recite*. Answer (14) *review questions* and write a (15) *summary* using your own words.

How can SQ3R help me read a textbook? Although answers will vary, in general, SQ3R breaks the reading assignment into three phases of previewing, reading, and reviewing information. By asking questions, recording ideas, and reciting information, I am more likely to understand and remember information.

PRACTICE 3

The following selection is a section of a chapter from a geography textbook. Use SQ3R to comprehend the passage. Skim the passage and answer the "Before Reading" questions. During reading, underline key concepts and definitions. After reading, complete the three-column notes with information from the passage. Some answers may vary.

Before Reading—Survey and Question:

1. What do I need to know? I need to be able to name and identify the different types of rocks. I need to know the meaning of the following terms: sima, sial, and shields.

2. What is my purpose? My purpose is to be able to identify the types of rocks and understand the role of minerals in rock formation.

Rock Formation

[1]Although by human standards Earth's surface moves very slowly—by at most a few centimeters per year—this movement produces Earth's great diversity of rocks. [2]As Earth's crust moves, its materials are eroded and deposited, heated and cooled, buried and exposed.

Types of rocks [3]Rocks can be grouped into three basic categories that reflect how they form:

[4]**Igneous rocks** are formed when molten crustal material cools and solidifies. [5]The name derives from the Greek word for fire, which is the same root as for the English word ignite. [6]Examples of igneous rocks are basalt, which is common in volcanic areas, including much of the ocean floor, and granite, which is common in continental areas.

[7]**Sedimentary rocks** result when rocks eroded from higher elevations (mountains, hills, plains) accumulate at lower elevations (like swamps and ocean bottoms). [8]When subjected to high pressure and the presence of cementing materials to bind their grains together, rocks like sandstone, shale, conglomerate, and limestone are formed.

[9]**Metamorphic rocks** are created when rocks are exposed to great pressure and heat, altering them into more compact, crystalline rocks. [10]In Greek the name means "to change form." [11]Examples include marble (which metamorphosed from limestone) and slate (which metamorphosed from shale).

Minerals [12]Minerals are natural substances that comprise rocks. [13]Each type of mineral has specific chemical and crystalline properties. [14]Earth's rocks are diverse in part because the crust contains thousands of minerals. [15]The density of rocks depends on the kinds of materials they contain. [16]Denser rocks are dominated by compounds of silicon, magnesium, and iron minerals; they are called **sima** (for *si*licon-*ma*gnesium). [17]Less dense rocks are dominated by compounds of silicon and aluminum minerals; they are called **sial** (for *si*licon-*al*uminum).

[18]Denser sima rocks make up much of the oceanic crust. [19]Less dense sial rocks make up much of the continental crust. [20]The lower density and greater thickness of sial rocks cause the continents to have higher surface elevations than the oceanic crust, just as a less dense dry log will float higher in water than a denser wet one.

[21]The formation and distribution of many minerals is caused by the movements of Earth's crust. [22]Vast areas of the continental crust, known as **shields**, have not been significantly eroded or changed for millions of years.

[23]Shield areas often contain rich concentrations of minerals, such as metal ores and fossil fuels. [24]Shields are located in the core of large continents such as Africa, Asia, and North America. [25]Many of the world's mining districts exist where these continental shields are exposed at the surface.

—From *Introduction to Geography: People, Places, and Environment*, 4th ed.,
pp. 101–103 by Edward Bergman and William H. Renwick. Copyright © 2008
by Pearson Education, Inc. Printed and Electronically reproduced by
permission of Pearson Education, Inc., Upper Saddle River, NJ.

After Reading: Review and Recite

Complete the following notes with information from the passage. Then, answer the summary question.

Chapter 3   Rock Formations   **Textbook Notes pages 102–103**

Term	Definition	Examples
3. Igneous rocks	are formed when molten crustal material cools and solidifies	basalt, granite
4. Sedimentary rocks	**5.** are formed when rocks erode from higher elevations and collect at lower elevations	sandstone, shale conglomerate, limestone

6. Metamorphic rocks	are formed when rocks are exposed to great pressure and heat, altering them into more compact, crystalline rocks	**7.** marble, slate
Minerals	are natural elements that comprise rocks	silicon, magnesium, aluminum, metal ores, fossil fuels
sima	**8.** are denser rocks dominated by compounds of silicon, magnesium and iron minerals	make up much of oceanic crust
9. sial	are less dense rocks dominated by compounds of silicon and aluminum minerals	make up much of continental crust
shields	vast areas of continental crust, contain rich concentrations of minerals	core of large continents such as Africa, Asia, North America

Summary: What role do minerals play in rock formation and what are the three types of rocks?

10. Minerals are the natural substances that make up rocks. Because the earth's crust contains so many minerals, Earth's rocks vary greatly in density and types. However, rocks can be grouped into three basic categories based on how they were formed: Igneous rocks, Sedimentary rocks, and Metamorphic rocks.

VISUAL VOCABULARY

Granite, a _____ rock, has become a popular building material for kitchen counter tops.

    a. an igneous
    b. a sedimentary
    c. a metamorphic

Application 1: Before, During, and After Reading

This activity is designed to give you an opportunity to apply the entire reading process to a short selection from a college health textbook. Survey the passage and answer the Before Reading question. Then, read the passage and answer the questions.

Types of Weight-Training Programs

Textbook
Skills

[1]Weight-training programs can be divided into three general categories classified by the type of muscle contraction involved: isotonic, isometric, and isokinetic.

Isotonic Programs [2]Isotonic programs, like isotonic contractions, involve the concept of contracting a muscle against a moveable load (usually a free weight or weights mounted by cables or chains to form a weight machine). [3]Isotonic programs are very popular and are the most common type of weight-training program in use today.

Isometric Programs [4]An isometric strength-training program is based on the concept of contracting a muscle at a fixed angle against an immovable object, using an isometric or static contraction. [5]Interest in strength training increased dramatically during the 1950s with the finding that maximal strength could be increased by contracting a muscle for 6 seconds at two-thirds of maximal tension once per day for 5 days per week! [6]Although subsequent studies suggested that these claims were exaggerated, it is generally agreed that isometric training can increase muscular strength and endurance.

[7]Two important aspects of isometric training make it different from isotonic training. [8]First, in isometric training, the development of strength and endurance is specific to the joint angle at which the muscle group is trained. [9]Therefore, if isometric techniques are used, isometric contractions at several different joint angles are needed to gain strength and endurance throughout a full range of motion. [10]In contrast, because isotonic contractions generally involve the full range of joint motion, strength is developed over the full movement pattern. [11]Second, the static nature of isometric muscle contractions can lead to breath holding (called a **valsalva maneuver**), which can reduce blood flow to the brain and cause dizziness and fainting. [12]In an individual at high risk for coronary disease, the maneuver could be extremely dangerous and should always be avoided. [13]Remember: Continue to breathe during any type of isometric or isotonic contraction!

Isokinetic Programs [14]Isokinetic contractions are isotonic contractions performed at a constant speed (*isokinetic* refers to constant speed of movement). [15]Isokinetic training is a relatively new strength training method, so limited research exists to describe its strength benefits compared with those of isometric and isotonic programs. [16]Isokinetic exercises require the use of machines that govern the speed of movement during muscle contraction. [17]The first isokinetic machines available were very expensive and were used primarily in clinical settings for injury rehabilitation. [18]Recently, less expensive machines use a piston device (much like a shock absorber on a car) to limit the speed of movement throughout the range of the exercise. [19]Today, these machines are found in fitness centers across the United States.

—From *Total Fitness and Wellness*, 4th ed., pp. 131–133 by
Scott K. Powers, Stephen J. Dodd and Virginia J. Noland.
Copyright © 2006 by Pearson Education, Inc. Printed and
Electronically reproduced by permission of Pearson
Education, Inc., Upper Saddle River, NJ.

Before Reading

1. What is your prior knowledge about strength training? Answers may vary.
Sample answer: I have lifted weights using weight machines for several years.

During and After Reading

2. What does an isotonic program involve? An isotonic program involves
contracting a muscle against a moveable load to improve strength.

3. What does an isometric program involve? An isometric program involves
strength training by contracting a muscle at a fixed angle against an
immoveable object, using an isometric or static contraction.

4. What is a *valsalva maneuver* and what are its effects? A *valsalva maneuver*
is holding the breath during an intense muscle contraction; it can reduce
blood flow to the brain and cause dizziness and fainting.

5. What does an isokinetic program involve? An isokinetic program involves
strength training through isotonic contractions performed at a constant speed.

After Reading

6. Write a one- or two-sentence summary. <u>Wording may vary. Possible answer:</u>

<u>Strength-training programs can be divided into three types. First, isotonic</u>

<u>programs include exercises with moveable loads; second, isometric training</u>

<u>includes exercises in which a muscle contracts at a fixed angle against an</u>

<u>immoveable object; and third, isokinetic exercises involve machines that</u>

<u>govern the speed of movement during muscle contraction.</u>

7. Write a paragraph that states your personal views about what you have

read. <u>Answers may vary. Sample response: My friend Joel works out every day</u>

<u>and keeps asking me to join him. Since I've never done any weight training, I fear</u>

<u>I will (a) hurt myself or (b) make a fool of myself. If I could train secretly, I would.</u>

VISUAL VOCABULARY

Jonathan Horton of the United States performs an <u>b</u> muscle contraction as he competes in the rings event during the men's team gymnastics final at the 2008 Olympics in Beijing China.

   a. isotonic
   b. isometric
   c. isokinetic

Textbook
Skills

Application 2: Previewing a Textbook

Preview a textbook by completing the following textbook and chapter survey forms. Consider previewing *The Master Reader* or a textbook from another course you are taking. Answers may vary.

Textbook Survey Form

Academic subject: Reading

Textbook: *The Master Reader, 3rd ed.*

Author(s): D. J. Henry

Most recent copyright date: 2011

This textbook contains the following (where appropriate, write in the blank the number of versions of the feature):

__2__ Table of Contents   __x__ Index   __36__ Vocabulary Preview

__x__ Preface   __0__ Appendices   __10__ Additional Readings

Number of units or parts: __3__   Number of Chapters: __13__

Average length of chapters: 40 to 50 pages

Other features: Reading Scorecards

How will I use the textbook features in my reading process? Answers may vary.

_____

_____

_____

Chapter Survey Form

This chapter contains the following (where appropriate, write in the blank the number of times an item appears in the chapter):

Chapter Number and Title: Chapter 3 Stated Main Ideas

Number of pages:

__x__ Introduction   __x__ Preview list of key ideas   __x__ Preview list of learning objectives

__5__ Headings   __6__ Subheadings   __3__ Information Boxes

__x__ Summaries   __x__ Review Questions   __x__ **Bold** or *italic* type

__4__ Photographs   __10__ Charts, tables, graphs   __1__ Illustrations, drawings

Other special features: practices, explanations, and tests _____

How will I use the chapter features in my reading process? Answers may vary. _____

_____

How many flash cards are needed for key terms and ideas? 3 _____

Before reading, I will preview the chapter by completing the "Before Reading About" activities.

During reading, I will annotate the text by underlining key ideas; I will take

notes and I will make flash cards for the information boxes. _____

After reading I will test my reading skills by my performance on the review and mastery

tests. I will use the "After Reading About" activity to keep track of what I am learning.

REVIEW TEST 1   Score (number correct) _____ × 10 = _____%

Before, During, and After Reading

A. Before you read, survey the following passage from a college health textbook, and then answer the questions listed here.

1. What is the topic of this passage? three types of eating disorders

_____

2. What are the ideas in **bold** type? anorexia nervosa, bulimia nervosa, binge

eating disorder

3. What do I already know about this idea? Answers may vary.

_____

4. What do I need to remember? Answers may vary.

Textbook
Skills

_____

B. Read the passage. As you read, answer the questions in the box.

5. What does obsessiveness mean?

Obsessiveness is the act of

being compulsive about

something, in this case, diet.

12.9 GE/248 words   **Eating Disorders**

¹On occasion, over one-third of all Americans fit the description of obesity and diet obsessiveness. ²For an increasing number of people, particularly young women, this obsessive relationship with food develops into an eating disorder.

6. What are the traits of anorexia nervosa?

Anorexia nervosa is a persistent, chronic eating disorder characterized by deliberate food restriction and severe, life-threatening weight loss.

7. What are the traits of bulimia nervosa?

People with bulimia binge and then take inappropriate measures, such as secret vomiting, to lose the calories they have just acquired.

8. What are the traits of binge eating disorder?

People who suffer with BED binge like their bulimic counterparts, but they do not take excessive measures to lose the weight that they gain; thus they are often obese.

[3]**Anorexia nervosa** is a persistent, chronic eating disorder characterized by deliberate food restriction and severe, life-threatening weight loss. [4]Anorexia involves self-starvation motivated by an intense fear of gaining weight along with an extremely distorted body image. [5]Usually people with anorexia achieve their weight loss through initial reduction in total food intake, particularly of high-calorie foods. [6]What they do eat, they often purge through vomiting or using laxatives.

[7]**Bulimia nervosa** often involves binging and purging. [8]People with bulimia binge and then take inappropriate measures, such as secret vomiting, to lose the calories they have just acquired. [9]People with bulimia are obsessed with their bodies, weight gain, and how they appear to others. [10]Unlike those with anorexia, people with bulimia are often "hidden" from the public eye because their weight may vary only slightly or fall within normal range.

[11]**Binge eating disorder** (BED) also involves frequent bouts of binge eating. [12]People who suffer with BED binge like their bulimic counterparts, but they do not take excessive measures to lose the weight that they gain. [13]Often they are clinically obese, and they tend to binge much more often than the typically obese person who may consume too many calories but spaces his or her eating over a more normal daily eating pattern.

—Adapted from *Health: The Basics,* 7th ed., pp. 299–301 by Rebecca J. Donatelle. Copyright © 2007 by Pearson Education, Inc. Printed and Electronically reproduced by permission of Pearson Education, Inc., Upper Saddle River, NJ.

After Reading

9. What are the differences among the three types of eating disorders?

Answers may vary. Possible answer: Anorexia is the act of starvation; bulimia is overeating and purging; binge eating is overeating without purging.

10. What is the main cause of eating disorders? Answers may vary. Possible answer: Poor body image or low self-esteem is a main cause of eating disorders.

REVIEW TEST 2

Score (number correct) _____ × 10 = _____%

SQ3R

Read the following two passages from a chapter in a college geography textbook. The first passage is the chapter's preview; the second passage is the chapter's summary. Use the appropriate steps in SQ3R to read the material and complete the activities. Wording of answers may vary.

Before Reading: Survey and Question
1. What is the topic? Earth's Resources and Environmental Protection

2. How many subheadings are in the chapter? 3

11.2 GE/592 words

Chapter 9 Earth's Resources and Environmental Protection

A Look Ahead (Preview)

What is a Natural Resource?

[1]A natural resource is something that is useful to people. [2]Usefulness is determined by a mix of cultural, technological, and economic factors in addition to the properties of a given resource. [3]We often substitute one resource for another as our needs change.

Mineral and Energy Resources

[4]Mineral resources include metals and nonmetals. [5]As mineral resources are depleted, they are usually replaced with substitute materials. [6]Landfills accumulate used materials and may one day be a source of materials for reuse. [7]One principal energy resource comes from three fossil fuels—oil, coal, and gas. [8]As fossil fuels are depleted, they are likely to be replaced with nuclear and renewable energy.

Air and Water Resources

[9]Pollution results when a substance is discharged into the air or water faster than it can be dispersed or removed by natural processes. [10]Recycling and pollution prevention are growing in importance as methods for solving pollution problems.

Chapter Summary

[1]A *natural resource* is an element of the physical environment that is useful to people. [2]Cultural values determine how resources are used.

[3]Technological factors limit our use of some resources by determining the particular applications to which certain materials can be put. [4]Economic factors such as resource prices and levels of affluence influence whether a resource is used, and how much. [5]Renewable natural resources include air, water, soil, plants, and animals. [6]Nonrenewable resources include fossil fuels and nonenergy minerals. [7]Most resources are substitutable to some degree, so that if one resource is less available or more expensive another resource is available to take its place.

[8]We depend on a great many different materials in our daily lives. [9]Wealthy countries use large quantities of resources, causing depletion of some *mineral resources*. [10]Mineral wastes and other materials accumulate in landfills. [11]Recycling can help conserve landfill space as well as reducing resource use.

[12]Over time, society has changed its use of *energy resources* from wood to coal, oil and gas. [13]At present the world is dependent on fossil fuels for energy. [14]The United States has abundant coal resources. [15]Although the United States is a major oil producer it must import most its oil from other countries. [16]Growing worldwide demand has caused large increases in energy prices. [17]As fossil fuels are depleted, we will need to use energy more efficiently and develop other sources of energy. [18]Nuclear power, renewable electricity, and energy conservation are promising new sources of energy.

[19]*Air pollution* is a concentration of trace substances at a greater level than occurs in average air. [20]Acid deposition and pollution of urban areas are particularly harmful forms of contemporary air pollution. [21]Acid deposition is a regional problem that is most acute in areas that burn large amounts of coal, or have large numbers of automobiles and fossil-fuel fired power plants. [22]Air pollution is particularly severe in urban areas where there is a large concentration of pollution sources. [23]*Water pollution* results from both point and nonpoint sources. [24]Industrial facilities and municipal sewage plants are important point sources while agricultural and urban runoff are significant non point sources. [25]Pollution prevention is a promising approach to reducing water pollution.

[26]Forests are an example of a resource with many different uses, and conflicts over which uses are most important often arise. [27]Among the important uses of forests are timber products such as lumber and paper, recreation, biodiversity preservation, and carbon storage. [28]Sustained yield management is a strategy that attempts to balance the productive use of a resource while not depleting its supply.

—From *Introduction to Geography: People, Places, and Environment,* 4th ed., pp. 352–353, 388–389 by Edward Bergman and William H. Renwick. Copyright © 2008 by Pearson Education, Inc. Printed and Electronically reproduced by permission of Pearson Education, Inc., Upper Saddle River, NJ.

After Reading: Complete the following SQ3R Study Guide with information from the passages.

SQ3R Study Guide: *Earth's Resources and Environmental Protection*	
Natural resource	3. An element of the physical environment . . . useful to people
Renewable resources	4. Air, water, soil, plants, and animals
5. Nonrenewable resources	6. Fossil fuels and nonenergy minerals
Energy sources	7. Wood, coal, oil and gas
New energy sources	8. Nuclear power, renewable electricity, and energy conservation
Air pollution	9. A concentration of trace substances at a greater level than occurs in average air
Water pollution	10. Results from both point and non point sources

VISUAL VOCABULARY

Steam rises from bore holes at Nesjavellir Geothermal Power Plant in Iceland. Geothermal power is a

b _____ energy source.

  a. nonrenewable
  b. renewable

REVIEW TEST 3

Score (number correct) _____ × 25 = _____%

Reading Textbook Selections

Before Reading: Survey the following passage from a college education textbook. Study the words in the Vocabulary Preview; then skim the passage, noting terms in **bold** or *italic* type. Answer the Before Reading questions that follow the passage. Then, read the passage and answer the After Reading questions that follow.

Textbook
Skills

Vocabulary Preview

preferences (sentence 9): favored choices
solitary (sentence 11): private, alone, independent
distinction (sentence 19): difference, trait
dimension (sentence chart): aspect, feature, trait
facets (sentence 21): aspect, feature, trait
cognitive (sentence 21): mental
spatial (sentence 21): physical space

10.8 GE/514 words   **Learning Preferences**

[1]Since the late 1970s, a great deal has been written about differences in students' learning preferences. [2]Learning preferences are often called *learning styles* in these writings, but I believe preferences is a more accurate label because the "styles" are determined by your preferences for particular learning environments—for example, where, when, with whom, or with what lighting, food, or music you like to study. [3]I like to study and write during large blocks of time—all day, if I don't have classes. [4]I usually make some kind of commitment or deadline every week so that I have to work in long stretches to finish the work before that deadline. [5]Then I take a day off. [6]When I plan or think, I have to see my thinking in writing. [7]I have a colleague who draws diagrams of relationships when she listens to a speaker or plans a paper. [8]You may be similar or very different, but we all may work effectively. [9]But are these **preferences** important for learning?

[10]Some proponents of learning styles believe that students learn more when they study in their preferred setting and manner. [11]And there is evidence that very bright students need less structure and prefer quiet, **solitary** learning. [12]But most educational psychologists are skeptical about the value of learning preferences. [13]"The reason researchers roll their eyes at learning styles research is the utter failure to find that assessing children's learning styles and matching to instructional methods has any effect on their learning" (Stahl, 2002, p. 99).

[14]Students, especially younger ones, may not be the best judges of how they should learn. [15]Sometimes, students, particularly those who have difficulty, prefer what is easy and comfortable; real learning can be hard and uncomfortable. [16]Sometimes, students prefer to learn in a certain way because they have no alternatives; it is the only way they know how to approach the task. [17]These students may benefit from developing new—and perhaps more effective—ways to learn. [18]One final consideration: Many of the learning styles advocates imply that the differences in the learner are what matter.

Visual/Verbal Distinctions

[19]There is one learning styles **distinction** that has research support. [20]Richard Mayer has been studying the distinction between visual and verbal learners, with a focus on learning from computer-based multimedia. [21]He is finding that there is a visualizer-verbalizer dimension and that it has three **facets:** *cognitive spatial* ability (low or high), *cognitive style* (visualizer vs. verbalizer), and *learning preference* (verbal learner vs. visual learner), as shown in the following table.

Three Facets of the Visualizer-Verbalizer Dimension

There are three **dimensions** to visual versus verbal learning: ability, style, and preference. Individuals can be high or low on any or all of these dimensions.

Facet	Types of Learners	Definition
Cognitive Ability	High spatial ability	Good abilities to create, remember, and manipulate images and spatial information
	Low spatial ability	Poor abilities to create, remember, and manipulate images and spatial information
Cognitive Style	Visualizer	Thinks using images and visual information
	Verbalizer	Thinks using words and verbal information
Learning Preference	Visual learner	Prefers instruction using pictures
	Verbal learner	Prefers instruction using words

—From "Types of Learners Table" and "Three Facets of the Visualizer-Verbalizer Dimension" by Richard E. Mayer from *Journal of Educational Psychology*, 2003. Copyright © 2003 by the American Psychological Association. Adapted and Reprinted by permission of author and American Psychological Association, Washington, D.C.

[22]The picture is more complex than simply categorizing a student as either a visual or a verbal learner. [23]Students might have preferences for learning with pictures, but their low spatial ability could make using pictures to learn less effective. [24]These differences can be reliably measured, but research has not identified the effects of teaching to these styles.

—From *Educational Psychology,* 10th ed., pp. 124–127 by Anita E. Woolfolk.
Copyright © 2007 by Pearson Education, Inc. Reproduced
by permission of Pearson Education, Inc., Boston, MA.

Before Reading

1. What do I already know about learning styles? <u>Answers may vary. I don't</u>
<u>know very much about learning styles. I know I need to hear something to</u>
<u>remember it, so I like to go to class and listen to the teacher's explanations.</u>

2. What do I need to learn? <u>Answers may vary. Possible answers: learning</u>
<u>preferences, visualizer, verbalizer, what my learning style is.</u>

After Reading

3. According to the chart, the three dimensions to visual versus verbal learning
are <u>ability</u>, <u>style</u>, and <u>preference</u>.

4. Which of the terms—verbalizer or visualizer—describes you as a learner?
Explain why. <u>Answers may vary. Possible answer: I am a visualizer. Charts,</u>
<u>graphs, and drawings really help me learn.</u>

WHAT DO YOU THINK?

What do you think is the best environment for learning? What kind of support and teaching do you need, based on your learning preference? Assume you have been asked to become a peer counselor in the learning center of your college or university. As part of the training program for peer counselors, you are required to go through some of the same activities required of students who seek academic support. You have been asked to prepare a report about your understanding and use of learning preferences. Based on the chart in the passage, identify and describe the ways in which you or someone you know is a visualizer-verbalizer. Be sure to give examples based on your experiences or observations of others.

REVIEW TEST 4

Score (number correct) _____ × 10 = _____%

Textbook
Skills

Before Reading: Survey the following passage from the college textbook *Criminal Justice Today*. Study the words in the Vocabulary Preview. Then, skim the passage and answer the Before Reading questions that follow the passage. Next, read the passage and answer the After Reading questions that follow.

Vocabulary Preview

ingestible (sentence 2): able to be absorbed into the body
social convention (sentence 6): rule, principle, standard, custom
inherent (sentence 6): basic, natural, inbuilt
legitimate (sentence 25): legal, lawful
psychoactive (sentence 29): drugs or medications having a significant effect on mood or behavior
anesthetic (sentence 31): substance that dulls pain
advocated (sentence 33): supported, promoted
strictures (sentence 35): limits, restrictions, severe criticism

13.2 GE/713 words   **What Is a Drug?**

¹Before we begin any comprehensive discussion of drugs, we must first grapple with the concept of what a drug is. ²In common usage, a *drug* may be any **ingestible** substance that has a noticeable effect on the mind or body. ³Drugs may enter the body via injection, inhalation, swallowing, or even direct absorption through the skin or mucous membranes. ⁴Some drugs, like penicillin and tranquilizers, are useful in medical treatment, while others, like heroin and cocaine, are attractive only to *recreational drug* users or to those who are addicted to them.

⁵In determining which substances should be called "drugs," it is important to recognize the role that social definitions of any phenomenon play in our understanding of it. ⁶Hence, what Americans today consider to be a drug depends more on **social convention** or agreed-on

definitions than it does on any **inherent** property of the substance itself. [7]The history of marijuana provides a case in point. [8]Before the early twentieth century, marijuana was freely available in the United States. [9]Although alcohol was the recreational drug of choice at the time, marijuana found a following among some artists and musicians. [10]Marijuana was also occasionally used for medical purposes to "calm the nerves" and to treat hysteria. [11]Howard Becker, in his classic study of the early Federal Bureau of Narcotics (forerunner of the Drug Enforcement Administration, or DEA), demonstrates how federal agencies worked to outlaw marijuana in order to increase their power. [12]Federally funded publications voiced calls for laws against the substance. [13]And movies like *Reefer Madness* led the drive toward classifying marijuana as a dangerous drug. [14]The 1939 Marijuana Tax Act was the result, and marijuana has been thought of as a drug worthy of federal and local enforcement efforts ever since.

[15]Both the law and social convention make strong distinctions between drugs that are socially acceptable and those that are not. [16]Some substances with profound effects on the mind and body are not even thought of as drugs. [17]Gasoline fumes, chemical vapors of many kinds, perfumes, certain vitamins, sugar-rich foods, and toxic chemicals may all have profound effects. [18]Even so, most people do not think of these substances as drugs. [19]And they are rarely regulated by the criminal law.

[20]Recent social awareness has reclassified alcohol, caffeine, and nicotine as "drugs." [21]However, before the 1960s it is doubtful that most Americans would have applied that word to these three substances. [22]Even today, alcohol, caffeine, and nicotine are readily available throughout the country, with only minimal controls on their manufacture and distribution. [23]As a result, these three drugs continue to enjoy favored status in both our law and culture. [24]Nonetheless, alcohol abuse and addiction are commonplace in American society, and anyone who has tried to quit smoking knows the power that nicotine can wield.

[25]Occupying a middle ground on the continuum between acceptability and illegality are substances that have a **legitimate** medical use and are usually available only with a prescription. [26]Antibiotics, diet pills, and, in particular, tranquilizers, stimulants, and mood-altering chemicals (like the popular drug Prozac) are culturally acceptable but typically can be attained legally only with a physician's prescription.

²⁷The majority of Americans clearly recognize these substances as drugs, albeit useful ones.

²⁸Powerful drugs, those with the ability to produce substantially altered states of consciousness and with a high potential for addiction, occupy the forefront in social and legal condemnation. ²⁹Among them are *psychoactive* substances like heroin, peyote, mescaline, LSD, and cocaine. ³⁰Even here, however, legitimate uses for such drugs may exist. ³¹Cocaine is used in the treatment of certain medical conditions and can be applied as a topical **anesthetic** during medical interventions. ³²LSD has been employed experimentally to investigate the nature of human consciousness, and peyote and mescaline may be used legally by members of the Native American Church in religious services. ³³Even heroin has been **advocated** as beneficial in relieving the suffering associated with some forms of terminal illness. ³⁴Hence, answers to the question of "What is a drug?" depend to a large extent on the social definitions and conventions operating at a given time and in a given place. ³⁵Some of the clearest definitional statements relating to controlled substances can be found in the law, although informal **strictures** and definitions guide much of everyday drug use.

—From *Criminal Justice Today: An Introductory Text for the 21st Century*, 10th ed., p. 578 by Frank J. Schmalleger. Copyright © 2009 by Pearson Education, Inc. Printed and Electronically reproduced by permission of Pearson Education, Inc., Upper Saddle River, NJ.

Before Reading

1. What is the topic? The definition of "drug"

2. What is the purpose for reading? To understand the definition of the term "drug" in terms of criminal justice.

After Reading

Complete the following chart with information from the passage

The Continuum of Acceptability and Illegality of Drugs

Socially Acceptable	Middle Ground	Illegal
3. alcohol	6. prescription drugs, diet pills, tranquilizers, stimulants,	8. heroin
4. caffeine		9. cocaine
5. nicotine	7. mood-altering drugs	10. marijuana

WHAT DO YOU THINK?

Would you be in favor of "reclassifying" any drugs that are currently considered illegal? Would you be in favor of reclassifying any drugs that are currently considered legal? Which ones and why? Have the government efforts to curtail use of illegal drugs been effective? Why or why not? Assume you are interested in a career in criminal justice and you are serving as a volunteer with your local police department. One of your duties is to help educate the public about important local issues. Your assignment today is to speak at a middle school about drugs. Based on the passage you just read, what do you want to share with the students? Write an essay in which you discuss the drug issue with this group of youth.

After Reading About a System for Master Readers

Before you move on to the Mastery Tests on a reading system for master readers, take time to reflect on your learning and performance by answering the following questions. Write your answers in your notebook.

- How has my knowledge base or prior knowledge changed about a reading system such as SQ3R?
- Based on my studies, how do I think I will perform on the Mastery Test(s)? Why do I think my scores will be above average, average, or below average?
- Would I recommend this chapter to other students who want to learn more about a reading system such as SQ3R. Why or why not?

Test your understanding of what you have learned about a Reading System for Master Readers by completing the Chapter 1 Review Card in the insert near the end of your text.

CONNECT TO **myreadinglab**

To check your progress in meeting Chapter 1's learning outcomes, log in to **www.myreadinglab.com** and try the following activities.

- The "Memorization and Concentration" section of MyReadingLab ties the use of prior knowledge to your ability to focus on and remember what you have read. To access this resource, click on the "Study Plan" tab. Then click on "Memorization and Concentration." Under the heading "Review Materials," choose option #3 "Model: Concentration and Memorization."

- The "Active Reading Strategies" section of MyReadingLab offers an overview, model, slide show, practices, and tests about the reading process. To access this resource, go to MyReadingLab.com. Click on the "Study Plan" tab. Then choose "Active Reading Strategies" from the menu.

- The "Reading Textbooks" section of MyReadingLab offers an overview, model, slide show, practices, and tests about the reading process and textbooks. For example, to learn about how to survey a textbook, click on "Reading Textbooks." Then, under the heading "Review Materials," choose option #2 "Model: Reading Textbooks." To learn more about applying SQ3R to textbook reading, choose option #3 "Model: SQ3R."

- To measure your mastery of the content of this chapter, complete the tests in the "Reading Textbooks" section and click on Gradebook to find your results.

Using SQ3R, read the following passage from a college economics textbook.

Textbook Skills   10.2 GE/442 words   **A Nation on the Move**

[1]World War II had a greater impact than the Depression on the future of American life. [2]While American soldiers and sailors fought abroad, the nation underwent sweeping social and economic changes at home.

[3]The war led to a vast migration of the American population. [4]Young men left their homes for training camps and then for service overseas. [5]Defense workers and their families, some nine million people in all, moved to work in the new booming shipyards, munitions factories, and aircraft plants. [6]Rural areas lost population while coastal regions, especially along the Pacific and the Gulf of Mexico, drew millions of people. [7]The location of army camps in the South and West created boom conditions in the future Sunbelt, as did the concentration of aircraft factories and shipyards in this region. [8]California had the greatest gains, adding nearly two million to its population in less than five years.

[9]This movement of people caused severe social problems. [10]Housing was in short supply. [11]Migrating workers crowded into house trailers and boardinghouses, bringing unexpected windfalls to landlords. [12]In one boomtown, a reporter described an old Victorian house that had five bedrooms on the second floor. [13]"Three of them," he wrote, "held two cots apiece, the two others held three cots." [14]But the owner revealed that "the third floor is where we pick up the velvet. . . . We rent to workers in different shifts . . . three shifts a day . . . seven bucks a week apiece."

[15]Family life suffered under these crowded living conditions. [16]An increase in the number of marriages, as young couples searched for something to hang on to in the midst of wartime turmoil, was offset by a rising divorce rate. [17]The baby boom that would peak in the 1950s began during the war and brought its own set of problems. [18]Only a few publicly funded day-care centers were available, and working mothers worried about their "latchkey children."

[19]Despite these problems, women found the war a time of economic opportunity. [20]The demand for workers led to a dramatic rise in women's employment, from fourteen million working women in 1940 to nineteen million by 1945. [21]Most of the new women workers were married and many were middle-aged, thus broadening the composition of the female workforce, which in the past had been composed primarily of young single women. [22]Women entered industries once viewed as exclusively male; by the end of the war, they worked alongside men tending blast furnaces in steel mills and welding hulls in shipyards. [23]Women enjoyed the hefty weekly paychecks, which rose by

50 percent from 1941 to 1943, and they took pride in their contributions to the war effort.

—From *The American Story,* 1st ed. pp. 886, 888, 890 by Robert A. Divine, George M. Fredrickson, R. Hal Williams and T. H. Breen. Copyright © 2002 by Pearson Education, Inc. Reprinted by permission of Pearson Education, Inc., Upper Saddle River, NJ.

1. What is the topic of this passage? The topic is shifts in the American population during World War II.

2–5. Complete the concept map that follows with information from the passage.

A Nation on the Move

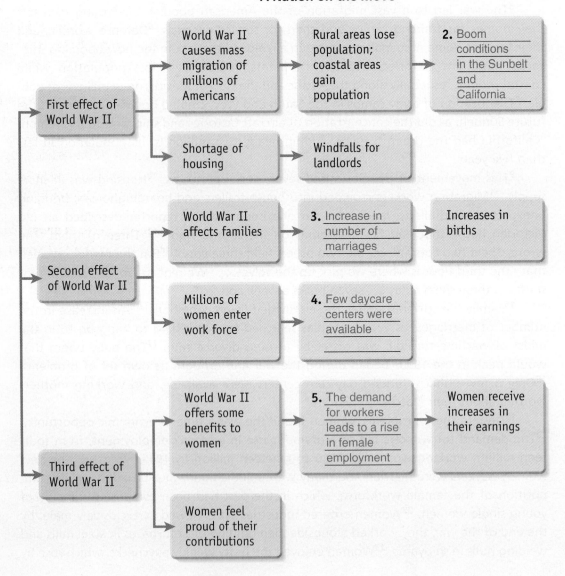

First effect of World War II

World War II causes mass migration of millions of Americans → Rural areas lose population; coastal areas gain population → **2.** Boom conditions in the Sunbelt and California

Shortage of housing → Windfalls for landlords

Second effect of World War II

World War II affects families → **3.** Increase in number of marriages → Increases in births

Millions of women enter work force → **4.** Few daycare centers were available

Third effect of World War II

World War II offers some benefits to women → **5.** The demand for workers leads to a rise in female employment → Women receive increases in their earnings

Women feel proud of their contributions

Using SQ3R, read the following passage taken from a college literature textbook.

Textbook
Skills

10.1 GE/325 words

Saying and Suggesting

[1]To write so clearly that they might bring "all things as near the mathematical plainness" as possible—that was the goal of scientists according to Bishop Thomas Sprat, who lived in the seventeenth century. [2]Such an effort would seem bound to fail, because words, unlike numbers, are ambiguous indicators. [3]Although it may have troubled Bishop Sprat, the tendency of a word to have multiplicity of meaning rather than mathematical plainness opens broad avenues to poetry.

[4]Every word has at least one **denotation**: a meaning as defined in a dictionary. [5]But the English language has many a common word with so many denotations that a reader may need to think twice to see what it means in a specific context. [6]The noun *field*, for instance, can denote a piece of ground, a sports arena, the scene of a battle, part of a flag, a profession, and a number system in mathematics. [7]Further, the word can be used as a verb ("he *fielded* a grounder") or an adjective (*field trip, field glasses*).

[8]A word also has **connotations**: overtones or suggestions of additional meaning that it gains from all the contexts in which we have met it in the past. [9]The word *skeleton*, according to a dictionary, denotes "the bony framework of a human being or other vertebrate animal, which supports the flesh and protects the organs." [10]But by its associations, the word can rouse thoughts of war, of disease and death, or (possibly) of one's plans to go to medical school. [11]Think, too, of the difference between "Old Doc Jones" and "Abner P. Jones, M.D." [12]In the mind's eye, the former appears in his shirtsleeves; the latter has a gold nameplate on his door. [13]That some words denote the same thing but have sharply different connotations is pointed out in this anonymous Victorian jingle:

[14]Here's a little ditty that you really ought to know:
Horses "sweat" and men "perspire," but ladies only "glow."

—From *Literature: An Introduction to Fiction, Poetry, and Drama,*
4th Compact Edition by X. J. Kennedy and Dana Gioia. Copyright
© 2005 by Pearson Education, Inc. Reprinted by permission of
Pearson Education, Inc., Glenview, IL.

1. What is the topic of this passage? The topic of this passage is the differences between saying something directly and suggesting it.

Term	Definition	Example
2. Denotation	**3.** a meaning as defined in the dictionary	*Field* can denote a piece of ground, a sports arena, the scene of a battle, part of a flag, a profession, and a number system in mathematics.
Connotation	**4.** overtone or suggestion of meanings based on associations of context	**5.** Skeleton can rouse thoughts of war, disease, and death.

Using SQ3R, read the following passage from a college psychology textbook.

Textbook
Skills

13.1 GE/293 words

Nonassertiveness, Aggressiveness, and Assertiveness

1. What are the traits of nonassertive behavior?

failure to assert rights,

unquestioning obedience, need

for permission, "you win, I lose"

philosophy, anxiety, low self-

esteem

2. What are the traits of aggressive behavior?

self-focused, disrespectful of

others, "I win, you lose"

philosophy, overly sensitive,

argumentative

3. What are the traits of assertive behavior?

firm, fair, "I win, you win" philoso-

phy, positive, respectful of others

[1]The nature of assertive communication can be better understood by distinguishing it from nonassertiveness and aggressiveness.

[2]**Nonassertiveness** refers to a lack of assertiveness in certain types of or in all communication situations. [3]People who are nonassertive fail to assert their rights. [4]In many instances, these people do what others tell them to do—parents, employers, and the like—without questioning and without concern for what is best for them. [5]They operate with a "You win, I lose" philosophy. [6]Nonassertive people often ask permission from others to do what is their perfect right. [7]Social situations create anxiety for these individuals, and their self-esteem is generally low.

[8]**Aggressiveness** is the other extreme. [9]Aggressive people operate with an "I win, you lose" philosophy; they care little for what the other person wants and focus only on their own needs. [10]Some people communicate aggressively only under certain conditions or in certain situations (for example, after being taken advantage of over a long period of time) while others communicate aggressively in all or at least most situations. [11]Aggressive communicators think little of the opinions, values, or beliefs of others and yet are extremely sensitive to others' criticism of their own behaviors. [12]Consequently, they frequently get into arguments with others.

[13]**Assertive behavior**—behavior that enables you to act in your own best interests without denying or infringing upon the rights of others—is the generally desired alternative to nonassertiveness or aggressiveness. [14]Assertive people operate with an "I win, you win" philosophy; they assume that both people can gain something from an interpersonal

4. What is the purpose of this passage?

To inform the reader about the

difference between nonassertive,

aggressive, and assertive behav-

ior; to convince the reader that

assertive behavior is the most

positive of the three behaviors

interaction. [15]Assertive people are willing to assert their own rights. [16]Unlike their aggressive counterparts, however, they don't hurt others in the process. [17]Assertive people speak their minds and welcome others' doing likewise.

—From *The Interpersonal Communication Book,* 10th ed., p. 149 by Joseph A. DeVito. Copyright © 2004 by Pearson Education, Inc. Reproduced by permission of Pearson Education, Inc., Boston, MA.

VISUAL VOCABULARY

Road rage is an example of which type of behavior?

c _____

a. assertive
b. nonassertive
c. aggressive

Read the following passage from a college science textbook. As you read, answer the questions in the box.

10.2 GE/237 words

Textbook
Skills

1. What is a food chain?

A food chain is a descriptive

diagram that represents the flow

of food energy from prey (the

consumed) to predator (the

consumer).

2. What are basal species?
Give an example.

Basal species, such as grass,

feed on no other species but are

fed upon by others.

3. What are intermediate
species? Give an example.

Intermediate species, such as

grasshoppers, feed on other

species, and they are prey

of other species.

4. What are top predators?
Give an example.

Top predators, such as the hawk,

are not subjected to predators

and prey on intermediate and

basal species.

Food Webs Describe Species Interactions

[1]Perhaps the most fundamental process in nature is the acquisition of food, or the energy and nutrients required for assimilation. [2]Ecologists studying the structure of communities often focus on the feeding relationships of the various species, or the manner in which species interact in the process of acquiring food.

[3]An abstract representation of feeding relationships within a community is the food chain. [4]A **food chain** is a descriptive diagram: a series of arrows, each pointing from one species to another. [5]The diagram represents the flow of food energy from prey (the consumed) to predator (the consumer). [6]For example, grasshoppers eat grass; clay-colored sparrows eat grasshoppers; and marsh hawks prey on the sparrows. [7]We write this relationship as follows:

grass ⟶ grasshopper ⟶ sparrow ⟶ hawk

[8]Feeding relationships in nature, however, are not simple, straight-line food chains. [9]Rather, they involve numerous food chains meshed into a complex food web with links leading from primary producers through an array of consumers. [10]Such food webs are highly interwoven. [11]Links represent a wide variety of species interactions.

[12]The species in a food web are distinguished by whether they are basal species, intermediate species,

or top predators. [13]**Basal species** feed on no other species but are fed upon by others. [14]**Intermediate species** feed on other species, and they are prey of other species. [15]Top **predators** are not subjected to predators and prey on intermediate and basal species.

> —Adapted from *Elements of Ecology*, 6th ed., pp. 340–341 by Thomas M. Smith and Robert Leo Smith. Copyright © 2006 by Pearson Education, Inc. Reprinted by permission of Pearson Education, Inc., Glenview, IL.

VISUAL VOCABULARY

This photograph illustrates the three levels in the food chain: The grass is the ^b_____. The zebra are members of the ^c_____. And the lion is the ^a_____.

    a. top predator.
    b. basal species.
    c. intermediate species.

Vocabulary Skills

2

LEARNING OUTCOMES

After studying this chapter, you should be able to do the following:

1. Define vocabulary. [Knowledge]
2. Classify context clues using SAGE. [Analysis]
3. Describe how to comprehend new words as you read. [Knowledge]
4. Assess your comprehension of context clues. [Evaluate]
5. Analyze the meaning of a word based on word parts. [Analysis]
6. Use a glossary. [Application]
7. Evaluate the importance of what you have learned about vocabulary skills. [Evaluate]
8. Apply what you have learned about vocabulary skills to your reading process. [Application]

 ## Before Reading About Vocabulary Skills

Chapter 1 taught you the importance of surveying material before you begin reading by skimming the information for **bold** or *italic* type. Throughout this textbook, key ideas are emphasized in bold or italic print where they appear in the passage; often they are also set apart visually in a box that gives the definition or examples of the term. Skim the chapter for key ideas in boxes that will help you understand vocabulary skills. Refer to these boxes and create at least six questions that you can answer as you read the chapter. Write your questions in the following spaces (record the page number for the key term in each question):

What is vocabulary _____? (page __48__)

What is a context clue _____? (page __49__)

What are signal words for synonyms _____? (page __49__)

What are the signal words for antonyms _____? (page __51__)

What are the signal words for examples _____? (page ___54___)

What is a glossary _____? (page ___55___)

Compare the questions you created with the following questions. Then, write the ones that seem most helpful in your notebook, leaving enough space after each question to record the answers as you read and study the chapter.

What is vocabulary? (page 48) What is a context clue? (page 49) What are the signal words for synonyms? (page 49) What are the signal words for antonyms? (page 51) What are the signal words for examples? (page 54) What is a glossary? (page 55) What are roots, prefixes, and suffixes? (page 59) How will knowing about these vocabulary skills help me develop my vocabulary? (pages 48 and 59)

Words Are Building Blocks

Words are the building blocks of meaning. Have you ever watched a child with a set of building blocks such as Legos? Hundreds of separate pieces can be joined together to create buildings, planes, cars, or even spaceships. Words are like that, too. A word is the smallest unit of thought. Words properly joined create meaning.

> **Vocabulary** is all the words used or understood by a person.

How many words do you have in your **vocabulary**? If you are like most people, by the time you are 18 years old, you know about 60,000 words. During your college studies, you will most likely learn an additional 20,000 words. Each subject you study will have its own set of words. There are several ways to study vocabulary.

Context Clues: A SAGE Approach

Master readers interact with new words in a number of ways. One way is to use **context clues**. The meaning of a word is shaped by its context. The word *context* means "surroundings." The meaning of a word is shaped by the words surrounding it—its context. Master readers use context clues to learn new words.

> A **context clue** is the information that surrounds a new word, used to understand its meaning.

There are four types of context clues:

- Synonyms
- Antonyms
- General context
- Examples

Notice that, put together, the first letter of each context clue spells the word SAGE. The word *sage* means "wise." Using context clues is a wise—a SAGE—reading strategy.

Synonyms

A **synonym** is a word that has the same or nearly the same meaning as another word. Many times, an author will place a synonym near a new or difficult word as a context clue to the word's meaning. Usually, a synonym is set off with a pair of commas, a pair of dashes, or a pair of parentheses before and after it.

Synonym Signal Words	
or	that is

EXAMPLES Each of the following sentences has a key word in **bold** type. In each sentence, underline the signal words and then circle the synonym for the word in **bold**.

1. To ensure personal safety, be **cognizant,** or aware, of your surroundings.

2. Many crimes are committed against women who are **oblivious,** that is, uninformed and ignorant, about how to protect themselves.

VISUAL VOCABULARY

Self-defense training makes women _b_____ of tactics they can use to ensure their safety.

   a. fearful
   b. cognizant
   c. skilled

EXPLANATIONS

1. The signal word *or* clues the reader that the synonym for *cognizant* is *aware*.

2. The signal words *that is* clue the reader that the synonyms for *oblivious* are *uninformed* and *ignorant*.

PRACTICE 1

Each of the following sentences contains a word that is a synonym for the word in **bold** type. Underline the signal words and circle the synonym in each sentence.

1. Idris is known for his **discreet**, or tactful, manner of handling personnel issues.

2. **Indigent**, that is, poverty-stricken, people do not have access to health care.

3. Rocky's poetry has a **lyrical**, or musical, quality.

Antonyms

An **antonym** is a word that has the opposite meaning of another word. Antonyms help you see the shade of a word's meaning by showing you what the original word is *not*. The following contrast words often act as signals that an antonym is being used.

Antonym Signal Words		
but	not	unlike
however	on the other hand	yet
in contrast		

Sometimes antonyms can be found next to the new word. In those cases, commas, dashes, or parentheses set them off. At other times, antonyms are placed in other parts of the sentence to emphasize the contrast between the ideas.

EXAMPLES In each sentence, underline the signal words and circle the antonym for the word in **bold** type. In the blank, write the letter of the word that best defines the word in **bold.**

_____a_____ **1.** Marcel **facilitated** the study group's progress with his thoughtful questions; in contrast, Randy hindered their ability to concentrate with his inappropriate jokes.
   a. assisted   c. deepened
   b. impeded   d. recorded

_____b_____ **2.** After purchasing a painting by the famous artist Monet, Charlene discovered the piece was a **facsimile**, not an original.
   a. innovation   c. rarity
   b. copy   d. spare

EXPLANATIONS

1. The signal words *in contrast* clue the reader to the antonym hindered. The best definition of the word *facilitated* is (a) *assisted.*

2. The signal word *not* clues the reader to the antonym *original.* The best definition of the word *facsimile* is (b) *copy.*

PRACTICE 2

In each sentence, underline the signal words and circle the antonym for the word in **bold** type. In the blank, write the letter of the word that best defines the word in **bold.**

_____c_____ **1.** The explanation the defense offered for the crime seems **credible.** It is not at all far-fetched, as the prosecution accuses.
   a. mature   c. trustworthy
   b. absurd   d. crazy

___d___   **2.** The candidate gave a long, **discursive** speech when instead she
should have made the speech short and direct.
  a. entertaining   c. important
  b. boring   d. rambling

___c___   **3.** Before cosmetic surgery, Rory's face was **craggy** with age lines, but
now after surgery, his complexion is smooth again.
  a. sagging   c. rough
  b. damaging   d. ugly

General Context

Often you will find that the author has not provided a synonym clue or an
antonym clue. In that case, you will have to rely on the general context of the
passage to figure out the meaning of the unfamiliar word. This requires you to
read the entire sentence, or to read ahead for a few sentences, for information
that will help you understand the new word.

Information about the word can be included in the passage in several
ways. Sometimes a definition of the word may be provided. Vivid word pictures
or descriptions of a situation can provide a sense of the word's meaning.
Sometimes you may need to figure out the meaning of an unknown word by
using logic and reasoning skills.

EXAMPLES   In the blank, write the letter of the word that best defines the
word in **bold** type.

Textbook
Skills

___b___   **1. Chronically** ill people may never regain the full level of health they
experienced before the onset of their illnesses, and they may face a
continuing loss of function and the constant threat of ever more
serious medical problems as their illness progresses.

> —From *Healthstyles: Decisions for Living Well,* 2nd ed., p. 344 by B. E.
> Pruitt and Jane J. Stein. Copyright © 1999 by Pearson Education, Inc.
> Printed and Electronically reproduced by permission of Pearson
> Education, Inc., Upper Saddle River, NJ.

  a. slightly   c. briefly
  b. permanently   d. effectively

___c___   **2.** Nitrogen is one of the most **essential** nutrients for life, and it
increases the fertility of soil and water.

> —From *Elements of Ecology,* 4th ed., p. 349 by Thomas M. Smith
> and Robert Leo Smith. Copyright © 2000 by Pearson Education, Inc.
> Reprinted by permission of Pearson Education, Inc., Glenview, IL.

  a. minor   c. necessary
  b. optional   d. possible

EXPLANATIONS

1. The best meaning of the word *chronically* is (b) *permanently*. Clues from the sentence are the words and phrases *never regain, continuing loss, constant, ever more serious,* and *progresses*.

2. The best meaning of the word *essential* is (c) *necessary*. A clue word is *most*, which describes the word *essential*. The way the word *essential* is used in the sentence also provides a clue, for it describes *nutrients*. Even if the meaning of *nutrients* is not clear, the reader knows from the rest of the sentence that nutrients improve soil and water (by increasing its fertility). Thus the reader can conclude that the *most essential nutrients* are necessary.

PRACTICE 3

Each of the following sentences has a word in **bold** type. In the blank, write the letter of the word that best defines the word in **bold.**

Textbook
Skills

___b___ 1. Parental restrictiveness and harsh criticism are also associated with a greater likelihood of a teenager smoking. **Conversely,** affection, emotional support, and participation in meaningful conversations at home more often result in the teenager not smoking.

—From *HealthStyles: Decisions for Living Well,* 2nd ed., p. 181 by B. E. Pruitt and Jane J. Stein. Copyright © 1999 by Pearson Education, Inc. Printed and Electronically reproduced by permission of Pearson Education, Inc., Upper Saddle River, NJ.

a. additionally   c. surprisingly
b. in contrast   d. as a result

___c___ 2. Fear **galvanized** my entire body, and I ran faster than I have ever run before, my heart thumping wildly.
a. froze   c. stimulated
b. broke   d. strained

___b___ 3. The statement "Bill is **at least** 21 years old" can also be expressed or translated into the following mathematical language: $b > 21$.
a. less than or equal to   c. less than
b. greater than or equal to d. equal to

Examples

Many times an author will show the meaning of a new or difficult word by providing an example. Signal words indicate that an example is coming.

Example Signal Words				
consists of	for example	for instance	including	such as

Colons and dashes can also indicate examples.

EXAMPLE Using example clues, choose the correct meaning of the words in **bold** type.

_____ c **1.** Some people believe that the pesticides used on foods cause serious physical **impairments** such as weakened kidneys and a more fragile immune system.

    a. improvements   c. injuries

    b. laws   d. pairings

_____ d **2.** Some students find **collaborative** learning helps them understand and retain information; for example, Nicole, Vejay, and Chad meet every Tuesday and Thursday in the library to compare notes and help each other prepare for tests.

    a. additional   c. independent

    b. intense   d. shared

EXPLANATIONS

    1. The best meaning of the word *impairments* is (c) *injuries*.

    2. The best meaning of the word *collaborative* is (d) *shared*.

PRACTICE 4

Using example clues, choose the correct meaning of the word in **bold** type.

Textbook
Skills

_____ c **1.** Your **habitat** could be the country you live in, your state and city of residence, or the location of your home. Depending on your activity, such as eating, it could be your kitchen. The same is true for other organisms.

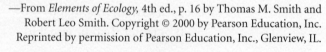
—From *Elements of Ecology*, 4th ed., p. 16 by Thomas M. Smith and Robert Leo Smith. Copyright © 2000 by Pearson Education, Inc. Reprinted by permission of Pearson Education, Inc., Glenview, IL.

Textbook
Skills

    a. lifestyle   c. territory

    b. work   d. reward

_____ a **2.** **Figurative** language (also known as a figure of speech) departs from the literal meanings of words, usually by comparing very different ideas or objects; for instance, "thorny problems" compares the pain of a problem or situation to the pricking pain of a thorn in the flesh.

—Adapted from *The Little, Brown Handbook,* 9th ed., p. 560 by H. Ramsey Fowler and Jane E. Aaron. Copyright © 2004 by Pearson Education, Inc. Reprinted by permission of Pearson Education, Inc., Glenview, IL.

a. symbolic   c. old-fashioned

b. factual   d. basic

Textbook
Skills

Reading a Textbook: Using a Glossary

Each subject or content area, such as science, mathematics, or English, has its own specialized vocabulary. As you learned in Chapter 1 (p. 16), some textbooks provide an extra section in the back of the book called a *glossary* that alphabetically lists all the specialized terms with their definitions as they were used throughout the textbook. Other textbooks may provide short glossaries within each chapter; in these cases, the glossaries may appear in the margins or in highlighted boxes, listing the words in the order that they appear on the page. The meanings given in a glossary are limited to the way in which the word or term is used in that content area.

> A **glossary** is a list of selected terms with their definitions as used in a specific area of study.

Glossaries provide excellent opportunities to use strategies before and after reading. Before reading, skim the section for specialized terms (usually these words are in **bold** or *italic* print). Checking the words and their meanings triggers prior knowledge or establishes meaning that will deepen your comprehension. In addition, you can create vocabulary review lists using glossary terms by paraphrasing or restating the definition in your own words. These vocabulary lists can be used after reading to review and test your recall of the material.

Textbook
Skills

EXAMPLE The following selection is from a college psychology textbook. Before reading, use the glossary to complete your vocabulary review list. Then, read the passage. After reading, answer the questions.

Physiological Stress Reactions

[1]How would you respond if you arrived at a class and discovered that you were about to have a pop quiz? [2]You would probably agree that

Glossary

Acute stress A transient state of arousal with typically clear onset and offset patterns.

Chronic stress A continuous state of arousal in which an individual perceives demands as greater than the inner and outer resources available for dealing with them.

Fight-or-flight response A sequence of internal activities triggered when an organism is faced with a threat; prepares the body for combat and struggle or for running away to safety; recent evidence suggests that the response is characteristic only of males.

this would cause you some stress, but what does that mean for your body's reactions? ³Many of the physiological responses we described for emotional situations are also relevant to day-to-day instances of stress. ⁴Such transient states of arousal, with typically clear onset and offset patterns, are examples of **acute stress.** ⁵**Chronic stress,** on the other hand, is a state of enduring arousal, continuing over time, in which demands are perceived as greater than the inner and outer resources available for dealing with them. ⁶An example of chronic stress might be a continuous frustration with your inability to find time to do all the things you want to do.

Emergency Reactions to Acute Threats

⁷In the 1920s, Walter Cannon outlined the first scientific description of the way animals and humans respond to danger. ⁸He found that a sequence of activity is triggered in the nerves and glands to prepare the body either to defend itself and struggle or to run away to safety. ⁹Cannon called this dual stress response the **fight-or-flight response.** ¹⁰At the center of this stress response is the *hypothalamus,* which is involved in a variety of emotional responses. ¹¹The hypothalamus has sometimes been referred to as the *stress center* because of its twin functions in emergencies: (1) it controls the autonomic nervous system (ANS) and (2) it activates the pituitary gland.

—From *Psychology and Life,* 16th ed., p. 6 by Richard J. Gerrig and Philip G. Zimbardo. Copyright © 2002 by Pearson Education, Inc. Reproduced by permission of Pearson Education, Inc., Boston, MA.

Before Reading

1. The process that readies the body to deal with danger and conflict is known as <u>fight-or-flight</u>.

2. <u>Acute stress</u> is a temporary state that arises from day-to-day instances of stress.

3. Ongoing stress that challenges available resources is known as <u>chronic stress</u>.

After Reading

___a___   **4.** The hypothalamus is also known as the
    a. stress center.
    b. autonomic nervous system.
    c. the pituitary gland.

___b___   **5.** Physiological stress reactions primarily involve
    a. the mind.
    b. the body.
    c. the emotions.

EXPLANATION

1. The process that readies the body to deal with danger and conflict is known as *fight-or-flight*. Note that the paraphrase (restatement) of the definition for fight-or-flight draws on information given in the glossary.

2. *Acute stress* is a temporary state that arises from day-to-day instances of stress.

3. Ongoing stress that challenges available resources is known as *chronic stress*.

4. The hypothalamus is also known as the (a) stress center.

5. Physiological stress reactions primarily involve (b) the body.

PRACTICE 5

The following selection is from a college psychology textbook. Before reading, use the glossary to complete your vocabulary review list. Then, read the passage. After reading, answer the questions.

Textbook Skills

Dependence and Addiction

Glossary

Psychoactive drugs
Chemicals that affect mental processes and behavior by temporarily changing conscious awareness of reality.

[1]**Psychoactive drugs** are chemicals that affect mental processes and behavior by temporarily changing conscious awareness. [2]Once in the brain, they attach themselves to synaptic receptors, blocking or stimulating certain reactions. [3]By doing so, they profoundly alter the brain's communication system, affecting perception, memory, mood, and behavior. [4]However, continued use of a given drug creates **tolerance**—greater dosages are required to achieve the same effect. . . . [5]Hand in

Glossary
Tolerance A situation that occurs with continued use of a drug in which an individual requires greater dosages to achieve the same effect.
Physiological dependence The process by which the body becomes adjusted to and dependent on a drug.
Addiction A condition in which the body requires a drug in order to function without physical and psychological reactions to its absence; often the outcome of tolerance and dependence.
Psychological dependence The psychological need or craving for a drug.

hand with tolerance is **physiological dependence,** a process in which the body becomes adjusted to and dependent on the substance, in part because neurotransmitters are depleted by the frequent presence of the drug. [6]The tragic outcome of tolerance and dependence is **addiction.** [7]A person who is addicted requires the drug in his or her body and suffers painful withdrawal symptoms (shakes, sweats, nausea, and, in the case of alcohol withdrawal, even death) if the drug is not present.

[8]When an individual finds the use of a drug so desirable or pleasurable that a *craving* develops, with or without addiction, the condition is known as **psychological dependence.** [9]Psychological dependence can occur with any drug. [10]The result of drug dependence is that a person's lifestyle comes to revolve around drug use so wholly that his or her capacity to function is limited or impaired. [11]In addition, the expense involved in maintaining a drug habit of daily—and increasing—amounts often drives an addict to robbery, assault, prostitution, or drug peddling. [12]One of the gravest dangers currently facing addicts is the threat of getting AIDS by sharing hypodermic needles—intravenous drug users can unknowingly share bodily fluids with those who have this deadly immune deficiency disease.

[13]Teenagers who use illicit drugs to relieve emotional distress and to cope with daily stressors suffer long-term negative consequences.

—From *Psychology and Life,* 16th ed., p. 174 by Richard J. Gerrig and Philip G. Zimbardo. Copyright © 2002 by Pearson Education, Inc. Reproduced by permission of Pearson Education, Inc., Boston, MA.

Before Reading

1. <u>Addiction</u>   The body requires a drug and suffers painful withdrawal symptoms if the drug is not present.

2. <u>Psychoactive drugs</u> Chemicals that affect an individual's thought processes and actions by temporarily altering the person's awareness of reality.

3. <u>Psychological dependence</u> The mental and emotional need or craving for a drug.

4. <u>Physiological dependence</u>   The body's need for a drug.

5. <u>Tolerance</u>   Greater amounts of the drug are needed for the same effect.

After Reading

Complete the following summary. Fill in the blanks with the appropriate word from the glossary.

Continued use of (6) <u>psychoactive drugs</u> leads to several serious outcomes. First, psychoactive drugs alter a person's sense of reality, "affecting perception, memory, mood, and behavior." Ongoing use of the drug causes (7) <u>tolerance</u>, a state in which the body needs more of the drug to produce the same effect. As the body develops tolerance, the body also develops (8) <u>physiological dependence</u> upon the drug. Tragically, the result of tolerance and dependence is (9) <u>addiction</u>. In addition, a person can suffer from (10) <u>psychological dependence</u>, when a "craving" for a drug "develops with or without addiction."

 ## Word Parts

Just as ideas are made up of words, words also are made up of smaller parts. *Word parts* can help you learn vocabulary more easily and quickly. In addition, knowing the meaning of the parts of words helps you understand a new word when you see it in context.

Many words are divided into the following three parts: *roots*, *prefixes*, and *suffixes*.

Root	The basic or main part of a word. Prefixes and suffixes are added to roots to make a new word. Example: *derm* means "skin."
Prefix	A group of letters with a specific meaning added to the beginning of a word (root) to make a new word. Example: the ***hypo*** in ***hypo****dermic* means "under."
Suffix	A group of letters with a specific meaning added to the end of a word (root) to make a new word. Example: the ***ic*** in *hyperderm**ic*** means "of, like, related to, being."

Master readers understand how the three word parts join together to make additional words.

Roots

The **root** is the basic or main part of a word. Many times a root combined with other word parts will create a whole family of closely related words. Even when the root word is joined with other word parts to form new words, the meaning of the root does not change. Knowing the commonly used roots will help you master many new and difficult words. A list of common roots is available on MyReadingLab.

EXAMPLES Study the following word parts. Using the meaning of the root *clamere* and the context of each sentence, put each word into the sentence that best fits its meaning. Use each word once.

Prefix: *re-*   (again, back)

Root: *clamere, claim, clam*   (call out, shout)

Suffix: *-ant*   (one who does)

claimant	reclaim

1. The city may ask to ___reclaim_____ the land it had leased to the shoe factory.

2. A ___claimant_____ is a person who files a loss with an insurance company.

EXPLANATIONS Both words contain the root *clamere* ("call out," "shout"), and each word uses the meaning differently. The additional word parts—the prefix and the suffix—created the different meanings.

1. The word *reclaim* combines the prefix *re-*, which means "again" or "back" with the root *claim*, which means "call out." *Reclaim* means "call back." The city may want to reclaim or call back control of the land it had leased.

2. The word *claimant* combines the root *claim*, which means "call out" with the suffix *-ant*, which means "one who does." A claimant is "one who calls out" for the insurance company to pay for the loss.

PRACTICE 6

Study the following word parts. Using the meaning of the root *dexter* and context clues, put each word into the sentence that best fits its meaning. Use each word once. Slight changes in spelling may be necessary.

Prefix: *ambi-* (both)
Root: *dexter* (on the right, skillful)
Suffix: *-ous* (of, like, related to, being)
  -ity (a quality)

ambidextrous	dexterity	dexterous

1. Jolene is <u>ambidextrous</u>; she can write and pitch a ball with either her right or her left hand.

2. Miguel, a <u>dexterous</u> mechanic, can rapidly rebuild an engine.

3. An Olympic gymnast must possess extraordinary <u>dexterity</u>.

Prefixes

A **prefix** is a group of letters with a specific meaning added to the beginning of a word or root to make a new word. Although the basic meaning of a root is not changed, a prefix changes the meaning of the word as a whole.

The importance of prefixes can be seen in the family of words that comes from the root *struct*, which means "build." Look over the following examples of prefixes and their meanings. Note the change in the meaning of the whole word based on the meaning of the prefix.

Prefix	Meaning	Root	Meaning	Example
con-	with, together	*struct*	build	*construct* (to build)
de-	down away, reverse			*destruct* (to destroy)
in-	in, into			*instruct* (to teach)

EXAMPLES Using the meanings of the prefixes, root, and context clues, put each word into the sentence that best fits its meaning. Use each word once.

Prefix	Meaning	Root	Meaning
dis-	apart, in different directions	*sect*	cut
inter-	among, between, in the midst		

dissect	intersect

1. Some ethicists believe that biology students should learn to <u>dissect</u> using a computer program instead of real animals, such as frogs or cats.

2. My house sits on the corner where the roads New Trail and Rio Pinar <u>intersect</u>.

EXPLANATIONS Compare your answers to the explanations below.

1. Some ethicists believe that biology students should learn how to cut apart, dissect, animals such as frogs and cats by using a computer program.

2. My house sits on the corner of two roads, New Trail and Rio Pinar, where they intersect, cross one another.

PRACTICE 7

Study the meaning of each of the following prefixes and roots.

Prefix	Meaning	Root	Meaning
circum-	around	spect	to look
intro-	inside, to the inside	stance	stand, position
retro-	backward		

Create at least three words by joining these prefixes and roots.

1. <u>Answers may vary, but include *circumstance, retrospect,*</u>

2. <u>*circumspect, introspect*</u>

3. _____

Suffixes

A **suffix** is a group of letters with a specific meaning added to the end of a word or root to make a new word. Although the basic meaning of a root does not change, a suffix can change the type of word and the way a word is used. (A list of common suffixes is available on MyReadingLab.) Look at the following set of examples.

Root	Meaning	Suffix	Meaning	Word
psych	mind	-ical	quality	*psychological*
		-ist	person	*psychologist*
		-ology	study of	*psychology*

Note that sometimes a word will use more than one suffix. For example, the word *psychologist* combines the root *psych* ("mind") with two suffixes: *-ology* ("study of") and *-ist* ("person"). Thus *psychologist* means "a person who studies the mind." The word *psychological* combines the root *psych* ("mind") with two suffixes: *-ology* ("study of") and *-ical* ("quality"). Thus the word *psychological* means "the study of the qualities of the mind." Note also that the *y* in the suffix *-ology* is dropped because the additional suffixes begin with an *i*, which takes the place of the *y*.

EXAMPLES   Using the meanings of the root and the suffixes, and the context clues, put each of the words in the box below into the sentence that best fits its meaning. Use each word once.

Root	Meaning	Suffix	Meaning
err	wander, stray, deviate	*-ancy*	quality or state of
		-ant	one who, that which
		-or	a condition

errant	errors

1. News reporters are expected to avoid <u>errors</u> in their reports.

2. Acting the part of the <u>errant</u> son, Nathan often rebelled against his parents' wishes.

EXPLANATIONS

1. News reporters are expected to avoid *errors*, that is, wandering or deviating from the facts that serve as a basis for the report.

2. Acting the part of the *errant* son, Nathan often strayed or deviated from his parents' wishes.

PRACTICE 8

Using the meanings of the roots and the suffixes, and the context clues, put each word in the box into the sentence that best fits its meaning. Use each word once. Slight changes in spelling may be necessary.

Root	Meaning	Suffix	Meaning
icon	image, symbol	*-graph*	writing
		-ic	of, like, related to, being
		-ology	study of, science

iconic	iconography	iconology

1. Ted's interest in <u>iconology</u> has taken him to Egypt to visit the pyramids.

2. Lady Gaga's musical abilities and controversial behaviors have turned her into an <u>iconic</u> pop figure.

3. Ancient Egyptians practiced <u>iconography</u> by creating a writing system using pictures for concepts instead of letters for sounds; their writing system is known as hieroglyphics.

Textbook
Skills

Reading a Textbook: Discipline-Specific Vocabulary

During your college career, you will take classes in a variety of different course areas, or disciplines. Each discipline has special words that it uses to describe the concepts of its area of study. In other words, each discipline has its own vocabulary. This is part of the reason why reading a biology textbook may seem like a very different experience than reading an economics textbook. Courses in different disciplines may use the same words, but the words sometimes take on new or different meanings within the context of each course area. For example, when a biology textbook talks about a "consumer," it is referring to any organism that eats either plants or animals for food; but when an economics textbook talks about a "consumer," it is referring to any individual who uses a product or service. Although the word is used similarly, the different definitions are a result of their discipline-specific applications.

To help you incorporate these new words into your vocabulary, textbooks usually provide context clues. Word parts can also be an essential tool for deciphering discipline-specific vocabulary. Many academic disciplines, especially in the sciences, use a language that relies heavily on Latin roots, suffixes, and prefixes.

EXAMPLE Read the following text from the college textbook *Life on Earth*. Then, answer the questions, using context clues and the information about word parts as needed.

Textbook
Skills

Energy Enters Community Through Photosynthesis

[1]During photosynthesis, pigments such as chlorophyll absorb specific wavelengths of sunlight. [2]This solar energy is then used in reactions that store energy in chemical bonds, producing sugar and other high-energy molecules. [3]Photosynthetic organisms, from mighty oak trees to single-celled diatoms in the ocean, are called autotrophs or producers, because they produce food for themselves using nonliving nutrients and sunlight. [4]In doing so, they directly or indirectly produce food for nearly all other forms of life as well. [5]Organisms that cannot photosynthesize, called heterotrophs or consumers, must acquire energy and many of their nutrients prepackaged in the molecules that comprise the bodies of other organisms.

—From *Biology: Life on Earth*, 8th ed., p. 561 by Teresa Audesirk, Gerald Audesirk, and Bruce E. Byers. Copyright © 2008 by Pearson Education, Inc. Printed and Electronically reproduced by permission of Pearson Education, Inc., Upper Saddle River, NJ.

Prefix	Meaning	Root	Meaning	Suffix	Meaning
auto-	self	*tithenai*	to do		
dia-	two	*tome*	segment	*-s*	more than one
eco-	habitat, environment	*troph*	to nourish	*-sis*	action, production
hetere-	other, different			*-ic*	pertaining to
photo-	light				
syn-	together				

_____d_____ **1.** What is the best meaning of the word **photosynthesis**?
    a. high-energy molecules   c. solar energy
    b. organisms that use light to   d. the action of using light
       produce food   to produce food

_____b_____ **2.** What is the best meaning of **diatoms**?
    a. multi-cell organisms   c. sea creatures
    b. single-cell organisms with   d. mineral deposits
       two-sided cell walls

_____a_____ **3.** What is the best meaning of **ecosystem**?
    a. environment   c. nutritional
    b. security   d. plants

_____c_____ **4.** What is the best meaning of **trophic**?
    a. environment   c. feeding level
    b. light levels   d. energy supply

5. How would you define **autotrophs** and **heterotrophs**? Explain how you came to your definitions. _Autotrophs are organisms that can produce their own_ food. The suffix *auto* means "self" and the root *troph* means "to nourish."

Heterotrophs are organisms that are fed by others. Heterotrophs cannot

photosynthesize.

EXPLANATION

1. Word parts and the general sense of the passage reveal the meaning of *photosynthesis*. The prefix *photo* means light; the prefix *syn* means "together"; the root *tithenai* means "to do," and the suffix *sis* indicates that the action of producing something is occurring. In addition, the author offers a defining phrase "use solar energy to make food." When combined, these word parts mean (d) "the action of using light to produce food."

2. Word parts and the general sense of the passage reveal the meaning of *diatoms*: the prefix *dia* means "two"; the root *tome* means "segment," and the suffix *s* indicates "more than one." The author states that diatoms are single-celled organisms, so the word parts indicate that the single cell must have two parts. Thus, the best meaning of *diatoms* is (b) "single-cell organisms with two-sided cell walls. "

3. Word parts reveal the meaning of *ecosystem*. The prefix *eco* means "habitat or environment." Thus (a) "environment" is the correct answer.

4. Word parts reveal the meaning of *trophic*. The root *troph* means "to nourish," and the suffix *ic* means "pertaining to." Thus (c) "feeding level" is the correct answer.

5. Although the wording of your answers may vary, you should have come to the following conclusion: "Autotrophs are organisms that can produce their own food." The suffix *auto* means "self" and the root *troph* means "to nourish." "Heterotrophs are organisms that are fed by others." The prefix *hetere* means "other," and the root *troph* means "to nourish."

PRACTICE 9

Textbook
Skills

Study the following text from the college textbook *Biology: Life on Earth*. Then, complete the activity "Key Term Review," using context clues and the information given about word parts, as needed.

Leaves and Chloroplasts Are Adaptations
for Photosynthesis

[1]The leaves of most land plants are only a few cells thick; their structure is elegantly adapted to the demands of photosynthesis. [2]The flattened shape of leaves exposes a large surface area to the sun, and their thinness ensures that sunlight can penetrate them to reach the light-trapping

chloroplasts inside. [3]Both the upper and lower surfaces of a leaf consist of a layer of transparent cells, the **epidermis**. [4]The outer surface of both epidermal layers is covered by the **cuticle**, a waxy, waterproof covering that reduces the evaporation of water from the leaf.

[5]A leaf obtains CO_2 for photosynthesis from the air; adjustable pores in the epidermis, called **stomata** (singular stoma; Greek for "mouth"), open and close at appropriate times to admit air carrying CO_2.

[6]Inside the leaf are layers of cells collectively called **mesophyll**. [7]The mesophyll cells contain most of a leaf's chloroplasts, and consequently photosynthesis occurs principally in these cells. [8]**Vascular bundles** supply water and minerals to the mesophyll cells and carry the sugars they produce to other parts of the plant.

[9]A single mesophyll cell can have from 40 to 200 chloroplasts, which are sufficiently small that 2000 of them lined up would just span your thumbnail. . . . [10]Chloroplasts are organelles that consist of a double outer membrane enclosing a semifluid medium, the stroma. [11]Embedded in the stroma are disk-shaped, interconnected membranous sacs called **thylakoids**. [12]The chemical reactions of photosynthesis that depend on light (light-dependent reactions) occur within the membranes of the thylakoids, while the photosynthetic reactions that can continue for a time in darkness (light-independent reactions) occur in the surrounding stroma.

—From *Biology: Life on Earth*, 8th ed., pp. 118–119 by Teresa Audesirk, Gerald Audesirk, and Bruce E. Byers. Copyright © 2008 by Pearson Education, Inc. Printed and Electronically reproduced by permission of Pearson Education, Inc., Upper Saddle River, NJ.

Prefix	Meaning	Root	Meaning	Suffix	Meaning
epi-	on	*cutis*	skin	*-ar*	of, like, related to
meso-	middle	*dermi*	skin	*-le*	of, like, related to
		phyllon	leaf	*-oid*	resembling
		thylakos	sack		
		vas	vessels		

Key Term Review Match the following terms to their definitions:

_____d_____ **1.** cuticle

_____a_____ **2.** epidermis

_____e_____ **3.** mesophyll

_____b_____ **4.** thylakoids

_____c_____ **5.** vascular bundles

a. outer cell layer of plant; outer layer of skin

b. sacs in which photosynthesis takes place

c. veins, fluid carrying vessels

d. waxy or fatty covering on the exposed surfaces of plants

e. middle of leaf

Complete the Summary Fill in the blanks with terms in the Key Term Review. A plant is made for the demands of photosynthesis. The waxy **(6)** cuticle covers the broad, thin **(7)** epidermis of the leaf. This flat expanse of the leaf epidermis takes in sunlight and its pores (called stomata) open and close to absorb CO_2. **(8)** Vascular bundles carry water and CO_2 to the **(9)** mesophyll cells, which contain chloroplasts; inside the chloroplasts are the **(10)** thylakoids , where photosynthesis occurs.

Reading a Textbook: Visual Vocabulary

Textbook Skills

Textbooks often make information clearer by giving a visual image such as a graph, chart, or photograph. Take time to study the visual images and captions in this section to figure out how each one ties in to the information given in words.

EXAMPLE Study the following image and its caption. Then answer the questions that follow. If necessary, review the passage "Leaves and Chloroplasts Are Adaptations for Photosynthesis" (page 66).

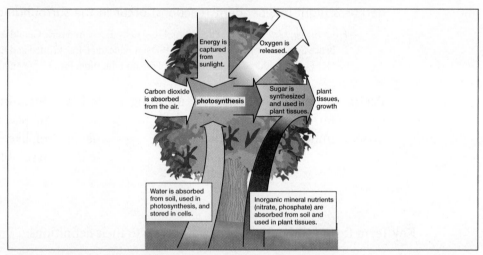

Figure 28-2 Primary productivity

Photosynthetic organisms, which capture solar energy and acquire inorganic nutrients from their environment, ultimately provide essentially all of the energy and most of the nutrients for organisms in higher trophic levels.

___c___ Which term best completes the caption?
a. Ecosystem   c. Photosynthetic
b. Trophic   d. Heterotrophic

2. How does this image add to your understanding of the passage?

Answers may vary. The image illustrates how a photosynthetic organism captures

solar energy and provides nutrients in the ecosystem.

EXPLANATION

1. Photosynthetic best completes the caption.

2. This image illustrates how a photosynthetic organism captures solar energy and provides nutrients in the ecosystem.

PRACTICE 10

Study the following image and its caption. Then answer the questions that follow. If necessary, review the passage "Leaves and Chloroplasts Are Adaptations for Photosynthesis" (page 66).

Interconnections between Photosynthesis and Cellular Respiration

Chloroplasts in green plants use the energy of sunlight to synthesize the high-energy carbon compounds such as glucose from low-energy molecules of water (H_2O) and carbon dioxide (CO_2). Plants themselves, and other organisms that eat plants or one another, extract energy from these organic molecules by cellular **respiration**, yielding water and carbon dioxide once again. This energy in turn drives all the reactions of life.

—From *Biology: Life on Earth*, 8th ed., Figure 28-2 from page 561 by Teresa Audesirk, Gerald Audesirk, and Bruce E. Byers. Copyright © 2008 by Pearson Education, Inc. Printed and Electronically reproduced by permission of Pearson Education, Inc., Upper Saddle River, NJ.

_____a_____   **1.** The best definition of **respiration** in this context is the
  a. energy-producing process in cells.
  b. process of making glucose.
  c. breathing process in animals.
  d. death of a cell.

2. How does this graphic add to your understanding of the passage? Answers may vary. The graphic provides a visual illustration of the relationship between the sun, the leaf's chloroplasts, and the flow of energy.

APPLICATIONS

Application 1: Context Clues and Glossary

The following passage from the college textbook *Psychology and Life* provides context clues and a glossary. Study the glossary. Read the passage, and circle the synonyms given for three of the words in **bold** type. Then, answer the questions.

> **Glossary**
>
> **Convergence** coming together
> **Depth perception** ability to perceive spatial relationships, especially distances between objects, in three dimensions
> **Foveae** a small cuplike depression or pit in a bone or organ
> **Retina** the membrane that lines the back of the eye; receives the image created by the eye's lens
> **Retinal disparity** the difference between the horizontal positions of matching images in two eyes

Textbook Skills

Depth Perception: Binocular Cues

[1]Have you ever wondered why you are **binocular**, or two-eyed, instead of **monocular**, or one-eyed? [2]The second eye is more than just a spare—it provides some of the best, most compelling information about depth. [3]The two sources of binocular depth information are *retinal disparity* and *convergence*. [4](The retina is the membrane that lines the back of the eye which receives the image created by the eye's lens.)

[5]Because the eyes are about 2 to 3 inches apart horizontally, they receive slightly different views of the world. [6]To convince yourself of this, try the following experiment. [7]First, close your left eye and use the right one to line up your two index fingers with some small object in the distance, holding one at arm's length and the other about a foot in front of your

face. ⁸Now keeping your fingers stationary, close your right eye and open the left one while continuing to fixate on the distant object. ⁹What happened to the position of your two fingers? ¹⁰The second eye does not see them lined up with the distant object because it gets a slightly different view.

¹¹This displacement between the horizontal positions of corresponding or matching images in your two eyes is called retinal disparity. ¹²It provides depth information because the amount of **disparity**, or difference, depends on the relative distance of objects from you.

¹³Other binocular information about depth comes from **convergence**. ¹⁴The two eyes turn inward to some extent whenever they are fixated on an object. ¹⁵When the object is very close—a few inches in front of your face—the eyes must turn toward each other quite a bit for the same image to fall on both foveae.

—From *Psychology and Life,* 16th ed., Figure 5.21 (p. 137) and text adapted from pp. 136–137 by Richard J. Gerrig and Philip G. Zimbardo. Copyright © 2002 by Pearson Education, Inc. Reproduced by permission of Pearson Education, Inc., Boston, MA.

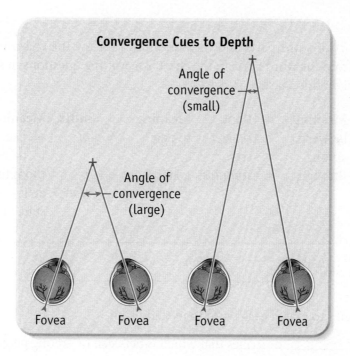

Convergence Cues to Depth

Angle of convergence (small)

Angle of convergence (large)

Fovea   Fovea   Fovea   Fovea

◄ When an object is close to you, your eyes must converge more than when an object is at a greater distance.

____b____ **1.** What kind of context clue does the word **monocular** provide for the word **binocular**?

    a. synonym   c. general context

    b. antonym   d. example

_____a_____ **2.** What is the best meaning of the word **convergence**?
  a. merging
  b. departure
  c. reunion
  d. fixated

_____c_____ **3.** What context clue did you use to determine the meaning of **convergence**?
  a. synonym
  b. antonym
  c. general context
  d. example

_____a_____ **4.** In the context of this reading selection, the words **disparity** and **convergence** are
  a. antonyms.
  b. synonyms.

Application 2: Word Parts

Study the chart of word parts and their meanings. Below the chart are three words made from the word parts in the chart. Answer the questions in sections A and B based on this chart.

Prefix	Meaning	Root	Meaning	Suffix	Meaning
inter-	between, among	*capere/ cept*	to take	*-al*	of, like, related to, being
per-	through	*stimulus*	goad, rouse, excite	*-i*	those that
				-tion	action or state of

interpersonal	perception	stimuli

A. Fill in the blanks to match each word to its definition.

  1. _Interpersonal_____ describes that which is between or among people.

  2. _Stimuli_____ are those conditions that motivate or provoke a response.

  3. _Perception_____ is one's understanding, awareness, or grasp.

B. **(4–6.)** Using word meanings and context clues, put each word into the sentence that best fits its meaning. Use each word once.

interpersonal	perception	stimuli

Textbook
Skills

The Stages of Perception

¹Perception_____ is the process by which you become aware of objects, events, and, especially, people through your senses: sight, smell, taste, touch, and hearing. ²Perception is an active, not a passive, process. ³Your perceptions result from what exists in the outside world and from your own experiences, desires, needs and wants, loves and hatreds. ⁴Among the reasons why perception is so important in interpersonal_____ communication is that it influences your communication choices. ⁵The messages you send and listen to will depend on how you see the world, on how you size up specific situations, on what you think of the people with whom you interact.

⁶Interpersonal perception is a continuous series of processes that blend into one another. ⁷For convenience of discussion we can separate them into five stages: (1) you sense, you pick up some kind of stimulation; (2) you organize the stimuli_____ in some way; (3) you interpret and evaluate what you perceive; (4) you store it in memory; and (5) you retrieve it when needed.

—From *Essentials of Human Communication*, 4th ed., p. 55 by Joseph A. DeVito. Copyright © 2002 by Pearson Education, Inc. Reproduced by permission of Pearson Education, Inc., Boston, MA.

REVIEW TEST 1   Score (number correct) _____ × 10 = _____ %

Context Clues

Read the following passage from the college textbook *Foundations of Earth Science*. Answer the questions that follow.

12.0 GE/775 words   **Earth's Internal Structure**

[1]Earth's interior has three basic divisions—the iron rich **core**; the thin primitive crust; and Earth's largest layer, called the **mantle**, which is located between the core and the crust.

Earth's Crust   [2]The crust, Earth's relatively thin, rocky outer skin, is of two types—**continental** crust and oceanic crust. [3]Both share the word crust, but the similarity ends there. [4]The oceanic crust is roughly 7 kilometers (4 miles) thick and composed of the dark igneous rock basalt. [5]By contrast, the continental crust averages 35 to 40 kilometers (22 to 25 miles) thick but may exceed 70 kilometers (40 miles) in some mountainous regions such as the Rockies and Himalayas. [6]Unlike the oceanic crust, which has a relatively **homogeneous** chemical composition, the continental crust consists of many rock types. [7]Although the upper crust has an average composition of a granitic rock called **granodiorite**, it varies considerably from place to place.

[8]Continental rocks have an average density of about 2.7 grams per cubic centimeter, and some are 4 billion years old. [9]The rocks of the oceanic crust are younger (180 million years or less) and denser (about 3.0 grams per cubic centimeter) than continental rocks.

Earth's Mantle   [10]More than 82 percent of Earth's volume is contained in the mantle, a solid, rocky shell that extends to a depth of about 2900 kilometers (1800 miles). [11]The boundary between the crust and mantle represents a marked change in chemical composition. [12]The dominant rock type in the uppermost mantle is **peridotite**, which is richer in the metals magnesium and iron than the minerals found in either the continental or oceanic crust.

[13]The upper mantle extends from the crust-mantle boundary down to a depth of about 660 kilometers (410 miles). [14]The upper mantle can be divided into three different parts. [15]The top portion of the upper mantle is part of the stiff **lithosphere**, and beneath that is the weaker asthenosphere. [16]The bottom part of the upper mantle is called the transition zone.

[17]The lithosphere (sphere of rock) consists of the entire crust and uppermost mantle and forms Earth's relatively cool, rigid outer shell. [18]Averaging about 100 kilometers (62 miles) in thickness, the lithosphere is more than 250 kilometers (155 miles) thick below the oldest portions of the continents (Figure 6.22). [19]Beneath this stiff layer to a depth of about 350 kilometers (217 miles) lies a soft, comparatively weak layer known as the asthenosphere ("weak sphere"). [20]The top portion of the asthenosphere has a temperature/pressure regime that results in a small amount of melting. [21]Within this very weak zone, the lithosphere is mechanically detached from

the layer below. [22]The result is that the lithosphere is able to move independently of the asthenosphere, a fact we will consider in the next chapter.

[23]It is important to emphasize that the strength of various Earth materials is a function of both their composition and the temperature and pressure of their environment. [24]The entire lithosphere does not behave like a brittle solid similar to rocks found on the surface. [25]Rather, the rocks of the lithosphere get progressively hotter and weaker (more easily deformed) with increasing depth. [26]At the depth of the uppermost asthenosphere, the rocks are close enough to their melting temperature that they are very easily deformed, and some melting may actually occur. [27]Thus, the upper most asthenosphere is weak because it is near its melting point, just as hot wax is weaker than cold wax.

[28]From 660 kilometers (410 miles) deep to the top of the core, at a depth of 2900 kilometers (1800 miles), is the lower mantle. [29]Because of an increase in pressure (caused by the weight of the rock above), the mantle gradually strengthens with depth. [30]Despite their strength however, the rocks within the lower mantle are very hot and capable of very gradual flow.

Earth's Core [31]The composition of the core is thought to be an iron-nickel alloy with minor amounts of oxygen, silicon, and sulfur-elements that readily form compounds with iron. [32]At the extreme pressure found in the core, this iron-rich material has an average density of nearly 11 grams per cubic centimeter and approaches 14 times the density of water at Earth's center.

[33]The core is divided into two regions that exhibit very different mechanical strengths. [34]The outer core is a liquid layer 2270 kilometers (1410 miles) thick. [35]It is the movement of metallic iron within this zone that generates Earth's magnetic field. [36]The inner core is a sphere with a radius of 1216 kilometers (754 miles). [37]Despite its higher temperature, the iron in the inner core is solid due to the immense pressures that exist in the center of the planet.

—From *Foundations of Earth Science*, 5th ed., pp. 176–177 by Frederick K. Lutgens, Edward J. Tarbuck, and Dennis Tasa. Copyright © 2008 by Pearson Education, Inc. Printed and Electronically reproduced by permission of Pearson Education, Inc., Upper Saddle River, NJ.

_____a_____ **1.** What is the best meaning of the word **continental** in sentence 2?
    a. of or related to land   c. of or related to oceans
    b. of or related to colonies   d. of or related to Europe

_____b_____ **2.** Identify the context clue used for **continental** in sentence 2.
    a. synonym   c. general sense of the passage
    b. antonym   d. example

_____c_____ **3.** What is the best meaning of **homogeneous** in sentence 6?

    a. different than   c. of the same kind

    b. liquid   d. solid

_____b_____ **4.** Identify the context clue used for **homogeneous** in sentence 6.

    a. synonym   c. general sense of the passage

    b. antonym   d. example

Match the following glossary words to their definitions

_____d_____ **5.** asthenosphere

_____c_____ **6.** core

_____e_____ **7.** granodiorite

_____a_____ **8.** mantle

_____f_____ **9.** lithosphere

_____b_____ **10.** peridotite

a. a solid rocky shell, extends about 1800 miles below crust

b. dominant rock in uppermost mantle; made of magnesium and iron

c. innermost layer of Earth; mostly of iron-nickel alloy

d. middle, weaker layer of the upper mantle

e. a granitic rock that composes the upper crust

f. rigid outer layer of Earth; includes the crust and upper mantle

REVIEW TEST 2

Score (number correct) _____ × 10 = _____ %

Context Clues

Choose the best definition for each word in **bold** type. Then, identify the context clue used in each passage. A clue may be used more than once.

Context Clues

> **S**ynonym
> **A**ntonym
> **G**eneral context
> **E**xample

_____c_____ **1.** Jerry and Marie were **incredulous** when they heard that they had purchased the sole winning lottery ticket; they were skeptical that they could have won the entire $34 million jackpot.

    a. excited   c. disbelieving

    b. secretive   d. hysterical

2. Context clue: _synonym_____

_____b_____ **3.** The Underground Railroad was a route made up of a series of **clandestine** safe houses for African Americans fleeing the injustice of slavery in the South.

    a. exposed   c. dangerous

    b. secret   d. poor

4. Context clue: _general context_____

_____d_____ **5.** Some people who are infected with West Nile virus develop mild flulike symptoms that disappear within a few days. However, in rare cases, West Nile virus leads to more **virulent** infections that could cause long-term disability or even death.

    a. weak   c. contagious

    b. hidden   d. dangerous

6. Context clue: _antonym_____

_____b_____ **7.** The play *The Taming of the Shrew* by William Shakespeare is known for its **trenchant,** or biting, wit about the battle of the sexes.

    a. subtle   c. bland

    b. cutting   d. rude

8. Context clue: _synonym_____

_____d_____ **9.** Often, humans are driven by their **temporal** needs for safety, food, housing, and other possessions and measure their success by how well these needs are met.

    a. long-term   c. spiritual

    b. sordid   d. worldly

10. Context clue: _example_____

REVIEW TEST 3   Score (number correct) _____ × 10 = _____ %

Vocabulary Skills

Before Reading: Study the glossary and survey the passage from a college sociology textbook. Locate the terms from the glossary in the passage; circle the terms and underline the definitions as they are worded in context. Then, read the passage and respond to the After Reading questions and activities.

Glossary: Vocabulary Preview

megalopolis: an urban area consisting of at least two metropolises and their many suburbs

megacity: a city of 10 million or more residents

metropolitan statistical area: a central city and the urbanized counties adjacent to it

metropolis: a central city surrounded by smaller cities and their suburbs

urbanization: the process by which an increasing proportion of the population live in cities and have growing influence on the culture

12.4 GE/637 words   **The Process of Urbanization**

[1]Although cities are not new to the world scene, urbanization is. [2]**Urbanization** refers to masses of people moving to cities, and these cities having a growing influence on society. [3]Urbanization is taking place all over the world. [4]In 1800, only 3 percent of the world's population lived in cities (Hauser and Schnore 1965). [5]Then in 2007, for the first time in history, more people lived in cities than in rural areas. [6]Urbanization is uneven across the globe. [7]For the industrialized world, it is 77 percent, and for the Least Industrialized Nations, it is 41 percent (Haub 2006; Robb 2007). [8]Without the Industrial Revolution, this remarkable growth could not have taken place, for an extensive infrastructure is needed to support hundreds of thousands and even millions of people in a relatively small area.

[9]To understand the city's attraction, we need to consider the "pulls" of urban life. [10]Because of its exquisite division of labor, the city offers incredible variety—music ranging from rap and salsa to country and classical, shops that feature imported delicacies from around the world and those that sell special foods for vegetarians and diabetics. [11]Cities also offer anonymity, which so many find refreshing in light of the tighter controls of village and small-town life. [12]And, of course, the city offers work.

[13]Some cities have grown so large and have so much influence over a region that the term city is no longer adequate to describe them. [14]The term **metropolis** is used instead. [15]This term refers to a central city surrounded by smaller cities and their suburbs. [16]They are linked by transportation and communication and connected economically, and sometimes politically, through county boards and regional governing bodies. [17]St. Louis is an example.

[18]Although this name, St. Louis, properly refers to a city of 340,000 people in Missouri, it also refers to another 2 million people

who live in more than a hundred separate towns in both Missouri and Illinois. [19]Altogether, the region is known as the "St. Louis or Bi-State Area." [20]Although these towns are independent politically, they form an economic unit. [21]They are linked by work (many people in the smaller towns work in St. Louis or are served by industries from St. Louis), by communications (they share the same area newspaper and radio and television stations), and by transportation (they use the same interstate highways, the Bi-State Bus system, and international airport). [22]As symbolic interactionists would note, shared symbols (the Arch, the Mississippi River, Busch Brewery, the Cardinals, the Rams, the Blues—both the hockey team and the music) provide the residents a common identity.

[23]Most of the towns run into one another, and if you were to drive through this metropolis, you would not know that you were leaving one town and entering another—unless you had lived there for some time and were aware of the fierce small town identifications and rivalries that coexist within this overarching identity.

[24]Some metropolises have grown so large and influential that the term **megalopolis** is used to describe them. [25]This term refers to an overlapping area consisting of at least two metropolises and their many suburbs. [26]Of the twenty or so megalopolises in the United States, the three largest are the Eastern seaboard running from Maine to Virginia, the area in Florida between Miami, Orlando, and Tampa, and California's coastal area between San Francisco and San Diego. [27]The California megalopolis extends into Mexico and includes Tijuana and its suburbs.

[28]This process of urban areas turning into a metropolis, and a metropolis developing into a megalopolis, occurs worldwide. [29]When a city's population hits 10 million, it is called a **megacity**. [30]In 1950, New York City was the only megacity in the world. [31]Today there are 19. [32]The figure entitled "How Many Millions of People Live in the World's Largest Megacities?" shows the world's 10 largest megacities. [33]Note that most megacities are located in the Least Industrialized Nations.

—From *Sociology: A Down-to-Earth Approach,* 9th ed., p. 606 by
James M. Henslin. Copyright © 2009 by James Henslin. Reproduced by
permission of Pearson Education, Inc., Boston, MA.

After Reading

Use the word parts and terms in the answer box to complete the word web based on information from the glossary and the passage.

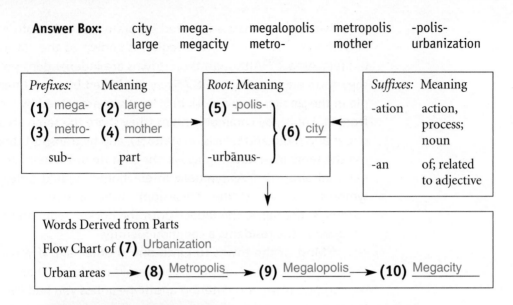

Answer Box: city   mega-   megalopolis   metropolis   -polis-
large   megacity   metro-   mother   urbanization

Prefixes:	Meaning		*Root:* Meaning	*Suffixes:*	Meaning
(1) mega-	**(2)** large		**(5)** -polis-	-ation	action, process; noun
(3) metro-	**(4)** mother		**(6)** city	-an	of; related to adjective
sub-	part		-urbānus-		

Words Derived from Parts
Flow Chart of **(7)** Urbanization
Urban areas ⟶ **(8)** Metropolis ⟶ **(9)** Megalopolis ⟶ **(10)** Megacity

VISUAL VOCABULARY

Fill in the blank with a word from the glossary that completes the caption.

The U.S. Census Bureau divides the country into 274 metropolitan statistical areas (MSAs). Each MSA consists of a central city of at least 50,000 people and the urbanized areas linked to it. About three of five Americans live in just fifty or so MSAs.

Tokyo	
2015	26
2000	26
1975	19

New York	
2015	17
2000	17
1975	16

Lagos	
2015	23
2000	13
1975	3

Los Angeles	
2015	14
2000	13
1975	9

Shanghai	
2015	15
2000	13
1975	11

Bombay	
2015	26
2000	18
1975	7

Mexico City	
2015	19
2000	18
1975	11

Sao Paulo	
2015	20
2000	18
1975	10

Buenos Aires	
2015	14
2000	13
1975	9

Calcutta	
2015	17
2000	13
1975	8

—From *Sociology: A Down-to-Earth Approach,* 9th ed., Figure 20.10 by James M. Henslin. Copyright © 2008 by James Henslin. Reproduced by permission of Pearson Education, Inc., Boston, MA.

WHAT DO YOU THINK?

What type of community do you live in—rural, suburban, or urban? What is the closest metropolis, megalopolis, and megacity near you? Reread the description of St. Louis. How has urbanization affected your area? Assume you are running for a local public office, such as a city commissioner or a mayor. Write an article for local publication that describes your vision for how the city should grow or control growth. Describe your community in terms of its urbanization, identify some strengths in your community, and identify one problem you would address.

REVIEW TEST 4   Score (number correct) _____ × 10 = _____%

Vocabulary Skills

Before Reading: Survey the following passage from the college textbook *World Civilizations: The Global Experience.* Study the words in the Vocabulary Preview; then skim the passage, noting the words in bold print. Answer the Before Reading questions that follow the passage. Then, read the passage. Finally, after reading, check the answers you gave before reading to make sure they are accurate. Respond to What Do You Think? to check your comprehension after reading.

Vocabulary Preview

Republic (sentence 2): State
Muslim (sentence 3): a believer of Islam
hold (sentence 21): the interior of a ship below deck; the cargo deck of a ship
singular (sentence 22): individual
11.4 GE/501 words

Textbook Skills

Africa and the Africans in the Age of the Atlantic Slave Trade

¹Sometimes a single, extraordinary life can represent the forces and patterns of a whole historical era. ²Born in the early 19th century, Mahommah Gardo Baquaqua was a young man from the trading town of Djougou in what is now the Benin **Republic** in west Africa. ³A **Muslim**, he could speak Arabic, Hausa, and a number of other languages, as was common among the trading peoples from which he came. ⁴At a young age, Baquaqua was captured and **enslaved** during a war with a neighboring

African state; after gaining his freedom, he was enslaved again, and around 1845 he was sold into the Atlantic slave trade.

[5]Baquaqua was taken first to northeastern Brazil and from there was purchased by a ship captain from Rio de Janeiro. [6]After a number of voyages along the Brazilian coast, his ship eventually sailed for New York. [7]After a failed attempt to use the American courts to gain his freedom (a strategy that many slaves attempted), Baquaqua fled to Boston with the help of local **abolitionists.** [8]In that city he was **befriended** by antislavery Baptist missionaries. [9]With them, he sailed for Haiti. [10]Eventually he learned French and English and studied at a college in upstate New York in order to prepare for missionary work in his native Africa. [11]His life was not easy. [12]Eventually, because of racial incidents, he moved to Canada.

[13]Although Baquaqua had left the Baptist college, he did not abandon his desire to return to Africa, and he continued to seek ways to make that voyage. [14]In 1854, in an attempt to get the money he needed to realize his dream, he published his **autobiography,** [15]*An Interesting Narrative: Biography of Mahommah G. Baquaqua.* [16]In it he was able to provide his personal observations on his experiences. [17]On the slave ship, he reported:

[18]O the loathsomeness and filth of that horrible place will never be **effaced** from my memory; nay as long as my memory holds her seat in this **distracted** brain, will I remember that. [19]My heart, even at this day, sickens at the thought of it. [20]Let those humane individuals, who are in favor of slavery, only allow themselves to take the slave's position in the noisome hold of a slave ship, just for one trip from Africa to America, and without going into the horrors of slavery further than this, if they do not come out thorough-going abolitionists, then I have no more to say in favor of abolition.

[21]The only place worse than the **hold** of a slave ship, said Baquaqua, was the place to which slave owners would be condemned in the next life. [22]We do not know whether Baquaqua finally returned to the land of his birth, but the life of this African, while **singular** in many aspects, represents the stories of millions of Africans in the age of the slave trade, and these make up an important part of world history.

—From *World Civilizations: The Global Experience, Combined Volume, Atlas Edition,* 5th ed., pp. 542–543 by Peter N. Stearns, Michael B. Adas, Stuart B. Schwartz, and Marc Jason Gilbert. Copyright © 2008 by Pearson Education, Inc. Printed and Electronically reproduced by permission of Pearson Education, Inc., Upper Saddle River, NJ.

Before Reading

A. Use context clues to state in your own words the definition of the following terms. Indicate the context clue you used.

1. In sentence 4, what does the word **enslaved** mean? <u>imprisoned</u>

2. Identify the context clue used for the word **enslaved** in sentence 4.
   <u>The antonym of enslaved is "gaining freedom."</u>

3. In sentence 7, what does the word **abolitionists** mean? <u>people who want</u>
   <u>to eliminate or end slavery</u>

4. Identify the context clue used for the word **abolitionists** in sentences 7 and 20.
   <u>general sense of the passage and the synonym for abolition is antislavery</u>

5. In sentence 8, what does the word **befriended** mean? <u>make friends with</u>

6. Identify the context clue used for the word **befriended** in sentence 8. <u>the</u>
   <u>general sense of the passage</u>

7. In sentence 18, what does the word **distracted** mean? <u>troubled, unhappy</u>

8. Identify the context clue used for the word **distracted** in sentence 18. <u>the</u>
   <u>general sense of the passage</u>

B. Study the following chart of word parts. Use context clues and the word parts to answer the questions that follow.

Prefix	Meaning	Root	Meaning	Suffix	Meaning
auto-	self	bio	life	-ed	completed action
ef-	out	fac	face	-y	quality, state
		graph	write		

<u>b</u> 9. What does the word **effaced** in sentence 18 mean?
   a. carved   c. seen
   b. wiped out   d. endured

10. What does the word **autobiography** in sentence 14 mean? <u>Wording</u>

<u>of answers may vary: A writing about one's own life</u>

WHAT DO YOU THINK?

The passage opens with the statement "Sometimes a single, extraordinary life can represent the forces and patterns of a whole historical era." Do you agree that Mahommah Gardo Baquaqua represents the experiences of millions of Africans in the age of slave trade? Why or why not? How does an autobiography or a biography add to our understanding of history? In what ways does your life or the life of someone you know represent an important aspect of our current era? Assume you have been invited to participate in a community-wide project to record aspects of current life for future generations. Your community has decided to create a time capsule in which items and writings from local people will be enclosed. This time capsule will be opened and publically shared by officials in the year 2060. Write an autobiographical or biographical essay to include in the time capsule.

After Reading About Vocabulary Skills

Before you move on to the Mastery Tests on vocabulary skills for master readers, take time to reflect on your learning and performance by answering the following questions. Write your answers in your notebook.

- How has my knowledge base or prior knowledge about vocabulary and glossary skills changed?
- Based on my studies, how do I think I will perform on the Mastery Test(s)? Why do I think my scores will be above average, average, or below average?
- Would I recommend this chapter to other students who want to learn more about vocabulary skills? Why or why not?

Test your understanding of what you have learned about Vocabulary Skills for Master Readers by completing the Chapter 2 Review Card in the insert near the end of your text.

CONNECT TO **myreadinglab**

To check your progress in meeting Chapter 2's learning outcomes, log in to **www.myreadinglab.com** and try the following activities.

- The "Vocabulary" section of MyReadingLab offers several tools that can help to accomplish this goal, including, the dictionary, vocabulary in context, synonyms and antonyms, and prefixes and suffixes. To access this resource, click on the "Study Plan" tab. Then click on "Vocabulary." Then click on the following links as needed:
  - "Overview"
  - "Model"
  - "Word Elements I: Root Words, Prefixes, and Suffixes (Flash Animation)"
  - "Compound Words (Flash Animation)"
  - "Word Elements II: Root Words, Prefixes, and Suffixes (Flash Animation)"
  - "Word Origins (Flash Animation)"
  - "Practice"
  - "Tests"

- The "Other Resources" section of MyReadingLab offers an overview of vocabulary and dictionary skills, along with an audio dictionary, activities, exercises and quizzes, spelling activities, and flashcards. To access resources for these skills, go to the "Other Resources" on the Home page of MyReadingLab. Click on the link labeled "Vocabulary Website." Under "select your level," choose the link labeled "Intermediate." Click on the following as needed: "Dictionary," "Context Clues," "Synonyms," "Antonyms," "Prefixes," "Roots," "Suffixes," and "Flashcards."

- To measure your mastery of the content of this chapter, complete the tests in the "Vocabulary" section and click on Gradebook to find your results.

Read the following passage from the college textbook *Psychology and Life.* Answer the questions that follow.

10.8 GE/197 words

Sleep Apnea

Textbook Skills

[1]Sleep apnea is a sleep disorder that causes the person to stop breathing while asleep. [2]When this happens, the blood's oxygen level drops and emergency hormones are **secreted**, which then causes the sleeper to awaken and begin breathing again. [3]Most people have a few apnea **episodes** a night. [4]However, someone with sleep apnea disorder can have hundreds of such cycles every night. [5]Sometimes apnea episodes frighten the sleeper. [6]But often they are so brief that the sleeper fails to credit **accumulating** or mounting sleepiness to them.

[7]Consider, for example, the case of a famous psychologist who, because of undetected sleep apnea, could not stay awake during research meetings and lectures. [8]When his wife made him aware of his disturbing nighttime behavior, he went to a sleep disorder clinic. [9]The treatment he received **reinvigorated** or revived his career (Zimbardo, personal communication, 1991). [10]In other cases, people have lost their jobs, friends, and even spouses.

[11]Sleep apnea is also frequent in premature infants. [12]These babies sometimes need physical **stimulation** to start breathing again. [13]Because of their immature respiratory system, these infants must remain attached to monitors in intensive care nurseries as long as the problem continues.

—From *Psychology and Life,* 16th ed., p. 165 by Richard J. Gerrig and Philip G. Zimbardo. Copyright © 2002 by Pearson Education, Inc. Reproduced by permission of Pearson Education, Inc., Boston, MA.

_____b_____ **1.** What is the best meaning of the word **secreted** in sentence 2?
a. hidden   c. suppressed
b. produced   d. disturbed

_____c_____ **2.** Identify the context clue used for **secreted** in sentence 2.
a. synonym   c. general context
b. antonym   d. example

_____b_____ **3.** What is the best meaning of the word **episodes** in sentence 3?
a. scares   c. reasons
b. events   d. treatments

_____c_____ **4.** Identify the context clue used for **episodes** in sentence 3.
    a. synonym   c. general context
    b. antonym   d. example

_____c_____ **5.** What is the best meaning of the word **accumulating** in sentence 6?
    a. lessening   c. increasing
    b. embarrassing   d. confusing

_____a_____ **6.** Identify the context clue used for **accumulating** in sentence 6.
    a. synonym   c. general context
    b. antonym   d. example

_____d_____ **7.** What is the best meaning of the word **reinvigorated** in sentence 9?
    a. repressed   c. cured
    b. ruined again   d. strengthened again

_____a_____ **8.** Identify the context clue used for **reinvigorated** in sentence 9.
    a. synonym   c. general context
    b. antonym   d. example

_____a_____ **9.** What is the best meaning of the word **stimulation** in sentence 12?
    a. encouragement   c. pain
    b. hindrance   d. relief

_____c_____ **10.** Identify the context clue used for **stimulation** in sentence 12.
    a. synonym   c. general context
    b. antonym   d. example

Read the following passage adapted from the college humanities textbook *The Creative Impulse: An Introduction to the Arts*. Using context clues, write the definition for each word in **bold** type. Choose definitions from the box. You will not use all the definitions. Then, identify the context clue you used to determine the meaning of each word.

13.1 GE/274 words

Textbook
Skills

Cave Painting

¹The Cave of Lascaux (lahs-KOH) in France lies slightly over a mile from the little town of Montignac, in the valley of the Vézère (vay-Zair) River. ²The cave itself was discovered in 1940 by a group of children who, while investigating a tree uprooted by a storm, scrambled down a **fissure** (crevice) into a world undisturbed for thousands of years. ³The cave was sealed in 1963 to protect it from **atmospheric** damage, and visitors now see Lascaux II, an exact replica, which is sited in a quarry 600 feet away.

⁴Perhaps a **sanctuary** for the performance of sacred rites and ceremonies, the Main Hall, or Hall of the Bulls, elicits a sense of power and grandeur. ⁵The thundering herd moves below a sky formed by the rolling contours of the stone ceiling of the cave, sweeping our eyes forward as we travel into the cave itself. ⁶At the entrance of the main hall, the 8-foot "unicorn" begins a larger-than-lifesize **montage** of bulls, horses, and deer, which are up to 12 feet tall. ⁷Their shapes intermingle with one another, and their colors radiate warmth and power. ⁸These magnificent creatures remind us that their creators were capable technicians, who, with artistic skills at least equal to our own, were able to capture the essence, that is heart, beneath the visible surface of their world. ⁹The paintings in the Main Hall were created over a long period of time and by a succession of artists. ¹⁰Yet their **cumulative** or combined effect in this 30- by 100-foot domed gallery is that of a single work, carefully composed for maximum dramatic and communicative impact.

—From *The Creative Impulse: An Introduction to the Arts*, 8th ed., pp. 38–39 by Dennis J. Sporre. Copyright © 2009 by Pearson Education, Inc. Reprinted by permission of Pearson Education, Inc., Upper Saddle River, NJ.

ancient	composite	environmental	spirit
collective	crack	shelter	sweeping

Context Clues

Synonym
Antonym
General context
Example

1. In sentence 2, **fissure** means crack   .

2. Context clue used for **fissure**: synonym

3. In sentence 3, **atmospheric** means environmental   .

4. Context clue used for **atmospheric**: general context

5. In sentence 4, **sanctuary** means shelter   .

6. Context clue used for **sanctuary**: general context

7. In sentence 6, **montage** means composite   .

8. Context clue used for **montage**: general context

9. In sentence 10, **cumulative** means collective   .

10. Context clue used for **cumulative**: synonym

VISUAL VOCABULARY

This painting in the Cave of Lascaux, France, is a montage   of larger-than-lifesize animals.

Read the following passage from the college textbook *Cultural Anthropology*. Answer the questions that follow the passage.

13.6 GE/330 words

Textbook
Skills

Intermarriage

[1]Fears of **ethnic** divide in the United States are being challenged by the rate at which couples of different races and ethnicities are marrying one another.

[2]Since 1970, the number of **interracial** marriages in the United States increased more than ten-fold, from less than 1 percent to more than 5 percent of the estimated 57 million couples recorded in the 2000 census. [3]This reflects both the population growth and an increased tendency to marry across racial lines. [4]At the same time, there have been dramatic improvements in the American attitudes toward race. [5]A Gallup poll conducted at the end of 2003 shows that 66 percent of White respondents said they would accept a child or grandchild marrying someone of a different race.

[6]Based on the 2000 census, interracial marriage has increased across most racial groups and is generating a growing population of **multiracial** Americans.

- [7]The typical interracial couple is a White person with a non-White spouse. [8]Intermarriage between two people from minority racial groups is relatively infrequent.
- [9]About one-fourth of Hispanic couples are inter-Hispanic, a rate that has been fairly stable since 1980.
- [10]Whites and Blacks have the lowest intermarriage rates while American Indians, Hawaiians, and multiple-race individuals have the highest.
- [11]Black men are more likely to **intermarry** than Black women, while Asian women are more likely to intermarry than Asian men. [12]Men and women from other racial groups are equally likely to intermarry.
- [13]Younger and better-educated Americans are more likely to intermarry than older and less-educated Americans.

[14]Intermarriage and the resulting mixed-race children they produce are gradually blurring the racial boundaries that have long divided the nation.

[15]Some **demographers** note that race could eventually lose much of its meaning in the United States, much as ethnicity has lost its meaning

among many Anglo Americans. [16]Interracial tolerance is increasing as the nation's Hispanic and Asian populations continue to grow. [17]Moreover, many new immigrants come from countries with mixed-race traditions, which may make them more open to interracial marriage.

—From *Cultural Anthropology,* 7th ed., p. 220 by Marvin Harris and Orna Johnson. Copyright © 2007 by Pearson Education, Inc. Printed and Electronically reproduced by permission of Pearson Education, Inc., Upper Saddle River, NJ.

Use context clues and the word parts in the chart below to state in your own words the definition of the following words from the passage.

Prefix	Meaning	Root	Meaning	Suffix	Meaning
im-	into	*demos*	people	*-al, ic*	related to, state
inter-	between, among	*ethnos*	race, nation	*-er*	one who is
multi-	many	*graph*	writing	*-y*	quality, trait
		marier	marry		
		migrare	move		
		razza	race		

1. In sentence 1, what does the word **ethnic** mean? related to a race or nation

2. In sentences 2, 7, 16, and 17, what does the word **interracial** mean? between races

3. In sentence 6, what does the word **multiracial** mean? being of many races

4. In sentences 11, 12, and 13, what does the word **intermarry** mean? the action of marrying a member from another race

5. In sentence 15, what does the word **demographers** mean? those who write about people

Name _____ Section _____

Date _____ **Score** (number correct) _____ × 10 = _____ %

A. Using context clues, select the letter of the best meaning for each word in **bold** type. Then, identify the context clue you used.

_____a_____ **1.** To obtain a driver's license, a person should offer **verification**, or evidence, of good eyesight, fast reflexes, and reasoning skills.

    a. proof   c. opinion

    b. test   d. denial

_____a_____ **2.** The context clue used for the word *verification* in sentence 1 is called

    a. a synonym.   c. the general context.

    b. an antonym.   d. an example.

_____c_____ **3.** For dramatic impact, artists often favor the use of **complementary** colors such as orange and blue, which share no common colors because orange is made with yellow and red.

    a. bold   c. contrasting

    b. related   d. mysterious

_____d_____ **4.** The context clue used for the word *complementary* in sentence 3 is called

    a. a synonym.   c. the general context.

    b. an antonym.   d. an example.

B. Using context clues, write the definition for each word in **bold** type. Choose definitions from the box. Use each definition once.

distorted	doubts	imperfect	practical	pride	reasonable

5. Ancient tragedy teaches that all humans are **fallible**, or faulty, in motives, thoughts, or deeds.

Fallible means ___imperfect_____.

6. Ancient tragic heroes lose power, respect, and even their lives due to **hubris**; for example, Oedipus arrogantly believes he can outwit the gods and control his own life.

Hubris means ___pride_____.

7. Even though he still had **qualms** that he would fail, Angelo scored a 95 on the test, which was the highest grade in the class.

   Qualms means <u>doubts</u>.

8. Due to the serious loss of life in manned space flights, some experts think that only unmanned missions should be thought of as **feasible** risks.

   Feasible means <u>reasonable</u>.

9. The loud evening songs of the cicada may sound **garbled** to the human ear, yet to the insects, they are clear messages.

   Garbled means <u>distorted</u>.

10. A personal finance course teaches **pragmatic** steps to managing money such as how to balance a bank book, use credit cards, and evaluate financial risks.

    Pragmatic means <u>practical</u>.

VISUAL VOCABULARY

Vincent van Gogh used <u>complementary</u> colors by placing brilliant orange flowers against a bright blue background.

Stated Main Ideas

3

LEARNING OUTCOMES

After studying this chapter you should be able to do the following:

1. Identify the following: traits of a main idea, the topic of a paragraph, a topic sentence. [Comprehension]
2. Distinguish the movement of ideas from general and specific. [Comprehension]
3. Define the following terms: *central idea* and *thesis statement*. [Knowledge]
4. Locate the stated main idea in a paragraph or longer passage. [Comprehension]
5. Assess your comprehension of locating stated main ideas. [Evaluation, Comprehension]
6. Evaluate the importance of locating stated main ideas. [Evaluation]

Before Reading About Stated Main Ideas

Effective use of the reading process relies on developing questions about the material that will guide you as you read. Using the chapter learning outcomes above, create at least five questions that you can answer as you study the chapter. Write your questions in the following spaces:

What are the traits of a main idea _____? (page __96__)

What is the difference between a topic and a topic sentence _____? (page __101__)

How is the flow of ideas related to the placement of topic sentences ? (page __105__)

What is the central idea _____? (page __113__)

What is the difference between the central idea and a topic sentence ? (page __113__)

Compare the questions you created based on the chapter learning outcomes with the following questions. Then, write the ones that seem the most helpful in your notebook, leaving enough space after each question to record the answers as you read and study the chapter.

What are the traits of a main idea? (p. 96) What is the difference between a topic and a topic sentence? (p. 101) How is the flow of ideas related to the placement of topic sentences? (p. 105) What is the central idea? (p. 113) What is the difference between the central idea and a topic sentence? (p. 113)

 ## The Traits of a Main Idea

> A **main idea** is the author's controlling point about the topic.
> It usually includes the topic and the author's attitude or
> opinion about the topic, or the author's approach to the topic.

To identify the main idea, ask yourself two questions:

- Who or what is the paragraph about? The answer is the *topic*. The topic can be stated in just a few words.

- What is the author's controlling point about the topic? The answer is the *main idea*. The main idea is stated in one sentence.

Consider these questions as you read the following paragraph from the college textbook *Essentials of Human Communication*.

Textbook
Skills

Communication Context

[1]The context of communication influences what you say and how you say it. [2]You communicate differently depending on the context you're in. [3]The communication context consists of at least four aspects. [4]The *physical context* refers to the tangible environment, the room, park, or auditorium; you don't talk the same way at a noisy football game as you do at a quiet funeral. [5]The *cultural context* refers to lifestyles, beliefs, values, behavior, and communication of a group; it is the rules of a group of people for considering something is right or wrong. [6]The *social-psychological context* refers to the status relationships among speakers, the formality of the situation; you don't talk the same way in the cafeteria as you would at a formal dinner at your boss's house. [7]The *temporal context* refers to the position in which a message fits into a sequence of events; you don't talk the same way after someone tells of the death of a close relative as you do after someone tells of winning the lottery.

—From *Essentials of Human Communication*, 4th ed., p. 7 by Joseph A. DeVito. Copyright © 2002 by Pearson Education, Inc. Reproduced by permission of Pearson Education, Inc., Boston, MA.

- *Who or what is the paragraph about?* The topic of the paragraph is "the communication context."
- *What is the author's controlling point about the topic?* The controlling point is that it "consists of at least four aspects." Putting topic and controlling point together, the main idea is "The communication context consists of at least four parts."

To better understand the traits of a main idea, compare a passage to a well-planned house of ideas. The *topic* or general subject matter is the roof. The roof covers all the rooms of the house. The *main idea* is the frame of the house, and the supporting details are the different rooms. The following diagram shows the relationship of the ideas:

Topic: the communication context

Main Idea (stated in a topic sentence):

The communication context consists of at least four aspects.

Supporting Details:

The physical context	The cultural context	The social-psychological context	The temporal context

Each of the supporting details explains one aspect of the communication process.

Identifying the Topic of a Paragraph

When you ask the question "Who or what is the paragraph about?" you must be sure that your answer is neither too general nor too specific. A general subject needs specific ideas to support or explain it. However, no single paragraph can discuss all the specific ideas linked to a general idea. So an author narrows the general subject to a topic that needs a specific set of ideas to support it. For example, the very general subject "humor" can be narrowed to "stand-up comics." And the specific details related to stand-up comics might include different comics, ranging from Chris Rock to Ellen DeGeneres to Dane Cook.

However, a piece of writing dealing with the general topic "humor" will include a very different set of specific ideas than the narrower topic of "stand-up comics." The more general category of humor might include jokes and television sitcoms, for example.

Often an author shows the relationship between the topic and the specific details by repeating the topic throughout the paragraph as new pieces of information are introduced. To identify the topic, a master reader often skims the material for this recurring idea. Skimming for the topic allows you to grasp the relationship among a general subject, the topic, and specific details.

EXAMPLE   Skim the following paragraph. Circle the topic as it recurs throughout the paragraph. Answer the question that follows.

A Question of Manners

¹Bad manners seem to dominate today's culture. ²In fact, bad manners have become so common in everyday life that even pop psychologist Dr. Phil devoted an entire segment of his television show to confronting people about their inconsiderate behaviors. ³Some people are rude enough to loudly conduct cell phone conversations about private matters in public places such as restaurants, stores, and theatres. ⁴Some customers feel no shame in speaking rudely, even abusively, to sales clerks and food servers. ⁵Frequently, automobile drivers change lanes or turn without signaling, ride too near to the bumpers of other cars, and make rude hand gestures as they pass.

_____b_____ Which of the following best states the topic?
    a. manners
    b. bad manners
    c. confronting people about their inconsiderate behaviors

EXPLANATION   "Manners" is too general, for it could cover good manners, business manners, or eating manners. "Confronting people about their inconsiderate behaviors" is too specific. This idea is a supporting detail, just one piece of evidence for the claim that bad manners dominate today's culture.

The topic of this paragraph is (b), "bad manners." You should have circled the following phrases: "Bad manners" (sentences 1 and 2), "inconsiderate behaviors" (sentence 2), "rudely" (sentence 4), and "rude" (sentences 3 and 5). Notice how the author uses the synonyms "rude" and "rudely" to restate the topic "bad manners."

PRACTICE 1

Skim each of the following paragraphs and circle the topic as it recurs throughout the paragraph. Then, identify the idea that correctly states the topic. (Hint: one idea is too general to be the topic; another idea is too specific.)

___c___ **1.**   [1]Reflexology is a form of natural healing based on the belief that reflexes in the hands, feet, and ears correspond to specific parts, glands, and organs of the body. [2]By applying pressure on these reflexes, reflexology aids the natural function of the related body areas by relieving tension and improving circulation. [3]Ancient humans stimulated reflexes naturally by working and building with their hands and walking barefoot over rough ground. [4]Modern humans have lost much of nature's way of maintaining a balanced and healthy equilibrium. [5]Reflexology aids natural health and vitality in several ways.

    a. glands and organs
    b. natural forms of healing
    c. reflexology

VISUAL VOCABULARY

A _reflexologist_ uses a method of massage that eases tension through the use of finger pressure, especially to the feet.

    a. reflex
    b. reflexologist
    c. reflexology

Textbook
Skills

___a___ **2.**   [1]Just as we must critically evaluate information we read, we must also use critical thinking skills as we view images. [2]Every day we are bombarded with images—pictures on billboards, commercials on television, graphs and charts in newspapers and textbooks, to name just a few examples. ³Most images slide by without our noticing them, or so we think. ⁴But images, sometimes even more than text, can influence us. ⁵Their creators have purposes, some worthy, some not. ⁶And understanding those purposes requires that we think critically. ⁷The methods of viewing images critically are the same as those we use for reading text critically. ⁸For example, we preview, analyze, interpret, and (often) evaluate images.

—From *The Little, Brown Compact Handbook,* 4th ed., p. 64 by Jane
E. Aaron. Copyright © 2001 by Pearson Education, Inc. Reprinted
by permission of Pearson Education, Inc., Glenview, IL.

a. viewing images critically
b. graphs and charts
c. images

Identifying a Topic Sentence

Most paragraphs have three parts:

- A topic (the general idea or subject)
- A main idea (the controlling point the author is making about the topic, often stated in a topic sentence)
- Supporting details (the specific ideas to support the main idea)

Think again of the house of ideas that a writer builds. Remember, the main idea *frames* the specific ideas. Think of all the different rooms in a house: the kitchen, bedroom, bathroom, living room. Each room is a different part of the house. The frame determines the space for each room and the flow of traffic between rooms. Similarly, the main idea determines how much detail is given and how each detail flows into the next. The main idea of a paragraph is usually stated in a single sentence called the **topic sentence**. The topic sentence—the stated main idea—is unique in two ways.

First, the topic sentence contains two types of information: the topic and the author's controlling point, which restricts or qualifies the topic. At times, the controlling point may be expressed as the author's opinion using biased words. (For more information on biased words see Chapter 9, "Fact and Opinion.") For example, in the topic sentence "Bad manners seem to dominate today's culture," the biased words "bad," "seem," and "dominate" limit and control the general topic "manners."

Other times, the controlling point may express the author's thought pattern, the way in which the thoughts are going to be organized. (For more information on words that indicate thought patterns, see Chapters 7 and 8.) For example, the topic sentence, "Just as we must critically evaluate information we read, we must also use critical thinking skills as we view images" uses the phrase "just as" to reveal that the author will control the topic by comparing our responses to text and images.

Often, an author will use both biased words and a thought pattern to qualify or limit the topic. For example, the topic sentence, "Reflexology aids natural health and vitality in several ways," combines the biased word "aids" and the phrase "several ways" to indicate a list of positive examples and explanations has been provided.

These qualifiers—words that convey the author's bias or thought pattern—helped you correctly identify the topic in the previous section. An important difference between the topic and the topic sentence is that the topic sentence states the author's main idea in a complete sentence.

> A **topic sentence** is a single sentence that states the topic and words that qualify the topic by revealing the author's opinion or approach to the topic.

The second unique trait of the topic sentence is its scope: the topic sentence is a general statement that all the other sentences in the paragraph explain or support. A topic sentence states an author's opinion or thought process, which must be explained further with specific supporting details. For example, in the paragraph about the communication context, the topic and the author's controlling point about the topic are stated in the first sentence. Each of the other sentences in the paragraph states and describes the four aspects of communication context:

Topic	Author's attitude	Author's thought pattern
↓	↓	↓

The *communication context* consists of *at least four aspects*.

First aspect	**Second aspect**	**Third aspect**	**Fourth aspect**
The physical context	The cultural context	The social-psychological context	The temporal context

> **Supporting details** are specific ideas that *develop, explain,* or *support* the main idea.

The supporting details of a paragraph are framed by the main idea, and all work together to explain or support the author's view of the topic. As a master reader, you will see that every paragraph has a topic, a main idea, and supporting details. It is much easier to tell the difference between these three parts of a passage once you understand how each part works. A topic, as the general subject of the paragraph, can be expressed in a word or phrase. The main idea contains both the topic and the author's controlling point about the topic and can be stated in one sentence called the topic sentence. The supporting details are all the sentences that state reasons and explanations for the main idea. To locate the topic sentence of a paragraph ask yourself two questions:

- Which sentence contains qualifiers that reveal the author's controlling point—that is, the author's attitude about the topic or approach to the topic?

- Do all the specific details in the passage support this statement?

EXAMPLES

A. The following group of ideas contains a topic, a main idea, and two supporting details. Circle the topic and underline the author's controlling point. Then, answer the questions.

   a. A (tsunami) (tsoo-nah-me) <u>can be the most disastrous of all ocean waves.</u>

   b. (Tsunamis) are powerful sea waves caused by seismic activity such as volcano eruptions, landslides, or earthquakes on the sea floor.

   c. (These waves), reaching heights over 100 feet and traveling as rapidly as 500 miles per hour, killed tens of thousands of people in the past century.

   ___a___ **1.** Which of the following best states the topic?

   　　a. a tsunami　　　　　　　　c. an ocean wave
   　　b. seismic activity

   ___a___ **2.** Which sentence is the stated main idea?

B. Read the following paragraph. Circle the topic and underline the author's controlling point. Then, answer the two questions that follow it.

Drugs in Our Lives

Textbook
Skills

¹Today, more than ever, (drugs) <u>affect our daily lives.</u> ²It is difficult to pick up a newspaper or to watch television without finding a report or program that concerns (drug use) or some issue associated with it. ³In your personal life, you have had to confront the reality of (drugs) around you. ⁴In school, you have probably been taught the risks involved in (drug use),

and very likely you have had to contend with pressure to share a (drug) experience with your friends or the possibility of (drugs) being sold to you. [5]High school students on a Monday morning may boast about how much beer they consumed at a keg party over the weekend. [6]For some students, (alcohol) consumption begins in junior high school or earlier. [7]Experimentation with marijuana and mind-altering pills of all sorts seems commonplace. [8](Tobacco) consumption among young people, despite the fact that it is illegal for those under eighteen years old to purchase tobacco products, remains a major societal problem. [9]Whether we like it or not, the decision to use (drugs) of all types and forms has become one of life's choices in American society and in communities around the world.

—Levinthal, *Drugs, Behavior, and Modern Society*, 3rd ed., p. 2.

1. What is the topic of the paragraph? drugs _____

2. Which sentence states the author's main idea? 1 _____

EXPLANATIONS

A. The topic is (a) "a tsunami." The first item (a) is the main idea. Note that the main idea is stated as a topic sentence, and contains both the topic "tsunami," and the author's controlling point about the topic, "most disastrous of all ocean waves." The second and third items give two details that support the main idea, by describing the disastrous traits of a tsunami.

B. Every idea in the paragraph has to do with drug usage. Sentence 1 states the main idea as a topic sentence: "Today, more than ever, drugs affect our daily lives." Notice that a topic sentence states the topic, and it states the author's controlling point about the topic. All the other sentences give reasons or evidence that "drugs affect our daily lives."

PRACTICE 2

Textbook
Skills

The following groups of ideas come from the college textbook *Biology: Life on Earth*. Each group contains a main idea and two supporting details. In each group, first identify the topic; then, identify the statement main idea. (Hint: circle the topic and underline the author's controlling point in each group.)

Group 1

a. (Living things) are defined by distinct characteristics.
b. (Living things) are composed of cells that have a complex organized structure.

    c. (Living things) acquire and use materials and energy from their environment and convert them into different forms.

> —From *Biology: Life on Earth,* 8th ed., p. 11 by Teresa Audesirk, Gerald Audesirk, and Bruce E. Byers. Copyright © 2008 by Pearson Education, Inc. Printed and Electronically reproduced by permission of Pearson Education, Inc., Upper Saddle River, NJ..

_____b_____ **1.** Which of the following best states the topic?
- a. cells
- b. traits of living things
- c. materials and energy
- d. living things

_____a_____ **2.** Which sentence is the stated main idea?

Group 2

a. All (cells) contain genes, units of heredity that provide the information needed to control the life of the cell and the small structures called organelles that are specialized to carry out specific functions such as moving the cell, obtaining energy, or synthesizing large molecules.

b. Even a single (cell) has an elaborate internal structure.

c. (Cells) are always surrounded by a thin plasma membrane that encloses the cytoplasm (organelles and the fluid surrounding them) and separates the cell from the outside world.

> —From *Biology: Life on Earth,* 8th ed., p. 11 by Teresa Audesirk, Gerald Audesirk, and Bruce E. Byers. Copyright © 2008 by Pearson Education, Inc. Printed and Electronically reproduced by permission of Pearson Education, Inc., Upper Saddle River, NJ.

_____d_____ **3.** Which of the following best states the topic?
- a. cells
- b. organelles
- c. hereditary information
- d. the internal structure of cells

_____b_____ **4.** Which sentence is the stated main idea?

Read the following paragraph from the college textbook *Biology: Life on Earth.* Circle the topic and underline the author's controlling point. Then, answer the questions that follow.

How Do Scientists (Categorize the Diversity of Life)?

[1]Although all living things share the general characteristics discussed earlier, evolution has produced an amazing variety of life-forms. [2](Organisms) can be (grouped into three major categories), called (domains): Bacteria, Archaea, and Eukarya. [3]This (classification) reflects fundamental differences among the cell types that compose these organisms. [4]Members of both the (Bacteria and the Archaea) usually consist of single, simple cells. [5]Members of the (Eukarya) have bodies composed of one or more

highly complex cells. [6]This (domain) includes three major (subdivisions or kingdoms): the Fungi, Plantae, and Animalia, as well as a diverse (collection) of mostly single-celled organisms collectively known as "protists." [7]There are exceptions to any simple set of criteria used to (characterize the domains and kingdoms), but three (characteristics) are particularly useful: cell type, the number of cells in each organism, and how it acquires energy.

—From *Biology: Life on Earth*, 8th ed., pp. 14–15 by Teresa Audesirk, Gerald Audesirk, and Bruce E. Byers. Copyright © 2008 by Pearson Education, Inc. Printed and Electronically reproduced by permission of Pearson Education, Inc., Upper Saddle River, NJ.

5. What is the topic of the paragraph? <u>The Diverse Categories of Life</u>

6. What is the topic sentence stating the main idea? <u>3</u>

VISUAL VOCABULARY

Trichophyton rubrum fungus This fungus infects tissues such as skin, nails, and hair in humans and other animals. This organism is classified as part of the <u>c</u>_____ domain.

   a. Bacteria
   b. Archaea
   c. Eukarya

 ## The Flow of Ideas and Placement of Topic Sentences

So far, many of the paragraphs you have worked on in this textbook have placed the topic sentence/main idea as the first sentence in the paragraph. However, not all paragraphs put the main idea first. In fact, a topic sentence can be placed at the **beginning** of a paragraph, **within** a paragraph, at the **end** of a paragraph, or at both the beginning and the end of a paragraph. The placement of the topic sentence controls the flow of ideas. In a sense, when a writer builds a house of ideas, the floor plan—the flow of ideas—changes based on where in the paragraph the topic sentence is located. One of the first things a master reader looks for is the location of the topic sentence.

Topic Sentence at the Beginning of a Paragraph

A topic sentence that begins a paragraph signals a move from general ideas to specific ideas. This flow from general to specific, in which an author begins with a general statement and moves to specific reasons and supports, is also known as deductive reasoning. Articles in encyclopedias and news stories in magazines and newspapers typically use the deductive flow of ideas. The following chart shows this flow from general to specific ideas.

Main idea: Topic sentence
Supporting detail
Supporting detail
Supporting detail
Supporting detail

EXAMPLE Read the paragraph, and identify its topic sentence. Remember to ask, "Does this sentence cover all the ideas in the passage?"

Textbook
Skills

Cancer

¹Cancer is a far-reaching malady. ²Statistics tell us that it affects three of four families. ³About a third of all Americans living today will contract cancer in their lifetime. ⁴And cancer kills more children between ages three and fourteen years than any other disease. ⁵Someone dies from cancer in the United States approximately every minute.

—Adapted from *Mind/Body Health: The Effects of Attitudes, Emotions,* and Relationships, 2nd ed., p. 13 by Keith J. Karren, Brent Q. Hafen, Lee Smith, and Kathryn J. Frandsen. Copyright © 2002 by Pearson Education, Inc. Reprinted by permission of Pearson Education, Inc., Upper Saddle River, NJ.

Topic sentence: ___1___

EXPLANATION The topic sentence of this paragraph is sentence 1: "Cancer is a far-reaching malady." All the other sentences explain the extent of cancer's effects.

Topic Sentence Within a Paragraph

Topic sentences within a paragraph can be near the beginning or in the middle of the paragraph.

Near the Beginning

A paragraph does not always start with the topic sentence. Instead, it may begin with a general overview of the topic. These introductory sentences are used to get the reader interested in the topic. They also lead the reader to the topic sentence. Sometimes introductory sentences tell how the ideas in one paragraph tie in to the ideas of earlier paragraphs. At other times, the introductory sentences give background information about the topic.

The flow of ideas remains deductive as it moves from general ideas (the introduction) and main idea (topic sentence) to specific ideas (supporting details). Human interest stories and editorials in magazines and newspapers, as well as academic papers, often rely on this flow of ideas. The following diagram shows this flow from general to specific ideas:

Introductory sentence(s)
Main idea: Topic sentence
Supporting detail
Supporting detail
Supporting detail

EXAMPLE Read the following paragraph, and identify its topic sentence. Remember to ask, "Does this sentence cover all the ideas in the passage?"

Textbook
Skills

Understanding and Meeting Guest Needs

[1]The first step in delivering high-quality service is to learn and fully understand what customers want in a particular tourism service. [2]Tourism managers can uncover specific needs and expectations of customers in a number of ways. [3]First, marketing research can be used to gather information from potential and existing customers. [4]Many companies regularly survey members of their target market to better understand the changing needs and desires of segments they hope to serve. [5]For example, when PepsiCo acquired Taco Bell, management conducted a study of fast-food customers (any fast-food customer, not simply customers who liked Mexican food). [6]From this survey, PepsiCo concluded that fast-food customers had expectations about four things, which can be remembered by the acronym FACT. [7]Customers wanted their fast food really *Fast;* they expected their orders to be *Accurately* delivered; they wanted the premises to be *Clean;* and they expected foods and beverages to be served at appropriate *Temperatures.* [8]With this knowledge, top management

redesigned the entire Taco Bell system to better deliver these expected qualities.

—From *Tourism: The Business of Travel*, 4th ed., pp. 69–70 by Roy A. Cook, Laura J. Yale and Joseph J. Marqua. Copyright © 2010 by Pearson Education, Inc. Printed and Electronically reproduced by permission of Pearson Education, Inc., Upper Saddle River, NJ.

Topic sentence: ___2___

EXPLANATION Sentence 2 is the topic sentence of this paragraph. Sentence 1 offers background information about the general topic "meeting guest needs." The purpose of sentence 1 is to get the reader's attention and tie the upcoming ideas with previously discussed ideas. Sentences 3 through 8 offer supporting details that explain and illustrate how a company can "meet guest needs."

In the Middle

At times, an author begins a paragraph with a few attention-grabbing details. These details are placed first to stir the reader's interest in the topic. The flow of ideas no longer follows the deductive pattern of thinking because the material now moves from specific ideas (supporting details) to a general idea (the topic sentence) to specific ideas (additional supporting details). Creative essays and special interest stories that strive to excite reader interest often employ this approach. Often television news stories begin with shocking details to hook the viewer and prevent channel surfing. The following diagram shows this flow of ideas:

> Supporting detail
> Supporting detail
> Main idea: Topic sentence
> Supporting detail
> Supporting detail

EXAMPLE Read the following paragraph, and identify its topic sentence. Remember to ask, "Does this sentence cover all the ideas in the passage?"

Adolescence

Textbook
Skills

[1]John and Jorge are two 16-year-old neighbors and friends of different ethnic backgrounds. [2]At the same time, they are so much alike. [3]They both wear adult-size clothes, both have a shadow of a mustache on their

upper lip, both play computer games for many hours a day, both contemplate getting a summer job, and both think of attending a local college in two years. [4]As adolescents, they both have reached sexual maturity but have not yet taken on the rights and responsibilities of the adult status. [5]Adolescence is viewed not only as a developmental stage but also as a cultural phenomenon. [6]For instance, extended schooling in many developed countries stretches the period from childhood to adulthood. [7]On the contrary, many non-industrialized cultures encourage their members to take on adult roles as early as possible. [8]Thus, the adolescent stage becomes almost indistinguishable. [9]In some countries, such as Brazil, many children begin to work full time and take care of other family members as early as 12 and sometimes even earlier. [10]In other societies such as India, a girl can marry in her early teens and move to her husband's home to accept the roles of wife and mother.

—Shiraev & Levy, *Cross-Cultural Psychology: Critical Thinking and Contemporary Applications*, 3rd ed., pp. 235–236.

Topic sentence: ____5____

EXPLANATION Sentences 1 through 4 offer introductory examples that capture the readers' interest, set up the topic, and give concrete examples of the developmental traits of adolescents. Sentence 5 is the topic sentence. Sentences 6 through 10 illustrate that adolescence is a cultural phenomenon.

Topic Sentence at the End of a Paragraph

Sometimes an author waits until the end of the paragraph to state the topic sentence and main idea. This approach can be very effective, for it allows the details to build up to the main idea. The pattern is sometimes called climactic order.

The flow of ideas is known as inductive as the author's thoughts move from specific (supporting details) to general (the topic sentence). Inductive reasoning is often used in math and science to generate hypotheses and theories, and to discover relationships between details. In addition, inductive reasoning is often used in argument (for more about argument, see Chapters 12 and 13). Politicians and advertisers use this approach to convince people to agree with their ideas or to buy their products. If a politician begins with a general statement such as "Taxes must be raised," the audience members may strongly disagree. If, however, the politician begins with the details and leads up to the main idea, people are more likely to agree. For example, people are more likely to agree that roads need to be repaired, even if it means raising taxes. Inductive reasoning is the process of arriving at a general understanding based on specific details. The following diagram shows the ideas moving from specific to general.

Supporting detail
Supporting detail
Supporting detail
Supporting detail
Main idea: Topic sentence

EXAMPLE Read the following paragraph, and identify its topic sentence. Remember to ask, "Does this sentence cover all the ideas in the passage?"

Roofies and Rape

¹Charlene sat perched on a bar stool as she sipped her drink and chatted flirtatiously with the cute stranger who had introduced himself as Roger. ²After a few minutes of conversation, she excused herself for a quick trip to the restroom. ³While she was gone, Roger dropped a little white pill into her glass and stirred until it dissolved. ⁴When she returned, she finished her drink. ⁵About ten minutes later, Charlene began to feel dizzy, disoriented, and nauseated; she felt simultaneously too hot and too cold. ⁶Roger asked her if she felt all right and offered to drive her home. ⁷Because she had difficulty speaking and moving, Roger easily guided her out of the bar and into his car. ⁸Shortly thereafter, she passed out. ⁹Roger took her to a remote wooded area, raped her, and left her there. ¹⁰The next morning, she had no memory of what had happened. ¹¹Charlene became one of the thousands of victims of Rohypnol, also known as "roofies." ¹²Rohypnol is used as a "date rape" drug, which causes a victim to pass out so she cannot resist or recall what happened to her.

Topic sentence: _____12_____

EXPLANATION Sentences 1 through 11 tell the story of one woman's experience with Rohypnol. Sentence 12 states the main idea. Starting the passage with the details of the incident draws readers into the situation and heightens their interest. Ending the passage with the main idea is very powerful.

Topic Sentence at the Beginning and the End of a Paragraph

A paragraph may start and end by stating one main idea in two different sentences. Even though these two sentences state the same idea, they usually word the idea in different ways. A topic sentence presents the main idea at the beginning of the paragraph. Then, at the end of the paragraph, the main idea is stated again, this time using different words. This flow of ideas is based on the age-old advice given to writers to "tell the reader what you are going to say; say it; then tell the reader what you said." Many essays written by college students rely on this presentation of ideas. The following diagram shows this flow of ideas:

Main idea: Topic sentence
Supporting detail
Supporting detail
Supporting detail
Supporting detail
Supporting detail
Supporting detail
Main idea: Topic sentence

EXAMPLE Read the following paragraph, and identify its topic sentences. Remember to ask, "Do these sentences cover all the ideas in the passage?"

Recreational Therapy

¹Recreational therapy benefits the physical and mental health of many patients. ²Recreational therapy includes music, art, drama, and dance. ³Patients who benefit from recreational therapy include those who suffer from substance abuse, eating disorders, violent abuse, homelessness, autism, and complications due to aging. ⁴This type of therapy improves a person's physical, mental, social, and emotional abilities. ⁵Recreational therapy promotes good health and well-being, which leads to a higher quality of life. ⁶This therapy also reduces the need for extended healthcare services by nurturing independent living skills. ⁷Recreational therapy is an excellent method to improve or maintain physical and mental health.

Topic sentences: __1, 7__

EXPLANATION Sentences 1 and 7 both state the main idea of the passage: Recreational therapy benefits patients. Notice how the wording changes at the end of the passage. Repeating the main idea makes the point much stronger and more likely to be remembered.

PRACTICE 3

Textbook
Skills

Read the following series of paragraphs taken from the same section of the college textbook *Business*. Identify the topic sentence of each paragraph. Remember to ask, "Which sentence covers all the details in each paragraph."

The Business Environment

¹No doubt business today is faster paced, more complex, and more demanding than ever before. ²In less than a decade, the hunt for new goods and services has been accelerated by product life cycles measured in weeks or months rather than years. ³Individual consumers and business customers want high-quality goods and services—often customized and with lower prices and immediate delivery. ⁴Sales offices, service providers, and production facilities are shifting geographically as new markets and resources emerge in other countries. ⁵Employees want flexible working hours and opportunities to work at home. ⁶Stockholder expectations also add pressure for productivity increases, growth in market share, and larger profits. ⁷At the same time, however, a more vocal public demands greater honesty, fair competition, and respect for the environment.

—From *Business*, 8th ed., p. 44 by Ricky W. Griffin and Ronald J. Ebert. Copyright © 2006 by Pearson Education, Inc. Printed and Electronically reproduced by permission of Pearson Education, Inc., Upper Saddle River, NJ.

Topic sentence(s): ____1____

Redrawing Corporate Boundaries

¹Successful companies are responding to these challenges in new, often unprecedented ways. ²To stay competitive, they are redrawing traditional organizational boundaries. ³Today, firms join together with other companies, even with competitors, to develop new goods and services. ⁴Some of these relationships are permanent. ⁵But others are temporary alliances formed on short notice so that, working together, partners can produce and deliver products with shorter lead times than either firm could manage alone. ⁶Increasingly, the most successful firms are getting leaner by focusing on their core competencies. ⁷Core competencies are the skills and resources with which they compete best and create the most value for owners. ⁸They *outsource* noncore business processes. ⁹They pay suppliers and distributors to perform these secondary processes

and thereby increase their reliance on suppliers. [10]These new business models call for unprecedented coordination—not only among internal activities, but also among customers, suppliers, and strategic partners.

—From *Business*, 8th ed., pp. 44–45 by Ricky W. Griffin and Ronald J. Ebert. Copyright © 2006 by Pearson Education, Inc. Printed and Electronically reproduced by permission of Pearson Education, Inc., Upper Saddle River, NJ.

Topic sentence(s): ___2, 9___

Outsourcing

[1]Outsourcing is the strategy of paying suppliers and distributors to perform certain business processes or to provide needed materials or services. [2]For example, the cafeteria at a large bank may be important to employees and some customers. [3]But running it is not the bank's main line of business and expertise. [4]Bankers need to focus on money management and financial services, not foodservice operations. [5]That's why most banks outsource cafeteria operations to foodservice management companies whose main line of business includes cafeterias. [6]The result, ideally, is more attention to banking by bankers, better food service for cafeteria customers, and formation of a new supplier-client relationship (foodservice company/bank). [7]Firms today outsource numerous activities. [8]These include payroll, employee training, and research and development. [9]Outsourcing is an increasingly popular strategy because it helps firms focus on their core activities and avoid getting sidetracked onto secondary activities.

—From *Business*, 8th ed., pp. 45–46 by Ricky W. Griffin and Ronald J. Ebert. Copyright © 2006 by Pearson Education, Inc. Printed and Electronically reproduced by permission of Pearson Education, Inc., Upper Saddle River, NJ.

Topic sentence(s): ___9___

 # The Central Idea and the Thesis Statement

Just as a single paragraph has a main idea, longer passages made up of two or more paragraphs also have a main idea. You encounter these longer passages in articles, essays, and textbooks. In longer passages, the main idea is called the **central idea**. Often the author will state the central idea in a single sentence called the **thesis statement**.

> The **central idea** is the main idea of a passage made up of two or more paragraphs.
> The **thesis statement** is a sentence that states the topic and the author's controlling point about the topic for a passage of two or more paragraphs.

You find the central idea of longer passages the same way you locate the main idea or topic sentence of a paragraph. The thesis statement is the one sentence that is general enough to include all the ideas in the passage.

EXAMPLE Read the following passage from a college health textbook, and identify the thesis statement, which states the central idea.

Textbook
Skills

Sunlight and Depression

¹Depression can strike anyone, and it has been known to affect people of all ages and from all walks of life. ²We do know that certain people are at increased risk for depression. ³One of the most significant factors is sunlight. ⁴Recent experiments at the National Institute of Mental Health have concluded that the ability to deal with stress—and thus to avoid depression—can be significantly influenced by the amount of sunlight received each day. ⁵Data from the studies indicate that a number of people seem better able to cope with stress, change, and challenge during the spring, summer, and early autumn months. ⁶As winter approaches and the days grow shorter and darker, many persons become lethargic, anxious, and depressed.

⁷Investigators at the National Institute of Mental Health noticed that during the winter, people tend to slow down, gain weight, and sleep more. ⁸Many also seem to struggle more with depression in the winter months, when there is less light. ⁹Some even develop serious problems more than just a mild case of the blues. ¹⁰Some become incapacitated. ¹¹Some even become suicidal.

¹²Believing that light played a role, investigators exposed persons predisposed to suffer from "light deprivation" to strong artificial, broad-spectrum light for at least five hours a day. ¹³For those exposed to light, symptoms of depression and distress were significantly reduced or even completely eliminated. ¹⁴The therapeutic light is broad-spectrum white light; yellow incandescent bulbs do not work. ¹⁵Since those early studies, the daily regimen has been much simplified and has produced much the same benefits. ¹⁶The usual regimen today is exposure to bright lights for 30 to 60 minutes in the early morning.

—From *Mind/Body Health: The Effects of Attitudes, Emotions, and Relationships*,
2nd ed., pp. 254–255 by Keith J. Karren, Brent Q. Hafen, Lee Smith, and
Kathryn J. Frandsen. Copyright © 2002 by Pearson Education, Inc. Reprinted by
permission of Pearson Education, Inc., Upper Saddle River, NJ.

Thesis statement: ____4____

EXPLANATION The first three sentences hook the reader's interest in the topic "sunlight and depression." Sentence 4 is the central idea of the passage.

Note that sentence 4 includes the topic "sunlight and depression" and the author's controlling point about the topic: "the ability to deal with stress—and thus to avoid depression—can be significantly influenced by the amount of sunlight received each day." Sentences 5 through 16 are supporting details that list the observations that investigators made about the role of light in depression.

PRACTICE 4

Read the following passage from a college history textbook. Identify the thesis statement, which states the central idea.

Textbook
Skills

God Kings

[1]Divine kingship was the cornerstone of Egyptian life. [2]Initially, the king was the incarnation of Horus, a sky and falcon god; later, the king was identified with the sun god Ra, as well as with Osiris, the god of the dead. [3]As divine incarnation, the king was obliged above all to care for his people. [4]It was he who ensured the annual flooding of the Nile, which brought water to the parched land. [5]His commands preserved *maat*, the ideal state of the universe and society, a condition of harmony and justice. [6]In the poetry of the Old Kingdom, the king was the divine herdsman, while the people were the cattle of god:

[7]Well tended are men, the cattle of god.

[8]He made heaven and earth according to their desire and repelled the demon of the waters . . .

[9]He made for the rulers (even) in the egg, a supporter to support the back of the disabled.

[10]Unlike the rulers in Mesopotamia, the kings of the Old Kingdom were not warriors but divine administrators. [11]Protected by the Sahara, Egypt had few external enemies and no standing army. [12]A vast bureaucracy of literate court officials and provincial administrators assisted the god-king. [13]They wielded wide authority as religious leaders, judicial officers, and when necessary, military leaders. [14]A host of subordinate overseers, scribes, metalworkers, stonemasons, artisans, and tax collectors rounded out the royal administration. [15]At the local level, governors administered provinces called *nomes*, the basic unit of Egyptian local government.

—Adapted from Kishlansky, Geary, & O'Brian, *Civilization in the West*, 4th ed., pp. 18–19.

Central idea: _____1_____

Reading a Textbook: Topics, Main Ideas, and Central Ideas

Textbooks identify topics in the title of each chapter. An excellent study strategy is to read a textbook's table of contents, including all of the chapters' titles, which list the general topics covered in the textbook. In addition to providing topics in chapter titles, textbooks also identify topics within each chapter. Other publications, such as newspapers and magazines, also use titles and headings to point out topics.

Textbook authors often state the topic of a passage or paragraph in a heading. For example, titles of graphs often help readers identify the main idea of the graph by stating the topic. Identifying the topic in a heading makes it easier to identify the central idea and supporting details.

EXAMPLE   Read the following passage from a psychology textbook. Then, answer the questions that follow it.

Workplace Violence: Aggression on the Job

¹City of Industry, California—A postal worker walked up to his boss, pulled a gun from a paper bag and shot him dead, the latest incident in an alarming increase in workplace violence. (*Los Angeles Times*, July 18, 1995)

²Portland, Oregon—A man accused of shooting two people and taking four others hostage in an office tower appeared in court on Friday. . . . ³Police initially said Rancor intended to shoot female office workers for having him fired from his job—but investigators said Friday that Rancor had problems with authority in general. (Associated Press, 1996)

⁴Reports of events such as these have appeared with alarming frequency in recent years. ⁵They appear to reflect a rising tide of violence in the workplace. ⁶In fact, more than eight hundred people are murdered at work each year in the United States (National Institute for Occupational Safety and Health, 1993). ⁷While these statistics seem to suggest that workplaces are becoming truly dangerous locations where disgruntled employees frequently attack or even shoot one another, two facts should be carefully noted. ⁸First, a large majority of violence occurring in work settings is performed by outsiders who do not work there but who enter a workplace to commit robbery or other crimes. ⁹Second, surveys indicate

that threats of physical harm or actual harm in work settings are actually quite rare. [10]In fact, for most occupations, the chances of being killed at work (by outsiders and coworkers combined) are something like 1 in 450,000.

[11]In sum, growing evidence suggests that while workplace violence is certainly an important topic worthy of careful study, it is relatively rare, and violence in work settings is, in fact, only the dramatic tip of the much larger problem of workplace aggression. [12]**Workplace aggression** is any form of behavior through which individuals seek to harm others in their workplace (Baron & Neuman, 1996; Neuman & Baron, 1998).

—Text and graph from *Social Psychology with Research Navigator*, 10th ed., pp. 460–461 and Figure 11.15 (p. 461) by Robert A. Baron and Donn Byrne. Copyright © 2004 by Allyn & Bacon, Inc. Reproduced by permission of Pearson Education, Inc., Boston, MA.

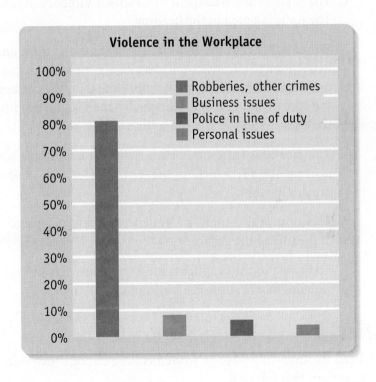

1. The topic of the paragraph is _Workplace Violence: Aggression on the Job_.

_a_   2. Sentence 11 is
      a. the central idea.   b. a supporting detail.

_____b_____ **3.** Sentence 10 is

    a. the central idea.   b. a supporting detail.

4. The topic of the graph is <u>Violence in the Workplace</u>.

5. ___b___ According to the graph, what percentage of workplace violence is tied to business problems?

    a. about 80%

    b. about 10%

    c. a bit more than 5%

    d. a bit less than 5%

EXPLANATION

1. The topic of the passage is "Workplace Violence: Aggression on the Job." The topic is stated in the heading.

2. Sentence 11 is (a) the central idea; it states the topic and the author's primary point about the topic: workplace violence is just part of the larger problem of aggression on the job. Note that this passage includes the central idea toward the end. The reader can use the heading, which identifies the topic, to help locate the central idea.

3. Sentence 10 is (b) a supporting detail. In fact, all the sentences leading up to sentence 11, which is the central idea, are supporting details that explain the topic.

4. The topic of the graph is "Violence in the Workplace." The topic is stated in the title of the graph.

5. According to the graph, business problems account for about 10% of the violence that occurs in the workplace.

PRACTICE 5

Read the following passage from a college biology textbook. Then, answer the questions that follow it.

Textbook
Skills

The Scientific Method Is the Basis of Scientific Inquiry

[1]A biologist's job is to answer questions about life. [2]What causes cancer? [3]Why are frog populations shrinking worldwide? [4]What happens

when a sperm and egg meet? [5]How does HIV cause AIDS? [6]When did the earliest mammals appear? [7]How do bees fly? [8]The list of questions is both endless and endlessly fascinating.

[9]Anyone can ask an interesting question about life. [10]A biologist, however, is distinguished by the manner in which he or she goes about finding answers. [11]A biologist is a scientist and accepts only answers that are supported by evidence, and then only by a certain kind of evidence. [12]Scientific evidence consists of observations or measurements that are easily shared with others and that can be repeated by anyone who has the appropriate tools. [13]The process by which this kind of evidence is gathered is known as the **scientific method.**

[14]The scientific method proceeds step-by-step. [15]It begins when someone makes an **observation** of an interesting pattern or phenomenon. [16]The observation, in turn, stimulates the observer to ask a **question** about what was observed. [17]Then, after a period of contemplation (that perhaps also includes reflecting on the scientific work of others who have considered related questions), the person proposes an answer to the question, an explanation for the observation. [18]This proposed explanation is a **hypothesis.** [19]A good hypothesis leads to a **prediction,** typically expressed in "if . . . then" language. [20]The prediction is tested with further observations or with experiments. [21]These experiments produce results that either support or refute the hypothesis, and a **conclusion** is drawn about it. [22]A single experiment is never an adequate basis for a conclusion; the experiment must be repeated not only by the original experimenter but also by others.

[23]You may find it easier to visualize the steps of the scientific method through an example from everyday life. [24]Imagine this scenario: Late to an appointment, you rush to your car and make the *observation* that it won't start. [25]This observation leads directly to a *question:* Why won't the car start? [26]You quickly form a *hypothesis:* The battery is dead. [27]Your hypothesis leads in turn to an if-then *prediction:* If the battery is dead, then a new battery will cause the car to start. [28]Next, you design an *experiment* to test your prediction: You replace your battery with the battery from your roommate's new car and try to start your car again. [29]Your car starts immediately, and you reach the *conclusion* that your dead battery hypothesis is correct.

—From *Life on Earth*, 5th ed., Figure 1-3 (p. 363) and pp. 3–4 by Teresa Audesirk, Gerald Audesirk and Bruce E. Byers. Copyright © 2009 by Pearson Education, Inc. Reprinted by permission of Pearson Education, Inc., Upper Saddle River, NJ.

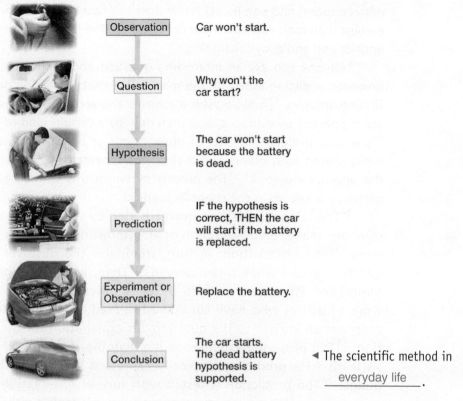

Observation — Car won't start.

Question — Why won't the car start?

Hypothesis — The car won't start because the battery is dead.

Prediction — IF the hypothesis is correct, THEN the car will start if the battery is replaced.

Experiment or Observation — Replace the battery.

Conclusion — The car starts. The dead battery hypothesis is supported.

◄ The scientific method in <u>everyday life</u>.

1. The topic of the passage is <u>the scientific method</u>

_____.

<u>b</u>   **2.** Sentence 1 is
     a. the central idea.   b. a supporting detail.

<u>b</u>   **3.** Sentence 8 is
     a. the central idea.   b. a supporting detail.

<u>b</u>   **4.** Sentence 11 is
     a. the central idea.   b a supporting detail.

<u>b</u>   **5.** Sentence 12 is
     a. the central idea.   b. a supporting detail.

<u>a</u>   **6.** Sentence 13 is
     a. the central idea.   b. a supporting detail.

7. Based on the information in the passage, state the main idea of the figure by completing the following caption for the figure: The scientific method in <u>everyday life</u>.

APPLICATIONS

Application 1: Identifying Topics

Read the following information that was posted on a government website. Circle the key terms that identify the topic as they recur throughout the paragraph. Then, answer the question that follows.

USAID Disaster Assistance Response Team: Haiti Earthquake

[1]The (U.S. Agency for International Development (USAID)) is an independent federal agency. [2](USAID) provides economic development and humanitarian assistance around the world in support of the foreign policy goals of the United States. [3]Within (USAID), a select group of staff is prepared to respond to disasters abroad, no matter when or where they occur. [4]This group is known as the (Disaster Assistance Response Team (DART)). [5]They are experienced professionals, dedicated to saving lives, easing suffering, and reducing the social and economic impact of disasters. [6]Within 24 hours of the 7.0 magnitude earthquake that rocked (Haiti) on January 12, 2010, the (DART arrived in Haiti). [7]They immediately set to work. [8](DART) conducted urban search and rescue (USAR) operations. [9]They organized logistics, established critical telecommunications support for the team and for the Government of (Haiti). [10]In addition, they provided information updates on the unfolding situation. [11]The (DART) coordinated the delivery of more than 40 planeloads of relief. [12]This included more than 111,000 water containers, nearly 75,000 hygiene kits, more than 10,000 rolls of plastic sheeting, and 5,000 kitchen sets. [13]In addition, the six (USAID)-funded USAR teams saved the lives of 47 people trapped in collapsed structures. [14]Within six weeks, (USAID) programmed more than $400 million to address immediate food, water, health, and shelter needs for (earthquake-affected) populations.

> —Adapted from "SUCCESS STORY: USAID Disaster Assistance Response Team: Haiti Earthquake." USAID 2 March 2010.
> http://www.usaid.gov/helphaiti/.

What is the topic of the paragraph? USAID Disaster Assistance Response Team: Haiti Earthquake

Application 2: The Topic and the Main Idea

Read the following paragraph. Then, answer the questions that follow it.

Computer Worms, Viruses, and Bugs

[1]Worms, viruses, and bugs have long been loathed by many in the natural world as annoying and even dangerous pests. [2]Likewise, the artificial world of computers constantly battles the infestation of worms, viruses, and bugs. [3]A computer virus is a programming code that is deliberately designed as a sneak attack on other people's computers. [4]A virus may be designed to deliver a harmless, silly message or to strike a destructive blow to files on hard drives. [5]Computer viruses depend on the aid of the unwitting computer user. [6]For example, viruses are usually spread by copying or transferring a file. [7]A computer worm is a program deliberately designed to reproduce itself on a network of computers. [8]Unlike a virus, a computer worm does not need the aid of the user to wreak havoc. [9]In contrast, a computer bug is an unintended flaw in a computer's program. [10]Often, a bug occurs because the rules of the programming language were broken or misunderstood. [11]Or, sometimes, a step or detail in the programming process was skipped.

1. What is the topic of the paragraph? <u>Computer Worms, Viruses, and Bugs</u>

<u>b</u>   **2.** Which sentence states the author's main idea?
   a. sentence 1
   b. sentence 2
   c. sentence 4

Application 3: Topics, Main Ideas, and Supporting Details

Each of the following groups of ideas has a main idea and two supporting details. In each group, first identify the topic. Then, identify the stated main idea. (Hint: circle the topic and underline the author's controlling point in each group.)

Group 1

a. A geyser is <u>a powerful eruption</u> of a hot spring into a column of hot water or steam.

b. For example, the geyser Old Faithful erupts into a 60-foot tower of 350-degree water.

c. Old Faithful erupts about every 30 minutes around the clock, and each eruption lasts approximately three or four minutes.

<u>b</u>   **1.** Which of the following best states the topic?
   a. Old Faithful   c. hot springs
   b. geysers

<u>a</u>   **2.** Which sentence is the stated main idea?

Group 2

a. The Emotional Competence Inventory is a testing tool that measures (emotional intelligence).

b. For example, the abilities to manage negative feelings and control impulses are signs of high (emotional intelligence).

c. (Emotional intelligence) is knowing what your feelings are and <u>making good decisions based on wise use of your emotions.</u>

___a___ **3.** Which of the following best states the topic?

    a. emotional intelligence   c. feelings

    b. The Emotional Competence Inventory

___c___ **4.** Which sentence is the stated main idea?

Application 4: Location of the Topic Sentence

Read the following paragraph from a college finance textbook and identify its topic sentence or sentences. Remember to ask, "Does this sentence (Do these sentences) cover all the ideas in the passage?"

Disadvantages of Using Credit

Textbook Skills

[1]<u>There can be a high cost to using credit.</u> [2]If you borrow too much money, you may have difficulty making your credit card payments. [3]It is easier to obtain credit than to pay it back. [4]And having a credit line can tempt you to make impulse purchases that you cannot afford. [5]Eighty-three percent of all students have at least one credit card, and almost a third have four or more. [6]The average credit card balance for 21 percent of undergraduates is between $3,000 and $7,000. [7]Many students make minimum payments on their credit cards while in school with the expectation that they will be able to pay off their balance once they graduate and are working full-time. [8]Yet the accumulating interest fees catch many by surprise, and the debt can quickly become difficult to manage. [9]Today's graduating students have an average of $24,567 in combined education loan and credit card balances. [10]If you are unable to repay the credit you receive, you may not be able to obtain credit again or will have to pay a very high interest rate to obtain it. [11]Your ability to save money will also be reduced if you have large credit payments. [12]If your spending and credit card payments exceed your net cash flow, you limit your ability to increase your personal wealth. [13]Credit can be costly.

—Adapted from *Personal Finance*, 3rd ed., pp. 174–175 by Jeff Madura. Copyright © 2007 by Pearson Education, Inc. Reproduced by permission of Pearson Education, Inc., Boston, MA.

Topic sentence(s): ___1, 13___

REVIEW TEST 1

Score (number correct) _____ × 20 = _____ %

Topics, Main Ideas, and Supporting Details

Textbook
Skills

A. Each of the following groups of ideas includes one topic, one main idea, and two supporting details. In each group, first identify the topic. Then, identify the stated main idea. (Hint: circle the topic and underline the author's controlling point in each group.)

Group 1

a. People use several methods to avoid conflict.
b. In addition, quick acceptance of a suggested solution avoids conflict.
c. For example, some stop themselves from raising controversial aspects of an issue.

—Adapted from Folger, Peale, & Stutman, *Working Through Conflict,* 4th ed., p. 24.

___c___ **1.** Which of the following best states the topic?
    a. avoiding controversial issues   c. avoiding conflict
    b. quick acceptance of a solution

___a___ **2.** Which sentence best states the main idea?

Group 2

a. The difference between sun and shade plants has practical importance.
b. Look in a nursery catalog and you will find plants keyed by symbols to indicate their adaptation to full sun, partial shade, and full shade.
c. Foresters and landscape designers base a part of their management plans on the shade tolerance or intolerance of plants.

—Adapted from Smith & Smith,
Elements of Ecology, 4th ed., p. 48.

___b___ **3.** Which of the following best states the topic?
    a. plants   c. landscape designers
    b. sun and shade plants

___a___ **4.** Which sentence best states the main idea?

B. Read the paragraph from a college education textbook. Then, answer the questions that follow it.

11.9 GE/101 words   **Classroom Tests**

[1]Teacher-made tests are a traditional and indispensable part of evaluation. [2]They serve several functions, including, of course, measuring achievement. [3]The items on a test provide the teacher with the opportunity to select for the student those aspects of the unit of study that are most important and thus reinforce learning of the material one last time during the study of the unit. [4]Furthermore, students' attention is entirely devoted to the test for the duration of the time, resulting in some of the most intense learning that occurs in a classroom. [5]This is a strong rationale for writing powerful tests.

—Wilen, Ishler, Hutchinson, & Kindsvatter, *Dynamics of Effective Teaching*, 4th ed., p. 354.

_____b_____ **5.** Which sentence states the main idea of the paragraph?
   a. sentence 1   c. sentence 3
   b. sentence 2   d. sentence 5

REVIEW TEST 2

Score (number correct) _____ × 10 = _____ %

The following passage is the summary of Chapter 4, "Biogeochemical Cycles in the Biosphere," in the college textbook *Geography: People, Places, and Environment*. Read the passage. Then, answer the questions that follow.

Textbook
Skills

12.7 GE/515 words   **Biogeochemical Cycles in the Biosphere:**
Chapter Summary

[1]Climate is the dominant control on local environmental processes, primarily through its influence on water availability and movement. [2]Knowledge of the water budget is essential to understanding both physical and biological processes because the water budget is a critical regulator of ecosystem activity. [3]This influence extends to human use of the landscape, through such issues as determining the natural vegetation cover or agricultural potential.

[4]Carbon is the basis of life on Earth; it cycles through the atmosphere, oceans, biosphere, and soil. [5]Photosynthesis transfers carbon from the atmosphere to the biosphere, and respiration returns it to the atmosphere. [6]Plant growth is most prolific in warm, humid climates where water and energy are plentiful. [7]Plant growth is less in dry or cool climates. [8]Large amounts of carbon are exchanged between the atmosphere and the oceans, and the oceans are a major sink for carbon dioxide that is added to the atmosphere by fossil-fuel combustion.

[9]The outermost layer of Earth's surface in land areas is soil, which is a mixture of mineral and organic matter formed by physical, chemical, and biological processes. [10]Climate is a major regulator of soil development, through its control on water movement. [11]Plant and animal activity in the soil produces organic matter and mixes the upper soil layers. [12]In humid regions, water moves downward through the soil, carrying dissolved substances lower in the profile or removing them altogether. [13]In arid regions, these substances are not so easily removed. [14]Soil characteristics reflect these processes, and there is close correspondence between the world climate map and the world soil map.

[15]Photosynthesis is the basis of food chains and ecological systems. [16]Plants compete for water, sunlight, and nutrients, and plants that are best adapted to compete for limiting factors will dominate a given environment. [17]Such adaptations help explain the world distribution of major vegetation types. [18]Disturbances modify ecological communities, and succession following disturbance is a fundamental process of landscape change. [19]Very large portions of the world's land surface have been modified by human activity, and humans are major players in most of the world's ecosystems.

[20]The world vegetation map closely mirrors the world climate map. [21]Ecologically diverse and complex forests occupy humid environments, storing most nutrients in their biomass. [22]In arid and semiarid regions, sparse vegetation is adapted to moisture stress. [23]Forests adapted to winter cold are in humid midlatitude climates, developing as broadleaf forests in warmer areas and coniferous forests in subarctic latitudes. [24]In high-latitude climates, cold-tolerant short vegetation occupies areas that have a mild summer season. [25]Vegetation is absent in ice-bound polar climates.

—From *Introduction to Geography: People, Places, and Environment*, 4th ed., p. 161 by Edward Bergman and William H. Renwick. Copyright © 2008 by Pearson Education, Inc. Printed and Electronically reproduced by permission of Pearson Education, Inc., Upper Saddle River, NJ.

_____b_____ **1.** Which of the following best states the topic of the first paragraph (sentences 1–3)?

    a. climate   c. human use of landscape

    b. water budget   d. agricultural potential

2. The topic sentence of the first paragraph (sentences 1–3) is ___2___.

_____a_____ **3.** Which of the following best states the topic of the second paragraph (sentences 4–8)?

    a. carbon   c. the oceans

    b. plant growth   d. the atmosphere

4. The topic sentence of the second paragraph (sentences 4–8) is ___4___.

__c__ **5.** Which of the following best states the topic of the third paragraph (sentences 9–13)?
    a. the Earth's surface   c. soil
    b. climate   d. plant and animal activity

6. The topic sentence of the third paragraph (sentences 9–14) is ___14___.

__d__ **7.** Which of the following best states the topic of the fourth paragraph (sentences 15–19)?
    a. photosynthesis   c. adaptations
    b. food chains   d. ecosystems

8. The topic sentence of the fourth paragraph (sentences 15–19) is ___16___.

__a__ **9.** Which of the following best states the topic of the fifth paragraph (sentences 20–25)?
    a. vegetation   c. world climate map
    b. forests   d. climates

10. The topic sentence of the fifth paragraph (sentences 20–25) is ___20___.

REVIEW TEST 3

Score (number correct) _____ × 10 = _____ %

Topics and Main Ideas

Before Reading: Survey the following passage adapted from the college textbook *Psychology and Life*. Skim the passage, noting the words in bold print. Answer the Before Reading questions that follow the passage. Then, read the passage. Next, answer the After Reading questions. Use the discussion and writing topics as activities to do after reading.

Textbook Skills

10.7 GE/315 words

Depression: A Mood Disorder

Vocabulary Preview

incredibly (1): extremely

mania (3): craze, obsession

[1]There have almost certainly been times in your life when you would have described yourself as terribly depressed or **incredibly** happy. [2]For some people, however, extremes in mood disrupt normal life experiences. [3]A mood disorder is an emotional disturbance, such as a severe depression or depression **alternating** with **mania**. [4]Researchers estimate that about 19 percent of adults have suffered from mood disorders.

psychopathy (6):
mental disorder

clinical (11):
medically shown or
proven by medical
testing

[5]One common type of mood disorder is the major depressive disorder.

[6]Depression has been characterized as the "common cold of **psychopathy**" for two reasons. [7]First, it occurs frequently, and, second, almost everyone has experienced elements of the full-scale disorder at some time in their life. [8]Everyone has, at one time or another, experienced grief after the loss of a loved one or felt sad or upset when failing to achieve a desired goal. [9]These sad feelings are only one symptom experienced by people suffering from a major depressive disorder.

[10]People suffering with depression differ in terms of the **severity** and duration of their symptoms. [11]Many people struggle with **clinical** depression for only several weeks at one point in their lives. [12]Others suffer depression **episodically** or chronically for many years. [13]Estimates of the prevalence of mood disorders reveal that about 21 percent of females and 13 percent of males suffer a major depression at some time in their lives.

[14]Depression takes an enormous toll on those who suffer, their families, and society. [15]One European study found that people with **chronic** depression spend a fifth of their entire adult lives in the hospital. [16]Twenty percent of sufferers are totally disabled by their symptoms and do not ever work again. [17]In the United States, depression accounts for the majority of all mental hospital admissions. [18]Still, many experts believe that the disorder is under-diagnosed and under-treated. [19]Fewer than half of those who struggle with major depressive disorder receive any professional help.

—From *Psychology and Life*, 16th ed., pp. 482–484 by Richard J. Gerrig and
Philip G. Zimbardo. Copyright © 2002 by Pearson Education, Inc.
Reproduced by permission of Pearson Education, Inc., Boston, MA.

Before Reading

Vocabulary in Context

___b___ **1.** The word **alternating** in sentence 3 means
   a. remaining.   c. shutting out.
   b. taking turns.   d. encouraging.

___d___ **2.** The word **severity** in sentence 10 means
   a. gentleness.   c. visibility.
   b. length.   d. harshness.

_____c_____ **3.** The word **episodically** in sentence 12 means
　　　　a. continually.　　　　　　c. regularly.
　　　　b. deeply.　　　　　　　　d. rarely.

_____a_____ **4.** The word **chronic** in sentence 15 means
　　　　a. constant.　　　　　　　c. treatable.
　　　　b. mild.　　　　　　　　　d. occasional.

Topics and Main Ideas

_____b_____ **5.** What is the topic of the passage?
　　　　a. grief　　　　　　　　　　c. normal life
　　　　b. major depressive disorder　d. mental hospital admissions

After Reading

Main Ideas and Supporting Details

_____b_____ **6.** Which sentence states the central idea of the passage?
　　　　a. sentence 1　　　　　　　c. sentence 10
　　　　b. sentence 5　　　　　　　d. sentence 14

_____b_____ **7.** What is the topic of the third paragraph (sentences 10–13)?
　　　　a. people suffering from depression
　　　　b. differences in the severity and duration of the symptoms of depression
　　　　c. the number of males and females suffering from depression

_____a_____ **8.** Which sentence states the main idea of the third paragraph?
　　　　a. sentence 10　　　　　　　c. sentence 12
　　　　b. sentence 11　　　　　　　d. sentence 13

9–10. Label each of the following two sentences from the fourth paragraph (sentences 14–19). Write **A** if it states the main idea or **B** if it supplies a supporting detail.

_____A_____ **9.** Depression takes an enormous toll on those who suffer, their families, and society.

_____B_____ **10.** Fewer than half of those who struggle with major depressive disorder receive any professional help.

WHAT DO YOU THINK?

What do you think are the major causes of depression? In what ways do you think depression affects a person's ability to work or learn? How do you think most people cope with depression? Assume you are taking a college course in psychology and your professor assigned the class to read the passage "Depression: A Mood Disorder." Your professor has also assigned you to begin the class discussion of the passage with a written response to the following prompt: "Predict or guess the difference between the terms **episodic depression** and **chronic depression**." Use details from the passage and from a dictionary to define each term. Can you think of possible examples to illustrate the differences? If so, include them in your written response.

REVIEW TEST 4   Score (number correct) _____ × 10 = _____ %

Topics and Main Ideas

Before Reading: Survey the following passage adapted from the college textbook *Cross-Cultural Psychology*. Skim the passage, noting the words in bold print. Answer the Before Reading questions that follow the passage. Then, read the passage. Next, answer the After Reading questions. Use the discussion and writing topics as activities to do after reading.

Textbook
Skills

Vocabulary Preview

psychological (1): mental, emotional

formulated (2): made, created

assumptions (3): beliefs, ideas

phenomenon (3): event, occurrence

10.2 GE/434 words

Cross-Cultural Sensitivity

[1]One type of **psychological** knowledge represents a collection of *popular beliefs,* often called *folk theories.* [2]This knowledge is a type of "everyday **psychology**" that is **formulated** by the people and for the people. [3]These popular beliefs are shared **assumptions** about certain aspects of human psychological **phenomena.** [4]These assumptions vary from being general, such as the belief in the ability of dreams to predict the future, to quite specific, that a particular item of clothing will bring good luck. [5]We can increase our cross-cultural sensitivity by understanding the psychological power of popular beliefs.

[6]When Jeff, an exchange student from Oregon, was invited to a birthday party, he was thrilled. [7]This was the first party he would attend in Russia, and he knew how well

Russians mastered the art of celebration. [8]The day of the birthday, he dug out a nice souvenir from his suitcase, then caught a taxicab and decided to stop by a flower market to buy a nice bouquet—he was invited by a female student and he thought flowers would be a nice addition to the souvenir he brought from Portland. [9]He could not anticipate that the flowers would cause so much anxiety and frustration an hour later. [10]He bought a dozen roses—a nice gesture according to U.S. standards. [11]But when he presented flowers to the host, he noticed how visibly upset she became when she put the flowers into a vase. [12]He even saw her crying in the kitchen. [13]A couple of friends were trying to comfort her. [14]Jeff began to wonder if his behavior had been the cause of the young woman's crying. [15]What he learned, as he later said, was one of the strangest experiences in his life. [16]He said that the young woman was extremely upset because he brought an even number of flowers. [17]**Coincidentally,** she had recently survived a deadly illness and was extremely sensitive to the issue of death and dying. [18]Apparently, Russians bring an even number of flowers to funerals, memorial services in church, and cemeteries. [19]An odd number of flowers is designed for dates, weddings, and other happy celebrations. [20]Apparently the flowers— the number of them, in fact—that Jeff brought to the party became a disturbing signal that brought the woman's traumatic experience back to her memory.

[21]In general, Russians will not react in the same dramatic way if you bring an even number of flowers to their celebrations. [22]However, you will notice that one flower—out of the dozen or half-a-dozen you bring—disappears from the vase. [23]Fears, phobias, and superstitions are at times rooted in folk customs and practices.

—Adapted from Shiraev & Levy, *Cross-Cultural Psychology: Critical Thinking and Contemporary Applications,* 3rd ed., pp. 11, 264.

Before Reading

Vocabulary in Context

Use your own words to define each of the following terms. Identify the context clue you used to make meaning of the word.

1. The word **theories** in sentence 1 means ___beliefs or ideas___ .

2. Context clue used for **theories:** ___synonym___

3. The word **coincidentally** in sentence 17 means <u>by chance</u>.

4. Context clue used for **coincidentally:** <u>general sense of the passage</u>

Topics and Main Ideas

5. What is the topic of the passage? <u>cross-cultural sensitivity and popular beliefs</u>

After Reading

Main Ideas and Supporting Details

6. Which sentence states the central idea of the passage? <u>5</u>

<u>b</u>   **7.** What is the topic of the second paragraph (sentences 6–20)?
   a. the young woman's near death experience
   b. Jeff's strange experience
   c. a birthday party

8–10. Label each of the following sentences from the third paragraph (sentences 21–23). Write **A** if it states the main idea or **B** if it supplies a supporting detail.

<u>B</u>   **8.** In general, Russians will not react in the same dramatic way if you bring an even number of flowers to their celebrations.

<u>B</u>   **9.** However, you will notice that one flower—out of the dozen or half-a-dozen you bring—disappears from the vase.

<u>A</u>   **10.** Fears, phobias, and superstitions are at times rooted in folk customs and practices.

WHAT DO YOU THINK?

Was Jeff wrong to bring flowers to the birthday party? Why or why not? Why was the young woman so upset? Why didn't she tell Jeff why she was upset? How would you define "cross-cultural sensitivity"? Assume you are a mentor to the young woman who became upset with Jeff's gesture of giving a dozen roses. Write a letter to her in which you give her advice and comfort.

After Reading About Stated Main Ideas

Before you move on to the Mastery Tests on stated main ideas, take time to reflect on your learning and performance by answering the following questions. Write your answers in your notebook.

- How has my knowledge base or prior knowledge about stated main ideas changed?

- Based on my studies, how do I think I will perform on the Mastery Test(s)? Why do I think my scores will be above average, average, or below average?

- Would I recommend this chapter to other students who want to learn more about stated main ideas? Why or why not?

Test your understanding of what you have learned about Vocabulary Skills for Master Readers by completing the Chapter 3 Review Card in the insert near the end of your text.

CONNECT TO **myreadinglab**

To check your progress in meeting Chapter 3's learning outcomes, log in to **www.myreadinglab.com** and try the following activities.

- The "Main Idea section of MyReadingLab provides review materials, practice activities, and tests about topics and main ideas. To access this resource, click on the "Study Plan" tab. Then click on "Main Idea." Then click on the following links as needed: "Overview," "Model," "Practice," and "Tests."

- To measure your mastery of the content of this chapter, complete the tests in the "Main Idea" section and click on Gradebook to find your results.

Name _____ Section _____

Date _____ **Score** (number correct) _____ × 25 = _____%

A. Skim each of the following paragraphs and circle the topic as it recurs throughout the paragraph. Then, identify the idea that correctly states the topic. (Hint: one idea is too general to be the topic; another idea is too specific.)

Textbook Skills

GE 11.3/136 words

Animals

[1]It is difficult to devise a concise definition of the term "animal." [2]No single feature fully characterizes animals, so the group is defined by a list of characteristics. [3]None of these characteristics is unique to animals, but together they distinguish animals from members of other kingdoms:

- [4]Animals are multicellular.
- [5]Animals obtain their energy by consuming the bodies of other organisms.
- [6]Animals typically reproduce sexually. [7]Although animal species exhibit a tremendous diversity of reproductive styles, most are capable of sexual reproduction.
- [8]Animal cells lack a cell wall.
- [9]Animals are motile (able to move about) during some stage of their lives. [10]Even the relatively stationary sponges have a free-swimming larval stage (a juvenile form).
- [11]Most animals are able to respond rapidly to external stimuli as a result of the activity of nerve cells, muscle tissue, or both.

—From *Biology: Life on Earth,* 8th ed., p.301, by Teresa Audesirk, Gerald Audesirk, and Bruce E. Byers. Copyright © 2008 by Pearson Education, Inc. Printed and Electronically reproduced by permission of Pearson Education, Inc., Upper Saddle River, NJ.

____c____ **1.**

    a. animals
    b. animal kingdoms
    c. characteristics of animals

VISUAL VOCABULARY

Sponges, such as the Erect Rope sponge and the Encrusting sponge, are often described as the most primitive of <u>c</u>_____.

   a. life forms.
   b. creatures.
   c. animals.

B. The following group of ideas is from a college psychology textbook. Read the ideas, and answer the questions that follow.

Textbook
Skills

   a. Implicit memories are of three major types.
   b. An implicit memory is a memory that cannot be voluntarily called to mind but still influences behavior or thinking in certain ways.
   c. One type of implicit memory is habits, which are well-learned responses that are carried out without conscious thought.

—From Stephen M. Kosslyn & Robin S. Rosenberg, *Psychology: The Brain, The Person, The World,* p. 206. Published by Allyn and Bacon, Boston, MA. Copyright © 2002 by Pearson Education. Reprinted by permission of the publisher.

_____<u>a</u>_____ **2.** Statement (a) is
    a. the main idea.   b. a supporting detail.

_____<u>b</u>_____ **3.** Statement (b) is
    a. the main idea.   b. a supporting detail.

_____<u>b</u>_____ **4.** Statement (c) is
    a. the main idea.   b. a supporting detail.

Identify the topic sentence in each of the following paragraphs.

A. Paragraph from a college accounting textbook

GE 12.0/235 words

Textbook
Skills

Estate Planning: Living Wills and Power of Attorney

[1]A living will is a simple legal document in which individuals state their preferences if they become mentally or physically disabled. [2]For example, many individuals have a living will that expresses their desire not to be placed on life support if they become terminally ill. [3]In this case, a living will also has financial implications because an estate could be charged with large medical bills resulting from life support. [4]In this way, those who do not want to be kept alive by life support can ensure that their estate is used in the way that they prefer. [5]A power of attorney is a legal document granting a person the power to make decisions for you in the event that you are incapacitated. [6]For example, you may name a family member or a close friend to make your investment and housing decisions if you become ill. [7]A durable power of attorney for health care is a legal document granting a person the power to make specific health care decisions for you. [8]While a living will states many of your preferences, a situation may arise that is not covered by your living will. [9]A durable power of attorney for health care means that the necessary decisions will be made by someone who knows your preferences, rather than by a health care facility. [10]Estate planning involves these decisions about a living will and power of attorney.

—Adapted from *Personal Finance,* 3rd ed., p. 543 by Jeff Madura. Copyright © 2007 by Pearson Education, Inc. Reproduced by permission of Pearson Education, Inc., Boston, MA.

Topic sentence(s): ___10___

B. Paragraph from a college health textbook

10.4 GE/142 words

Textbook
Skills

Caffeine Addiction

[1]As the effects of caffeine wear off, users may feel let down. [2]They may feel mentally or physically depressed, exhausted, and weak. [3]To offset this, people commonly choose to drink another cup of coffee. [4]Habitual

use leads to tolerance and psychological dependence. [5]Until the mid-1970s, caffeine was not medically recognized as addictive. [6]Chronic caffeine use and the behaviors linked to it was called "coffee nerves." [7]This syndrome is now recognized as caffeine intoxication, or **caffeinism**. [8]Symptoms of caffeinism include chronic insomnia, jitters, irritability, nervousness, anxiety, and involuntary muscle twitches. [9]Withdrawing the caffeine may make the effects worse and lead to severe headaches. [10](Some physicians ask their patients to take a simple test for caffeine addiction: don't consume anything containing caffeine, and if you get a severe headache within four hours, you are addicted.) [11]Caffeine meets the requirements for addiction, which are tolerance, psychological dependence, and withdrawal symptoms; thus, it can be classified as addictive.

—Adapted from *Health: The Basics*, 5th ed., p. 215 by Rebecca J. Donatelle. Copyright © 2003 by Pearson Education, Inc. Printed and Electronically reproduced by permission of Pearson Education, Inc. Upper Saddle River, NJ.

Topic sentence(s): ___11___

C. Paragraph from a college psychology textbook

11.0 GE/105 words   **Touch and Skin Senses**

Textbook
Skills

[1]The skin is a remarkably versatile organ. [2]In addition to protecting you against surface injury, holding in body fluids, and helping control body temperature, it contains nerve endings that produce sensations of pressure, warmth, and cold. [3]These sensations are called cutaneous senses (skin senses). [4]Because you receive so much sensory information through your skin, many different types of receptor cells operate close to the surface of the body. [5]Two examples are the *Meissner corpuscles* and *Merkel disks*. [6]The Meissner corpuscles respond best when something rubs against the skin, and the Merkel disks are most active when a small object exerts steady pressure against the skin.

—From *Psychology and Life*, 16th ed., pp. 108–109 by Richard J. Gerrig and Philip G. Zimbardo. Copyright © 2002 by Pearson Education, Inc. Reproduced by permission of Pearson Education, Inc., Boston, MA.

Topic sentence(s): ___1___

Read the passage below. Then, answer the questions that follow it.

GE 11.6/314 words

Textbook
Skills

The Theater of Sophocles

[1]For the citizens of Athens, Greece, in the fifth century B.C., theater was both a religious and a civic occasion. [2]Seated in the open air in a hillside amphitheater, as many as 17,000 spectators could watch a performance that must have somewhat resembled an opera or musical. [3]Plays were presented only twice a year on religious festivals. [4]These festivals were related to Dionysius, the god of wine and crops; in January there was the Lenaea, the festival of the winepress, when plays, especially comedies, were performed. [5]But the major theatrical event of the year came in March at the Great Dionysia. [6]This was a citywide celebration that included sacrifices, prize ceremonies, and spectacular processions as well as three days of drama.

[7]Each day at dawn a different author presented a trilogy of tragic plays. [8]A trilogy was made up of three related dramas that depicted an important mythic or legendary event. [9]Each intense tragic trilogy was followed by a satyr play, an obscene parody of a mythic story. [10]In a satyr play the chorus dressed as satyrs, unruly followers of Dionysius who were half goat or horse and half human.

[11]The Greeks loved competition and believed it fostered excellence; even theater was a competitive event—not unlike the Olympic games. [12]A panel of five judges voted each year at the Great Dionysia for the best dramatic presentation, and a substantial cash prize was given to the winning poet-playwright (all plays were written in verse). [13]Any aspiring writer who has ever lost a literary contest may be comforted to know that Sophocles, who triumphed in the competition twenty-four times, seems not to have won the annual prize for *Oedipus the King*. [14]Although this play ultimately proved to be the most celebrated Greek tragedy ever written, it lost the award to a revival of Aeschylus, a playwright who had recently died.

—Adapted from *Literature: An Introduction to Fiction, Poetry, and Drama*, 8th ed., p. 1375 by X. J. Kennedy and Dana Gioia. Copyright © 2002 by Pearson Education, Inc. Reprinted by permission of Pearson Education, Inc., Glenview, IL.

1. What is the topic of the passage? Greek theater

_____a_____   **2.** Which sentence (or sentences) states the central idea of the passage?
 a. sentence 1   c. sentence 10
 b. sentence 3   d. sentences 1 and 14

_____a_____   **3.** Which sentence (or sentences) state(s) the main idea of the second paragraph?
 a. sentence 7   c. sentence 9
 b. sentence 8   d. sentence 10

_____b_____   **4.** Which sentence (or sentences) state(s) the main idea of the third paragraph?
 a. sentences 11 and 14   c. sentence 12
 b. sentence 11   d. sentence 14

VISUAL VOCABULARY

This ancient ^b_____ is the Theatre of Dionysus, built between 342–326 B.C., Athens, Greece.

 a. competition
 b. amphitheater
 c. region

Read the following passage from a college psychology textbook. Answer the questions that follow.

GE 12.3/450 words

Textbook
Skills

Biological Approaches to Motivation

[1]Perhaps you have heard the term instinct used to explain why spiders spin webs or birds fly south in the winter. [2]An instinct is a fixed behavior pattern that is characteristic of every member of a species and is assumed to be genetically programmed. [3]Thus, instincts represent one kind of biological motivation. [4]Psychologists generally agree that no true instincts motivate human behavior. [5]However, most also agree that biological forces underlie some human behaviors.

[6]One biological approach to motivation, drive-reduction theory, was popularized by Clark Hull (1943). [7]According to Hull, all living organisms have certain biological needs that must be met if they are to survive. [8]A need gives rise to an internal state of tension called a drive, and the person or organism is motivated to reduce it. [9]For example, when you are deprived of food or go too long without water, your biological need causes a state of tension in this case, the hunger or thirst drive. [10]You become motivated to seek food or water to reduce the drive and satisfy your biological need.

[11]Drive-reduction theory is derived largely from the biological concept of homeostasis—the tendency of the body to maintain a balanced, internal state to ensure physical survival. [12]Body temperature, blood sugar level, water balance, blood oxygen level—in short, everything required for physical existence must be maintained in a state of equilibrium, or balance. [13]When such a state is disturbed, a drive is created to restore the balance.

[14]Drive-reduction theory assumes that humans are always motivated to reduce tension. [15]Other theorists argue just the opposite, that humans are sometimes motivated to increase tension. [16]These theorists use the term arousal to refer to a person's state of alertness and mental and physical activation. [17]Arousal levels can range from no arousal (when a person is comatose), to moderate arousal (when pursuing normal day-to-day activities), to high arousal (when excited and highly stimulated). [18]Arousal theory states that people are motivated to maintain an optimal level of arousal. [19]If arousal is less than the optimal level, we do something to stimulate it; if arousal exceeds the optimal level, we seek to reduce the stimulation.

[20]When arousal is too low, stimulus motives—such as curiosity and the motives to explore, to manipulate objects, and to play—cause humans and other animals to increase stimulation. [21]Think about sitting in an airport or at a bus stop or any other place where people are waiting. [22]How many people do you see playing games on their cellphones or personal digital assistants (PDAs)? [23]Waiting is boring; in other words, it provides no sources of arousal. [24]Thus, people turn to electronic games to raise their level of arousal.

_____a_____ **1.** Which of the following best states the topic of the first paragraph (sentences 1–5)?
- a. instinct
- b. motivation
- c. human behavior
- d. psychologists

2. The topic sentence of the first paragraph (sentences 1–5) is ___3___.

_____c_____ **3.** Which of the following best states the topic of the second paragraph (sentences 6–10)?
- a. Clark Hull
- b. needs
- c. drive-reduction theory
- d. drives

4. The topic sentence of the second paragraph (sentences 6–10) is ___6___.

_____b_____ **5.** Which of the following best states the topic of the third paragraph (sentences 11–13)?
- a. drive-reduction theory
- b. homeostasis
- c. motivation
- d. physical survival

6. The topic sentence of the third paragraph (sentences 11–13) is ___11___.

_____d_____ **7.** Which of the following best states the topic of the fourth paragraph (sentences 14–19)?
- a. drive-reduction theory
- b. tension
- c. stimulation
- d. arousal theory

8. The topic sentence of the fourth paragraph (sentences 14–19) is ___18___.

_____a_____ **9.** Which of the following best states the topic of the fifth paragraph (sentences 20–24)?
- a. stimulus motives
- b. arousal
- c. boredom
- d. games

10. The topic sentence of the fifth paragraph (sentences 20–24) is ___20___.

Implied Main Ideas and Implied Central Ideas

LEARNING OUTCOMES

After studying this chapter you should be able to do the following:

1. Define the term *implied main idea*. [Knowledge]
2. Analyze supporting details to identify and state a topic of a passage. [Analysis]
3. Determine an implied main idea of a passage based on the topic, supporting details, and thought patterns of a passage. [Synthesis]
4. Create a topic sentence that states the implied main idea of a paragraph. [Application]
5. Determine the implied central idea of a longer passage. [Synthesis]
6. Create a thesis statement that states the implied central idea of a passage. [Application]
7. Evaluate the importance of stating implied main ideas. [Evaluation]

Before Reading About Implied Main Ideas and Implied Central Ideas

Take a moment to study the chapter learning outcomes. Underline key words that refer to ideas you have already studied in previous chapters. Each of these key words represents a great deal of knowledge upon which you will build as you learn about implied main ideas and implied central ideas. These key terms have been listed below. In the given spaces, write what you already know about each one. Answers may vary.

- Main ideas: Main ideas are stated in a topic sentence. A topic sentence includes a topic and the author's controlling point.

- Supporting details: Supporting details explain the main idea. There are two types of supporting details. Major supporting details directly explain the topic sentence (or thesis statement), and minor supporting details explain the major supporting details.

- A summary: A summary condenses a paragraph or passage to its main idea.

- Central ideas: Central ideas are the main ideas of longer passages. Stated

central ideas are called thesis statements.

Compare what you wrote to the following paragraph, which summarizes this vital prior knowledge:

> Main ideas are stated in a topic sentence. A topic sentence includes a topic and the author's controlling point. Supporting details explain the main idea. There are two types of supporting details. Major supporting details directly explain the topic sentence (or thesis statement), and minor supporting details explain the major supporting details. A summary condenses a paragraph or passage to its main idea. Central ideas are the main ideas of longer passages. Stated central ideas are called thesis statements.

Recopy the list of key words in your notebook; leave several blank lines between each idea. As you work through this chapter, record how you apply each idea in the list to the new information you learn about implied main ideas and implied central ideas.

 ## What Is an Implied Main Idea?

As you learned in Chapter 3, sometimes authors state the main idea of a paragraph in a topic sentence. However, other paragraphs do not include a stated main idea. Even though the main idea is not stated in a single sentence, the paragraph still has a main idea. In these cases, the details clearly suggest or imply the author's main idea.

> An **implied main idea** is a main idea that is not stated directly but is strongly suggested by the supporting details in the passage.

When the main idea is not stated, you must figure out the author's controlling point about a topic. One approach is to study the facts, examples, descriptions, and explanations given—the supporting details. Another approach is to identify the author's thought pattern. A master reader often uses both approaches. Learning how to develop a main idea based on the supporting details and thought patterns will help you develop several skills. You will learn how to study information, value the meaning of supporting details, recognize the relationships among ideas, and use your own words to express an implied main idea.

Many different types of reading material use implied main ideas. For example, you will often need to formulate the implied main idea when you read literature. Short stories, novels, poems, and plays rely heavily on vivid details to suggest the author's point. The following short story is taken from a college literature textbook. Read the story, asking yourself, "What is the main idea?"

The Appointment in Samarra

W. Somerset Maugham

[1]*Death speaks*: There was a merchant in Baghdad who sent his servant to market to buy provisions and in a little while the servant came back, white and trembling, and said, Master, just now when I was in the marketplace, I was jostled by a woman in the crowd and when I turned I saw it was Death that jostled me. [2]She looked at me and made a threatening gesture; now, lend me your horse, and I will ride away from this city and avoid my fate. [3]I will go to Samarra and there Death will not find me. [4]The merchant lent him his horse, and the servant mounted it, and he dug his spurs in its flanks and as fast as the horse could gallop he went. [5]Then the merchant went down to the marketplace and he saw me standing in the crowd and he came to me and said, Why did you make a threatening gesture to my servant when you saw him this morning? [6]That was not a threatening gesture I said, it was only a start of surprise. [7]I was astonished to see him in Baghdad, for I had an appointment with him tonight in Samarra.

—"An Appointment in Samarra" From *Sheppey* by W. Somerset Maugham, copyright 1933 by W. Somerset Maugham. Used by permission of Doubleday, a division of Random House, Inc., and A.P. Watt Ltd.

Did you notice that every sentence in this paragraph is a supporting detail? No single sentence covers all the other ideas. To figure out the implied main idea, ask the following questions:

Questions for Finding the Implied Main Idea

- What is the topic, or subject, of the paragraph?
- What are the major supporting details?
- Based on the details about the topic, what point or main idea is the author trying to get across?

Apply these three questions to the Somerset Maugham story by writing your responses to each question in the following blanks. Wording of answers may vary.

1. What is the topic of the story? the appointment in Samarra, which is an

appointment with Death

In this case, the title of the story tells us that the topic is an appointment, and each detail in the story leads to the understanding that the appointment was to be with Death.

2. What are the major supporting details?

The servant of a merchant went to a market in Baghdad.

The servant was jostled by Death.

The servant saw Death make a threatening gesture at him and became

afraid.

The servant tried to avoid Death by fleeing on his master's horse to

Samarra.

The merchant went to the Baghdad market and asked Death why she

made a threatening gesture at his servant.

Death replied that she was only surprised to see the servant, for she had an

appointment with him that night in Samarra.

3. What is the main idea the author is trying to get across? We each have

an appointed time of death that cannot be avoided, and our decisions lead

us to our appointed time of death.

In order to formulate a main idea statement for this story, you had to consider each of the details within it. First, the author has made Death a humanlike character. Next, when the servant has an encounter with Death in the marketplace, he misunderstands her gesture and in fear runs from her. Third, consider the difference between the ways the merchant and his servant interact with Death. The servant fears and misunderstands Death and runs away; the merchant faces Death and seeks to understand Death's intentions. Interestingly, the servant's fear of Death and his decision to run from Death drives him to meet Death, his death, at the appointed time and place.

This story is an excellent example of the different shades of meaning an author can imply through the use of supporting details. Implying the main idea allows the reader to use creative and critical thinking skills to make meaning of the piece.

Asking and answering these questions allows you to think about the impact of each detail and how the details fit together to create the author's most important point. Searching for an implied main idea is like a treasure hunt. You must carefully read the clues provided by the author. The following examples and practices are designed to strengthen this important skill.

Using Supporting Details and Thought Patterns to Find Implied Main Ideas

Remember that the main idea of a paragraph is like a frame of a house. Just as a frame includes all the rooms, a main idea must cover all the details in a paragraph. Therefore, the implied main idea will be general enough to cover all the details, but it will not be so broad that it becomes an overgeneralization or a sweeping statement that suggests details not given; nor can it be so narrow that some of the given details are not covered. Instead, the implied main idea must cover *all* the details given.

Having the skill of identifying a stated main idea will also help you grasp the implied main idea. You learned in Chapter 3 that the stated main idea (the topic sentence) has two parts. A main idea is made up of the topic and the author's controlling point about the topic. One trait of the controlling point is the author's opinion or bias. A second trait is the author's thought pattern. Consider, for example, the topic sentence "Older people benefit from volunteer work for several reasons." "Older people" and "volunteer work" make up the topic. "Benefit" states the opinion, and "several reasons" states the thought pattern. When you read material that implies the main idea, you should mentally create a topic sentence based on the details in the material.

Textbook Skills

EXAMPLE Read the following list of supporting details from a criminal justice textbook. Circle the topic as it recurs throughout the list of details. Underline transition words and double underline the biased (opinion) words. Then, choose the statement that best expresses the author's controlling point about the topic.

- Lay witnesses are non-expert witnesses who may be called to testify in court for either the prosecution or the defense.

- Lay witness may be eyewitnesses who saw the crime being committed or who came upon the crime scene shortly after the crime had occurred.
- Another type of lay witness is the character witness.
- A character witness frequently provides information about the personality, family life, business acumen, and so on of the defendant.
- Of course the victim may also be a lay witness, providing detailed and sometimes lengthy testimony about the defendant and the crime.

> —From *Criminal Justice Today: An Introductory Text for the 21st Century,* 10th ed.,
> p. 338 by Frank J. Schmalleger. Copyright © 2009 by Pearson Education, Inc.
> Printed and Electronically reproduced by permission of Pearson
> Education, Inc., Upper Saddle River, NJ.

____c____ Which statement best expresses the implied main idea?
  a. Character witnesses offer important information on behalf of the defendant.
  b. Witnesses are important to both the prosecution and the defense.
  c. Several types of lay witnesses, or non-expert witnesses, may be called to testify for the prosecution or the defense.
  d. Eyewitnesses and victims frequently provide details about the defendant and the crime.

EXPLANATION The best statement of the implied main idea is (c) Several types of lay witnesses, or non-expert witnesses, may be called to testify for the prosecution or the defense. Option (a) is too general, and options (b) and (d) state specific details. The terms *lay witness, witness, eyewitness, character witness,* and *victim* state the various forms of the topic and should have been circled. The words *another type, frequently, also,* and *sometimes* are transition words that should have been underlined. The phrase *another type* suggests that this list of details describes types of lay witnesses. The word *may* is a biased word that suggests a possibility rather than a factual event and, therefore, should be double underlined.

PRACTICE 1

Read the following groups of supporting details. Circle the topic as it recurs throughout the list of details. Underline transition words to help you locate the major details. Also, double underline the biased words to determine the author's opinion. Then, select the sentence that best expresses the implied main idea.

Group 1

- <u>Many</u> people (volunteer) within their communities <u>because</u> they <u>want</u> to make a difference.
- Others (volunteer) so that they <u>can</u> develop <u>new</u> skills.
- One reason some (volunteer) is to <u>explore</u> career paths.
- In addition, (volunteering) is a <u>good</u> way for young people to have <u>fun</u> working with friends.
- Finally, (volunteers) <u>feel</u> <u>good</u> about themselves.

_____c_____ **1.** Which statement best expresses the implied main idea?
   a. Volunteer work is a good way to build a résumé.
   b. Volunteering provides an excellent opportunity to meet new people.
   c. People engage in volunteer work for several reasons.
   d. Volunteer work is very rewarding.

Textbook
Skills

Group 2

- (Ancient Roman) entertainment included public fights between (gladiators).
- Many (gladiators) were volunteers who <u>willingly</u> gave up their rights and property and pledged <u>not only</u> to <u>suffer intensely</u> but to die fighting.
- (Romans) <u>valued</u> a concept called *virtus* (<u>honor above</u> life).
- *Virtus* was a <u>specifically</u> male trait and was <u>most often</u> applied to a (gladiator) who had fought <u>well</u> or continued to <u>struggle</u> even after defeat.
- If a (gladiator) displayed *virtus* but was <u>clearly</u> losing, he <u>could</u> raise one finger in a <u>plea</u> for mercy.
- Usually, (Romans) granted *missio* or <u>mercy</u> for gladiators who displayed virtus <u>so that</u> they could live to fight another day.

—Adapted from *The Creative Impulse: An Introduction to the Arts,* 8th ed.,
p. 133, by Dennis J. Sporre. Copyright © 2009 by Pearson Education, Inc.
Reprinted by permission of Pearson Education, Inc., Upper Saddle River, NJ.

_____b_____ **2.** Which statement best expresses the implied main idea?
   a. Ancient Romans enjoyed violent entertainment.
   b. Ancient Romans valued honor above life.
   c. Ancient Romans were often merciful.
   d. Ancient Romans were virtuous.

Group 3

Textbook
Skills

- A person who is supporting a family will <u>normally</u> incur <u>more</u> ⟨expenses⟩ <u>than</u> a single person without dependents.
- As people get older, they <u>tend</u> to ⟨spend⟩ <u>more</u> ⟨money⟩ on <u>expensive</u> houses, cars, and vacations.
- In addition, people's ⟨consumption behavior⟩ varies <u>greatly</u>.
- For example, at one <u>extreme</u> are people who ⟨spend⟩ their <u>entire</u> paycheck within a few days of receiving it; at the <u>other</u> <u>extreme</u> are "<u>big savers</u>" who reduce their ⟨spending⟩ and focus on saving for the future.

—Adapted from *Personal Finance,* 2nd ed., p. 32 by Jeff Madura. Copyright © 2004 by Pearson Education, Inc. Reproduced by permission of Pearson Education, Inc., Boston, MA.

<u>   c   </u>   **3.** Which statement best expresses the implied main idea?
   a. Some people are better at managing their money than others.
   b. The size of one's family affects cash outflows.
   c. Several factors affect cash outflows.
   d. People spend more money as they age.

Group 4

- Nomadic ⟨Native American tribes⟩ followed migratory prey and the seasonal changes of plant life.
- Nomadic ⟨Native American tribes⟩ needed ⟨housing structures⟩ that were <u>easily erected and dismantled</u>.
- For example, ⟨tipis⟩ were <u>easily erected and dismantled</u>.
- Agricultural ⟨Native American tribes⟩, on the other hand, could enjoy more permanent ⟨dwellings⟩, like ⟨pueblos⟩.

<u>   b   </u>   **4.** Which statement best expresses the implied main idea?
   a. Native American tribes were constantly on the move.
   b. The lifestyle of a Native American tribe influenced the types of dwellings they inhabited.
   c. Native American tribes were excellent architects.
   d. Native American tribes lived in substandard housing.

 ## Finding the Implied Main Ideas of Paragraphs

So far, you have learned to recognize the implied main idea by studying the specific details in a group of sentences. In this next step, the sentences will form a paragraph, but the skill of recognizing the implied main idea is exactly the same.

The implied main idea of paragraphs must not be too broad or too narrow, so study the supporting details and look for thought patterns and opinions that suggest the main idea.

EXAMPLE Read the following paragraph. Circle the topic as it recurs throughout the paragraph. Underline transition words to help you locate the major details. Also, double underline biased words to determine the author's opinion. Then, select the sentence that best expresses the implied main idea.

Textbook
Skills

The Faces of Fetal Alcohol Syndrome

¹"The guilt is tremendous . . . I did it again and again . . . I don't know how to tell them. ²It was something I could have prevented." ³Debbie has had seven children. ⁴One of her older daughters, Corey, has been diagnosed with fetal alcohol syndrome (FAS), the most serious type of alcohol damage. ⁵At age three she was hyperactive and talked like a one-year-old. ⁶Doctors believe that Debbie's youngest child Sabrina is almost certainly a victim as well. ⁷Her face bears the characteristic features of FAS, including small eyes, a short nose, and a small head. ⁸At 7 months, she was weak, began having seizures, and could not eat solid food because she was unable to close her mouth around the spoon. ⁹As this pregnant mother repeatedly got drunk, so did her developing children.

—From *Life on Earth*, 5th ed., p. 486 by Teresa Audesirk, Gerald Audesirk, and Bruce E. Byers. Copyright © 2009 by Pearson Education, Inc. Printed and Electronically reproduced by permission of Pearson Education, Inc., Upper Saddle River, NJ..

_____ c _____ Which sentence best states the implied main idea?
- a. The effects of Fetal Alcohol Syndrome can be avoided.
- b. Pregnant women can consume alcohol in moderate amounts.
- c. Pregnant mothers who frequently consume alcohol cause preventable physical and mental damage to their developing children.

EXPLANATION Implied main ideas require that the reader be actively involved in the meaning-making process. The author states the damage caused to developing children by their mothers' prenatal consumption of alcohol in the following expression: "most serious type of alcohol damage." The author reinforces the point by describing the physical and mental traits of FAS in sentences 5 and 7. Item (c) is the best statement of the implied main idea of this paragraph. Item (a) is too narrow, and item (b) jumps to the wrong conclusion based on the evidence in the paragraph. Nowhere in the paragraph does the author imply that occasional or moderate consumption of alcohol is safe or leads to FAS.

PRACTICE 2

Read the following paragraphs. In each paragraph, circle the topic as it recurs throughout the paragraph. Underline transition words to help you locate the major details. Also, double underline the biased words to determine the author's opinion. Then, select the sentence that best expresses the implied main idea.

Textbook
Skills

Opposition to Capital Punishment

¹The first recorded effort to eliminate the death penalty occurred at the home of Benjamin Franklin in 1787. ²At a meeting there on March 9 of that year, Dr. Benjamin Rush, a signer of the Declaration of Independence and a leading medical pioneer, read a paper against capital punishment to a small but influential audience. ³Although his immediate efforts came to nothing, his arguments laid the groundwork for many debates that followed. ⁴Michigan, widely regarded as the first abolitionist state, joined the Union in 1837 without a death penalty. ⁵A number of other states, including Alaska, Hawaii, Massachusetts, Minnesota, West Virginia, and Wisconsin, have since spurned death as a possible sanction for criminal acts. ⁶However, the death penalty remains a sentencing option in 38 of the states and in all federal jurisdictions.

—Adapted from *Criminal Justice Today: An Introductory Text for the 21st Century*, 10th ed., p. 409 by Frank J. Schmalleger. Copyright © 2009 by Pearson Education, Inc. Printed and Electronically reproduced by permission of Pearson Education, Inc., Upper Saddle River, NJ.

_____d_____ **1.** Which sentence best states the implied main idea?
   a. Many oppose capital punishment.
   b. Capital punishment should not be a viable sanction for criminal acts.
   c. Dr. Benjamin Rush was the first to publically oppose capital punishment.
   d. Attempts have been made to abolish capital punishment since the founding of the United States.

¹The *personal* aspects of emotional intelligence are a set of components that include awareness and management of our own emotions. ²People who are able to monitor their feelings as they arise are less likely to be ruled by them. ³However, managing emotions does not mean suppressing them; nor does it mean giving free rein to every feeling. ⁴Instead, effective management of emotions involves expressing them appropriately. ⁵Emotion management also involves engaging in activities that cheer us up, soothe our hurts, or reassure us when we feel anxious. ⁶The *interpersonal*

aspects of (emotional intelligence) make up the second set of components. [7]Empathy, or sensitivity to others' feelings, is one such component. [8]One key indicator of empathy is the ability to read others' nonverbal behavior— the gestures, vocal inflections, tones of voice, and facial expressions of others. [9]Another of the interpersonal components is the capacity to manage relationships. [10]However, it is related to both the personal aspects of (emotional intelligence) and to empathy. [11]In other words, to effectively manage the (emotional) give-and-take involved in social relationships, we have to be able to manage our own feelings and be sensitive to those of others.

—Adapted from *Mastering the World of Psychology*, 3rd ed., p. 237 by Samuel E. Wood, Ellen Green Wood, and Denise Boyd. Copyright © 2008 by Pearson Education, Inc. Reproduced by permission of Pearson Education, Inc., Boston, MA.

_____a_____   **2.** Which sentence best states the implied main idea?
   a. Emotional intelligence includes two sets of components.
   b. Emotional intelligence is made up of personal aspects.
   c. Emotional intelligence is made up of interpersonal aspects.
   d. Emotional intelligence is the ability to manage emotions effectively.

Creating a Summary from the Supporting Details

You have developed the skill of figuring out implied main ideas, which will serve you well throughout college. The next step is to state the implied main idea in your own words. When you are reading and studying, you must be able to summarize the most important details in a one-sentence statement; in other words, you must create a topic sentence.

To formulate this one-sentence summary, find the topic, determine the author's opinion by examining the biased words, and use the thought pattern to locate the major details. Then, combine these ideas in a single sentence. The summary sentence includes the topic and the author's controlling point, just like a topic sentence. The statement you come up with must not be too narrow, for it must cover all the details given. On the other hand, it must not be too broad or go beyond the supporting details.

Remember that a main idea is always written as a complete sentence.

EXAMPLE Read the following paragraph. Circle the topic as it recurs throughout the paragraph. Underline words that reveal thought patterns and bias to discover the controlling point. Then, write a sentence that best states the implied main idea. Remember: not too narrow, not too broad—find that perfect fit!

The Cost of Owning a Horse

¹People invest in horses for a variety of reasons, including riding for pleasure or therapy, competing in shows, farming, breeding, and racing. ²The first cost incurred is, of course, the purchase of the horse. ³Depending on the pedigree, health, and prior training of the horse, prices vary from a few hundred to several thousand dollars. ⁴The ongoing cost of boarding the horse must be considered as well. ⁵Boarding costs vary based on location and the type of services. ⁶For example, some facilities offer just a pasture while others offer full-service stall boarding and daily exercise. ⁷A third major expense involved in owning a horse is feed. ⁸Horses are usually fed a grain mix, grass hay, and salt and minerals. ⁹Next, health care costs include dewormings four times a year and a variety of vaccinations. ¹⁰In addition, medical attention associated with breeding and emergencies can cause sizeable increases in expenses. ¹¹Farrier costs must also be considered; this expense includes at a minimum trimming the hooves every couple of months, but may require, depending on the type of activity and the owner's taste, shoeing the horse or resetting the horse's shoes. ¹²Another cost that must be taken into account is the cost of stall bedding. ¹³The dollar amount varies based on different bedding sources and quantity used. ¹⁴Finally, the costs for equipment most often include items needed for grooming, feeding, and cleaning such as brushes, buckets, shovels, and forks; in addition, tack must be bought and kept in good repair.

Implied main idea: Answers may vary. One possible answer: Many expenses are involved in owning a horse.

VISUAL VOCABULARY

A synonym for *farrier* is

c_____.

   a. veterinarian.
   b. groomer.
   c. blacksmith.

▶ A farrier making a horse shoe.

EXPLANATION The following sentence is one way to state the main idea of the paragraph: "Many expenses are involved in owning a horse." Keep in mind that using your own words to formulate an implied main idea means that the wording of answers will vary.

PRACTICE 3

Read the following paragraphs. Annotate the text. Then, write a sentence that states the implied main idea.

From *Narrative of the Life of Frederick Douglass, an American Slave. Written by Himself*

¹I was born in Tuckahoe, near Hillsborough, and about twelve miles from Easton, in Talbot county, Maryland. ²I have no accurate knowledge of my age, never having seen any authentic record containing it. ³By far the larger part of the slaves know as little of their ages as horses know of theirs, and it is the wish of most masters within my knowledge to keep their slaves thus ignorant. ⁴I do not remember to have ever met a slave who could tell of his birthday. ⁵They seldom come nearer to it than planting-time, harvest-time, cherry-time, spring-time, or fall-time. ⁶A want of information concerning my own was a source of unhappiness to me even during childhood. ⁷The white children could tell their ages. ⁸I could not tell why I ought to be deprived of the same privilege. ⁹I was not allowed to make any inquiries of my master concerning it. ¹⁰He deemed all such inquiries on the part of a slave improper and impertinent, and evidence of a restless spirit. ¹¹The nearest estimate I can give makes me now between twenty-seven and twenty-eight years of age. ¹²I come to this, from hearing my master say, some time during 1835, I was about seventeen years old.

—From Douglass, Frederick, *Narrative of the Life of Frederick Douglass, an American Slave. Written by Himself,* 1845. pp. 1–2.

1. Implied main idea: Answers may vary. One possible answer: Slaves were unjustly denied their basic human right to know their exact dates of birth.

From *A Personal Journal of an American Woman*

¹For eons and in many societies, it seems, most women have been fastened to the traditional roles dictated by biology and culture. ²However, women such as Oprah Winfrey, Diane Sawyer, Toni Morrison, Sally Ride,

and Sandra Day O'Connor prove to me that I am free. [3]As so many American freedoms, my freedom—the freedom of my American sisters— was bequeathed to me—to us—by warrior women who fought for the right to vote, the right to education, the right to fair wages, the right to birth control. [4]Women such as Harriet Tubman, Elizabeth Cady Stanton, Lucretia Mott, and Margaret Sanger possessed the riches of vision, courage, and fortitude, and they invested their wealth in our lives long before we were born. [5]And now as I live in the 21st century, I am free to be me: educator, author, entrepreneur, wife, and mother.

2. Implied main idea: Answers may vary. One possible answer: As an American woman living in the cusp of the 21st century, the writer is the heir to freedoms and attitudes that seem unprecedented.

The Implied Central Idea

Just as a single paragraph can have an implied main idea, longer passages made up of two or more paragraphs can also have an implied main idea. As you learned in Chapter 3, the stated main idea or central idea of these longer passages is called the *thesis statement*. When the main idea of several paragraphs is implied, it is called the **implied central idea**. You use the same skills to formulate the implied central idea of a longer passage that you use to formulate the implied main idea of a paragraph.

> **The implied central idea** is the main idea suggested by the details of a passage made up of two or more paragraphs.

Annotating the text is a helpful tool in determining the implied central idea. Just as you did to grasp the implied main idea for paragraphs, circle the topic. Underline the signal words for thought patterns. Remember, transition words introduce supporting details. An author often pairs a transition word with a major supporting detail. Consider the following examples: *the first reason, a second cause, the final effect, another similarity, an additional difference,* and so on. When you see phrases such as these, your one-sentence summary may include the following kinds of phrases: *several effects, a few differences,* and so on.

A longer passage often contains paragraphs with stated main ideas. The stated main idea of a paragraph is a one-sentence summary of that paragraph and can be used as part of your summary of the implied central idea.

EXAMPLE   Read the following passage from a college humanities textbook. Annotate the text. Then, select the sentence that summarizes its implied central idea.

Textbook
Skills

Hesiod

¹Born at the end of the eighth century B.C.E., Hesiod (HEE-see-uhd) was the son of an emigrant farmer from Asia Minor. ²He depicts this hard life in his poem *Works and Days*. ³Hesiod's lesson is that men must work, and he sketches the work that occupies a peasant throughout the year, recounting how an industrious farmer toils and how work brings prosperity, in contrast to the ruin brought about by idleness. ⁴He captures the changing seasons and countryside with vivid word pictures. ⁵He also describes life at sea, and concludes with a catechism detailing how people should deal with each other. ⁶His style is similar to Homer's, but his subject matter is quite different, for rather than telling of heroes and gods, Hesiod dwells on the mundane and mortal.

⁷Hesiod's most famous work, however, is the *Theogony*, in which he traces the mythological history of the Greek gods. ⁸He describes the rise of the earth out of chaos, the overthrow of the Titans by Zeus, and the emergence of each god and goddess. ⁹Scholars attempting to understand Greek art and religion have found this work invaluable as a source of information.

—From The Creative *Impulse: An Introduction to the Arts,* 8th ed., p. 70 by Dennis J. Sporre. Copyright © 2009 by Pearson Education, Inc. Reprinted by permission of Pearson Education, Inc., Upper Saddle River, NJ.

Implied central idea: Answers may vary. One possible answer: Born in the eighth century B.C.E., the Greek writer Hesiod wrote about both the struggles of everyday life and the history of the Greek gods.

EXPLANATION   Hesiod, a Greek writer, is the topic of this passage. The topic sentences of each paragraph tell the reader the two major points the author is using to limit the topic. In the first paragraph, sentence 2 is the topic sentence, and it focuses on the subject matter in one of Hesiod's writings: "hard life in his poem *Works and Days.*" The additional details make clear that the poem is about everyday Greek life. In the second paragraph, sentence 7 is the topic sentence, and it focuses on another type of subject that Hesiod wrote about in a different work: "*Theogony,* in which he traces the mythological history of the Greek gods." By combining these two main ideas, a master reader creates a one-sentence summary of the passage.

Though answers will vary, one possible answer is "Born in the eighth century B.C.E., the Greek writer Hesiod wrote about both the struggles of everyday life and the history of the Greek gods." This sentence covers all the major supporting details but does not go beyond the information given in the passage.

PRACTICE 4

Textbook
Skills

Read the following passage from a college sociology textbook. Write a sentence that states the implied central idea.

[1]Prostitution is illegal because it is a social problem that has a corrosive effect on society—it has widespread implications that go beyond prostitutes and their customers. [2]Prostitution keeps pimps and madams (who are constantly on the lookout for new employees) in business and can corrupt police officers who are bribed to look the other way. [3]Most importantly, it can feed into larger, more harmful organized crimes, such as the drug trade.

[4]Any neighborhood with the presence of prostitution will be hurt. [5]Property values will decrease substantially. [6]Not only will the prostitution activity be unwanted, but it will also attract undesirable people to the neighborhood. [7]Residents who have children will relocate, and prospective home buyers will look elsewhere.

[8]Prostitution can rapidly spread disease and is an enormous health risk. [9]Because of the many sexual partners that a prostitute encounters on a regular basis, one prostitute who carries an STD could infect dozens of people. [10]If the disease goes undetected and those clients have other sexual partners, more could be infected as well.

[11]Prostitution is immoral and undermines an accepted sense of decency. [12]The selling of sex and the sex acts that are performed by prostitutes violate long-held beliefs about intimacy and sexuality. [13]Prostitution ruins marriages, tears families apart, and leads to corruption in the home and community.

[14]Women are often treated in a manner in which they are objectified, and prostitution only serves to continue—and even enhance this mind-set. [15]The profession itself is degrading to women, and because of the stigma attached to prostitution, women are often seen and treated as second class citizens.

Implied central idea: _Answers may vary. Prostitution should remain illegal_

for several reasons.

Reading a Textbook: How to Read a Map

Textbook
Skills

Many academic courses, particularly in the social sciences, rely on maps to communicate important geographical, political, social, and economic information. Maps provide information about what occurs in time and space. Not only do maps show the exact locations of particular places, but they also document the movements of civilizations, people, ideas, and trade. To analyze a map, follow these basic steps:

- **Read the title and caption to identify the main topic of the map**. Is the map illustrating a political idea, physical features, or a particular theme? Read the title and caption before you study the map to focus your attention on the cartographer's purpose for the map.

- **Activate your prior knowledge**. What do you already know about the topic, the region, and the time period? How does this map fit in with what you already know? What do you need to know to understand the map?

- **Discern the orientation of the map**. The orientation, the direction in which the map is pointed, is usually shown by a compass. Most current maps place north at the top of the map.

- **Identify the date of the map**. Because our world (and our understanding of our world) is ever-changing politically and socially, older maps may not be relevant. In addition, a map may be illustrating a historical perspective.

- **Understand and apply the legend**. The legend, or key, which shows the meaning of the colors, symbols, and other markings on the map, is crucial to understanding what the map represents.

- **Understand and apply the scale**. The scale tells you the relationship between the distance on the map and the corresponding distance on the ground. For example, one inch may represent 100 miles. Understanding the scale enables the reader to visualize the size of and distance between places.

EXAMPLE The following map is from the textbook *World Civilizations: The Global Experience*. Read the map and answer the questions. Then, state the implied main idea of the map in one sentence.

European Population Density, c.1600

—From *World Civilizations: The Global Experience, Combined Volume, Atlas Edition,* 5th ed, Map 22.2 (p. 490) by Peter N. Stearns, Michael B. Adas, Stuart B. Schwartz, and Marc Jason Gilbert. Copyright © 2008 by Pearson Education, Inc. Printed and Electronically reproduced by permission of Pearson Education, Inc., Upper Saddle River, NJ.

1. What is the title and date of the map? <u>European Population Density, c. 1600</u>

2. According to the legend, what do the colors represent? <u>People per square mile</u>

3. Name three densely populated regions of Europe. <u>Answers may vary.</u>
   <u>Ireland, England, and France.</u>

4. Why might most of the most heavily populated areas be located alongside rivers, oceans, or seas? <u>Answers may vary. Waterways make trade easier, and</u> <u>people settle along trade routes.</u>

Implied main idea of the map: <u>Answers may vary. In 1600, European</u> <u>population density was greater alongside rivers, oceans, and seas.</u>

EXPLANATION Compare your answers to the following.

(1) The date of the map is included in its title "European Population Density, c. 1600." Based on the date, the reader understands that this map offers a historical view of the region. (2) The legend indicates four levels of "people per square mile." (3) The map indicates more than three regions that are densely populated, so answers may vary, but should include three of the following: Ireland, England, France, United Netherlands, Holy Roman Empire, and Papal States. (4) Answers may vary, but prior knowledge supports the idea that during this time water provided the major means of transportation of people and trade, so the following statement is an appropriate answer: "Waterways make trade easier, and people settle along trade routes." Although your interpretation of the main idea of the map may vary, based on the title, the legend, and the answers to the preceding questions, the implied main idea of the map is as follows: "In 1600, European population density was greater alongside rivers, oceans, and seas." Quite often, to properly analyze a map, a master reader uses prior knowledge (see page 8 in this textbook for more information about this term).

PRACTICE 5

Study the map from the textbook *Introduction to Geography: People, Places, and Environment.* Answer the questions, and write a sentence that states the implied main idea of the map.

1. What prior knowledge is needed to understand the implied main idea of the map? <u>Answers may vary. One possible response may be world regions.</u>

2. According to the caption, what is the topic of the map? <u>World Merchandise</u> <u>Trade by Region</u>

3. According to the legend, what is the unit of measurement? <u>U.S. dollars</u>

<u>by billions</u>

4. What is the implied main idea of the map? <u>Answers may vary. North</u>

<u>America, Europe, and Asia dominate world merchandize trade.</u>

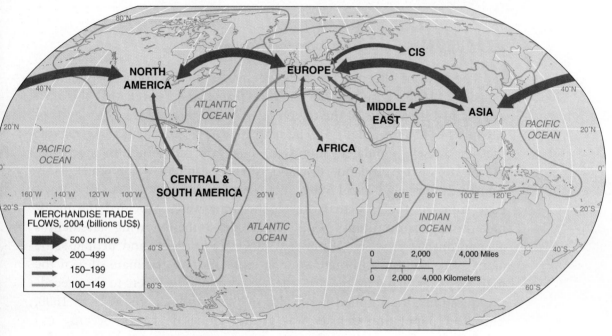

"Figure 12.32 World Merchandize trade by Region"
—From *Introduction to Geography: People, Places, and Environment,* 4th ed., Figure 12.32 by
Edward Bergman and William H. Renwick. Copyright © 2008 by Pearson Education, Inc.
Reprinted by permission of Pearson Education, Inc., Upper Saddle River, NJ.

 A Final Note About Experience and Perspective

As you have worked through this chapter, hopefully you have had some lively
discussions about the possible answers for activities that asked you to state implied
main ideas. Often a set of details will suggest many things to many people.
Determining main ideas requires that the reader bring personal understandings
and experience to the task. Thus people with different perspectives may disagree about what the details suggest. Another complex aspect of determining
main ideas is that authors may choose to give a collection of details because
the idea suggested is difficult to sum up in one sentence. The author intends
several meanings to coexist. The important point to remember is that the main

idea you formulate should be strongly supported by the details in the paragraph or longer passage.

APPLICATIONS

Application 1: Creating a Summary from Supporting Details

A. Read each group of supporting details. Annotate the text by circling the topic and underlining key words of support and transition. In the spaces provided, use your own words to write the implied main idea for each group.

Supporting details from a college health textbook:

Textbook
Skills

- For (men), (excessive fat) is concentrated in the waist, abdomen, and upper body.
- For (women), (excessive fat) is concentrated in the hips and thighs.
- (Excessive fat) concentrated in the waist, abdomen, and upper body is <u>less healthy than</u> fat located in the hips and thighs.
- Experts are not sure what accounts for these <u>differences</u> in (fat) distribution between (men) and (women).

—Adapted from McGuigan, *Encyclopedia of Stress,* 1999, p. 77.

Implied main idea: <u>Answers may vary. One possible answer: The location of</u>

<u>excessive fat mysteriously differs between men and women and is relevant to</u>

<u>health concerns.</u>

B. Read the following two paragraphs from a college history textbook. Annotate the text. In the spaces provided, write a sentence that states the implied main idea for each paragraph.

Education for Democracy

Textbook
Skills

[1]During the mid-1800s, except on the edge of the frontier and in the South, most youngsters between the ages of 5 and 10 attended (school) for at least a couple of months of the year. [2]These (schools), however, were privately run and charged fees. [3]Attendance was not required and fell off sharply once children learned to read and do their sums well enough to get along in day-to-day life. [4]The teachers were usually young men waiting for something better to do. [5]All this changed with the rise of the common (school movement). [6]At the heart of the movement was the belief, widely expressed in the first days of the Republic, that a government based on <u>democratic rule</u> must provide the means, as Jefferson put it, to

"diffuse knowledge throughout the mass of the people." [7]This meant free tax-supported schools, which all children were expected to attend. [8]It also came to mean that such an educational system should be administered on a statewide basis and that teaching should become a profession that required formal training.

—Adapted from *The American Nation: A History of the United States to 1877: Volume 1,* 10th ed., pp. 316–317 by John A. Garraty and Mark A. Carnes. Copyright © 2000 by Pearson Education, Inc. Printed and Electronically reproduced by permission of Pearson Education, Inc., Upper Saddle River, NJ.

1. Implied main idea: <u>Answers may vary. One possible answer: The common</u>

<u>school movement of the mid-1800s, based on the belief that education of the</u>

<u>"masses of the people" is necessary for democracy, changed the educational</u>

<u>system in the United States.</u>

Textbook
Skills

The Blue and the Gray

[1]At the beginning of the Civil War, more than 20 million people lived in the northern states (excluding Kentucky and Missouri, where opinion was divided). [2]In contrast, only 9 million people lived in the South, and of those about 3.5 million were slaves whom the whites hesitated to trust with arms. [3]In addition, the North's economic capacity to wage war was even more impressive. [4]It was manufacturing nine times as much as the Confederacy (including 97 percent of the nation's firearms) and had a far larger and more efficient system than the South. [5]Northern control of the merchant marine and the navy made possible a blockade of the Confederacy. [6]A blockade was a potent threat to a region so dependent on foreign markets.

—Adapted from *The American Nation: A History of the United States to 1877: Volume 1,* 10th ed., p. 405 by John A. Garraty and Mark A. Carnes. Copyright © 2000 by Pearson Education, Inc. Printed and Electronically reproduced by permission of Pearson Education, Inc., Upper Saddle River, NJ.

2. Implied main idea: <u>Answers may vary. One possible answer: The North was</u>

<u>better equipped than the South to wage war.</u>

Application 2: Implied Central Idea

Read each of the following passages from a college science textbook. Annotate the text. Then, answer the questions that follow each excerpt.

Gambling

[1]Compulsive—or addictive—behavior often fits a positive feedback model. [2]In this model there is repeated uncontrolled acting out of the

behavior pattern until the abuser's system goes out of control. ³For example, a cocaine addict may ingest a substance until death, an alcoholic may similarly experience blackout, and a gambler may run out of money or collateral. ⁴Compulsive gamblers usually continue gambling regardless of whether they are winning or losing. ⁵However, lack of control is more serious when they are losing, perhaps because they are obsessed with the notion that a big win is just one bet away. ⁶Some gamblers typically believe that the laws of probability, which are certain to lead to losses, do not apply to them. ⁷But even if they understand that they will eventually lose, their control is less than that of non-compulsive gamblers.

⁸Compulsive gamblers often destroy their families as they ignore family needs and lose money to gambling. ⁹The compulsion to make up for their losses often leads them to run up large debts and then even to steal. ¹⁰The compulsive gambler is also often self-destructive. ¹¹For example, one-third of the compulsive gamblers sampled in one study had serious weight problems, 42 percent were drug abusers, 38 percent had cardiovascular problems, and 50 percent had violated laws.

—Adapted from *Encyclopedia of Stress*, 1st ed., by F. J. McGuigan. Copyright © 1999 by Pearson Education, Inc. Printed and Electronically reproduced by permission of Pearson Education, Inc., Upper Saddle River, NJ.

___d___   **1.** Which sentence is the best statement of the implied main idea?
- a. Compulsive gamblers are self-destructive.
- b. Many people are compulsive gamblers.
- c. Compulsive gamblers lack self-control.
- d. Compulsive gambling is a serious disorder that harms the gambler and his family.

Insomnia

¹The term insomnia typically means "sleeplessness" or "inability to sleep." ²More precisely, common patterns are (1) resistance to falling asleep, (2) difficulty in remaining asleep, (3) poor sleep quality, and (4) waking up too early.

³Common problems related to chronic insomnia are fatigue, irritability, inability to concentrate, poor short-term memory, drowsiness, and abuse of stimulants. ⁴Short-term insomnia occurs in most people who are under great distress or emotional upheaval. ⁵Women tend to be more affected than men. ⁶The frequency of both increases with age. ⁷Chronic insomnia can begin at any age. ⁸However, most patients experience ongoing difficulty prior to age 40.

⁹Physical factors that may affect sleep include heart disease, high blood pressure, "heartburn" associated with a hernia, and chronic

breathing problems. [10]However, most cases lack any obvious physical basis. [11]Stressful experiences that create unresolved excess tension are the main factors that cause insomnia. [12]Psychological factors such as anxiety and anger can keep a person "on alert." [13]And a highly active imagination and the reviewing of the day's activities can hinder one's ability to fall asleep.

—Adapted from *Encyclopedia of Stress,* 1st ed., p. 119 by F. J. McGuigan. Copyright © 1999 by Pearson Education, Inc. Printed and Electronically reproduced by permission of Pearson Education, Inc., Upper Saddle River, NJ.

2. Implied central idea: Answers may vary. One possible answer: Insomnia is a

sleep disorder with various causes and effects.

Application 3

The following passage is taken from a chapter review of a college psychology textbook. This portion of the review covers the first major section of the chapter. This major section has four subdivisions as indicated. Complete the study outline that follows the passage. First, determine the implied main idea of each subdivision. Then, determine the implied central idea of the entire section. Wording of answers may vary.

Textbook
Skills

Explaining Motivation

A. How do the three components of motivation work together to influence behavior?

Activation is the component of motivation in which an individual takes the first steps toward a goal. Persistence is the component of motivation that enables a person to continue to work toward the goal even when he or she encounters obstacles. The intensity component of motivation refers to the energy and attention a person must employ to reach a goal.

B. What is the difference between intrinsic and extrinsic motivation?

With intrinsic motivation, an act is performed because it is satisfying or pleasurable in and of itself. With extrinsic motivation, an act is performed to bring a reward or to avert an undesirable sequence.

C. How do drive-reduction and arousal theory explain motivation?

Drive-reduction theory suggests that a biological need creates an unpleasant state of emotional arousal that impels the organism to engage in behavior that will reduce the arousal level. Arousal theory suggests that the aim of motivation is to maintain an optimal level of arousal.

D. **According to Maslow, how do individuals attain self-actualization?**
   Maslow claimed that individuals must satisfy physiologic, safety needs before addressing needs for love, esteem, and self-actualization.

—From *Mastering the World of Psychology*, 3rd ed., p. 314 by Samuel E. Wood, Ellen Green Wood, and Denise Boyd. Copyright © 2008 by Pearson Education, Inc. Reproduced by permission of Pearson Education, Inc., Boston, MA.

1. Implied Central Idea: Motivation can be explained by its components, the difference between intrinsic and extrinsic motivation, biological needs, and Maslow's theory of self-actualization.

   A. Implied main idea: Three components work together to influence behavior.

   B. Implied main idea: Intrinsic motivation differs from extrinsic motivation.

   C. Implied main idea: Drive-reduction and arousal theories are two explanations for motivation.

   D. Implied main idea: Maslow developed a theory to explain how individuals attain self-actualization.

REVIEW TEST 1

Score (number correct) _____ × 25 = _____%

Implied Main Ideas

A. Read each group of supporting details. Annotate the text. Then, choose the sentence that best expresses the implied main idea for each group.
   11.0 GE/128 words

   1. Supporting details:

   ■ **Education.** About 1 in 4 adults with an advanced degree engage in a high level of overall physical activity, compared with 1 in 7 of those with less than a high school diploma.

   ■ **Income.** Adults with incomes below the poverty level are three times as likely to be physically inactive as adults in the highest income group.

- **Marital Status.** Married women are more likely than never-married women to engage in a high level of overall physical activity.

- **Geography.** Adults in the South are more likely to be physically inactive than adults in any other region.

- This information is based on approximately 32,000 interviews with adults ages 18 and over, regardless of employment status, from the National Health Interview Survey, conducted by CDC's National Center for Health Statistics (NCHS).

> —"HHS Issues New Report on Americans' Overall Physical Activity Levels,"
> National Center for Health Statistics, 14 May 2003, Centers for Disease
> Control and Prevention. 2 Dec 2003 http://www.cdc.gov/nchs/
> releases/03news/physicalactivity.htm

___a___   Which statement best expresses the implied main idea?
  a. According to the National Center for Health Statistics, several factors affect the levels of physical activity of Americans.
  b. People who live in the South are lazier than those who live in any other region.
  c. Married women are in better physical condition than single women.
  d. Exercise is an important aspect of a healthy lifestyle.

2. Supporting details:

- Graffiti consists of inscriptions, slogans and drawings scratched, scribbled or painted on a wall or other public or private surface.

- Graffiti is most often thought of as an eyesore.

- Graffiti generates fear of neighborhood crime and instability.

- It is costly, destructive, and lowers property values.

- Graffiti sends a message that people of the community are not concerned about the appearance of their neighborhoods.

- It is also against the law!

> —Adapted from "What Is Graffiti?" Graffiti Control Program, The City of
> San Diego. 2 Dec. 2003 http://www.sannet.gov/graffiti/whatis.shtml

___b___   Which sentence best states the implied main idea?
  a. Graffiti should be considered as a right to free speech.
  b. Graffiti is not art; it is vandalism.
  c. Graffiti lowers the value of property.
  d. Graffiti is illegal.

B. Read the following paragraph. Annotate the text. In the space provided, write the letter of the best statement of the implied main idea.

11.9 GE/197 words   **Building Healthy Bones**

¹The main mineral in bones is calcium, one of whose functions is to add strength and stiffness to bones, which they need to support the body. ²To lengthen long bones during growth, the body builds a scaffold of protein and fills this scaffold in with calcium-rich mineral. ³From the ages of 11 through 24, an individual needs about 1,200 milligrams (mg) of calcium each day. ⁴Bone also needs vitamin D, to move calcium from the intestine to the bloodstream and into bone. ⁵Vitamin D can be obtained from short, normal day-to-day exposure of arms and legs to sun and from foods fortified with the vitamin. ⁶Also needed are vitamin A, vitamin C, magnesium and zinc, as well as protein for the growing bone scaffold. ⁷Many foods provide these nutrients. ⁸Growing bone is especially sensitive to the impact of weight and pull of muscle during exercise, and responds by building stronger, denser bones. ⁹That's why it's especially important to be physically active on a regular basis. ¹⁰Bone building activities include sports and exercise such as football, basketball, baseball, jogging, dancing, jumping rope, inline skating, skateboarding, bicycling, ballet, hiking, skiing, karate, swimming, rowing a canoe, bowling, and weight-training.

—Adapted from Farely, Dixie. "Bone Builders: Support Your Bones with Healthy Habits." *FDA Consumer Magazine*. September–October 1997. U. S. Food and Drug Administration. 19 March 2004. http://www.fda.gov/fdac/features/1997/697_bone.html

_____c_____ **3.** The best statement of the implied main idea is
a. Healthy diet leads to healthy bones.
b. Calcium is necessary to building healthy bones.
c. One must eat a well-balanced diet and exercise regularly to build healthy bones.
d. Many people develop weak bones due to poor diet and lack of exercise.

C. Study the following map from the textbook *Cultural Anthropology*. Write a sentence that states the implied main idea of the map.

12.4 GE/
64 words

4. Implied main idea: <u>Answers may vary. The</u> <u>ancient city of Jerusalem is a place of great</u> <u>significance for three major religions:</u> <u>Judaism, Islam, and Christianity.</u>

◀ Sacred Sites in the Old City of Jerusalem, Israel. Jerusalem is the holiest city of Judaism, the third holiest city of Islam, and holy to some Christian denominations. The section called the Old City is surrounded by walls that have been built, razed, relocated, and rebuilt over several hundred years. The Old City contains four quarters: Armenian, Christian, Jewish, and Muslim, and many sacred sites such as the Kotel and the via Dolorosa.

—From *Cultural Anthropology*, 4th ed., Map 13.5 (p. 356) by Barbara Miller. Copyright © 2007 by Pearson Education, Inc. Printed and Electronically reproduced by permission of Pearson Education, Inc., Upper Saddle River, NJ.

REVIEW TEST 2

Score (number correct) _____ × 25 = _____%

Read the following passage from an American history college textbook. Answer the questions that follow the passage.

Textbook
Skills

13.1 GE/671 words   **Taking Sides: Constitutional Principles**

¹What is the best way of understanding the Constitution? ²Does it embody universal values, or should it be understood in terms of contemporary society? ³Is there a difference between the founding conceptions of equality and those of today? ⁴Does a natural rights understanding assume more individual freedom?

Overview

[5]When the Constitution was ratified in June 1788, the United States had a population of roughly 3.9 million, with an urban population of less than 500,000 citizens (approximately 11 percent). [6]The overwhelmingly dominant religion was Protestantism, and the right to vote was held principally by those who owned property. [7]In 2005, the United States had a population of nearly 300 million, with an urban population of roughly 225 million (72.5 percent). [8]How is it that the Constitution can incorporate the differing social and political views of a multicultural and diverse nation?

[9]Some scholars argue that the Constitution has been a successful document. [10]Its success is based upon the principles of natural law and natural rights—principles holding that all human beings are created equal and endowed with certain inalienable rights. [11]These principles do not change over time. [12]And political institutions can be created to reflect natural equality and human dignity.

[13]Others argue that the Constitution is a flexible instrument created to adapt to social, historical, and political change. [14]This view—positivism—holds that constitutions and laws should reflect prevailing social convention and thought, and it is in this way that the Constitution has been able to be interpreted to allow for equality and social justice. [15]Just what does the Constitution mean and how will this question determine the near future of American history?

Supporting a Natural Rights Interpretation of the Constitution

[16]**Natural rights theory assumes a higher moral law**. [17]The founders were correct in their supposition that it is through liberty and justice that individuals can realize their potential and approach happiness, and the Constitution was created to embody these values. [18]These values do not change over time.

[19]**A natural rights interpretation assumes the use of reason**. [20]Alexander Hamilton argues in the Federalist Papers that the Constitution represents "good government" created by "reflection and choice." [21]The founders used reflection and reason to create a new form of government based on the natural rights principle that all political power is derived from the people exercising their right to create government and to live under laws of their own choosing.

[22]**Natural rights theory embodies the principle of political equality**. [23]The Constitution should be interpreted as incorporating the principle found in the Declaration of Independence that "all men are created

equal" and should have equal political rights. [24]This allows the rich and the poor, the highly educated and the ignorant, the secular and the religious, and the interested and the apathetic to have a say and a share in government.

Against a Natural Rights Interpretation of the Constitution

[25]**The founders simply used the prevailing philosophies of their times.** [26]There is no way to determine if natural rights theory is true. [27]The founders lived in a certain moment in history and they had no way of knowing what the future held in the way of new philosophies and science of government. [28]For example, they did not consider that government could be used for social purposes, such as ensuring social welfare through government policy.

[29]**The Constitution must be interpreted in light of advances in technology and social organization.** [30]The United States of 2008 is a different nation than the America of 1788. [31]It is highly unlikely that the founders could envision the complex evolution of human society and technology—how could they consider freedom of speech issues and the Internet? [32]To apply constitutional law to Internet speech issues necessarily means interpreting the Constitution in a way undreamed of by the founders.

[33]**Natural rights theory as understood by the founders leads to inequality.** [34]For example, the Declaration of Independence declares all men are equal, yet it allowed for slavery and unregulated free markets. [35]The Constitution must be interpreted with a view to new understandings of social and political equality.

—From *Think American Government*, 2nd ed., p. 53 by Neal R. Tannahill. Copyright © 2011 by Pearson Education, Inc. Reprinted by permission of Pearson Education, Inc., Glenview, IL.

_____c_____ **1.** Which sentence best states the implied main idea of paragraph 2 (sentences 5–8)?
   a. The United States was founded on Protestant religious values.
   b. The Constitution is based on universal values that do not change.
   c. The United States has changed dramatically in size and culture since the Constitution was ratified.
   d. The Constitution is outdated.

_____b_____ **2.** Which sentence best states the implied central idea of paragraphs 5 through 7 (sentences 16–24)?
   a. Natural rights theory is based on the moral law of values that do not change.

b. Natural rights theory is the foundation of the Constitution.

c. The Constitution is a well-thought out document.

d. The Constitution states "all men are created equal."

_____d_____ **3.** Which sentence best states the implied central idea of paragraphs 8 through 10 (sentences 25–35)?

a. Technology and social organization have outpaced natural rights.

b. Natural rights is a theory of the founders who were limited by their own culture and ideas.

c. The natural rights theory did not prevent slavery.

d. Natural rights theory is an outdated interpretation of the Constitution for three reasons.

_____b_____ **4.** Which sentence best states the implied central idea of the entire passage?

a. Positivism views the Constitution as a flexible document.

b. The Constitution is based on universal values of natural rights and natural law that do not change.

c. The meaning of the Constitution is a matter of debate.

d. Scholars debate the meaning of the Constitution based on the conflicting theories of natural rights and positivism.

REVIEW TEST 3

Score (number correct) _____ × 10 = _____ %

Implied Main Ideas

Before you read, skim the following passage. Answer the Before Reading questions. Read the passage and annotate the text. Then, answer the After Reading questions. 10.0 GE/630 words

The Awe in Autumn: Why Leaves Change Their Color

Vocabulary Preview

ornamental (5): decorative, attractive

pigments (10): colors

spectrum (12): range

synthesize (17): manufacture

foliage (35): plant life

¹Did you know that the state of Maine is the most heavily forested state in the union? ²It's true. ³Over 90 percent of the state's land mass is devoted to growing trees. ⁴That's 17 million acres! ⁵In addition, we have a wide variety of trees, with over 50 native species, and many more **ornamental** trees in various neighborhoods. ⁶With such an abundance of trees, it is no wonder that we have such a breathtaking season.

⁷Every autumn, magic **transformations** begin as trees begin to prepare for winter. ⁸In certain regions, such as our

own, the shedding of leaves is preceded by a spectacular color show. [9]Formerly green leaves turn to brilliant shades of yellow, orange, and red. [10]These color changes are the result of transformations in leaf **pigments**.

[11]All during the spring and summer, leaves serve as factories where most of the foods necessary for the trees' growth are manufactured. [12]This food-making process takes place inside the leaf in numerous cells that contain the pigment chlorophyll, which actually masks the true color of the leaf by absorbing all other light colors and reflecting only the green light **spectrum**—thus the leaves appear to our eyes as green.

[13]The energy of the light absorbed by chlorophyll is converted into chemical energy stored in carbohydrates (sugars and starches). [14]By the plant absorbing water and nutrients through its roots, and absorbing carbon dioxide from the air, the chemical process of photosynthesis takes place. [15]This chemical change drives the biochemical reactions that cause plants to grow, flower, and produce seed. [16]Chlorophyll is not a very stable compound; bright sunlight causes it to **decompose**. [17]To maintain the amount of chlorophyll in their leaves, plants continuously **synthesize** it. [18]The synthesis of chlorophyll in plants requires sunlight and warm temperatures. [19]During the summer months, chlorophyll is continuously broken down and regenerated in the leaves of the trees.

[20]The shortening of the days and the cooler temperatures at night trigger several changes within the tree. [21]One of these changes is the growth of a corky membrane between the branch and the leaf stem. [22]This membrane interferes with the flow of nutrients into the leaf. [23]As this nutrient flow is interrupted, the production of chlorophyll in the leaf declines, and the green color begins to fade.

[24]The different chemical components that are always present inside the structure of the individual leaf will determine its fleeting brilliant color in the fall. [25]But weather also plays a factor in determining color. [26]The degree of color may vary from tree to tree. [27]For example, leaves directly exposed to the sun may turn red, while those on the shady side of the same tree may appear yellow or orange. [28]Also, the colors on the same tree may vary from year to year, depending upon the combination of weather conditions.

[29]According to the tree experts at several universities, including North Carolina State, the U.S. Department of Agriculture, and the U.S. Forestry Service, the most vivid colors appear after a warm, dry summer

and early autumn rains, which will help prevent early leaf fall. [30]Long periods of wet weather in late fall will produce a rather drab coloration. [31]Droughts favor the chemical formation of anthocyanin, which is the chemical that is most responsible for the brilliant reds and purples. [32]Drought conditions, especially in late summer, also favor red pigment formation due to the reduction of nitrate absorption through the tree's roots.

[33]The best colors seem to be displayed when relatively warm and sunny days are followed by cold nights through early October. [34]Light frost will enhance the colors, but a hard, killing frost will hasten the actual fall of the leaves from the trees. [35]The right combination of temperature, rainfall, and sunshine can prolong the autumn **foliage** brilliance by as much as two weeks.

—"The Awe in Autumn: Why Leaves Change Their Color," *Maine-ly Weather,*
Fall/Winter 2002–2003, National Weather Service, NOAA. 2 Dec. 2003
http://www.erh.noaa.gov/er/car/WCM/Winter0203/page6.html

Before Reading

Vocabulary in Context

_____ b   **1.** The best definition of the word **transformations** in sentence 7 is
　　　a. mysteries.　　　　　　　c. shows.
　　　b. changes.　　　　　　　d. seasons.

_____ c   **2.** The best meaning of the word **decompose** in sentence 16 is
　　　a. stabilize.　　　　　　　c. decay.
　　　b. grow.　　　　　　　　d. stink.

Thought Patterns

_____ a   **3.** What is the thought pattern suggested by the title of the passage?
　　　a. cause and effect　　　　c. spatial order
　　　b. classification　　　　　d. comparison

Stated Main Ideas

_____ b   **4.** Which sentence is the topic sentence in the fifth paragraph (sentences 20–23)?
　　　a. sentence 20　　　　　　c. sentence 22
　　　b. sentence 21　　　　　　d. sentence 23

After Reading

Supporting Details

____c____ **5.** According to tree experts from universities and government agencies,
  a. autumn is a breathtaking season.
  b. trees go through magic transformations.
  c. the most vivid colors appear after a warm, dry summer.
  d. carbohydrates are sugars and starches.

____c____ **6.** Based on the passage, chlorophyll
  a. causes the color of the leaves to turn brilliant colors.
  b. is a stable compound.
  c. is a pigment which masks the true color of the leaf.
  d. is a corky membrane between the branch and the leaf stem.

Concept Maps and Charts

7. Complete the concept map with information from the passage.

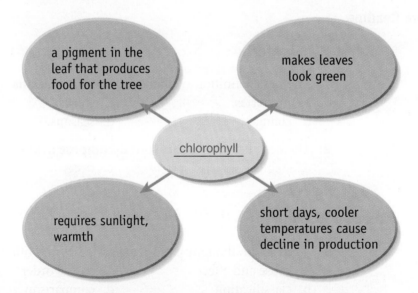

Implied Main Ideas and Implied Central Idea

____a____ **8.** Which sentence best states the implied main idea of the third, fourth, and fifth paragraphs (sentences 11–23)?
  a. The production of chlorophyll affects the color of the leaves on a tree.

b. Chlorophyll produces food for the tree.

c. When chlorophyll production declines, leaves lose their green color.

d. Cooler weather slows down the production of chlorophyll.

_____c_____ **9.** Which sentence best states the implied main idea of the eighth paragraph (sentences 33–35)?

a. A hard frost will cause autumn leaves to fall from trees early in the season.

b. Warm and sunny days produce brilliant colors.

c. Climate plays a significant role in the brilliance of the autumn colors.

d. Many factors affect the brilliance of the autumn colors.

_____c_____ **10.** Which sentence best states the implied central idea of the reading passage?

a. Autumn is a beautiful season.

b. Chlorophyll is a major component in the process of leaves turning colors.

c. Several factors work together to produce the awe-inspiring colors of fall.

d. Weather is a major factor that affects the quality of the color of autumn leaves.

WHAT DO YOU THINK?

Do you think the change of seasons affects humans physically? Emotionally? Why or why not? Assume you are a real estate salesperson. Your firm is planning a national advertising campaign to persuade people to move to your region to buy a home or commercial property. Write a couple of paragraphs that describe the appealing aspects of a particular season or all the seasons in your area.

REVIEW TEST 4   Score (number correct) _____ × 10 = _____ %

Implied Main Ideas

Before you read, skim the following passage. Answer the Before Reading questions. Read the passage and annotate the text. Then, answer the After Reading questions.

12.5 GE/478 words **The Food-Producing Revolution**

¹For the first thousands of millennia of their existence, modern humans, known as *Homo sapiens sapiens* ("most intelligent people"), did not produce food. ²Between 200,000 and 100,000 years ago, *Homo sapiens sapiens* first appeared in Africa and began to spread to other continents. ³Scientists refer to this stage of human history as the Paleolithic Age, or Old Stone Age, because people made tools by cracking rocks and using their sharp edges to cut and chop. ⁴*Homo sapiens sapien's* use of tools demonstrated adaptation to new environments and practical needs. ⁵They **scavenged** for wild food and became shrewd observers of the natural environment. ⁶They followed **migrating** herds of animals, hunting with increasing efficiency as their weapons improved. ⁷They also created beautiful works of art by carving bone and painting on cave walls. ⁸By 45,000 years ago, these humans had reached most of Earth's **habitable** regions, except for Australia, the islands of the South Pacific, and North and South America.

⁹The end of the last Ice Age about 15,000 years ago ushered in an era of momentous change: the food-producing revolution. ¹⁰As the Earth's climate became warmer, causing changes in vegetation, humans began to interact with the natural environment in new ways. ¹¹The warmer climate allowed cereal grasses to spread quickly over large areas; hunter-gatherers learned to collect these wild grains and grind them up for food. ¹²Some groups of hunter-gatherers settled in semi-permanent camps near rivers and wetlands, where wild grains grew. ¹³When people learned that the seeds of wild grasses could be transplanted and grown in new areas, the domestication of plants was under way (see Map).

¹⁴At the same time that people discovered the benefits of planting seeds, they also began domesticating pigs, sheep, goats, and cattle, which eventually replaced wild game as the main source of meat. ¹⁵Domestication occurs when humans **manipulate** the breeding of animals in order to serve their own purposes—for example, making wool (lacking on wild sheep), laying extra eggs (not done by undomesticated chickens), and producing extra milk (wild cows produce only enough milk for their offspring). ¹⁶The first signs of goat domestication occurred about 8900 B.C.E. in the Zagros Mountains in Southwest Asia. Pigs, which adapt very well to human settlements because they eat garbage, were first domesticated around 7000 B.C.E. ¹⁷By around 6500 B.C.E. domesticated cattle, goats, and sheep had become widespread.

[18]Farming and herding required hard work. [19]Even simple agricultural methods could produce about fifty times more food than hunting and gathering. [20]Thanks to the increased food supply, more newborns survived past infancy. [21]Populations expanded, and so did human settlements. [22]With the mastery of food production, human societies developed the **mechanisms** not only to feed themselves, but also to produce a surplus, which could then be traded for other resources. [23]Such economic activity allowed for economic specialization and fostered the growth of social, political, and religious **hierarchies**.

—Adapted from *The West: Encounters & Transformation, Atlas Edition,* Combined Edition, 2nd ed., Map 1.1, pp. 13–14, 27 by Brian Levack, Edward Muir, Meredith Veldman and Michael Maas. Copyright © 2008 by Pearson Education, Inc. Printed and Electronically reproduced by permission of Pearson Education, Inc., Upper Saddle River, NJ.

The Beginnings of Food Production

The Beginnings of Food Production

Before Reading

Vocabulary in Context

1–2. Study the following chart of word parts and the context in which the words are used. Then, use your own words to define the terms.

Root	Meaning	Suffix	Meaning
habitare	possess	*-able*	quality, degree
domus	house	*-ation*	action, process

1. In sentence 8, **habitable** means <u>a place that one can possess or live in.</u>

<u> </u>

2. In sentence 15, **domestication** means <u>taming of a plant or animal for</u>

<u>household use.</u>

After Reading

Thought Patterns

<u> a </u> **3.** The overall thought pattern used in this passage is
   a. time order.   c. definition and example.
   b. comparison and contrast.   d. space order.

Stated Main Ideas

<u> a </u> **4.** The sentence that states the main idea of the second paragraph (sentences 9–13) is
   a. sentence 9.   c. sentence 11.
   b. sentence 10.   d. sentence 12.

Supporting Details and Concept Maps

5–7. Complete the following concept map with details from the passage and the map.

Chronology: Beginnings of Civilization

200,000 to 100,000 years ago   Modern humans first appear in Africa.

45,000 years ago   **5.** <u>Modern humans spread through</u>

<u>Africa, Asia, and Europe.</u>

15,000 years ago	Ice Age ends.
	6. <u>Food-producing revolution begins.</u>
8900 B.C.E.	First signs of goat domestication occurred.
7000 B.C.E.	Pigs were domesticated.
6500 B.C.E.	**7.** <u>Domestication of cattle, goats, and</u> <u>sheep was widespread.</u>

Implied Main Ideas and Implied Central Ideas

_b_   **8.** Which sentence best states the implied main idea of the fourth paragraph (sentences 18–23)?
   a. Domesticating plants and animals was a difficult process.
   b. The benefits of farming and herding were worth the effort.
   c. Farming and herding increased trade.
   d. Farming and herding lengthened the life expectancy of infants.

_d_   **9.** Which sentence best states the implied central idea of the passage?
   a. Food production requires great effort.
   b. Domestication of plants and animals occurred about 15,000 years ago.
   c. Increased food supplies lengthened the life of humans.
   d. Food production made civilization possible.

Reading a Map

10. Study the map. State in one sentence the implied main idea of the map.

<u>Answers may vary. One possible answer: This map shows early farming sites</u>

<u>where the first known production of food occurred in ancient Southwest Asia.</u>

WHAT DO YOU THINK?

With the advancement of technology, humans now have the ability to feed the entire world. Why do you think, then, that famine and hunger are still a global problem? Which regions of the world are most affected by famine and starvation? What steps can we take as a country or as individuals to offer relief? Assume you are a concerned citizen who wants to help a particular group of people who are suffering from hunger. Write a letter to the editor of your local newspaper that calls on the public to help this group of people. Explain the problem and ask for action.

After Reading About Implied Main Ideas and Implied Central Ideas

Before you move on to the Mastery Tests on implied main ideas and implied central ideas, take time to reflect on your learning and performance by answering the following questions. Write your answers in your notebook.

- How has my knowledge base or prior knowledge about implied main ideas changed?

- Based on my studies, how do I think I will perform on the Mastery Test(s)? Why do I think my scores will be above average, average, or below average?

- Would I recommend this chapter to other students who want to learn more about implied main ideas? Why or why not?

Test your understanding of what you have learned about Implied Main Ideas for Master Readers by completing the Chapter 4 Review Card in the insert near the end of your text.

CONNECT TO myreadinglab

To check your progress in meeting Chapter 4's learning outcomes, log in to **www.myreadinglab.com** and try the following activities.

- The "Main Idea" section of MyReadingLab provides review materials, practice activities, and tests about topics and main ideas. To access this resource, click on the "Study Plan" tab. Then click on "Main Idea." Then click on the following links as needed: "Overview," "Model," "Practice," and "Tests."

- To measure your mastery of the content in this chapter, complete the tests in the "Main Idea" section and click on Gradebook to find your results.

A. Study the map and its caption from a college history textbook. Then, write a sentence that states the implied main idea of the map.

Textbook Skills

▲ Islam originated in the early seventh century among the inhabitants of the Arabian peninsula. Through conquest and expansion, Muslims created a single Islamic Empire stretching from Spain to central Asia by 750.

—Adapted from *The West: Encounters & Transformations, Atlas Edition, Combined Edition*, 2nd ed., Map 7.3, pp. 219, 221 by Brian Levack, Edward Muir, Meredith Veldman and Michael Maas. Copyright © 2008 by Pearson Education, Inc. Printed and Electronically reproduced by permission of Pearson Education, Inc., Upper Saddle River, NJ.

1. Implied main idea of map: Islam became the dominant religion in the vast empire, which extended from Spain, along the top of Africa from Morocco through Arabia and into Iran.

B. Determine the central idea stated in a thesis sentence for the following passage from a college history textbook. Annotate the text. Using your own words, write the central idea in the space provided.

Textbook
Skills

11.3 GE/227 words   **The Struggles of Free Blacks**

¹In addition to the 4 million blacks in bondage, there were approximately 500,000 free African Americans in 1860, about half of them living in slave states. ²Public facilities were strictly segregated, and after the 1830s, blacks in the United States could vote only in four New England states. ³Nowhere but in Massachusetts could they testify in court cases involving whites.

⁴Free blacks had difficulty finding decent jobs; most employers preferred immigrants or other whites over blacks. ⁵The blacks were usually relegated to menial and poorly paid occupations. ⁶Many states excluded blacks entirely from public schools, and the federal government barred them from serving in the militia, working for the postal service, and laying claim to public lands. ⁷Free blacks were even denied U.S. passports. ⁸In effect, they were stateless persons even before the 1857 Supreme Court ruling that no Negro could claim American citizenship.

⁹In the South, free blacks were subject to a set of direct controls that tended to make them semi-slaves. ¹⁰They were often forced to register or to have white guardians who were responsible for their behavior. ¹¹They were required to carry papers proving their free status, and in some states, they had to obtain official permission to move from one county to another. ¹²Licensing laws excluded blacks from several occupations, and authorities often blocked attempts by blacks to hold meetings or form organizations.

—Adapted from *The American Story*, 1st ed., pp. 427–428 by Robert A. Divine, George M. Fredrickson, R. Hal Williams and T. H. Breen. Copyright © 2002 by Pearson Education, Inc. Reprinted by permission of Pearson Education, Inc., Upper Saddle River, NJ.

2. Central idea stated in a thesis sentence: Whether they were in the North or in the South, "free Negroes" were treated as social outcasts and denied legal and political equality with whites.

Read the following textbook passages. Annotate the texts. Then, either write the letter of the best statement of the implied main idea or use your own words to state the implied main idea.

11.1 GE/165 words

Textbook
Skills

Interpersonal Relationships and the Media

[1]Whether for good or ill, millions of people tune in to the ever-present talk show to learn about friendship, romantic, family, and workplace relationships. [2]Talk shows often present themselves as educational, as therapy, and as authoritative about how you, your parents, and your friends should develop and maintain relationships. [3]Especially in the speech that closes many of the shows, talk show hosts with little to no professional training give out interpersonal advice. [4]For instance, they often give communication advice with no basis in scientific research. [5]They foster myths about communication. [6]Perhaps the most common myth is the idea that the more communication a couple has the better the relationship will be.

[7]Newspaper and magazine columnists offer advice without knowing even a scrap of information about who you are. [8]They do not know what difficulties you may be facing, nor do they know what you really want and need. [9]And astrology columns and psychic hotlines give you advice that has no basis in research.

—From *The Interpersonal Communication Book,* 10th ed., p. 274 by Joseph A. DeVito. Copyright © 2004 by Pearson Education, Inc. Reproduced by permission of Pearson Education, Inc., Boston, MA.

_____a_____ **1.** Which sentence best states the implied central idea?
- a. The media are currently teaching millions of people ideas about interpersonal relationships that are not based on research.
- b. Television talk shows foster myths about communication.
- c. The more communication a couple has the better their relationship will be.
- d. Newspaper and magazine columnists offer advice to millions of people.

10.7 GE/140 words

Textbook
Skills

Writing and Speaking

[1]Writing and speechmaking have much in common: both require careful thought about your subject, purpose, and audience. [2]Thus the

mental and physical activities that go into the writing process can also help you prepare and deliver a successful speech.

³Despite many similarities, however, writing for readers is not the same as speaking to listeners. ⁴Whereas a reader can go back and reread a written message, a listener cannot stop a speech to rehear a section. ⁵Several studies have reported that immediately after hearing a short talk, most listeners cannot recall half of what was said.

⁶Effective speakers adapt to their audience's listening ability by restating and repeating their ideas. ⁷They use simple words, short sentences, personal pronouns, and informal language. ⁸In formal writing, these strategies might seem out of place and too informal. ⁹But in speaking, they improve listeners' comprehension.

> —Adapted from *The Little, Brown Handbook,* 9th ed., p. 905 by H. Ramsey Fowler and Jane E. Aaron. Copyright © 2004 by Pearson Education, Inc. Reprinted by permission of Pearson Education, Inc., Glenview, IL.

2. Implied central idea of paragraphs 1 and 2: Answers may vary. One possible answer: Despite the similarities between writing and speaking, important differences exist between the two.

3. Implied main idea of paragraph 3: Answers may vary. One possible answer: Speakers use different strategies than writers to reach their audience.

Textbook
Skills

11.1 GE/107 words   Advertisements' Purpose

¹Business ads try to influence people's attitudes and behaviors toward the product and services a business sells. ²Most of these ads try to persuade consumers to buy something. ³But sometimes a business tries to improve its image through advertising.

⁴Public service ads promote behaviors and attitudes that are beneficial to society and its members. ⁵These ads may be either national or local and usually are the product of donated labor and media time or space.

⁶Political ads aim to persuade voters to elect a candidate to political office or to influence the public on legislative matters. ⁷These advertisements are run at the local, state, and national levels.

> —Adapted from Folkerts & Lacy, *The Media in Your Life,* 2nd ed., p. 428.

4. Implied central idea: Answers may vary. One possible answer: Advertisements can be divided into three categories based on purpose: business ads, service ads, and political ads.

Read the following selections. Annotate the texts. In the spaces provided, use your own words to state the implied main idea of each one.

A poem

Dark house, by which once more I stand (1850)
by Alfred Lord Tennyson

Dark house, by which once more I stand
    Here in the long unlovely street,
    Doors, where my heart was used to beat
So quickly, waiting for a hand,

A hand that can be clasped no more—
    Behold me, for I cannot sleep,
    And like a guilty thing I creep
At earliest morning to the door.

He is not here; but far away
    The noise of life begins again,
    And ghastly through the drizzling rain
On the bald street breaks the blank day.

—Tennyson, Alfred Lord. *In Memoriam* (London: E Moxon, 1850).

1. Implied main idea: ___Answers may vary. One possible answer: Grief over the___

___loss of a friend overshadows the joy of life.___

Paragraph from a college science textbook

Lives Up in Smoke

Textbook
Skills

[1]Mark Twain once said "Quitting smoking is easy, I've done it a thousand times." [2]Researchers have found that, like cocaine and heroin, nicotine activates the brain's reward center. [3]The brain adjusts by becoming less sensitive, requiring larger quantities of nicotine to experience the same rewarding effect, and causing the reward center to feel understimulated when nicotine is withdrawn. [4]Withdrawal symptoms include nicotine craving, depression, anxiety, irritability, difficulty concentrating, headaches, and disturbed sleep. [5]Although at least 70% of smokers would like to quit, only about 2.5% of smokers are successful each year.

—From *Life on Earth*, 5th ed., p. 390 by Teresa Audesirk, Gerald Audesirk, and Bruce E. Byers. Copyright © 2009 by Pearson Education, Inc. Printed and Electronically reproduced by permission of Pearson Education, Inc., Upper Saddle River, NJ.

2. Implied main idea: Answers may vary. Nicotine is a powerfully addictive drug, as likely to lead to addiction as cocaine or heroin.

Paragraph from a college history textbook

10.3 GE/83 words

Textbook
Skills

Abraham Lincoln's Humble Beginnings

¹Born to poor, illiterate parents on the Kentucky frontier in 1809, Abraham Lincoln received a few months of formal schooling in Indiana after the family moved there in 1816. ²But mostly, he educated himself. ³He read and reread a few treasured books by firelight. ⁴In 1831, when the family moved to Illinois, he left home to make a living for himself in the struggling settlement of New Salem. ⁵After failing as a merchant, he found a path to success in law and politics.

—Adapted from *The American Story,* 1st ed., p. 468 by Robert A. Divine, George M. Fredrickson, R. Hal Williams and T. H. Breen. Copyright © 2002 by Pearson Education, Inc. Reprinted by permission of Pearson Education, Inc., Upper Saddle River, NJ.

3. Implied main idea: Answers may vary. One possible answer: Abraham Lincoln was a self-educated man who overcame difficulties before becoming successful in law and politics.

Visual graphic or concept map from a college health textbook

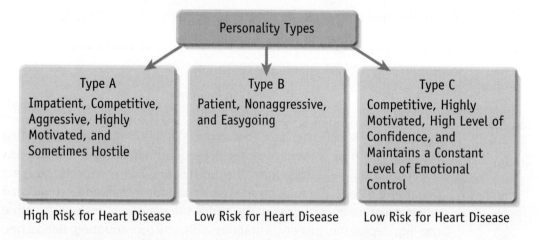

4. Implied main idea: Personality types affect an individual's risk for heart disease.

Read the passage and answer the questions that follow.

12.8 GE/573 words

History of Drug Abuse

[1]Drug use is nothing new to the human race. [2]As long as fruit has fermented and been consumed, our species has experienced the effects of drugs, substances that have psychological or physical effects. [3]Intentional fermentation—the process used to make alcohol—dates back to the Stone Age. [4]Beer jugs from the Neolithic period serve as evidence that alcoholic beverages were produced as early as 10,000 B.C.E. [5]Narcotics, drugs that are considered illegal today, also date back thousands of years.

Drug Use in Ancient Times [6]Citizens of Sumer, the first true civilization, used opium for medical and recreational purposes as early as 3000 B.C.E.; early tablets reveal that Sumerians referred to the substance as "Gil Hul" or "joy plant." [7]Ancient texts such as the Torah describe the early origins of winemaking in the Middle East, and the Ebers Papyrus, a medical document from ancient Egypt, outlines the many medicinal uses of opium.

Drug Use in the 18th Century [8]Although opium was originally used as a medicine, it was also one of the first drugs to be abused for recreational purposes. [9]Opium addiction became a serious social problem in China during the 18th century. [10]Initially, it was used to sedate patients and relieve tension amid pain. [11]However, by 1729, opium use became so rampant that the emperor outlawed the cultivation, sale, and use of the drug.

Early Drug Use in the United States [12]During the Civil War in the United States, both opium and its derivative morphine were regularly given to soldiers to relieve the pain of battle wounds. [13]But dependence on the drugs lasted long after the wounds were healed, leading the addiction to become known as "army disease." [14]In 1898, Bayer, the German company known for producing aspirin, developed heroin. [15]Ironically, this drug was marketed as a non-addictive substitute for morphine, as well as a cough suppressant. [16]Heroin was in fact stronger than morphine, and by 1900, approximately 1 percent of the U.S. population was addicted to some form of opiates.

[17]In the early 1900s, harmful and addictive drugs were readily available to consumers. [18]Drugstores were free to sell virtually anything they wished as

long as a person had a prescription, and many over-the-counter drugs contained heroin, morphine, and other opiates. [19]Even Coca-Cola—a seemingly harmless product—contained cocaine until the company switched to caffeine in 1906. [20]However, around the same time, temperance movements for alcohol and drugs began to arise. [21]The first federal law to restrict the sale, manufacturing, and distribution of drugs was the Harrison Narcotic Act of 1914.

> —From *Think Social Problems*, p. 142 by John D. Carl.
> Copyright © 2011 by Pearson Education, Inc. Reproduced
> by permission of Pearson Education, Inc., Boston, MA.

___d___ **1.** Which sentence best states the implied main idea of paragraphs 1 and 2 (sentences 1–7)?
   a. Narcotics have been in use for thousands of years.
   b. The earliest drug to be produced and used was beer.
   c. Drug use first developed for medical and religious reasons.
   d. Humans have used drugs since the beginning of civilization.

___a___ **2.** Which sentence best states the implied central idea of paragraph 3 (sentences 8–11)?
   a. Opium was not intended to be used as a recreational drug.
   b. Outlawing a drug does not stop its abuse.
   c. Opium was first used as a recreational drug in the 18th century.
   d. The Chinese were the first to outlaw the use of opium.

___b___ **3.** Which sentence best states the implied central idea of paragraphs 4 and 5 (sentences 12–21)?
   a. Drug use was prevalent during the Civil War.
   b. Drug abuse in the United States is a historical problem.
   c. In the past, the United States encouraged the use of harmful and addictive drugs.
   d. The social problem of drug use is a significant current issue in the United States.

___c___ **4.** Which sentence best states the implied central idea of the entire passage?
   a. The United States struggles to address the social problems of drug use.
   b. People have always used drugs.
   c. The social problems caused by drug use began in ancient times and continue throughout history.
   d. Drug abuse cannot be eliminated.

Supporting Details

5

LEARNING OUTCOMES

After studying this chapter you should be able to do the following:

1 Define *major supporting details, minor supporting details*, and *summary*. [Knowledge]

2 Create questions to locate supporting details. [Analysis, Synthesis]

3 Distinguish between major and minor supporting details. [Comprehension]

4 Complete a simple chart that outlines the topic, main idea, and supporting details of a passage. [Application]

5 Annotate a passage to create a summary. [Application]

6 Create a summary of a passage. [Synthesis]

7 Evaluate the importance of supporting details. [Evaluation]

 ## Before Reading About Supporting Details

In Chapter 3, you learned several important ideas that will help you as you work through this chapter. Use the following questions to call up your prior knowledge about supporting details.

What is a main idea? (page 96) A main idea is the author's controlling point about the topic. It usually includes the topic and the author's attitude or opinion about the topic or the author's approach to the topic.

What are the three parts of most paragraphs? (page 100) the topic, the main idea, and the supporting details.

Define supporting details. (page 101) Supporting details are the specific ideas that develop, explain, or support the main idea.

What are the different possible locations of topic sentences? (pages 105–111.)

Topic sentences can be located at the beginning of a paragraph, within a paragraph,

at the end of a paragraph, or at the beginning and the end of a paragraph.

What is a central idea? (page 113.) The central idea is the main idea of a passage

made up of two or more paragraphs.

 ## Questions for Locating Supporting Details

To locate supporting details, a master reader turns the main idea into a question by asking one of the following reporter's questions: *who, what, when, where, why,* or *how.* The answer to this question will yield a specific set of supporting details. For example, the question *why* is often answered by listing and explaining reasons or causes. The question *how* is answered by explaining a process. The answer to the question *when* is based on time order. An author strives to answer some or all of these questions with the details in the paragraph. You may want to try out several of the reporter's questions as you turn the main idea into a question. Experiment to discover which question is best answered by the details.

> **Supporting details** explain, develop, and illustrate the main idea.

Take, for example, the subject "youth joining gangs." For this topic an author might choose to write about ways parents can prevent their child from becoming involved in gangs. The main idea of such a paragraph may read as follows:

Main idea: To prevent their children from joining gangs, parents must take the following two steps.

Using the word *how* turns the main idea into this question: "How can parents prevent their children from joining gangs?" Read the following paragraph for the answers to this question.

Parental Love:
The First Line of Defense in the War Against Gangs

[1]To prevent their children from joining gangs, parents must take the following two steps. [2]First, and most important, parents should

spend time with their children. ³One-on-one time with a parent who is giving undivided attention builds trust, establishes communication, and fosters self-esteem. ⁴Likewise, family trips to parks, libraries, museums, or the beach create a sense of belonging so that children are not tempted to seek acceptance elsewhere. ⁵Second, parents should set and abide by reasonable rules. ⁶Establishing boundaries that ensure safety and teach respect for authority is an expression of love. ⁷Parents who expect children to value an education, abide by a curfew, and choose friends wisely are thwarting the chances that their children will join a gang.

The supporting details for this main idea answer the question "how?" by listing the two steps that are likely to prevent a child from joining a gang. Then, the paragraph discusses why these steps may help.

Note the relationship between the author's controlling point and the supporting details.

Notice that the details about situations directly explain the main idea. However, additional supporting details were given in the paragraph that are not listed. Each of the main supporting details needed further explanation. This paragraph shows us that there are two kinds of supporting details: details that explain the main idea and details that explain other details.

EXAMPLE Read the paragraph. Turn the topic sentence into a question using one of the reporter's questions (Who? What? When? Where? Why? How?). Write the question in the space. Fill in the chart with the answers to the questions you have created.

The Traits of Attention Deficit Hyperactivity Disorder

[1]Attention Deficit Hyperactivity Disorder (ADHD) has three basic traits. [2]One trait of ADHD children is **inattention.** [3]They have a hard time keeping their minds on any one thing and may get bored with a task after only a few minutes. [4]If they are doing something they really enjoy, they have no trouble paying attention. [5]But focusing deliberate, conscious attention to organizing and completing a task or learning something new is difficult. [6]Homework is particularly hard for these children. [7]They will forget to write down an assignment, or leave it at school. [8]They will forget to bring a book home, or bring the wrong one. [9]The homework, if finally finished, is full of errors and erasures. [10]Homework is often accompanied by frustration for both parent and child. [11]Another trait of ADHD children is **hyperactivity.** [12]These children seem to be constantly in motion. [13]They dash around touching or playing with whatever is in sight, or talk incessantly. [14]Sitting still at dinner or during a school lesson or story can be a difficult task. [15]They squirm and fidget in their seats or roam around the room. [16]Or they may wiggle their feet, touch everything, or noisily tap their pencil. [17]The third trait of ADHD children is **impulsivity.** [18]They seem unable to curb their immediate reactions or think before they act. [19]They will often blurt out inappropriate comments, display their emotions without restraint, and act without regard for the later consequences of their conduct. [20]Their impulsivity may make it hard for them to wait for things they want or to take their turn in games. [21]They may grab a toy from another child or hit when they're upset. [22]Even as teenagers or adults, they may impulsively choose to do things that have an immediate but small payoff rather than engage in activities that may take more effort yet provide much greater but delayed rewards.

—Adapted from "Attention Deficit Hyperactivity Disorder."
National Institute of Mental Health. 9 April 2004. 13 Dec 2007
http://www.nimh.nih.gov/publicat/adhd.cfm#symptoms

Question based on topic sentence: What are the three basic traits of ADHD?

Topic sentence: ADHD has three basic traits.

First trait   **Second trait**   **Third trait**

(**1**) Inattention   (**2**) Hyperactivity   (**3**) Impulsivity

EXPLANATION Using the reporter's question *What?*, you should have turned the topic sentence into the following question: *What are the three basic traits of*

ADHD? The answer to this question yields the supporting details. Compare your answers to the following: (1) Inattention, (2) Hyperactivity, and (3) Impulsivity.

PRACTICE 1

Read the paragraph. Turn the topic sentence into a question using one of the reporter's questions (Who? What? When? Where? Why? How?). Write the question in the space. Fill in the chart with the answers to the question you have created.

Ozone and Your Health

[1]Ozone is a gas that occurs both in the Earth's upper atmosphere and at ground level. [2]Ozone can be helpful or harmful, depending on where it is found. [3]The helpful ozone occurs naturally in the Earth's upper atmosphere—10 to 30 miles above the Earth's surface. [4]At this level, it shields us from the sun's harmful ultraviolet rays. [5]The harmful ozone is found in the Earth's lower atmosphere, near ground level. [6]Harmful ozone is formed when pollutants emitted by cars, power plants, industrial boilers, refineries, chemical plants, and other sources react chemically in the presence of sunlight. [7]Ozone at the ground level can harm your health. [8]First, ozone can irritate your respiratory system, causing you to start coughing, feel an irritation in your throat or experience an uncomfortable sensation in your chest. [9]Second, ozone can reduce lung function and make it more difficult for you to breathe as deeply and vigorously as you normally would. [10]When this happens, you may notice that breathing starts to feel uncomfortable. [11]If you are exercising or working outdoors, you may notice that you are taking more rapid and shallow breaths than normal. [12]Third, ozone can aggravate asthma. [13]When ozone levels are high, more people with asthma have attacks that require a doctor's attention or the use of additional medication. [14]One reason this happens is that ozone makes people more sensitive to allergens, which are the most common triggers for asthma attacks. [15]Also, asthmatics are more severely affected by the reduced lung function and irritation that ozone causes in the respiratory system. [16]Fourth, ozone can inflame and damage cells that line your lungs. [17]Within a few days, the damaged cells are replaced and the old cells are shed—much in the way your skin peels after a sunburn. [18]Fifth, ozone may aggravate chronic lung diseases such as emphysema and bronchitis and reduce the immune system's ability to fight off bacterial infections in the respiratory system. [19]Sixth, ozone may cause permanent lung damage. [20]Repeated

short-term ozone damage to children's developing lungs may lead to reduced lung function in adulthood. [21]In adults, ozone exposure may accelerate the natural decline in lung function that occurs as part of the normal aging process.

> —Adapted from "Ozone and Your Health." *AIRNow.* The Environmental Protection Agency. 15 Dec 2004. 13 Dec 2007 http://www.airnow.gov/index.cfm?action=static.brochure

Question based on topic sentence: How does ozone at the ground level harm your health?

Topic sentence: Ozone at the ground level can harm your health.

Harmful Effects:

(1) irritate respiratory system	(2) reduce lung function	(3) aggravate asthma	(4) inflame, damage cells that line lungs	(5) aggravate chronic lung disease	(6) cause permanent lung damage

Major and Minor Details

A supporting detail will always be one of two types:

> A **major detail** directly explains, develops, or illustrates the *main idea.*
> A **minor detail** explains, develops, or illustrates a *major detail.*

A **major detail** is directly tied to the main idea. Without the major details, the author's main idea would not be clear because the major details are the principal points the author is making about the topic.

In contrast, a **minor detail** explains a major detail. The minor details could be left out, and the main idea would still be clear. Thus minor details are not as important as major details. Minor details are used to add interest and to give further descriptions, examples, testimonies, analysis, illustrations, and reasons for the major details. To better understand the flow of ideas, study the following diagram:

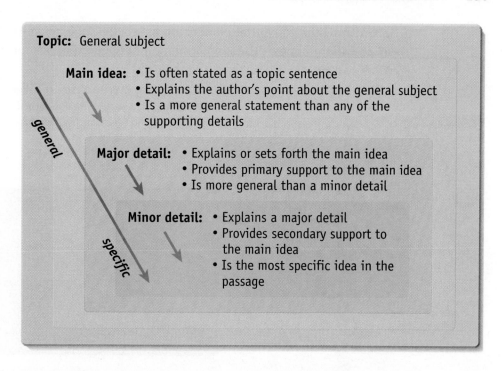

As ideas move from general to specific details, the author often uses signal words to introduce a new detail. These signal words—such as *first, second, next, in addition*, or *finally*—can help you identify major and minor details.

EXAMPLE See if you can tell the difference between major and minor details. Read the following paragraph. Then, complete the exercise that follows.

Terrestrial and Jovian Planets

[1]Planets fall quite nicely into two groups: the terrestrial (Earthlike) planets (Mercury, Venus, Earth, and Mars), and the Jovian (Jupiter-like) planets (Jupiter, Saturn, Uranus, and Neptune). [2]Pluto was recently demoted to a dwarf planet—a new class of solar system objects that have an orbit around the Sun but share their space with other celestial bodies. [3]The most obvious difference between the terrestrial and the Jovian planets is their size. [4]The largest terrestrial planets (Earth and Venus) have diameters only one quarter as great as the diameter of the smallest Jovian planet (Neptune). [5]Also, their masses are only 1/17 as great as Neptune's. [6]Hence, the Jovian planets are often called giants. [7]In addition to their size, planets are distinguished based on their location. [8]Because of their relative locations, the four Jovian planets are also referred to as the **outer planets**.

[9]In contrast, the terrestrial planets are called the **inner planets**. [10]As we will see, there appears to be a correlation between the location of these planets within the solar system and their sizes.

—From *Foundations of Earth Science,* 5th ed., p. 407 by Frederick K. Lutgens, Edward J. Tarbuck, and Dennis Tasa. Copyright © 2008 by Pearson Education, Inc. Printed and Electronically reproduced by permission of Pearson Education, Inc., Upper Saddle River, NJ.

VISUAL VOCABULARY

Saturn, known for its rings of debris and ice, is classified as a

b _____ planet and also referred to as an

d _____ planet.

  a. Terrestrial
  b. Jovian
  c. inner
  d. outer

Complete the following outline of the paragraph by supplying the appropriate major and minor details.

Stated main idea: Planets fall quite nicely into two groups: the terrestrial (Earthlike) planets (Mercury, Venus, Earth, and Mars), and the Jovian (Jupiter-like) planets (Jupiter, Saturn, Uranus, and Neptune).

A. The most obvious difference between the terrestrial and the Jovian planets is their size.

  1. The largest terrestrial planets (Earth and Venus) have diameters only one quarter as great as the diameter of the smallest Jovian planet (Neptune).

  2. Also, their masses are only 1/17 as great as Neptune's.

  3. Hence, the Jovian planets are often called giants.

B. In addition to their size, planets are distinguished based on their location.

  1. Because of their relative locations, the four Jovian planets are also referred to as the outer planets.

2. In contrast, the terrestrial planets are called the inner planets.

3. As we will see, there appears to be a correlation between the location of these planets within the solar system and their sizes.

EXPLANATION This paragraph provides two major supporting details that help explain the main idea: sentences 3 and 7 state these two major supporting details that describe the classification of planets based on size and location. Sentences 4, 5, and 6 are minor details that explain the differences between the two types of planets based on size. Sentences 8 and 9 are minor details; they explain the differences between the types of planets based on location. Sentence 10 is a minor detail; it suggests a relationship between the size and location of a planet. Interestingly, sentence 2 is a detail that does not directly relate to the two types of planets discussed in the paragraph. The author may have felt this detail was necessary, however, since Pluto, long thought of as a planet, has just recently been reclassified and is no longer considered a planet at all. Thus, sentence 2 acknowledges that some readers have prior knowledge about Pluto's former status as a planet. Sentence 2 preempts reader confusion and readjusts prior knowledge to current scientific standards.

PRACTICE 2

Read the following paragraph. Then, identify the major and minor details by completing the outline that follows it.

Weight Loss in Our Pets

[1]Weight management is an important aspect of ensuring a long, healthy, and happy life for our pets. [2]As a caring pet owner, you need to be aware of the various reasons pets lose weight and when weight loss signals trouble. [3]Of course, at times, some weight loss is expected. [4]For example, dropping a pound or so may be perfectly normal, particularly if your pet has put on a few extra pounds over the years. [5]In addition, some pets lose weight during those hot summer months when soaring temperatures can curb an appetite. [6]Likewise, some pets lose weight during the frigid winter months as they burn more calories to keep warm. [7]And female pets who are nursing mothers may lose weight as they burn calories to produce milk. [8]Another major cause of weight loss is the environment. [9]Even healthy pets that are boarded may lose weight because of the stress of a different environment. [10]What you feed your pet is a key aspect of the animal's environment; diet plays a vital role in weight

management because poor quality, spoiled, or inedible food can result in undernourishment and weight loss. [11]Finally, many underlying medical conditions are often signaled by sudden or dramatic weight loss. [12]A few examples of conditions to be on guard against are dental disease, gastrointestinal disorders (which may include parasites), diabetes, liver or kidney disease, heart disease, and cancer. [13]Any one of these conditions can interfere with eating and the absorption of nutrients.

Stated main idea: As a caring pet owner, you need to be aware of the various reasons pets lose weight and when weight loss signals trouble.

A. Of course, at times, some weight loss is expected.

    1. For example, dropping a pound or so may be perfectly normal, particularly if your pet has put on a few extra pounds over the years.

    2. In addition, some pets lose weight during those hot summer months when soaring temperatures can curb an appetite.

    3. Likewise, some pets lose weight during the frigid winter months as they burn more calories to keep warm.

    4. And female pets who are nursing mothers may lose weight as they burn calories to produce milk.

B. Another major cause of weight loss is the environment.

    1. Even healthy pets that are boarded may lose weight because of the stress of a different environment.

    2. What you feed your pet is a key aspect of the animal's environment; diet plays a vital role in weight management because poor quality, spoiled, or inedible food can result in undernourishment and weight loss.

C. Finally, many underlying medical conditions are often signaled by sudden or dramatic weight loss.

    1. A few examples of conditions to be on guard against are dental disease, gastrointestinal disorders (which may include parasites), diabetes, liver or kidney disease, heart disease, and cancer.

    2. Any one of these conditions can interfere with eating and the absorption of nutrients.

Creating a Summary from Annotations

Reading for main ideas and major supporting details is an excellent study technique. Writing down main ideas and major supporting details in a summary after you read is an effective strategy that will deepen your understanding and provide you with study notes for review and reflection. (Chapter 1 presented a number of reading strategies.) A **summary** condenses a paragraph or passage down to only its primary points by restating the main idea, major supporting details, and important examples. Often, you will want to paraphrase or restate the ideas in your own words; other times, you may need to use the exact language of the text to ensure accuracy. For example, scientific or medical terms have precise meanings that must be memorized; thus your summaries of these types of ideas would include the original language of the text.

> A **summary** is a brief, clear restatement of the most important points of a paragraph or passage.

Different lengths of text require different lengths of summaries. For example, a paragraph can be summarized in one sentence or a few sentences. A passage of several paragraphs can be reduced to one paragraph, and a much longer selection such as a chapter in a textbook may require a summary of a page or two in length.

To help create a summary after reading, you can **annotate**, or mark, your text *during reading*. For example, as you read, circle the main idea and underline the major supporting details and important examples. To learn more about annotating a text see pages 594–595 in Part Two.

 EXAMPLE Read the following paragraph from a college accounting textbook. Annotate the text by circling the main idea and underlining the major supporting details and the important examples. Then, complete the summary by filling in the blanks with information from the passage.

Textbook Skills

Income Method and Life Insurance

Main idea — [1]The **income method** is a general formula for determining how much life insurance you should maintain based solely on your income. [2]This method normally specifies the life insurance amount as a multiple of your income, such as 10 times your annual income. [3]For example, if you have

Major supporting details

Important
example

an annual income of $40,000, this formula would suggest that you need $400,000 in life insurance. ⁴This method is very easy to use. ⁵The disadvantage is that it does not consider your age and your household situation. ⁶Thus, it does not make a distinction between a household that has no children and one with four children. ⁷The household with four children will likely need more life insurance because its expenses will be higher.

—Adapted from *Personal Finance,* 3rd ed., p. 372 by Jeff Madura. Copyright © 2007 by Pearson Education, Inc. Reproduced by permission of Pearson Education, Inc., Boston, MA.

Summary

The **income method** is a general formula for determining how much life insurance you should maintain based on a multiple of your income, such as 10 times your annual income.

For example, for an annual income of $40,000, you probably need $400,000 in life insurance.

EXPLANATION   The main idea of the paragraph is "The income method is a general formula for determining how much life insurance you should maintain based solely on your income." Including important details in your summary clarifies the way the necessary amount of insurance is calculated. The disadvantages of this formula are minor details that you do not need to include since the main idea states that the formula is based solely on income.

Compare your summary to the following: The **income method** is a general formula for determining how much life insurance you should maintain based on a multiple of your income, such as 10 times your annual income. For example, for an annual income of $40,000, you probably need $400,000 in life insurance.

PRACTICE 3

Read the following passage from a college textbook about tourism. Annotate the text by circling the central idea and underlining the major supporting details and important examples. Then, compose a summary of the passage.

Textbook
Skills

[1]For decades, tourism researchers have grouped tourist motivations as push or pull factors. [2]The notion is that travelers are both "pushed" to travel by personality traits or individual needs and wants, and "pulled" to travel by appealing attributes of travel destinations. [3]Traditionally, the push motivations have been thought useful for explaining the desire for travel while the pull motivations have been thought useful for explaining the actual destination choice.

[4]This "theory" of travel motivation highlights the fact that tourists are pushed (motivated) to travel by many factors simultaneously, and destinations pull (attract) visitors with a combination of resources. [5]For instance, a tourist generates the desire to escape from his mundane day-to-day routine and seeks a destination that seems to offer the "ticket" to that escape. [6]Research has shown that push and pull factors are matched by travelers. [7]For example, studies have found a large percentage of travelers are motivated to travel by a desire to be pampered, comfortable, and entertained. [8]Destinations that generate the most "pull" for this group of travelers are cities and beach resorts.

[9]Several "push" factors have been identified and researched as personality traits (such as novelty seeking). [10]An additional and particularly appropriate personality trait theory that relates to tourism is optimal arousal theory. [11]Briefly, the core of this theory is that each of us has some optimal level of arousal at which we feel most comfortable. [12]For some, that level is quite low, leading to a relaxed, slower-paced lifestyle, whereas for many, the optimal arousal level is very high, driving individuals constantly to seek new and challenging activities. [13]A person who is stressed out by work may desire to reduce arousal by seeking a quiet seaside resort to spend some quiet time with a loved one. [14]Another who is bored by the routine of his job and life may instead decide to travel to Europe and test his mettle on the ski slopes of the Alps.

—From *Tourism: The Business of Travel*, 4th ed, pp. 34–35 by Roy A. Cook, Laura J. Yale and Joseph J. Marqua. Copyright © 2010 by Pearson Education, Inc. Printed and Electronically reproduced by permission of Pearson Education, Inc., Upper Saddle River, NJ.

In tourism, the push and pull theory explains that tourists match their motivation

or "push" to travel to the "pull" or attraction of the resources of a destination.

Furthermore, push factors are often based on optimal arousal theory that is the level

of stimulation with which we feel most comfortable. For example, the push to relieve

stress may lead to a vacation with loved ones in a quiet ocean resort.

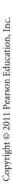

Creating a Summary: Implied Main Ideas

At times, an author may choose to imply a main idea instead of directly stating it. As you learned in Chapter 4, you can use supporting details to create a topic sentence or thesis statement when the main idea or central point is implied. Annotating your text will also help you create a summary for passages with an implied main idea.

First, identify the topic of the passage. Underline recurring words or phrases. Locate each heading or major supporting detail in the passage. (Remember, minor details explain or support major details. Thus, when creating a summary, you can ignore these minor details.) Assign a number or letter to each of the headings or major details you identified. Next, for each piece of information you have marked, ask the question "What controlling point or opinion about the topic does this detail reveal?" Often, a main heading can be turned into a question that will help you determine the implied main idea. Then, write a brief answer to each question in the margin next to the detail you marked. Next, after you finish reading, create a topic sentence or thesis statement for the passage. Finally, use only a few brief sentences to create the entire summary.

EXAMPLE Read the following passage taken from a college psychology textbook. As you read, complete the following steps. Then, create a summary of the passage in the space provided after the passage. Answers may vary.

Step 1. Annotate the text: Underline the recurring key terms or phrases and label the major supporting details with a number or letter.

Step 2. Turn the main heading into a question to determine the implied main idea. If needed, turn major details into questions that reveal the author's controlling point.

Step 3. Answer each question in your own words.

Step 4. Create a thesis statement based on the main heading and/or supporting details.

Step 5. Write a summary that combines the thesis statement and the major supporting details into one sentence or a few brief sentences.

Textbook
Skills

Three Ways to Measure Memory

[1]We have all had the embarrassing experience of being unable to recall the name of a person whom we are sure that we have already met. [2]This happens to everyone because recognition is an easier memory task than recall. [3]In ① **recall**, a person must produce required information

What are the three ways to measure memory? Recall, recognition, and relearning.

What is re-
call? Recall is
the process
of searching
memory.

simply by searching memory. [4]Trying to remember someone's name, the items on a shopping list, or the words of a speech or a poem is a recall task. [5]A recall task may be made a little easier if cues are provided to jog memory. [6]A **retrieval cue** is any stimulus or bit of information that aids in retrieving a particular memory. [7]Think about how you might respond to these two test questions:

What is a
retrieval cue?
A retrieval
cue is a bit of
information
that stimu-
lates recall.

[8]What are the four basic memory processes?

[9]The four processes involved in memory are e_____, s_____, c_____, and r_____.

[10]Both questions require you to recall information. [11]However, most students would find the second question easier to answer because it includes four retrieval cues.

What is
recognition?
Recognition
occurs when
a person
identifies
information
as familiar.

②[12]**Recognition** is exactly what the name implies. [13]A person simply recognizes something as familiar—a face, a name, a taste, a melody. [14]Multiple-choice, matching, and true false questions are examples of test items based on recognition. [15]The main difference between recall and recognition is that a recognition task does not require you to supply the information but only to recognize it when you see it. [16]The correct answer is included along with other items in a recognition question.

[17]There is another, more sensitive way to measure memory. [18]With

What is the
relearning
method?
The relearn-
ing method
measures
the amount
of time re-
quired to
relearn
information
relative to
the amount
of time it
took to learn
the material
originally.

the ③**relearning method**, retention is expressed as the percentage of time saved when material is relearned relative to the time required to learn the material originally. [19]Suppose it took you 40 minutes to memorize a list of words, and one month later you were tested on those words, using recall or recognition. [20]If you could not recall or recognize a single word, would this mean that you had absolutely no memory of anything on the list? [21]Or could it mean that the recall and recognition tasks were not sensitive enough to measure what little information you may have stored? [22]How could a researcher measure such a remnant of former learning? [23]Using the relearning method, a researcher could time how long it would take you to relearn the list of words. [24]If it took 20 minutes to relearn the list, this would represent a 50% savings over the original learning time of 40 minutes. [25]The percentage of time saved—the savings score—reflects how much material remains in long-term memory.

[26]College students demonstrate the relearning method each semester when they study for comprehensive final exams. [27]Relearning material for a final exam takes less time than it took to learn the material originally.

—Adapted from *Mastering the World of Psychology*, 3rd ed., pp. 184–185 by Samuel E. Wood, Ellen Green Wood and Denise Boyd. Copyright © 2008 by Pearson Education, Inc. Reproduced by permission of Pearson Education, Inc., Boston, MA.

Summary: The three ways to measure memory include recall, recognition, and the relearning method. Recall is the task of producing information by searching memory. Often a retrieval cue, a bit of information or stimulus, aids in the recall of information from long-term memory. Recognition is the task of identifying material as familiar. Finally, the relearning method measures the percentage of time saved when material is relearned compared to the time needed to learn the material originally.

EXPLANATION Think about the following question based on the title of the passage: "What are the three ways to measure memory?" To answer this question, you should have located and numbered the major supporting details, which also state the central idea of the passage. The author used bold print to highlight the three major details that answer the question. By using your own words to combine the thesis statement and the major supporting details, you create your summary. Compare your summary to the following: The three ways to measure memory include recall, recognition, and the relearning method. Recall is the task of producing information by searching memory. Often a retrieval cue, a bit of information or stimulus, aids in the recall of information from long-term memory. Recognition is the task of identifying material as familiar. Finally, the relearning method measures the percentage of time saved when material is relearned compared to the time needed to learn the material originally.

PRACTICE 4

Read the following passage from a college textbook about human anatomy. Then, create a summary of the passage in the space provided after the passage.

Muscle Tissue

Textbook
Skills

[1]Muscle tissues are highly specialized to contract, or shorten, to produce movement.

[2]**Skeletal muscle** tissue is packaged by connective tissue sheets into organs called skeletal muscles, which are attached to the skeleton. [3]These muscles, which can be controlled voluntarily (or consciously), form the flesh of the body, the so-called muscular system. [4]When the skeletal muscles contract, they pull on bones or skin. [5]The result of their action is gross body movements—or changes in our facial expressions. [6]The cells of skeletal muscle are long, cylindrical, multinucleate, and they have obvious striations (stripes). [7]Because skeletal muscle cells are elongated to provide a long axis for contraction, they are often called muscle fibers.

What is muscle tissue? How many types of muscle tissue are there? Muscle tissues contract to create movement. There are three specialized types of muscle tissue: skeletal muscle, cardiac muscle, and smooth muscle.

What are skeletal muscles? Skeletal muscles are attached to the skeleton and move bones and skin.

What are cardiac muscles? Cardiac muscles cause the heart to pump blood.

[8]**Cardiac muscle** is found only in the heart. [9]As it contracts, the heart acts as a pump and propels blood through the blood vessels. [10]Like skeletal muscle, cardiac muscle has striations, but cardiac cells are uninucleate, relatively short, branching cells that fit tightly together (like clasped fingers) at junctions called intercalated disks. [11]These intercalated disks contain gap junctions that allow ions to pass freely from cell to cell, resulting in rapid conduction of the exciting electrical impulse across the heart. [12]Cardiac muscle is under involuntary control, which means that we cannot consciously control the activity of the heart. [13](There are, however, rare individuals who claim they have such an ability.)

What are smooth muscles? Smooth muscles are visceral muscles found in the walls of organs.

[14]**Smooth muscle**, or visceral muscle, is so called because no striations are visible. [15]The individual cells have a single nucleus and are spindle-shaped (pointed at each end). [16]Smooth muscle is found in the walls of hollow organs such as the stomach, uterus, and blood vessels. [17]As smooth muscle in its walls contracts, the cavity of an organ alternately becomes smaller (constricts on smooth muscle contraction) or enlarges (dilates on smooth muscle relaxation) so that substances are propelled through the organ along a specific pathway. [18]Smooth muscle contracts much more slowly than the other two muscle types. [19]Peristalsis (per"ĭstal'sĭs), a wavelike motion that keeps food moving through the small intestine, is typical of its activity.

—From *Essentials of Human Anatomy and Physiology*, 9th ed., pp. 66, 98 by Elaine N. Marieb. Copyright © 2009 by Pearson Education, Inc. Reprinted by permission of Pearson Education, Inc., Glenview, IL.

Summary: Answers may vary. Muscle tissue is highly specialized tissue that contracts to produce movement. There are three types of muscle tissue: skeletal muscles move bones and skin; cardiac muscle pumps the heart; and smooth muscle, also known as visceral muscles, causes the walls of organs to move substances through the organs.

Textbook Skills

Reading a Textbook: Chapter-end Questions

Textbooks often provide questions at the end of a chapter or section to help you identify and remember the most important points. These questions typically ask you to summarize the main idea and major supporting details. The chapter-end questions may also ask you to note one or two minor supporting details as examples. Annotating your text by circling the main idea and underlining major supporting details and examples as you read will help you answer chapter-end questions and summarize what you are learning.

EXAMPLE Read the following paragraph and chapter-end question about the paragraph from a college communications textbook. Circle the topic sentence and underline the major supporting details and the important examples. Then, answer the question.

Textbook
Skills

Types of Media

¹The mass media fall broadly into two categories or groups. ²These two groups have certain elements in common, yet they possess different physical traits. ³The first group, **print**, includes newspapers, magazines, newsletters, and books. ⁴Their words create images in the mind as well as convey information. ⁵The second group is **electronics and film**. ⁶This group includes radio, recordings, television, still and motion pictures, and video. ⁷These media send their messages through visual and audio impact on the senses, sometimes with great emotional power.

Chapter-end Question: What are the two basic categories of media? Name at least two media in each category.

—Adapted from Agee, Ault, & Emery, *Introduction to Mass Communication*, 12th ed., pp. 6, 20.

Answer:

The two basic categories of media are (1) **print**, which includes magazines and

books, and (2) **electronics and film**, which includes radio and television .

EXPLANATION By answering this question, you are restating the main idea and the major supporting details. In the second part of the question, the textbook author asks you to name two examples. All of this information can be stated in one sentence: "The two basic categories of media are (1) print, which includes magazines and books, and (2) electronics and film, which includes radio and television."

PRACTICE 5

Read the following paragraph and chapter-end question about the paragraph from a college communications textbook. Circle the topic sentence and underline the major supporting details. Then, answer the question.

Textbook
Skills

Friendship

¹Friendship is an interpersonal relationship between two persons that is mutually productive and is characterized by mutual positive regard.

²Several types of friendships exist. ³One type of friendship is known as 1st type reciprocity, characterized by loyalty, self-sacrifice, mutual affection, 2nd type and generosity. ⁴A second type is based on receptivity, characterized by a comfortable and positive imbalance in the giving and receiving of rewards; each person's needs are satisfied by the exchange. ⁵Another 3rd type type of friendship identified as association is a transitory relationship, more like a friendly relationship than a true friendship. ⁶Friendships meet our needs and give us a variety of values, among which are the values of utility, affirmation, ego support, stimulation, and security. ⁷Interestingly, women share more and are more intimate with same-sex friends than are men. ⁸Men's friendships are often built around shared activities rather than shared intimacies. ⁹By understanding the nature and function of friendship, the types of friendships, and the ways in which friendships differ between men and women, we can improve the effectiveness of our interpersonal communication with our friends.

Chapter-end Question: What is friendship, its types and purposes, and the ways it differs between men and women?

—From *The Interpersonal Communication Book*, 11th ed., pp. 282–283 by Joseph A. DeVito. Copyright © 2007 by Pearson Education, Inc. Reproduced by permission of Pearson Education, Inc., Boston, MA.

Answer:

Friendship, a mutually beneficial relationship marked by respect, can be classified

by reciprocity, receptivity, and association; friendships offer the values of utility,

affirmation, ego support, stimulation, and security. Unlike women, men form

friendships based on activities rather than intimacy.

APPLICATIONS

Application 1: Main Ideas, Major Supporting Details, and Minor Supporting Details

Read the following paragraph, and then, answer the questions.

Acne

¹Acne is a skin condition characterized by whiteheads, blackheads, and inflamed red pimples. ²The condition occurs when tiny holes on the surface of the skin, called pores, become plugged. ³Each pore is an

opening to a canal called a follicle, which contains a hair and an oil gland. [4]Normally, the oil glands help keep the skin lubricated and help remove old skin cells. [5]When glands produce too much oil, the pores can become blocked, accumulating dirt, debris, and bacteria. [6]The blockage or plug is often called a comedone. [7]The top of the plug may be white (whitehead) or dark (blackhead). [8]If the comedone ruptures, the material inside, including oil and bacteria, can spread to the surrounding area and cause an inflammatory reaction. [9]The inflammation usually takes the form of pimples or "zits." [10]If the inflammation is deep in your skin, the pimples may enlarge to form firm, painful cysts. [11]Acne commonly appears on the face and shoulders, but may also occur on the trunk, arms, legs, and buttocks.

> —Adapted from "Acne," *Medical Encyclopedia*, 10 Oct. 2003, MedlinePlus,
> U.S. Library of Medicine. National Institutes of Health. 10 Oct 2007
> http://www.nlm.nih.gov/medlineplus/ency/article/000873.htm

    __a__   **1.** Sentence 1 is a
                        a. main idea.   c. minor supporting detail.
                        b. major supporting detail.

    __c__   **2.** Sentence 4 is a
                        a. main idea.   c. minor supporting detail.
                        b. major supporting detail.

    __b__   **3.** Sentence 9 is a
                        a. main idea.   c. minor supporting detail.
                        b. major supporting detail.

Application 2: Using the Main Idea and Supporting Details to Summarize

Read the following paragraph taken from a government Web site. Annotate the paragraph by circling the topic sentence and underlining the major supporting details. Then, write a one or two sentence summary of the information.

The Rights and Responsibilities of Citizenship

[1]Citizens of the United States have the right and the responsibility to participate in their government. [2]This process of self-government insures that power will always remain where it belongs—with the people. [3]The most important right citizens have is the right to vote. [4]By voting, the people have a voice in the government. [5]Officials can be voted in or out of office. [6]Every person's vote counts the same as another person's vote.

[7]It is important for all citizens to vote in every election to make sure that the democratic, representative system of government is maintained. [8]Before voting in an election, each citizen should be well informed about the issues and candidates. [9]A citizen of the United States also has the responsibility to serve on a jury if called to do so by the government. [10]If an individual is chosen for jury duty, he or she must stop work and attend the trial as long as he or she is needed. [11]The members of the jury need to decide the case in as fair a way as they can. [12]In addition, every person is responsible for obeying the laws of the community, state and country in which he or she lives, and all persons living in the United States are expected to pay the income taxes and other taxes honestly and on time. [13]Another duty of citizenship is to serve in the armed forces as needed. [14]During times of war, any man who is physically able can be called upon to fight for the United States; in peaceful times, there can be a draft, or men and women can enlist voluntarily.

—Adapted from "Responsibilities of Citizenship," *Ben's Guide to U.S. Government for Kids*, 1 Dec. 1999, U.S. Government Printing Office. 18 Nov 2007
http://bensguide.gpo.gov/6-8/citizenship/responsibilities.html

Summary: Citizens of the United States have the following rights and responsibilities: the right to vote, the responsibility to serve on a jury, and the responsibilities to obey laws and to pay taxes; physically able citizens have the responsibility to serve in the armed forces, as needed.

Textbook Skills

What are the characteristics of successful stepfamilies? How many traits are there? Successful stepfamilies share 6 characteristics.

Application 3: Using Supporting Details to Summarize a Passage with an Implied Central Idea

Read the following information from a college textbook about marriage and families. Annotate the passage and write a summary of the passage.

Characteristics of Successful Stepfamilies

[1]Overcoming the challenges associated with stepfamily life is not an easy task, and many families fall apart under the pressure. [2]Approximately 60 percent of remarriages end in divorce. [3]Despite the risks, many stepfamilies do function successfully. [4]Consider the following information

about successful stepfamilies provided by marriage and family therapists Emily Visher and John Visher:

- (1) [5]They allow losses to be mourned. [6]Adults grieve for the loss of a previous relationship and allow children to share feelings of anger, fear, and guilt about their parents' divorce.
- (2) [7]They have realistic expectations. [8]Adults and children come to realize that their stepfamily will be different from their first family and that expectations of instant love and adjustment are not realistic. [9]They understand that relationships develop over time.
- (3) [10]Adult couples have a strong relationship. [11]Remarried adults find time away from the children to nurture their relationship.
- (4) [12]They establish family traditions. [13]Successful remarried families develop their own rituals and traditions to help them bond as a family.
- (5) [14]They develop step-relationships. [15]Stepparents gradually take on a disciplinary role, allowing the biological parent to perform primary parenting duties until a solid relationship with the stepparent is formed.
- (6) [16]They cooperate with the absent parent. [17]Stepfamilies are able to collaborate over child care arrangements, enabling children to transfer between households without being caught in the crossfire between parents and stepparents.

—From *Think Marriages & Families*, p. 263 by Jenifer Kunz. Copyright © 2011 by Pearson Education, Inc. Reproduced by permission of Pearson Education, Inc., Boston, MA.

Summary: Answers may vary. According to marriage and family therapists Emily Visher and John Visher, successful stepfamilies share six traits. Successful stepfamilies mourn the loss of previous relationships, have realistic expectations, build a strong relationship among the adults, establish family traditions, develop step-relationships, and cooperate with the absent parent.

REVIEW TEST 1   Score (number correct) _____ × 20 = _____ %

Main Ideas and Supporting Details

Read the paragraph, and then, answer the questions.

13.9 GE/291 words

A Primer on Gasoline Prices

[1]The cost to produce and deliver gasoline to consumers includes the cost of crude oil to refiners, taxes, refinery processing costs, marketing and distribution costs, and finally the retail station costs. [2]In 2005 the price of crude oil averaged $50.23 per barrel, and crude oil accounted for about 53 percent of the cost of a gallon of regular grade gasoline. [3]In comparison, the average price for crude oil in 2004 was $36.98 per barrel, and it comprised 47 percent of the cost of a gallon of regular gasoline. [4]Federal, state, and local taxes are a large component of the retail price of gasoline. [5]Taxes (not including county and local taxes) account for approximately 19 percent of the cost of a gallon of gasoline. [6]Within this national average, federal excise taxes are 18.4 cents per gallon and state excise taxes average about 21 cents per gallon. [7]Also, eleven states levy additional state sales and other taxes. [8]Additional local county and city taxes can have a significant impact on the price of gasoline. [9]Refining costs and profits comprise about 19 percent of the retail price of gasoline. [10]Distribution, marketing and retail dealer costs and profits combined make up 9 percent of the cost of a gallon of gasoline. [11]From the refinery, most gasoline is shipped first by pipeline to terminals near consuming areas, then loaded into trucks for delivery to individual stations. [12]Some retail outlets are owned and operated by refiners, while others are independent businesses that purchase gasoline for resale to the public. [13]The price on the pump reflects the retailer's purchase cost for the product, the other costs of operating the service station, and local market conditions, such as the desirability of the location and the marketing strategy of the owner.

—Adapted from "A Primer on Gasoline Prices." May 2006. Energy Information Administration, U.S. Department of Energy 1 Oct. 2007 http://www.eia.doe.gov/pub/oil_gas/ petroleum/analysis_publications/primer_on_gasoline_ prices/html/petbro.html.

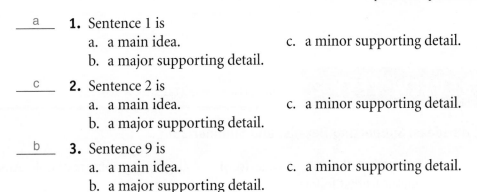

_____a_____ **1.** Sentence 1 is
    a. a main idea.
    b. a major supporting detail.
    c. a minor supporting detail.

_____c_____ **2.** Sentence 2 is
    a. a main idea.
    b. a major supporting detail.
    c. a minor supporting detail.

_____b_____ **3.** Sentence 9 is
    a. a main idea.
    b. a major supporting detail.
    c. a minor supporting detail.

_____b_____ **4.** Sentence 10 is
  a. a main idea.   c. a minor supporting detail.
  b. a major supporting detail.

_____c_____ **5.** Sentence 13 is
  a. a main idea.   c. a minor supporting detail.
  b. a major supporting detail.

VISUAL VOCABULARY

Complete the graphic based on the information in the passage. Fill in the blanks with the appropriate labels that identify what we pay for when we buy a gallon of gasoline.

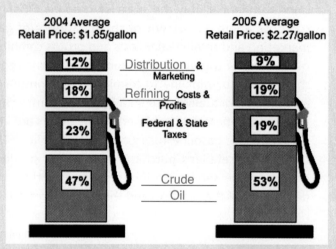

Source: A Primer on Gasoline Prices. Energy Information Administration, U.S. Department of Energy, May 2006

REVIEW TEST 2

Score (number correct) _____ × 10 = _____ %

Main Ideas, Supporting Details, and Summarizing

Read the following passage from a college geography textbook. Answer the questions that follow.

12.2 GE/262 words

Textbook
Skills

The Differences between Folk Culture
and Popular Culture

[1]The term **folk culture** refers to a culture that preserves traditions. [2]Folk groups are often bound by a distinctive religion, national background, or language, and are conservative and resistant to change. [3]Most folk-culture groups are rural, and relative isolation helps these groups maintain their integrity. [4]Folk-culture groups, however, also include urban neighborhoods of immigrants struggling to preserve their native cultures in their new homes. [5]Folk culture suggests that any culture identified by the term is a lingering remnant of something that is embattled by the tide of modern change.

[6]Folk geographic studies in the United States range from studies of folk songs, folk foods, folk medicine, and folklore to objects of folk material as diverse as locally produced pottery, clothing, tombstones, farm fencing, and even knives and guns. [7]In North America, the Amish provide an example of a folk culture. [8]The Amish are notable because they wear plain clothing and shun modern education and technology.

[9]**Popular culture**, by contrast, is the culture of people who embrace innovation and conform to changing norms. [10]Popular culture may originate anywhere. [11]And it tends to diffuse rapidly, especially wherever people have time, money, and inclination to indulge in it.

[12]Popular material culture usually means mass culture. [13]For example, items such as clothing, processed food, CDs, and household goods are mass produced for mass distribution. [14]Whereas folk culture is often produced or done by people at-large (folk singing and dancing, cooking, costumes, woodcarving, etc.), popular culture, by contrast, is usually produced by corporations and purchased.

—Adapted from *Introduction to Geography: People, Places, and Environment*, 4th ed., pp. 221–223 by Edward Bergman and William H. Renwick. Copyright © 2008 by Pearson Education, Inc. Printed and Electronically reproduced by permission of Pearson Education, Inc., Upper Saddle River, NJ.

_____ a   **1.** Sentence 1 states _____ of the first paragraph (sentences 1–5).
　　　　a. the main idea　　　　　　　c. a minor supporting detail
　　　　b. a major supporting detail

_____ b   **2.** Sentence 2 states _____ of the first paragraph (sentences 1–5).
　　　　a. the main idea　　　　　　　c. a minor supporting detail
　　　　b. a major supporting detail

_____ c   **3.** Sentence 7 states _____ of the second paragraph (sentences 6–8).
　　　　a. the main idea　　　　　　　c. a minor supporting detail
　　　　b. a major supporting detail

_____a_____ **4.** Sentence 9 states _____ of the third paragraph (sentences 9–11).
    a. the main idea   c. a minor supporting detail
    b. a major supporting detail

_____b_____ **5.** Sentence 13 states _____ of the fourth paragraph (sentences 12–14).
    a. the main idea   c. a minor supporting detail
    b. a major supporting detail

Complete the following summary with information from the passage.

    (6) <u>Folk culture</u> differs from **(7)** <u>popular culture</u>. On the one hand folk culture refers to a culture that **(8)** <u>preserves tradition and resists change</u>. On the other hand, popular culture refers to the culture that **(9)** <u>accepts change and conforms to changing norms</u>. Folk culture is produced by local people in rural regions while popular culture is mass produced, mass distributed, and sold to the masses by **(10)** <u>corporations</u>.

REVIEW TEST 3

Score (number correct) _____ × 10 = _____ %

Main Ideas, Supporting Details, and Summarizing

Textbook
Skills

Before you read the following passage from a college sociology textbook, skim the material and answer the Before Reading questions. Read the passage. Then, answer the After Reading questions.

Vocabulary Preview

incompatible (1): mismatched, opposed

fragile (10): weak, unstable, breakable

perceptions (16): views, insights, understandings

interpersonal (19): between people

relative (20): in relation to

11.2 GE/501 words

Conflict Defined

[1]Conflict is the interaction of interdependent people who perceive **incompatible** goals and interference from each other in achieving those goals. [2]This definition has the advantage of providing a much clearer focus than definitions that view conflict simply as disagreement, as competition, or as the presence of opposing interests.

[3]The most important feature of conflict is that it is based in interaction. [4]Conflicts are formed and sustained by the behaviors of the parties involved and their verbal and nonverbal reactions to one another. [5]Conflict interaction takes many forms, and each form presents special problems and requires special handling. [6]The most familiar type of conflict interaction

is marked by shouting matches or open competition in which each party tries to defeat the other. [7]But conflicts may also be more subtle. [8]People may react to conflict by suppressing it. [9]A husband and wife may communicate in ways that allow them to avoid confrontation. [10]Either they are afraid the conflict may damage a **fragile** relationship, or they convince themselves that the issue "isn't worth fighting over." [11]This response is as much a part of the conflict process as fights and shouting matches.

[12]People in conflict perceive that they have incompatible goals or interests; they also believe that others are a barrier to achieving their goals. [13]The key word here is *perceive*. [14]Regardless of whether goals are actually incompatible, if the parties believe them to be incompatible, then conditions are ripe for conflict. [15]Regardless of whether one employee really stands in the way of a co-worker's promotion, if the co-worker interprets the employee's behavior as interfering with his promotion, then a conflict is likely to occur. [16]Communication is important; it is the key to shaping and maintaining the **perceptions** that guide conflict behavior.

[17]Communication problems can be an important cause of conflict. [18]Conflict may result from misunderstandings that occur when people have different communication styles. [19]For example, Tannen argues that men and women have different approaches to **interpersonal** communication. [20]Men are mostly task-oriented; they are concerned with establishing their position **relative** to others in conversations. [21]In contrast, women use conversations to build relationships and establish connections with others. [22]As a result, men and women may interpret the same act in very different ways. [23]When a man makes a demand during a conflict, he might mean to signal that he is strong and has a definite position. [24]A woman hearing this demand is likely to focus more on its **implications** for their relationship. [25]Thus she may interpret it as a signal that it will be very difficult to deal with this man. [26]As a result, the woman may become more competitive toward her male partner than she would have had she seen his demand in the man's terms. [27]According to Tannen, stylistic differences of this sort create communication barriers that make misunderstanding—and the conflict that results from it— **inevitable** in male-female relationships. [28]Similar communication problems can occur across almost any social divide, such as those between people of different cultures, ages, educational backgrounds, and socioeconomic classes.

—Adapted from Folger, Poole, & Stutman, *Working Through Conflict*, 4th ed., pp. 5–6.

Before Reading

Vocabulary in Context

_____b_____ **1.** In sentence 24 of the passage, the word **implications** means
- a. conflicts.
- b. meanings.
- c. accusations.
- d. levels.

_____d_____ **2.** In sentence 27 of the passage, the word **inevitable** means
- a. delayed.
- b. long term.
- c. hidden.
- d. unavoidable.

After Reading

Main Ideas

_____a_____ **3.** Which sentence states the central idea of the passage?
- a. sentence 1
- b. sentence 2
- c. sentence 3
- d. sentence 4

_____a_____ **4.** Which sentence is the topic sentence of the fourth paragraph (sentences 17–28)?
- a. sentence 17
- b. sentence 18
- c. sentence 20
- d. sentence 27

Supporting Details

_____a_____ **5.** Sentence 7 is
- a. a major supporting detail.
- b. a minor supporting detail.

_____b_____ **6.** Sentence 9 is
- a. a major supporting detail.
- b. a minor supporting detail.

_____b_____ **7.** Sentence 15 is
- a. a major supporting detail.
- b. a minor supporting detail.

8–10. Complete the summary with information from the passage.

Conflict is the _interaction_ of interdependent people who perceive incompatible goals and interference from each other in achieving those goals. Perceptions based on _verbal_ reactions, nonverbal reactions, and differing interpersonal _communication_ styles are key sources of conflict.

WHAT DO YOU THINK?

Do you agree with Tannen's description of the different approaches to communication used by men and women? Why or why not? What are some other interactions between people that often lead to conflict? How can communication add to or ease conflict? Assume you are a supervisor of a sales staff at a local retail store, and two employees under your supervision are in conflict with each other. Assume you have met with them both privately and individually to understand and resolve the conflict. Write a memo to be sent to both employees and placed in their personnel files. Describe the conflict and suggest steps that you expect both to take to resolve the issue.

REVIEW TEST 4   Score (number correct) _____ × 10 = _____ %

Main Ideas and Supporting Details

Textbook
Skills

Before Reading: Survey the following passage adapted from the college textbook *World Civilizations: The Global Experience*. Skim the passage, noting the words in bold print. Answer the Before Reading questions that follow the passage. Then, read the passage. Next, answer the After Reading questions. Use the discussion and writing topics as activities to do after reading.

Vocabulary Preview

periodically (1): every so often

militants (3): violent protestors

authoritarian (5): controlling

alliance (5): partnership

justifiable (8): acceptable, valid, proper

fundamentalist (13): a person who strictly follows a set of basic ideas or principles

12.9 GE/336 words   **A Very Present Problem**

[1]American interests had **periodically** been the targets of terrorist attacks since the 1960s. [2]Hijacking of airplanes and other moves frequently expressed hostility to U.S. policies. [3]But the massive attacks on the World Trade Center and the Pentagon by Islamic **militants** on September 11, 2001, created a new level of threat. [4]The attacks reflected concern about specific U.S. policies in the Middle East. [5]These concerns included support for **authoritarian** governments, the **alliance** with Israel, and the stationing of troops on "sacred ground" in Saudi Arabia. [6]The terrorists were also hostile to wider U.S. power, or as they termed it, arrogance. [7]Their response, hijacking airliners to crash into buildings that symbolized American financial and military might, killed about 3,000 people. [8]The terrorists regarded this as **justifiable** action against a nation they could not hope to fight by conventional means.

Vocabulary Preview

harbored (13): protected

Al Qaeda (13): a radical Sunni Muslim organization dedicated to the elimination of a Western presence in Arab countries

erroneous (17): wrong, incorrect

ensuing (20): resulting, following

⁹The attacks clearly altered U.S. policy and focused the administration on a war against terrorism. ¹⁰"War on Terror" was the new catchphrase. ¹¹And a number of measures were taken, including heightened screening of international visitors. ¹²The problem dominated American foreign policy. ¹³A first response involved a military attack that successfully toppled the Islamic **fundamentalist** regime in Afghanistan that had **harbored** the **Al Qaeda** group behind the September 11 attacks. ¹⁴World opinion largely supported this move. ¹⁵The United States established new military bases near several possible centers of terrorist activity.

¹⁶In 2003 U.S. attention turned to Iraq, which was accused of amassing dangerous weaponry and aiding terrorists. ¹⁷Evidence for these charges proved largely **erroneous.** ¹⁸And world opinion turned heavily against the American move, with millions of demonstrators protesting the impending war in February 2003. ¹⁹But the United States, joined by several **allies,** including Britain, invaded and quickly conquered the country. ²⁰The **ensuing** occupation, however, was extremely troubled, as the United States could not clearly restore order against a variety of **insurgents.** ²¹The results of this war, in terms of Iraq's future, broader global reactions to the United States, and the flexibility of the American policy itself, are not yet clear.

—From *World Civilizations: The Global Experience, Combined Volume, Atlas Edition,* 5th ed., pp. 966–967 by Peter N. Stearns, Michael B. Adas, Stuart B. Schwartz, and Marc Jason Gilbert. Copyright © 2008 by Pearson Education, Inc. Printed and Electronically reproduced by permission of Pearson Education, Inc., Upper Saddle River, NJ.

Before Reading

Vocabulary in Context

1–2. Use your own words to define the following term. Identify the context clue you used to make meaning of the word.

The word **allies** in sentence 19 means <u>partners.</u>

Context clue used for **allies** <u>example and general sense of the passage</u>

3. Study the following chart of word parts.

Prefix	Meaning	Root	Meaning	Suffix	Meaning
in-	in, into, on	*surge*	rise up	*-ent*	one who, one that

Use context clues and the word parts to state the definition of the word **insurgent** in sentence 20: one who rises up or rebels, fighter

Topic

4. What is the topic of the passage? anti-American terrorism and response

After Reading

Main Ideas and Supporting Details

Complete the following study notes with information from the passage.

Thesis Statement: The attacks clearly altered U.S. policy and focused the administration on a war against terrorism.

Major Supports	Minor Supports
American interests had been targets of terrorist attacks since **(5)** 1960s.	Hijacking of airplanes and other moves frequently expressed hostility to U.S. policies.
	6. September 11, 2001, attacks on World Trade Center and the Pentagon killed around 3,000 people.
7. Attacks reflected concern about U.S. policies in the Middle East.	U.S. "arrogance" revealed by the following: Support of authoritarian governments; the alliance with Israel;
	8. the stationing of troops on "sacred ground" in Saudi Arabia.
9. Attacks altered U.S. policy and focused on war against terrorism.	"War on Terror" is a new catchphrase. Military attack topples Islamic regime that harbored Al Qaeda in Afghanistan.
	U.S. established military bases near centers of terrorist activities.

10. U.S. and allies invade and conquer
Iraq.

Ensuing occupation could not restore order against insurgents.

WHAT DO YOU THINK?

September 11, 2001 stands as a significant event in United States history. Did you or someone you know witness the event or the news coverage of the events surrounding 9/11? Do you think many people still think about 9/11? Should September 11, 2001 be officially recognized as a day to remember? Why or why not? Assume your college or university holds an annual day of observance every September 11. Also assume you are a member of the Student Government Association, and you have been asked to speak at this year's college-wide memorial service. A copy of your speech will also be printed in the student newspaper.

After Reading About Supporting Details

Before you move on to the Mastery Tests on supporting details, take time to reflect on your learning and performance by answering the following questions. Write your answers in your notebook.

- How has my knowledge base or prior knowledge about supporting details changed?

- Based on my studies, how do I think I will perform on the Mastery Test(s)? Why do I think my scores will be above average, average, or below average?

- Would I recommend this chapter to other students who want to learn more about supporting details? Why or why not?

Test your understanding of what you have learned about Supporting Details for Master Readers by completing the Chapter 5 Review Card in the insert near the end of your text.

CONNECT TO **myreadinglab**

To check your progress in meeting Chapter 5's learning outcomes, log in to **www.myreadinglab.com** and try the following activities.

- The "Supporting Details" section of MyReadingLab offers more information about supporting details. You will find an overview, model, review materials, practice activities, and tests. To access this resource, click on the "Study Plan" tab. Then click on "Supporting Details." Then click on the following links as needed: "Overview," "Model," "Practice," and "Tests."

- The "Outlining and Summarizing" section of MyReadingLab gives an overview about memory and active reading. This section also provides a model for summarizing. You will find practice activities and tests. To access this resource, click on the "Study Plan" tab. Then click on "Outlining and Summarizing." Then click on the following links as needed: "Overview," "Model: Summarizing," "Practice," and "Tests."

- To measure your mastery of the content in this chapter, complete the tests in the "Supporting Details" section and click on Gradebook to find your results.

Read the passage from a college communications textbook. Then, complete the summary that follows it.

Textbook
Skills

10.8 GE/324 words

The Context of Communication

¹Communication always takes place within a context that influences the form and the content of communication. ²At times this context is so natural that you ignore it, like street noise. ³At other times the context stands out, and the ways in which it affects the flow of your communications are obvious. ⁴Think, for example, of the different ways you'd talk at a funeral, in a quiet restaurant, and at a rock concert.

⁵The context of communication has at least four dimensions. ⁶The room, workplace, or park in which communication takes place—the concrete environment—is the *physical dimension.* ⁷When you communicate face-to-face you're both in the same physical environment. ⁸In computer-based communication, you may be in very different environments. ⁹One of you may be on a beach in San Juan while another is in a Wall Street office. ¹⁰The *cultural dimension* is passed from one generation to another and refers to the rules, the beliefs, and the attitudes of the people communicating. ¹¹For example, in some cultures it's considered polite to talk to strangers. ¹²In others it's something to be avoided. ¹³In some cultures, direct eye contact between child and adult shows directness and honesty; in others it shows defiance and arrogance. ¹⁴The *social-psychological dimension* includes several aspects. ¹⁵For example, it refers to the status relationships among the participants, such as who is the employer and who is the employee or who is the salesperson and who is the store owner. ¹⁶The formality or informality, friendliness or hostility, and cooperativeness or competitiveness of the interaction are also part of this dimension. ¹⁷The *temporal* or *time dimension* refers to where a particular message fits into the sequence of communication events. ¹⁸For example, if you tell a joke about sickness immediately after your friend tells you she is sick, the joke will be seen differently than the same joke told as one of a series of similar jokes to your friends in the locker room of the gym.

—From *Messages: Building Interpersonal Communication Skills,*
4th ed., pp. 16–17 by Joseph A. DeVito. Copyright © 1999
by Pearson Education, Inc. Reproduced by permission
of Pearson Education, Inc., Boston, MA.

___c___ **1.** Sentence 4 states a
    a. main idea.   c. minor supporting detail.
    b. major supporting detail.

___a___ **2.** Sentence 5 states a
    a. main idea.   c. minor supporting detail.
    b. major supporting detail.

___b___ **3.** Sentence 6 states a
    a. main idea.   c. minor supporting detail.
    b. major supporting detail.

___c___ **4.** Sentence 9 states a
    a. main idea.   c. minor supporting detail.
    b. major supporting detail.

___b___ **5.** Sentence 17 states a
    a. main idea.   c. minor supporting detail.
    b. major supporting detail.

6–10. Complete the summary with information from the paragraph.

The context of communication has at least **(6)** _four_ dimensions. The physical dimension is the **(7)** _concrete_ environment, such as communicating via computers from different physical locations. The **(8)** _cultural_ dimension is passed from one generation to another and refers to attitudes, beliefs, and cultural rules. The social-psychological dimension includes the **(9)** _status_ of the people communicating and the tone and purpose of the communication. The **(10)** _temporal_ or time dimension refers to the sequence of the communication, such as the proper time to tell a joke.

Read this passage from a college communications textbook. Then, answer the questions that follow it.

10.7 GE/281 words **Guidelines for Communicating Emotions**

Textbook
Skills

[1]Communicating your emotions and responding appropriately to the emotional expressions of others are as important as they are difficult. [2]There are, however, a variety of suggestions that will make these tasks easier and more effective. [3]Expressing emotions effectively begins with understanding your emotions and then deciding if and how you wish to express them.

[4]Your first task is to understand the emotions you're feeling. [5]For example, consider how you would feel if your best friend just got the promotion that you wanted or if your brother, a police officer, was shot while breaking up a street riot. [6]Think about your emotions as objectively as possible. [7]Think about both the bodily reactions you'd be experiencing as well as the interpretations and evaluations you'd be giving to these reactions. [8]Further, identify the prior conditions (in as specific terms as possible) that may be influencing your feelings. [9]Try to answer the question, "Why am I feeling this way?" or "What happened to lead me to feel as I do?"

[10]Your second task is to decide if, in fact, you want to express your emotions. [11]It will not always be possible to stop to think about whether you wish to express your emotions—at times you may respond almost automatically. [12]More often than not, however, you will have the time and the chance to ask yourself whether you wish to express your emotions. [13]When you do have this chance, remember that it isn't always necessary or wise to express every feeling you have. [14]Remember, too, the irreversibility of communication; once you communicate something, you cannot take it back. [15]Therefore, consider carefully the arguments for and against expressing your emotions for each decision you have to make.

—From *Messages: Building Interpersonal Communication Skills, 4th ed.*, p. 184 by Joseph A. DeVito. Copyright © 1999 by Pearson Education, Inc. Reproduced by permission of Pearson Education, Inc., Boston, MA.

____a____ **1.** Sentence 4 is
    a. a main idea.
    b. a major supporting detail.
    c. a minor supporting detail.

____c____ **2.** Sentence 5 is
    a. a main idea.
    b. a major supporting detail.
    c. a minor supporting detail.

_____c_____   **3.** Sentence 7 is
     a. a main idea.   c. a minor supporting detail.
     b. a major supporting detail.

_____a_____   **4.** Sentence 10 is
     a. a main idea.   c. a minor supporting detail.
     b. a major supporting detail.

_____a_____   **5.** Sentence 15 is
     a. a main idea.   c. a minor supporting detail.
     b. a major supporting detail.

Read the following passage from a museum's website. Then, complete the summary. (**Hint:** As you read, annotate the information.)

13.9 GE/167 words   **Mexican Genius: Artist Diego Rivera**

[1]Diego María Rivera (1886–1957) is one of the most prominent Mexican artists of the twentieth century. [2]He gained international acclaim as a leader of the Mexican mural movement that sought to bring art to the masses through large-scale works on public walls. [3]In his murals of the 1920s and 1930s, Rivera developed a new, modern imagery to express Mexican national identity. [4]His style featured stylized representations of the working classes and indigenous cultures and supported revolutionary ideals. [5]During his time abroad, Rivera drew upon the radical innovations of cubism, inaugurated a few years earlier by Pablo Picasso and Georges Braque. [6]Rivera adopted their dramatic fracturing of form; he used multiple perspective points and flattened the picture plane. [7]He also borrowed favorite cubist motifs, such as liqueur bottles, musical instruments, and painted wood grain. [8]Yet Rivera's cubism is formally and thematically distinctive. [9]Characterized by brighter colors and a larger scale than many early cubist pictures, his work also features highly textured surfaces executed in a variety of techniques.

    —"Introduction" from *The Cubist Paintings of Diego Maria Rivera.* http://www.nga.gov/exhibitions
    /2004/rivera/intro.shtm. Reproduced by permission of National Gallery of Art, Washington, D.C.

6–10. Complete the summary with information from the paragraph.

    Diego María Rivera (1886–1957), a prominent **(6)** _Mexican artist_ of the twentieth century, is celebrated for his large-scale **(7)** _murals_ on public walls that brought **(8)** _art to the masses_. Influenced by **(9)** _Picasso_ and Braque, Rivera adopted **(10)** _cubist_ motifs and techniques. However, in contrast to early cubist artists, Rivera used brighter colors, highly textured surfaces, and a larger scale to express Mexican national identity.

Read this passage from a college history textbook. Then, answer the questions that follow it.

Textbook
Skills

11.7 GE/300 words

The Jazz Age

[1]"The music from the trumpet at the Negro's lips is honey mixed with liquid fire." [2]With these words, Langston Hughes described the new music called jazz. [3]But among black intellectuals, Hughes's opinion was in the minority. [4]Many black Americans distanced themselves from the sensuous music that brought white attention to black culture. [5]Jazz music's improvisational style, they argued, only reinforced the stereotype that black people were impetuous and lacked intellectual discipline. [6]Other black people criticized this "folk art" because it was born in brothels and performed in speakeasies—illegal bars that opened during the decade of Prohibition, when the government outlawed alcohol. [7]But jazz was not just a musical innovation. [8]At a time when all other social institutions in the United States were segregated, a few jazz clubs brought together music lovers of all races.

[9]Some historians consider jazz the only truly American art form. [10]Rather than deriving from another culture, it was born in the United States from a blend of European and African percussion, horn, and piano melodies. [11]Many jazz artists were trained in the disciplined formality of classical piano. [12]Most jazz was feel-good music, embracing a bewildering array of forms—from spirituals and the mournful tones of the blues to the aggressive percussion of marching band rhythms, from the asymmetry of ragtime to the staid patterns of European tradition. [13]Jazz offered deep, throaty voices, and provocative brass, woodwind, and percussion sounds. [14]Building on written scores, band members improvised during performances. [15]Thus jazz was always in motion, always transforming something familiar into something new. [16]Hughes felt that jazz embodied a cultural richness that opened new doors for black Americans. [17]Through jazz, Hughes commented, "Josephine Baker goes to Paris, Robeson to London, Jean Toomer to a Quaker Meeting House, Garvey to Atlanta Federal Penitentiary . . . and Duke Ellington to fame and fortune."

—Carson, Lapsansky-Werner, & Nash, *The Struggle for Freedom: A History of African Americans, Volume II*, p. 363.

___a___   **1.** Sentence 1 is
  a. a main idea.   c. a minor supporting detail.
  b. a major supporting detail.

___a___   **2.** Sentence 3 is
  a. a main idea.   c. a minor supporting detail.
  b. a major supporting detail.

___b___   **3.** Sentence 10 is
  a. a main idea.   c. a minor supporting detail.
  b. a major supporting detail.

___c___   **4.** Sentence 13 is
  a. a main idea.   c. a minor supporting detail.
  b. a major supporting detail.

___a___   **5.** Sentence 16 is
  a. a main idea.   c. a minor supporting detail.
  b. a major supporting detail.

VISUAL VOCABULARY

Jazz percussionist Hamid Drake performs at the 2008 New Orleans Jazz and Heritage Festival.

A percussionist __b_____.

  a. plays the drums.
  b. makes music by striking instruments.
  c. is a set of drums.

Read the following passage from a college history textbook. Answer the questions that follow.

Textbook Skills

11.9 GE/213 words

The Iroquois of the Northeast Woodlands

¹Europeans arriving in what is now upper New York State found various groups speaking dialects of a common Iroquoian language. ²They had created a distinctive culture by 1000 C.E. and subsequently formed the League of the Five Nations. ³They used the metaphor of the longhouse, their traditional communal dwelling, to describe their political alliance: the Mohawk along the Hudson were the "keepers of the eastern door," adjoined in sequence by the Oneida, Onondaga, and Cayuga, with the Seneca, "keepers of the western door." ⁴When the Tuscarora joined in the early eighteenth century, the confederacy became known as the Six Nations. ⁵The Iroquois eventually extended their control from the Great Lakes toward the Atlantic by subjugating the nomadic, food-gathering Algonquin people.

⁶The Iroquois had the advantage of being agriculturists with permanent villages. ⁷Some of these had several hundred residents and extensive fields where maize, beans, squash, and tobacco were grown. ⁸Fish traps were built across streams, and smokehouses preserved joints of game. ⁹Related families lived in the longhouses, long rectangular buildings protected by high wooden palisades. ¹⁰Women played a notable part: they owned the homes and gardens, and, since descent was matrilineal, chose the leaders. ¹¹If the men chosen did not provide good leadership, they could be replaced.

—From *Civilizations Past & Present, Combined Volume,* 12th ed., p. 357 by Robert R. Edgar, Neil J. Hackett, George F. Jewsbury, Barbara S. Molony, Matthew Gordon. Copyright © 2008 by Pearson Education, Inc. Reprinted by permission of Pearson Education, Inc., Upper Saddle River, NJ.

___a___ **1.** Sentence 1 states _____ of paragraph 1 (sentences 1–5).
    a. the main idea   c. a minor supporting detail
    b. a major supporting detail

___b___ **2.** Sentence 2 states _____ of paragraph 1 (sentences 1–5).
    a. the main idea   c. a minor supporting detail
    b. a major supporting detail

___c___ **3.** Sentence 5 states _____ of paragraph 1 (sentences 1–5).
    a. the main idea   c. a minor supporting detail
    b. a major supporting detail

_____a_____ **4.** Sentence 6 states _____ of paragraph 2 (sentences 6–11).
      a. the main idea   c. a minor supporting detail
      b. a major supporting detail

_____c_____ **5.** Sentence 11 states _____ of paragraph 2 (sentences 6–11).
      a. the main idea   c. a minor supporting detail
      b. a major supporting detail

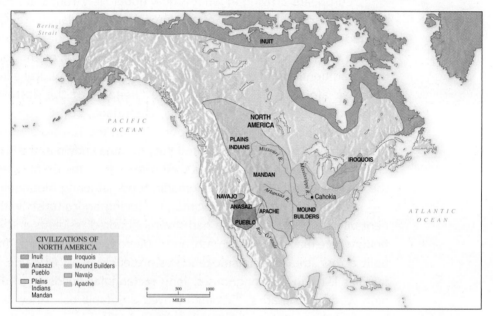

In the vastness of the North American continent, the varied environmental challenges led to the development of hundreds of different Indian tribes—more than 252 alone in the present-day state of California.

    —From *Civilizations Past & Present, Combined Volume,* 12th ed., p. 357 by Robert R. Edgar, Neil J. Hackett, George F. Jewsbury, Barbara S. Molony, Matthew Gordon. Copyright © 2008 by Pearson Education, Inc. Reprinted by permission of Pearson Education, Inc., Upper Saddle River, NJ.

According to the legend, which group of Native Americans developed in the closest location to the Iroquois? _____d_____
      a. Inuit   c. Navajo
      b. Plains Indians   d. Mound Builders

Outlines and Concept Maps

6

LEARNING OUTCOMES

After studying this chapter you should be able to do the following:

1 Define the terms *outline* and *concept map*. [Knowledge]

2 Create an outline. [Analysis, Synthesis]

3 Create a concept map. [Analysis, Synthesis]

4 Evaluate the importance of outlines and concept maps. [Evaluation]

 ## Before Reading About Outlines and Concept Maps

In Chapter 5, you learned several important ideas that will help you use outlines and concept maps effectively. To review, reread the diagram about the flow of ideas on page 197 in Chapter 5. Next, skim this chapter for key ideas in boxes about outlines, concept maps, and the table of contents in a textbook. Refer to the diagrams and boxes and create at least three questions that you can answer as you read the chapter. Write your questions in the following spaces (record the page number for the key term in each question):

How does an outline show the relationships among the main idea, major supporting

details, and minor supporting details _____? (page __234__)

Where are major supporting details used in an outline, concept map, and table of

contents _____? (pages __234, 237, 241__)

What is the difference between a formal outline and an informal outline? (page __234__)

Compare the questions you created with those that follow. Then, write the ones that seem most helpful in your notebook, leaving enough space after each question to record the answers as you read and study the chapter.

How does an outline show the relationships among the main idea, major supporting details, and minor supporting details? Where are main ideas used in an outline, concept map, and table of contents? Where are major supporting details used in an outline, concept map, and table of contents? Where are minor supporting details used in an outline, concept map, and table of contents? What is the difference between a formal outline and an informal outline?

 ## Outlines

An outline shows how information in a paragraph or passage moves from a general idea to specific supporting details; thus it helps you make sense of the ways ideas relate to one another. A master reader uses an outline to see the main idea, major supporting details, and minor supporting details.

> An **outline** shows the relationships among the main idea, major supporting details, and minor supporting details.

Outlines can be formal or informal. A **formal** or **traditional outline** uses Roman numerals to indicate the main idea, capital letters to indicate the major details, and Arabic numbers to indicate minor details. It can be composed of full sentences or of topics or sentence parts that begin with a capital letter. A formal outline is particularly useful for studying complex reading material. Sometimes, you may choose to use an **informal outline** and record only the main ideas and the major supporting details. Because these outlines are informal, they may vary according to each student's notetaking style. Elements may or may not be capitalized. Also, one person might label the main idea with the number 1 and the major supporting details with letters *a, b, c, d,* and so on. Another person might not label the main idea at all and might label each major supporting detail with either letters or numbers.

EXAMPLE Read the following paragraph from a college finance textbook. Fill in the details to complete the outline. Then, answer the questions that follow it.

Income and Types of Jobs

Textbook
Skills

[1]Income varies by job type. [2]Jobs that require specialized skills tend to pay much higher salaries than those that require skills that can be obtained very quickly and easily. [3]The income level associated with specific skills is also affected by the demand for those skills. [4]For example, the demand for people with a nursing license has been very high in recent years, so hospitals have been forced to pay high salaries to outbid other

hospitals for nurses. ⁵Conversely, the demand for people with a history or English literature degree is low because more students major in these areas than there are jobs.

—From *Personal Finance,* 3rd ed., p. 27 by Jeff Madura. Copyright © 2007 by Pearson Education, Inc. Reproduced by permission of Pearson Education, Inc., Boston, MA.

Outline

I. (Main idea) Income varies by job type.

   A. Jobs that require specialized skills tend to pay much higher salaries than those that require skills that can be obtained very quickly and easily.

   B. The income level associated with specific skills is also affected by the demand for those skills.

      1. For example, the demand for people with a nursing license has been very high in recent years, so hospitals have been forced to pay high salaries to outbid other hospitals for nurses.

      2. Conversely, the demand for people with a history or English literature degree is low because more students major in these areas than there are jobs.

Questions

  b   **1.** Sentences 4 and 5 are
     a. major supporting details.
     b. minor supporting details.

  b   **2.** The outline used in this activity is an example of
     a. an informal outline.
     b. a formal outline.

EXPLANATION The main idea of this paragraph is stated in sentence 1: "Income varies by job type." The author suggests that a list of supporting details will be presented and explained with the phrase "varies by job type." The second major detail, stated in sentence 3, is signaled with the word *also*. Sentences 4 and 5 are minor supporting details, introduced with the words *for example* and *conversely*. This outline is an example of a formal outline that includes the main idea, the major supporting details, and the minor supporting details of one paragraph.

An informal outline of the information looks like the following:

Stated main idea: Income varies by job type.

1. Jobs that require specialized skills tend to pay much higher salaries than those that require skills that can be obtained very quickly and easily.

2. The income level associated with specific skills is also affected by the demand for those skills.

Notice how this informal outline of the main idea and the major supporting details—without the minor supporting details—condenses the material into a summary of the author's primary points.

PRACTICE 1

Read the following paragraph from a college communications textbook. Then, answer the questions that follow it.

Textbook
Skills

Active Listening

[1]Active listening serves several important functions. [2]First, it helps you as a listener to check your understanding of what the speaker said and, more important, what he or she meant. [3]Reflecting perceived meanings back to the speaker gives the speaker an opportunity to offer clarification and correct any misunderstandings. [4]Second, through active listening you let the speaker know that you acknowledge and accept his or her feelings. [5]An active learner accepts and identifies feelings with statements such as "You sound angry and upset." [6]Third, active listening stimulates the speaker to explore feelings and thoughts. [7]Elaborating on feelings helps you deal with them by talking them through with responses such as "I am upset and afraid, but I am not angry."

—From *The Interpersonal Communication Book,* 10th ed., p. 126 by Joseph A. DeVito. Copyright © 2004 by Pearson Education, Inc. Reproduced by permission of Pearson Education, Inc., Boston, MA.

1–5. Complete the following outline. Wording of answers may vary.

I. (Stated main idea) Active listening serves several important functions.

   A. It clarifies and corrects.

      1. First, it helps you as a listener to check your understanding of what the speaker said and, more important, what he or she meant.

  2. <u>Reflecting perceived meanings back to the speaker gives the speaker an</u>

  <u>opportunity to offer clarification and correct any misunderstandings.</u>

B. It offers acceptance.

  1. Second, through active listening you let the speaker know that you acknowledge and accept his or her feelings.

  2. <u>An active learner accepts and identifies feelings with statements such as</u>

  <u>"You sound angry and upset."</u>

C. It deals with feelings.

  1. Third, active listening stimulates the speaker to explore feelings and thoughts.

  2. <u>Elaborating on feelings helps you deal with them by talking them through</u>

  <u>with responses such as "I am upset and afraid, but I am not angry."</u>

VISUAL VOCABULARY

The best synonym for *empathy* is <u>a</u> _____.

  a. understanding.
  b. pity.
  c. sorrow.

▶ Active listening communicates empathy for the feelings of another.

 ## Concept Maps

An outline is one way to see the details that support a main idea. Another way to see details is through the use of a concept map. A **concept map** is a diagram that shows the flow of ideas from the main idea to the supporting details. Think of what you already know about a map. Someone can tell you how to get somewhere, but it is much easier to understand the directions if you can see how each road connects to the others by studying a map. Likewise, a concept map shows how ideas connect to one another.

> A **concept map** is a diagram that shows the flow of ideas from the main idea to the supporting details.

To make a concept map, a master reader places the main idea in a box or circle as a heading and then places the major supporting details in boxes or circles beneath the main idea. Often arrows or lines are used to show the flow of ideas.

EXAMPLE Read the following passage. Then, complete the concept map by filling in the major and minor supporting details from the paragraph. Wording of answers may vary.

The Dangers of Texting While Driving

[1]Putting the brakes on the distracted driving epidemic will require both dedication and creative thinking, and the FCC is committed to doing its part to address this growing crisis.

Distracted Driving Is Dangerous

[2]The popularity of mobile devices has had some unintended and even dangerous consequences. [3]We now know that mobile communications is linked to a significant increase in distracted driving, resulting in injury and loss of life. [4]The National Highway Traffic Safety Administration reported in 2008 that driver distraction was the cause of 16 percent of all fatal crashes—5,800 people killed—and 21 percent of crashes resulting in an injury—515,000 people wounded. [5]According to AAA, nearly 50 percent of teens admit to texting while driving. [6]Distracted driving endangers life and property and the current levels of injury and loss are unacceptable.

What You Can Do

[7]*Give Clear Instructions* [8]Give teen drivers simple, clear instructions not to use their wireless devices while driving. [9]According to CTIA, the easiest way to say it is: "On the road, off the phone." [10]Before new drivers get their licenses, discuss the fact that taking their eyes off the road—even for a few seconds—could cost someone injury or even death.

11*Lead by Example* **12**Children learn from their parent's behavior. No one should text and drive. **13**Be an example for your children and if you need to text or talk on the phone, pull over to a safe place.

14*Become Informed and Be Active* **15**Review the information in our Clearinghouse and the literature on the web sites mentioned above. **16**Set rules for yourself and your household regarding distracted driving. **17**Tell family, friends and organizations to which you belong about the importance of driving without distractions. **18**Take information to your children's schools and ask that it be shared with students and parents.

—Federal Communications Commission. "FCC Consumer Advisory: The Dangers of Texting while Driving." Consumer & Government Affairs Bureau. 17 March 2010. http://www.fcc.gov/cgb/consumerfacts/drivingandtexting.html.

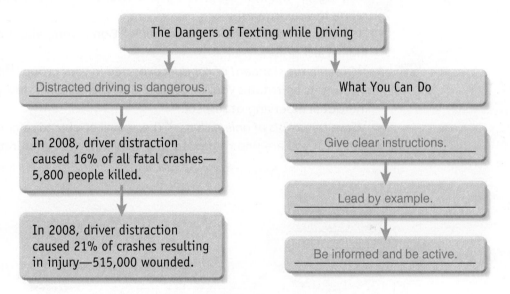

EXPLANATION The author of this passage used bold and italic print to emphasize the important ideas in the passage. The title of the passage states the topic and the author's controlling point. The two subheadings in bold print state the two major supporting details. The details in italic print highlight important minor details—action steps citizens can take in response to the dangers of texting while driving.

PRACTICE 2

Read the following passage from a college English handbook. Then, fill in the concept map with the central idea and major supporting details from the reading. Wording of answers may vary.

Textbook
Skills

Using Online Chat

[1]You may be familiar with chat conversations from using instant messaging with friends and family. [2]In academic settings, chat will likely occur with coursework such as *WebCT* or *Blackboard*. [3]Collaborating via chat discussions will be more productive if you follow these tips:

- [4]*Use the chat space for brainstorming topics and exchanging impressions.* [5]The pace of online chat rarely allows lengthy consideration and articulation of messages.
- [6]*Focus on a thread or common topic.* [7]Online chat can be the electronic equivalent of a busy hallway outside a classroom, with different conversations occurring in the same space. [8]If you have trouble keeping up with all the messages, concentrate on the ones that relate to your interest.
- [9]*Write as quickly and fluidly as possible.* [10]Don't worry about producing perfect prose.
- [11]*Observe the standard of conduct expected in your group.* [12]If someone upsets or irritates you, remember that the person is, like you, an individual deserving of respect.
- [13]*Save transcripts of online chats.* [14]Then you'll be able to refer to them later. [15](If you are unsure how to save transcripts, ask your instructor.)

—Fowler & Aaron, *The Little, Brown Handbook,* 9th ed., p. 233.

Reading a Textbook: The Table of Contents in a Textbook

The table of contents is a special kind of outline that is based on topics and subtopics. A **topic** is the *general subject,* so a **subtopic** is a *smaller part* of the topic. The general subject of the textbook is stated in the textbook's title. For example, the title *Health in America: A Multicultural Perspective* tells us that the book is about health concerns from the view of different cultures. Textbooks divide the general subject into smaller sections or subtopics. These subtopics form the chapters of the textbook. Because a large amount of information is found in each chapter, chapters are further divided into smaller parts or subtopics, and each subtopic is labeled with a heading. The table of contents lists the general subjects and subtopics of each chapter. Many textbooks provide a brief table of contents that divides the textbook into sections and lists the chapter titles for each section. There also may be a separate detailed table of contents that lists the subtopics for each chapter. A master reader examines the table of contents of a textbook to understand how the author has organized the information and to determine where specific information can be found.

EXAMPLE Survey, or look over, the following brief table of contents. Then, answer the questions.

1. What is the general topic of this textbook? Messages: Building Interpersonal Communication Skills

2. How many parts did the author use to divide the general topic? 3

3. How many chapters are in each part? 4 What is the approximate length of each chapter? 20–30 pages.

4. Write a one-sentence summary using the topic and subtopics for Part Two.
Spoken and unspoken messages include verbal messages, nonverbal messages, emotional messages, and conversation messages.

EXPLANATION The general topic of this textbook is stated in its title: *Messages: Building Interpersonal Communication Skills.* The author divides the general topic into three parts: "Messages about the Self and Others," "Messages: Spoken and Unspoken," and "Messages in Context." Each part is divided into

Messages: Building Interpersonal Communication Skills, 6th ed.

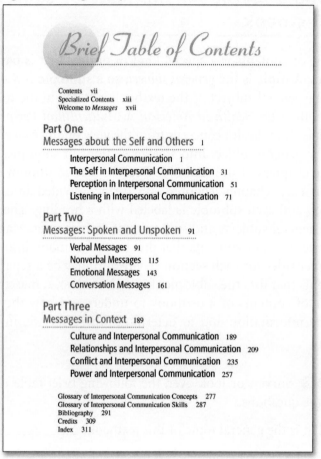

—From *Messages: Building Interpersonal Communication Skills,* 6th ed, pp. v–vi by Joseph A. DeVito. Boston: Allyn & Bacon, 2005.

four chapters. Knowing the length of each chapter helps you set aside the proper amount of time needed to read and study. In this textbook, each chapter is about twenty to thirty pages in length. One way to get a general sense of the ideas in a chapter or part is by writing a summary. Compare your summary to the following: Spoken and unspoken messages include verbal messages, nonverbal messages, emotional messages, and conversation messages.

PRACTICE 3

Study the following detailed table of contents for Chapter 1 of *Messages: Building Interpersonal Communication Skills,* 6th ed.

1. What is the topic of the chapter? _Interpersonal Communication_

2. How many subtopics are listed for the section "Principles of Interpersonal Communication"? 6_____

3. On what page does the discussion about competence in interpersonal communication begin? 13_____

4. What are the major supporting details of this chapter? The major supporting details of this chapter include the nature of interpersonal communication, the principles of interpersonal communication, and culture and interpersonal communication.

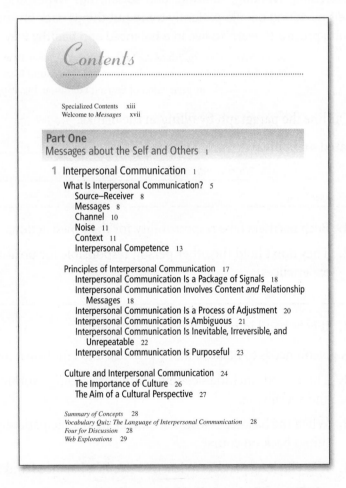

Contents

—From *Messages: Building Interpersonal Communication Skills,* 6th ed, p. vii by Joseph A. DeVito. Boston: Allyn & Bacon, 2005.

APPLICATIONS

Application 1: Major Supporting Details and Outlines

Read the following paragraph from a college health textbook.

Balanced Living

Textbook
Skills

[1]Accountability and self-nurturance are very important to a good relationship. [2]**Accountability** means that both partners take responsibility for their own actions. [3]They don't hold the other person responsible for positive or negative experiences. [4]**Self-nurturance** goes hand in hand with accountability. [5]In order to make good choices in life, a person needs to balance many physical and emotional needs. [6]These needs include sleeping, eating, exercising, working, relaxing, and socializing. [7]When the balance is lost, self-nurturing people patiently try to put things back on course. [8]It is a lifelong process to learn to live in a balanced and healthy way.

—From *Access to Health*, 7th ed., p. 144 by Rebecca J. Donatelle and Lorraine G. Davis. Copyright © 2002 by Pearson Education, Inc. Printed and Electronically reproduced by permission of Pearson Education, Inc., Upper Saddle River, NJ.

1–3. Outline the paragraph by filling in the blanks.

I. **(Stated main idea)** Accountability and self-nurturance are very important to a good relationship.

  A. Accountability

    1. Both partners take responsibility for their own actions.

    2. They don't hold the other person responsible for positive or negative experiences.

  B. Self-nurturance

    1. It goes hand in hand with accountability.

  C. A person needs to balance many physical and emotional needs.

    1. These needs include sleeping, eating, exercising, working, relaxing, and socializing.

    2. When the balance is lost, self-nurturing people patiently try to put things back on course.

    3. It is a lifelong process to learn to live in a balanced and healthy way.

    _____b_____ **4.** The outline above is an example of
      a. an informal outline.
      b. a formal outline.

<u>　b　</u>   **5.** Sentence 6 is a
         a. major supporting detail.
         b. minor supporting detail.

VISUAL VOCABULARY

The best antonym for

nurturance is <u>　a　</u>.

  a. neglect.
  b. challenge.
  c. loving care.

▸ Self-nurturance means taking
time to exercise and have fun.

Application 2: Major Details, Minor Supporting Details, and Outlines

Read the following paragraph from a college sociology textbook.

Textbook
Skills

Can Deviance Really Be Functional for Society?

¹When we think of deviance, its dysfunctions are likely to come to mind. ²Functionalists, in contrast, are as likely to stress the functions of deviance as they are to emphasize its dysfunctions. ³Most of us are upset by deviance, especially crime, and assume that society would be better off without it. ⁴The classic functionalist theorist Emile Durkheim, however, came to a surprising conclusion. ⁵Deviance, he said, including crime, is functional for society, for it contributes to the social order. ⁶Its three main functions include the following. ⁷*Deviance clarifies moral boundaries and affirms norms.* ⁸A group's ideas about how people should act and think mark its *moral boundaries.* ⁹Deviant acts challenge those boundaries. ¹⁰To call a member into account is to say, in effect, "You broke an important rule, and we cannot tolerate that." ¹¹To punish deviants affirms the group's norms and clarifies what it means to be a member of the group. ¹²*Deviance promotes social unity.* ¹³To affirm the group's moral boundaries by punishing deviants fosters a "we" feeling among the group's members. ¹⁴In saying, "You can't get by with that," the group collectively

affirms the rightness of its own ways. [15]*Deviance promotes social change.* [16]Groups do not always agree on what to do with people who push beyond their accepted ways of doing things. [17]Some group members may even approve of the rule-breaking behavior. [18]Boundary violations that gain enough support become new, acceptable behaviors. [19]Thus, deviance may force a group to rethink and redefine its moral boundaries, helping groups—and whole societies—to change their customary ways.

> —From *Essentials of Sociology: A Down-to-Earth Approach,* 7th ed., p. 148 by James M. Henslin. Copyright © 2007 by Pearson Education, Inc. Reproduced by permission of Pearson Education, Inc., Boston, MA.

1–5. Complete the outline of the paragraph by filling in the blanks. Wording of answers may vary.

Stated main idea: The three main functions of deviance include the following.

A. Deviance clarifies moral boundaries and affirms norms.

    1. A group's ideas about how people should act and think mark its moral boundaries. Deviant acts challenge those boundaries.

    2. To call a member into account is to say, in effect, "You broke an important rule, and we cannot tolerate that."

    3. To punish deviants affirms the group's norms and clarifies what it means to be a member of the group.

B. Deviance promotes social unity.

    1. To affirm the group's moral boundaries by punishing deviants fosters a "we" feeling among the group's members.

    2. In saying, "You can't get by with that," the group collectively affirms the rightness of its own ways.

C. Deviance promotes social change.

    1. Groups do not always agree on what to do with people who push beyond their accepted ways of doing things.

    2. Some group members may even approve of the rule-breaking behavior.

    3. Boundary violations that gain enough support become new, acceptable behaviors.

4. Thus, deviance may force a group to rethink and redefine its moral boundaries, helping groups—and whole societies—to change their customary ways.

Application 3: Concept Maps and Signal Words

Read the following paragraph. Then, complete the concept map with the missing information from the paragraph.

A Caste System

Textbook
Skills

[1]A **caste system** is a type of social stratification in which status is determined by birth and is life-long. [2]Someone who is born into a low-status group will always have low status, no matter how much that person may accomplish in life. [3]Achieved status cannot change an individual's place in this system. [4]India provides the best example of a caste system. [5]Based not on race but on religion, India's caste system has existed for nearly 3,000 years. [6]India's four main castes are subdivided into thousands of subcastes or jati. [7]Each subcaste specializes in a particular occupation. [8]For example, one jati washes clothes, another sharpens knives, and yet another repairs shoes. [9]Of the four main castes, the highest caste, the **Brahman**, is made up of priests and teachers. [10]Next is the **Kshatriya** caste of rulers and soldiers; followed by the **Vaishya** of merchants and traders while the lowest caste of the four is the **Shudra** comprised of peasants and laborers. [11]The lowest group in India's caste system is the **Dalit**, who make up India's "untouchables." [12]If a Dalit touches someone of a higher caste, that person becomes unclean. [13]Although the Indian government formally abolished the caste system in 1949, centuries-old practices cannot be eliminated so easily, and the caste system remains a part of everyday life in India.

—Adapted from *Essentials of Sociology: A Down-to-Earth Approach*, 7th ed., p. 171 by James M. Henslin. Copyright © 2007 by Pearson Education, Inc. Reproduced by permission of Pearson Education, Inc., Boston, MA.

Application 4: Summary

Read the following paragraph from a college biology textbook. Complete the summary. Wording of answers may vary.

Textbook Skills

Energy Passes from One Trophic Level to Another

[1]Energy flows through communities from producers through several levels of consumers. [2]Each category of organism is called a **trophic level.** [3]The producers are the first trophic level, generally obtaining their energy directly from sunlight. [4]Consumers occupy several trophic levels. [5]Some consumers feed directly on producers, the most abundant living energy source in any ecosystem. [6]These **primary consumers,** or **herbivores** (plant eaters), ranging from grasshoppers to giraffes, form the second trophic level. [7]The third trophic level consists of **secondary consumers** or **carnivores** (meat eaters), predators such as the spider, eagle, and wolf that feed mainly on primary consumers. [8]Some carnivores occasionally eat other carnivores. [9]When doing so, they occupy the fourth trophic level, **tertiary consumers.**

—From *Life on Earth,* 5th ed., p. 578 and Figure 29–4a (p. 578) by Teresa Audesirk, Gerald Audesirk, and Bruce E. Byers. Copyright © 2009 by Pearson Education, Inc. Printed and Electronically reproduced by permission of Pearson Education, Inc., Upper Saddle River, NJ.

Complete the illustration with information from the passage. Then, complete the summary that follows.

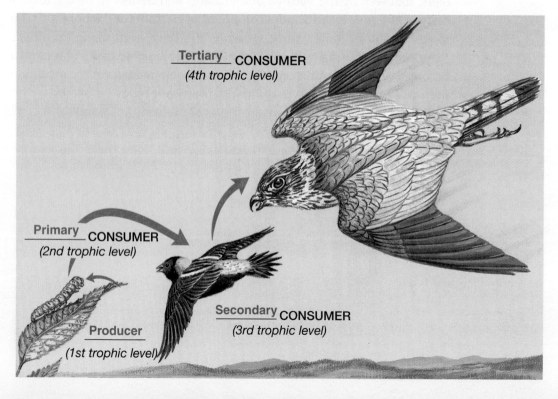

Tertiary CONSUMER
(4th trophic level)

Primary CONSUMER
(2nd trophic level)

Secondary CONSUMER
(3rd trophic level)

Producer
(1st trophic level)

Summary

Energy flows through communities from producers through several levels of consumers. Each category of organism is called a trophic_____ level. Producers, or plants, which get their energy directly from the sun_____, make up the first trophic level. The second trophic level is made up of primary consumers called herbivores_____ or plant eaters; the third trophic level consists of secondary consumers called carnivores or meat eaters_____. The fourth_____ trophic level includes tertiary consumers which consist of carnivores that eat other carnivores_____.

REVIEW TEST 1

Score (number correct) _____ × 10 = _____%

Main Ideas, Major and Minor Supporting Details, and Outlines

Read the following passage from a college business textbook. Then, complete the outline with the major and minor details from the passage.

11.5 GE/435 words

Textbook Skills

Consumer Rights

[1]Much of the current interest in business responsibility toward customers can be traced to the rise of consumerism-social activism dedicated to protecting the rights of consumers in their dealings with businesses. [2]The first formal declaration of consumer rights protection came in the early 1960s when President John F. Kennedy identified four basic consumer rights. [3]Since that time, general agreement on two additional rights has also emerged; these rights are also backed by numerous federal and state laws. Legally, consumers have six basic rights:

- [4]*Consumers have a right to safe products.* [5]Businesses can't knowingly sell products that they suspect of being defective. [6]For example, a central legal argument in the recent problems involving Firestone tires was whether or not company officials knew in advance that the firm was selling defective tires.
- [7]*Consumers have a right to be informed about all relevant aspects of a product.* [8]For example, apparel manufacturers are now required to provide full disclosure on all fabrics used (cotton, silk, polyester, and so forth) and instructions for care (dry-clean, machine wash, hand wash).

- [9]*Consumers have a right to be heard.* [10]Labels on most products sold today have either a telephone number or address through which customers can file complaints or make inquiries.
- [11]*Consumers have a right to choose what they buy.* [12]Customers getting auto-repair service are allowed to know and make choices about pricing and warranties on new versus used parts. [13]Similarly, with the consent of their doctors, people have the right to choose between name-brand medications versus generic products that might be cheaper.
- [14]*Consumers have a right to be educated about purchases.* [15]All prescription drugs now come with detailed information regarding dosage, possible side effects, and potential interactions with other medications.
- [16]*Consumers have a right to courteous service.* [17]This right, of course, is hard to legislate. [18]But as consumers become increasingly knowledgeable, they're more willing to complain about bad service. [19]Consumer hotlines can also be used to voice service-related issues.

[20]American Home Products provides an instructive example of what can happen to a firm that violates one or more of these consumer rights. [21]For several years the firm aggressively marketed the drug Pondimin, a diet pill containing fenfluramine. [22]During its heyday, doctors were writing 18 million prescriptions a year for Pondimin and other medications containing fenfluramine. [23]The FDA subsequently discovered a link between the pills and heart-valve disease. [24]A class action lawsuit against the firm charged that the drug was unsafe and that users had not been provided with complete information about possible side effects. [25]American Home Products eventually agreed to pay $3.75 billion to individuals who had used the drug.

—From *Business,* 8th ed., p. 75 by Ricky W. Griffin and Ronald J. Ebert. Copyright © 2006 by Pearson Education, Inc. Printed and Electronically reproduced by permission of Pearson Education, Inc., Upper Saddle River, NJ.

Stated central idea: **(1)**   Legally, consumers have six basic rights:

A. (2) Consumers have a right to safe products.

1. (3) Businesses can't knowingly sell products that they suspect of being defective.

2. For example, a central legal argument in the recent problems involving Firestone tires was whether or not company officials knew in advance that the firm was selling defective tires.

B. (4) Consumers have a right to be informed about all relevant aspects of a product.

   1. For example, apparel manufacturers are now required to provide full disclosure on all fabrics used (cotton, silk, polyester, and so forth).

   2. Also required are instructions for care (dry-clean, machine wash, hand wash).

C. (5) Consumers have a right to be heard.

   1. Labels on most products sold today have either a telephone number or address.

   2. Thus, customers can file complaints or make inquiries.

D. (6) Consumers have a right to choose what they buy.

   1. Customers getting auto-repair service are allowed to know and make choices about pricing and warranties on new versus used parts.

   2. (7) Similarly, with the consent of their doctors, people have the right to choose between name-brand medications versus generic products that might be cheaper.

E. (8) Consumers have a right to be educated about purchases.

   1. All prescription drugs now come with detailed information.

   2. Information may include dosage, possible side effects, and potential interactions with other medications.

F. (9) Consumers have a right to courteous service.

   1. (10) This right, of course, is hard to legislate.

   2. But as consumers become increasingly knowledgeable, they're more willing to complain about bad service.

   3. Consumer hotlines can also be used to voice service-related issues.

REVIEW TEST 2   Score (number correct) _____ × 25 = _____ %

Supporting Details, Outlines, and Concept Maps

Read the following paragraph from a college ecology textbook. Complete the concept map with the main idea and the major supporting details from the paragraph.

Textbook
Skills

10.2 GE /155 words   **Coral Reefs**

[1]Lying in the warm, shallow waters about tropical islands and continental land masses are colorful rich oases, the coral reefs. [2]They are a unique buildup of dead skeletal material from a variety of organisms, including coral, certain types of algae, and mollusks. [3]Built only underwater at shallow depths, coral reefs need a stable foundation upon which to grow. [4]Such foundations are provided by shallow continental shelves and submerged volcanoes. [5]Coral reefs are of three types. [6](1) *Fringing reefs* grow seaward from the rocky shores of islands and continents. [7](2) *Barrier reefs* parallel shorelines of continents and islands and are separated from land by shallow lagoons. [8](3) *Atolls* are horseshoe-shaped rings of coral reefs and islands surrounding a lagoon, formed when a volcanic mountain subsided. [9]Such lagoons are about 40m deep, usually connect to the open sea by breaks in the reef, and may hold small islands of patch reefs. [10]Reefs build up to sea level.

—Adapted from Smith & Smith, *Elements of Ecology*, 4th ed. update, p. 504.

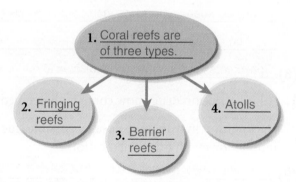

1. Coral reefs are of three types.

2. Fringing reefs

3. Barrier reefs

4. Atolls

VISUAL VOCABULARY

Belize's Lighthouse Reef is
c _____ that
surrounds the Blue Hole, a
sunken cave system that is a
haven for marine life and scuba
divers.

   a. a fringe
   b. a barrier
   c. an atoll

REVIEW TEST 3

Score (number correct) _____ × 10 = _____ %

Supporting Details and Outlines

Before you read the following passage from a college textbook about tourism, skim the material and answer the Before Reading questions. Read the passage. Then, answer the After Reading questions and activities.

Textbook Skills   11.6 GE/538 words

The Art of Travel Writing

by William R. Gray

Vocabulary Preview

reportorial (1): having the traits of reporting news or facts

vanguard (4): the leading position in a movement, field, or trend

platoons (4): bodies of people with a common purpose or goal

atmospherics (10): the mood, tone, environment, climate

raucous (15): loud, noisy

[1]Over the past three decades or so, travel writing—like other nonfiction—has undergone a transformation from a more **reportorial** style to one that is propelled by the literary voice of the author. [2]This approach is personal and features the active participation of the writer in the subject matter—and thus is highly involving for readers, who feel they are being taken on a journey of discovery.

[3]Writers such as Edward Abbey, John McPhee, William Least Heat-Moon (particularly in *Blue Highways*), and Paul Theroux were in the **vanguard** of this approach to nonfiction writing, and today there are literally **platoons** of excellent writers following their lead. [4]And the great travel magazines overflow each issue with generally superb writing.

[5]In teaching my writing courses—including travel writing—and speaking at conferences, I try to instill the key elements that contribute to quality nonfiction writing, and all of these apply most emphatically to travel. [6]Focusing on these attributes helps elevate the quality of the writing, the personal involvement of the author, and draws readers in—and as writers we always need to keep our readers in the forefront of our minds.

- [7]Keen Observer: always seek the descriptive element, the penetrating detail that truly brings your subject to life and illuminates its uniqueness. [8]When interviewing someone, avoid the obvious descriptors such as color of hair and eyes; instead focus on timbre of voice, tilt of head, the gesture or mannerism that reveals character, the way light and shadow play across the face. [9]Likewise with place, use imagery—to evoke essential qualities; **atmospherics** and color are integral—the play of clouds, the tone of wind; use color dramatically—a cobalt sky; a sunset the color of apricots.

- **10**Active Participant: be both dynamically and intimately involved with your subject; follow every lead and participate in every activity appropriate to the place you are writing about. **11**Get up early, stay up late, and experience new things all day long.

- **12**Depth of Feeling: develop empathy for your subject; seek to experience it emotionally and do not hesitate to reveal something of yourself—how events and people affect you.

- **13**Openness to Experience: seek the **harrowing**, the exhilarating, the unusual. **14**Canoe through the crocodile-infested waters; climb the treacherous cliff; stay up all night with the **raucous** carnival celebrants. **15**In other words, be open to doing everything that might contribute to your understanding of the place you are writing about. **16**Be spontaneous—one of these activities may form the basis of the lead to your story.

- **17**Desire to Seek Knowledge and Understanding: strive to know your subject deeply; it's the way it is today because of the **confluence** of history, geology, exploration, warfare, cultural traditions, racial configuration, tourism, and a dozen other factors. **18**Understanding these elements will give perspective to your writing and help make it insightful and profound.

- **19**Desire to Seek a High Level in the Craft of Writing: use a strong first person point of view and a clear literary style to elevate and distinguish your writing. **20**Begin with an effective, original lead and end meaningfully. **21**Always be aware of **diction**, sentence variety, and quality of transitions. **22**Write so creatively and imaginatively that you leave your readers impatiently waiting to devour your next piece of writing.

Before Reading

Vocabulary in Context

_____c_____   **1.** In sentence 13 of the passage, the word **harrowing** means
  a. fun.   c. frightening.
  b. pleasant.   d. fulfilling.

_____a_____   **2.** In sentence 17 of the passage, the word **confluence** means
  a. meeting.   c. departure.
  b. multitude.   d. being.

___b___   **3.** In sentence 21 of the passage, the word **diction** means
a. speech.   c. accent.
b. wording.   d. organization.

After Reading

Main Ideas and Supporting Details

4–10. Complete the following outline with the main idea and major supporting
details of the passage.

Stated central idea: (4) _Focusing on these attributes helps elevate the quality of_

the writing, the personal involvement of the author, and draws readers in—and as

writers we always need to keep our readers in the forefront of our minds.

  - **(5)** _Keen Observer_

  - **(6)** _Active Participant_

  - **(7)** _Depth of Feeling_

  - **(8)** _Openness to Experience_

  - **(9)** Desire to Seek Knowledge and Understanding

  - **(10)** Desire to Seek a High Level in the Craft of Writing

WHAT DO YOU THINK?

Do you have a favorite travel destination? If you could go anywhere in the world,
where would you go and why? What place do you think everyone should visit at
least once in her or his lifetime? Assume you are a travel writer and an online
travel blog has asked you to write an article about a place of your choosing.
Consider the following possibilities: your home town; a tourist attraction such
as Disney World or Universal Studios; a state or national park. As you write and
revise, use the elements of effective travel writing suggested by William R. Gray.

REVIEW TEST 4   Score (number correct) _____ × 10 = _____ %

Supporting Details and Concept Maps

Before Reading: Survey the following passage adapted from the college textbook *The Interpersonal Communication Book*. Skim the passage, noting the

words in bold print. Answer the Before Reading questions that follow the passage. Then, read the passage. Next, answer the After Reading questions. Use the discussion and writing topics as activities to do after reading.

12.3 GE/488 words

Textbook
Skills

Repairing Conversational Problems: The Excuse

[1]At times you may say the wrong thing; then, because you can't erase the message (communication really is irreversible), you may try to account for it. [2]Perhaps the most common method for doing so is the excuse. [3]You learn early in life that when you do something that others will view negatively, an excuse is in order to justify your performance. [4]*Excuses*, central to all forms of communication and interaction, are "explanations or actions that lessen the negative **implications** of an actor's performance, thereby maintaining a positive image for oneself and others" (Snyder, 1984; Snyder, Higgins, & Stucky, 1983).

[5]Excuses seem especially in order when you say or are accused of saying something that runs **counter** to what is expected, sanctioned, or considered "right" by the people with whom you're talking. [6]Ideally, the excuse lessens the negative impact of the message.

Vocabulary Preview

implications (4): meanings

counter (5): opposite

subsequent (8): following, later

alibi (16): explanation, excuse

assurance (17): promise, guarantee

Some Motives for Excuse Making

[7]The major motive for excuse making seems to be to maintain your self-esteem, to project a positive image to yourself and to others. [8]Excuses also represent an effort to reduce stress: You may feel that if you can offer an excuse—especially a good one that is accepted by those around you—it will reduce the negative reaction and the **subsequent** stress that accompanies a poor performance.

[9]Excuses also may enable you to maintain effective interpersonal relationships even after some negative behavior. [10]For example, after criticizing a friend's behavior and observing the negative reaction to your criticism, you might offer an excuse such as, "Please forgive me; I'm really exhausted. [11]I'm just not thinking straight." [12]Excuses enable you to place your messages—even your possible failures—in a more favorable light.

Types of Excuses

[13]Think of the recent excuses you have used or heard. [14]Did they fall into any of these three classes (Snyder, 1984)?

■ **15**_I didn't do it:_ Here you deny that you have done what you're being accused of. **16**You may then bring up an **alibi** to prove you couldn't have done it, or perhaps you may accuse another person of doing what you're being blamed for ("I never said that" or "I wasn't even near the place when it happened"). **17**These "I didn't do it" types are the worst excuses, because they fail to acknowledge responsibility and offer no **assurance** that this failure will not happen again.

■ **18**_It wasn't so bad:_ Here you admit to doing it but claim the offense was not really so bad or perhaps that there was justification for the behavior ("I only padded the expense account, and even then only modestly" or "Sure, I hit him, but he was asking for it").

■ **19**_Yes, but:_ Here you claim that **extenuating circumstances** accounted for the behavior; for example, that you weren't in control of yourself at the time or that you didn't intend to do what you did ("It was the liquor talking" or "I never intended to hurt him; I was actually trying to help").

—Adapted from _The Interpersonal Communication Book,_ 11th ed., pp. 210–211 by Joseph A. DeVito. Copyright © 2007 by Pearson Education, Inc. Reproduced by permission of Pearson Education, Inc., Boston, MA.

Before Reading

Vocabulary in Context

Use your own words to define the following terms. Identify the context clue you used to make meaning of the word.

1. The word **counter** in sentence 5 means <u>to act in opposition.</u>

2. Context clue used for **counter** <u>antonym (expected, sanctioned, or considered</u>
<u>"right")</u>

3. The phrase **extenuating circumstances** in sentence 19 means <u>uncontrollable</u>
<u>events that excuse or explain.</u>

4. Context clue used for **extenuating circumstances** <u>examples and general</u>
<u>sense of the passage</u>

After Reading

Main Ideas and Supporting Details

Complete the following graphic organizer with information from the passage.

Stated main idea: **5.** Excuses are explanations of our actions that lessen the negative complications of an actor's performance, thereby maintaining a positive image for oneself and others.

6. Motives and Excuse Making

Types of Excuses

To maintain self-esteem, to project a positive image for yourself and to others

8. I didn't do it.

9. It wasn't so bad.

7. To reduce stress.

10. Yes, but

To maintain effective inter-personal relationships even after some negative behavior

WHAT DO YOU THINK?

What kinds of excuses do you hear in informal groups on your campus? Do excuses on the job differ from excuses heard at school? Why or why not? Assume you are a manager of a local retail store. Tardiness to work is a growing problem among a significant number of employees in your department. At a manager's meeting, you discover that managers in other departments are experiencing the same problem. Write an article for your company's newsletter to educate workers about excuse making. Explain possible motivations, types of excuses, and the possible impact of excuse making on their chances for promotion. Also suggest a solution to avoid the need for excuses.

After Reading About Outlines and Concepts

Before you move on to the Mastery Tests on outlines and concept maps, take time to reflect on your learning and performance by answering the following questions. Write your answers in your notebook.

- How has my knowledge base or prior knowledge about outlines and concept maps changed?

- Based on my studies, how do I think I will perform on the Mastery Test(s)? Why do I think my scores will be above average, average, or below average?

- Would I recommend this chapter to other students who want to learn more about outlines and concept maps? Why or why not?

Test your understanding of what you have learned about Outlines and Concept Maps for Master Readers by completing the Chapter 6 Review Card in the insert near the end of your text.

CONNECT TO **myreadinglab**

To check your progress in meeting Chapter 6's learning outcomes, log in to **www.myreadinglab.com** and try the following activities.

- The "Outlining and Summarizing" section of MyReadingLab gives an overview about memory and active reading. This section also provides a model for outlining and a model for mapping. You will also find practice activities and tests. To access this resource, click on the "Study Plan" tab. Then click on "Outlining and Summarizing." Then click on the following links as needed: "Overview," "Model: Outlining," "Model: Mapping," "Practice," and "Tests."

- To measure your mastery of the content of this chapter complete the tests in the "Outlining and Summarizing" section and click on Gradebook to find your results.

A. Read the following passage from a college communications textbook.

Textbook
Skills

12.3 GE/187 words   **Networking Relationships**

¹**Networking** is a process of using other people to try to help you solve your problems, or at least offer insights that bear on your problem—for example, how to publish your manuscript, where to look for low-cost auto insurance, how to find an affordable apartment, or how to empty your cache. ²Networking comes in two forms: informal and formal. ³*Informal* networking is what we do every day when we find ourselves in a new situation or unable to answer questions. ⁴Thus, for example, if you're new at school, you might ask someone in your class where to eat or shop for new clothes, or who's the best teacher. ⁵In the same way, if you enter a new work environment, you might ask more experienced workers how to perform certain tasks or whom you should avoid or approach when you have questions. ⁶*Formal* networking is the same thing except that it's much more systematic and strategic. ⁷It's the establishment of connections with people who can help you—answer your questions, get you a job, help you get promoted, help you relocate, or accomplish any task you want to accomplish.

—Adapted from *The Interpersonal Communication Book,* 11th ed., pp. 305–306 by Joseph A. DeVito. Copyright © 2007 by Pearson Education, Inc. Reproduced by permission of Pearson Education, Inc., Boston, MA.

1–2. Complete the summary with information from the paragraph.

Networking is (1) a process of using other people to try to help you solve your

problems, or at least offer insights that bear on your problem —for example, **(2)**

informal problems; networking is everyday problem solving, and formal networking is

systematic and strategic connections with people who can help you.

_____ a   **3.** Sentence 1 is a
      a. main idea.   c. minor supporting detail.
      b. major supporting detail.

_____ c   **4.** Sentence 4 is a
      a. main idea.   c. minor supporting detail.
      b. major supporting detail.

5. What signal phrase introduces the second minor supporting detail for informal networking? <u>In the same way</u>

B. Read the following paragraph from a college government textbook.

Textbook Skills

11.5 GE/124 words   **News by Trial Balloon**

¹Those who make the news depend on the media to spread certain information and ideas to the general public. ²Sometimes they feed stories to reporters in the form of **trial balloons**: information leaked to see what the political reaction will be. ³For example, a few days prior to President Clinton's admission that he had an "inappropriate relationship" with Monica Lewinsky, top aides to the president leaked the story to Richard Berke of the *New York Times*. ⁴The timing of the leak was obvious; the story appeared just before Clinton had to decide how to testify before Kenneth Starr's grand jury. ⁵When the public reacted that it was about time he admitted this relationship, it was probably easier for him to do so—at least politically.

—Edwards, Wattenberg, & Lineberry, *Government in America*, 5th ed., Brief Version, p. 171.

6–7. Complete the summary with information from the paragraph.

(**6**) <u>Trial balloons are made up of information leaked to see what the political</u>

<u>reaction will be</u> —for example, (**7**) <u>a few days prior to President Clinton's</u>

<u>admission that he had an "inappropriate relationship" with Monica Lewinsky, top</u>

<u>aides to the president leaked the story to Richard Berke of the *New York Times*.</u>

<u>b</u>   **8.** In the paragraph, sentence 3 is
   a. a main idea.
   b. a major supporting detail.
   c. a minor supporting detail.

<u>c</u>   **9.** In the paragraph, sentence 4 is
   a. a main idea.
   b. a major supporting detail.
   c. a minor supporting detail.

10. What signal word introduces the find minor supporting detail? <u>When</u>

Textbook
Skills

Read the following paragraph from a college psychology textbook. Then, answer the questions that follow it.

10.0 GE/211 words

What Is Substance Abuse?

¹What is the difference between drug use and substance abuse? ²The impact on people's lives is one way to gauge use versus abuse. ³People who experience negative effects as a result of their drug use cross the line into substance abuse. ⁴A **substance abuser** is a person who overuses and relies on drugs to deal with everyday life. ⁵Most substance abusers use alcohol or tobacco, but the whole range of psychoactive drugs and combinations of these drugs presents possibilities for substance abuse. ⁶A person is a substance abuser if all three of the following statements apply:

- ⁷The person has used the substance for at least a month.
- ⁸The use has caused legal, personal, social, or vocational problems.
- ⁹The person repeatedly uses the substance even in situations when doing so is hazardous, such as when driving a car.

¹⁰Missing work or school, spending too much money on drugs, damaging personal relationships, and getting into legal trouble are all signs of substance abuse. ¹¹When substance abusers try to decrease or quit their drug use, they may experience withdrawal symptoms. ¹²**Withdrawal symptoms** are the reactions experienced when a substance abuser stops using a drug with dependence properties. ¹³For example, an alcoholic may experience the "shakes" as he or she attempts to quit drinking alcohol.

—Adapted from Lefton & Brannon, *Psychology*, 8th ed., pp. 215–216.

___b___ **1.** Which sentence states the main idea of the passage?
- a. sentence 1
- b. sentence 2
- c. sentence 3
- d. sentence 8

___d___ **2.** In general, the major details of this passage are
- a. facts that show the number of people who are substance abusers.
- b. ways to avoid substance abuse.
- c. reasons for substance abuse.
- d. definitions of substance abuse, substance abuser, and withdrawal symptoms.

___b___ **3.** In the passage, sentence 4 is
- a. a main idea.
- b. a major supporting detail.
- c. a minor supporting detail.

_____c_____   **4.** In the passage, sentence 7 is
        a. a main idea.   c. a minor supporting detail.
        b. a major supporting detail.

5–10. Complete the informal outline with the key terms, definitions, and examples from the paragraph.

Main idea: Drug abuse can be measured by the impact on the lives of users.

A. _Substance abuse_ :   Negative effects as a result of drug use

    Example: Missing work or school, spending too much money on drugs, damaging personal relationships, and getting into legal trouble are all signs of substance abuse.

B. Substance abuser: A person who overuses and relies on drugs to deal with everyday life

    Example: Most substance abusers use alcohol or tobacco, but the whole range of psychoactive drugs and combinations of these drugs presents possibilities for substance abuse.

C. _Withdrawal symptoms_ :   The reactions experienced when a substance abuser stops using a drug with dependence properties

    Example: An alcoholic may experience the "shakes" as he or she attempts to quit drinking alcohol.

VISUAL VOCABULARY

Which word or phrase best states the meaning of *psychoactive*?

_____a_____

    a. mind-altering
    b. satisfying
    c. addictive

▶ Caffeine is one example of a commonly used *psychoactive* drug.

Read the following passage from a college humanities textbook.

Textbook
Skills

11.1 GE/209 words   **The Difference Between Problems and Issues**

¹To be able to think clearly and effectively, you must be able to understand and recognize problems and issues. ²Problems and issues differ in some respects. ³A problem is a situation that we regard as unacceptable. ⁴In contrast, an issue is a matter about which intelligent, informed people disagree to some extent. ⁵Solving problems, therefore, means deciding what action will change the situation for the best. ⁶On the other hand, resolving issues means deciding what belief or viewpoint is the most reasonable.

⁷Whenever you are uncertain whether to treat a particular challenge as a problem or an issue, apply this test: Ask whether the matter involved tends to arouse partisan feelings and to divide informed, intelligent people. ⁸If it does not, treat it as a problem. ⁹If it does, treat it as an issue. ¹⁰Here are some sample problems: a student trying to study in a noisy dormitory, a child frightened by the prospect of going to the hospital, a businesswoman dealing with sexual harassment. ¹¹Here are some sample issues: a public school teacher leading students in prayer in a public school classroom, a member of Congress proposing a cut in Social Security benefits for the elderly, an anthropologist stating that human beings are violent by nature.

—Adapted from Ruggiero, *The Art of Thinking*, 7th ed., p. 109.

_____a_____ **1.** Sentence 2 is a
    a. main idea.   c. minor supporting detail.
    b. major supporting detail.

_____b_____ **2.** Sentence 3 is a
    a. main idea.   c. minor supporting detail.
    b. major supporting detail.

_____b_____ **3.** Sentence 4 is a
    a. main idea.   c. minor supporting detail.
    b. major supporting detail.

_____c_____ **4.** Sentence 8 is a
    a. main idea.   c. minor supporting detail.
    b. major supporting detail.

_____c_____ **5.** Sentence 11 is a
           a. main idea.
           b. major supporting detail.
           c. minor supporting detail.

6–10. Complete the concept map (a contrast chart) with information from the passage. Wording of some answers may vary.

Differences between:	6. ___Problems___	Issues
Definitions	an unacceptable situation	**7.** a matter about which intelligent, informed people disagree to some extent
Goals	positive actions	**8.** reasonable beliefs
Traits	**9.** do not arouse feelings and do not divide people	arouse feelings and divide people
Examples	**10.** a student trying to study in a noisy dormitory, a child frightened by the prospect of going to the hospital, a businesswoman dealing with sexual harassment	a public school teacher leading students in prayer in a public classroom, a member of Congress proposing a cut in Social Security benefits for the elderly, an anthropologist stating that human beings are violent by nature

VISUAL VOCABULARY

This photograph entitled "Pro-Life Demonstrators Face Pro-Choice Demonstrators" illustrates a significant

____b_____ in the United States.

    a. problem
    b. issue

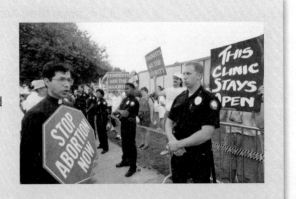

Read the following passage from a college textbook. Complete the concept map with information from the passage.

Textbook
Skills

13.1 GE/413 words   **Popular Areas of Small-Business Enterprise**

¹Not surprisingly, small businesses are more common in some industries than in others. ²The major small-business industry groups are *services, construction, finance and insurance, wholesaling,* and *transportation and manufacturing.* ³Each industry differs in its needs for employees, money, materials, and machines. ⁴But as a general rule, the more resources required, the harder it is to start a business and the less likely an industry is dominated by small firms.

⁵Remember, too, that small is a relative term. ⁶The criteria (number of employees and total annual sales) differ from industry to industry and are often meaningful only when compared with truly large businesses. ⁷The following discussion focuses on U.S. businesses across industry groups employing fewer than 20 employees.

Services ⁸Small-business services range from marriage counseling to computer software, from management consulting to professional dog walking. ⁹Partly because they require few resources, service providers are the fastest-growing segment of small business. ¹⁰A retailer, for example, sells products made by other firms directly to consumers. ¹¹Usually, people who start small retail businesses favor specialty shops—say, big men's clothing or gourmet coffees—that let them focus limited resources on narrow market segments.

Construction ¹²About 10 percent of businesses with fewer than 20 employees are involved in construction. ¹³Because many construction jobs are small local projects, local firms are often ideal contractors.

Finance and Insurance ¹⁴Financial and insurance firms also account for about 10 percent of all firms with fewer than 20 employees. ¹⁵Most of these businesses are affiliates of or agents for larger national firms.

Wholesaling ¹⁶Small-business owners often do well in wholesaling. ¹⁷About 8 percent of businesses with fewer than 20 employees are wholesalers. ¹⁸Wholesalers buy products from manufacturers or other producers and sell them to retailers. ¹⁹They usually purchase goods in bulk and store them in quantities at locations convenient for retailers. ²⁰For a given volume of business, therefore, they need fewer employees than manufacturers, retailers, or service providers.

Transportation and Manufacturing [21]Some small firms—about 5 percent of all companies with fewer than 20 employees—do well in transportation and related businesses. [22]These include taxi and limousine companies, charter airplane services, and tour operators. [23]More than any other industry, manufacturing lends itself to big business. [24]But this doesn't mean that no small businesses do well in manufacturing; rather, about 5 percent of firms with fewer than 20 employees are involved in manufacturing. [25]Indeed, small manufacturers sometimes outperform big ones in such innovation-driven industries as electronics, toys, and computer software.

—Adapted from *Business*, 8th ed., pp. 92–93 by Ricky W. Griffin and Ronald J. Ebert. Copyright © 2006 by Pearson Education, Inc. Printed and Electronically reproduced by permission of Pearson Education, Inc., Upper Saddle River, NJ.

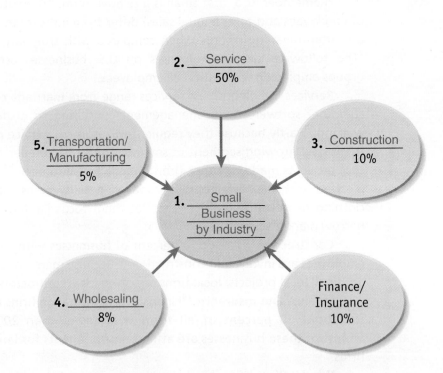

Transitions and Thought Patterns

7

LEARNING OUTCOMES

After studying this chapter you should be able to do the following:

1. Define the terms *transitions* and *thought patterns*. [Knowledge]
2. Determine the relationships of ideas within a sentence. [Analysis]
3. Determine the relationships of ideas between sentences. [Analysis]
4. Recognize the following thought patterns and their signal words: *time order*, *space order*, *listing*, *classification*. [Knowledge]
5. Determine the thought pattern used to organize a passage. [Analysis]
6. Evaluate the importance of transitions and thought patterns. [Evaluation]

 ## Before Reading About Transitions and Thought Patterns

Using the reporter's questions (Who? What? When? Where? Why? and How?), refer to the chapter learning outcomes and create at least three questions that you can answer as you study the chapter. Write your questions in the following spaces:

What are transitions? What are thought patterns?

What is the relationship between transitions and thought patterns?

How do thought patterns use transition words?

Now take a few minutes to skim the chapter for ideas and terms that you have studied in previous chapters. List those ideas in the following spaces:

main idea, supporting details, outlines

Compare the questions you created based on the chapter learning outcomes with the following questions. Then, write the ones that seem the most helpful in your notebook, leaving enough space after each question to record the answers as you read and study the chapter.

What are transitions? What are thought patterns? What is the relationship between transitions and thought patterns? How do thought patterns use transition words?

On page 274, the terms *main idea* and *supporting details* are discussed in relationship to transitions and thought patterns. Consider the following study questions based on these ideas: How can transitions help me understand the author's main idea? How can transitions help me create an outline?

 ## Transition Words: Relationships Within a Sentence

Read the following set of ideas. Which word makes the relationship between the ideas clear?

Marcus was asked to leave the movie <u>because</u> he was talking loudly.

 a. however b. because c. finally

The word that makes the relationship between ideas within the sentence clear is (b) *because*. The first part of the sentence states what happened to Marcus. The second part of the sentence explains why he was asked to leave the theatre. The word *because* best signals the cause and effect relationship between Marcus's behavior and the result of his behavior.

Transitions are key words and phrases that signal the logical relationships both within a sentence and between sentences. **Transitions** help you make sense of an author's idea in two basic ways. First, transitions join ideas within a sentence. Second, transitions establish **thought patterns** so readers can understand the logical flow of ideas between sentences.

> **Transitions** are words and phrases that signal thought patterns by showing the logical relationships both within a sentence and between sentences.
> A **thought pattern** is established by using transitions to show the logical relationship between ideas in a paragraph or passage.

Some transition words have similar meanings. *For example, also, too,* and *furthermore* all signal the relationship of addition or listing. Sometimes a single word can serve as two different types of transitions, depending on how it is used. For example, the word *since* can reveal time order, or it can signal a cause. Notice the difference in the following two sentences.

Since I began studying every day, my understanding and my grades have improved dramatically.

Since you have the flu, please stay home from work to avoid spreading the disease.

EXAMPLE Complete the following ideas with a transition that shows the relationship within each sentence. Fill in each blank with a word from the box. Use each word once.

adjacent	another	during	one type

1. In the ancient Aztec culture, priests offered cacao seeds and chocolate drinks to their gods <u>during</u> sacred ceremonies.

2. One way to shop for a vehicle is to visit local dealerships; <u>another</u> way is to use online resources such as AutoTrader.com.

3. Fear of failure is <u>one type</u> of attitude that drives academic cheating.

4. The registrar's office is <u>adjacent</u> to the financial aid office.

EXPLANATION

1. The word *during* indicates *when* the Aztec priests offered the cacao seeds and chocolate drinks to their gods.

2. *Another* signals the *addition* of the second idea in this sentence.

3. The phrase *one type* suggests that other types of thinking also motivate academic cheating.

4. The word *adjacent* signals that the registrar's office is located *next to* the financial aid office.

PRACTICE 1

Complete the following ideas with a transition that shows the relationship within each sentence. Fill in each blank with a word from the box. Use each word once.

furthermore	in the foreground	one category	subsequently

1. An American citizen is entitled to a fair and speedy trial whether ___subsequently___ found guilty or innocent.

2. Walking—a safe, efficient, and popular method of attaining and maintaining physical fitness—strengthens the heart and lungs; ___furthermore___, it builds bones and tones muscles.

3. In Monet's 1877 painting *Arrival of a Train,* the smoke of the trains ___in the foreground___ of the painting blurs the cathedral, which is barely visible past the smoke.

4. The white lie is only ___one category___ of the myriad types of lies that do much harm.

Master readers look for transition words, study their meaning in context, and use them as keys to unlock the author's thought pattern.

 ## Thought Patterns: Relationships Between Sentences

Not only do transitions reveal the relationships among ideas within a sentence, they also show the relationship of ideas between sentences.

Walking strengthens the heart and lungs. It *also* builds and tones muscles.

EXAMPLE   Complete each of the following ideas with a transition that makes the relationship between the sentences clear. Fill in each blank with a word from the box. Use each word once.

as a result	finally	for example	next

1. According to the National Weather Service, frostbite is the damage caused to body tissue due to freezing. ___As a result___, frostbite causes a loss of feeling and white or pale coloring of the affected areas.

2. Your family should have an emergency or disaster kit on hand. <u>For example</u>, you should have water, non-perishable food, and first aid supplies.

3. Four test-taking tips may prove helpful if you experience test anxiety. First, keep a positive attitude. <u>Next</u>, to gain confidence and build up points, answer the easy questions before you answer tougher ones.

4. Third, don't let the hard questions stump you; circle them, move on, and come back to them later if you can. <u>Finally</u>, take time to proof-read for careless errors.

The root **dermis** means

c
_____.

   a. degree.
   b. skin.
   c. layer of skin or tissue.

▶ **Cross-Section of the Three Layers of Human Skin**
First-degree frostbite injuries involve the epidermis, and fourth-degree injuries involve the epidermis, dermis, and subcutaneous tissue.

—Adapted from *Occupational Dermatoses*, Page 3, Slide 14, 21 Apr. 2001; National Institute for Occupational Safety and Health Photolibrary, CDC. http://www.cdc.gov/niosh/ocderm3.html

EXPLANATION

1. The transition *as a result* indicates that the second sentence offers specific symptoms of frostbite.

2. The transition phrase *for example* logically introduces example items to include in a family disaster kit.

3–4. Items 3 and 4 list four test-taking tips. In item 3, the transition *next* logically introduces the second tip, and in item 4, the transition *finally* introduces the last of the four test-taking tips.

PRACTICE 2

Complete the following ideas with transitions. Fill in each blank with a word from the box. Use each word once.

| immediately | meanwhile | next | on | out |

Andre began choking. **(1)** <u>Immediately</u> Daine wrapped his arms around Andre's waist. **(2)** <u>Next</u>, Daine made a fist with his right hand. He then placed the thumb side of his fist **(3)** <u>on</u> the middle of Andre's abdomen just above his navel and well below the lower tip of his breastbone. **(4)** <u>Meanwhile</u>, he grasped the fist with the other hand. He pressed his fist into Andre's abdomen with a quick upward thrust. After several quick, hard thrusts, the piece of food that had been blocking Andre's airway flew **(5)** <u>out</u> of his mouth.

You will recall that a paragraph is made up of a group of ideas. Major details support the main idea, and minor details support the major details. Transitions make the relationship between these three levels of ideas clear, smooth, and easy to follow.

Before beginning to write, an author must ask, "What thought pattern best expresses these ideas?" or "How should these ideas be organized so that the reader can follow and understand my point?" A **thought pattern** (also called a **pattern of organization**) allows the author to arrange the supporting details in a clear and smooth flow by using transition words.

> **Thought patterns** (or **patterns of organization**) are signaled by using transitions to show the logical relationship between ideas in a paragraph, passage, or textbook chapter.

As you learned in Chapter 3, a main idea is made up of a topic and the author's controlling point about the topic. One way an author controls the topic is by using a specific thought pattern. Read the following paragraph. Identify the topic sentence by circling the topic and underlining the controlling point.

Textbook
Skills

Interpersonal Perception

[1]Perception takes place in three stages that flow into one another and overlap. [2]At the first stage, you sense the stimuli. [3]At the second phase, you organize the stimulations. [4]The third stage in the process is interpretation-evaluation. [5]These stages are not separate; they're continuous and blend into and overlap one another.

—Adapted from *Messages: Building Interpersonal Communication Skills,* 4th ed.,
p. 66 by Joseph A. DeVito. Copyright © 1999 by Pearson Education, Inc.
Reproduced by permission of Pearson Education, Inc., Boston, MA.

The topic is "perception" and the controlling point is the phrase "three stages that flow into one another and overlap." The phrase "that flow into one another and overlap" states the author's opinion. The words "three stages" state the author's thought pattern. The author's controlling point limits the supporting details to listing and describing the three stages of perception. The transition phrases *first stage, second phase,* and *third stage* signal each of the supporting details. Authors often introduce supporting details with transition words based on the controlling point. Creating an outline using transition words is an excellent way to grasp an author's thought pattern.

EXAMPLE Read the following paragraph. Complete the informal outline, then answer the question.

Textbook
Skills

Types of Coping Styles

[1]Each of us can learn to control stress by adopting coping strategies that are consistent with our lifestyles. [2]According to Lazarus and Folkman (1984; Folkman and Lazarus, 1991), there are two types of coping responses. [3]The first type of coping style, **problem-focused coping,** is directed toward the source of the stress. [4]For example, if the stress is job-related, a person might try to change conditions at the job site or take courses to acquire skills that would enable him or her to obtain a different job. [5]The second type of coping style, **emotion-focused coping,** is directed toward a person's own personal reaction to a stressor. [6]For example, a person might try to relax and forget about the problem or find solace in the company of friends.

—Adapted from Carlson & Buskist, *Psychology: The Science of Behavior,* 5th ed., p. 552.

Topic sentence: <u>There are two types of coping responses.</u>

A. <u>Problem-focused coping is directed toward the source of the stress.</u>

> For example, if the stress is job-related, a person might try to change conditions at the job site or take courses to acquire skills that would enable him or her to obtain a different job.

B. Emotion-focused coping is directed toward a person's own personal reaction

to a stressor.

> For example, a person might try to relax and forget about the problem or find solace in the company of friends.

_____b_____ What is the author's thought pattern?
    a. time order   b. classification

EXPLANATION Compare your outline to the following:

Topic sentence: There are two types of coping responses.

A. Problem-focused coping is directed toward the source of the stress.

> For example, if the stress is job-related, a person might try to change conditions at the job site or take courses to acquire skills that would enable him or her to obtain a different job.

B. Emotion-focused coping is directed toward a person's own personal reaction to a stressor.

> For example, a person might try to relax and forget about the problem or find solace in the company of friends.

The topic is "coping responses." The thought pattern is signaled by the phrase "two types." The transitions clearly carry out the thought pattern by introducing the major supporting details (the two types of coping responses) with the phrases "first type" and "second type." In addition, the author provides minor details in the form of examples, and each example is introduced with the phrase "for example." In this paragraph, these transitions establish the (b) classification thought pattern, which is discussed later in the chapter.

PRACTICE 3

Read the following paragraph. Then, complete the informal outline.

Textbook
Skills

Biodiversity Loss and Species Extinction

¹Biodiversity at all levels is being lost to human impact, most irretrievably in the extinction of species. ²Once vanished, a species can never

return. [3]**Extinction** occurs when the last member of a species dies and the species ceases to exist, as apparently was the case with Monteverde's golden toad. [4]The disappearance of a particular population from a given area, but not the entire species globally, is referred to as **extirpation**. [5]For example, the tiger has been extirpated from most of its historic range, but it is not yet extinct. [6]However, extirpation is an erosive process that can, over time, lead to extinction.

> —From *Essential Environment: The Science Behind the Stories*, 3rd ed., p. 165 by Jay H. Withgott and Scott R. Brennan. Copyright © 2009 by Pearson Education, Inc. Reprinted by permission of Pearson Education, Inc., Upper Saddle River, NJ.

Topic sentence: Biodiversity at all levels is being lost to human impact, most irretrievably in the extinction of species.

   a. **Extinction** occurs when the last member of a species dies and the species ceases to exist, as apparently was the case with Monteverde's golden toad.

   b. The disappearance of a particular population from a given area, but not the entire species globally, is referred to as **extirpation**.

      1. For example, the tiger has been extirpated from most of its historic range, but it is not yet extinct.

      2. However, extirpation is an erosive process that can, over time, lead to extinction.

In this chapter, we discuss four common thought patterns and the transition words and phrases used to signal each:

- The time order pattern
- The space order pattern
- The listing pattern
- The classification pattern

Some additional common thought patterns are covered in Chapter 8.

The Time Order Pattern

The **time order** thought pattern generally shows a chain of events. The actions or events are listed in the order in which they occur. This is called *chronological* *order.* Two types of chronological order are narration and process. An author uses narration to describe a chain of points such as a significant event in history or a story. The second type of chronological order is process. Process is used to give directions to a task in order, like in steps, stages, or directions.

Narration: A Chain of Events

Transitions of **time** signal that the writer is describing when things occurred and in what order. The writer presents an event and then shows when each of the additional details or events flowed from the first event. Thus the details follow a logical order based on time.

Stretching your muscles *before* they are warmed up may cause injury.

Notice that this sentence warns about the relationship between stretching muscles, warming up muscles, and possible injury to muscles. The transition word tells us the order in which certain actions should occur and why. Muscles should be warmed up *before* they are stretched to avoid injury.

Transitions Used in the Time Order Pattern for Events or Stages				
after	during	last	often	then
afterward	eventually	later	previously	ultimately
as	finally	meanwhile	second	until
before	first	next	since	when
currently	immediately	now	soon	while

EXAMPLE Determine the logical order of the following seven sentences from a college history textbook. Write **1** in front of the sentence that should come first, **2** by the sentence that should come second, **3** by the sentence that should come third, and so on. (**Hint:** Circle the time transition words.)

The Beringia Land Bridge

___4___ (Eventually), this process dramatically lowered ocean levels.

___5___ (Ultimately), a land bridge emerged in the area of the Bering Strait.

___7___ (Today), 56 miles of ocean separate Siberia from Alaska.

___6___ (At times) this land bridge between Asia and America, *Beringia*, may have been 1,000 miles wide.

___3___ (In turn), these ice caps spread over vast reaches of land.

___2___ Year (after) year water being drawn from the oceans formed into mighty ice caps.

___1___ The world was a much colder place 75,000 years ago; a great ice age, known as the Wisconsin glaciation, had begun.

—Adapted from Martin et al., America and Its People, 3rd ed., p. 5.

EXPLANATION Compare your answers to the sentences arranged in the order used by the author of a college history textbook. The transitions are in **bold** type.

Textbook
Skills

The Beringia Land Bridge

[1]The world was a much colder place 75,000 years ago; a great ice age, known as the Wisconsin glaciation, had begun. [2]**Year after year** water being drawn from the oceans formed into mighty ice caps. [3]**In turn**, these ice caps spread over vast reaches of land. [4]**Eventually**, this process dramatically lowered ocean levels. [5]**Ultimately**, a land bridge emerged in the area of the Bering Strait. [6]**At times** this land bridge between Asia and America, *Beringia*, may have been 1,000 miles wide. [7]**Today**, 56 miles of ocean separate Siberia from Alaska.

—Adapted from America and Its Peoples, Volume 1: A Mosaic in the Making, 3rd ed.,
p. 5 by James Kirby Martin, Randy J. Roberts, Steven Mintz, Linda O. McMurry and
James H. Jones. Copyright © 1997 by Pearson Education, Inc. Printed and Electronically
reproduced by permission of Pearson Education, Inc., Upper Saddle River, NJ.

PRACTICE 4

Determine the logical order for the following six sentences. Write **1** by the sentence that should come first, **2** by the sentence that should come second, **3** by the sentence that should come third, and so on. (**Hint:** Circle the time transition words.)

Textbook
Skills

Initiating

___1___ (During) the first stage of a relationship, we make conscious and unconscious judgments about others.

___2___ Although we are cautious at (this stage), we have usually sized up the other person within 15 seconds.

___4___ (Immediately), he stereotyped and classified available women according to his own personal preferences.

___6___ (Finally), he began a conversation by asking, "Would you like a drink?" "Are you waiting for someone?" "You look like you need company," or "It was nice of you to save me this seat."

___3___ For example, David entered a singles' bar and scanned the room for prospective dancing partners.

___5___ (After) narrowing the field to two women, David planned his approach.

—Adapted from Barker and Gaut,
Communication, 8th ed., p. 131.

Process: Steps, Stages, or Directions

The process thought pattern for steps, stages, or directions shows actions that can be repeated at any time with similar results. This pattern is used to provide steps or give directions for completing a task.

Process: Steps, stages, or directions

Step 1

Step 2

Step 3

Read the following topic sentences. Circle the words that signal process time order.

1. Follow six simple (steps) to lose weight.

2. Photosynthesis is the (process) by which plants harness light energy from the sun.

3. Effective communication occurs through the (cycle) of sending and receiving messages.

Sentence 1 uses the word *steps* to introduce directions for the reader to follow. Sentence 2 uses the word *process* to indicate that these are stages plants undergo in photosynthesis. Sentence 3 signals a pattern of giving and receiving messages in communication using the word *cycle*. In paragraphs that developed these topic sentences, transitions of time order would likely signal the supporting details.

Transitions Used in the Time Order Pattern for Process				
after	during	later	previously	ultimately
afterward	eventually	meanwhile	second	until
as	finally	next	since	when
before	first	now	soon	while
currently	last	often	then	

EXAMPLE The following passage from the government website Small Business Administration uses the time order process to offer advice to people who are starting up their own small businesses. Read the passage and list the major steps to time management for small business owners. (**Hint:** Circle the time order transition words.)

Making Time

¹The (first step) in learning how to manage your time is to develop a general work schedule. ²Your work schedule should include time for yourself as well as time for the maintenance of your business.

³(After) you've defined the major elements of your workload, the (next step) is to prioritize them by identifying critical deadlines, routine maintenance items, and fun/relaxation time. ⁴Answering questions like "How much time do I have to make this decision, finish this task, or contact this person?" will help you to start identifying what needs to be done immediately versus what can wait. ⁵Setting priorities depends on deadlines, how many people you must call to get the information you need, and whether you can delegate or get assistance from others. ⁶If you are involved in group projects, reserve additional time for communication and problem-solving.

⁷(Once) you have identified your priorities, look at all of your options for achieving them. ⁸Evaluate and move forward with the ones you feel are the most useful for you. ⁹The only time to consider changing approaches mid-task is when you know the change will save time. ¹⁰If you are in doubt, it is usually best to consider staying in the direction you started.

[11]By setting up your work schedule and identifying your priorities, you have already started down the road to more effective time management.

—U.S. Small Business Association. "Manage Your Business." 18 March 2010.

VISUAL VOCABULARY

A successful business person must **prioritize** goals. The best synonym for prioritize is b_____.

a. complete.
b. rank.
c. identify.

I. The first step in learning how to manage your time is to develop a general work schedule.

II. After you've defined the major elements of your workload, the next step is to prioritize them by identifying critical deadlines, routine maintenance items, and fun/relaxation time.

III. Once you have identified your priorities, look at all of your options for achieving them.

EXPLANATION Compare your answers to the following:

I. The first step in learning how to manage your time is to develop a general work schedule.

II. After you've defined the major elements of your workload, the next step is to prioritize them by identifying critical deadlines, routine maintenance items, and fun/relaxation time.

III. Once you have identified your priorities, look at all of your options for achieving them.

PRACTICE 5

The following paragraph uses the time order pattern for steps or directions to organize its ideas. Complete the list of steps that follows it by giving the missing details in their proper order. (**Hint:** Circle the time order transition words.)

Seirta's System to Collect and Organize Information

¹During her first week of attending her composition, psychology, and history classes, Seirta noted that each course required class discussion and papers based on current events and how those events relate to the information studied in each course. ²Seirta liked the idea of connecting class work to real life; thus she devised and carried out the following plan. ³First, she skimmed the two newspapers delivered to her home, looking for headlines that tied in to the topics discussed that week in her classes (one paper was the local newspaper; the other was *USA Today*). ⁴As she skimmed, if a piece seemed relevant, she placed a large check with a red pencil next to that headline. ⁵Later, after all her family members had read the papers, she cut out each article she had checked. ⁶While doing so, she was also careful to record the following information directly on the cut-out article: the name of the newspaper, the date of the newspaper, and the section and page number(s) where the article appeared. ⁷Next, she carefully read each article and underlined relevant details with a yellow highlighter. ⁸Often she quickly wrote a paragraph explaining how the article related to a particular concept covered in class. ⁹She stapled her response to the article. ¹⁰Then she placed the article in a file folder labeled with the topic of the article. ¹¹For example, one file folder was labeled "Women in Politics," another was labeled "Gang Violence," and a third was labeled "Stress." ¹²As the semester progressed, she added more articles to each folder or created new folders for new topics. ¹³Seirta deliberately worked quickly so the entire process took less than 30 minutes. ¹⁴Every day, Seirta carried her folders of information with her to class and referred to them during class discussion. ¹⁵When the time came to write an essay, Seirta used much of the information she had collected in her file.

Seirta's System to Collect and Organize Information

Step 1: She skimmed the two newspapers delivered to her home, looking for headlines that tied in to the topics discussed that week in her classes.

Step 2: As she skimmed, if a piece seemed relevant, she placed a large check with a red pencil next to that headline.

Step 3: Later, after all her family members had read the papers, she cut out each article she had checked.

Step 4: While doing so, she was also careful to record the following information directly on the cut-out article: the name of the newspaper, the date of the newspaper, and the section and page number(s) where the article appeared.

Step 5: Next, she carefully read each article and underlined relevant details with a yellow highlighter.

Step 6: Often she quickly wrote a paragraph explaining how the article related to a particular concept covered in class.

Step 7: She stapled her response to the article.

Step 8: Then she placed the article in a file folder labeled with the topic of the article.

Step 9: As the semester progressed, she added more articles to each folder or created new folders for new topics.

Step 10: Every day, Seirta carried her folders of information with her to class and referred to them during class discussion.

Step 11: When the time came to write an essay, Seirta used much of the information she had collected in her file.

The Space Order Pattern

The **space order pattern** allows authors to describe a person, place, or thing based on its location or the way it is arranged in space. In the space order pattern, also known as spatial order, the writer often uses descriptive details to help readers create vivid mental pictures of the subject being described. An author may choose to describe an object from top to bottom, from bottom to top, from right to left, from left to right, from near to far, from far to near, from inside to outside, or from outside to inside.

> ## Space Order: Descriptive Details
> Descriptive detail 1 ➡ Descriptive detail 2 ➡ Descriptive detail 3

Transition words of **space order** signal that the details follow a logical order based on two elements: (1) how the object, place, or person is arranged in space, and (2) the starting point from which the author chooses to begin the description.

Transition Words Used in the Space Order Pattern

above	at the side	below	center	front	middle	there
across	at the top	beneath	close to	here	nearby	under
adjacent	back	beside	down	in	next to	underneath
around	backup	beyond	far away	inside	outside	within
at the bottom	behind	by	farther	left	right	

EXAMPLE Determine a logical order for the following six sentences. Write **1** by the sentence that should come first, **2** in front of the sentence that should come second, **3** in front of the sentence that should come third, **4** in front of the sentence that should come fourth, **5** in front of the sentence that should come fifth, and **6** in front of the sentence that should come last. (**Hint:** Circle the space order transition words.)

___1___ (In) a tropical rain forest, vertical stratification, or layering, provides several discernible strata or layers of plant growth.

___2___ (At the upper) canopy level, the treetops range from 100 to 160 feet, (out of) which emergents may soar to 200 feet.

___4___ The (middle) layer contains another level of treetops that are covered with vines and air plants.

___6___ The (lowest) and the thinnest layer is the forest (floor) of seedlings, shoots, and herbaceous plants.

___5___ (Between the middle layer and the forest floor) is the shrub (understory); thus very little light passes through the dense middle layer to the forest floor.

___3___ This (upper) canopy is uneven, allowing sunlight to filter through treetops to the middle layer.

EXPLANATION Compare your answers to the sentences arranged in the proper order in the paragraph below. The transition words are in **bold** print.

> [1]**In** a tropical rain forest, vertical stratification, or layering, provides several discernible strata or layers of plant growth. [2]**At the upper** canopy level, the treetops range from 100 to 160 feet, **out of** which emergents may soar to 200 feet. [3]This **upper** canopy is uneven, allowing sunlight to filter through treetops to the middle layer. [4]The **middle** layer contains another level of treetops that are covered with vines and air plants. [5]**Between the middle layer and the forest floor** is the shrub **understory;** thus very little light passes through the dense **middle** layer to the forest floor. [6]The **lowest** and the thinnest layer is the forest **floor** of seedlings, shoots, and herbaceous plants.

PRACTICE 6

Textbook
Skills

Determine a logical order for the following five sentences. Write **1** in front of the sentence that should come first, **2** in front of the sentence that should come second, **3** in front of the sentence that should come third, **4** in front of the sentence that should come fourth, and **5** in front of the sentence that should come last. (**Hint:** Circle the space order transition words.)

The Anatomy of a Generalized Cell

____4____ In turn, the cytoplasm is enclosed by the plasma membrane.

____5____ The plasma membrane forms the outer cell boundary.

VISUAL VOCABULARY

Label the three regions of a generalized cell.

a. cytoplasm
b. nucleus
c. plasma membrane

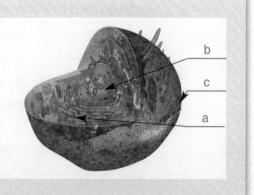

   3   The nucleus is (surrounded by) the semifluid cytoplasm.

   2   The nucleus is usually located (near the center) of the cell.

   1   In general, all cells have three main (regions); the *nucleus* (nu´kle-us), *cytoplasm* (si´to-plazm´´), and a plasma membrane.

—From *Essentials of Human Anatomy and Physiology,* 9th ed., p. 66 and figure by Elaine N. Marieb. Copyright © 2009 by Pearson Education, Inc. Reprinted by permission of Pearson Education, Inc., Glenview, IL.

The Listing Pattern

Often authors want to present an orderly series or set of reasons, details, or points. These details are listed in an order that the author has chosen. Changing the order of the details does not change their meaning. Transitions of addition, such as *and, also,* and *furthermore,* are generally used to indicate a *listing pattern.*

Listing Pattern
Idea 1
Idea 2
Idea 3

Transitions of **addition** signal that the writer is adding to an earlier thought. The writer presents an idea and then *adds* other ideas to deepen or clarify the first idea. Thus, transitions of addition are used to establish the listing pattern.

Addition Transitions Used in the Listing Pattern				
also	final	for one thing	last of all	second
and	finally	furthermore	moreover	third
another	first	in addition	next	
besides	first of all	last	one	

EXAMPLE Refer to the box of addition transitions used in the listing pattern. Complete the following paragraph with transitions that show the appropriate relationship between sentences. Answers may vary.

Benefits of Weightlifting

Weightlifting is an exercise that offers many benefits. **(1)** First_____, increased muscle mass causes the body to burn fat, and lowered body fat reduces several health risks. **(2)** In addition_____, weightlifting builds bone density and thus reduces the risk of osteoporosis (brittle bones). **(3)** Finally_____, weightlifting increases strength, independence, and self-confidence.

EXPLANATION   Compare your answers to the following:

Benefits of Weightlifting

[1]Weightlifting is an exercise that offers many benefits. [2]**First**, increased muscle mass causes the body to burn fat, and lowered body fat reduces several health risks. [3]**In addition**, weightlifting builds bone density and thus reduces the risk of osteoporosis (brittle bones). [4]**Finally**, weightlifting increases strength, independence, and self-confidence.

The paragraph on the benefits of weightlifting begins with a general idea that is then followed by three major supporting details. Each detail requires a transition to show addition.

PRACTICE 7

The following paragraph adapted from a college health textbook uses the listing thought pattern. Finish the outline that follows it by listing the major supporting details in their proper order. (**Hint:** Circle the addition transition words.)

Life Style Assessment

Textbook
Skills

[1]Life style assessment is an important life skill. [2]First, life style assessment raises "awareness of areas that increase risk of disease, injury, and possibly premature death." [3]For example, examining specific patterns of behavior such as eating and sleeping allows us to be sure we are acting in healthy ways. [4]In addition, life style assessment increases the likelihood of making more positive life style choices in areas that have been unhealthy. [5]For example, smokers who think seriously about how many cigarettes they smoke in a day, how much money they spend weekly on smoking, and whether they have a chronic smoker's cough will understand the costs and risks of smoking better. [6]Once the risks become

real, our behaviors are easier to change. [7](Besides) assessing eating, sleeping, (and) patterns of addiction, life style assessment looks at other patterns of behavior related to stress, relationships, physical fitness, (and) so on. [8]The (final) point to remember is that you have control over your life style choices.

—Adapted from Powers & Dodd, *Behavior Change Log Book*, 3rd ed., pp. 1–3.

Life Style Assessment

Life style assessment is an important life skill.

A. First, life style assessment raises "awareness of areas that increase risk of

disease, injury, and possibly premature death."

B. In addition, life style assessment increases the likelihood of making more

positive life style choices in areas that have been unhealthy.

C. Besides assessing eating, sleeping, and patterns of addiction, life style

assessment looks at other patterns of behavior related to stress, relationships,

physical fitness, and so on.

D. The final point to remember is that you have control over your life style choices.

The Classification Pattern

Authors use the **classification pattern** to sort ideas into smaller groups and describe the traits of each group. Each smaller group, called a *subgroup*, is based on shared traits or characteristics. The author lists each subgroup and describes its traits.

Because groups and subgroups are listed, transitions of addition are also used in this thought pattern. These transitions are coupled with words that indicate classes or groups. Examples of classification signal words are *first type, second kind, another group, order,* and *traits.*

Transitions Used in the Classification Pattern	
another (group, kind, type)	first (group, category, kind, type)
characteristics	second (group, class, kind, type)

EXAMPLE   Determine a logical order for the following sentences. Write **1** in front of the sentence that should come first, **2** in front of the sentence that should come second, **3** in front of the sentence that should come third, and **4** in front of the sentence that should come last. (**Hint:** Circle the classification signal words.)

Types of Process Addictions

Textbook
Skills

___3___ (Another type) of process addiction is money addiction, which includes gambling, spending, and borrowing; money addicts develop tolerance and also experience withdrawal symptoms such as depression, anxiety, and anger.

___2___ (One type) of process addiction is work addiction, marked by the compulsive use of work and the work persona to fulfill needs of intimacy, power, and success.

___4___ A (third type) of this kind of addiction is exercise addiction; addictive exercisers abuse exercise the same way that alcoholics abuse alcohol and face effects similar to those found in other addictions: alienation of family and friends, injuries from overdoing it, and a craving for more.

___1___ Process addictions are behaviors known to be addictive because they are mood-altering.

—Adapted from *Access to Health*, 7th ed., pp. 317–320 by Rebecca J. Donatelle and Lorraine G. Davis. Copyright © 2002 by Pearson Education, Inc. Printed and Electronically reproduced by permission of Pearson Education, Inc., Upper Saddle River, NJ.

EXPLANATION   Compare your answers to the sentences arranged in their proper order in the paragraph below. The transition words are in **bold** type.

Types of Process Addictions

[1]Process addictions are behaviors known to be addictive because they are mood-altering. [2]**One type** of process addiction is work addiction, marked by the compulsive use of work and the work persona to fulfill

needs of intimacy, power, and success. **³Another type** of process addiction is money addiction, which includes gambling, spending, and borrowing; money addicts develop tolerance and also experience withdrawal symptoms such as depression, anxiety, and anger. **⁴A third type** of this kind of addiction is exercise addiction; addictive exercisers abuse exercise the same way that alcoholics abuse alcohol and face effects similar to those found in other addictions: alienation of family and friends, injuries from overdoing it, and a craving for more.

In this paragraph, transitions of addition work with the classification signal words. In this case, *one*, *another*, and *third* convey the order of the types listed.

PRACTICE 8

The following passage uses the classification pattern of organization. Fill in the outline that follows by giving the missing major details in their proper order. (**Hint:** Circle the classification transition words.)

Types of Volcanoes

¹Geologists generally group volcanoes into four main kinds—cinder cones, composite volcanoes, shield volcanoes, and lava domes. ²The first type, the cinder cone volcanoes, are the simplest type of volcano. ³They are built from particles and blobs of congealed lava ejected from a single vent. ⁴As the gas-charged lava is blown violently into the air, it breaks into small fragments that solidify and fall as *cinders* around the vent to form a circular or oval cone. ⁵Most cinder cones have a bowl-shaped *crater* at the summit and rarely rise more than a thousand feet or so above their surroundings.

⁶The second type of volcano is the *composite* volcano. ⁷The essential feature of a composite volcano is a conduit system through which magma from a reservoir deep in the Earth's crust rises to the surface. ⁸The volcano is built up by the accumulation of material erupted through the conduit and increases in size as lava, cinders, ash, and so on, are added to its slopes. ⁹Most composite volcanoes have a crater at the summit which contains a central vent or a clustered group of vents. ¹⁰Lavas either flow through breaks in the crater wall or issue from fissures on the flanks of the cone. ¹¹Lava, solidified within the fissures, forms dikes that act as ribs, which greatly strengthen the cone.

¹²Shield volcanoes, the third type of volcano, are built almost entirely of fluid lava flows. ¹³Flow after flow pours out in all directions from a central

summit vent, or group of vents, building a broad, gently sloping cone of flat, domical shape, with a profile much like that of a warrior's shield. [14]They are built up slowly by the accretion of thousands of highly fluid lava flows called basalt lava that spread widely over great distances, and then cool as thin, gently dipping sheets. [15]Lavas also commonly erupt from vents along fractures (rift zones) that develop on the flanks of the cone.

[16]The (fourth type), volcanic or lava domes, are formed by relatively small, bulbous masses of lava too viscous to flow any great distance; consequently, on extrusion, the lava piles over and around its vent. [17]A dome grows largely by expansion from within. [18]As it grows, its outer surface cools and hardens, then shatters, spilling loose fragments down its sides. [19]Some domes form craggy knobs or spines over the volcanic vent, whereas others form short, steep-sided lava flows known as "coulees." [20]Volcanic domes commonly occur within the craters or on the flanks of large composite volcanoes.

—Adapted from Tilling, "Volcanoes," 6 Feb. 1997, U.S. Geological Survey. 22 Dec. 2003 http://pubs.usgs.gov/gip/volc/types.html

Types of Volcanoes

I.   Cinder cones _____

II. Composite volcanoes _____

III. Shield volcanoes _____

IV. Volcanic or lava domes _____

VISUAL VOCABULARY

Which type of volcano is this Hawaiian volcano?

a _____

a. cinder cone
b. shield
c. composite
d. lava dome

Reading a Textbook: Thought Patterns in Textbooks

Textbook authors often use transitions to make relationships between ideas clear and easy to understand. However, often an author will use more than one type of transition. For example, classification combines words that indicate addition and types. Sometimes addition and time words are used in the same paragraph or passage for a specific purpose. Furthermore, authors may mix thought patterns in the same paragraph or passage. Finally, be aware that relationships between ideas still exist even when transition words are not explicitly stated. The master reader looks for the author's primary thought pattern.

EXAMPLE Read the following paragraphs from college textbooks. Circle the transitions or signal words used in each paragraph. Then, identify the primary thought pattern used in the paragraph.

A.   **Reinforcement**

¹A positive reinforcement is a reward that is given to increase the likelihood that a behavior change will occur. ²Most positive reinforcers can be classified under five headings. ³The first type is consumable reinforcers, which are delicious edibles, such as candy, cookies, or gourmet meals. ⁴Second, activity reinforcers are opportunities to do something enjoyable, such as to watch TV, go on a vacation, or go swimming. ⁵Third, manipulative reinforcers are incentives, such as getting a lower rent in exchange for mowing the lawn or the promise of a better grade for doing an extra-credit project. ⁶A fourth type of positive reinforcer is the possessional reinforcers, which are tangible rewards, such as a new TV or a sports car. ⁷The final type consists of social reinforcers that express signs of appreciation, approval, or love, such as loving looks, affectionate hugs, and praise.

—Adapted from *Health: The Basics*, 5th ed., p. 21 by Rebecca J. Donatelle. Copyright © 2003 by Pearson Education, Inc. Printed and Electronically reproduced by permission of Pearson Education, Inc. Upper Saddle River, NJ.

_____b_____ The primary thought pattern of the paragraph is
    a. time order.   b. classification.

B.   **Interpersonal Perception**

¹Interpersonal perception is a continuous series of processes that blend into one another. ²For convenience of discussion we can separate them into five stages. ³During the first stage, you sense, you pick up some

kind of stimulation. ⁴Next, you organize the stimuli in some way. ⁵Third, you interpret and evaluate what you perceive. ⁶Then, you store it in memory, and finally, in stage five, you retrieve it when needed.

—Adapted from *The Interpersonal Communication Book*, 10th ed., p. 91 by Joseph A. DeVito. Copyright © 2004 by Pearson Education, Inc. Reproduced by permission of Pearson Education, Inc., Boston, MA.

___a___ The primary thought pattern of the paragraph is
  a. time order.   b. listing.

EXPLANATION Compare your answers to the following answers.

Passage A, "Reinforcement," is organized by (b) classification.

Passage B, "Interpersonal Perception," is organized by (a) time order.

PRACTICE 9

Read the following paragraph taken from a college communications textbook. Circle the transitions or signal words used in the passage. Then, identify the primary thought pattern used in the paragraph.

Skill Acquisition

Textbook
Skills

¹You may develop communication apprehensions largely because you see yourself as having inadequate skills. ²So you logically fear failing. ³The following suggestions will enable you to acquire the skills necessary to master your fears. ⁴First, prepare and practice. ⁵The more preparation and practice you put into something, the more comfortable you feel with it, and, thus, the less anxious you feel. ⁶Second, focus on success. ⁷Think positively. ⁸Concentrate your energies on doing the very best job you can in whatever situation you are in. ⁹Visualize yourself succeeding, and you stand a good chance of doing just that. ¹⁰Third, familiarize yourself with the situation. ¹¹The more familiar you are with the situation, the better. ¹²The reason is simple: When you're familiar with the situation and with what will be expected of you, you're better able to predict what will happen.

—Adapted from *The Interpersonal Communication Book*, 10th ed., p. 87 by Joseph A. DeVito. Copyright © 2004 by Pearson Education, Inc. Reproduced by permission of Pearson Education, Inc., Boston, MA.

___b___ The primary thought pattern used in the paragraph is
  a. time order.   b. listing.

APPLICATIONS

Application 1: Identifying Transitions

Fill in each blank with one of the words from the box below. Use each word once.

during	eventually	now	within

(1) <u>During</u> the last ice age (about 10,000 years ago), the Sahara was largely savanna and supported animals like giraffes, lions, and elephants, which are now found in East Africa, plus wandering bands of hunters. With the warming and drying trend of the past 10,000 years, the savanna gave way to desert grassland, which supported herds of cattle. The herders and the cattle (2) <u>eventually</u> disappeared as the desert reclaimed the land, from about 8,000 years ago to the present.

In Roman times, however, the region just east of the Atlas Mountains was still able to support irrigated fields of wheat, and the area which is (3) <u>now</u> stark desert was known as the bread basket of the Roman Empire.

Today, an estimated 2 million people live (4) <u>within</u> the Sahara Desert. About two-thirds of these people are concentrated in oases, and the remaining one-third are nomadic people who travel throughout the desert.

—Adapted from "People," *Sahara*, PBS. org, December 29, 2003, http://www.pbs.org/sahara/people/people.htm Reprinted by permission of Telenova Productions.

Application 2: Identifying Thought Patterns

Identify the thought pattern suggested by each of the following topic sentences taken from college textbooks.

a   **1.** It is convenient to divide up conversation into chunks or stages and view each stage as a choice as to what you'll say and how you'll say it.

—Adapted from *The Interpersonal Communication Book,* 10th ed., p. 214 by Joseph A. DeVito. Copyright © 2004 by Pearson Education, Inc. Reproduced by permission of Pearson Education, Inc., Boston, MA.

    a. time order   b. space order

b   **2.** The use of genetically modified organisms in agriculture is controversial for two major reasons.

—From *Life on Earth,* 5th ed., p. 207 by Teresa Audesirk, Gerald Audesirk, and Bruce E. Byers. Copyright © 2009 by Pearson Education, Inc. Printed and Electronically reproduced by permission of Pearson Education, Inc., Upper Saddle River, NJ.

    a. time order   b. listing

b   **3.** The most popular types of insurance are term insurance, whole life insurance, and universal life insurance.

—From *Personal Finance,* 2nd ed., p. 345 by Jeff Madura. Copyright © 2004 by Pearson Education, Inc. Reproduced by permission of Pearson Education, Inc., Boston, MA.

    a. time order   b. classification

a   **4.** The civilization that would become the Roman Empire arose at the same time as that of ancient Greece.

—From *The Creative Impulse: An Introduction to the Arts,* 8th ed., p. 113 by Dennis J. Sporre. Copyright © 2009 by Pearson Education, Inc. Reprinted by permission of Pearson Education, Inc., Upper Saddle River, NJ.

    a. time order   b. listing

b   **5.** English builds all sentences on five basic sentence patterns.

—Fowler and Aaron, *The Little, Brown Handbook,* 9th ed., p. 243.

    a. space order   b. classification

REVIEW TEST 1   Score (number correct) _____ × 10 = _____ %

Transitions and Thought Patterns

Fill in each blank with a transition from the box. Use each transition once. Then, answer the questions that follow the paragraph.

already	and	in addition	when
also	another	one	

Textbook Skills

10.5 GE/149 words

Barriers to Memory

It is likely that you will remember things that support your position **(1)** _and_ forget or distort information that contradicts your current beliefs. **(2)** _One_ reason, of course, may be selective attention; you focus on things you want to hear or things you expect to hear. Distortion can **(3)** _also_ be explained, in part, through schema theory. Ideas that fit into your existing framework are stored more readily than bits of information that don't make sense in light of what you **(4)** _already_ know. **(5)** _In addition_, threatening or unpleasant experiences are often blocked, or repressed, while positive images remain vivid. **(6)** _Another_ reason why you forget is that the information you are trying to store in long-term memory becomes mixed with information already in your memory system. **(7)** _When_ these two information sets become confused, there is a "backward" impact of new learning on the material stored earlier.

—Adapted from *Listening: Attitudes, Principles, and Skills*, 2nd ed. pp. 155–156 by Judi Brownell. Copyright © 2002 by Pearson Education, Inc. Reproduced by permission of Pearson Education, Inc., Boston, MA.

_____a_____ **8.** The relationship signaled by the word **already** is
   a. time order.   b. classification.

_____a_____ **9.** The relationship signaled by the transition word **one** is
   a. addition.   b. space order.

_____a_____ **10.** The overall thought pattern of the paragraph is
   a. listing.   b. time order.

REVIEW TEST 2   Score (number correct) _____ × 10 = _____ %

Transitions

Select a transition word for each of the blanks. Then, identify the type of transition you chose.

A. The thief had bought thousands of dollars worth of goods with Aimee's credit card _____ she even knew it was missing.

____c____ **1.** The best transition word for sentence A is
     a. meanwhile.   c. before.
     b. after.

____b____ **2.** The relationship between the ideas in sentence A is one of
     a. classification.   b. time order.

B. Every cell has a plasma membrane which forms its _____ border and sets the cell off from its fluid environment.

____b____ **3.** The best transition word for the sentence above is
     a. another.   c. one.
     b. outside.

____a____ **4.** The relationship between the ideas above is one of
     a. space order.   b. addition.

C. Everything inside a cell _____ the plasma membrane and the nucleus is called the cytoplasm.

____a____ **5.** The best transition word for the sentence above is
     a. between.   c. since.
     b. before.

____b____ **6.** The relationship between the ideas above is one of
     a. listing.   b. space order.

D. Poetry can be broken into two very broad groups. The first type, dramatic poetry, tells a story using characters, setting, and conflict. The _____, lyric poetry, directly expresses the emotions of the poet.

____b____ **7.** The best transition word or phrase for the sentences in section D is
     a. additional part.   c. later time.
     b. second type.

_____a_____ **8.** The relationship between the ideas in the sentences in section D is one of

  a. classification.   b. time order.

E.   ¹For producing electricity, hydropower has two clear advantages over fossil fuels. ²First, it is renewable; as long as precipitation falls from the sky and fills rivers and reservoirs, we can use water to turn turbines. ³The _____ advantage of hydropower over fossil fuels is its cleanliness. ⁴No carbon compounds are burned in the production of hydropower, so no carbon dioxide or other pollutants are emitted into the atmosphere. ⁵Of course, fossil fuels are used in constructing and maintaining dams. ⁶Moreover, recent evidence indicates that reservoirs release the greenhouse gas methane as a result of anaerobic decay in deep water. ⁷Overall, hydropower accounts for only a fraction of the greenhouse gas emissions typical of fossil fuel combustion.

—From *Essential Environment: The Science Behind the Stories*, 3rd ed., p. 363 by Jay H. Withgott and Scott R. Brennan. Copyright © 2009 by Pearson Education, Inc. Reprinted by permission of Pearson Education, Inc., Upper Saddle River, NJ.

_____c_____ **9.** The best transition word for the blank in sentence 3 is

  a. later.   c. second.
  b. addition.

_____b_____ **10.** The main thought pattern of the paragraph is

  a. time order.   b. listing.

VISUAL VOCABULARY

The Grand Coulee Dam in Washington State, the largest electric power-producing facility in the United States, is an example of hydropower. The best meaning of hydro is

_____d_____.

  a. electric.
  b. pressure.
  c. wind.
  d. water.

REVIEW TEST 3   Score (number correct) _____ × 5 = _____ %

Transitions and Thought Patterns

Textbook Skills

The following passage appears in a college psychology textbook. Before you read, skim the passage and answer the Before Reading questions. Read the passage. Then, answer the After Reading questions.

Categorizing Personality by Types

12.9 GE/584 words

[1]We are always categorizing people according to distinguishing features. [2]These include college class, academic major, sex, and race. [3]Some personality theorists also group people into distinct, nonoverlapping categories that are called personality **types**. [4]Personality types are all-or-none **phenomena**, not matters of degree: If a person is assigned to one type, he or she could not belong to any other type within that system. [5]Many people like to use personality types in everyday life because they help simplify the complex process of understanding other people.

[6]One of the earliest type theories was originated in the 5th century B.C. by Hippocrates, the Greek physician who gave medicine the Hippocratic Oath. [7]He theorized that the body contained four basic fluids, or **humors**, each associated with a particular temperament, a pattern of emotions and behaviors. [8]In the 2nd century A.D., a later Greek physician, Galen, suggested that an individual's personality depended on which humor was predominant in his or her body. [9]Galen paired Hippocrates's body humors with personality temperaments according to the following scheme:

- [10]**Blood**. Sanguine temperament: cheerful and active
- [11]**Phlegm**. **Phlegmatic** temperament: apathetic and sluggish
- [12]**Black bile**. Melancholy temperament: sad and brooding
- [13]**Yellow bile**. Choleric temperament: irritable and excitable

[14]The theory proposed by Galen was believed for centuries, up through the Middle Ages, although it has not held up to modern scrutiny.

[15]In modern times, William Sheldon (1898–1977) originated a type theory that related physique to temperament. [16]Sheldon (1942) assigned people to three categories based on their body builds: *endomorphic* (fat, soft, round), *mesomorphic* (muscular, rectangular, strong), or *ectomorphic* (thin, long, fragile). [17]Sheldon believed that endomorphs are relaxed, fond of eating, and sociable. [18]Mesomorphs are physical people, filled with energy, courage, and assertive tendencies. [19]Ectomorphs are brainy, artistic, and introverted; they would think about life, rather than consuming it or acting

on it. [20]For a period of time, Sheldon's theory was sufficiently influential that nude "posture" photographs were taken of thousands of students at U.S. colleges like Yale and Wellesley to allow researchers to study the relationships between body type and life factors. [21]However, like Hippocrates's much earlier theory, Sheldon's notion of body types has proven to be of very little value in predicting an individual's behavior (Tyler, 1965).

[22]More recently, Frank Sulloway (1996) has proposed a contemporary type theory based on birth order. [23]Are you the firstborn child (or only child) in your family, or are you a laterborn child? [24]Because you can take on only one of these birth positions, Sulloway's theory fits the criteria for being a type theory. [25](For people with unusual family constellations—for example, a very large age gap between two children—Sulloway still provides ways of categorizing individuals.) [26]Sulloway makes birth-order predictions based on Darwin's idea that organisms diversify to find niches in which they will survive. [27]According to Sulloway, firstborns have a ready-made niche: They immediately command their parents' love and attention; they seek to maintain that initial attachment by identifying and complying with their parents. [28]By contrast, laterborn children need to find a different niche—one in which they don't so clearly follow their parents' example. [29]As a consequence, Sulloway characterizes laterborns as "born to rebel": "they seek to excel in those domains where older siblings have not already established superiority. [30]Laterborns typically cultivate openness to experience—a useful strategy for anyone who wishes to find a novel and successful niche in life" (Sulloway, 1996, p. 353).

—From *Psychology and Life*, 19th ed., pp. 407–408 by Richard J. Gerrig and Philip G. Zimbardo. Copyright © 2010 by Pearson Education, Inc. Reproduced by permission of Pearson Education, Inc., Boston, MA.

Before Reading

Vocabulary in Context

_b_   **1.** The word **phenomena** in sentence 4 means
    a. spectacles.   c. facts.
    b. experiences.   d. features.

_c_   **2.** The best meaning of the word **humors** in sentence 7 is
    a. funny qualities.   c. effects of body fluids.
    b. emotions.   d. behaviors.

_a_   **3.** The best synonym for the word **phlegmatic** in sentence 10 is
    a. unmotivated.   c. calm.
    b. sickly.   d. determined.

After Reading

Concept Maps and Graphic Organizers

4–15. Complete the following two-column notes with information from the passage.

Categorizing Personality by Types	
Theorist	**Theories of Personality Type**
4. Hippocrates and Galen	**5.** Blood. Sanguine temperament: cheerful and active
	6. Phlegm. Phlegmatic temperament: apathetic and sluggish
	Black bile. Melancholy temperament: sad and brooding
	7. Yellow bile. Choleric temperament: irritable and excitable
8. William Sheldon	**9.** Endomorphic (fat, soft, round)
	10. Mesomorphic (muscular, rectangular, strong)
	11. Ectomorphic (thin, long, fragile)
12. Frank Sulloway	**13.** Firstborn command parents' love and attention; identify and comply with parents
	14. Laterborn are born to rebel; they seek to excel in those domains where older siblings have not already established superiority

Central Ideas

_____ c **15.** Which sentence states the central idea of the essay?
- a. sentence 1
- b. sentence 2
- c. sentence 3
- d. sentence 5

Supporting Details

_____c_____ **16.** Sentence 20 states a

    a. a main idea.   c. minor supporting detail.

    b. major supporting detail.

Transitions and Thought Patterns

_____b_____ **17.** What thought pattern does the word **types** in sentence 3 signal?

    a time order   c. space order

    b. classification

_____a_____ **18.** What is the relationship of ideas within sentence 16?

    a. listing   c. space order

    b. time order

_____a_____ **19.** What is the relationship of ideas between sentence 7 and sentence 8?

    a. time order   c. listing

    b. classification

_____c_____ **20.** Based on the title, the main thought pattern of the passage is

    a. time order.   c. classification.

    b. space order.

WHAT DO YOU THINK?

Do you know people whom you would label as particular "types"? What particular "type" are you? Does "type" include all there is to know about the person? Assume you are taking a college level psychology class, and your professor has given you the following assignment: Choose a fictional character from a television show, movie, book, graphic novel, etc. Analyze the character using each of the personality types described in the passage. Describe the moods and behaviors of the character to support your use of each label.

REVIEW TEST 4

Score (number correct) _____ × 10 = _____ %

Transitions and Thought Patterns

Textbook Skills

Before Reading: Survey the following passage from the college textbook _Life on Earth_. Skim the passage, noting the words in **bold** print. Answer the Before Reading questions that follow the passage. Then, read the passage. Next, answer the After Reading questions. Use the discussion and writing topics as after reading activities.

11.0 GE/830 words

Vocabulary Preview

mammalian (3): related to mammals, animals that have a spine and milk glands

mechanoreceptor (3): a nerve ending that responds to a mechanical stimulus (as in a change of pressure)

auditory (12): hearing

cerebellum (12): located at the back of the brain, the control center for muscle tone, balance, and coordination of movement

pharynx (14): a hollow tube that begins behind the nose and ends at the top of the windpipe

membrane (17): a thin barrier that surrounds a cell or parts of a cell

receptors (20): receivers

basilar (21): located at the base of a structure

cilia (22): short, hairlike projections from the surface of certain cells. The movement of cilia aids the movement of cells and fluids

The Perception of Sound Is a Specialized Type of Mechanoreception

[1]Sound is produced by any vibrating object—a drum, vocal cords, or the speaker of your CD player. [2]These vibrations, or sound waves, are transmitted through the air and intercepted by our ears, which convert them to signals that our brains interpret as the direction, pitch, and loudness of sound. [3]The **mammalian** ear consists of a variety of structures (for example, the outer ear and eardrum) that transmit vibrations to specialized **mechanoreceptor** cells deep in the inner ear.

The Ear Converts Sound Waves into Electrical Signals

[4]The ear of humans and most other vertebrates consists of three parts: the outer, middle, and inner ear. [5]The *outer ear* consists of the *pinna* and *auditory canal.* [6]The pinna is the flap of skin-covered cartilage attached to the surface of the head. [7]The pinna collects sound waves and modifies them in various ways. [8]Humans and other fairly large animals determine sound direction by differences in *when* sound arrives at the two ears and in *how loud* it is in each ear. [9]The shape and mobility of the pinna further contribute to sound localization. [10]Bats have probably the most precise sound localization in the animal kingdom. [11]Insect-eating bats emit extremely high-pitched shrieks that reflect off moths and other insect prey. [12]Large ears, a highly developed **auditory** cortex, and an enormous **cerebellum** (for precise control of flying) combine to allow the bats to intercept their flying prey in pitch darkness.

[13]The air-filled auditory canal conducts the sound waves to the *middle ear,* consisting of the *tympanic membrane,* or *eardrum;* three tiny bones called the *hammer, anvil,* and *stirrup;* and the auditory tube (also called the *Eustachian tube*). [14]The auditory tube connects the middle ear to the **pharynx** and equalizes the air pressure between the middle ear and the atmosphere.

[15]Sound waves traveling down the auditory canal vibrate the tympanic membrane, which in turn vibrates the hammer, the anvil, and the stirrup. [16]These bones transmit vibrations to

embedded (23): fixed in, set in

gelatinous (23): a jelly-like texture, quality, or consistency

potentials (25): stored energies

axons (26): large extensions of nerve cells, reaching from the cell body to the ends of other nerve cells or muscles

the *inner ear,* which contains the spiral-shaped *cochlea.* [17]The stirrup bone transmits vibrations to the fluid within the cochlea by vibrating a **membrane** on the cochlea called the *oval window.* [18]The *round window* is a second membrane that allows fluid within the cochlea to shift back and forth as the stirrup bone vibrates the oval window.

Sound Is Converted into Electrical Signals in the Cochlea

[19]The cochlea, in cross section, consists of three fluid-filled canals. [20]The central canal houses the **receptors** and the supporting structures that activate them in response to sound vibrations. [21]The floor of this central canal is the *basilar membrane,* on top of which sit mechanoreceptors called *hair cells.* [22]Hair cells have small cell bodies topped by hairlike projections that resemble stiff **cilia**. [23]Some of these hairs are **embedded** in a **gelatinous** structure called the *tectorial membrane.*

[24]The oval window passes vibrations from the bones of the middle ear to the fluid in the cochlea, which in turn vibrates the basilar membrane relative to the tectorial membrane. [25]This movement bends the hairs of the hair cells, producing receptor **potentials**. [26]The hair cells _____ release **neurotransmitters** onto neurons whose **axons** form the auditory nerve. [27]Action potentials triggered in these axons travel to auditory processing centers within the brain.

[28]The structures of the inner ear allow us to perceive *loudness* (the magnitude of sound vibrations) and *pitch* (the frequency of sound vibrations). [29]Soft sounds cause small vibrations, which bend the hairs only slightly and result in a small receptor potential and a low rate of action potentials in axons of the auditory nerve. [30]Loud sounds cause large vibrations, which cause greater bending of the hairs, a larger receptor potential, and a high rate of action potentials in the axons of the auditory nerve. [31]Loud sounds sustained for a long time can damage the hair cells, resulting in hearing loss, a fate suffered by many rock musicians and their fans. [32]In fact, many sounds in our everyday environment have the potential to damage hearing, especially if exposure to them is prolonged.

[33]The perception of pitch is a little more complex. [34]The basilar membrane resembles a harp in shape and stiffness: narrow and stiff at the end near the oval window but wider and more flexible near the tip of the cochlea. [35]In a harp, the short, tight strings produce high notes and the long, looser strings produce low notes. [36]In the basilar membrane, the **progressive** change in shape and stiffness causes each portion to

vibrate most strongly to a particular frequency of sound: high notes near the oval window and low notes near the tip of the cochlea. [37]The brain interprets signals from hair cells near the oval window as high-pitched sound, whereas signals from hair cells located progressively closer to the tip of the cochlea are interpreted as increasingly lower in pitch. [38]Young people with undamaged cochleas can detect sounds from about 30 vibrations per second (very low pitched) to about 20,000 vibrations per second (very high pitched).

—From *Life on Earth*, 5th ed., pp. 476–477 by Teresa Audesirk, Gerald Audesirk and Bruce E. Byers. Copyright © 2009 by Pearson Education, Inc. Reprinted by permission of Pearson Education, Inc., Upper Saddle River, NJ.

Before Reading

Vocabulary

1–2. Study the following chart of word parts. Read the sentences in which the words appear for context clues. Then, use your own words to define the terms.

Prefix	Meaning	Root	Meaning	Suffix	Meaning
pro-	before	gress	to step	-er	doer
trans-	across	mitt	to send	-ive	of, relating to, the quality or nature of
		neuron	nerve cell		

1. In sentence 26, **neurotransmitters** are <u>senders of information from one nerve cell to another nerve cell</u>.

2. In sentence 36, **progressive** means <u>moving forward, advancing</u>

After Reading

3–5. Central Idea and Supporting Details

Complete the following study notes with information from the passage and the illustration of the ear in the Visual Vocabulary activity.

Thesis Statement: (3) <u>The ear of humans and most other vertebrates consists of three parts: the outer, middle, and inner ear</u>.

Questions Based on Major Supporting Details	Answers Based on Minor Supporting Details
What does the outer ear consist of?	the flap-like pinna and the auditory canal
What does the middle ear consist of?	the tympanic membrane (eardrum); three bones called the hammer, (4) _____anvil_____, and stirrup; and the auditory tube (Eustachian tube)
What does the inner ear consist of?	the (5) _____cochlea_____ (three fluid-filled chambers); the basilar membrane; hair cells, and the auditory nerve

Transitions and Thought Patterns

_____b_____   **6.** The main thought pattern for the fifth paragraph (sentences 19–23) is
   a. time order.   c. listing.
   b. space order.

VISUAL VOCABULARY

▲ The Human Ear

—From *Life on Earth*, 5th ed., Figure 24-16a (p. 476) by Teresa Audesirk, Gerald Audesirk and Bruce E. Byers. Copyright © 2009 by Pearson Education, Inc. Reprinted by permission of Pearson Education, Inc., Upper Saddle River, NJ.

___c___   **7.** What is the relationship of ideas within sentence 4?
a. time order   c. classifications
b. space order

___a___   **8.** What is the main relationship of ideas between sentences 13 and 14?
a. space order   c. listing
b. time order

___a___   **9.** Which is the best transition word(s) for the blank in sentence 26?
a. then   c. in addition
b. after

___b___   **10.** What is the relationship of ideas in sentence 34?
a. time order   c. classification
b. space order

WHAT DO YOU THINK?

How could the study of biology affect our lifestyle choices? For example, what lifestyle choices would or should the following people make after reading this passage: construction worker, factory worker, music lovers who use ear buds or attend concerts, airport baggage carriers. Assume you are writing a series of articles for your college newspaper about the relationship between classroom learning and real life. This week, you are writing about biology's relevance to the real world. Write about particular lifestyle choices that may damage human hearing. Use details from the passage to explain the dangers, and list several actions your readers should take to protect their hearing.

 ## After Reading About Transitions and Thought Patterns

Before you move on to the Mastery Tests on transitions and thought patterns, take time to reflect on your learning and performance by answering the following questions. Write your answers in your notebook.

- How has my knowledge base or prior knowledge about transitions and thought patterns changed?

- Based on my studies, how do I think I will perform on the Mastery Test(s)? Why do I think my scores will be above average, average, or below average?

- Would I recommend this chapter to other students who want to learn more about transitions and thought patterns? Why or why not?

Test your understanding of what you have learned about Transitions and Thought Patterns for Master Readers by completing the Chapter 7 Review Card in the insert near the end of your text.

CONNECT TO ᴘᴇᴀʀꜱᴏɴ **myreadinglab**

To check your progress in meeting Chapter 7's learning outcomes, log in to **www.myreadinglab.com** and try the following exercises.

- The "Patterns of Organization" section of MyReadingLab gives additional information about transitions and patterns of organization. The section provides a model, practices, activities, and tests. To access this resource, click on the "Study Plan" tab. Then click on "Patterns of Organization." Then click on the following links as needed: "Overview," "Model," "Signal Words (Flash Animation)," "Other Patterns of Organization (Flash Animation)," "Practice," and "Tests."

- To measure your mastery of the content of this chapter, complete the tests in the "Transitions" section and click on Gradebook to find your results.

A. The following information is from a college science textbook. Determine a logical order for the ideas to create a paragraph that makes sense. Indicate the proper order of ideas by writing **1, 2, 3, 4,** and **5** in the spaces provided.

Textbook
Skills

__1__ Prey have evolved a number of defense mechanisms.

__5__ A fourth and more subtle defense is the timing of reproduction so that most of the offspring are produced in a short period of time.

__2__ One defense mechanism is cryptic coloration, which includes colors, patterns, shapes, and postures that allow prey to blend into the background.

__4__ A third defense mechanism employs physical means; for example, clams, armadillos, turtles, and numerous beetles all withdraw into their armor coat or shell when danger approaches.

__3__ Another defense is behavioral, such as alarm calls and distraction displays.

—Adapted from Smith and Smith, *Elements of Ecology*, updated 4th ed., pp. 198–199.

__b__ **6.** What overall thought pattern is shown in the paragraph?
　　a. time order
　　b. listing

VISUAL VOCABULARY

The best synonym for the phrase **cryptic coloration** is

__a__ _____.

　　a. camouflage.
　　b. hidden.
　　c. colorful.

▶ An excellent example of cryptic coloration is the Peppered Moth.

B. Read the following paragraph from a college communications textbook. Fill in each blank (**7–9**) with the correct transition from the box. Use each transition once.

also	in addition	last

Textbook
Skills

10.4 GE/119 words   **Persuasive Proof**

In a persuasive speech, your support is proof, and your proof is material that offers evidence, argument, and motivational appeal. **(7)** <u>In addition</u>, your support establishes your credibility and reputation. You can persuade your audience with several types of support. First, logical support is built on specific examples and general concepts. Logical supports **(8)** <u>also</u> come from comparisons and contrasts, from causes and effects, and from signs. Second, motivational support appeals to the emotions of your audience. These supports appeal to their desire for status, financial gain, or increased self-esteem. The **(9)** <u>last</u> type, credibility appeals, are built on your own personal reputation or trustworthiness. This type of appeal rests on your skill, high moral character, and personal charm.

—Adapted from *Essentials of Human Communication*, 4th ed., p. 308 by
Joseph A. DeVito. Copyright © 2002 by Pearson Education, Inc.
Reproduced by permission of Pearson Education, Inc., Boston, MA.

<u> a </u> **10.** What thought pattern is used in the paragraph?
    a. classification
    b. time order

A. Read the following paragraph from a college biology textbook.

Textbook
Skills

11.6 GE/91 words   **How Do Biologists Study Life?**

[1]Biology is the science of life. [2]Knowledge in biology is acquired through the scientific method. [3]First, an observation is made, which leads to a question. [4]Then a hypothesis is formulated that suggests a possible answer to the question. [5]The hypothesis is used to predict the outcome of further observations or experiments. [6]A conclusion is then drawn about the hypothesis. [7]Conclusions are based only on results that can be shared, verified, and repeated. [8]A scientific theory is a general explanation of natural phenomena, developed through extensive and reproducible experiments and observations.

—From *Life on Earth*, 5th ed., p. 13 by Teresa Audesirk, Gerald Audesirk, and Bruce E. Byers. Copyright © 2009 by Pearson Education, Inc. Printed and Electronically reproduced by permission of Pearson Education, Inc., Upper Saddle River, NJ.

___a___ **1.** The relationship between sentence 3 and sentence 4 is based on
     a. time.   b. addition.

___b___ **2.** The overall thought pattern that organizes the paragraph is
     a. classification.   b. time order.

B. Read the following information from a college mathematics textbook.

Textbook
Skills

10.0 GE/155 words   **Types of Real Numbers**

[1]The set of real numbers is the set of all numbers corresponding to points on the number line. [2]In addition, real numbers consist of several levels of relationships among various kinds of numbers. [3]First, real numbers are divided into two subsets: rational numbers and irrational numbers. [4]Rational numbers are next classified either as rational numbers that are not integers (such as 2/3, −4/5, and 8.2) or as integers. [5]Three types of integers exist: positive integers (1, 2, 3 . . .), zero (0), and negative integers (−1, −2, −3 . . .). [6]Every rational number has a point on the number line. [7]However, there are points on the line for which there are no rational numbers. [8]These points correspond to the second subset of real numbers—irrational numbers. [9]One example is the number π, which is used to

find the area and the circumference of a circle. [10]Another_____ example of an irrational number is the square root of 2, named $\sqrt{2}$.

____c____ **3.** Which transition word best fits the blank in sentence 10?
    a. First   c. Another
    b. Third

____a____ **4.** What is the thought pattern used in the paragraph?
    a. classification
    b. time order

Complete the concept map with the information from the passage.

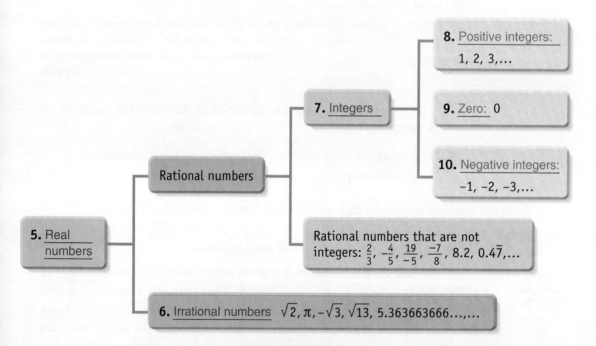

A. Read the following poem by Elizabeth Barrett Browning, originally poem XLIII in *Sonnets from the Portuguese*.

How Do I Love Thee? Let Me Count the Ways

1 How do I love thee? Let me count the ways.
2 I love thee to the depth and breadth and height
3 My soul can reach, when feeling out of sight
4 For the ends of Being and ideal Grace.
5 I love thee to the level of every day's
6 Most quiet need, by sun and candle-light.
7 I love thee freely, as men strive for Right.
8 I love thee purely, as they turn from Praise.
9 I love thee with the passion put to use
10 In my old griefs, and with my childhood's faith.
11 I love thee with a love I seemed to lose
12 With my lost saints—I love thee with the breath,
13 Smiles, tears, of all my life!—and, if God choose,
14 I shall but love thee better ^after_____ death.

____a____ **1.** What is the relationship between the ideas in line 2?
   a. listing   b. time

____a____ **2.** Which transition word best fits the blank in line 14?
   a. after   c. through
   b. when

____b____ **3.** In this paragraph, the author
   a. explains step by step how to fall in love.
   b. gives a list of descriptions to express the quality of her love.

B. Read the following passage from a college government textbook.

11.5 GE/265 words   **Interest Groups**

Textbook
Skills

¹Interest groups are everywhere in the American political system. ²Political scientists loosely categorize interest groups into clusters. ³An examination of the four distinct types of interest groups gives a good picture of much of the American interest group system.

[4]One type of group focuses on economic interests. [5]All economic interests are ultimately concerned with wages, prices, and profits. [6]In the American economy, the government does not determine these directly. [7]More commonly the government affects economic interests through regulations and taxes, among other things. [8]Business executives, factory workers, and farmers seek to affect government's impact on their livelihoods.

[9]Another type of interest group is made up of the environmentalists. [10]Environmental groups have promoted pollution-control policies, wilderness protection, and population control. [11]They have fought against strip mining, supersonic aircraft, the Alaskan oil pipeline, offshore oil drilling, and nuclear power plants.

[12]The next kind of interest group fights for equality interests. [13]The Fourteenth Amendment assures equal protection under the law. [14]American history, though, shows that this is easier said than done. [15]Interest groups representing minorities and women have made equal rights their main policy goal.

[16]The fourth type of interest group deals with consumers and public interests. [17]Today, over 2,000 organized groups are championing various causes or ideas in the public interest. [18]If products are made safer by the lobbying of consumer protection groups, it is not the members of such groups alone that benefit; everyone should be better off. [19]In addition to consumer groups, other groups speaking for those who cannot speak for themselves seek to protect children, animals, and the mentally ill.

—Adapted from Edwards, Wattenberg, & Lineberry, *Government in America*, Brief 5th ed., pp. 253–258.

_____b_____ **4.** The overall thought pattern for the passage is
   a. time order.   b. classification.

5. The second major supporting detail is signaled by the transition word(s)
Another type
_____.

6–10. Complete the outline with information from the paragraph.

Main idea stated in a topic sentence: An examination of the four distinct types of interest groups gives a good picture of much of the American interest group system.

Major supporting details:

a. Economic interests

b. Environmental interests

c. Equality interests

d. Consumer and public interests

Read the following passage from a college world history textbook. Answer the questions that follow.

Textbook Skills

11.8 GE/545 words

Out of the Mud: Farming and Herding after the Ice Age

[1]We can divide environments suited to early agriculture into three broad types: swampy wetlands, uplands, and alluvial plains, where flooding rivers or lakes renew the topsoil. [2](Cleared woodlands and irrigated drylands are also suitable for agriculture, but as far as we know, farming never originated in these environments. [3]Rather, outsiders brought it to these areas from someplace else.) [4]Each of the three types developed with peculiar characteristics and specialized crops. [5]It is worth looking at each in turn.

Swampland [6]Swamp is no longer much in demand for farming. [7]Nowadays, in the Western world, if we want to turn bog into farmland we drain it. [8]But it had advantages early on. [9]Swamp soil is rich, moist, and easy to work with simple technology. [10]At least one staple grows well in waterlogged land—rice. [11]We still do not know where or when rice was first cultivated, or even whether any of these wetland varieties preceded the dryland rice that has gradually become more popular around the world. [12]Most evidence, however, suggests that people were producing rice at sites on the lower Ganges River in India and in parts of Southeast Asia some 8,000 years ago, and in paddies in the Yangtze River valley in China not long afterward.

Uplands [13]Like swamplands, regions of high altitude are not places that people today consider good for farming. [14]Farmers have usually left these regions to the herdsmen and native upland creatures, such as sheep, goats, yaks, and llamas. [15]There are three reasons for doing so. [16]First, as altitude increases, cold and the scorching effects of solar radiation in the thin atmosphere diminish the variety of viable plants. [17]Second, slopes are subject to erosion (although this has a secondary benefit because relatively rich soils collect in valley bottoms). [18]Finally, slopes in general are hard to work once you have come to rely on plows, but this does not stop people who do not use plows from farming them. [19]Nonetheless, in highlands suitable for plant foods, plant husbandry or mixed farming did develop.

Alluvial Plains [20]Although swamps and rain-fed highlands have produced spectacularly successful agriculture, farmers get the best help from nature in alluvial plains, flat lands where mud carried by overflowing rivers or lakes renews the soil. [21]If people can channel the floods to keep crops from being swept away on these

—Adapted from *The World: A History, Combined Volume*, 2nd ed., pp. 41–47 by Felipe Fernandez-Armesto. Copyright © 2010 by Pearson Education, Inc. Reprinted by permission of Pearson Education, Inc., Upper Saddle River, NJ.

plains, alluvium, made up of sediment and other organic matter, restores nutrients and compensates for lack of rain. [22]Alluvial soils in arid climates sustained some of the world's most productive economies until late in the second millennium B.C.E. [23]Wheat and barley grew in the black earth that lines Egypt's Nile, the floodplains of the lower Tigris and Euphrates rivers in what is now Iraq, and the Indus River in what is now Pakistan. [24]People first farmed millet on alluvial soils in a somewhat cooler, moister climate in China, in the crook of the Yellow River and the Guanzhong Basin around 7,000 years ago. [25]And in the warm, moist climate of Indochina in what is now Cambodia, three crops of rice a year could grow on soil that the annual counter flow of the Mekong River created. [26]The Mekong becomes so torrential that the delta—where the river enters the sea—cannot funnel its flow, and water is forced back upriver.

    _____b_____ **1.** The relationship of ideas within sentence 23 is
          a. listing.   c. time order.
          b. space order.

    _____a_____ **2.** The relationship of ideas between sentence 15 and sentence 16 is
          a. addition.   c. classification.
          b. time order.

    _____b_____ **3.** The thought pattern of the third paragraph (sentences 13–19) is
          a. space order.   c. classification.
          b. listing.

    _____c_____ **4.** The main thought pattern of the passage is
          a. time order.   c. classification.
          b. space order.

5–10. Complete the following study notes with information from the passage.

Central Idea (Thesis statement): (5) We can divide environments suited to early

agriculture into three broad types: swampy wetlands, uplands, and alluvial plains,

where flooding rivers or lakes renew the top soil.

Type	Trait
I. **(6)** Swampland	**(9)** Wording may vary: Rich, moist soil; grew rice well
II. **(7)** Uplands	High altitudes; harsh, thin atmosphere; subject to erosion; hard to plow; left to herdsmen
III. **(8)** Alluvial Plains	Flood waters **(10)** renew soil; mud made up of sediment and organic matter; sustained economies; grew wheat, barley, millet, and rice

More Thought Patterns

8

LEARNING OUTCOMES

After studying this chapter you should be able to do the following:

1 Recognize the following relationships or thought patterns: *comparison, contrast, cause, effect, generalization-and-example, definition-and-example.* [Knowledge]

2 Determine the relationships of ideas within a sentence. [Analysis]

3 Determine the relationships of ideas between sentences. [Analysis]

4 Determine the thought pattern used to organize a passage. [Analysis]

5 Evaluate the importance of transitions and thought patterns. [Evaluation]

 ## Before Reading About More Thought Patterns

In Chapter 7, you learned several important ideas that will help you as you work through this chapter. Use the following questions to call up your prior knowledge about transitions and thought patterns.

What are transitions? (Refer to page 270.) Transitions are words and phrases that signal thought patterns by showing the logical relationship within and between sentences.

What are thought patterns? (Refer to page 270.) Thought patterns are created by using transitions to show the logical relationship between ideas in a paragraph or passage.

What is important to know about mixed thought patterns? Give an example from Chapter 7. (Refer to page 293.) Authors often mix patterns. For example, classification identifies traits and uses addition words to list the traits. So when a variety of transition words are used, a reader must determine the author's primary thought pattern.

You have learned that transitions and thought patterns show the relationships of ideas within sentences as well as between sentences and paragraphs, and you studied four common types: time order, space order, listing, and classification. In this chapter, we will explore some other common thought patterns:

- The comparison-and-contrast patterns
- The cause-and-effect pattern
- The generalization-and-example pattern
- The definition-and-example pattern

The Comparison-and-Contrast Patterns

Many ideas become clearer when they are thought of in relation to one another. For example, comparing the prices of different phone plans makes us smarter shoppers. Likewise, noting the difference between mature and immature behavior helps us grow. The comparison-and-contrast patterns enable us to see these relationships. This section discusses both comparison and contrast, starting with comparison. The discussion then turns to the important and effective comparison-and-contrast pattern, in which these two basic ways of organizing ideas are combined when writing an explanation, a description, or an analysis.

Comparison

Comparison points out the ways in which two or more ideas are alike. Sample signal words are listed in the box.

Words and Phrases of Comparison				
a kind of	comparable	in like manner	likewise	same
alike	equally	in the same way	matching	similar
as	in a similar fashion	just as	near to	similarity
as well as	in character with	like	resemble	similarly

When comparison is used to organize an entire paragraph, the pattern looks like this.

Comparison Pattern		
Idea 1		**Idea 2**
Idea 1	*like*	Idea 2
Idea 1	*like*	Idea 2
Idea 1	*like*	Idea 2

Words and phrases of comparison state the relationship of ideas within and between sentences.

EXAMPLE Fill in each blank with a word or phrase that shows comparison. Wording may vary.

1. Earning a promotion is <u>like</u> running a marathon.

2. An aspiring employee must work to achieve <u>in the same way</u> a competitive athlete trains to win.

3. A raise in rank and salary is <u>a kind of</u> trophy.

EXPLANATION   Each of the example sentences compares two topics to make a point: *earning a promotion* and *running a marathon*. Note that the relationship within each sentence helps to establish a comparison pattern for a three-sentence paragraph as illustrated in the following chart. Compare your choice of words of comparison with the ones given in the chart.

Comparison Pattern: Promotion and Marathon		
Idea 1		**Idea 2**
earning a promotion	(1) *like*	running a marathon
aspiring employee works	(2) *in the same way*	competitive athlete trains
raise	(3) *a kind of*	trophy

PRACTICE 1

Determine the logical order for the following four sentences. Write **1** by the sentence that should come first, **2** by the sentence that should come second, **3** by the sentence that should come third, and **4** by the sentence that should come last. Then, use the information to fill in the chart. Wording for the chart may vary.

___1___ The careers of Jennifer Lopez and Beyoncé Knowles are similar in several respects.

___4___ An overall similarity between these two mega-stars is their financial success; both are extraordinarily rich with growing incomes.

___3___ Both women also enjoy success as singers, record producers, actors, and fashion icons.

___2___ Both Lopez and Knowles are known world-wide by their single names: J-Lo and Beyoncé.

Similarities between Jennifer Lopez and Beyoncé Knowles	
Jennifer Lopez	**Beyoncé Knowles**
5. known world-wide by single name: J-Lo	6. known world-wide by single name: Beyoncé
7. successful singer, record producer, actor, and fashion icon	8. successful singer, record producer, actor, and fashion icon
9. financial success	10. financial success

Contrast

Contrast points out the ways in which two or more ideas are different. Sample signal words are listed in the box below.

Words and Phrases of Contrast				
all	counter to	differently	instead	than
although	despite	even though	nevertheless	to the contrary
as opposed to	differ	however	on the contrary	unlike
at the same time	difference	in contrast	on the one hand	while
but	different	in spite of	on the other hand	yet
conversely	different from	incompatible with	still	

When contrast is used to organize an entire paragraph, the pattern looks like this.

Contrast Pattern		
Idea 1		**Idea 2**
Idea 1	*differs from*	Idea 2
Idea 1	*differs from*	Idea 2
Idea 1	*differs from*	Idea 2

Words and phrases of contrast state the relationship of ideas within and between sentences.

EXAMPLE Fill in each blank with a word or phrase that shows contrast. Wording may vary.

Brain development **(1)** differ̲s̲̲̲̲̲̲̲̲̲̲̲̲ between girls and boys. Girls develop the right side of the brain faster **(2)** t̲h̲a̲n̲̲̲̲̲̲̲̲̲ boys. **(3)** I̲n̲ ̲c̲o̲n̲t̲r̲a̲s̲t̲̲̲̲, boys develop the left side faster **(4)** t̲h̲a̲n̲̲̲̲̲̲̲̲̲̲̲ girls. So girls may talk and read earlier **(5)** t̲h̲a̲n̲̲̲̲̲̲̲̲̲ boys **(6)** w̲h̲i̲l̲e̲̲̲̲̲̲̲̲ boys may figure out how to build block towers and solve puzzles earlier **(7)** t̲h̲a̲n̲̲̲̲̲̲̲̲̲̲ girls. Girls and boys also **(8)** d̲i̲f̲f̲e̲r̲̲̲̲̲̲̲̲ in what they talk about. **(9)** O̲n̲ ̲t̲h̲e̲ ̲o̲n̲e̲ ̲h̲a̲n̲d̲, girls tend to talk about other people; secrets in order to bond friendships; and school, wishes, and needs. **(10)** O̲n̲ ̲t̲h̲e̲ ̲o̲t̲h̲e̲r̲ ̲h̲a̲n̲d̲, boys talk about things and activities such as what they are doing and who is best at the activity.

EXPLANATION

Every sentence in the paragraph contrasts two topics to make a point. Note that the relationships within and between sentences establish a contrast pattern for the paragraph as illustrated in the following chart. Compare your choice of words of contrast with the ones given in the chart.

Contrast Pattern: Difference between Girls and Boys in Brain Development		
Idea 1		**Idea 2**
Brain development of girls		**Brain development of boys**
Right side develops faster (2) *than*	(1) *differs*	Left side develops faster (4) *than*
Talk and read earlier (5) *than*	(3) *in contrast*	Build block towers and solve puzzles earlier (7) *than*
	(6) *while*	
What they talk about	(8) *differ*	What they talk about
People, secrets, school, wishes, needs	(9) *on the one hand*	Other people, secrets, school, wishes, needs
	(10) *on the other hand*	Things and activities such as what they are doing and who is best

PRACTICE 2

Determine a logical order for the following five sentences. Write **1** by the sentence that should come first, **2** in front of the sentence that should come second, **3** by the sentence that should come third, and so on. Then, use the information to fill in the chart.

Textbook
Skills

Cultural Differences and Touch

___4___ Thus, on the one hand, southern Europeans may view the Japanese as cold, distant, and uninvolved.

___5___ On the other hand, the Japanese may view the southern Europeans as pushy, aggressive, and too intimate.

___2___ Members of a contact culture, such as southern Europeans, maintain close distances and touch each other in conversation, face each other directly, and maintain eye contact.

___3___ In contrast, members of a noncontact culture, such as the Japanese, maintain greater distances in their interactions, rarely touch each other, avoid facing each other, and have much less direct eye contact.

___1___ Some cultures are contact cultures, as opposed to others that are noncontact cultures.

—From *The Interpersonal Communication Book*, 10th ed., p. 193.
by Joseph A. DeVito. Copyright © 2004 by Pearson Education, Inc.
Reproduced by permission of Pearson Education, Inc., Boston, MA.

Cultural Differences and Touch

Contact Cultures	Noncontact Cultures
1. Southern European	1. Japanese
2. maintain close distances and touch each other in conversation, face each other directly, and maintain eye contact	2. maintain greater distances, rarely touch each other, avoid facing each other, and have much less direct eye contact
3. Southern Europeans may view the Japanese as cold, distant, and uninvolved	3. The Japanese may view the southern Europeans as pushy, aggressive, and too intimate.

Comparison and Contrast

The **comparison-and-contrast pattern** shows how two things are similar and how they are different.

A is like B, but A also differs from B.

| Comparison | Contrast |
| A *is like* B | A *is different from* B |

The following short paragraph offers an example of a comparison-and-contrast between two types of weight training. Read the paragraph and circle the comparison and contrast words and phrases.

> ¹Although exercising with free weights is similar to exercising with machine weights, important differences exist between the two methods. ²Both methods offer resistance training, and both improve posture, build bones and muscles, and improve one's overall well-being. ³However, free weights and machine weights differ in cost and convenience. ⁴On the one hand, free weights are inexpensive and portable. ⁵On the other hand, machines, such as Bowflex and Nautilus, costs hundreds of dollars and require a fixed location.

Did you circle the following nine signal words and phrases: *although*, *similar*, *differences*, *both*, *both*, *however*, *differ*, *on the one hand*, and *on the other hand*. These signal words and phrases state the relationship within and between sentences and establish the paragraph's thought pattern.

EXAMPLE Read the following paragraph from a college sociology textbook. Circle the comparison-and-contrast words; then, answer the questions that follow the paragraph.

Men and Women and Hormones

¹Scientists don't know why women and men differ but believe that hormones provide part of the explanation. ²All males and females share three sex hormones. ³Estrogen is dominant in females and is produced by the ovaries. ⁴Progesterone is present in high levels during pregnancy and

Textbook
Skills

is also secreted by the ovaries. ⁵Testosterone is dominant in males, where it is produced by the testes. ⁶All of these hormones are produced in very small quantities in both sexes before puberty.

⁷After puberty, different levels of these hormones in females and males produce different changes in bodily processes. ⁸For example, testosterone, the main male sex hormone, strengthens muscles but threatens the heart. ⁹Thus males are at twice the risk of heart disease as are females. ¹⁰The main female sex hormones, especially estrogen, make blood vessels more elastic and strengthen the immune system. ¹¹Thus females are more resistant to infection.

—Adapted from *Marriages and Families: Changes, Choices, and Constraints*, 4th ed., p. 75 by Nijole V. Benokraitis. Copyright © 2002 by Pearson Education, Inc. Reproduced by permission of Pearson Education, Inc., Boston, MA.

1. What two ideas are being compared and contrasted? <u>men's hormones and</u>

<u>women's hormones</u>

2. List four different comparison-and-contrast words or phrases in the paragraph. <u>differ, but, share, both, all, different, as, more</u>

EXPLANATION (1) The paragraph compares and contrasts men's hormones and women's hormones. (2) You were correct to choose any four of these comparison-and-contrast words: *differ, but, share, both, all, different, as, more.*

PRACTICE 3

This paragraph from a college sociology textbook uses comparison and contrast. Read the paragraph and then, answer the questions that follow.

Textbook Skills

¹The *authoritative* parent and the *authoritarian* parent may seem similar in purpose but differ in style. ²The similar spelling of the terms *authoritative* and *authoritarian* requires that you read these terms carefully. ³The first part of both words, which comes from the word authority, suggests that these parents are willing to "take charge" of their children. ⁴However, they take charge in quite different ways. ⁵On the one hand, authoritative parents are warm (accepting) and firm (controlling). ⁶They use reason to gain compliance. ⁷They explain rules and encourage verbal give-and-take with their children. ⁸They are flexible in setting limits and

are responsive to their children's needs. ⁹They encourage independent thinking and are accepting of opposing points of view. ¹⁰During a conflict, an authoritative parent might ask a child, "What do you think we should do?" ¹¹In contrast, authoritarian parents value obedience above all. ¹²They limit their child's freedom by imposing many rules, which they strictly enforce. ¹³They favor punishment and forceful measures and mainly use power to gain compliance. ¹⁴They value order and tradition and do not compromise. ¹⁵They do not encourage verbal give-and-take with their children. ¹⁶During a conflict, this parent is likely to assert power with statements such as "Because I said so."

—Adapted from Jaffe, *Understanding Parenting*, 2nd ed., pp. 158, 160.

1. What two ideas are being discussed? <u>authoritative parents</u>

and <u>authoritarian parents</u>

2. How are authoritative and authoritarian parents similar? <u>They both</u>

<u>"take charge" of their children.</u>

3. Complete the following chart with information from the passage:

The *authoritative* parent and the *authoritarian* parent may seem similar in purpose but differ in style.

Comparison	Contrast	
Both **authoritative** and **authoritarian** parents "take charge" of a child.	**Authoritative Parents**	**Authoritarian Parents**
	encourage independent thinking	value obedience above all
	use reason to gain compliance	use forceful measures and power to gain compliance
	are flexible	are inflexible
	say, "What do you think we should do?"	say, "Because I said so."

The Cause-and-Effect Pattern

Sometimes an author talks about *why* something happened or *what* results came from an event. A **cause** states why something happens; an **effect** states a result or outcome. Sample signal words are listed in the box.

Cause-and-Effect Words			
accordingly	by reason	leads to	so
as a result	consequently	on account of	thereby
because	due to	results in	therefore
because of	if . . . then	since	thus

Here are some examples:

> **Because** Zahira is the oldest of eight siblings, she has developed many leadership skills.

> **Due to** a collision involving 34 vehicles, all lanes of Interstate 4 have been shut down for hours.

Each of the example sentences has two topics: one topic causes or has an effect on the second topic. The cause or effect is the author's main point. For example, the two topics in the first sentence are Zahira's birth order and her leadership skills. The stated main idea is that being the oldest of eight siblings is the cause of her leadership skills. The cause is introduced by the word *because*. In the second sentence the two topics are the collision of 34 vehicles and the closing of Interstate 4; the author focuses on the cause by using the signal phrase *due to*.

Note that cause and effect has a strong connection to time, and many of the transitions for this pattern have a time element. Although many cause-and-effect transition words have similar meanings and may be interchangeable, authors carefully choose the transition that best fits the context.

EXAMPLE Read the following paragraph. Fill in each blank (**1–5**) with a cause-and-effect word or phrase from the box. Each is used only once. Answers may vary.

because	due to	leads to	result	therefore

The State of Knowledge about Climate Science

Scientists know with virtual certainty several causes and effects of climate change. The composition of Earth's atmosphere is changing (1) <u>because</u> of human activities. Increasing levels of greenhouse gases like carbon dioxide (CO_2) in the atmosphere since pre-industrial times are well-documented and understood. The atmospheric buildup of CO_2 and other greenhouse gases is largely the (2) <u>result</u> of human activities such as the burning of fossil fuels. An "unequivocal" warming trend of about 1.0 to 1.7°F occurred from 1906–2005. Warming occurred in both the Northern and Southern Hemispheres, and over the oceans. The major greenhouse gases emitted **(3)** ___due to_____ human activities remain in the atmosphere for periods ranging from decades to centuries. It is **(4)** ___therefore_____ virtually certain that atmospheric concentrations of greenhouse gases will continue to rise over the next few decades. Increasing greenhouse gas concentrations **(5)** ___leads to_____ the warming of the planet.

—U. S. Environmental Protection Agency. "Climate Change: State of Knowledge." 28 Sept. 2009.
http://www.epa.gov/climatechange/science/stateofknowledge.html.

Copyright © 2011 Pearson Education, Inc.

VISUAL VOCABULARY

The best meaning of radiation is ___c_____.

a. gases.
b. atmosphere.
c. heat.

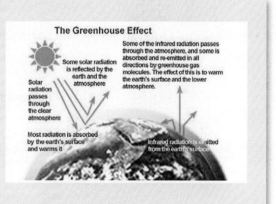

The Greenhouse Effect

Some solar radiation is reflected by the earth and the atmosphere

Solar radiation passes through the clear atmosphere

Most radiation is absorbed by the earth's surface and warms it

Some of the infrared radiation passes through the atmosphere, and some is absorbed and re-emitted in all directions by greenhouse gas molecules. The effect of this is to warm the earth's surface and the lower atmosphere.

Infrared radiation is emitted from the earth's surface

EXPLANATION   Compare your answers to the following: (1) because, (2) result, (3) due to, (4) therefore, (5) leads to.

Common Cause-and-Effect Patterns

The writer using cause and effect introduces an idea or event, then provides supporting details to show how that idea *results in* or *leads to* another idea. Many times, the second idea comes about because of the first idea. Thus the first idea is the cause, and the following ideas are the effects.

For example, read the following topic sentence:

Music therapy leads to the improvement of a person's physical and psychological well-being.

Often an author will begin with an effect and then give the causes.

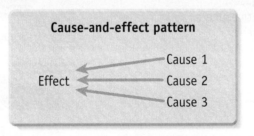

For example, read the following topic sentence.

Some people turn to music therapy due to a loss of physical or psychological well-being.

Sometimes the author may wish to emphasize a chain reaction.

Cause-and-effect chain reaction

Cause

↓

  Effect 1

   ↓

    Effect 2

     ↓

      Effect 3

For example, read the following topic sentence.

Music therapy reduces stress and anxiety, which leads to positive emotional states and can ultimately result in feelings of control and empowerment.

Cause-and-effect chain reaction

Cause: music therapy ➝ Effect: reduces stress and anxiety ➝ Effect: positive emotional states ➝ Effect: feelings of control and empowerment

EXAMPLE Determine a logical order for the following three sentences from a college health textbook. Write **1** by the sentence that should come first, **2** in front of the sentence that should come second, and **3** by the sentence that should come last.

Textbook
Skills

  2   First, CRH instructs the pituitary gland and the adrenal glands to secrete special stress hormones.

  1   Hostility causes the body to release corticotrophin-releasing-hormone (CRH), which starts the whole sequence of stress hormones.

  3   The result is a classic stress response: blood pressure rises, the heart beats harder and faster, blood volume is increased, blood moves from the skin and organs to the brain and muscles, the liver releases stored sugar, and breathing speeds up.

—From *Mind/Body Health: The Effects of Attitudes, Emotions, and Relationships,* 2nd ed.,
p. 218 by Keith J. Karren, Brent Q. Hafen, Lee Smith, and Kathryn J. Frandsen.
Copyright © 2002 by Pearson Education, Inc. Reprinted by permission of
Pearson Education, Inc., Upper Saddle River, NJ.

EXPLANATION Here are the sentences arranged in their proper order. The transition and signal words are in bold type.

The Bodily Effects of Hostility

[1]Hostility **causes** the body to release corticotrophin-releasing-hormone (CRH), which starts the whole sequence of stress hormones. [2]**First**, CRH instructs the pituitary gland and the adrenal glands to secrete special stress hormones. [3]The **result** is a classic stress response: blood pressure rises, the heart beats harder and faster, blood volume is increased, blood moves from the skin and organs to the brain and muscles, the liver releases stored sugar, and breathing speeds up.

—From *Mind/Body Health: The Effects of Attitudes, Emotions, and Relationships*, 2nd ed., p. 218 by Keith J. Karren, Brent Q. Hafen, Lee Smith, and Kathryn J. Frandsen. Copyright © 2002 by Pearson Education, Inc. Reprinted by permission of Pearson Education, Inc., Upper Saddle River, NJ.

In this paragraph, the cause-and-effect signal words are *causes* and *result*. The listing word *first* indicates the order of the cause-and-effect discussion. The addition word *and* is used to list the bodily effects of hostility. This paragraph actually uses two thought patterns to make the point—listing, as well as cause and effect. Even though two patterns are used, the cause-and-effect pattern is the primary organizing pattern.

PRACTICE 4

This excerpt from a college health textbook uses the cause-and-effect thought pattern to organize information. Read the paragraph, circle the cause-and-effect signal words in it, and complete the concept map that follows.

Causes of Loneliness

Textbook
Skills

[1]According to researchers with the Department of Health and Human Services, loneliness has several basic causes. [2]First, many lonely people have distinctive social traits that make it difficult for them to form and keep relationships. [3]They may be shy or lack self esteem and are unable to be assertive. [4]In addition, certain situations can lead to loneliness. [5]Time, distance, and money may hinder a person from becoming involved in meaningful relationships. [6]Cultural values may also lead to loneliness; American culture encourages us to be independent and mobile. [7]The nature of relationships is another cause of loneliness. [8]Lonely people have fewer social contacts and relationships than people who are not lonely; thus they

spend less time with other people and are likely to spend time with people they are not close to rather than with good friends. [9]Finally, countless events in life (many beyond our control) can make us feel lonely, rejected, alone, or inadequate. [10]Examples of the most frequent events (that cause) loneliness are the death of a spouse, divorce, or a geographical move.

—Adapted from *Mind/Body Health: The Effects of Attitudes, Emotions, and Relationships,* 2nd ed., pp. 346–348 by Keith J. Karren, Brent Q. Hafen, Lee Smith, and Kathryn J. Frandsen. Copyright © 2002 by Pearson Education, Inc. Reprinted by permission of Pearson Education, Inc., Upper Saddle River, NJ.

 The Generalization-and-Example Pattern

Curiosity can quickly lead to danger: Rayanne, a curious five year old, found a hairpin on the floor and stuck it in an electrical outlet to see what would happen.

Some people may read this sentence and think that the author's focus is on Rayanne. However, the author's general point is about curiosity, not Rayanne. In the first part of the sentence the author has made a generalization: "Curiosity can quickly lead to danger." Adding an **example word** or phrase makes it clear that the author is using Rayanne as only one example of the general dangers of curiosity.

Read the sentence about Rayanne again. Note how the use of the signal word makes the relationship between ideas clear.

> Curiosity can quickly lead to danger; *for instance,* Rayanne, a curious five year old, found a hairpin on the floor and stuck it in an electrical outlet to see what would happen.

In the generalization-and-example thought pattern, the author makes a general statement and then offers an example or a series of examples to clarify the generalization.

The Generalization-and-Example Pattern
Statement of a general idea
Example
Example

Example words signal that a writer is giving an instance of a general idea.

Words and Phrases That Introduce Examples			
an illustration	for instance	once	to illustrate
for example	including	such as	typically

EXAMPLE Read each of the following items and fill in the blanks with an appropriate example word or phrase. Answers may vary.

1. History is full of people who overcame significant challenges and went on to achieve success; <u>for example</u>, Abraham Lincoln lost at least six major elections for various political offices before becoming the sixteenth president of the United States.

2. Women can now earn some of the highest salaries. <u>For instance</u>, in 2009, Forbes reported that Tyra Banks earned $30 million.

3. Television programs <u>such as</u> *Sesame Street* and *Blue's Clues* have helped educate millions of children.

EXPLANATION Many words and phrases that introduce examples are easily interchanged. Compare your choices with the following: (1) *for example,* (2) *For instance,* and (3) *such as.* Notice that in the first two of these three examples, the phrases *for example* and *for instance* are similar in meaning, signaling that at least one example will be offered. The use of the transition phrase *such as* in the third example, however, tends to signal a list. Even though transition words or phrases have similar meanings, authors carefully choose transitions based on style and meaning.

PRACTICE 5

Determine a logical order for the following three sentences. Write a **1** by the sentence that should come first, a **2** in front of the sentence that should come second, and **3** by the sentence that should come last.

___3___ The $250,000–$450,000 million loss in crops that occurred in 2010 further exemplifies the damage of such a Florida freeze.

___1___ Sunny, warm Florida can experience crop-damaging cold spells.

___2___ In one instance, the temperature in agricultural areas during January 2010 dipped as low as 17 degrees.

The Definition-and-Example Pattern

Textbooks are full of new words and special terms. Even if the word is common, it can take on a special meaning in a specific course. To help students understand the ideas, authors often include a definition of the new or special term. Then, to make sure the meaning of the word or concept is clear, the author will also give examples.

Textbook Skills

Euphemisms are rephrasings of harsh terms; they attempt to avoid offending or to skirt an unpleasant issue. For instance, the Federal Reserve Board is fond of calling a bad market "a market imbalance." A bereaved person might rather hear, "I was sorry to hear of your grandmother's passing" than "I was sorry to hear your grandmother died."

—Faigley, *The Penguin Handbook,* 2003, p. 506.

In the paragraph above, the term *euphemisms* is defined first. Then, the author gives two examples to make the term clear to the reader.

The Definition Pattern
Term and definition
Example
Example

- The **definition** explains the meaning of new, difficult, or special terms. Definitions include words like *is, are,* and *means*: "Euphemisms *are* rephrasings of harsh terms; they attempt to avoid offending or to skirt an unpleasant issue."

- The **examples** follow a definition to show how the word is used or applied in the content course. Examples are signaled by words like *for example* and *such as:* "For instance, the Federal Reserve Board is fond of calling a bad market 'a market imbalance.'"

Textbook Skills

EXAMPLE Determine a logical order for the following three sentences. Write a **1** by the sentence that should come first, a **2** in front of the sentence that should come second, and a **3** by the sentence that should come last. Then, read the explanation.

__2__ They also help clarify and intensify your verbal messages.

_____1_____ *Illustrators* are physical gestures that go along with and literally illustrate the verbal message; they make your communications more vivid and help to maintain your listener's attention.

_____3_____ In saying, "Let's go up," for example, you probably move your head and perhaps your finger in an upward direction.

—From *The Interpersonal Communication Book,* 10th ed., p. 182 by Joseph A. DeVito. Copyright © 2004 by Pearson Education, Inc. Reproduced by permission of Pearson Education, Inc., Boston, MA.

EXPLANATION The sentences have been arranged in the proper order in the paragraph below. The definition, example, and transition words are in **bold** type.

Illustrators, One Type of Body Gesture

Illustrators **are** physical gestures that go along with and literally illustrate the verbal message; they make your communications more vivid and help to maintain your listener's attention. They **also** help clarify and intensify your verbal messages. In saying, "Let's go up," **for example,** you probably move your head and perhaps your finger in an upward direction.

This sequence of ideas begins by introducing the term *illustrators.* The term is linked to its definition with the verb *are.* The author signals two additional traits of illustrators with the addition word *also.* The sentence that contains *for example* logically follows the definition and additional traits of the term *illustrators.*

PRACTICE 6

Read the paragraph. Finish the definition concept table that follows it by adding the missing details in the proper order.

Textbook
Skills

Affect Displays, A Type of Gesture

[1]Affect displays are the movements of the face that convey emotional meaning—the expressions that show anger and fear, happiness and surprise, eagerness and fatigue. [2]They're the facial muscles that give you away when you try to present a false image and that lead people to say "You look angry. [3]What's wrong?" [4]We can, however, consciously control affect displays, as actors do when they play a role. [5]Affect displays

may be unintentional (as when they give you away) or intentional (as when you want to show anger, love, or surprise).

—From *The Interpersonal Communication Book*, 10th ed., p. 182 by Joseph A. DeVito. Copyright © 2004 by Pearson Education, Inc. Reproduced by permission of Pearson Education, Inc., Boston, MA.

Term: affect displays

Definition: the movements of the face that convey emotional meaning

Example: expressions that show anger and fear, happiness and surprise, eagerness and fatigue

Example: unintentional (as when they give you away)

Example: intentional (as when you want to show anger, love, or surprise)

VISUAL VOCABULARY

Provide captions for the two photographs that correctly label the types of gestures represented by each of the images.

Affect display

Illustrator

Reading a Textbook: Thought Patterns and Textbooks

Textbook authors rely heavily on the use of transitions and thought patterns to make information clear and easier to understand.

EXAMPLE   The following topic sentences have been taken from college textbooks. Identify the *primary* thought pattern that each sentence suggests.

___a___   **1.** After 1660, the Virginia economy steadily declined for several reasons.
  a. cause and effect
  b. comparison and contrast
  c. definition and example

___c___   **2.** Domain-specific knowledge is knowledge that pertains to a particular task or subject; for example, knowing that the shortstop plays between second and third base is specific to the domain of baseball.
  a. cause and effect
  b. comparison and contrast
  c. definition and example

EXPLANATION   Topic sentence 1, taken from a history textbook, uses (a) cause and effect, signaled by the phrase *for several reasons*. Topic sentence 2, from an education textbook, is organized according to (c) definition and example, using the verb *is* in the definition and the phrase *for example* to introduce the example.

PRACTICE 7

The following topic sentences have been taken from college textbooks (in mathematics, social science, health, and literature). Identify the primary thought pattern that each sentence suggests.

___a___   **1.** A stereotype, a fixed impression about a group, may influence your views of individual group members because you may see individuals only as members of a group rather than as unique individuals.
  a. cause and effect
  b. comparison and contrast
  c. definition and example

___b___   **2.** Note that the expressions $x + y$ and $y + x$ have the same values no matter what the variables stand for; they are equivalent.
  a. cause and effect
  b. comparison and contrast
  c. generalization and example

_____a_____ **3.** Excessive time pressure, excessive responsibility, lack of support, or excessive expectations of yourself and those around you may result in overload.
a. cause and effect c. definition and example
b. comparison and contrast

_____c_____ **4.** Poets have long been fond of retelling myths, narrowly defined as traditional stories about the deeds of immortal beings; myths tell us stories of gods or heroes—their battles, their lives, their loves, and often their suffering—all on a scale of magnificence larger than our life.
a. cause and effect c. definition and example
b. comparison and contrast

APPLICATIONS

Application 1: Identifying Thought Patterns

Read the following paragraph and identify the thought pattern used in its organization. Fill in the concept map that follows with the missing details.

Yoga or Pilates?

[1]Pilates and Yoga seem similar in many ways. [2]They both strengthen the muscles of the arms, legs, abdomen, and back. [3]Both demand concentration, rely on proper breathing techniques, and result in better posture. [4]However, Yoga and Pilates differ in their origins, purposes, methods, and outcomes. [5]The differences between these activities are grounded in their origin. [6]Yoga originated around 5,000 years ago in India as an Eastern philosophy. [7]Yoga, which means "discipline," refers to a method of meditation to gain release from the bondage of Karma (or fate) and achieve rebirth. [8]In contrast, Pilates is an exercise system developed 80 years ago by Joseph Pilates, a Western athlete from Germany, to rehabilitate injured soldiers. [9]The difference in their origins is also seen in the different purposes of the activities. [10]While Yoga is a holistic spiritual discipline, based on meditation to create a life of balance and composure, Pilates is aimed at physical fitness that develops coordination between muscles to stabilize the body. [11]Yoga emphasizes the union of body, mind, and spirit; Pilates strengthens the core and lengthens the spine. [12]Given these core differences in origin and purpose, it makes sense that their methods vary as well. [13]Many styles of Yoga exist, yet all are performed on a mat and may use props such as blocks and straps to foster fluid movement into and out of poses that stretch and strengthen the body. [14]In contrast, Pilates can be performed in two basic ways: on a mat as callisthenic exercises or on

special machines for movement against resistance. [15]Although both activities increase flexibility and improve posture, they do differ in some outcomes. [16]Yoga lubricates the joints and massages the internal glands and organs, as well as detoxifies and tones the body. [17]On the other hand, Pilates develops a flat abdomen and strong back.

1. What is the main thought pattern? comparison and contrast

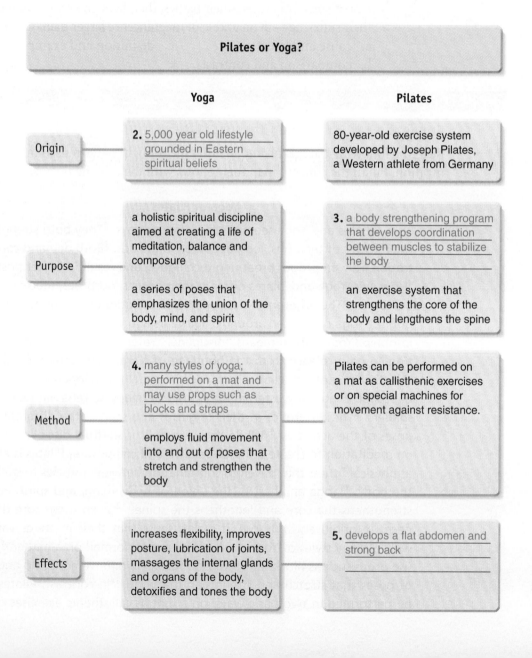

Pilates or Yoga?	
Yoga	**Pilates**

Origin

| 2. 5,000 year old lifestyle grounded in Eastern spiritual beliefs | 80-year-old exercise system developed by Joseph Pilates, a Western athlete from Germany |

Purpose

| a holistic spiritual discipline aimed at creating a life of meditation, balance and composure | 3. a body strengthening program that develops coordination between muscles to stabilize the body |
| a series of poses that emphasizes the union of the body, mind, and spirit | an exercise system that strengthens the core of the body and lengthens the spine |

Method

| 4. many styles of yoga; performed on a mat and may use props such as blocks and straps | Pilates can be performed on a mat as callisthenic exercises or on special machines for movement against resistance. |
| employs fluid movement into and out of poses that stretch and strengthen the body | |

Effects

| increases flexibility, improves posture, lubrication of joints, massages the internal glands and organs of the body, detoxifies and tones the body | 5. develops a flat abdomen and strong back |

Application 2: Using Several Thought Patterns in One Passage

Read the following passage from a college social science textbook. Answer the questions that follow.

Comparable Worth

[1]**Comparable worth** is an idea that calls for equal pay for males and females doing work that requires the same skill, effort, level of responsibility, and working conditions. [2]Supporters of this idea argue that jobs can be measured in terms of needed education, skills, experience, mental demands, and working conditions. [3]The basic worth of the job can also be assessed based on its importance to society. [4]Assigning point values to these and other traits, several communities found that women were making much lower salaries than men, even though their jobs had high points. [5]For example, a legal secretary was paid $375 a month less than a carpenter, but both received the same number of job evaluation points. [6]Since 1984, a few states (for example, Minnesota, South Dakota, New Mexico, and Iowa) have raised women's wages after conducting comparable worth studies.

—Adapted from *Marriages and Families: Changes, Choices, and Constraints*, 4th ed., p. 485 by Nijole V. Benokraitis. Copyright © 2002 by Pearson Education, Inc. Reproduced by permission of Pearson Education, Inc., Boston, MA.

1. What is the main organizing thought pattern? <u>definition and example</u>

2. What is the relationship of ideas *within* sentence 4? <u>contrast</u>

3. What is the relationship *between* sentence 4 and sentence 5? <u>example</u>

4. What is the relationship of ideas *within* sentence 5? <u>comparison and</u>
<u>contrast</u>

VISUAL VOCABULARY

Comparable worth calls for

<u>c</u>_____ pay for men and women based on skill, effort, responsibility, and working conditions.
Which term best completes the idea?
  a. discriminating
  b. selective
  c. equivalent

REVIEW TEST 1

Score (number correct) _____ × 10 = _____%

Transition Words and Thought Patterns

A. Circle the signal words used in these sentences from a college psychology text. Then, identify the organizational pattern in each, as follows:

    a. cause and effect   c. definition and example

    b. comparison or contrast or both

Textbook
Skills

___c___ **1.** Social negotiation is an aspect of the learning process that relies on collaboration with others and respect for different points of view. For example, during class discussions, while students talk and listen to each other, they learn to establish and defend their own positions and respect the opinions of others.

> —Adapted from *Educational Psychology*, 8th ed., p. 335, 369–370 by Anita E. Woolfolk. Copyright © 2001 by Pearson Education, Inc. Reproduced by permission of Pearson Education, Inc., Boston, MA.

___a___ **2.** Higher mental processes develop through social negotiation and interaction, so collaboration in learning is valued.

> —Adapted from Woolfolk, p. 335.

___b___ **3.** A reward is an attractive object or event supplied as a result of a particular behavior. In contrast, an incentive is an object or event that encourages or discourages the behavior. The promise of an A may be an incentive for a student to work hard at studying, while actually receiving the A is her reward.

> —Adapted from Woolfolk, pp. 369–370.

___a___ **4.** If we are consistently reinforced for certain behaviors, then we may develop habits or tendencies to act in certain ways.

> —Adapted from Woolfolk, p. 370.

B. Read the following passage from a college health textbook. Then, answer the questions that follow.

10.5 GE/268 words

Beliefs and Attitudes

Textbook
Skills

    [1]Even if you know why you should change a specific behavior, your beliefs and attitudes about the value of your actions will significantly affect what you do. [2]We often assume that if rational people realize there is a risk in what they are doing, then they will act to reduce that risk. [3]But this is not necessarily true. [4]Consider, for example, the number of physicians

and other health professionals who smoke, fail to manage stress, consume high-fat diets, and act in other unhealthy ways. [5]They surely know better, but their "knowing" is disconnected from their "doing." [6]Why is this so? [7]Two strong influences on behaviors are beliefs and attitudes.

[8]A **belief** is an appraisal of the relationship between some object, action, or idea and some attribute of that object, action, or idea (for example ___, smoking is expensive, dirty, causes cancer—or it is relaxing). [9]Beliefs may develop from direct experience (such as whether you have trouble breathing after smoking for several years). [10]Or they may develop from secondhand experience or knowledge conveyed by other people (for example, if you see your grandfather die of lung cancer after he smoked for years). [11]Although most of us have a general idea about what makes up a belief, we may be a bit unsure about what makes up an attitude. [12]We often hear or say comments such as "He's got a rotten attitude" or "She needs an attitude adjustment." [13]However, we may still be unable to define attitude. [14]**Attitude** is a relatively stable set of beliefs, feelings, and behaviors in relation to something or someone.

—Adapted from *Access to Health*, 7th ed., pp. 19–20 by Rebecca J. Donatelle and Lorraine G. Davis. Copyright © 2002 by Pearson Education, Inc. Printed and Electronically reproduced by permission of Pearson Education, Inc., Upper Saddle River, NJ.

5. Fill in the blank in sentence 2 with a transition word or phrase that makes sense.

___c___ **6.** The relationship of ideas within sentence 2 is one of
   a. generalization and example.   c. cause and effect.
   b. comparison and contrast.

___c___ **7.** The primary thought pattern of organization for the first paragraph is
   a. generalization and example.   c. cause and effect.
   b. comparison and contrast.

8. Fill in the blank in sentence 8 with a transition word or phrase that makes sense.

___b___ **9.** The relationship of ideas between sentence 12 and sentence 13 is one of
   a. definition and example.   c. cause and effect.
   b. comparison and contrast.

___a___ **10.** The primary thought pattern for the second paragraph is
   a. definition and example.   c. cause and effect.
   b. comparison or contrast or both.

REVIEW TEST 2

Score (number correct) _____ × 20 = _____ %

Read the passage and complete the concept map with information from the passage.

10.2 GE/177 words

Textbook
Skills

Sleep Deprivation

[1]What is the longest you have ever stayed awake? [2]Most people have missed no more than a few consecutive nights of sleep, perhaps studying for final exams. [3]If you have ever missed two or three nights of sleep, you may remember having had difficulty concentrating, lapses in attention, and general irritability. [4]Research indicates that even the rather small amount of sleep deprivation associated with delaying your bedtime on weekends leads to decreases in cognitive performance and increases in negative mood on Monday morning. [5]Thus, the familiar phenomenon of the "Monday morning blues" may be the result of staying up late on Friday and Saturday nights. [6]Moreover, sleep loss is known to impair learning in both children and adults.

[7]How does a lack of sleep affect the brain? [8]The effects of sleep deprivation go beyond simply feeling tired. [9]In fact, research has shown that failing to get enough sleep affects your ability to learn. [10]So, if you stay up all night to study for a test, you may actually be engaging in a somewhat self-defeating behavior.

—From *Mastering the World of Psychology*, 3rd ed., p. 123 by Samuel E. Wood, Ellen Green Wood, and Denise Boyd. Copyright © 2008 by Pearson Education, Inc. Reproduced by permission of Pearson Education, Inc., Boston, MA.

1–5. Complete the following cause-and-effect concept map with information from the passage.

REVIEW TEST 3

Score (number correct) _____ × 10 = _____%

Transitions and Thought Patterns

Textbook
Skills

Before you read the following essay from the college textbook *Psychology and Life*, skim the passage and answer the Before Reading questions. Read the essay. Then, answer the After Reading questions.

10.9 GE/466 words

A Hierarchy of Needs

Vocabulary Preview

affiliate (7): associate, connect with

aesthetic (12): artistic

hierarchy (1, 13): ladder, series of levels

actualization (14): realization, fulfillment

transcendence (16): the state of going beyond usual limits

[1]Humanist psychologist Abraham Maslow (1970) formulated the theory that basic motives form a **hierarchy** of needs. [2]In Maslow's view, the needs are arranged in a sequence from primitive to advanced, and the needs at each level must be satisfied before the next level can be reached. [3]At the bottom (primitive level) of this hierarchy are the basic biological needs, such as hunger and thirst. [4]They must be met before any other needs can begin to operate. [5]When *biological needs* are pressing, other needs are put on hold and are unlikely to influence your actions. [6]When they are reasonably well satisfied, the needs at the next level—*safety needs*—motivate you. [7]When you are no longer concerned about danger, you become motivated by *attachment needs*—needs to belong, to **affiliate** with others, to love, and to be loved. [8]If you are well fed and safe and if you feel a sense of belonging, you move up to *esteem needs*—to like oneself, to see oneself as **competent** and effective, and to do what is necessary to earn the esteem of others.

[9]Humans are thinking beings, with complex brains that demand the stimulation of thought. [10]You are motivated by strong *cognitive needs* to know your past, to comprehend the puzzles of current existence, and to predict the future. [11]It is the force of these needs that enables scientists to spend their lives discovering new knowledge. [12]At the next level of Maslow's hierarchy comes the human desire for beauty and order, in the form of *aesthetic needs* that give rise to the creative side of humanity.

[13]At the top of the **hierarchy** are people who are nourished, safe, loved and loving, secure, thinking, and creating. [14]These people have moved beyond basic human needs in the quest for the fullest development of their abilities, or *self-actualization*. [15]A self-actualizing person has many positive traits such as being self-aware, self-accepting, socially responsive, creative, and open to change. [16]*Needs for transcendence* may lead to higher states of

awareness and a cosmic vision of one's part in the universe. [17]Very few people move beyond the self to achieve union with spiritual forces.

[18]Maslow's theory is a particularly upbeat view of human motivation. [19]At the core of the theory is the need for each individual to grow and actualize his or her highest potential. [20]Can we maintain such an unfailingly positive view? [21]The data suggests that we cannot. [22]Alongside the needs Maslow recognized, we find that people express power, dominance, and aggression. [23]You also know from your own experience that Maslow's strict hierarchy breaks down. [24]You're likely, for example, to have ignored hunger on occasion to follow higher-level needs. [25]Even with these limitations, however, Maslow's scheme may enable you to bring some order to different aspects of your motivational experiences.

—From *Psychology and Life*, 16th ed., pp. 388–389 by Richard J. Gerrig and Philip G. Zimbardo. Copyright © 2002 by Pearson Education, Inc. Reproduced by permission of Pearson Education, Inc., Boston, MA.

VISUAL VOCABULARY

Which level of Maslow's hierarchy of needs is represented by the picture?

attachment

Before Reading

Vocabulary in Context

_____c_____ **1.** The word **competent** in sentence 8 means
    a. prideful.   c. capable.
    b. happy.   d. clear.

_____b_____ **2.** The best synonym for **cognitive** in sentence 10 is
    a. emotional.   c. demanding.
    b. thinking.   d. planning.

After Reading

Concept Maps

3–4. Finish the concept map that follows with information from the passage.

Transcendence
Spiritual needs for
cosmic identification

Self-Actualization
Needs to fulfill potential,
have meaningful goals

Aesthetic
4. Needs for order, beauty
_____

Cognitive
Needs for knowledge,
understanding, novelty

Esteem
Needs for confidence, sense
of worth and competence, self-
esteem and respect of others

Attachment
Needs to belong, to affiliate,
to love and be loved

Safety
Needs for security, comfort,
tranquility, freedom from fear

3. Biological _____
Needs for food, water, oxygen, rest,
sexual expression, release from tension

▲ **Maslow's Hierarchy of Needs**
According to Maslow, needs at the lower level of the hierarchy dominate an individual's motivation as long as they are unsatisfied. Once these needs are adequately met, the higher needs occupy the individual's attention.

—From *Psychology and Life*, 16th ed., Figure 12.7 (p. 390) by Richard J. Gerrig and Philip G. Zimbardo. Copyright © 2002 by Pearson Education, Inc. Reproduced by permission of Pearson Education, Inc., Boston, MA.

Central Idea and Main Idea

___a___ **5.** Which sentence states the central idea of the passage?
   a. sentence 1   c. sentence 17
   b. sentence 2   d. sentence 24

Supporting Details

___a___ **6.** Sentence 7 is
   a. a major supporting detail.
   b. a minor supporting detail.

Transitions

___b___ **7.** The word *if* in sentence 8 is a signal word that shows
   a. comparison.   c. time order.
   b. cause and effect.

___b___ **8.** The word *however* in sentence 25 signals
   a. cause and effect.   c. addition.
   b. contrast.

Thought Patterns

___a___ **9.** The primary thought pattern for the entire passage is
   a. classification.   c. comparison and contrast.
   b. cause and effect.

___a___ **10.** The thought pattern for the second paragraph (sentences 9–12) is
   a. cause and effect.   c. listing.
   b. definition and example.

WHAT DO YOU THINK?

Do you agree with the order or sequence of needs in Maslow's hierarchy? Why or why not? Do you agree with the textbook author's view that Maslow's hierarchy is an optimistic view of human development? Why or why not? Assume you are taking a college course in psychology, and your professor has assigned a weekly essay response to your textbook reading. Choose one of the following topics and write a few paragraphs in response to Maslow's hierarchy: Describe your motivations or the motivations of someone you know based on Maslow's hierarchy of needs. Describe a public figure who has reached self-actualization. Use generalizations, definitions, and examples in your response.

REVIEW TEST 4

Score (number correct) _____ × 10 = _____%

Transitions and Thought Patterns

Before Reading: Survey the following passage adapted from the college textbook *The Interpersonal Communication Book*. Skim the passage, noting the words in bold print. Answer the Before Reading questions that follow the passage. Then, read the passage. Next, answer the After Reading questions. Use the discussion and writing topics as activities to do after reading.

12.6 GE/460 words

Gossip

Vocabulary Preview

solidifies (6): strengthens

camaraderie (6): friendship

exhortation (11): urging, advice, warning

ethical (17): moral, principled, right

[1]Gossip is social talk that involves making evaluations about persons who are not present during the conversation; it generally occurs when two people talk about a third party (Eder & Enke, 1991). [2]As you obviously know, a large part of your conversation at work and in social situations is spent gossiping (Lachnit, 2001; Waddington, 2004; Carey, 2005). [3]In fact, one study estimates that approximately two-thirds of people's conversation time is devoted to social topics, and that most of these topics can be considered gossip (Dunbar, 2004). [4]Gossiping seems universal among all cultures (Laing, 1993), and among some it's a commonly accepted ritual (Hall, 1993).

[5]Lots of reasons have been suggested for the popularity and persistence of gossip. [6]One reason often given is that gossip bonds people together and **solidifies** their relationship; it creates a sense of **camaraderie** (Greengard, 2001; Hafen, 2004). [7]At the same time, of course, it helps to create an in-group (those doing the gossiping) and an out-group (those being gossiped about). [8]Gossip also serves a persuasive function in teaching people the cultural rules of their society. [9]That is, when you gossip about the wrong things that so-and-so did, you're in effect identifying the rules that should be followed and perhaps even the consequences that follow when the rules are broken. [10]Gossip enables you to learn what is and what is not acceptable behavior (Baumeister, Zhang, & Vohs, 2004). [11]Within an organization, gossip helps to regulate organization behavior: Gossip enables workers to learn who the organizational heroes are, what they did, and how they were rewarded—and carries an implicit **exhortation** to do likewise. [12]And, of course, negative gossip enables workers to learn who broke the rules and what punishments resulted from such rule-breaking-again,

with an accompanying implicit **admonition** to avoid such behaviors (Hafen, 2004).

[13]People often engage in gossip for some kind of reward; for example, to hear more gossip, gain social status or control, have fun, cement social bonds, or make social comparisons (Rosnow, 1977; Miller & Wilcox, 1986; Leaper & Holliday, 1995; Wert & Salovey, 2004). [14]Research is not consistent on the consequences of gossip for the person gossiping. [15]One research study argues that gossiping leads others to see you more negatively, regardless of whether your gossip is positive or negative and whether you're sharing this gossip with strangers or friends (Turner, Mazur, Wendel, & Winslow, 2003). [16]Another study finds that positive gossip leads to acceptance by your peers and greater friendship intimacy (Cristina, 2001).

[17]As you might expect, gossiping often has **ethical** implications, and in many instances gossip would be considered unethical. [18]Some such instances: when gossip is used to unfairly hurt another person, when you know it's not true, when no one has the right to such personal information, or when you've promised secrecy (Bok, 1983).

—From *The Interpersonal Communication Book,* 11th ed., pp. 212–213 by Joseph A. DeVito. Copyright © 2007 by Pearson Education, Inc. Reproduced by permission of Pearson Education, Inc., Boston, MA.

Before Reading

Vocabulary in Context

1. In sentence 12, **admonition** means <u>warning</u>
2. Context clue used for **admonition** <u>synonym (exhortation) and general</u>
   <u>sense of the passage</u>

After Reading

3–6. Central Idea, Supporting Details, and Outlines

Complete the following outline with information from the passage. Wording may vary.

Thesis Statement: (3) <u>Gossiping occupies a large part of our conversational time</u>

<u>and can create problems when some simple principles are not followed.</u>

I. Gossip

  A. Definition: (**4**) <u>Gossip is social talk that involves making evaluations</u>

     <u>about persons who are not present during the conversation.</u>

    1. Two-thirds of conversation time is considered gossip.

    2. Gossip is a universal ritual among all cultures.

  B. Reasons for gossip

    1. Gossip bonds people and solidifies relationships.

    2. Gossip creates an in-group and an out-group.

    3. (**5**) <u>Gossip teaches people the cultural roles of their society.</u>

  C. (**6**) <u>Consequences of gossip debated</u>

    1. Gossiping may lead others to see you negatively.

    2. Gossiping may lead to acceptance and intimacy.

Transitions and Thought Patterns

   c   **7.** The main thought pattern for the first paragraph (sentences 1–4) is
      a. comparison.   c. definition and example.
      b. cause and effect.

   b   **8.** The main thought pattern for the second paragraph (sentences 5–12) is
      a. comparison.   c. definition and example.
      b. cause and effect.

   c   **9.** What is the relationship of ideas between sentences 8 and 9?
      a. cause and effect   c. generalization and example
      b. contrast

   b   **10.** What is the relationship of ideas within sentence 13?
      a. definition and example   c. contrast
      b. generalization and example

WHAT DO YOU THINK?

Why do people gossip? When is gossip unethical or harmful? Can gossip ever be beneficial? How or why? Have you or someone you know been the subject of gossip? How did being the topic of gossip make you or that person feel? What role does gossip play in online social networks like Facebook and Twitter? Assume you have taken the role of a mentor to a younger person through your public service work with a youth organization such as the Boys Club, the Girls Club, Boys Scouts, Girl Scouts, or the YMCA. Write an article to post on the organization's local Web page about the causes and effects of gossip—particularly in the context of online social networks.

 ## After Reading About More Thought Patterns

Before you move on to the Mastery Tests on thought patterns, take time to reflect on your learning and performance by answering the following questions. Write your answers in your notebook.

- How has my knowledge base or prior knowledge about more thought patterns changed?

- Based on my studies, how do I think I will perform on the Mastery Test(s)? Why do I think my scores will be above average, average, or below average?

- Would I recommend this chapter to other students who want to learn about thought patterns? Why or why not?

Test your understanding of what you have learned about Thought Patterns for Master Readers by completing the Chapter 8 Review Card in the insert near the end of your text.

CONNECT TO **myreadinglab**

To check your progress in meeting Chapter 8's learning outcomes, log in to www.myreadinglab.com and try the following exercises.

- The "Patterns of Organization" section of MyReadingLab gives additional information about transitions and patterns of organization. The section provides a model, practices, activities, and tests. To access this resource, click on the "Study Plan" tab. Then click on "Patterns of Organization." Then click on the following links as needed: "Overview," "Model," "Signal Words (Flash Animation)," "Other Patterns of Organization (Flash Animation)," "Practice," and "Tests."

- To measure your mastery of the content of this chapter, complete the tests in the "Patterns of Organization" section and click on Gradebook to find your results.

Read the following paragraph from a college social science textbook. Fill in the blanks (**1–5**) with transition words from the box. Then, answer the questions following the paragraph.

differences	effect	more	same	than

Textbook
Skills

11.0 GE/172 words

Differences in the Effects of Drugs

Some differences in drug effects may be related to an interaction between the drug itself and the specific traits of the person taking the drug. One characteristic is a person's weight. In general, a heavier person will require a greater amount of a drug **(1)** <u>than</u> a lighter person to receive the same drug **(2)** <u>effect</u>. It is for this reason that drug dosages are expressed as a ratio of drug amount to weight. Another characteristic is gender. Even if a man and a woman are exactly the **(3)** <u>same</u> weight, differences in drug effects can still result on the basis of gender **(4)** <u>differences</u> in body composition and sex hormones. Women have, on average, a higher proportion of fat, due to a greater fat-to-muscle ratio, and a lower proportion of water than men. When we look at the effects of alcohol consumption in terms of gender, we find that the lower water content in women makes them feel **(5)** <u>more</u> intoxicated than men, even if the same amount of alcohol is consumed.

—Adapted from Levinthal, *Drugs, Behaviors, and Modern Society*, 3rd ed., pp. 58–59.

_____c_____ **6.** The transition used to fill blank (1) signals
   a. cause and effect.
   b. generalization and example.
   c. comparison and contrast.

_____a_____ **7.** The transition used to fill blank (2) signals
   a. cause and effect.
   b. generalization and example.
   c. comparison and contrast.

_____c_____ **8.** The transition used to fill blank (3) signals
   a. cause and effect.
   b. definition and example.
   c. comparison and contrast.

_____c_____ **9.** The transition used to fill blank (4) signals
   a. cause and effect.
   b. generalization and example.
   c. comparison and contrast.

_____c_____ **10.** The transition used to fill blank (5) signals
   a. cause and effect.
   b. definition.
   c. comparison and contrast.

A. Write the numbers **1** to **9** in the spaces provided to identify the correct order of the ideas. Then, answer the question that follows the list.

Textbook Skills

Physical Effects of Modern Life

__2__ One of the most pervasive problems is shortened muscles, tendons, and ligaments.

__5__ For example, continual sitting at work and leisure results in shortened muscles, tendons, and ligaments and eventually results in restricted movements.

__4__ However, our daily activities have changed drastically.

__1__ Our modern living patterns are directly responsible for a host of health problems.

__3__ First, our basic body structure and function have not changed since the days of prehistoric humans.

__6__ It is not unusual for adults in their mid-twenties to be so restricted that touching their toes while keeping the knees straight is impossible or painful.

__7__ In addition to restricted movement, chronic sitting affects the spine.

__9__ The result will be a sitting-type posture when one is standing or walking; this posture produces pain and tension because body parts are not positioned naturally.

__8__ The spine will condition itself to the demand of chronic sitting and lose its ability to remain erect.

—Adapted from Girdano, Everly, & Dusek, *Controlling Stress and Tension*, 6th ed., p. 248.

__c__ **10.** The primary thought pattern is
   a. generalization and example.
   b. comparison and contrast.
   c. cause and effect.

B. Read the following paragraph from a college social science textbook. Then, answer the questions and complete the concept map.

12.4 GE/71 words

Insomnia

[1]The term *insomnia* typically means "sleeplessness" or the "inability to sleep." [2]Insomnia has several causes and effects. [3]Common effects of insomnia include fatigue, irritability, poor concentration, poor short-term memory, drowsiness, and abuse of stimulants. [4]Several factors that contribute to insomnia are physical, such as heart disease, high blood pressure, "heartburn," and chronic breathing problems. [5]However, mental factors such as tension caused by anxiety and anger are the main causes of insomnia.

—Adapted from *Encyclopedia of Stress*, 1st ed., p. 119 by F. J. McGuigan. Copyright © 1999 by Pearson Education, Inc. Printed and Electronically reproduced by permission of Pearson Education, Inc., Upper Saddle River, NJ.

_____ **11.** The relationship between sentence 3 and sentence 4 is
   a. cause and effect.
   b. addition.
   c. contrast.

Causes and Effects of Insomnia

Main idea (stated in the topic sentence): Insomnia has several causes and effects.

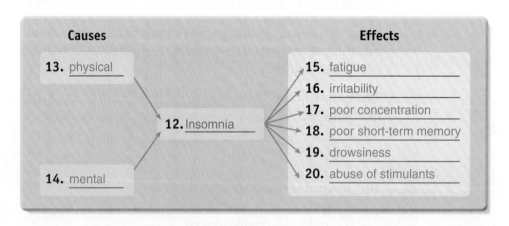

Causes

13. physical

14. mental

12. Insomnia

Effects

15. fatigue

16. irritability

17. poor concentration

18. poor short-term memory

19. drowsiness

20. abuse of stimulants

Read the following paragraphs from college textbooks. Then, answer the questions and complete the outline and the concept table.

10.0 GE/177 words

Road Rage

[1]"Road rage" is the term used to describe the attitude of extremely angry, hostile, and aggressive drivers. [2]Several factors are linked to road rage. [3]First, road congestion has become worse in the past 10 years due to an increase in both the number of cars and total miles driven, without an expansion in the amount of road space available. [4]Road congestion adds to the amount of time a driver spends on the road and frequently causes delay as well as late or missed appointments. [5]This is an added stressor for people whose schedules are already overloaded due to work and family demands. [6]Thus, poor time management skills may contribute to road rage. [7]Finally, a lack of anger control often leads to road rage. [8]Demands on time increase the tendency to overreact to what otherwise might be considered slight inconveniences. [9]Thus, the angry, stressed driver is likely to see the presence of others on the road as "unreasonable" behavior and an excuse to disregard legal and safety rules so that she or he can get past the "morons."

—Adapted from *Encyclopedia of Stress*, 1st ed., pp. 185–186 by F. J. McGuigan. Copyright © 1999 by Pearson Education, Inc. Printed and Electronically reproduced by permission of Pearson Education, Inc., Upper Saddle River, NJ.

_____a_____ **1.** The thought pattern suggested by sentence 1 is
   a. definition and example.
   b. comparison and contrast.
   c. cause and effect.

_____b_____ **2.** The primary thought pattern
   a. discusses the similarities between normal drivers and "morons."
   b. explains some of the causes of road rage.
   c. compares individual responses to road rage.

3–5.   **Road Rage**

Main idea (stated in the topic sentence): Several factors are linked to road rage.

   A. road congestion _____

   B. poor time management skills _____

   C. lack of anger control _____

357

Textbook
Skills

10.2 GE/196 words   **Semantic versus Episodic Memory**

[1]In your long-term memory (LTM), you store two different types of information: semantic and episodic memories. [2]Semantic memories are memories of the meanings of words (a pine is an evergreen tree with long needles), concepts (heat moves from a warmer object to a cooler one), and general facts about the world (the original 13 colonies were established by the British). [3]For the most part, you don't remember when, where, or how you learned this information. [4]In contrast, episodic memories are memories of events that are linked to a time, place, and situation (when, where, and how). [5]In other words, episodic memories provide a context. [6]The meaning of the word *memory* is no doubt firmly implanted in your semantic memory; whereas the time and place you first began to read this book are most likely in your episodic memory. [7]Brain scanning studies have given evidence that semantic and episodic memories are distinct. [8]The frontal lobe of the brain, for instance, plays a key role in looking up stored information. [9]However, when we recall semantic memories, the left frontal lobe tends to be more active than the right. [10]The reverse is true when we recall episodic memories.

—Adapted from Kosslyn & Rosenberg, *Fundamentals of Psychology*, p. 163.

_____a_____ **6.** The relationship between sentences 7 and 8 is
  a. generalization and example.
  b. cause and effect.
  c. comparison and contrast.

Semantic versus Episodic Memory

(7) Main idea (Stated in the topic sentence): In your long-term memory (LTM), you store two different types of information: semantic and episodic memories.

	Semantic Memory	Episodic Memory
First difference	(8) Memories of the meaning of words	Memories of events that are linked to time, place, and situation
Second difference	(9) You don't remember when, where, or how you learned information.	Episodic memories are learned in context.
Third difference	The left frontal lobe is more active than the right frontal lobe when we recall semantic memories.	(10) The right frontal lobe is more active than the left when we recall episodic memories.

Read the following passage from a college science textbook. After reading, complete the concept map with information from the passage. Wording may vary.

12.1 GE/485 words

Human Use and Impact: Oceans

[1]Our species has a long history of interacting with the oceans. [2]We have traveled across their waters, clustered our settlements along their coastlines, and been fascinated by their beauty, power, and vastness. [3]We have also left our mark upon them by exploiting oceans for their resources and polluting them with our waste.

Marine pollution threatens resources [4]People have long made the oceans a sink for waste and pollution. [5]Oil, plastic, industrial chemicals, sewage, excess nutrients, and abandoned fishing gear all eventually make their way into the oceans.

Nets and plastic debris [6]Plastic bags and bottles, fishing nets, gloves, fishing line, buckets, floats, abandoned cargo, and much else that people transport on the sea or deposit into it can harm marine organisms. [7]Because most plastic is not biodegradable, it can drift for decades before washing up on beaches. [8]Marine mammals, seabirds, fish, and sea turtles may mistake floating plastic debris for food and can die as a result of ingesting material they cannot digest or expel. [9]Fishing nets that are lost or intentionally discarded may continue snaring animals for decades. [10]We can all help minimize this type of harm by reducing our use of plastics and by picking up trash on beaches.

Oil pollution [11]Major oil spills—such as the one that occurred in 1989 when the Exxon Valdez struck a reef in Prince William Sound, Alaska, and spilled 42 million L (11 million gal) of crude oil—make headlines and cause serious environmental problems. [12]Yet the majority of oil pollution in the oceans accumulates from innumerable widely spread small sources, including leakage from small boats and runoff from human activities on land. [13]Moreover, the amount of petroleum spilled into the oceans in recent years is equaled by the amount that seeps up from naturally occurring seafloor deposits. [14]Nonetheless, minimizing the amount of oil we release into coastal waters is important. [15]Petroleum can physically coat and kill marine organisms and, when ingested, can poison them. [16]Oil spills can devastate fisheries and the local economies dependent on them.

Excess nutrients [17]Pollution from fertilizer runoff or other nutrient inputs can create dead zones in coastal marine ecosystems, as with the Gulf of Mexico. [18]Excessive nutrient concentrations also may give rise to population explosions among several species of marine algae that produce powerful toxins that attack the nervous systems of vertebrates. [19]Blooms of these algae are known as harmful algal blooms. [20]Some algal species produce reddish pigments that discolor surface waters, and blooms of these species are nicknamed red tides. [21]Harmful algal blooms can cause illness and death among zooplankton, birds, fish, marine mammals, and people as their toxins are passed up the food chain. [22]They also cause economic loss for communities dependent on fishing or beach tourism.

[23]As severe as the impacts of all these types of marine pollution can be, however, most marine scientists concur that the more worrisome dilemma is overharvesting.

—Adapted from *Essential Environment: The Science behind the Stories*, 3rd ed., pp. 275–276
by Jay H. Withgott and Scott R. Brennan. Copyright © 2009 by Pearson Education, Inc.
Reprinted by permission of Pearson Education, Inc., Upper Saddle River, NJ.

1. Causes	Marine Pollution	Effects
Trash	2. Nets and plastic debris	poisons, snares, and kills marine life
Oil spills	Oil pollution	poisons, coats, kills marine life
3. Leakage from small boats		
Runoff from land		
Natural seafloor deposits		
Fertilizer runoff	4. Excess nutrients	creates dead zones;
		population explosion of toxic algae and algal blooms
		5. sickens and kills life up the food chain

Fact and Opinion

LEARNING OUTCOMES

After studying this chapter you should be able to do the following:

1. Define the following terms: *fact* and *opinion*. [Knowledge]
2. Ask questions to identify facts. [Comprehension]
3. Analyze biased words to identify opinions. [Analysis]
4. Analyze supposed "facts." [Analysis]
5. Distinguish between fact and opinion. [Analysis]
6. Evaluate the importance of facts and opinions. [Evaluation]
7. Interpret fact(s) and opinion(s) to improve comprehension. [Application, Comprehension]

Before Reading About Fact and Opinion

You are most likely already familiar with the commonly used words *fact* and *opinion*, and you probably already have an idea about what each one means. Take a moment to clarify your current understanding about fact and opinion by writing a definition for each one in the spaces below:

Fact: Answers may vary. _____

_____

Opinion: _____

_____

_____

As you work through this chapter, compare what you already know about fact and opinion to new information that you learn using the following method:

On a blank page in your notebook draw a line down the middle of the page to form two columns. Label one side "Fact" and the other "Opinion." Below each heading, copy the definition you wrote for each one. As you work through the chapter, record new information you learn about facts and opinions in their corresponding columns.

 ## What Is the Difference Between Fact and Opinion?

Fact: The average American child will witness 12,000 violent acts on television each year, amounting to about 200,000 violent acts by age 18.

Opinion: American television programming is too violent.

Master readers must sort fact from opinion to properly understand and evaluate the information they are reading.

> A **fact** is a specific detail that is true based on objective proof. A fact is discovered.
> An **opinion** is an interpretation, value judgment, or belief that cannot be proved or disproved. An opinion is created.
> **Objective proof** can be physical evidence, an eyewitness account, or the result of an accepted scientific method.

Most people's points of view and beliefs are based on a blend of fact and opinion. Striving to remain objective, many authors rely mainly on facts. The main purpose of these authors is to inform. For example, textbooks, news articles, and medical research rely on facts. In contrast, editorials, advertisements, and fiction often mix fact and opinion. The main purpose of these types of writing is to persuade or entertain.

Separating fact from opinion requires you to think critically because opinion is often presented as fact. The following clues will help you separate fact from opinion.

Fact	Opinion
Is objective	Is subjective
Is discovered	Is created
States reality	Interprets reality
Can be verified	Cannot be verified
Is presented with unbiased words	Is presented with biased words
Example of a fact	*Example of an opinion*
Spinach is a source of iron.	Spinach tastes awful.

A fact is a specific, objective, and verifiable detail; in contrast, an opinion is a biased, personal view created from feelings and beliefs.

EXAMPLE Read the following statements, and mark each one **F** if it states a fact or **O** if it expresses an opinion.

<u> O </u>   **1.** The most beautiful spot on earth is a serene lake nestled in the foothills of the Appalachian Mountains.

<u> F </u>   **2.** Tippah Lake is located just outside of the small town of Ripley, Mississippi, in the foothills of the Appalachian Mountains.

EXPLANATION The first sentence expresses an opinion in the form of a personal interpretation about what is beautiful. The second sentence is a statement of fact that gives the location of the lake.

PRACTICE 1

Read the following statements and mark each one **F** if it states a fact or **O** if it expresses an opinion.

<u> O </u>   **1.** Living in a large city is detrimental to one's psychological well-being.

<u> F </u>   **2.** New York City offers an array of cultural experiences including Broadway theatre, historic sites such as Ellis Island and the Statue of Liberty, and many museums such as the Children's Museum of Manhattan.

Ask Questions to Identify Facts

To test whether a statement is a fact, ask these three questions:

- Can the statement be proved or demonstrated to be true?
- Can the statement be observed in practice or operation?
- Can the statement be verified by witnesses, manuscripts, or documents?

If the answer to any of these questions is no, the statement is not a fact. Instead, it is an opinion. Keep in mind, however, that many statements blend both fact and opinion.

EXAMPLE Read the following statements and mark each one **F** if it states a fact or **O** if it expresses an opinion.

_____ F   **1.** In the 1700s women sewed lead weights into the bottoms of their bathing gowns to prevent the gowns from floating up and exposing their legs.

_____ O   **2.** Bikinis reveal too much skin and are indecent.

_____ F   **3.** Arnold Schwarzenegger, governor of California, was born in Austria.

_____ O   **4.** Arnold Schwarzenegger's distinguished film career and admirable devotion to public service make him a unique American hero.

EXPLANATION Compare your answers to the ones below.

1. F: This statement can be easily verified by doing research.

2. O: This is a statement of personal opinion. Words and phrases such as *too much* and *indecent* are judgments that vary from person to person.

3. F: These facts are common knowledge and easily verified.

4. O: Several words in this statement, such as *distinguished, admirable,* and *unique,* reveal that it is a statement of opinion based on personal views.

PRACTICE 2

Read the following statements, and mark each one **F** if it states a fact or **O** if it expresses an opinion or **F/O** if it expresses both a fact and an opinion.

_____ F   **1.** Ninety-five percent of the world's consumers live outside the United States.

_____ F   **2.** During the creation of his novel *Carrie*, Stephen King threw the novel into the trash, and his wife dug it out and convinced him to finish it.

_____ O   **3.** Low-carbohydrate diets such as Atkins and South Beach are ineffective and dangerous.

_____ F   **4.** Balto was a dog who, in the winter of 1925, led a dogsled team through a blizzard to get medicine to Nome, Alaska, because of a fatal diphtheria epidemic; a statue stands in his honor in Central Park, New York, at 67th Street and Fifth Avenue, just inside the Park.

_____ O   **5.** Cats can be irritating pets because they are independent and unaffectionate.

___O___ **6.** Newspapers are the most reliable source for news.

___F___ **7.** Danica Sue Patrick is an American auto racing driver, currently competing in the IndyCar Series, the ARCA Racing Series, and the NASCAR Nationwide Series.

___F/O___ **8.** Danica Patrick is also a beautiful woman who has appeared on the cover of *Sports Illustrated*.

___F___ **9.** Regular dental flossing reduces gum disease.

___O___ **10.** People who live in the Northeast part of the United States are much more open-minded and liberal than people who live in the South.

 ## Note Biased Words to Identify Opinions

Be on the lookout for biased words. **Biased words** express opinions, value judgments, and interpretations. They are often loaded with emotion. The box contains a small sample of these kinds of words.

Biased Words					
amazing	best	favorite	great	miserable	stupid
awful	better	frightful	greatest	more	ugly
bad	disgusting	fun	handsome	most	unbelievable
beautiful	exciting	good	horrible	smart	very

Realize that a sentence can include both facts and opinions. The part of the sentence that includes a biased word may be an opinion about another part of the sentence that is a fact.

EXAMPLE Read the following sentences. Underline the biased words.

1. John Coltrane was a jazz musician whose quartet produced hit albums that remain the <u>most innovative and expressive</u> jazz music of our time.

2. Even though marijuana use is widespread in America, <u>it should not be legalized</u>.

EXPLANATION In the first sentence, the first part "John Coltrane was a jazz musician whose quartet produced hit albums" is a fact that can be proved. The second part of the sentence, however, expresses an opinion about his music using the biased words *most innovative* and *expressive*. In the second sentence, the widespread use of marijuana is well documented, but the idea that "it should not be legalized" is an opinion.

Read the following two sentences. Underline the biased words.

1. The works of Joan Didion, one of the <u>most brilliant</u> writers of this generation, <u>should be</u> required reading in a <u>liberal</u> arts education.

2. Writing is a <u>satisfying</u> process that can lead to <u>alarming</u> self-discoveries, <u>comforting</u> insights, and <u>much needed</u> wisdom.

Note Qualifiers to Identify Opinions

Be on the lookout for words that qualify an idea. A qualifier may express an absolute, unwavering opinion using words like *always* or *never*. Other times a qualifier expresses an opinion in the form of a command as in *must*, or the desirability of an action with a word like *should*. Qualifiers may indicate different degrees of doubt with words such as *seems* or *might*. The box contains a few examples of these kinds of words.

Words That Qualify Ideas					
all	could	likely	never	possibly, possible	sometimes
always	every	may	often	probably, probable	think
appear	has/have to	might	only	seem	usually
believe	it is believed	must	ought to	should	

Remember that a sentence can include both fact and opinion. Authors use qualifiers to express opinions about facts.

EXAMPLE Read the following sentences. Underline the qualifiers.

1. Dissatisfaction with work <u>often</u> spills over into relationships; <u>most</u> people are not able to separate work problems from their relationship lives.

2. In his book *Messages: Building Interpersonal Communication Skills*, Joseph A. DeVito states, "Commitment <u>may</u> take <u>many</u> forms; it <u>may</u> be an engagement or a marriage; it <u>may</u> be a commitment to help the person or be with the person, or a commitment to reveal your deepest secrets." (1999, p. 264)

EXPLANATION

1. The qualifiers in this sentence are *often* and *most*.

2. The qualifiers in this sentence are *may* and *many*.

PRACTICE 4

Read the following sentences. Underline the qualifiers.

1. Oral hygiene is the <u>only</u> way to avoid <u>possible</u> gum disease; you <u>must</u> brush your teeth three times a day and floss at least once daily.

2. All citizens <u>should</u> save some portion of their earnings for their <u>probable</u> retirement.

 # Think Carefully About Supposed "Facts"

Beware of **false facts,** or statements presented as facts that are actually untrue. At times, an author may mislead the reader with a false impression of the facts. Political and commercial advertisements often present facts out of context, exaggerate the facts, or give only some of the facts. For example, Governor People boasts that under his leadership, his state has attained the highest literacy rates ever achieved. Although his state's literacy rates did reach their highest historical levels, the actual rise was slight, and his state's literacy levels remained the lowest in the country. The governor misled people by leaving out important facts.

Sometimes an author deliberately presents false information. Journalist Jayson Blair concocted a host of false facts in many of the articles he wrote for the *New York Times*. For example, in his five articles about the capture and rescue of Private Jessica Lynch, Blair fabricated many facts. First, he wrote his stories as if he had conducted face-to-face interviews, yet he never traveled to meet the family, and he conducted all of his interviews by telephone. Then, in a March 27, 2003, article, he described Lynch's father as being "choked up as he stood on his porch here overlooking the tobacco fields and cattle pastures." The statement was false: He never witnessed such a scene, and the Lynch home does not overlook tobacco fields or cattle pastures. Blair's use of false facts ruined his career and damaged the reputation of the prestigious *New York Times*.

Most often, however, false facts are mere errors. Read the following two examples of false facts:

1. Thomas Alva Edison invented the first light bulb.

2. The common cold is most commonly spread by coughing and sneezing.

Research quickly proves the first statement to be a false fact; light bulbs were being used 50 years before Edison patented his version of the light bulb. The second statement is a false fact because studies show that a cold is more likely to be spread by physical contact such as shaking hands or sharing a phone than by inhaling particles in the air. Often some prior knowledge of the topic is needed to identify false facts. The more you read, the more masterful you will become at evaluating facts as true or false.

False facts can be used to mislead, persuade, or entertain. For example, read the following claims about a nutritional supplement that allegedly prevents a wide range of illnesses including colds, flus, cancer, irritable bowel syndrome, *Candida Albicans,* and heart disease.

BodyWise

[1]Every day your body is under attack and the results can be deadly. [2]The best thing you can do is to bolster your immune system so it can defend itself from infection and foreign invaders. [3]We believe BodyWise International's all natural AG-Immune formula is the most powerful product ever created to promote a healthy immune system . . . and a healthier future. [4]And while it's [sic] primary ingredient, Ai/E10™, has proven to be clinically effective for use with both immune and autoimmune disorders, you don't have to be immune system challenged to enjoy the amazing benefits of this exciting new supplement. [5]Think of it as a prudent preventative measure that promotes optimal health by increasing the activity of natural killer (NK) cells—your body's last line of defense against illness and disease. [6]AG-Immune has already changed the lives of thousands of people across North America. [7]Imagine what it could do for you: [8]"One day I happened to notice that, on the cover of The Ultimate Nutrient booklet, *candida* was listed as one of the areas Ai/E10 was clinically successful in treating. [9]I began taking two a day and literally—within 36 hours—the pain began to dissipate. [10]After only three weeks, my symptoms were completely gone! [11]I have been on BodyWise for almost eight years and at the risk of sounding over-dramatic, I have to say, the products have definitely changed my quality of life."

—Adapted from *United States of America, Plaintiff, v. Body Wise International, Inc.,* and *Jesse A. Stoff, M.D., Defendants,* United States District Court, Central District of California, Southern Division. Civil Action No.: SACV-05-43 (DOC) (Anx) 5 Nov. 2007. http://www.ftc.gov/os/caselist/bodywise/050118compbodywise.pdf

The Federal Trade Commission sued and won a settlement against the company for false advertisement. The company could not support its claims to prevent or improve disease symptoms with scientific evidence. Note the biased words the author used to describe the effectiveness of the supplement: *attack, deadly, best, bolster, most powerful, healthier, amazing benefits, exciting, prudent,* and *optimal,* to name a few.

Copyright © 2011 Pearson Education, Inc.

VISUAL VOCABULARY

The best synonym for "clinically" is b_____.

a. accidentally.
b. scientifically.
c. humanly.

▶ Ai/E10™ has proven to be clinically effective for use with both immune and autoimmune disorders.

In addition to thinking carefully about false facts, beware of opinions worded to sound like facts. Remember that facts are specific details that can be researched and verified as true. However, opinions may be introduced with phrases like *in truth, the truth of the matter,* or *in fact.* Read the following two statements:

1. In truth, reproductive cloning is expensive and highly inefficient.

2. More than 90% of cloning attempts fail to produce viable offspring, and cloned animals tend to have much weaker immune function and higher rates of infection, tumor growth, and other disorders; in fact, reproductive cloning is expensive and highly inefficient.

—Adapted from "Cloning Fact Sheet," 19 Nov. 2003, *Human Genome Program,* U.S. Department of Energy. 29 Jan. 2004, http://www.ornl.gov/sci/techresources/Human_ Genome/elsi/cloning.shtml#risks

The first statement is a general opinion that uses the biased words *expensive, highly,* and *inefficient.* The second statement is a blend of fact and opinion.

It begins with the facts, but then uses the phrase *in fact* to introduce the opinion.

EXAMPLES Read the following statements, and mark each one as follows:

F if it states a fact

O if it states an opinion

F/O if it combines fact and opinion

_____F_____ **1.** Public funding for art education, at both national and local levels, has declined in recent years.

_____O_____ **2.** Diet Pepsi tastes better than Diet Coke.

_____F/O_____ **3.** Microwave popcorn is a nutritious, low-calorie, and tasty snack food.

_____F_____ **4.** T'ai Chi and Yoga include relaxation and breathing techniques that improve mental and physical health.

_____F/O_____ **5.** With humankind's ability to produce synthetic fibers that can clothe us with beauty and comfort, humans should refrain from murdering animals so their hides, coats, or furs can be used as clothing.

EXPLANATIONS

1. This is a statement of fact that can be researched.

2. This is a statement of opinion that includes the biased word *better*. Taste preferences are a matter of personal opinion.

3. This is a blend of fact and opinion. Popcorn is a low-calorie snack food, and its nutritional value can be verified; however, the value word *tasty* states an opinion.

4. This is a statement of fact that can be verified through research.

5. This is a statement that blends fact and opinion. The biased words *beauty, should*, and *murdering* are used.

EXAMPLE Look at the following cartoon. Then, write one fact and one opinion about the cartoon.

© Jeff Parker 1/14/04 *Florida Today* and Cagle Cartoons, Inc.

Fact: Many Americans ignore the Surgeon General's warning against smoking.

              The percentage of Americans who smoke has declined since 1964.

Opinion: The Surgeon General's warning against smoking has had a significant

              effect on American smoking behaviors. People who smoke are foolish.

EXPLANATION Compare your answers to the ones below. Answers may vary.

Fact: Many Americans ignore the Surgeon General's warning against smoking. The percentage of Americans who smoke has declined since 1964.

Opinion: The Surgeon General's warning against smoking has had a significant effect on American smoking behaviors. People who smoke are foolish.

PRACTICE 5

A. Read the following statements and mark each one as follows:

F if it states a fact

O if it expresses an opinion

F/O if it combines fact and opinion

___O___ **1.** I believe capital punishment is a crime against humanity.

___O___ **2.** Executives of large corporations receive outrageously large salaries that unfairly reward them for successes created by lower paid rank-and-file workers.

_____F_____ **3.** *E. coli*, influenza, tuberculosis, measles, mumps, and smallpox are just a few of the diseases that are preventable through vaccinations.

_____F/O_____ **4.** More than 8 million Africans are infected with tuberculosis, with nearly 3 million dying each year; wealthier and more developed countries, such as the United States, should help fund widespread vaccination programs in Africa.

_____O_____ **5.** Astrology offers information that is effective in making important life decisions.

B. Read the following short reviews of destinations, restaurants, movies, and plays. Mark each one as follows:

F if it states a fact

O if it expresses an opinion

F/O if it combines fact and opinion

_____O_____ **6.** The 14th Street Bar and Grill in Boulder, Colorado, offers excellent food, average service, and a spectacular view of the Rocky Mountains.

_____F_____ **7.** Drago's Seafood in Metairie, Louisiana, offers Creole cuisine ranging from $21 to $24, with lobster and seafood as the main entrees.

_____F/O_____ **8.** Judson College, the nation's sixth-oldest women's college, offers a challenging and high-quality liberal arts education.

_____F_____ **9.** One bat can eat as many as one thousand insect pests, such as mosquitoes, in an hour.

_____F/O_____ **10.** *TMZ TV,* a television magazine show that delves into the private lives of celebrities, stands as an embarrassing example of the public's interest in gossip and the misfortune of other people.

Read Critically: Evaluate Details as Fact or Opinion in Context

Because the printed word seems to give authority to an idea, many of us accept what we read as fact. Yet much of what is published is actually opinion. Master readers question what they read. Reading critically is noting the use of fact and opinion in the context of a paragraph or passage, the author, and the type of source in which the passage is printed.

Evaluate the Context of the Passage

EXAMPLE Read the passage, and identify each sentence as follows:

F if it states a fact

O if it expresses an opinion

F/O if it combines fact and opinion

Vermicomposting

¹Composting is an excellent way to recycle organic materials like food scraps and yard clippings. ²Vermicomposting uses red worms to decompose organic material and create fertilizer for gardens. ³In addition, it provides an easy, clean, odor-free, and environmentally correct way to get rid of garbage. ⁴The worms are able to eat over half their body weight in one day, and their waste material, known as castings, is full of nutrients and microbes that promote plant growth. ⁵Everyone should use vermicomposting.

1. __F/O__   2. __F__   3. __F/O__   4. __F__   5. __O__

EXPLANATION Compare your answers to the ones below.

1. **F/O:** Composting is a way to recycle organic materials like food scraps and yard clippings; however, the word *excellent* is a biased word.

2. **F:** This statement can be verified.

3. **F/O:** Vermicomposting is a way to get rid of garbage; however, the words *easy, clean*, and *environmentally correct* are biased words or phrases.

4. **F:** This statement can be checked and verified as true.

5. **O:** This statement expresses an opinion with the words *everyone* and *should*.

PRACTICE 6

Read the passage, and identify each sentence as follows:

F if it states a fact

O if it expresses an opinion

F/O if it combines fact and opinion

What Makes a Home Energy Star?

[1]ENERGY STAR is the government-backed symbol for energy efficiency; homes that earn the ENERGY STAR are significantly more energy efficient than standard homes. [2]ENERGY STAR builders achieve this high efficiency for you by selecting from a variety of features such as the following:

Tight Construction and Ducts

[3]Advanced techniques for sealing holes and cracks in the home's "envelope" and in heating and cooling ducts help reduce drafts, moisture, dust, pollen, pests, and noise. [4]A tightly sealed home improves comfort and indoor air quality while lowering utility and maintenance costs.

Effective Insulation Systems

[5]Properly installed and inspected insulation in floors, walls, and attics ensures even temperatures throughout the house, while using less energy. [6]The result is lower utility costs and a quieter, more comfortable home.

Efficient Heating and Cooling Equipment

[7]An energy-efficient, properly installed heating and cooling system uses less energy to operate, which reduces your utility bills. [8]This system can also be quieter, reduce indoor humidity, and improve the overall comfort of your home.

High Performance Windows

[9]Energy-efficient windows employ advanced technologies, such as protective coatings and improved frame assemblies, to help keep heat in during the winter and out during the summer. [10]These windows also block damaging ultraviolet sunlight that can discolor carpets and furnishings.

—Adapted from U. S. Environmental Protection Agency. *Energy Star*®
Qualified New Homes. EPA 430-F-09-053 March 2009. http://www
.energystar.gov/ia/partners/downloads/consumer_brochure.pdf.

1. __F__   2. __F__   3. __F__   4. __F/O__   5. __F__

6. __F/O__   7. __F__   8. __F/O__   9. __F__   10. __F__

VISUAL VOCABULARY

Energy construction materials, including insulation, replaces a tornado destroyed home.
The best definition of **insulation** is material that <u>c</u> heat, electricity, or sound.

   a. isolates
   b. enhances
   c. blocks

Evaluate the Context of the Author

Even though opinions can't be proved true like facts can, many opinions are still sound and valuable. To judge the accuracy of the opinion, you must consider the source: the author of the opinion. Authors offer two types of valid opinions: informed opinions and expert opinions.

> An author develops an **informed opinion** by gathering and analyzing evidence.
> An author develops an **expert opinion** through much training and extensive knowledge in a given field.

EXAMPLE Read the topic and study the list of authors who have written their opinions about the topic. Identify each person as **IO** if he or she is more likely to offer an informed opinion and **EO** if he or she is more likely to offer an expert opinion.

How to Lose Weight Safely and Effectively

<u>EO</u> **1.** Michael F. Roizen, MD, and Mehmet C. Oz, MD, authors of *You: On a Diet.*

<u>IO</u> **2.** An advice columnist such as Ann Landers or Dear Abby responding to a reader's question.

____EO____ **3.** Martha Stewart giving cooking tips on her nationally syndicated talk show.

____IO____ **4.** A student essay based on research.

EXPLANATION

1. Drs. Roizen and Oz are considered experts in the field of weight loss. One way to identify an expert opinion is to note if the person giving the opinion holds an advanced degree or title or has published articles or books about the topic being discussed. Both Roizen and Oz have the education and the achievement of being successful authors about this topic.

2. Advice columnists offer informed opinions on a wide range of topics. They often cite experts in their advice.

3. Martha Stewart has had extensive experience cooking and writing cookbooks and can provide an expert opinion about food preparation.

4. A student offers an informed opinion based on research.

Evaluate the Context of the Source

Often people turn to factual sources to find the factual details needed to form informed opinions and expert opinions. A medical dictionary, an English handbook, and a world atlas are a few excellent examples of factual sources.

EXAMPLE Read the following passage from a college psychology textbook. Answer the questions that follow.

Interpreting Dreams

Textbook
Skills

¹You may have wondered whether dreams, especially those that frighten us or that recur, have hidden meanings. ²Sigmund Freud believed that dreams function to satisfy unconscious sexual and aggressive desires. ³Because such wishes are unacceptable to the dreamer, they have to be disguised and therefore appear in dreams in symbolic forms. ⁴Freud claimed that objects such as sticks, umbrellas, tree trunks, and guns symbolize the male sex organ; objects such as chests, cupboards, and boxes represent the female sex organ. ⁵Freud differentiated between the **manifest content** of a dream—the content of the dream as recalled by the

dreamer—and the **latent content**—or the underlying meaning of the dream—which he considered more significant.

[6]Beginning in the 1950s, psychologists began to move away from the Freudian interpretation of dreams. [7]For example, Hall (1953) proposed a **cognitive theory of dreaming**. [8]He suggested that dreaming is simply thinking while asleep. [9]Advocates of Hall's approach argued for a greater focus on the manifest content. [10]The actual dream itself is seen as an expression of a broad range of the dreamer's concerns rather than as an expression of sexual impulses (Webb, 1975).

[11]Well-known sleep researcher J. Allan Hobson (1988) rejects the notion that nature would equip humans with the capability of having dreams that would require a specialist to interpret. [12]Hobson and McCarley (1977) advanced the **activation-synthesis hypothesis of dreaming**. [13]This hypothesis suggests that dreams are simply the brain's attempt to make sense of the random firing of brain cells during REM-sleep. [14]Just as people try to make sense of input from the environment during their waking hours, they try to find meaning in the conglomeration of sensations and memories that are generated internally by this random firing of brain cells. [15]Hobson (1989) believes that dreams also have psychological significance, because the meaning a person imposes on the random mental activity reflects that person's experiences, remote memories, associations, drives, and fears.

—From *Mastering the World of Psychology*, 3rd ed., p. 127 by Samuel E. Wood, Ellen Green Wood, and Denise Boyd. Copyright © 2008 by Pearson Education, Inc. Reproduced by permission of Pearson Education, Inc., Boston, MA.

___b___ **1.** Sentence 1 states
    a. a fact.   c. a fact and an opinion.
    b. an opinion.

___b___ **2.** Sentence 3 states
    a. a fact.   c. a fact and an opinion.
    b. an opinion.

___a___ **3.** Sentence 6 states a
    a. a fact.   c. a fact and an opinion.
    b. an opinion.

___b___ **4.** Overall, the theories of Freud, Hall, Hobson, and McCarley offer
    a. informed opinions.   c. factual details.
    b. expert opinions.

EXPLANATION Compare your answers to the following:

1. Sentence 1 states (b) an opinion. Many readers may have never "wondered" about dreams. This statement cannot be verified or proven.

2. Sentence 3 states the expert (b) opinion of Sigmund Freud—which is a partial explanation of his theory of dream interpretation.

3. Sentence 6 states (a) fact—an event in the history of dream interpretation.

4. Overall, the theories of Freud, Hall, Hobson, and McCarley offer (b) expert opinions. Scientific theories are plausible explanations for a fact or occurrence that can be observed. Thus, theories are not themselves facts, but reasonable explanations by experts supported by facts. As seen in this passage, conflicting theories about an occurrence can exist.

PRACTICE 7

Read the passage, and then, answer the questions that follow it.

Phobias

[1]All of us have experienced that gnawing feeling of fear in the pit of our stomach. [2]Perhaps we feared failing a test, losing a job, or disappointing a loved one, and each of these circumstances caused us to experience legitimate fear. [3]In contrast, a significant number of us experience fear for no known or logical reason. [4]According to the National Institute of Mental Health, millions of Americans, as many as one out of ten, suffer from phobias. [5]F. J. McGuigan, in his book *Encyclopedia of Stress,* defines a phobia as "an irrational, obsessive, and intense fear that is focused on a specific circumstance, idea, or thing." [6]Experts discuss phobias in terms of three subgroups: agoraphobia, social phobia, and specific phobia. [7]Agoraphobia is defined by *Merriam-Webster's Collegiate Dictionary* as the "abnormal fear of being helpless in an embarrassing or unescapable situation that is characterized especially by the avoidance of open or public places." [8]For example, McGuigan states that people who suffer agoraphobia tend to avoid crowds, tunnels, bridges, public transportation, and elevators. [9]In the textbook *Psychology and Life,* authors Richard Gerrig and Philip Zimbardo write that social phobia occurs as a person anticipates a public situation in which he or she will be observed by others. [10]People who suffer from social phobias fear public embarrassment. [11]"Finally, specific phobias occur in response to a specific object or situation." [12]For example, some people have an irrational fear of snakes, insects, or heights.

_b_   **1.** Sentence 1 is
    a. a fact.   b. an opinion.

_a_   **2.** In sentence 4, the National Institute of Mental Health is offered as
    a. a factual resource.   b. an informed opinion.

_a_   **3.** In sentence 5, the *Encyclopedia of Stress* offers
    a. a factual resource.   b. an opinion.

_b_   **4.** In sentence 7, *Merriam-Webster's Collegiate Dictionary* acts as
    a. an expert opinion.   b. a factual resource.

_b_   **5.** In sentence 9, Gerrig and Zimbardo's definition is
    a. an informed opinion.   b. an expert opinion.

_b_   **6.** Overall, this paragraph is
    a. a factual resource.   c. an expert opinion.
    b. an informed opinion.

VISUAL VOCABULARY

1. Identify the meaning of the word parts:

agora means <u>open or public places</u>

phobia means <u>irrational fear</u>

2. What type of phobia is agoraphobia? <u>fear of open or public places</u>

▲ Maya overcame agoraphobia and now enjoys city life.

Textbook Skills

Reading a Textbook: The Use of Graphics, Fact, and Opinion in a Textbook

Most textbook authors are careful to present only ideas based on observation, research, and expert opinion.

In addition, textbook authors often use pictures, drawings, or graphics to make the relationship between the main idea and supporting details clear. These graphics, most of which are based on factual data and expert opinions, require careful analysis to discern fact from opinion as you interpret them.

EXAMPLE Read the following passage and graphic illustration from a college nutrition textbook. Identify the sentences in the passage and the statements about the graphic as follows:

F if it states a fact

O if it states an opinion

F/O if it combines fact and opinion

¹The Best Way to Meet Your Nutrient Needs Is with a Well-Balanced Diet

²Many foods provide a variety of nutrients. ³For example, low-fat milk is high in carbohydrates and protein and provides a small amount of fat; milk is also a good source of the vitamins A, D, and riboflavin, as well as the minerals potassium and calcium, and is approximately 90 percent water by weight. ⁴Whereas milk contains a substantial variety of all six classes of nutrients, as a single food item it doesn't have to provide all nutrients in order to be good for you. ⁵Rather, a well-balanced diet composed of a variety of foods can provide you with all of these important nutrients (see Figure 1). ⁶Also the delicious texture and aroma of foods coupled with the social interaction of meals are lost when you pop a pill to meet your nutrient needs; that said, some individuals should take a supplement if food alone can't meet their needs.

—From *Nutrition and You*, 1st ed., p. 12 by Joan Salge Blake. Copyright © 2008 by Pearson Education, Inc. Printed and Electronically reproduced by permission of Pearson Education, Inc., Upper Saddle River, NJ.

1. _O_   **2.** _F_   **3.** _F/O_   **4.** _F/O_   **5.** _F_   **6.** _O_

_F_   **7.** According to Figure 1, popcorn popped in oil is empty in nutritional value.

_F_   **8.** Broccoli is a low-fat, high-fiber food.

_O_   **9.** Chicken is probably more nutritional without the skin.

_F_   **10.** Broccoli contains more nutritional value than popcorn.

Chicken with skin

Popcorn popped in oil

Broccoli (raw)

▨ Carbohydrates	▨ Vitamins	
▨ Fiber	▨ Minerals	
▨ Protein	▨ Water	
▨ Fats	▨ Phytochemicals	◄ **Nutrients in Foods**

—From *Nutrition and You,* 1st ed., Figure 1.2 (p. 12) by Joan Salge Blake. Copyright © 2008 by Pearson Education, Inc. Printed and Electronically reproduced by permission of Pearson Education, Inc., Upper Saddle River, NJ.

EXPLANATION   Compare your answers to the ones that follow:

1. **O:** The word *Best* states a value judgment, which is based on expert opinion and facts. The last sentence actually contradicts this opinion by stating that some people cannot meet their nutritional needs through food alone.

2. **F:** This sentence states a commonly known and accepted fact.

3. **F/O:** Although the information in this sentence can be verified, the author includes the value word *good.* Some might say that milk is an *excellent* or *adequate* source of these nutrients.

4. **F/O:** Again, the author includes value words such as *substantial* and *good.* Again, these value judgments are based on facts and expert opinions, but these words are vague, subjective, and arguable in their meaning.

5. **F:** This sentence states a commonly known and accepted fact supported by the graphic illustration.

6. **O:** This sentence offers the author's opinion as indicated by the subjective tone words *delicious, pop a pill,* and *should.*

7. **F:** This is a false fact. As the graphic illustrates, popcorn does have nutritional value.

8. **F:** This is a factual statement as illustrated by the graphic.

9. **O:** Although our prior knowledge may lead us to believe this statement is factual, it is an opinion not supported by the paragraph or the illustration.

10. **F:** This is a factual statement as illustrated by the graphic.

PRACTICE 8

A. Read the following passage from a history textbook. Mark selected sentences as follows:

F if it states a fact

O if it expresses an opinion

F/O if it combines fact and opinion

Textbook
Skills

Women and World War II

[1]World War II had a dramatic impact on women. [2]Easily the most visible change involved the sudden appearance of large numbers of women in uniform. [3]The military organized women into auxiliary units with special uniforms, their own officers, and amazingly, equal pay. [4]By 1945, more than 250,000 women had joined the Women's Army Corps (WAC), the Army Nurses Corps, the Women Accepted for Voluntary Emergency Service (WAVES), the Navy Nurses Corps, the Marines, and the Coast Guard. [5]Most women who joined the armed services either filled traditional women's roles, such as nursing, or replaced men in noncombat jobs.

[6]Women also substituted for men on the home front. [7]For the first time in history, married working women outnumbered single working women, as 6.3 million women entered the workforce during the war. [8]The war challenged the conventional image of female behavior, as "Rosie the Riveter" became the popular symbol of women who abandoned traditional female occupations to work in defense industries.

[9]Women paid a price for their economic independence, though. [10]Outside employment did not free wives from domestic duties. [11]The same women who put in full days in offices and factories went home to cook, clean, shop, and care for their children. [12]They had not one job, but two, and the only way they could fill both was to sacrifice relaxation, recreation, and sleep. [13]Outside employment also raised the problem of

child care. [14]A few industries, such as Kaiser Steel, offered day-care facilities, but most women had to make their own informal arrangements.

—Adapted from *America and Its Peoples, Volume II: A Mosaic in the Making,* 3rd ed., pp. 875–876 by James Kirby Martin, Randy J. Roberts, Steven Mintz, Linda O. McMurry and James H. Jones. Copyright © 1997 by Pearson Education, Inc. Printed and Electronically reproduced by permission of Pearson Education, Inc., Upper Saddle River, NJ.

___F/O___ **1.** Sentence 1   ___F/O___ **5.** Sentence 8

___F/O___ **2.** Sentence 2   ___O___ **6.** Sentence 9

___F/O___ **3.** Sentence 3   ___F/O___ **7.** Sentence 12

___F___ **4.** Sentence 4

B. Study the image of "Rosie the Riveter." Then, identify each sentence, based on the picture, as follows:

F if it states a fact

O if it expresses an opinion

F/O if it combines fact and opinion

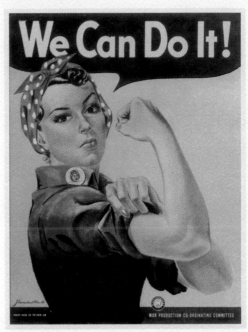

—"We Can Do It!" poster by J. Howard Miller. *Produced by Westinghouse for the War Production Co-Ordinating Committee, NARA Still Picture Branch (NWDNS-179-WP-1563)*, National Archives and Records Administration. © Courtesy of National Archives, photo war & conflict #798_we_can_do_it.

___F___ **8.** Some women gave up their traditional feminine dress to enter the workforce.

_____F/O_____ **9.** "Rosie the Riveter" has the look of a strong, competent woman dressed in overalls and bandanna.

_____O_____ **10.** "Rosie the Riveter" is the ideal patriotic woman.

APPLICATIONS

Textbook Skills

Application 1: Fact and Opinion

The following graph comes from a health textbook. Study the graph, and label each statement, based on the graph, as follows:

F if it states a fact

O if it expresses an opinion

F/O if it combines fact and opinion

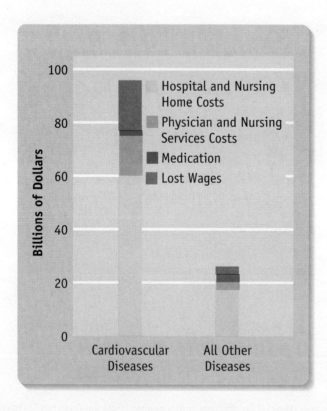

◄ Annual Economic Costs of Cardiovascular Diseases and All Other Diseases in the United States

—From *Total Fitness and Wellness Student Textbook Component,* 3rd ed. by Scott K. Powers and Stephen L. Dodd. Copyright © 2003 by Pearson Education, Inc. Printed and Electronically reproduced by permission of Pearson Education, Inc., Upper Saddle River, NJ.

_____F/O_____ **1.** The economic costs of cardiovascular diseases are alarmingly higher than the costs for all other diseases in the United States.

_____F_____ **2.** The yearly costs of cardiovascular diseases run more than $90 billion.

_____F_____ **3.** In contrast to all other diseases, more dollars are lost in wages to cardiovascular diseases.

_____O_____ **4.** Developing a national strategy to reduce the risk of cardiovascular disease should be a major health priority.

Application 2: Opinions, Biased Words, and Qualifiers

Read the following statements. Underline any biased words or qualifiers that are used. Then, mark each statement as follows:

F if it states a fact

O if it expresses an opinion

F/O if it combines fact and opinion

Textbook
Skills

_____F_____ **1.** Hybrid electric vehicles (HEVs) combine the internal combustion engine of a conventional vehicle with the battery and electric motor of an electric vehicle; the <u>proven</u> result is twice the fuel economy of conventional vehicles.

_____F/O_____ **2.** The <u>practical</u> benefits of HEVs include not only <u>improved</u> fuel economy but also <u>lower</u> emissions, making HEVs the <u>best</u> cars on the market.

_____F_____ **3.** By combining gasoline with electric power, hybrids have the <u>same or greater</u> range than traditional combustion engines.

_____F_____ **4.** The 2008 Toyota Pruis gets between 43–56 miles per gallon.

_____O_____ **5.** HEVs <u>should</u> be the <u>only</u> cars on the market.

—Adapted from United States Environmental Protection Agency.
"Hybrid Vehicles." 5 Nov. 2007 http://www.fueleconomy.gov/

Application 3: Informed and Expert Opinions

Read the list of ten sources from which information can be obtained. Label each source as follows:

IO if it offers an informed opinion

EO if it offers an expert opinion

FS if it is a factual source

_____FS_____ **1.** The National Archives and Records Administration (NARA), an independent federal agency that preserves our nation's history by overseeing the management of all federal records

_____IO_____ **2.** A physical education instructor's recommendation for a knee injury

_____EO_____ **3.** A physician's recommendation for a knee injury

_____IO_____ **4.** A family member who has researched features and prices for several brands of dishwashers

_____FS_____ **5.** A medical dictionary

_____FS_____ **6.** *The Little, Brown Handbook,* a textbook used in college writing courses

_____FS_____ **7.** A college course syllabus

_____EO_____ **8.** About communication: Deborah Tannen, Professor of Linguistics, Georgetown University; author of several books and dozens of articles about communication

_____EO_____ **9.** Lance Armstrong, six-time winner of the Tour de France, on the sport of cycling

_____FS_____ **10.** The Web site *howstuffworks,* a commercial online resource for explanations about how things work

REVIEW TEST 1   Score (number correct) _____ × 20 = _____%

Read the following article from a college health textbook. Answer the questions that follow.

Textbook
Skills

10.9 GE/443 words   **Do Restaurants and Food Marketers Encourage Overeating?**

¹When you go out to your local restaurant, do you think your dinner looks the same as one your grandmother might have ordered 50 years ago? ²Would you be surprised to learn that today's serving portions are significantly larger than those of past decades? ³Today's popular restaurant foods dwarf their earlier counterparts. ⁴A 25 ounce prime-rib dinner served at one local steak chain, for example, contains nearly 3,000 calories and 150 grams of fat in the meat alone. ⁵Add a baked potato with

sour cream or butter, a salad loaded with creamy dressing, and fresh bread with real butter, and the meal may surpass the 5,000-calorie mark and ring in at close to 300 grams of fat. In other words, it exceeds what most adults should eat in 2 days!

[6]And that is just the beginning. [7]Soft drinks, once commonly served in 12-ounce sizes, now come in "big gulps" and 1-liter bottles. [8]Cinnamon buns used to be the size of a dinner roll; now one chain sells them in giant, butter-laden, 700-calorie portions.

[9]What accounts for the increased portion sizes of today? [10]Restaurant owners might say that they are only giving customers what they want. [11]While there may be some merit to this claim, it's also true that bigger portions can justify higher prices, which help increase an owner's bottom line.

[12]A quick glance at the fattening of Americans provides growing evidence of a significant health problem. [13]According to Donna Skoda, a dietitian and chair of the Ohio State University Extension Service, "People are eating a ton of extra calories. [14]For the first time in history, more people are overweight in America than are underweight. [15]Ironically, although the U.S. fat intake has dropped in the past 20 years from an average of 0 to 33 percent of calories, the daily calorie intake has risen from 1,852 calories per day to over 2,000 per day. [16]In theory, this translates into a weight gain of 15 pounds a year." [17]Skoda and others say that the main reason Americans are gaining weight is that people no longer recognize a normal serving size. [18]The National Heart, Lung, and Blood Institute has developed a pair of "Portion Distortion" quizzes that show how today's portions compare with those of 20 years ago. [19]Test yourself online at http://hin.nhlbi.nih.gov/portion to see whether you can guess the differences between today's meals and those previously considered normal. [20]Just one example is the difference between an average cheeseburger 20 years ago and the typical cheeseburger of today. [21]According to the "Portion Distortion" quiz, today's cheeseburger has 590 calories—257 more calories than the cheeseburger of 20 years ago!

—Adapted from *Access to Health*, 11th ed., Green Edition, p. 292 by Rebecca Donatelle. Copyright © 2010 by Pearson Education, Inc. Printed and Electronically reproduced by permission of Pearson Education, Inc., Upper Saddle River, NJ.

_____c_____ **1.** Sentence 3 states

    a. a fact.   c. a fact and an opinion.

    b. an opinion.

_____b_____ **2.** Sentence 10 states
    a. a fact.   c. a fact and an opinion.
    b. an opinion.

_____b_____ **3.** Sentence 11 states
    a. a fact.   c. a fact and an opinion.
    b. an opinion.

_____a_____ **4.** Sentence 14 states
    a. a fact.   c. a fact and an opinion.
    b. an opinion.

_____b_____ **5.** In the article, Donna Skoda offers
    a. an informed opinion based on personal experience.
    b. an expert opinion based on education and professional experience.
    c. factual details only.

REVIEW TEST 2

Score (number correct) _____ × 10 = _____%

Fact and Opinion

Read the review, and answer the questions that follow it.

13.3 GE/255 words   **From the Pen of the Mighty King**

[1]Stephen King, with his fantastical imagination, has built an impressive body of literary work worthy of recognition.[2]The scope of his writing includes short stories, novels, screenplays for movies and television series, nonfiction, illustrated novels, a comic book, and a children's cookbook. [3]However, he may be most widely known for those stories that explore the darkness of our fury and fears. [4]In fact, an editor for Barnes & Noble stated on the bookseller's website, "Stephen King proves once again why he is the reigning master of dark fiction" in their review of his novel *Dreamcatcher*. [5]His first novel, *Carrie*, the novel he allegedly threw in the trash, reveals the macabre side of his imagination. [6](Thank God his wife allegedly dug it out, flung it back and said, "finish it!") [7]*Carrie* is a dark, dark tale fueled by the ferocity of an adolescent experience;

the story encompasses outcasts, bullies, guilt, anger, sin, mayhem, death, justice, and fear. [8]In *Carrie*, King revealed his ability to make nightmares seem real. [9]In contrast, King also has the ability to probe into common human experiences with wit and tenderness, as in his short story "The Body," also made into a Hollywood movie, *Stand By Me*. [10]In this story, King's pen renders a compelling portrait of a young boy's end of innocence, his conflict with mortality, and his induction into adulthood. [11]Stephen King's body of work has made him the 2003 recipient of *The National Book Foundation Medal for Distinguished Contribution to American Letters*.

_____b_____ **1.** Sentence 1 is a statement of
    a. fact.   c. a combination of fact and opinion.
    b. opinion.

_____a_____ **2.** Sentence 2 is a statement of
    a. fact.   c. a combination of fact and opinion.
    b. opinion.

_____b_____ **3.** Sentence 3 is a statement of
    a. fact.   c. a combination of fact and opinion.
    b. opinion.

_____c_____ **4.** Sentence 5 is a statement of
    a. fact.   c. a combination of fact and opinion.
    b. opinion.

_____c_____ **5.** Sentence 6 is a statement of
    a. fact.   c. a combination of fact and opinion.
    b. opinion.

_____c_____ **6.** Sentence 7 is a statement of
    a. fact.   c. a combination of fact and opinion.
    b. opinion.

_____c_____ **7.** Sentence 9 is a statement of
    a. fact.   c. a combination of fact and opinion.
    b. opinion.

_____c_____ **8.** Sentence 10 is a statement of
    a. fact.   c. a combination of fact and opinion.
    b. opinion.

___a___ **9.** Sentence 11 is a statement of
  a. fact.
  b. opinion.
  c. a combination of fact and opinion.

___b___ **10.** The editor from Barnes & Noble in sentence 4 offers
  a. an informed opinion.
  b. an expert opinion.
  c. a fact.

REVIEW TEST 3

Score (number correct) _____ × 10 = _____ %

Fact and Opinion

Before you read this passage from a psychology textbook, skim the passage and answer the Before Reading questions. Read the passage. Then, answer the After Reading questions.

Textbook
Skills

11.3 GE/825 words

Gambling and Sports

Vocabulary Preview

sanctioning (2):
permitting,
authorizing

enterprise (7):
venture, project

priorities (40): main
concerns

[1]Objections to the legalization of sports gambling appear to fall into two classes, moral and financial. [2]Many people do not like the idea of legally **sanctioning** a vice like gambling. [3]Part of the reason major sports organizations object is the justified fear that gambling would taint the image of professional sports. [4]Image is an important financial asset to sports teams and leagues. [5]A public suspicion that games might be "fixed" by crooked gambling interests could result in lowered gate receipts and a reduced TV audience (Prey, 1985, p. 210).

[6]Curiously, gambling interests, even legal gambling interests, may oppose legalization of sports gambling (as did the Canadian provinces) to prevent a loss of their share of the gambling market. [7]For example, lawful off-track betting parlors could be expected to lose business to a newly legalized sports bookmaking **enterprise**.

[8]The argument that legal gambling might somehow threaten the integrity of sports appears to be wrong. [9]Over 95 percent of the sports betting in the United States, about $24 billion worth, is handled by illegal bookmakers (Prey, 1985, p. 196). [10]Legalization of sports gambling could be expected to draw money away from these underworld bookies toward aboveboard, legally regulated bookies. [11]It seems naive to believe that gamblers placing bets with legal bookmakers would be

likely to try to fix games while those already betting with illegal, possibly mob-controlled bookmakers would not. [12]Insofar as gambling threatens the integrity of sports, sports are already thoroughly threatened. [13]Legalization of sports gambling could only be expected to reduce this threat (Smith, 1990).

[14]Legal and illegal sports bookies serve as brokers of bets on highly visible sports events. [15]To bet on the outcome of a professional football game a person must stop by the bookie's office. [16]The office may be a bar, a magazine store, a gas station, or some other front business. [17]Good customers can place their bets by telephone, in effect taking a loan from the bookmaker. [18]To place a $100 wager, the bettor hands the bookie $110 or so. [19]The extra $10 is a commission paid to the bookmaker for his or her services. [20]This commission is only paid on losses. [21]Winners get their $110 back, plus $100 in winnings.

[22]The successful bookmaker must have several business skills. [23]The bookmaker makes a 5 percent commission on all bets handled if an equal amount is bet on each team. [24]To encourage equal wagering the bookie creates a line that requires bettors to predict not only the winning team but the point differential as well. [25]Thus, "Chicago over Minnesota by 9" means a Chicago backer wins only if Chicago wins by 9 points or more. [26]If not enough people bet on Minnesota and Chicago wins by 9 or more points, the bookie loses money. [27]It is important that the line attract an equal amount of wagering on the two teams. [28]A successful bookie has the knowledge to do this.

[29]A successful bookmaker may occasionally "take a bath" by accepting too many bets on the losing side of a game or, more correctly, a number of games, thereby having to pay out more money to winners than he or she collected from losers. [30]This temporary cash-flow problem cannot as a rule be quickly covered by a legitimate bank loan. [31]Herein lies one of the reasons bookmakers are likely to be linked with organized crime. [32]The best, and perhaps the only, source of a short-term, no-questions-asked loan is the local loan shark. [33]Loan sharking is a standard organized crime business that makes loans to "friends" at **exorbitant** (20 percent per week) interest, but this may seem a good deal to a bookie with temporary cash-flow problems. [34]Bookmakers may also occasionally require debt-collection services, which loan sharks can provide.

[35]A second tie-in with organized crime is protection from authorities. [36]Bookmaking operations, like any service business, must be accessible to the public if they are to make money. [37]This means remaining at one location with one telephone number for a long time. [38]If a would-be bettor can find a bookmaker, so can an arresting officer. [39]No illegal

bookmaking operation can succeed without somehow avoiding police in-terference. [40]Law-enforcement officials may choose to overlook a harm-less, honest bookie in that no one is being hurt, otherwise law-abiding citizens are involved in placing bets, and police have more important **priorities** than to prosecute a bookmaker who may well be acquitted even if the case against the bookie is strong. [41]They may also refrain from interfering thanks to payoffs or favors to political leaders.

[42]These payoffs may be provided by an organized crime figure. [43]Few bookmakers are so successful that they can afford to pay off mayors and city council members, but an organized crime figure may assure pro-tection of smalltime bookies in return for a share of the profits. [44]The natural tie-in with organized crime and government corruption provides the strongest argument for the legalization of gambling as well as some other vices (Barnes & Teeters, 1959).

—From *Sociology of Sport*, pp. 243–245 by John C. Phillips. Copyright © 1993 by Allyn & Bacon. Reproduced by permission of Pearson Education, Inc., Boston, MA.

Before Reading

Vocabulary in Context

_____a_____ **1.** What does the word **exorbitant** mean in sentence 33?
a. excessive   c. expected
b. reasonable   d. low

After Reading

Main Idea and Implied Central Idea

_____a_____ **2.** The main idea of paragraph 1 (sentences 1–7) is stated in
a. sentence 1.   c. sentence 6.
b. sentence 2.   d. sentence 7.

_____c_____ **3.** Which of the following sentences best states the implied central idea of the passage?
a. Sports bookmaking is a billion dollar industry in the United States.
b. Sports gambling should be legalized to end the link to organized crime and government corruption.
c. Sports gambling, a billion dollar business, is a controversial issue for several reasons.

Supporting Details

_c_   **4.** According to the author, lawful off-track betting parlors oppose the legalization of sports gambling because
   a. gambling is a vice.
   b. of the tie between sports gambling and organized crime.
   c. they could lose money to newly legalized sports bookmaking businesses.
   d. they fear damage to their image.

Transitions

_d_   **5.** The relationship of ideas between sentence 6 and sentence 7 is one of
   a. cause and effect.   c. contrast.
   b. time order.   d. generalization and example.

_a_   **6.** The relationship between the ideas within sentence 26 is one of
   a. cause and effect.   c. contrast.
   b. time order.   d. addition.

Thought Patterns

_a_   **7.** The primary thought pattern that organizes paragraph 6 (sentences 35–41) is
   a. cause and effect.   c. examples.
   b. time order.   d. contrast.

Fact and Opinion

_c_   **8.** Sentence 1 is
   a. a fact.   c. both fact and opinion.
   b. an opinion.

_c_   **9.** Sentence 3 is
   a. a fact.   c. a mixture of fact and opinion.
   b. an opinion.

_a_   **10.** Sentence 9 is
   a. a fact.   c. a mixture of fact and opinion.
   b. an opinion.

WHAT DO YOU THINK?

Is gambling a vice or just another form of entertainment? In what ways do you think cell phones and wireless computers have affected the bookmaking business? Assume that your city government wants to legalize gambling in your area. Write a letter to the editor of your local newspaper, which you also plan to mail to the mayor and city council members. In your letter, express your support of or opposition to legalized gambling in your area.

REVIEW TEST 4

Score (number correct) _____ × 10 = _____%

Fact and Opinion

(Textbook Skills) **Before Reading:** Survey the following passage adapted from a college nutrition textbook. Skim the passage, noting the words in bold print. Answer the Before Reading questions that follow the passage. Then, read the passage. Next, answer the After Reading questions. Use the discussion and writing topics as activities to do after reading.

12.5 GE/525 words

What Is *Trans* Fat and Where Do You Find It?

Vocabulary Preview

saturated (1): of or relating to an organic compound, especially a fatty acid, containing the maximum number of hydrogen atoms and only single bonds between the carbon atoms

unsaturated (2): of or relating to an organic compound with a double or triple bond that links two atoms, usually of carbon

[1]At one time, saturated fats from animal sources, like lard, and highly **saturated** tropical plant oils, like coconut and palm oils, were staples in home cooking and commercial food preparation. [2]These saturated fats work well in commercial food products because they provide a rich, flaky texture to baked goods and are more resistant to **rancidity** than the **unsaturated** fats found in oils. [3](The double bonds in unsaturated fats make them more susceptible to being damaged by oxygen, and thus, becoming rancid.) [4]Then, in the early twentieth century, a German chemist discovered the technique of **hydrogenation** of oils, which caused the unsaturated fatty acids in the oils to become more saturated. [5]*Trans fats* were born.

[6]The process of hydrogenation involves heating an oil and exposing it to **hydrogen** gas, which causes some of the double bonds in the unsaturated fatty acid to become saturated with hydrogen. [7]Typically, the hydrogens of a double bond are lined up in a *cis (cis* = same) **configuration**, that is,

hydrogenation (4): the adding of hydrogen to an unsaturated fatty acid to make it more saturated and solid at room-temperature

hydrogen (6): a colorless, tasteless, odorless, flammable gaseous substance that is the simplest and most abundant element

configuration (7): pattern, design

reformulated (13): changed, remade

cholesterol (17): a soft, waxy substance found among the lipids (fats) in the bloodstream and in the body's cells

they are all on the same side of the carbon chain in the fatty acid. [8]During hydrogenation, some hydrogens cross to the opposite side of the carbon chain, resulting in a *trans* (*trans* = cross) configuration. [9]The newly configured fatty acid is now a *trans fatty acid.*

[10]*Trans* fats provide a richer texture, a longer shelf life, and better resistance to **rancidity** than unsaturated fats, so food manufacturers use them in many commercially made food products. [11]The first partially hydrogenated shortening, Crisco, was made from cottonseed oil, and became available in 1911.

[12]*Trans* fats came into even more widespread commercial use when saturated fat fell out of favor in the 1980s. [13]Research had confirmed that saturated fat played a role in increased risk of heart disease, so food manufacturers **reformulated** many of their products to contain less saturated fat. [14]The easiest solution was to replace the saturated fat with *trans* fats. [15]Everything from cookies, cakes, and crackers to fried chips and doughnuts used *trans* fats to maintain their texture and shelf life. [16]*Trans* fats were also frequently used for frying at fast-food restaurants.

[17]We now know that *trans* fats are actually worse for heart health than saturated fat because they not only raise the LDL **cholesterol** levels, but they also lower HDL cholesterol in the body. [18]*Trans* fat currently provides an estimated 2.5 percent of the daily calories in the diets of adults in the United States. [19]Of this amount, about 25 percent of them are coming from naturally occurring *trans* fats that are found in meat and dairy foods. [20]We don't yet know if the naturally occurring *trans* fats have the same heart-unhealthy effects as do those that are created through hydrogenation. [21]*Trans* fats use should be kept as low as possible in the diet.

[22]The major sources of *trans* fats are commercially prepared baked goods, margarines, fried potatoes, snacks, shortenings, and salad dressings. [23]Whole grains, fruits, and vegetables don't contain any *trans* fats, so consuming a plant-based diet with minimal commercially prepared foods will go a long way toward preventing *trans* fat (and saturated fat) from overpowering your diet.

—Adapted from *Nutrition and You,* 1st ed., p. 147 by Joan Salge Blake. Copyright © 2008 by Pearson Education, Inc. Printed and Electronically reproduced by permission of Pearson Education, Inc., Upper Saddle River, NJ.

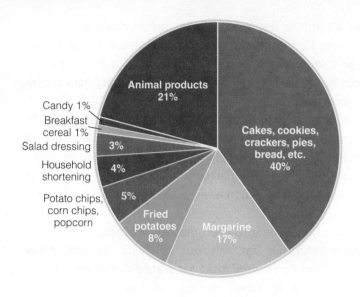

◄ **Major Food Sources of Trans Fat for U.S. Adults** Commercially made baked goods and snack items are the major contributors of trans fat in the diet.
—Source FDA, Questions and Answers About Trans Fat Nutrition Labeling, 2003.

Before Reading

Vocabulary in Context

Use context clues to state in your own words the definition of the following terms. Indicate the context clue you used.

1. In sentences 2 and 10 what does the word **rancidity** mean? spoiled, offensive in odor or flavor

2. Identify the context clue used for the word **rancidity** in sentences 2 and 10. general sense of the passage

After Reading

Implied Central Idea

3. Using your own words, write a sentence that best states the implied main idea of the passage. Trans fats, found in most commercially prepared foods, are created by hydrogenating unsaturated fats and their use should be kept as low as possible in the diet.

Main Idea and Supporting Details

_____c_____ **4.** In paragraph 4 (sentences 12–16), sentence 16 is a
   a. main idea.
   b. major supporting detail.
   c. minor supporting detail.

Transitions

_____b_____ **5.** The relationship of ideas between sentence 15 and sentence 16 is one of
   a. cause and effect.
   b. listing.
   c. time order.
   d. definition and example.

_____c_____ **6.** The relationship of ideas within sentence 23 is one of
   a. time order.
   b. contrast.
   c. cause and effect.
   d. definition and example.

Thought Patterns

_____a_____ **7.** The overall thought pattern for this passage is
   a. time order.
   b. definition and example.
   c. space order.
   d. comparison and contrast.

Fact and Opinion

_____a_____ **8.** Sentence 4 is a statement of
   a. fact.
   b. opinion.
   c. fact and opinion.

_____b_____ **9.** Sentence 14 is a statement of
   a. fact.
   b. opinion.
   c. fact and opinion.

_____a_____ **10.** Read the caption for the graphic. The caption is a statement of
   a. fact.
   b. opinion.
   c. fact and opinion.

WHAT DO YOU THINK?

Why are trans fats so harmful to human health? Assume you taking a college-level health course. Your professor has assigned weekly written responses to what you are learning through your studies. This week, you have decided to respond to what you have learned about a healthful diet and trans fats. You have narrowed your written response to two topics. Choose one of these topics and write several paragraphs using information from the passage about trans fats: (1) Evaluate your own diet and discuss ways in which your diet is healthful or needs to change to become healthful. (2) Persuade people who consume a diet high in trans fats to change to a diet balanced with grains, fruits, vegetables, and protein.

After Reading About Fact and Opinion

Before you move on to the Mastery Tests on fact and opinion, take time to reflect on your learning and performance by answering the following questions. Write your answers in your notebook.

- How has my knowledge base or prior knowledge about fact and opinion changed?

- Based on my studies, how do I think I will perform on the Mastery Test(s)? Why do I think my scores will be above average, average, or below average?

- Would I recommend this chapter to other students who want to learn about fact and opinion? Why or why not?

Test your understanding of what you have learned about fact and opinion by completing the Chapter 9 Review Card in the insert near the end of your text.

CONNECT TO **myreadinglab**

To check your progress in meeting Chapter 9's learning outcomes log in to **www.myreadinglab.com** and try the following exercises.

- The "Critical Thinking" section of MyReadingLab gives additional information about fact and opinion. The section provides a model, practices, activities, and tests. To access this resource, click on the "Study Plan" tab. Then click on "Critical Thinking." Then click on the following links as needed: "Overview," "Model," "Critical Thinking: Facts and Opinions (Flash Animation)," "Practice," and "Tests."

- To measure your mastery of this chapter, complete the tests in the "Critical Thinking" section and click on Gradebook to find your results.

A. Read the following statements, and mark each one as follows:

F if it states a fact

O if it expresses an opinion

F/O if it combines fact and opinion

___O___ **1.** The barbell squat is the best exercise to sculpt beautiful, toned, firm legs.

___F___ **2.** The barbell squat develops the quadriceps muscles (the front upper leg), the hamstring muscles (back of upper leg), and the gluteal muscles (the buttocks).

___O___ **3.** In today's fast-paced, high-stress society, too many people eat to satisfy emotional needs.

___F/O___ **4.** Because nutritional supplements prevent nutritional deficiencies, everyone should take supplements.

___F/O___ **5.** Vitamin C is a water-soluble vitamin that may aid dieters by suppressing cortisol, a hormone that aids in fat storage and breaks down muscle tissue.

B. Read the following short reviews. Mark each one as follows:

F if it states a fact

O if it expresses an opinion

F/O if it combines fact and opinion

___F/O___ **6.** *Animal Farm* by George Orwell, Penguin, 1951.

12.9 GE/111 words

Animal Farm is easily the most famous work of political allegory ever written. The animals take over the running of a farm, and everything is wonderful for a while—until the pigs get out of hand. It is a brilliant description of what happens when the revolution goes astray. Allegory is hard to do gracefully, but Orwell manages it superbly: while true appreciation of *Animal Farm* requires an understanding of the history of the Russian revolution, those without it will still get the point. And *Animal Farm* can even be appreciated as a story by children with no understanding of the political message at all!

—Yee, *Danny Yee's Book Reviews*, 10 Aug. 1992. 4 Feb. 2004
http://dannyreviews.com/s/romance.html

399

F/O **7.** *Beyond a Boundary* by C. L. R. James, Duke University Press, 1993.

10.8 GE/125 words

Beyond a Boundary blends personal memoir, social history, and sports commentary. James's subject is cricket and its role in his own life and in the history of the West Indies and England. He begins with the place of cricket in his family history, in his childhood and schooling in Trinidad, and in the social stratification of West Indian society. He then recounts his personal experiences of some of the great West Indian cricketers, among them George John, Wilton St Hill, and above all Learie Constantine, who was a personal friend. In the three essays on Constantine, James also discusses league cricket and his own move to England and involvement with West Indian politics.

—Yee, *Danny Yee's Book Reviews*, 1998. 31 Jan. 2003
http://dannyreviews.com/h/Beyond_Boundary.html

F **8.** *Statistical Abstract of the United States, 2007.*

College level/52 words

The *Statistical Abstract of the United States,* published since 1878, is the authoritative and comprehensive summary of statistics on the social, political, and economic organization of the United States. Sources of data include the Census Bureau, Bureau of Labor Statistics, Bureau of Economic Analysis, and many other Federal agencies and private organizations.

—United States. *The 2007 Statistical Abstract: The National Data Book.* U.S. Census
Bureau. 5 Nov. 2007. http://www.census.gov/compendia/statab/

F **9.** The *Encyclopedia of Earth,* <http://www.eoearth.org/>.

14.3 GE/51 words

The *Encyclopedia of Earth* is an electronic reference about the Earth, its natural environments, and their interaction with society. The *Encyclopedia* is a free, fully searchable collection of articles. Articles are written by scholars, professionals, educators, and experts who collaborate and review each other's work.

F/O **10.** Gladwell, Malcolm, *What the Dog Saw*, Little, Brown, and Co.,
10.3 GE/102 words
2009, $27.99.

Gladwell's latest book, *What the Dog Saw*, a package of his favorite articles from the *New Yorker* since he joined as a staff writer in 1996, is divided into three sections: The first deals with what he calls obsessives and minor geniuses; the second with flawed ways of thinking; the third on how we make predictions about people: will they make a good employee, are they capable of great works of art, or are they the local serial killer? Brought together, the pieces form a dazzling record of Gladwell's art, according to Ian Sample of the *Guardian*.

A. Read the list of statements, and mark each one as follows:

F if it states a fact; **O** if it expresses an opinion; **F/O** if it combines fact and opinion

___O___ **1.** Capital punishment is immoral and cruel. It should be outlawed in a civilized society.

___O___ **2.** Any criminal, no matter how hardened, can be and should be rehabilitated to reenter society.

___F___ **3.** As of January 2007, 3,350 men and women were on death rows across the United States.

___O___ **4.** Capital punishment is the only form of justice for heinous crimes against humanity.

___F___ **5.** A majority of nations have ended capital punishment in law or practice.

B. Read the paragraph from a college history textbook. Identify the numbered sentences as follows:

F if it states a fact; **O** if it expresses an opinion; **F/O** if it combines fact and opinion

Textbook
Skills

13.1 GE/70 words   **Settling the Far West**

⁶During the 1840s thousands of pioneers headed westward toward California and Oregon. ⁷In 1841, the first party of 69 pioneers left Missouri for California, led by an Ohio schoolteacher named John Bidwell. ⁸The hardships the party endured were nearly unbearable. ⁹They were forced to abandon their wagons and eat their pack animals, "half roasted, dripping with blood." ¹⁰Over the next 25 years, 350,000 more made the trek along the overland trails.

—From *America and Its Peoples, Volume I: A Mosaic in the Making*, 3rd ed., pp. 423–424 by James Kirby Martin, Randy J. Roberts, Steven Mintz, Linda O. McMurry and James H. Jones. Copyright © 1997 by Pearson Education, Inc. Printed and Electronically reproduced by permission of Pearson Education, Inc., Upper Saddle River, NJ.

6. ___F___   **7.** ___F___   **8.** ___F/O___   **9.** ___F___   **10.** ___F___

C. Read the following passage from a college history textbook. Identify each numbered sentence as follows:

F if it states a fact; **O** if it expresses an opinion; **F/O** if it combines fact and opinion

401

Textbook Skills

10 GE/103 words

Trailblazing

¹¹In 1811 and 1812 fur trappers marked out the Oregon Trail, the longest and most famous pioneer route in American history. ¹²This trail crossed about 2000 miles from Independence, Missouri, to the Columbia River country of Oregon. ¹³During the 1840s, 12,000 pioneers traveled the Trail's entire length to Oregon.

¹⁴Travel on the Oregon Trail was a tremendous test of human endurance. ¹⁵The journey by wagon train took six months. ¹⁶Settlers encountered prairie fires, sudden blizzards, and impassable mountains. ¹⁷Cholera and other diseases were common; food, water, and wood were scarce. ¹⁸Only the stalwart dared brave the physical hardship of the westward trek.

—From *America and Its Peoples, Volume I: A Mosaic in the Making,* 3rd ed., p. 425 by James Kirby Martin, Randy J. Roberts, Steven Mintz, Linda O. McMurry and James H. Jones. Copyright © 1997 by Pearson Education, Inc. Printed and Electronically reproduced by permission of Pearson Education, Inc., Upper Saddle River, NJ.

11. _F/O_   12. _F_   13. _F_   14. _F/O_   15. _F_

16. _F_   17. _F_   18. _O_

D. Study the picture and its caption. Mark each idea as follows:

F if it states a fact; **O** if it expresses an opinion; **F/O** if it combines fact and opinion

◄ Life along the westward trails was a tremendous test of human endurance.

_F/O_ **19.** Pioneers encountered arid desert, difficult mountain passes, dangerous rivers, and quicksand.

_O_ **20.** Still, despite the hardships of the experience, few emigrants ever regretted their decision to move west.

—Text and image adapted from *America and Its Peoples, Volume I: A Mosaic in the Making,* 3rd ed., p. 425 by James Kirby Martin, Randy J. Roberts, Steven Mintz, Linda O. McMurry and James H. Jones. Copyright © 1997 by Pearson Education, Inc. Printed and Electronically reproduced by permission of Pearson Education, Inc., Upper Saddle River, NJ.

A. The following passage and the figure in section B were published together in a health textbook. Read the passage, and identify the numbered sentences as follows:

F if it states a fact

O if it expresses an opinion

F/O if it combines fact and opinion

Textbook Skills

12.0 GE/83 words   **Content and Information Regulation**

¹Direct content regulation emerged from government efforts to balance the free flow of information and ideas against the negative effects of media products. ²Part of the news media's role, as H. L. Mencken said, "is to comfort the afflicted and afflict the comfortable." ³Content regulation tries to reduce unjustified, unnecessary, and unreasonable harm to people from media content. ⁴Such regulation can occur before or after distribution. ⁵Some types of speech, such as political speech, are more protected than others, such as commercial speech.

—Folkerts & Lacy, *The Media in Your Life*, 2nd ed., p. 327.

1. __F__   2. __O__   3. __F__   4. __F__   5. __F__

VISUAL VOCABULARY

The business conversation of this real estate agent is an example of __b__ _____ speech.

   a. political
   b. commercial

B. Study the graph. Read the statements that are based on the figure. Then, identify each one as follows:

F if it states a fact

O if it expresses an opinion

Textbook Skills   **F/O** if it combines fact and opinion

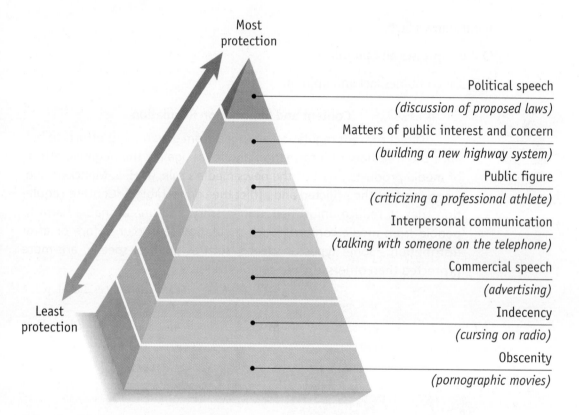

▲ **Levels of Protected Communication**
—From Folkerts & Lacy, *The Media in Your Life*, p. 327. Published by Allyn and Bacon. Copyright © 2001. "Levels of Protected Communication" by Todd F. Simon. Reprinted by permission of author.

_F_   **6.** Political speech includes discussions of proposed laws.

_F_   **7.** This chart outlines the levels of protected speech.

_F_   **8.** Talking with someone on a telephone has a degree of protection.

_O_   **9.** Obscenity should not be protected communication.

_F/O_   **10.** According to the graphic, political communication receives more protection than commercial communication; thus a politician's speech is a more important form of communication than is a commercial.

Read the following information posted on the website of the Smithsonian Institute. Answer the questions that follow.

12.7 GE/651 words   **Tattoos: The Ancient and Mysterious History**

[1]Humans have marked their bodies with tattoos for thousands of years. [2]These permanent designs are sometimes plain, sometimes elaborate, always personal. [3]They have served as amulets, status symbols, declarations of love, signs of religious beliefs, adornments and even forms of punishment. [4]Joann Fletcher, research fellow in the department of archaeology at the University of York in Britain, describes the history of tattoos and their cultural significance to people around the world.

The earliest evidence of tattoos

[5]In terms of tattoos on actual bodies, the earliest known examples were for a long time Egyptian, and tattoos were present on several female mummies dated to c. 2000 B.C. [6]But the more recent discovery of the Iceman from the area of the Italian-Austrian border in 1991 and his tattoo patterns serves as an earlier example. [7]He was carbon-dated at around 5,200 years old.

Description of the tattoos on the Iceman
and their significance

[8]According to Professor Don Brothwell of the University of York, one of the specialists who examined him, the distribution of the tattooed dots and small crosses on his lower spine and right knee and ankle joints correspond to areas of strain-induced degeneration. [9]This pattern suggests that the tattoos may have been applied to alleviate joint pain, and they were therefore essentially therapeutic. [10]This would also explain their somewhat "random" distribution in areas of the body. [11]The marks would not have been that easy to display had they been applied as a form of status marker.

Evidence that ancient Egyptians had tattoos

[12]There's certainly evidence that women had tattoos on their bodies and limbs from figurines from 4000-3500 B.C. [13]Occasional female figures are represented in tomb scenes around 1200 B.C. [14]And tattoos are evident in figurine form around 1300 B.C. All these had tattoos on their thighs. [15]Also small bronze implements identified as tattooing tools were discovered at the town site of Gurob in northern Egypt and dated 1450 B.C. [16]And then, of course, there are the

mummies with tattoos. [17]Included are the three women already mentioned and dated to c. 2000 B.C. [18]And several later examples of female mummies with these forms of permanent marks were found in Greco-Roman burials at Akhmim.

The function served by tattoos: Who and why

[19]Because this seemed to be an exclusively female practice in ancient Egypt, mummies found with tattoos were usually dismissed by the (male) excavators who seemed to assume the women were of "dubious status." [20]They were described in some cases as "dancing girls." [21]The female mummies had nevertheless been buried at Deir el-Bahari (opposite modern Luxor) in an area associated with royal and elite burials. [22]And we know that at least one of the women described as "probably a royal concubine" was actually a high-status priestess named Amunet, as revealed by her funerary inscriptions.

[23]And although it has long been assumed that such tattoos were the mark of prostitutes or were meant to protect the women against sexually transmitted diseases, I personally believe that the tattooing of ancient Egyptian women had a therapeutic role and functioned as a permanent form of amulet during the very difficult time of pregnancy and birth. [24]This is supported by the pattern of distribution, largely around the abdomen, on top of the thighs and the breasts. [25]This would also explain the specific types of designs, in particular the net-like distribution of dots applied over the abdomen. [26]During pregnancy, this specific pattern would expand in a protective fashion in the same way bead nets were placed over wrapped mummies to protect them and "keep everything in." [27]The placing of small figures of the household deity Bes at the tops of their thighs would again suggest the use of tattoos as a means of safeguarding the actual birth. [28]Bes was the protector of women in labor, and his position at the tops of the thighs is a suitable location. [29]This would ultimately explain tattoos as a purely female custom.

—Adapted from Lineberry, "Tattoos: The Ancient and Mysterious History." Smithsonian.com 1 Jan. 2007. 23 March 2010. http://www.smithsonianmag.com/history-archaeology/tattoo.html.

_____a_____ **1.** Sentence 1 states
a. a fact.   b. an opinion.   c. both fact and opinion.

_____a_____ **2.** Sentence 5 states
a. a fact.   b. an opinion.   c. both fact and opinion.

_____c_____ **3.** Sentence 23 states
a. a fact.   b. an opinion.   c. both fact and opinion.

_____c_____ **4.** Sentence 27 states
a. a fact.   b. an opinion.   c. both fact and opinion.

Tone and Purpose

LEARNING OUTCOMES

After studying this chapter you should be able to do the following:

1. Define the following terms: *tone* and *purpose*. [Knowledge]
2. Understand how tone is established. [Comprehension]
3. Identify subjective and objective tone words. [Knowledge]
4. Determine the general purpose in the main idea. [Analysis]
5. Determine the primary purpose. [Analysis]
6. Evaluate a passage for the use of irony. [Evaluation]
7. Use tone and purpose to improve comprehension. [Application, Comprehension]

Before Reading About Tone and Purpose

Study the chapter learning outcomes and underline words that relate to ideas you have already studied. Did you underline the following terms: subjective, objective, and main idea? What you already know about these topics will help you learn about tone and purpose. Use the blanks that follow to write a short one- or two-sentence summary about each topic:

Subjective words: Answers may vary. _____

_____.

Objective words: _____

_____.

Main idea: _____

_____.

What Are Tone and Purpose?

Read the following two paragraphs. As you read, think about the difference in the tone and purpose of each one:

> Youth substance abuse can lead to many other problems, including the development of delinquent behavior, anti-social attitudes, and health-related issues. These problems not only affect the child, but can also influence the child's family, community, and ultimately society.
>
> —Executive Office of the President of the United States, "Juveniles and Drugs."
> Executive Office of the President. Office of National Drug Control Policy. 2 Nov. 2007.
> http://www.whitehousedrugpolicy.gov/drugfact/juveniles/index.html

> My name is Sheanne; I am 17 years old, and I am an alcoholic. I began drinking when I was 9 years old. My older cousins used to party pretty hard, and it seemed so cool, like they were having so much fun. They always got a kick out of giving me a beer on the sly, and I loved being part of the scene. By the time I was 11, I was guzzling hard booze. I fought with my family all the time, and school was a blur. Then last year, drunk as usual, I insisted on driving home from a late-night party. My twin sister, Shannon, rode with me. I don't remember what happened; I blacked out. Shannon died in that crash. I have been sober for 305 days. Every day is a struggle. Take my advice: Don't drink! If you do, don't drink and drive!
>
> —Sheanne's speech to a high school audience

The differences in the tone and purpose of these two paragraphs are obvious. The first paragraph was written by the government to inform the public about juveniles and drug abuse, using unbiased words and an objective, formal tone. The second paragraph approaches the same subject, drug abuse, with a different purpose—to persuade youth to avoid alcohol abuse. Sheanne conveys a painful personal experience using biased words and a subjective, informal tone.

Every text is created by an author who has a specific attitude toward the chosen topic and a specific reason for writing and sharing that attitude. The author's attitude is conveyed by the tone. **Tone** is the emotion or mood of the author's written voice. Understanding tone is closely related to understanding the author's reason for writing about the topic. This reason for writing is known as the author's **purpose.** Tone and purpose work together to convey the author's meaning.

Tone and purpose are greatly influenced by the audience the author is trying to reach. The audience for the first paragraph is members of the general public who need factual information; the objective presentation of facts best serves such a wide-ranging audience. The audience for the second example is teenagers who need to be persuaded; the informal, personal approach is much more likely to reach this audience. Tone and purpose are established with word choice. Master readers read to understand the author's tone and purpose. To identify tone and purpose, you need to build on several skills you have already studied: vocabulary, fact and opinion, and main ideas.

> **Tone** is the author's attitude toward the topic.
> **Purpose** is the reason the author writes about a topic.

 ## Understand How Tone Is Established

The author's attitude is expressed by the tone of voice he or she assumes in the passage. An author carefully chooses words that will make an impact on the reader. Sometimes an author wants to appeal to reason by using an objective tone, and just gives facts and factual explanations. At other times, an author wants to appeal to emotions by using a subjective tone to stir the reader to feel deeply.

Study the following list of words that describe the characteristics of tone.

Characteristics of Tone Words			
Objective Tone	**Shows no feelings for or against a topic**	**Subjective Tone**	**Shows favor for or against a topic**
unbiased	—remains impartial	biased	—makes it personal
neutral	—focuses on facts	emotional	—focuses on feelings
formal	—uses higher level words	informal	—uses conversational language
	—avoids personal pronouns *I* and *you*		—uses personal pronouns *I* and *you*
	—creates distance between writer and reader		—creates a connection between writer and reader
An objective tone is impartial, unbiased, neutral and most often formal.		A subjective tone is personal, biased, emotional, and often informal.	

For example, in an effort to share reliable information, textbooks strive for an objective tone, one that is matter-of-fact and neutral. The details given in an objective tone are likely to be facts. In contrast, sharing an author's personal world view through fiction and personal essays often calls for a subjective tone. A subjective tone uses words that describe feelings, judgments, or opinions. The details given in a subjective tone are likely to include experiences, senses, feelings, and thoughts.

EXAMPLES Look at the following list of quotations. Based on word choice, choose the tone word that best describes each statement.

___b___ **1.** "Permanent success cannot be achieved except by incessant intellectual labour, always inspired by the ideal."
Sarah Bernhardt (1845–1923), French actor

> —From *The Art of the Theatre*, ch. 3 (1924); qtd. in *The Columbia World of Quotations*, 1996. *Bartleby.com*, 2001. 7 Nov. 2007 www.bartleby.com/66/

    a. objective   b. subjective

___a___ **2.** "It is . . . to my three children [that] I owe my very being. In attempting to fulfill my duty to them as a mother, I met the challenge of their helplessness, their innocence, their dependence. Despising cowardice in others, I wished to prove myself no coward. Believing in the good, the gentle, the beautiful things of life, I addressed myself to the sweet duty of keeping these attributes for my children's sake and my own. And in striving to provide a living for them, I found a success beyond my wildest dreams."
Alice Foote MacDougall (1867–1945), U.S. businesswoman

> —From *The Autobiography of a Business Woman*, ch. 4 (1928); qtd. in *The Columbia World of Quotations*, 1996. *Bartleby.com*, 2001. 7 Nov. 2007 www.bartleby.com/66/

    a. emotional   b. neutral

___b___ **3.** "Success is a great deodorant. It takes away all your past smells."
Elizabeth Taylor, American film actor

> —From ABC-TV interview April 6, 1977; qtd. in *The Columbia World of Quotations*, 1996. *Bartleby.com*, 2001. 7 Nov. 2007 www.bartleby.com/66/

    a. formal   b. informal

EXPLANATIONS

1. (b) subjective: Sarah Bernhardt establishes a subjective tone through the use of biased language with words such as *incessant, intellectual, labor, inspire,* or *ideal.*

2. (a) emotional: MacDougall expresses a passionate drive for success.

3. (b) informal: Taylor uses colloquial language (commonly spoken words) for a witty effect.

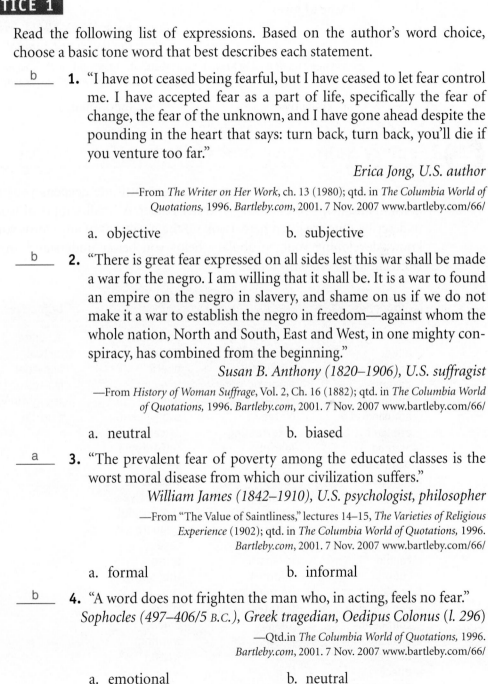

PRACTICE 1

Read the following list of expressions. Based on the author's word choice, choose a basic tone word that best describes each statement.

_b_   **1.** "I have not ceased being fearful, but I have ceased to let fear control me. I have accepted fear as a part of life, specifically the fear of change, the fear of the unknown, and I have gone ahead despite the pounding in the heart that says: turn back, turn back, you'll die if you venture too far."

Erica Jong, U.S. author

—From *The Writer on Her Work*, ch. 13 (1980); qtd. in *The Columbia World of Quotations*, 1996. *Bartleby.com*, 2001. 7 Nov. 2007 www.bartleby.com/66/

a. objective   b. subjective

_b_   **2.** "There is great fear expressed on all sides lest this war shall be made a war for the negro. I am willing that it shall be. It is a war to found an empire on the negro in slavery, and shame on us if we do not make it a war to establish the negro in freedom—against whom the whole nation, North and South, East and West, in one mighty conspiracy, has combined from the beginning."

Susan B. Anthony (1820–1906), U.S. suffragist

—From *History of Woman Suffrage*, Vol. 2, Ch. 16 (1882); qtd. in *The Columbia World of Quotations*, 1996. *Bartleby.com*, 2001. 7 Nov. 2007 www.bartleby.com/66/

a. neutral   b. biased

_a_   **3.** "The prevalent fear of poverty among the educated classes is the worst moral disease from which our civilization suffers."

William James (1842–1910), U.S. psychologist, philosopher

—From "The Value of Saintliness," lectures 14–15, *The Varieties of Religious Experience* (1902); qtd. in *The Columbia World of Quotations*, 1996. *Bartleby.com*, 2001. 7 Nov. 2007 www.bartleby.com/66/

a. formal   b. informal

_b_   **4.** "A word does not frighten the man who, in acting, feels no fear."
Sophocles (497–406/5 B.C.), Greek tragedian, Oedipus Colonus (l. 296)

—Qtd. in *The Columbia World of Quotations*, 1996. *Bartleby.com*, 2001. 7 Nov. 2007 www.bartleby.com/66/

a. emotional   b. neutral

___b___   **5.** Around us fear, descending
Darkness of fear above
And in my heart how deep unending
Ache of love!

James Joyce (1882–1941), Irish writer,
"On the Beach at Fontana" (l. 9–12)

—From *Oxford Book of Modern Verse*, Yeats, ed. (1936); qtd. in *The Columbia World of*
Quotations, 1996. *Bartleby.com*, 2001. 7 Nov. 2007 www.bartleby.com/66/

a. objective   b. emotional

 # Identify Subjective and Objective Tone Words

Recognizing tone and describing an author's attitude deepens your comprehension and helps you become a master reader. A small sample of words used
to describe tone are listed here. Look up the meanings of any words you do not
know; developing your vocabulary helps you better understand an author's
word choice to establish tone.

Subjective			Objective
admiring	disbelieving	persuasive	accurate
angry	discouraged	pleading	factual
annoyed	disdainful	poetic	impartial
anxious	dramatic	reverent	matter-of-fact
approving	earnest	rude	straightforward
argumentative	elated	sad	truthful
arrogant	entertaining	sarcastic	
assured	fearful	self-pitying	
belligerent	friendly	serious	
biting	funny	sincere	
bitter	gloomy	supportive	
bored	happy	suspenseful	
bubbly	hostile	sympathetic	
calm	humorous	tender	
candid	idealistic	tense	
cold	informal	thoughtful	
comic	informative	threatening	
complaining	irritated	timid	
confident	joking	urgent	
cynical	jovial	warning	
demanding	joyful	wistful	
direct	lively	wry	
disappointed	loving		

EXAMPLE   Read the following quotations. Choose a word that best describes the tone of each statement.

cautionary	confident	critical	joyous	reverent

1. "Queenliness is an attitude that starts on the inside and works its way out. The way you hold your head up makes you a queen . . . I know who I am. I am confident. I know God. I can take care of myself. I share my life with others, and I love—I am worthy of the title Queen."

Queen Latifah, actress, singer, rap artist

—Source: From *Ladies First: Revelations of a Strong Woman* by Queen Latifah and Karen Hunter. Copyright 1999 by Queen Latifah, Inc.

Tone: confident

2. "Music puts me in touch with something beyond the intellect, something otherworldly, something sacred."

Sting, musician

—"Mystery and Religion of Music," Berklee College of Music, 1994.

Tone: reverent

3. "After a century of striving, after a year of debate, after a historic vote, health care reform is no longer an unmet promise. It is the law of the land. It is the law of the land."

President Barack Obama

—Remarks by the President on Health Insurance Reform at the Department of the Interior, 23 March 2010 whitehouse.gov/the-press-office.

Tone: joyous

4. "Americans wanted us to get at the root of this problem, which is cost. Instead, Democrats are spending trillions more on a system that already costs too much and forcing seniors, small business owners and middle class families to pay for it. You can call that a lot of things. You might even call it historic. But you can't call it reform."

Senator Mitch McConnell, Republican-Kentucky, Minority Leader

—Remarks in press release regarding health care bill, 23 March 2010 http://mcconnell.senate.gov/public/index.cfm?p=PressReleases& ContentRecord_id=3ae19c9a-060b-47e3-9558-60e262b02427.

Tone: critical

5. "As though a deep gulf were yawning below, As crossing thin ice, Take heed how ye go."

Confucius

—*The Sayings of Confucius.* Vol. XLIV, Part 1. *The Harvard Classics.* New York: P.F. Collier & Son, 1909–14; Bartleby.com, 2001. www.bartleby.com/44/1/. [24 March 2010].

Tone: cautionary

VISUAL VOCABULARY

Use a tone word to describe the mood of President Obama and his team as they work to pass the health care reform bill in 2010.

Answers may vary: worried,

serious, tense

EXPLANATION Compare your answers to the following: (1) confident, (2) reverent, (3) joyous, (4) critical, (5) cautionary.

PRACTICE 2

Read the following items. Based on the author's word choice, choose a word from the box that best describes the tone of each statement.

emotional	humble	matter-of-fact	reflective	respectful

1.
Harvard University, Cambridge, May 28, 1896
President Booker T. Washington

MY DEAR SIR: Harvard University desires to confer on you at the approaching Commencement an honorary degree; but it is our custom to confer degrees only on gentlemen who are present. Our Commencement occurs this year on June 24, and your presence would be desirable from about noon till about five o'clock in the afternoon. Would it be possible for you to be in Cambridge on that day?

> Believe me, with great regard,
> Very truly yours,
> CHARLES W. ELIOT.

—From Washington, Booker, *Up from Slavery: An Autobiography,*
ch. XVII, p. 4 (1901); *Bartleby.com*, 2000. 24 Feb. 04
www.bartleby.com/1004/

Tone: respectful _____

2. "This was a recognition that had never in the slightest manner entered into my mind, and it was hard for me to realize that I was to be honoured by a degree from the oldest and most renowned university in America."

Booker T. Washington, President of Tuskegee College

—From *Up from Slavery: An Autobiography,* ch. XVII, p. 5 (1901);
Bartleby.com, 2000. 24 Feb. 04 www.bartleby.com/1004/

Tone: humble _____

3. "As I sat upon my veranda, with this letter in my hand, tears came into my eyes. My whole former life—my life as a slave on the plantation, my work in the coal-mine, the times when I was without food and clothing, when I made my bed under a sidewalk, my struggles for an education, the trying days I had had at Tuskegee, days when I did not know where to turn for a dollar to continue the work there, the ostracism and sometimes oppression of my race,—all this passed before me and nearly overcame me."

Booker T. Washington, President of Tuskegee College

—From *Up from Slavery: An Autobiography,* ch. XVII, p. 5 (1901);
Bartleby.com, 2000. 24 Feb. 04 www.bartleby.com/1004/

Tone: emotional _____

4. "As this was the first time that a New England university had conferred an honorary degree upon a Negro, it was the occasion of much newspaper comment throughout the country."

Booker T. Washington, President of Tuskegee College

—From *Up from Slavery: An Autobiography,* ch. XVII, p. 10 (1901);
Bartleby.com, 2000. 24 Feb. 04 www.bartleby.com/1004/

Tone: matter-of-fact _____

5. "If my life in the past has meant anything in the lifting up of my people and the bringing about of better relations between your race and mine, I assure you from this day it will mean doubly more."

Booker T. Washington, President of Tuskegee College

—From *Up from Slavery: An Autobiography,* ch. XVII, p. 9 (1901); *Bartleby.com,* 2000. 24 Feb. 04 www.bartleby.com/1004/

Tone: reflective or emotional

Discover the General Purpose in the Main Idea

In Chapter 3, you learned that a main idea is made up of a topic and the author's controlling point. You identified the controlling point by looking for thought patterns and biased (tone) words. The next two sections will build on what you have learned. First, you will study the relationship between the general purpose and the author's main idea. Then, you will apply what you have learned to figure out an author's primary purpose.

Many reasons can motivate a writer. These can range from the need to take a stand on a hotly debated issue to the desire to entertain an audience with an amusing story. Basically, an author writes to share a main idea about a topic. An author's main idea, whether stated or implied, and the author's purpose are directly related. One of the following three general purposes will drive a main idea: to inform, to persuade, and to entertain.

- **To inform.** When a writer sets out to inform, he or she shares knowledge and information or offers instruction about a particular topic. A few tone words typically used to describe this purpose include *objective, matter-of-fact,* and *straightforward.* Authors use facts to explain or describe the main idea to readers. Most textbook passages are written to inform. The following topic sentences reflect the writer's desire to inform.

  1. A sensible weight management program combines a healthful diet and regular exercise.
  2. *Narrative of the Life of Frederick Douglass, an American Slave, Written by Himself* records Douglass's life as a slave in the United States.

In sentence 1, the topic is weight management, and the words that reveal the controlling point are *sensible, healthful,* and *regular.* The author uses a tone that is unbiased and objective, so the focus is on the information. In sentence 2, the topic is Frederick Douglass's autobiography, and the words that reveal the controlling point are *records, life,* and *slave.* Again, the author chooses words that are matter-of-fact and suggest that factual details will follow. Both topic sentences indicate that the author's purpose is to provide helpful information.

- **To persuade.** A writer who sets out to persuade tries to bring the reader into agreement with his or her view on the topic. A few of the tone words typically used to describe this purpose include *argumentative, persuasive, forceful, controversial, positive, supportive, negative,* and *critical.* Authors combine facts with emotional appeals to sway the reader to their point of view. Politicians and advertisers often write and speak to persuade. The following topic sentences reflect the writer's desire to persuade.

    3. Resistance training is the best method of shaping the body.
    4. *Narrative of the Life of Frederick Douglass, an American Slave, Written by Himself* should be required reading in American public high schools.

In sentence 3, the topic is resistance training. The word that reveals the author's controlling point is *best.* In sentence 4, the topic is Douglass's auto-biography. The words that reveal the controlling point are *should be,* which are followed by a recommendation for action. The author is offering a debat-able personal opinion about what should be required high school reading. In both of these sentences, the authors are out to convince others to agree with them.

- **To entertain.** A writer whose purpose is to entertain sets out to captivate or interest the audience. A few of the tone words typically used to describe this purpose include *amusing, entertaining, lively, humorous,* and *suspenseful.* To entertain, authors often use expressive language and creative thinking. Most readers are entertained by material that stirs an emotional reaction such as laughter, sympathy, or fear. Thus, authors engage readers creatively through vivid images, strong feelings, or sensory details (such as sights, sounds, tastes, textures, and smells). Both fiction and nonfiction writers seek to entertain. The following topic sentences reflect the writer's desire to entertain.

    5. Leona had the fashion style of a cantaloupe.
    6. Anton woke up to the cozy aromas of coffee, bacon, and freshly baked bread, just as he had every day of his twenty years, yet today promised to be very different. He just knew it.

You may have found identifying the topic and controlling point a little more challenging in these two sentences. Often, when writers entertain, they imply the main idea. And when they use an implied main idea, they rely much more heavily on tone words. Sentence 5 deals with the topic of Leona and her fashion style. In this sentence, the author focuses the topic with the phrase "style of a cantaloupe." The use of *cantaloupe* (a biased word when used in this context) offers a strong clue that the author's purpose is to entertain. The author seeks to amuse the reader with the contrast between style and cantaloupe. Surprising contrasts often amuse the reader. Authors also use other methods to entertain, including exaggerations, vivid details, and dramatic descriptions.

Sentence 6 deals with the topic of Anton's experience. In this case, the words that reveal the author's controlling point are *cozy, aromas, freshly baked,* which are pleasant sensory details, and *promised* and *different*. However, the main idea is not really about Anton's experience. The point seems to be about a change or hope for change in Anton's life.

These six sentences show that a topic can be approached in a variety of ways. The author chooses a topic and a purpose. The purpose shapes the focus of the main idea. The author carefully chooses tone words to express the main idea in light of the purpose. Each of these choices then controls the choices of supporting details and the thought pattern used to organize them.

EXAMPLES Read each of the following paragraphs. Annotate them for main idea and tone. Then, identify the author's purpose as follows:

I = to inform   **P** = to persuade   **E** = to entertain

___E___ **1.** ¹Darla shivered, pulled her jacket's fuzzy collar up to the tops of her ears, and tucked her chin into its warmth; her arms and legs felt heavy and difficult to move as she started across the street. ²It was only November, and already she longed for the bright, long days of June and July. ³She dreaded the looming blackness of January and February. ⁴She did not mesh well with the rhythm of their abbreviated days and unending nights.

⁵Ah, she thought to herself, I am so incredibly tired. ⁶She felt the familiar cravings for something sweet and crunchy; she mentally pictured the box of Cocoa Puffs sitting on the pantry shelf, and she longed to be home. ⁷She didn't care that she was already beginning to show her dreaded winter weight, she was going to have a bowl, or maybe two, as soon as she could.

___I___ **2.** ¹Some people suffer from symptoms of depression during the winter months, with symptoms subsiding during the spring and summer months. ²This may be a sign of Seasonal Affective Disorder (SAD).

³SAD is a mood disorder linked to two factors: episodes of depression and the seasonal variations of daylight.

⁴Some experts believe as seasons change, a shift in our "biological internal clocks" occurs, partly because of the changes in sunlight patterns. ⁵This may cause our biological clocks to be out of "step" with our daily schedules. ⁶The most difficult months for some SAD sufferers seem to be January and February. ⁷In addition, younger persons and women seem to be at higher risk.

—Adapted from "Seasonal Affective Disorder," Mental Health America, Copyright 2010 Mental Health America, http://www.mentalhealthamerica.net/go/sad

_P_   **3.** ¹If you suffer from seasonal affective disorder (SAD), also known as winter depression, you should implement the following lifestyle as a remedy. ²First, you need to spend at least thirty minutes outside every morning, even when it's very cloudy, for the effects of daylight are very beneficial. ³You must eat a well-balanced diet that includes sufficient amounts of vitamins and minerals as recommended by the FDA. ⁴You should exercise for 30 minutes a day, three times a week. ⁵Proper diet and exercise give you more energy, even though your body is craving starchy and sweet foods. ⁶Just as importantly, you must develop an active social life and become involved with regular activities. ⁷Of course, you should also seek professional counseling if needed, during the winter months.

—Adapted from "What Is Seasonal Disorder?" The Cleveland Clinic Health Information Center. 22 Feb. 2004 http://www.clevelandclinic.org/health/health-info/docs/2300/2361.asp?index=9293

4. Study each of the photographs of people in public speaking situations. Label the purpose of each speaker with one of the following:

E = to entertain   **I** = to inform   **P** = to persuade

a. ___P___   b. ___I___   c. ___E___

EXPLANATIONS

Passages 1 through 3 used the same topic: seasonal affective disorder (SAD). However, the purpose of each passage differed. Note how the difference in purpose affected the selection and presentation of supporting details.

1. The topic is Darla's experience with SAD. This topic is implied. In the first paragraph, the author uses vivid details, descriptions, and appeals to the senses *to entertain* the reader through an unfolding dramatic event.

2. In the second paragraph, the author's purpose is simply *to inform* the reader about the symptoms of seasonal affective disorder (SAD).

3. However, in the third paragraph, the author attempts *to persuade* the reader that the only solution to SAD is a change in lifestyle. The persuasive tone is established and carried through by using the verbs *should, need to,* and *must.*

4. a. P, to persuade   b. I, to inform   c. E, to entertain

PRACTICE 3

Read the following topic sentences. Label each according to its purpose:

I = to inform   **P** = to persuade   **E** = to entertain

____P____ 1. Understanding the aging process and those who seem to defy it is vital to our future.

____I____ 2. According to Elisabeth Kubler-Ross, people go through five stages of grief.

____P____ 3. To experience the hospitality and delights of a true summer resort away from the daily stresses, take a trip back in time to Mackinac Island in Michigan.

____E____ 4. The sun spilled its brilliance from above so that every leaf, blade of grass, and ripple of water on the lake shimmered with no regard for my great grief.

 Figure Out the Primary Purpose

In addition to the three general purposes, authors often write to fulfill a more specific purpose. The following table offers several examples of specific purposes.

General and Specific Purposes		
To Inform	**To Entertain**	**To Persuade**
to analyze	to amuse	to argue for
to clarify	to delight	to argue against
to discuss	to frighten	to criticize
to establish		to convince
to explain		to inspire (motivate a change)

Often a writer has two or more purposes in one piece of writing. Blending purposes adds interest and power to a piece of writing. Take, for example, the award-winning documentary *Sicko* by Michael Moore. This film attempts to inform and entertain, but its primary purpose is to argue. The film uses facts, personal bias, and humor to take a strong stand against the current system of health care in America. When an author has more than one purpose, only one purpose is in control overall. This controlling purpose is called the **primary purpose.**

You have studied several reading skills that will help you grasp the author's primary purpose. For example, the author's primary purpose is often suggested by the main idea, the thought pattern, and the tone of the passage. Read the following topic sentence. Identify the author's primary purpose by considering the main idea, thought pattern, and tone.

___b___ Spanking must be avoided as a form of discipline due to its long-term negative effects on the child.
   a. to discuss the disadvantages of spanking
   b. to argue against spanking as a means of discipline
   c. to make fun of those who use spanking as a means of discipline

This topic sentence clearly states a main idea "against spanking" using the tone words *must* and *negative*. The details will be organized using the thought pattern "long-term effects." Based on the topic sentence, the author's primary purpose is (b) to argue against spanking as a means of discipline. Even when the main idea is implied, tone and thought patterns point to the author's primary purpose.

You should also take into account titles, headings, and prior knowledge about the author. For example, it's easy to see that Jay Leno's primary purpose is to entertain us with his book *If Roast Beef Could Fly*. The title is funny, and we know Jay Leno is a comedian. A master reader studies the general context of the passage to find out the author's primary purpose.

> **Primary purpose** is the author's main reason for writing the passage.

EXAMPLE Read the following paragraphs. Identify the primary purpose of each.

1. **Coacoochee**

Coacoochee. A Seminole warrior, nicknamed "Wildcat" and "Shrieky Scream," led raids against Americans, including Captain Dummett and Sergeant Ormond on the Halifax River. Famous for escaping jail in St. Augustine [Florida], he was banished to Mexico where he died at 49 of smallpox. His mother said he was made of Florida sands.

—Images of America: Ormond Beach, published by
The Ormond Beach Historical Trust, 1999, p. 15.

_____a_____ The main purpose of this paragraph is
   a. to share historical information about Coacoochee, a Seminole Indian.
   b. to amuse the reader with entertaining details about Coacoochee.
   c. to convince readers that Coacoochee was a hero.

2. **Early Biological Thought Did Not Include the Concept of Evolution**

Textbook
Skills

[1]Pre-Darwinian science, heavily influenced by theology, held that all organisms were created simultaneously by God and that each distinct life-form remained fixed and unchanging from the moment of its creation. [2]This explanation of how life's diversity arose was elegantly expressed by the ancient Greek philosophers especially Plato and Aristotle. [3]Plato (427–347 B.C.) proposed that each object on Earth was merely a temporary reflection of its divinely inspired "ideal form." [4]Plato's student Aristotle (384–322 B.C.) categorized all organisms into a linear hierarchy that he called the "ladder of Nature."

[5]These ideas formed the basis of the view that the form of each type of organism is permanently fixed. [6]This view reigned unchallenged for nearly 2,000 years. [7]By the eighteenth century, however, several lines of newly emerging evidence began to erode the dominance of this static view of creation.

—From Life on Earth, 5th ed., pp. 211–212 by Teresa Audesirk, Gerald Audesirk, and Bruce
E. Byers. Copyright © 2009 by Pearson Education, Inc. Printed and Electronically
reproduced by permission of Pearson Education, Inc., Upper Saddle River, NJ.

___c___ The main purpose of this passage is

    a. to offer entertaining details about the idea of fixed species.

    b. to convince the reader that the idea of fixed species is a proven fact.

    c. to explain the origin of the idea of fixed species.

3.   **Should Children Pledge Allegiance?**

Textbook
Skills

[1]A government that is built upon respect for the dignity and the rights of every human being deserves the allegiance or loyalty of its citizens. [2]The United States is built upon respect for the dignity and the rights of every human being. [3]Therefore, the United States deserves the allegiance of its citizens. [4]In addition, an effort to develop in citizens an appreciation for such an allegiance is acceptable. [5]That effort, however, must not harm the dignity of the individual. [6]In addition, the effort must not cause the individual to act against his or her personal beliefs. [7]Sadly, requiring students to recite the pledge of allegiance in school does, in some cases, cause students to act against their personal beliefs. [8]And, in some cases, when students refuse to act against their beliefs in this way, they have been abused. [9]Therefore, requiring students to recite the pledge of allegiance is not acceptable.

—Adapted from *The Art of Thinking: A Guide to Critical and Creative Thought*, 7th ed., p. 200 by Vincent R. Ruggiero. Copyright © 2004 by Pearson Education, Inc. Reprinted by permission of Pearson Education, Inc., Glenview, IL.

___a___ The main purpose of this paragraph is

    a. to argue against requiring students to recite the pledge of allegiance.

    b. to entertain the reader with a clever view about requiring students to recite the pledge of allegiance.

    c. to inform the reader about the pledge of allegiance.

EXPLANATION

1. The first paragraph is taken from a book produced by the historical society of the small coastal town of Ormond Beach, Florida. The purpose is (a), to share historical information about Coacoochee, a Seminole Indian.

2. The second paragraph comes from a college biology textbook. The main purpose is (c), to explain the origin of the idea of fixed species.

3. The third paragraph is taken from a college textbook on critical thinking. Its main purpose is (a), to argue against requiring students to recite the pledge of allegiance.

PRACTICE 4

A. Read the passage from a college finance textbook. Answer the questions that follow it.

Personal Financial Planning

Textbook
Skills

¹Where does it all go? ²It seems like the last paycheck is gone before the next one comes in. ³Money seems to burn a hole in your pocket, yet you don't believe that you are living extravagantly. ⁴Last month you made a pledge to yourself to spend less than the month before. ⁵Somehow, though, the weeks seem to go by, and you are again in the same position as you were last month. ⁶Your money is gone. ⁷Is there any way to plug the hole in your pocket?

⁸As with any campaign, the first step is to gather information. ⁹How much income do you earn? ¹⁰How much is left after withholding taxes? ¹¹What are your expenses? ¹²For many people, the first obstacle is to correctly assess their true expenses. ¹³Calculating your net income is easy; just look at your pay statement. ¹⁴But expenses are sly little creatures. ¹⁵Each one seems so harmless and worthwhile, but combined together they can be a pack of piranhas that quickly gobble up your modest income. ¹⁶What can you do to gain control of your personal finances?

¹⁷The solution is simple, but not easy. ¹⁸The solution is simple because others have blazed the path; however, your task is not easy, because it takes self-discipline and there may be no immediate reward. ¹⁹The result is often like a diet: easy to get started, but hard to carry through.

²⁰Your tools are the personal balance statement, the personal cash flow statement, and a budget. ²¹These three personal financial statements show you where you are, predict where you will be after three months or a year, and help you control those pesky expenditures; the potential benefits are reduced spending, increased savings and investments, and peace of mind from knowing that you are in control.

—From *Personal Finance*, 2nd ed., pp. 27–28 by Jeff Madura. Copyright © 2004 by Pearson Education, Inc. Reproduced by permission of Pearson Education, Inc., Boston, MA.

_____a_____ **1.** The purpose of sentence 8 in the second paragraph is
   a. to inform the reader that financial planning is similar to any operating plan.
   b. to state a point against extravagant spending.
   c. to entertain the reader with a vivid detail about planning.

_____b_____ **2.** The main purpose of the second paragraph is
   a. to explain to the reader that everyone struggles with financial problems.

    b. to convince the reader that personal financial planning is necessary.

    c. to amuse the reader with a real-life story.

_b_ **3.** The main purpose of the passage overall is

    a. to explain and illustrate the process of personal financial planning.

    b. to offer an amusing approach with real life details to the topic "personal financial planning."

    c. to argue against extravagant spending.

 ## Recognize Irony Used for Special Effects

Irony is a tone often used in both conversation and written text. An author uses **irony** when he or she says one thing but means something else. Irony is the contrast between what is stated and what is implied, or between actual events and expectations.

Irony is often used to entertain and enlighten. For example, in the novel *Huckleberry Finn* by Mark Twain, the boy Huckleberry Finn believes he has done something wrong when he helps his older friend Jim escape slavery. The ironic contrast lies between what Huckleberry Finn thinks is wrong and what really is wrong: slavery itself. Twain set up this ironic situation to reveal the shortcomings of society.

Irony is also used to persuade. In her essay "I Want a Wife," Judy Brady seems to be saying she wants a wife to take care of the children, do the household chores, and perform all the other countless duties expected of a wife in the mid-twentieth century. However, she doesn't really want a wife; she wants equality with men. As she describes the role of a wife as a submissive servant, she argues against the limitations that society has placed on women.

Due to the powerful effects of irony, authors use it in many types of writing. You may come across irony in fiction, essays, poetry, comedy routines, and cartoons. When authors use irony, they imply their main ideas and rely heavily on tone. Thus you need to understand two common types of irony so that you can see and enjoy their effects: verbal irony and situational irony.

> **Verbal irony** occurs when the author's words state one thing but imply the opposite.

- During a disagreement, your friend says, "I can't wait to hear your next great idea!"
- After eating large portions of a full-course meal, a diner says, "Good thing I wasn't hungry."
- After completing a challenging exam, a student says, "Well, that was easy."

> **Situational irony** occurs when the events of a situation differ from what is expected.

- A popular singer suffers from severe stage fright.
- The person voted "most likely to succeed" in high school becomes a homeless drifter.
- A wealthy person who has never taken a vacation.

EXAMPLES   Read the items, and identify the type of irony used in each.

____a____   **1.** Referring to Katharine Hepburn, in a theater review of *The Lake*, Dorothy Parker wrote, "She runs the gamut of emotions from A to B."

> —In *The Columbia World of Quotations,* 1996; *Bartleby.com,*
> 2001. 7 Nov. 2007 www.bartleby.com/66/

    a. verbal irony   c. no irony
    b. situational irony

____b____   **2.** "Talkative people who wish to be loved are hated; when they desire to please, they bore; when they think they are admired, they are laughed at; they injure their friends, benefit their enemies, and ruin themselves."

> —*Plutarch, Greek essayist and biographer (46–119 A.C.E.)*
>
> —From *The International Dictionary of Thoughts,* Comp.
> Bradley, Daniels, and Jones, 1969, p. 707.

    a. verbal irony   c. no irony
    b. situational irony

____c____   **3.** "C-O-P-D [Chronic Obstructive Pulmonary Disease] is the fourth leading cause of death in the United States. It is a serious lung disease that takes away the breath of 12 million Americans."

> —*Kenneth P. Moritsugu, Acting Surgeon General,*
> *U.S. Department of Health and Human Services*
>
> —From Remarks at 52nd International Respiratory Congress.
> 11 Nov. 2006. Washington, D.C. 7 Nov. 2007
> http://www.surgeongeneral.gov/news/speeches/12112006.html.

    a. verbal irony   c. no irony
    b. situational irony

EXPLANATIONS Compare your answers with these:

1. (a) verbal irony: Dorothy Parker is known for her ironic wit. In this case, Parker's biting wit arises out of the contrast between the word *gamut* and the phrase "A to B." The word *gamut* means "scope" or "range," and sets up the expectation that Parker is going to imply that Ms. Hepburn displays an impressive breadth of emotion; however, she surprisingly limits Hepburn's range of emotion to the first two letters of the alphabet. What initially seems to be a compliment ends as a humorous insult.

2. (b) situational irony: Most people who are talkative are trying to make a connection or make a difference through the power of talk. Plutarch points out the irony of the situation when their excessive talk brings about the opposite of their hopes.

3. (c) no irony: The author directly states facts without implying any other meaning than the one stated.

PRACTICE 5

Read the items below and identify the type of irony used in each.

___a___ 1. "I love working sixteen-hour days for minimum wage."
     a. verbal irony   c. no irony
     b. situational irony

___b___ 2. A recent college graduate takes a job as an intern in a company as a stepping-stone into a salaried position with full benefits. However, the intern's supervisor feels threatened by the efficiency and skill of the intern and denies her the full-time position.
     a. verbal irony   c. no irony
     b. situational irony

___a___ 3. "Notice—By Order of the Author. Persons attempting to find a motive in this narrative will be prosecuted; persons attempting to find a moral in it will be banished; persons attempting to find a plot in it will be shot."

                                                    —Mark Twain, *Huckleberry Finn* (1884).

     a. verbal irony   c. no irony
     b. situational irony

_____c_____ **4.** A student studies for weeks for final exams and earns the highest grade point average in her classes.
    a. verbal irony   c. no irony
    b. situational irony

_____b_____ **5.** On his way home from an Alcoholics Anonymous meeting, a reformed alcoholic is killed in an automobile accident by a drunk driver who walks away from the accident with only minor injuries.
    a. verbal irony   c. no irony
    b. situational irony

Textbook
Skills

Reading a Textbook: Author's Tone and Purpose

Read the following passage from the textbook *Access to Health*. Then, answer the questions about the author's tone and purpose.

Societal Causes of Violence

[1]Although the underlying causes of violence and abuse are as varied as the individual crimes and people involved, several social, cultural, and individual factors seem to increase the likelihood of violent acts (see Figure 10.1). [2]Included among those factors most commonly listed are the following:

Poverty. [3]Low socioeconomic status and poor living conditions can create an environment of hopelessness, leaving one feeling trapped and seeing violence as the only way to obtain what is needed or wanted.

Unemployment. [4]It is a well-documented fact that when the economy goes sour, violent crime, suicide, assault, and other crimes increase.

Parental influence. [5]Violence is cyclical. [6]Children raised in environments in which shouting, slapping, hitting, and other forms of violence are commonplace are more apt to "act out" these behaviors as adults. [7]Horrifying reports in recent years have made this pattern impossible to ignore.

Cultural beliefs. [8]Cultures that objectify women and empower men to be tough and aggressive tend to have increased rates of violence in the home.

The media. [9]A daily dose of murder and mayhem can take a toll on even resistant minds.

Discrimination/oppression. [10]Whenever one group is oppressed by another, seeds of discontent are sown and hate crimes arise.

Religious differences. [11]Religious persecution has been a part of the human experience since the earliest times. [12]These battles between right and wrong, good and evil, and the attempt to impose beliefs on others have often led to violence.

Breakdown in the criminal justice system. [13]Overcrowded prisons, lenient sentences, early releases from prisons, and trial errors subtly encourage violence in a number of ways.

Stress. [14]People who suffer from inordinate amounts of stress or are in crisis are more apt to be highly reactive, striking out at others or acting irrationally.

—Text and graphic from *Access to Health*, 7th ed., pp. 94–95 and Figure 4.1 (p. 95) by Rebecca J. Donatelle and Lorraine G. Davis. Copyright © 2002 by Pearson Education, Inc. Printed and Electronically reproduced by permission of Pearson Education, Inc., Upper Saddle River, NJ.

a   **1.** The author's primary purpose for this section of the textbook is
    a. to inform.   c. to persuade.
    b. to entertain.

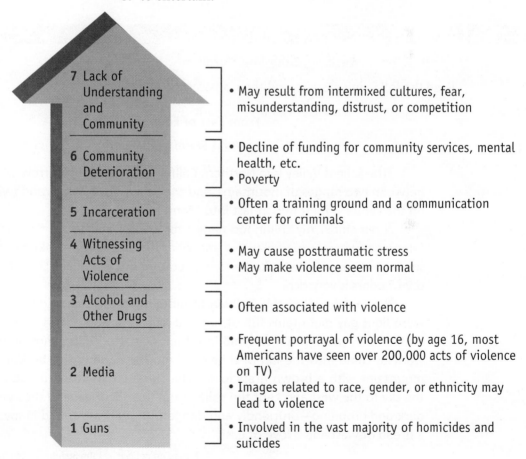

▲ **Figure 4.1**   Correlates to Violence

_____b_____   **2.** The overall tone of the text is
  a. biased.   b. objective.

_____a_____   **3.** The purpose of Figure 10.1, "Correlates to Violence," is
  a. to inform.   c. to persuade.
  b. to entertain.

_____d_____   **4.** The tone of sentence 6 is
  a. ironic.   c. sarcastic.
  b. angry.   d. matter-of-fact.

_____c_____   **5.** The tone of sentence 7 is
  a. irritated.   c. firm.
  b. matter-of-fact.   d. sarcastic.

APPLICATIONS

Application 1: Author's Tone and Purpose

Read the following passage, and then, answer the questions.

From *East of Eden*

by John Steinbeck

¹The Salinas Valley is in Northern California. ²It is a long narrow swale between two ranges of mountains, and the Salinas River winds and twists up the center until it falls at last into Monterey Bay.

³I remember my childhood names for grasses and secret flowers. ⁴I remember where a toad may live and what time the birds awaken in the summer—how people looked and walked and smelled even. ⁵The memory of odors is very rich.

⁶I remember that the Gabilan Mountains to the east of the valley were light gay mountains full of sun and loveliness and a kind of invitation, so that you wanted to climb into their warm foothills almost as you want to climb into the lap of a beloved mother. ⁷They were beckoning mountains with a brown grass love. ⁸The Santa Lucias stood up against the sky to the west and kept the valley from the open sea, and they were dark and brooding—unfriendly and dangerous. ⁹I always found in myself a dread of west and a love of east.

— From *East of Eden* by John Steinbeck. New York:
Penguin Group (USA) Inc., 1952, 1980.

_____a_____ **1.** The tone of sentences 1 and 2 is
    a. factual.   c. cold.
    b. reflective.

_____b_____ **2.** The tone of sentences 3 to 5 is
    a. encouraging.   c. sarcastic.
    b. reflective.

_____c_____ **3.** The tone of sentences 6 and 7 is
    a. matter-of-fact.   c. admiring.
    b. prideful.

_____b_____ **4.** The tone of sentence 8 is
    a. sarcastic.   c. objective.
    b. critical.

_____a_____ **5.** The purpose of the first paragraph is
    a. to inform the reader about certain aspects of the Salinas Valley.
    b. to entertain the reader with little-known facts about the Salinas Valley.
    c. to persuade the reader that the Salinas Valley is beautiful.

_____b_____ **6.** The overall purpose of the passage is
    a. to inform.   c. to persuade.
    b. to entertain.

Application 2: Irony

Read the items below. Identify the type of irony used, if any.

_____a_____ **1.** "The brain is a wonderful organ; it starts working the moment you get up, and does not stop until you get to the office."

—*Robert Frost*

—In Eldin, *Jokes & Quotes for Speeches*, 1989, p. 42.

    a. verbal irony   c. no irony
    b. situational irony

_____a_____ **2.** "The drive down to see you was just wonderful, simply wonderful! How boring it would have been if we had simply zipped down here in the usual one-hour drive time. We were thrilled by the three-hour traffic jam caused by a minor accident that every driver on the road just had to slow down to inspect."
    —*A son's response to his parents' inquiry about his drive to visit them*
    a. verbal irony   c. no irony
    b. situational irony

_____b_____ **3.** One of the surprising parts of maturing as a woman is the way in which one grows to resemble one's mother, both in looks and ways.
a. verbal irony
c. no irony
b. situational irony

ZITS © 2010 Zits Partnership, King Features Syndicate

_____a_____ **4.** What irony is used in the cartoon?
a. verbal irony
c. no irony
b. situational irony

REVIEW TEST 1
Score (number correct) _____ × 10 = _____ %

Author's Purpose

A. Read the topic sentences. Label each one according to its purpose as follows:

I = to inform   **P** = to persuade   **E** = to entertain

_____E_____ **1.** A wedding should be viewed as one of the happiest of events, and we worked very hard to behave as if that were true for us, too—but more and more, the day felt like a collision of families in slow motion.

_____I_____ **2.** Americans consume more calories per person than does any other group of people in the world.

_____P_____ **3.** The Federal Drug Administration has a moral responsibility to the public that includes regulating alternative or herbal medicines.

_____I_____ **4.** "The process by which money that you currently hold accumulates interest over time is referred to as compounding."

—From *Personal Finance*, 2nd ed., p. 61 by Jeff Madura. Copyright © 2004 by Pearson Education, Inc. Reproduced by permission of Pearson Education, Inc., Boston, MA.

P   **5.** A dollar received today is worth more than a dollar received to-morrow because it can be saved and invested; the time value of money is one of the strongest forces on earth—so save and invest.

> —Adapted from *Personal Finance,* 2nd ed., p. 59 by Jeff Madura. Copyright © 2004 by Pearson Education, Inc. Reproduced by permission of Pearson Education, Inc., Boston, MA.

P   **6.** Adults with higher levels of education and income generally have more favorable health behaviors in terms of cigarette smoking, leisure-time physical activity, and body weight status; therefore, it is imperative that all people are afforded the opportunity for higher education.

I   **7.** In 2000, a total of 2,403,351 deaths occurred in the United States; life expectancy at birth was 76.9 years, and the leading causes of death were as follows: heart disease, cancer, stroke, chronic lower respiratory diseases, accidents, diabetes, influenza and pneumonia, Alzheimer's disease, and kidney disease.

> —Adapted from "National Vital Statistics Reports," 50: 15, CDC, 11 June 2003. 3 May 2008 http://www.cdc.gov/nchs/data/nvsr/nvsr50/nvsr50_15.pdf

E   **8.** One way to achieve the status of expert on a subject is through firsthand experience; thus I think it honest and helpful to offer my-self as an expert of the highest order on the subject of smoking cessation, having quit over a dozen times.

B. Read the following items. Identify the primary purpose of each.

Editorial Cartoon Published in a Newspaper

© 2010 Clay Bennett Chattanooga Times Free Press

_____c_____ **9.** The primary purpose of this cartoon is

    a. to inform the reader about the quality of public education.

    b. to entertain the reader by mocking the public education system.

    c. to persuade the reader to oppose the emphasis on testing in public education.

Graphic from a Health Textbook

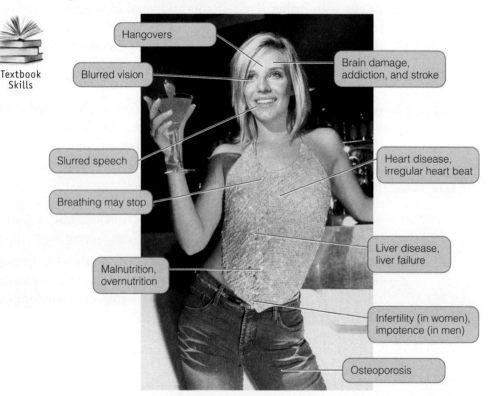

Textbook Skills

—From *Access to Health*, 7th ed., p. 380 by Rebecca J. Donatelle and Lorraine G. Davis. Copyright © 2002 by Pearson Education, Inc. Printed and Electronically reproduced by permission of Pearson Education, Inc., Upper Saddle River, NJ.

_____b_____ **10.** The primary purpose of this graphic is

    a. to persuade readers to abstain from alcohol consumption.

    b. to inform readers about the various negative effects of alcohol on the body.

    c. to interest readers with an interesting illustration.

REVIEW TEST 2

Score (number correct) _____ × 25 = _____ %

Read the following passage from a college history textbook. Answer the questions that follow.

Textbook
Skills

13.0 GE/505 words

Native Americans

[1]Native Americans are the first true Americans, and their status under U.S. law is unique. [2]Under the U.S. Constitution, Indian tribes are considered distinct governments. [3]This situation has affected Native Americans' treatment by the Supreme Court in contrast to other groups of ethnic minorities. [4]And, minority is a term that accurately describes American Indians. [5]It is estimated that there were as many as 10 million Indians in the New World at the time Europeans arrived in the 1400s. [6]The actual number of Indians is hotly contested. [7]Estimates vary from a high of 150–200 million to a low of 20–50 million throughout North and South America. [8]By 1900, the number of Indians in the continental United States had plummeted to less than 2 million. [9]Today, there are 2.8 million.

[10]Many commentators would agree that for years Congress and the courts manipulated Indian law to promote the westward expansion of the United States. [11]The Northwest Ordinance of 1787, passed by the Continental Congress, specified that "good faith should always be observed toward the Indians; their lands and property shall never be taken from them without their consent, and their property rights, and liberty, they shall never be invaded or disturbed, unless in just and lawful wars authorized by Congress." [12]These strictures were not followed. [13]Instead, over the years, "American Indian policy has been described as 'genocide-at-law' promoting both land acquisition and cultural extermination." [14]During the eighteenth and nineteenth centuries, the U.S. government isolated Indians on reservations as it confiscated their lands and denied them basic political rights. [15]Indian reservations were administered by the federal government. [16]And Native Americans often lived in squalid conditions.

[17]With passage of the Dawes Act in 1887, however, the government switched policies to promote assimilation over separation. [18]Each Indian family was given land within the reservation. [19]The rest was sold to whites, thus reducing Indian lands from about 140 million acres to about 47 million. [20]Moreover, to encourage Native Americans to assimilate, Indian children were sent to boarding schools off the reservation, and native languages and rituals were banned. [21]Native Americans didn't become U.S. citizens nor were they given the right to vote until 1924.

[22]At least in part because tribes were small and scattered (and the number of Indians declining), Native Americans formed no protest movement in reaction to these drastic policy changes. [23]It was not until the 1960s that Indians began to mobilize. [24]During this time, Indian activists,

many trained by the American Indian Law Center at the University of New Mexico, began to file hundreds of test cases in the federal courts involving tribal fishing rights, tribal land claims, and the taxation of tribal profits.

[25]Native Americans have won some very important victories concerning hunting, fishing, and land rights. [26]Native American tribes all over America have sued to reclaim lands they say were stolen from them by the United States, often more than 200 years ago. [27]Today, these land rights allow Native Americans to play host to a number of casinos across the country.

—Adapted from O'Connor and Sabato. *American Government: Continuity and Change*, 2008 ed., pp. 226–227.

  a   **1.** The overall purpose of the passage is to
    a. inform the reader with an overview of the history of Native Americans.
    b. amuse the reader with graphic details from the history of Native Americans.
    c. persuade the reader to support the Native American cause.

  b   **2.** The overall tone of the passage is
    a. informal.   b. formal.

  a   **3.** The overall tone of the passage is
    a. neutral.   b. biased.

  b   **4.** Overall, the difficulties faced by the Native American reveals
    a. verbal irony.   c. no irony.
    b. situational irony.

REVIEW TEST 3

Score (number correct) _____ × 10 = _____ %

Author's Purpose and Tone

Before Reading: Survey the following passage adapted from the college textbook *Atlas of Slavery*. Skim the passage, noting the words in **bold** print. Answer the Before Reading questions that follow the passage. Then, read the passage. Next, answer the After Reading questions. Use the discussion and writing topics

Textbook Skills

as activities to do after reading.

Vocabulary Preview

integral (2): essential

artifacts (3): manufactured objects

barter (4): exchange

dragooned (7): forced

legions (17): masses

retinue (19): servants, followers

ubiquitous (20): everywhere

11.4 GE/451 words   **Slavery in the Ancient World**

[1]Slavery was commonplace in a host of ancient and traditional societies. [2]For example, it played a major, **integral** role in societies from ancient Egypt to the wider world of classical **antiquity**. [3]Indeed, many of the surviving **artifacts** and buildings of those societies, now awash with millions of tourists, from the Pyramids to the urban fabric of ancient Greece, were built by slaves. [4]In all those societies, slaves were recruited from outside: by warfare, by raids and kidnapping and by trade and **barter** in humanity. [5]There were slave markets for the transfer and supply of fresh slaves arriving from the edges of trade and military conquest. [6]Throughout the history of ancient Egypt, large numbers of slaves were acquired by military means (though the slave population also grew of its own accord). [7]The New Kingdom (1560–1070 B.C.) expanded throughout the present day Middle East and Sudan; many thousands of Nubians from the Sudan were **dragooned** as slaves, working in agriculture, in manufacturing and in the military. [8]Females inevitably found their way into domestic slavery. [9]Other African slaves came to Egypt from the coast of Somalia.

[10]Greek civilization was equally bound up with slavery, and trade thrived in enslaved peoples, especially in the classical period (450–330 B.C.). [11]Slaves could be found in large numbers in all the major city-states, where they were bought and sold as objects, with men used in heavy work, women normally in domestic chores. [12]Again, slaves were recruited by violent expeditions. [13]Curiously, the rise of slavery paralleled the rise of Greek democracy, for the slaves gave citizens the freedom to take part in their civic duties. [14]Although slavery changed over time, it became a defining characteristic of Greek civilization. [15]Slaves from the East passed through the Greek slave markets of Chios, Delos and Rhodes.

[16]Slavery in the Roman Empire is better known (because it was more recent and therefore better documented). [17]The successes of the Roman legions throughout that far-flung empire provided **legions** of slaves for the Roman heartlands, from the northern boundaries of the empire in Britain to the southern limits in Africa. [18]It has been calculated that the golden age of Rome was maintained by the importation of upwards of half a million slaves in one year. [19]Indeed, Roman armies returned in triumph to the imperial capital ahead of their **retinue** of conquered slaves from as far afield as Germany, Britain and Gaul. [20]Slaves were **ubiquitous**: as domestics, as labourers in Roman agriculture, in the hell of the mines and, of course, for entertainment in the Colosseum. [21]Few areas of

Roman life remained untouched by slaves. [22]Rome may not have been built in a day, but it was certainly built by slaves.

—Adapted from Walvin, James. *Atlas of Slavery.* pp. 16, 18. © James Walvin, 2006. Reprinted by permission of Pearson Education Limited.

Before Reading

Vocabulary in Context

1. In sentence 2, what does the word **antiquity** mean? <u>ancient times</u>

    <u>   </u>

2. Identify the context clue used for the word **antiquity** in sentence 2. <u>the</u>
<u>synonym "ancient world" in the title</u>

After Reading

Central Idea

<u> a </u> **3.** Which sentence best states the central idea of the passage?
    a. sentence 1   c. sentence 2
    b. sentence 3   d. sentence 22

Supporting Details

<u> b </u> **4.** One of the benefits of slavery in Greek civilization was
    a. the construction of pyramids.
    b. the rise of democracy.
    c. entertainment in the Colosseum.
    d. the establishment of city-states.

Transitions

<u> b </u> **5.** The relationship of ideas within sentence 10 is
    a. cause and effect.   c. comparison.
    b. space order.   d. listing.

Thought Patterns

<u> c </u> **6.** The overall thought pattern for the passage is
    a. cause and effect.   c. time order.
    b. space order.   d. definition and example.

Fact and Opinion

_____c_____ **7.** Sentence 20, "Slaves were ubiquitous: as domestics, as labourers in Roman agriculture, in the hell of the mines and, of course, for entertainment in the Colosseum" is a statement of
    a. fact.
    b. opinion.
    c. fact and opinion.

Tone and Purpose

_____b_____ **8.** The tone of sentence 22 "Rome may not have been built in a day, but it was certainly built by slaves" is
    a. objective.   c. witty.
    b. sarcastic.

_____a_____ **9.** The overall tone of the passage is
    a. informative.   c. witty.
    b. argumentative.

_____c_____ **10.** The primary purpose of the passage is
    a. to persuade the reader that slavery in ancient times was inhumane.
    b. to engage the reader with interesting facts about slavery in ancient times.
    c. to inform the reader about the importance of slavery in ancient times.

WHAT DO YOU THINK?

Why were slaves important to developing civilization in the ancient world? What contributions were made by slaves in the ancient world? Assume you are taking a college history course, and your professor requires written responses to what you are reading. Choose one of the following topics and write a three-paragraph essay: (1) Assume the role of an Egyptian, Greek, or Roman citizen who opposes slavery. Write a draft of a speech you plan to give during a public forum; in your speech explain your reasons for opposing slavery. Include descriptions of daily tasks, working conditions, and inhumane treatment of a slave in ancient times. (2) Explain several reasons why slavery existed in ancient Egypt, Greece, and Rome.

REVIEW TEST 4

Score (number correct) _____ × 10 = _____ %

Author's Purpose and Tone

Textbook Skills

Before Reading: Survey the following passage adapted from the college text-book *The West: Encounters & Transformations*. Skim the passage, noting the words in **bold** print. Answer the Before Reading questions that follow the passage. Then, read the passage. Next, answer the After Reading questions. Use the discussion and writing topics as activities to do after reading.

11.7 GE/566 words

The Death Camps: Murder by Assembly Line

Vocabulary Preview

SS (2): abbreviation for the German *word Schutzstaffel*, which translates as Protective Squadron, a personal guard unit for Hitler, responsible for the mass murder of Jews and others deemed undesirable

Einsatzgruppen (3): strike or task force, SS units given the task of murdering Jews and Communist Party members in the areas of the Soviet Union occupied by Germany during World War II

indoctrinated (8): instructed, taught

Roma (12): gypsies

conglomerate (15): corporation, business

ghettos (20): in certain European cities, a section to which Jews were formerly restricted

[1]On January 20, 1942, senior German officials met in a villa in Wannsee, outside Berlin, to finalize plans for killing every Jew in Europe. [2]**SS** lieutenant colonel Adolf Eichmann (1906–1962) listed the number of Jews in every country; even the Jewish populations in neutral countries such as Sweden and Ireland showed up on the target list. [3]The Wannsee Conference marked the beginning of a more systematic approach to murdering European Jews, one that built on the experience gained by the **Einsatzgruppen** in the Soviet war.

[4]To accomplish mass murder, the Einsatzgruppen had become killing machines. [5]By trial and error, they discovered the most efficient ways of identifying and rounding up Jews, shooting them quickly, and burying the bodies. [6]But the Einsatzgruppen actions also revealed the limits of conventional methods of killing. [7]Shooting took time, used up valuable ammunition, and required large numbers of men.

[8]Moreover, even the best-trained and carefully **indoctrinated** soldiers eventually cracked under the strain of shooting unarmed women and children at close range. [9]A systematic approach was needed, one that would utilize advanced killing technology and provide a comfortable distance between the killers and the killed. [10]This perceived need resulted in a key Nazi innovation: the death camp.

[11]The death camp was a specialized form of a concentration camp. [12]From 1933 on, Hitler's government had sentenced communists, Jehovah's Witnesses, the **Roma**, and anyone else defined as an enemy of the **regime** to forced labor in concentration camps. [13]After the war began, the concentration camp system

extermination (21):
execution, death

culled (25): picked

expanded dramatically. [14]Scattered throughout Nazi-controlled Europe, concentration camps became an essential part of the Nazi war economy. [15]Some firms, such as the huge chemical **conglomerate** I. G. Farben, established factories inside or right next to camps, which provided vital supplies of forced labor. [16]All across Europe during the war, concentration camp inmates died in huge numbers from the brutal physical labor, torture, and diseases brought on by malnutrition and inadequate housing and sanitary facilities. [17]But it was only in Poland that the Nazis constructed death camps, specialized concentration camps with only one purpose—murder, primarily the murder of Jews.

[18]The death camps marked the final stage in a vast assembly line of murder. [19]In early 1942 the trains conveying victims to the death camps began to rumble across Europe.

[20]Jewish **ghettos** across Nazi-occupied Europe emptied as their inhabitants moved in batches to their deaths. [21]Individuals selected for **extermination** followed orders to gather at the railway station for deportation to "work camps" farther east. [22]They were then packed into cattle cars, more than 100 people per car, all standing up for the entire journey. [23]Deprived of food and water, with hardly any air, and no sanitary facilities, often for several days, many Jews died en route. [24]The survivors stumbled off the trains into a nightmare world. [25]At some camps, SS guards **culled** stronger Jews from each transport to be worked to death as slave laborers. [26]Most, however, walked straight from the transport trains into a reception room, where they were told to undress, and then herded into a "shower room"—actually a gas chamber. [27]Carbon monoxide gas or a pesticide called Zyklon-B killed the victims. [28]After the poison had done its work, Jewish slaves emptied the chamber and burned the bodies in vast crematoria, modeled after industrial bake ovens. [29]The Nazis thus constructed a vast machine of death.

—From *The West: Encounters & Transformations, Atlas Edition, Combined Edition*, 2nd edition., pp. 870–871 by Brian Levack, Edward Muir, Meredith Veldman and Michael Maas. Copyright © 2008 by Pearson Education, Inc. Printed and Electronically reproduced by permission of Pearson Education, Inc., Upper Saddle River, NJ.

Before Reading

Vocabulary in Context

1. In sentence 12, what does the word **regime** mean? the ruling party

2. Identify the context clue used for the word **regime** in sentence 12. <u>general</u> <u>sense of the passage</u>

After Reading

Central Idea

__d__ **3.** Which sentence best states the central idea of the passage?
   a. sentence 1   c. sentence 4
   b. sentence 3   d. sentence 29

Supporting Details

__b__ **4.** According to the passage, the death camps were constructed
   a. across Europe.   c. in Berlin.
   b. only in Poland.   d. in Jewish ghettos.

Transitions

__b__ **5.** The relationship between sentence 5 and sentence 6 is
   a. time order.   c. listing.
   b. contrast.   d. definition and example.

Thought Patterns

__d__ **6.** The thought pattern for paragraph 4 (sentences 11–17) is
   a. listing.   c. contrast.
   b. time order.   d. definition and example.

Fact and Opinion

__c__ **7.** Sentence 8 is a statement of
   a. fact.   c. fact and opinion.
   b. opinion.

Tone and Purpose

__a__ **8.** The tone of sentence 18 is
   a. matter-of-fact.   c. bitter.
   b. condemning.   d. understanding.

__c__ **9.** The overall tone of the passage is
   a. horrified.   c. condemning.
   b. neutral.   d. sorrowful.

   c   **10.** The primary purpose of the passage is

           a. to persuade the reader about the brutality of the Nazi death camps.

           b. to shock the reader with graphic details about the Nazi death camps.

           c. to inform the reader about the Nazi commitment to exterminating Jews and others they deemed undesirable.

WHAT DO YOU THINK?

Do you think that most of the citizens of Germany knew about the death camps? Do you think you would have had the courage to defy the Nazi regime and help the Jews and other "enemies of the state"? Assume that a local chapter of the American Jewish League is sponsoring an essay contest with a $250 prize in honor of those who suffered and died under the Nazi regime and to educate the next generation about the consequences of prejudice. Choose one of the following two topics and write a 500-word essay:

1. The Nazi regime exhibited the extreme effects of prejudice and hatred during the early twentieth century. Today, in the early twenty-first century, we also see the extreme effects of prejudice and hatred of certain regimes in the world. Identify and discuss a current regime and its actions of terror that should be stopped.

2. Both before and during the Nazi regime many German citizens did not raise objections to the actions of terror that occurred under Hitler's rule; other German citizens tried to secretly help those who were targeted for prison or death. Write an essay that discusses several steps the average German citizen could have taken to take a stand against Hitler and his reign of terror.

 ## After Reading About Tone and Purpose

Before you move on to the Mastery Tests on tone and purpose, take time to reflect on your learning and performance by answering the following questions. Write your answers in your notebook.

- How has my knowledge base or prior knowledge about tone and purpose changed?

- Based on my studies, how do I think I will perform on the Mastery Test(s)? Why do I think my scores will be above average, average, or below average?

- Would I recommend this chapter to other students who want to learn about tone and purpose? Why or why not?

Test your understanding of what you have learned about tone and purpose by completing the Chapter 10 Review Card in the insert near the end of your text.

CONNECT TO myreadinglab

To check your progress in meeting Chapter 10's learning outcomes, log in to **www.myreadinglab.com** and try the following exercises.

- The "Purpose and Tone" section of MyReadingLab provides an overview, model, practices, activities, and tests. To access this resource, click on the "Study Plan" tab. Then click on "Purpose and Tone." Then click on the following links as needed: "Overview," "Model," "Practice," and "Tests."

- To measure your mastery of this chapter, complete the tests in the "Purpose and Tone" section and click on Gradebook to find your results.

Read the poem, and then, answer the questions that follow it.

Fear Not the Fall

by Billie Jean Young

Fear not the fall.
Better to fall from the strength
of the sound of one's voice
speaking truth to the people
than to spend a lifetime
mired in discontent,
groveling in the sty of certainty
of acceptance,
of pseudo-love,
of muteness,
and easy-to-be-around-ness.

Better to fall screaming—
arms flailing,
legs askew
clawing in your intensity
for the right to be—
than silently,
like a weakened snowbird,
sentenced to the boredom of earth
too sick to sing.

— From *Fear Not the Fall: Poems and a Two-Act Drama* by Billie Jean Young,
Reprinted with permission of NewSouth Books, Montgomery, AL. p. 112.

_____a_____ **1.** In the first stanza, the words *strength*, *sound*, *speaking*, and *truth* are
best described by the tone word
a. confident.   c. afraid.
b. humble.   d. angry.

_____c_____ **2.** In the second stanza, the words *screaming*, *flailing*, *askew*, *clawing*,
and *intensity* are best described by the tone word
a. composed.   c. hostile.
b. defeated.   d. sad.

_____c_____   **3.** The tone of the last three lines of the second stanza is
      a. hateful.   c. solemn.
      b. cold.   d. neutral.

_____b_____   **4.** The phrase "fear not the fall" is ironic because
      a. the poem states "fear not" but implies the opposite.
      b. people often warn against falling or failing, but this poem advises "fear not."
      c. the poem suggests that failure is certain.

_____a_____   **5.** The overall purpose of this poem is
      a. to persuade the reader to risk living honestly and avoid settling for security.
      b. to inform the reader about the effect of fear and the need to directly face fear.
      c. to entertain the reader with a personal experience about the fear of falling.

Read the following passage from a college literature textbook. Then, answer the questions.

10.6 GE/334 words

Textbook
Skills

Blues

[1]Among the many song forms to have shaped the way poetry is written in English, no recent form has been more influential than the blues. [2]Originally a type of folk music developed by black slaves in the South, blues songs have both a distinctive form and tone. [3]They traditionally consist of three-line stanzas in which the first two identical lines are followed by a concluding, rhyming third line.

[4]To dream of muddy water—trouble is knocking at your door.
[5]To dream of muddy water—trouble is knocking at your door.
[6]Your man is sure to leave you and never return no more.

[7]Early blues lyrics almost always spoke of some sadness, pain, or deprivation—often the loss of a loved one. [8]The melancholy tone of the lyrics, however, is not only world-weary but also world-wise. [9]The blues expound the hard-won wisdom of bitter life experience. [10]They frequently create their special mood through down-to-earth, even gritty, imagery drawn from everyday life. [11]Although blues reach back into the nineteenth century, they were not widely known outside African American communities before 1920 when the first commercial recordings appeared. [12]Their influence on both music and song from that time was rapid and extensive. [13]By 1930 James Weldon Johnson could declare, "It is from the blues that all that may be called American music derives its most distinctive characteristic." [14]Blues have not only become an enduring category of popular music; they have helped shape virtually all the major styles of contemporary pop—jazz, rap, rock, gospel, country, and of course, rhythm-and-blues.

[15]The style and structure of blues have also influenced modern poets. [16]Not only African American writers like Langston Hughes, Sterling A. Brown, Etheridge Knight, and Sonia Sanchez have written blues poems, but white poets as dissimilar as W. H. Auden, Elizabeth Bishop, Donald Justice, and Sandra McPherson have employed the form. [17]The classic touchstones of the blues, however, remain the early singers like Robert Johnson, Ma Rainey, Blind Lemon Jefferson, Charley Patton, and—perhaps preeminently—Bessie Smith, "the Empress of the Blues."

—Kennedy & Gioia, *Literature: An Introduction to Fiction, Poetry, and Drama*, 3rd Compact ed., pp. 586–587.

447

_____b_____ **1.** Which term best describes the tone of sentence 1?
a. objective   b. subjective

_____a_____ **2.** The tone of sentence 2 and sentence 3 is
a. objective.   b. subjective.

_____d_____ **3.** The tone of the words *preeminently* and *Empress of the Blues* in sentence 17 is
a. mocking.   c. objective.
b. understated.   d. admiring.

_____c_____ **4.** Which word describes the overall tone of the passage?
a. humorous   c. academic
b. informal   d. argumentative

_____a_____ **5.** The overall purpose of this passage is
a. to inform the reader about the general importance, history, and characteristics of the blues.
b. to entertain the reader with lively details about the lives of blues singers and artists.
c. to persuade the reader that blues is the most important form of music and poetry in the English language.

Read the following passage from a college communications textbook. Then, answer the questions.

12.1 GE/282 words

Advertisement's Purpose

¹Although most advertisements promote a product or service, not all do. **²**Advertisements fall into three categories: business ads, public service ads, and political ads.

³Business ads try to influence people's attitudes and behaviors toward the product and services a business sells, toward the business itself, or toward an idea that the business supports. **⁴**Most of these ads try to persuade customers to buy something, but sometimes a business tries to improve its image through advertising. **⁵**This often occurs when a company has been involved in a highly publicized incident that might negatively affect its image. **⁶**Exxon had to rebuild its image after the *Valdez* accident in 1989, in which an Exxon tank spilled millions of gallons of oil in Prince William Sound and damaged the Alaska Coast.

⁷Public service ads promote behaviors and attitudes that are beneficial to society and its members. **⁸**These ads may be either national or local and usually are the product of donated labor and media time or space. **⁹**The Advertising Council produces the best known public service ads. **¹⁰**The council, which is supported by advertising agencies and the media, was formed during World War II to promote the war effort. **¹¹**It now runs about twenty-five campaigns a year. **¹²**These campaigns must be in the public interest, timely, noncommercial, nonpartisan, nonsectarian, and nonpolitical.

¹³Political ads aim to persuade voters to elect a candidate to political office or to influence the public on legislative issues. **¹⁴**These advertisements run at the local, state, and national levels. **¹⁵**They incorporate most forms of media but use newspapers, radio, television, and direct mail most heavily. **¹⁶**During a presidential election year, more than $1 billion is spent on political ads.

—Folkerts & Lacy, *The Media in Your Life*, 2nd ed., pp. 428–429.

_____a_____ **1.** The tone of the first paragraph (sentences 1–2) is
   a. neutral.   c. bitter.
   b. approving.   d. bored.

_____c_____ **2.** The purpose of sentence 6 is
  a. to condemn Exxon for spilling millions of gallons of oil.
  b. to keep the reader entertained with a vivid detail.
  c. to illustrate the need for a business ad to improve a company's image.

_____c_____ **3.** The tone of sentence 16 is
  a. shocked. c. matter-of-fact.
  b. shameful. d. abrupt.

_____a_____ **4.** Which word best describes the overall tone of this passage?
  a. unbiased b. biased

_____a_____ **5.** The overall purpose of this passage is
  a. to inform the reader about different types of advertising.
  b. to persuade the reader that advertising serves beneficial purposes.
  c. to entertain the reader with interesting details about advertising.

VISUAL VOCABULARY

This advertisement is an example of a _public service_ _____ advertisement.

—Library of Congress, Prints & Photography Division, Yanker Poster Collection, POS6-U.S., no. 1384

Read the following passage from a college social science textbook. Then, answer the questions.

Textbook
Skills

13.0 GE/387 words **Earth Watch: Tangled Troubles—Logging and Bushmeat**

¹The bushmeat trade in Africa is a prime example of how threats to biodiversity interact and amplify one another. ²Historically, rural Africans have supplemented their diet by hunting a variety of animals, collectively called "bushmeat." ³Traditional subsistence hunting by small tribes using primitive weapons did not pose a serious threat to animal populations.

⁴Now, however, as logging roads penetrate deeper into rain forests, hunters follow, using shotguns and snares to kill any animal large enough to eat. ⁵Communities that spring up along logging roads develop a culture of hunting and selling bushmeat, and become dependent on this new and profitable industry. ⁶Logging trucks are sometimes used to carry the meat to urban markets. ⁷The World Conservation Society estimates that the bushmeat harvest in equatorial Africa exceeds a million tons annually. ⁸Many of the hunted animals play an important role in dispersing tree seeds. ⁹Thus, loss of these animals reduces the ability of the logged forest to regenerate.

¹⁰Bushmeat hunters pay no attention to the sex, age, size, or rarity of the animal. ¹¹Therefore, many threatened species are declining rapidly. ¹²For example, despite estimates that only about 2,000 to 3,000 pygmy hippos remain in the wild, pygmy hippo meat has been found in bushmeat markets, as has meat from elephants and rhinos.

¹³The profitability of bushmeat has helped overcome traditional African taboos against eating primates. ¹⁴Although one-third of all primates (apes, monkeys, and lemurs) are threatened with extinction, in some bushmeat markets, 15% of the meat comes from primates. ¹⁵In Cameroon, Africa, endangered gorillas are a favored target of poachers because of their large size. ¹⁶Even endangered chimpanzees and bonobos, our closest relatives, end up in cooking pots. ¹⁷Experts now believe that bushmeat hunting is an even greater threat than habitat loss for Africa's great apes, and that the combined threats of hunting and habitat loss make extinction in the wild a very real possibility for some of these magnificent, intelligent species.

451

¹⁸Recognizing the threats to wildlife, several central African countries are working to reduce illegal timber harvesting and wildlife poaching. ¹⁹Together, they have established protected areas in the African rain forest of the Congo River Basin. ²⁰Although enormous logging enterprises continue along the borders of these reserves, protecting them is a crucial step toward preserving some of Africa's rich natural heritage.

—Adapted from *Life on Earth*, 5th ed., p. 631 by Teresa Audesirk, Gerald Audesirk, and Bruce E. Byers. Copyright © 2009 by Pearson Education, Inc. Printed and Electronically reproduced by permission of Pearson Education, Inc., Upper Saddle River, NJ.

_____a_____ **1.** The overall tone of the passage is
    a. biased against bushmeat hunters.
    b. biased for bushmeat hunters.
    c. neutral about bushmeat hunters.

_____b_____ **2.** The tone of sentence 16 is
    a. angry.   c. neutral.
    b. ironic.   d. mournful.

_____c_____ **3.** In sentence 17, the words that describe the apes are
    a. demeaning.   c. admiring.
    b. bitter.   d. sorrowful.

_____c_____ **4.** The overall purpose of the passage is to
    a. inform the reader about the bushmeat trade in Africa.
    b. entertain the reader with graphic details about the bushmeat trade in Africa.
    c. persuade the reader that the bushmeat trade in Africa is a serious problem that must be addressed.

Inferences

LEARNING OUTCOMES

After studying this chapter you should be able to do the following:

1. Define the term *inference*. [Knowledge]
2. Distinguish between a valid and an invalid inference. [Analysis]
3. Identify and apply the five steps for making a VALID inference. [Knowledge, Application]
4. Form valid inferences. [Analysis, Synthesis]
5. Define the following terms: *connotation, metaphor, personification, simile*, and *symbol*. [Knowledge]
6. Infer meanings based on connotations, metaphors, personification, simile, and symbol. [Analysis, Synthesis]
7. Evaluate the importance of inferences. [Evaluation]

Before Reading About Inferences

Predict what you need to learn based on the learning outcomes for this chapter by completing the following chart.

What I Already Know	What I Need to Learn
Answers may vary.	Answers may vary.

Copy the following study outline in your notebook. Leave ample blank spaces between each topic. Use your own words to fill in the outline with information about each topic as you study about inferences.

Reading Skills Needed to Make VALID Inferences

    I. **V**erify facts.

   II. **A**ssess prior knowledge.

  III. **L**earn from text.

       a. Context clues

       b. Thought patterns

       c. Implied main ideas

  IV. **I**nvestigate bias.

   V. **D**etect contradictions.

 ## Inferences: Educated Guesses

Read the following paragraph.

> As Professor De Los Santos handed out the graded essays, Kassie's stomach rumbled with a familiar queasiness. She avoided looking around and focused with intensity on the opened textbook, not really seeing the pages that were before her. Aaron, who sat next to her, exclaimed with pleasure as he received his paper. "Unbelievable," he said as he turned to Kassie in surprise, "I thought I had blown this assignment." Kassie did not look up or respond to him, but continued staring at her book as she listened intently for her name. A girl with short, spiky hair across the room frowned after she received her paper and asked, "Dr. De Los Santos, may we rewrite this assignment?" The professor shook her head. Finally, Kassie heard her name, looked up, and took her essay. "Good job, Kassie," Dr. De Los Santos said as she handed her the paper, "Your work shows much improvement." Kassie smiled and carefully read each suggestion the teacher had written on her essay.

Which of the following statements might be true, based on the ideas in the passage?

   ✔   Kassie is extremely nervous about her essay.

   ✔   The girl with short, spiky hair is not satisfied with the grade she received.

  _____ Aaron did not put much effort into his essay.

  _____ Kassie's grade was "A" on her essay.

Did you choose the first two statements? Congratulations! You just made a set of educated guesses, or **inferences**. An author suggests or **implies** an idea, and the reader comes to a conclusion and makes an inference about what the author means.

In the paragraph about Kassie, the first two statements are firmly based on the information in the passage. However, the last two statements are not backed by the supporting details. The facts only suggest that Aaron thought he hadn't performed well on the assignment. He could have put a great deal of effort into the work; perhaps he underestimated his abilities. We just don't have enough information to make either assumption. Likewise, the passage does not suggest that Kassie made an "A," only that her work had improved.

 ## What Is a Valid Inference?

People constantly draw conclusions about what they notice. We observe, gather information, and make inferences all the time.

> An **inference** or **conclusion** is an idea that is suggested by the facts or details in a passage.

For example, study the photo, and then answer the accompanying question.

VISUAL VOCABULARY

This business man is wearing a face mask because

of air pollution.

(Answers may vary.)

If you wrote *of air pollution*, you made an inference based on the clues given by the visual details of the situation.

A **valid inference** is a rational judgment based on details and evidence. The ability to make a valid inference is a vital life skill. Making valid inferences aids us in our efforts to care for our families, succeed in our jobs, and even guard our health.

For example, doctors strive to make inferences about our health based on our symptoms. In the case of a heart attack, a doctor notes the observable symptoms such as pressure or pain in the center of the chest, shortness of breath, a cold sweat, nausea, or lightheadedness. To confirm the diagnosis, the doctor checks the patient's heart rate and blood pressure, takes a blood sample and performs a test called an electrocardiogram. If her educated guess (a guess based on evidence) is correct, she prescribes the best treatment she deems necessary.

> A **valid inference** is a logical conclusion based on evidence.

EXAMPLE   Read the following passage. Write **V** beside the three valid inferences. (**Hint:** valid inferences are firmly supported by the details in the passage.)

Pollen and Allergies

[1]For the past two weeks a heavy dusting of yellow pollen from the pine trees coated all the cars in the parking lot at Robert's job site. [2]The thick layering of pine pollen masked the fact that the oak and juniper trees were also pollinating. [3]In addition, every yard in Robert's neighborhood was covered with the purple flowering heads of Bermuda grass. [4]Interestingly, Robert linked the obvious pine pollen to allergy flare-ups, until he read a scientific report that stated that the heaviness of pine pollen causes it to fall to the ground rather than be carried by the wind like most allergy-causing pollen. [5]The same report stated that some of the most widely known plants that cause allergic reactions are Kentucky bluegrass, Johnson grass, Bermuda grass, redtop grass, orchard grass, and sweet vernal grass. [6]Trees that produce allergenic pollen include oak, ash, elm, hickory, pecan, box elder, and mountain cedar. [7]An allergic reaction includes frequent sneezing, clear and watery nasal discharge and congestion, itchy eyes, nose, and throat, and watery eyes. [8]For over a week, Robert has been experiencing these symptoms.

   __V__   **1.** Robert is experiencing an allergic reaction to pollen.

   _____   **2.** Pine pollen is a major source of allergic reactions.

   __V__   **3.** Robert's yard consists of Bermuda grass.

   __V__   **4.** Robert's allergy attack is caused by the pollen from oak trees, juniper trees, or Bermuda grass.

_____ **5.** Kentucky bluegrass does not grow where Robert lives.

_____ **6.** Robert suffers with allergy attacks from pollen every year.

EXPLANATION Statements 1, 3, and 4 are firmly based on the information in the passage. It is reasonable to infer that Robert is experiencing an allergic reaction to pollen based on his symptoms and the fact that Robert's yard consists of Bermuda grass since "every" yard in his neighborhood does. It is also reasonable to infer that either one or some combination of the pollen from the oak trees, juniper trees, and Bermuda grass is causing his allergic reaction, based on the list of plants known to cause allergic reactions.

Statements 2, 5, and 6 are not based on the information in the passage. It is unreasonable to assume that pine pollen is a major source of allergic reactions because of information in the scientific report that explained that this pollen drops to the ground and is not carried by the wind and thus not breathed in by humans. It is also wrong to infer that Kentucky bluegrass does not grow where Robert lives simply because it is not present in the yards in his neighborhood or at his place of business. Finally, it is incorrect to infer that Robert experiences an allergic reaction to pollen every year. The passage only focuses on the last few weeks of Robert's life, so we do not have enough information to know whether he has suffered from these symptoms before.

PRACTICE 1

Each of the following items contains a short passage and three inferences. In each item, only one inference is valid. In the space provided, write the letter of the inference that is clearly supported by each passage.

_b_ **1.** Jermaine and his office coworkers all arrived at work at the same time Monday morning. As usual, Jermaine unlocked the only entrance to the building, and then everyone unlocked their offices to begin their work routine. Immediately, Jermaine and his coworkers discovered that their computers and printers were missing from their offices. Each one reported that they had locked their offices with their computers and printers securely inside before they left on Friday. As they looked around the office, nothing indicated a forced entry. Jermaine called the police to report the theft of the computers and printers.
   a. Jermaine stole the computers.
   b. The office computers and printers were stolen by someone who had access to the office keys.
   c. Jermaine and his coworkers were not surprised to find the computers and printers were missing.

_____b_____ **2.** Alex and Mindy sit opposite each other in a booth at a diner. Mindy's face is streaked with tears. Alex's face is turned away as if in deep thought. His mouth is drawn into a thin frown, and his arms are folded across his chest. They do not speak to one another. As the waitress fills their coffee cups, Alex's frown turns into a smile, and he orders a large breakfast. Mindy shakes her head to indicate that she does not want anything to eat. As fresh tears begin to flow, she quickly ducks her head.

   a. Alex and Mindy are having a fight.

   b. Mindy is more upset than is Alex.

   c. Alex is insensitive to Mindy's feelings.

_____c_____ **3.** The patrol officer flashes his lights to pull over the sedan that has been weaving across the center line that divides the two-way traffic. After inspecting the driving license of Laurel, the young woman behind the wheel, he asks her to step out of the car, stand with her arms outstretched, and touch the tip of her nose with an index finger. She loses her balance as she tries to do so.

   a. Laurel is drunk.

   b. The police officer is harassing Laurel.

   c. The police officer suspects that Laurel has been driving while under the influence of alcohol.

Making VALID Inferences and Avoiding Invalid Conclusions

Two of the most common pitfalls of making inferences are ignoring the facts and relying too much on personal opinions and bias. Often we are tempted to read too much into a passage because of our own prior experiences or beliefs. Of course, to make a valid inference, we must use clues based on logic and our experience. However, the most important resource must be the written text. As master readers, our main goal is to find out what the author is stating or implying. Master readers learn to use a VALID thinking process to avoid drawing false inferences or coming to invalid conclusions.

> An **invalid conclusion** is a false inference that is not based on the details, or facts in the text or on reasonable thinking.

The VALID approach is made up of 5 steps:

Step 1. **V**erify and value the facts.

Step 2. **A**ssess prior knowledge.

Step 3. **L**earn from the text.

Step 4. **I**nvestigate for bias.

Step 5. **D**etect contradictions.

Step 1: Verify and Value the Facts

Develop a devotion to finding the facts. In Chapter 9, you learned to identify facts and to beware of false facts. You learned that authors may mix fact with opinion or use false information for their own purposes. Just as authors may make this kind of mistake, readers may, too. Readers may draw false inferences by mixing the author's facts with their own opinions or by misreading the facts. So it is important to find, verify, and stick to factual details. Once you have all the facts, only then can you begin to interpret the facts by making inferences.

EXAMPLE   Read the following short passage. Then, write **V** next to the two valid inferences firmly supported by the facts.

Child Passenger Safety

[1]Motor vehicle injuries are the leading cause of death among children in the United States. [2]But many of these deaths can be prevented. [3]In the United States during 2005, 1,451 children ages 14 years and younger died as occupants in motor vehicle crashes, and approximately 203,000 were injured. [4]That's an average of 4 deaths and 556 injuries each day. [5]Of the children ages 0 to 14 years who were killed in motor vehicle crashes during 2005, nearly half were unrestrained.

[6]One out of four of all occupant deaths among children ages 0 to 14 years involve a drinking driver. [7]More than two-thirds of these fatally injured children were riding with a drinking driver. [8]Restraint use among young children often depends upon the driver's restraint use. [9]Almost 40% of children riding with unbelted drivers were themselves unrestrained. [10]Child restraint systems are often used incorrectly; one study found that 72% of nearly 3,500 observed child restraint systems were misused in a way that could be expected to increase a child's risk of injury during a crash. [11]All children under the age of 12 should ride in the back

seat. [12]Putting children in the back seat places children in the safest part of the vehicle in the event of a crash.

> —Adapted from United States, Department of Human and Health Services. "Child Passenger Safety: Fact Sheet." *National Center for Injury Prevention and Control, Centers for Disease Control and Prevention.* 2 Feb 2010. http://www.cdc.gov/ncipc/factsheets/childpas.htm

_____V_____ **1.** Most of the deaths and injuries related to motor vehicle crashes among children could be prevented.

_____V_____ **2.** Placing children 14 years and younger in age-appropriate restraint systems could reduce serious and fatal injuries by half.

_____ **3.** Parents are the chief cause of deaths and injuries related to motor vehicle crashes among children.

EXPLANATION The first two statements are correct inferences based on the facts. However, there is no hint or clue that parents are the chief cause of these injuries and deaths. Children often ride in vehicles with people other than their parents. The third statement goes beyond the facts without any reason to do so.

VISUAL VOCABULARY

Fill in the blanks with words from the passage "Child Passenger Safety" that best complete the caption.

This child is __improperly__ restrained, __increasing__ the child's risk of injury during a crash.

Step 2: Assess Prior Knowledge

Once you are sure of the facts, the next step is to draw on your prior knowledge. What you have already learned and experienced can help you make accurate inferences.

EXAMPLE 1 Read the following passage from a college science textbook. Identify the facts. Check those facts against your own experience and understanding. Write **V** next to the four inferences firmly supported by the facts in the passage.

Textbook
Skills

The Flow of Energy and the Food Chain

[1]Energy stored by plants moves through the ecosystem in a series of steps of eating and being eaten, the **food chain**. [2]Food chains are descriptive diagrams—a series of arrows, each pointing from one species to another for which it is a source of food. [3]For example, grasshoppers eat grass, clay-colored sparrows eat the grasshoppers, and marsh hawks prey upon the sparrows. [4]We write this relationship as follows:

[5]grass ⟶ grasshopper ⟶ sparrow ⟶ marsh hawk

[6]However, the food chain is not linear. [7]Resources are shared, especially at the beginning of the food chain. [8]The same plant is food for a variety of animals and insects, and the same animal is food for several predators. [9]Thus food chains link to form a **food web**, the complexity of which varies within and among ecosystems.

—Adapted from *Elements of Ecology*, 4th ed., p. 329 by Thomas M. Smith and Robert Leo Smith. Copyright © 2000 by Pearson Education, Inc. Reprinted by permission of Pearson Education, Inc., Glenview, IL.

____V____ **1.** An *ecosystem* is a community of organisms and its environment functioning as a unit.

_____ **2.** Grasshoppers eat only grass.

____V____ **3.** Plant life is the basis of the food chain used as an example.

____V____ **4.** The phrase *prey upon* in sentence 3 means "feed on."

____V____ **5.** The survival of the marsh hawk could be dependent upon the availability of grasshoppers.

_____ **6.** Grass is always a basic element in a food chain or food web.

EXPLANATION Items 1, 3, 4, and 5 are sound inferences based on information in the passage. However, we have no evidence that grasshoppers eat only grass (item 2), nor that grass is always a basic element in a food chain or food web (item 6). In fact, sentence 9 states that ecosystems vary as does their complexity. For example, the food chain in a lake or ocean would not necessarily include grass.

EXAMPLE 2 Study the editorial cartoon. In the space provided, write an inference that is firmly supported by the details. Answers may vary.

One possible response: Global use of fossil fuels by industries is killing the

planet.

EXPLANATION Consider the following inference solidly based on the cartoon (and prior knowledge about fossil fuels and the environment): Global use of fossil fuels by industries is killing the planet.

Step 3: Learn from the Text

When you value and verify facts, you are learning from the text. A valid inference is always based on what is stated or implied by the details in the text; in contrast, an invalid inference goes beyond the evidence. Thus, to make a valid inference, you must learn to rely on the information in the text. Many of the skills you have studied in previous chapters work together to enable you to learn from the text. For example, context clues unlock the meaning of an author's use of vocabulary. Becoming aware of thought patterns teaches you to look for the logical relationship between ideas. Learning about stated and implied main ideas trains you to examine supporting details. (In fact, you use inference skills to find the implied main idea.) In addition, tone and purpose reveal the author's bias and intent. (Again, you often use inference skills to grasp the author's tone and purpose.) As you apply these skills to your reading process, you are carefully listening to what the author has to say. You are learning from the text. Only after you have learned from the text can you make a valid inference. The following examples show you how you learn from the text.

EXAMPLE Read the following statement. Answer the questions that follow.

> Dr. Mehmet Oz, a consummate heart surgeon, deserves recognition as one of the most important figures in the 21st century because he's the most important and most accomplished celebrity doctor in history.

__a__ **1.** The best synonym for the word **consummate** is
   a. excellent.   c. demanding.
   b. expensive.

__b__ **2.** What is the primary relationship of ideas within the sentence?
   a. addition   c. generalization and example
   b. cause and effect

__c__ **3.** The author's tone is
   a. sarcastic.   c. flattering.
   b. neutral.

__c__ **4.** The author's purpose is to
   a. inform.   c. persuade.
   b. entertain.

__b__ **5.** Which of the following is a valid inference?
   a. Dr. Oz only treats celebrities.
   b. Dr. Oz has a large public following through the media.
   c. Most people agree that Dr. Oz is "one of the most important and accomplished celebrity doctors in history."

PRACTICE 2

Read the following passages from college textbooks. Then, answer the questions that follow.

Textbook
Skills

Alcohol, Cancer, and Heart Disease

[1]Heavy drinking is associated with an increased risk for several cancers—notably, cancer of the mouth, esophagus, pharynx, larynx, liver, and pancreas. [2]An analysis of multiple studies published in the mid-1990s found that having two alcoholic drinks per day (any type of alcohol) increased a woman's chances of developing breast cancer by nearly 25 percent. [3]The reasons for this are unclear. [4]However, researchers speculate that alcohol influences the metabolism of estrogen and that prolonged exposure to high levels of estrogen increases breast cancer risk, particularly for women on hormone replacement therapy (HRT). [5]The effect of

one drink per day on increased risk is a matter of debate. [6]Most experts feel that one drink per day does not increase risk. [7]But before you decide to toss out all your alcohol, you should know that there is increasing evidence that a glass of red wine seems to provide protection against heart disease.

> —From *Access to Health*, 7th ed., p. 442 by Rebecca J. Donatelle and Lorraine G. Davis. Copyright © 2002 by Pearson Education, Inc. Printed and Electronically reproduced by permission of Pearson Education, Inc., Upper Saddle River, NJ.

_____c_____ **1.** The best meaning of the word **speculate** in sentence 4 is
    a. know.   c. think.
    b. study.

_____c_____ **2.** What is the relationship of ideas between sentence 3 and sentence 4?
    a. listing   c. contrast
    b. cause and effect

_____b_____ **3.** What is the primary thought pattern of the paragraph?
    a. contrast   c. time order
    b. cause and effect

_____b_____ **4.** Which of the following best describes the author's tone and purpose?
    a. to convince the reader to avoid consuming wine
    b. to inform the general public about the possible link between alcohol and increased risk of cancer
    c. to entertain the reader with interesting facts about the possible effects of alcohol

Textbook
Skills

The Cracking Glass Ceiling

[1]What keeps women from breaking through the glass ceiling, the mostly invisible barrier that prevents women from reaching the executive suite? [2]Researchers have identified a "pipeline" that leads to the top: the marketing, sales, and production positions that directly affect the corporate bottom line. [3]Men, who dominate the executive suite, stereotype women as being less capable of leadership than they are. [4]Viewing women as good at "support," they steer women into human resources or public relations. [5]There, successful projects are not appreciated in the same way as those that bring corporate profits—and bonuses for their managers.

[6]Another reason the glass ceiling is so powerful is that women lack mentors—successful executives who take an interest in them and teach them the ropes. [7]Lack of a mentor is no trivial matter, for mentors can

provide opportunities to develop leadership skills that open the door to the executive suite.

[8]The glass ceiling is cracking, however. [9]A look at women who have broken through reveals highly motivated individuals with a fierce competitive spirit who are willing to give up sleep and recreation for the sake of career advancement. [10]They also learn to play by "men's rules," developing a style that makes men comfortable. [11]Most of these women also have supportive husbands who share household duties and adapt their careers to accommodate the needs of their executive wives. [12]In addition, women who began their careers 20 to 30 years ago are running many major divisions within the largest companies. [13]With this background, some of these women will emerge as the new top CEOs.

—From *Essentials of Sociology: A Down-to-Earth Approach,* 7th ed., pp. 271–272
by James M. Henslin. Copyright © 2007 by Pearson Education, Inc. Reproduced
by permission of Pearson Education, Inc., Boston, MA.

_____b_____ **1.** The best meaning of the word **mentor** in sentence 6 is
   a. employer.   c. men.
   b. adviser.

_____c_____ **2.** What is the relationship of ideas between sentence 7 and sentence 8?
   a. listing   c. contrast
   b. cause and effect

_____b_____ **3.** What is the primary thought pattern of the paragraph?
   a. classification   c. contrast
   b. cause and effect

_____a_____ **4.** Which of the following statements best describes the author's tone and purpose?
   a. to inform the reader about the causes of the glass ceiling
   b. to persuade the reader to protest the glass ceiling
   c. to entertain the reader with interesting facts about the glass ceiling

Step 4: Investigate for Bias

One of the most important steps in making a valid inference is confronting your biases. Each of us possesses strong personal views that influence the way we process information. Often our personal views are based on prior experiences.

For example, if we have had a negative prior experience with a used car salesperson, we may become suspicious and stereotype all used car salespeople as dishonest. Sometimes, our biases are based on the way in which we were raised. Some people register as Democrats or Republicans and vote for only Democratic or Republican candidates simply because their parents were dedicated supporters of one party. To make a valid inference, we must investigate our response to information for bias. Our bias can shape our reading of the author's meaning. To investigate for bias, note biased words and replace them with factual details as you form your conclusions.

EXAMPLE Reword each of the following statements to eliminate the use of biased words.

1. Simon Cowell is best known for his roles as a brutally honest judge on the silly TV talent shows *The X Factor* and *American Idol*.

    Simon Cowell is known for his roles as judge on the TV talent shows
    _____

    The X Factor and *American Idol*.
    _____

2. Surprisingly, Simon Cowell won the prestigious International Emmy award because he completely reshaped 21st century television and music around the world.

    Simon Cowell won the International Emmy award because he has influenced
    _____

    21st century television and music around the world.
    _____

EXPLANATION Compare your answers to the following:

1. Simon Cowell is known for his roles as judge on the TV talent shows *The X Factor* and *American Idol*. The following biased words were deleted: *best*, *brutally honest*, and *silly*.

2. Simon Cowell won the International Emmy award because he has influenced 21st century television and music around the world. The following biased words were deleted: *Surprisingly, prestigious, completely reshaped*.

PRACTICE 3

Study the photo and caption that appears in a college sociology textbook. Reword the caption to eliminate any bias.

◄ **Jackson Pollock,
Shimmering Substance.
(1946)** Many of Pollock's
postwar works—huge
paintings that pulse with
power—show an obses-
sion with heat and light,
surely no coincidence in
the dawn of the nuclear
age.
—From *The West: Encounters &
Transformations, Atlas Edition,
Combined Edition,* 2nd ed., p. 910
by Brian Levack, Edward Muir,
Meredith Veldman and Michael
Maas. Copyright © 2008 by Pearson
Education, Inc. Printed and
Electronically reproduced by
permission of Pearson Education,
Inc., Upper Saddle River, NJ.

Textbook
Skills

Many of Pollock's postwar works—large paintings—show an interest in heat
and light.

Step 5: Detect Contradictions

Have you ever misjudged a situation or had a wrong first impression? For example, have you ever assumed a person was conceited or rude only to find out later
that he or she was acutely shy? Many times, there may be a better explanation for
a set of facts than the first one that comes to mind. The master reader hunts for
the most reasonable explanation. The best way to do this is to consider other
explanations that could logically contradict your first impression.

EXAMPLE 1   Read the following list of symptoms. Then, in the blank, write as
many explanations for the symptoms as you can.

- Fatigue
- Muscle and joint pain
- Erythema migrans (bull's-eye skin rash)
- Swollen lymph nodes
- Chills and fever
- Headache

Answers may vary.

EXPLANATION Some people may think the symptoms describe the flu, but it is actually a list of symptoms for the first stage of Lyme disease. The symptom that clearly identifies Lyme disease is the bull's-eye rash; however, not everyone who has the disease has this symptom, and others may have this symptom but not have Lyme disease. Thus Lyme disease can be misdiagnosed in its earliest stage. A reader who does not think about other possible views can easily jump to a wrong conclusion. Master readers consider all the facts and all the possible explanations for those facts.

EXAMPLE 2 Study the graphic. In the space provided, write an inference that is firmly supported by the details. Answers may vary.

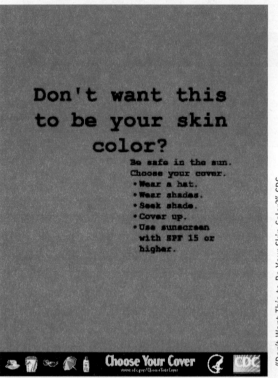

—"Don't Want This to Be Your Skin Color?" CDC
http://www.cdc.gov/cancer/skin/pdf/poster-red.pdf

You should protect yourself from severe sunburn and sun damage by covering up

with one or more of the following: a hat, clothing, sunscreen, and sunglasses.

EXPLANATION This poster implies that protection against the sun's harmful UV rays is necessary. Consider the following statement of an inference firmly based on the information in the poster: "You should protect yourself from severe sunburn and sun damage by covering up with one or more of the following: a hat, clothing, sunscreen, and sunglasses."

PRACTICE 4

Read the following passage. Investigate the list of inferences that follow for bias. Underline biased words. Mark each inference as follows: **V** for a valid inference firmly supported by the facts, **I** for an invalid inference.

Marching for the Vote:
The Woman Suffrage Parade of 1913

¹On Monday, March 3, 1913, clad in a white cape astride a white horse, lawyer Inez Milholland led the great woman suffrage parade down Pennsylvania Avenue in the nation's capital. ²Behind her stretched a long line with nine bands, four mounted brigades, three heralds, about twenty-four floats, and more than 5,000 marchers. ³The procession began late, but all went well for the first few blocks. ⁴Soon, however, the crowds, mostly men in town for the following day's inauguration of Woodrow Wilson, surged into the street making it almost impossible for the marchers to pass. ⁵Occasionally only a single file could move forward. ⁶Women were jeered, tripped, grabbed, shoved, and many heard "indecent epithets" and "barnyard conversation." ⁷Instead of protecting the parade, the police "seemed to enjoy all the ribald jokes and laughter and participated in them." ⁸One policeman explained that they should stay at home where they belonged. ⁹The men in the procession heard shouts of "Henpecko" and "Where are your skirts?" ¹⁰As one witness explained, "There was a sort of spirit of levity connected with the crowd. ¹¹They did not regard the affair very seriously."

—Adapted from Harvey, "Marching for the Vote: The Woman Suffrage Parade of 1913," *American Women*, 18 June 2003, Library of Congress. 12 Feb. 2004 http://memory.loc.gov/ammem/awhhtml/aw01e/aw01e.html#ack

___V___   **1.** The word *suffrage* in sentence 1 means "right to vote."

___I___   **2.** Nearly all of the 5,000 marchers were women.

___I___   **3.** The police supported women's right to vote.

_____I_____ **4.** Men opposed a woman's right to vote.

_____V_____ **5.** Many men in the crowd opposed the women's right to vote.

 ## Inferences in Creative Expression

As you have learned, nonfiction writing, such as in textbooks and news articles, directly states the author's point. Everything is done to make sure that the meanings are clear and unambiguous (not open to different interpretations). However, in many other types of writing, both fiction and nonfiction, authors use creative expression to suggest layers of meaning. Creative expressions are also known as literary devices. The following chart shows a few common literary devices, their meanings, and an example of each.

Creative Expression: Literary Devices		
Literary Device	**Meanings**	**Example**
Connotations of words	The emotional meaning of words	My home is for sale.
Metaphor	A direct comparison	Lies are sinkholes.
Personification	Giving human traits to things that are not human	The sun woke slowly.
Simile	An indirect comparison	Lies are like sticky webs.
Symbol	Something that stands for or suggests something else	A skull and crossbones is a symbol for poison and death.

By using these devices, a writer creates a vivid mental picture in the reader's mind. When a creative expression is used, a reader must infer the point the writer is making from the effects of the images. The following paragraph is the introduction to an essay about anger. Notice its use of literary devices. After you read, write a one-sentence statement of the author's main idea for this paragraph.

A Growing Anger

¹At first, Julio sat quietly shaking his head; then his forehead crumpled into a wadded frown, and his mouth flattened into a pencil-thin line. ²As the speaker continued, Julio's heartbeat sounded like drums beating in his ears, and his entire body flushed as a searing heat rushed up from his toes to the roots of his hair. ³His jaw tightened and his fists

clenched and unclenched as he constantly shifted his weight in his chair. [4]Finally, unable to contain himself any longer, he abruptly rose, jostling the table and tumbling the wine glasses. [5]His body trembled, and his voice shook as he exclaimed, "You have no idea what you are talking about." [6]Just as suddenly, he thudded back into his chair, fists still clenched, and stared without seeing at the white tablecloth bloodied with spilled wine.

Answers may vary: Julio became increasingly angry.

This paragraph uses several creative expressions. *Forehead crumpled into a wadded frown* and *mouth flattened into a pencil-thin line* are metaphors. The author is showing the physical effects of anger by directly comparing Julio's frown to a crumpled wad and his mouth to a thin pencil line. The phrase *heartbeat sounded like drums* is a simile that indirectly compares the sound of Julio's heartbeat to a drum. The author chooses words that have rich connotations in the phrase *flushed as a searing heat rushed,* suggesting that Julio is becoming inflamed and passionate about what he is hearing. And finally, the author uses personification with the phrase *tablecloth bloodied with spilled wine.* The phrase suggests that the tablecloth is injured rather than merely soiled and that the wine bled instead of spilled. All of these details work to create a vivid mental image, and based on these details, the reader must come to the conclusion that Julio becomes increasingly angry. To understand plays, novels, short stories, and poems, the master reader must use inference skills.

EXAMPLE   Read the following poem written by Langston Hughes. Answer the questions that follow.

I, Too

by Langston Hughes

I, too, sing America.

I am the darker brother.
They send me to eat in the kitchen
When company comes,
But I laugh,
And eat well,
And grow strong.

> Tomorrow,
> I'll be at the table
> When company comes.
> Nobody'll dare
> Say to me,
> "Eat in the kitchen,"
> Then.
>
> Besides,
> They'll see how beautiful I am
> And be ashamed–
>
> I, too, am American.

> —Hughes, Langston, "I, Too," from *The Collected Poems of Langston Hughes*, edited by
> Arnold Rampersad with David Roessel, Associate Editor, copyright © 1994 by The Estate of
> Langston Hughes. Used by permission of Alfred A. Knopf, a division of Random House, Inc.

1–3. Choose **three** inferences that are most firmly based on the information in the passage by writing a **V** next to each one.

____V____   a. When the speaker of the poem refers to himself as "the darker brother," he is implying that he is an African American.

____V____   b. The line "they send me to eat in the kitchen" refers to the historical unequal treatment of African Americans in America.

_____   c. The speaker of the poem is angry and resentful.

____V____   d. The speaker of the poem possesses pride and hope.

_____   e. The speaker does not believe that African Americans will ever be appreciated in America.

____a____   **4.** Based on the details of the poem, we can conclude that the implied main idea of the poem could be that
    a. the speaker is celebrating being an African American.
    b. the speaker is condemning America.
    c. the speaker is celebrating America.

EXPLANATION

1–3. The valid inferences are (a), (b), and (d).

4. Based on the details of the poem, we can conclude that the main idea of the poem could be (a) the speaker is celebrating being an African American.

PRACTICE 5

Textbook
Skills

Read the poem written by Robert Frost. Then, choose the inferences that are most logically based on the details in the poem.

The Road Not Taken

by Robert Frost

Two roads diverged in a yellow wood,
And sorry I could not travel both
And be one traveler, long I stood
And looked down one as far as I could
To where it bent in the undergrowth;

Then took the other, as just as fair,
And having perhaps the better claim,
Because it was grassy and wanted wear;
Though as for that the passing there
Had worn them really about the same,

And both that morning equally lay
In leaves no step had trodden black.
Oh, I kept the first for another day!
Yet knowing how way leads on to way,
I doubted if I should ever come back.

I shall be telling this with a sigh
Somewhere ages and ages hence:
Two roads diverged in a wood, and I—
I took the one less traveled by,
And that has made all the difference.

—From *Mountain Interval* by Robert Frost.
New York: Henry Holt, 1920.

_____a_____ **1.** The best meaning of the word **diverged** in the first line is
        a. parted.   c. merged.
        b. ended.

_____c_____ **2.** In the poem, the roads represent
        a. travelers.   c. choices.
        b. fears.

_____a_____ 3. The second verse describes the "other" road he took as
   a. less traveled than the first road.
   b. completely untraveled by others.
   c. worn with the constant travel of others.

_____b_____ 4. In the first two lines of the third verse, the speaker implies that
   a. others had traveled on both roads earlier that day.
   b. no other person had traveled on either road that day.
   c. he already regrets his decision to take the other road.

_____a_____ 5. The main idea of the poem is that the speaker
   a. is an individualist.
   b. has many regrets.
   c. conforms to the leadership of others.

Textbook
Skills

Reading a Textbook: Inferences and Visual Aids

Textbook authors often use pictures, photos, and graphs to imply an idea. These visuals are used to reinforce the information in that section of the textbook.

EXAMPLE Study this figure, taken from the textbook *Psychology and Life*. Then answer the question.

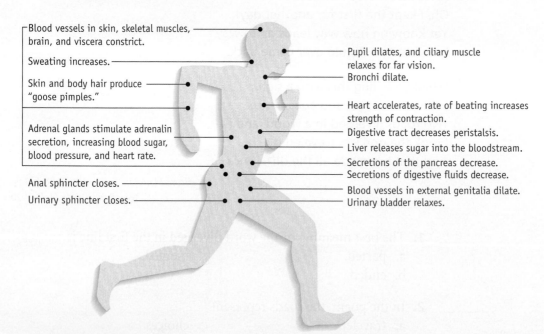

▲ **The Body's Reaction to Stress**
—From *Psychology and Life,* 19th ed., Figure 13.7, (p. 407) by Richard J. Gerrig and Philip G. Zimbardo. Copyright © 2010 by Pearson Education, Inc. Reproduced by permission of Pearson Education, Inc., Boston, MA.

_____c_____   **1.** What is the topic or title of the chapter?
a. Jogging and Fitness
b. Cardiovascular Health
c. Emotion, Stress, and Health

2. Write a caption in a complete sentence that best states the main idea of the figure.

Stress produces a wide range of physiological changes in the body.

_____

EXPLANATION

1. This figure appeared in a chapter with the title "Emotion, Stress, and Health," choice (c).

2. The figure shows at least 15 different ways in which stress affects the human body. Consider the following statement of the figure's main idea: Stress produces a wide range of physiological changes in the body.

PRACTICE 6

Study this figure, taken from the textbook *Life on Earth* and read the list of statements about the figure. Write a **V** in the blanks next to the four inferences that are most firmly based on the figure.

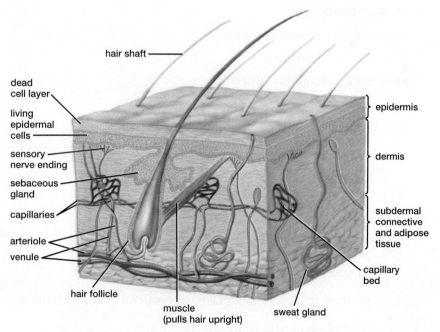

—From *Life on Earth*, 5th ed., Figure 19.9 (p. 363) by Teresa Audesirk, Gerald Audesirk and Bruce E. Byers. Copyright © 2009 by Pearson Education, Inc. Reprinted by permission of Pearson Education, Inc., Upper Saddle River, NJ.

_____V_____   **1.** This figure appears in the chapter titled "The Organization of the Animal Body."

_____   **2.** This figure appears in the chapter titled "Animal Behavior."

_____   **3.** The epidermis is one thin layer of living cells.

_____V_____   **4.** The epidermis is the outer layer of skin.

_____V_____   **5.** Mammalian skin is made up of three layers.

_____V_____   **6.** Skin contains muscle tissue.

_____   **7.** Human skin differs from mammalian skin.

_____   **8.** Skin is not an organ.

APPLICATIONS

Application 1: Making Inferences from a List

Read the following list of details. Write a **V** in the blank next to the three inferences that are most firmly based on the information.

Characteristics of Successful Marriages

- commitment
- interdependence
- reciprocity (desire to please)
- good communication
- integrity, credibility, and trust
- intimacy and self-disclosure
- emotional support and validation
- good conflict resolution skills, especially flexibility, negotiation, and compromise
- patience, sensitivity, and tolerance
- similar views of the relationship

—Adapted from Jaffe, *Understanding Parenting*, 2nd ed., p. 103.

_____   Partners in a successful marriage never disagree.

_____V_____   Partners in a successful marriage cooperate with each other.

_____V_____   Intimacy is enhanced by self-disclosure.

_____V_____ Flexibility and compromise are key elements in effectively resolving conflicts.

_____ Successful marriages are difficult to achieve and less and less common.

_____ The most important trait of a successful marriage is commitment.

Application 2: Making Inferences from a Visual

Textbook Skills

The following comic strip from *Frank and Earnest* appeared in a college sociology textbook in the chapter about socialization and gender. Read the cartoon; then write an inference about gender that is soundly based on the information in the comic strip.

Frank and Ernest

—©2002 Thaves/Dist. by NEA, Inc. www.frankandernest.com <http://www.frankandernest.com>

Answers may vary. Gender roles are learned during childhood.

Application 3: Making Inferences from Literature

Read the following excerpt from the well-known play *Hamlet*, written by William Shakespeare. Then, using inference skills, answer the questions. Wording of answers may vary.

> **Hamlet:** To be, or not to be: that is the question:
> Whether 'tis nobler in the mind to suffer
> The slings and arrows of outrageous fortune,
> Or to take arms against a sea of troubles,
> And by opposing end them? To die: to sleep;
> No more; and, by a sleep to say we end
> The heart-ache and the thousand natural shocks
> That flesh is heir to, 'tis a consummation
> Devoutly to be wish'd. To die, to sleep;
> To sleep: perchance to dream: ay, there's the rub;
> For in that sleep of death what dreams may come
> When we have shuffled off this mortal coil,

Must give us pause. There's the respect
That makes calamity of so long life;
For who would bear the whips and scorns of time,
The oppressor's wrong, the proud man's contumely,
The pangs of dispriz'd love, the law's delay,
The insolence of office, and the spurns
That patient merit of the unworthy takes,
When he himself might his quietus make
With a bare bodkin? who would fardels bear,
To grunt and sweat under a weary life,
But that the dread of something after death,
The undiscover'd country from whose bourn
No traveller returns, puzzles the will,
And makes us rather bear those ills we have
Than fly to others that we know not of?
Thus conscience does make cowards of us all;
And thus the native hue of resolution
Is sicklied o'er with the pale cast of thought,
And enterprises of great pith and moment
With this regard their currents turn awry,
And lose the name of action.

—From *Hamlet*. In *The Complete Works of William Shakespeare*.
Edited by W. J. Craig. London: Oxford University Press, 1914.

1. What action is Hamlet considering?

suicide

_____

2. To what does the metaphor "mortal coil" refer?

life

_____

3. To what does the metaphor "The undiscover'd country from whose bourn
No traveller returns" refer?

life after death

_____

4. What stops Hamlet from taking the action he is considering?

fear of the unknown, fear of death

REVIEW TEST 1

Score (number correct) _____ × 20 = _____ %

Making Inferences

Read the poem, and then answer the questions that follow.

My Heart Leaps up When I Behold

by William Wordsworth (1807)

My heart leaps up when I behold
　A rainbow in the sky:
So was it when my life began;
So is it now I am a man;
So be it when I shall grow old,
　Or let me die!
The Child is father of the Man;
　I could wish my days to be
Bound each to each by natural piety.

—Wordsworth, William, *The Complete Poetical Works.*
London: Macmillan and Co., 1888; Bartleby.com,
1999. www.bartleby.com/145/. 28 March 2010.

___c___ **1.** Based on the context of the poem, the best synonym for the word **piety** is
　　a. youthfulness.　　　　c. goodness.
　　b. courage.　　　　　　d. law.

___d___ **2.** What emotion does the title of the poem suggest?
　　a. fear　　　　　　　c. doubt
　　b. confidence　　　　d. joy

___a___ **3.** The rainbow represents
　　a. nature.　　　　　　c. youthfulness.
　　b. mankind.　　　　　d. old age.

___b___ **4.** In the line "The Child is the father of the Man," the poet suggests
　　a. mankind is as innocent as a child.
　　b. the person we are as an adult is connected to the person we are as a child.
　　c. life passes by too quickly.

_____b_____ **5.** Overall, the poet expresses
     a. faith in the goodness of human beings.
     b. a life-long love of nature.
     c. a fear of death.

REVIEW TEST 2

Score (number correct) _____ × 20 = _____ %

Textbook
Skills

Read the following passage from a college psychology textbook. Complete the activities that follow.

12.5 GE/356 words   **Episodic and Semantic Memories**

[1]When we discussed the functions of memories earlier, we made a distinction between declarative and procedural memories. [2]We can define another dimension along which declarative memories differ with respect to the cues that are necessary to retrieve them from memory. [3]Canadian psychologist Endel Tulving (1972) first proposed the distinction between episodic and semantic types of declarative memories.

[4]**Episodic memories** preserve, individually, the specific events that you have personally experienced. [5]For example, memories of your happiest birthday or of your first kiss are stored in episodic memory. [6]To recover such memories, you need retrieval cues that specify something about the time at which the event occurred and something about the content of the events. [7]Depending on how the information has been encoded, you may or may not be able to produce a specific memory representation for an event. [8]For example, do you have any specific memories to differentiate the tenth time ago you brushed your teeth from the eleventh time ago?

[9]Everything you know, you began to acquire in some particular context. [10]However, there are large classes of information that, over time, you encounter in many different contexts. [11]These classes of information come to be available for retrieval without reference to their multiple times and places of experience. [12]These **semantic memories** are generic, categorical memories, such as the meanings of words and concepts. [13]For most people, facts like the formula $E = MC^2$ and the capital of France don't require retrieval cues that make reference to the episodes, the original learning contexts, in which the memory was acquired.

[14]Of course, this doesn't mean that your recall of semantic memories is foolproof. [15]You know perfectly well that you can forget many facts that have become dissociated from the contexts in which you learned them. [16]A

good strategy when you can't recover a semantic memory is to treat it like an episodic memory again. [17]By thinking to yourself, "I know I learned the names of the Roman emperors in my Western civilization course," you may be able to provide the extra retrieval cues that will shake loose a memory.

—From *Psychology and Life,* 19th ed., p. 206 by Richard J. Gerrig and Philip G. Zimbardo. Copyright © 2010 by Pearson Education, Inc. Reproduced by permission of Pearson Education, Inc., Boston, MA.

1–3. Write **V** for valid by the three inferences that are most firmly supported by the ideas in the passage.

___V___ The term episodic refers to actions that occur in time.

___V___ The term semantic refers to language and symbols.

_____ Episodic and semantic memories never work together to retrieve information.

_____ Most people would rely on episodic memories to retrieve the dates of the Civil War.

___V___ There are at least four categories of long-term memories.

4–5. Complete the concept map with information from the passage. Wording may vary.

REVIEW TEST 3   Score (number correct) _____ × 10 = _____ %

Making Inferences

Textbook Skills

Before you read the following passage from a college health textbook, skim the passage. Answer the Before Reading questions. Then, read the passage and answer the After Reading questions.

10.2 GE/631 words   **Exercise Prescription**

Vocabulary Preview

incentive (8):
motivation, reason

**cardiorespiratory
(18):** of or relating to
the heart and
respiratory system

calisthenics (20):
exercises

elevate (21): raise

duration (23): length,
period of time

[1]Doctors often prescribe medications to treat certain diseases. [2]For every individual there is an appropriate dosage of medicine to cure an illness. [3]Similarly, for each individual, there is a correct dosage of exercise to best promote physical fitness. [4]An **exercise prescription** should be tailored to meet the needs of the individual. [5]It should include fitness goals, mode of exercise, a warm-up, a primary conditioning period, and a cool-down.

[6]Establishing short-term and long-term fitness goals is an important part of an exercise prescription. [7]Goals serve as motivation to start an exercise program. [8]Further, reaching your fitness goals improves self-esteem and provides the **incentive** to make a lifetime commitment to regular exercise. [9]A logical and common type of fitness goal is a performance goal. [10]Increased flexibility is an example of a performance goal. [11]You should set both long-term and short-term performance goals, and you should be tested to determine when you have achieved them. [12]In addition to performance goals, consider setting exercise **adherence** goals. [13]That is, set a goal to exercise a specific number of days per week. [14]Exercise adherence goals are important because fitness will improve only if you exercise regularly. [15]The most important rule in setting goals is that you must create realistic ones. [16]Set fitness goals that you can reach so you will be encouraged to continue exercising.

[17]Every exercise prescription includes at least one mode, or type, of exercise. [18]For example, to improve **cardiorespiratory** fitness, you could select from a wide variety of exercise modes such as running, swimming, or cycling.

[19]A warm-up is a brief (5–15 minute) period of exercise that occurs before the workout. [20]It generally involves light **calisthenics** or stretching. [21]The purpose of a warm-up is to **elevate** muscle temperature and increase blood flow to those muscles that will be used in the workout. [22]A warm-up can also reduce the strain on the heart and may reduce the risk of muscle and tendon injuries.

[23]The primary conditioning period includes the mode of exercise and the frequency, intensity, and **duration** of the workout. [24]The frequency of exercise is the number of times per week that you exercise. [25]In general, the suggested number is three to five times per week. [26]The intensity of exercise is the amount of stress or overload placed on the body during the exercise. [27]The method of measuring intensity

varies with the type of exercise. [28]For example, the heart rate is a standard means of tracking intensity during training to improve cardiorespiratory fitness. [29]In strength training, the number of repetitions that can be performed before muscle fatigue occurs is used. [30]In addition, flexibility is measured by the degree of tension or discomfort felt during the stretch.

[31]Another key **component** of the exercise prescription is the duration of exercise. [32]This is the amount of time spent in performing the primary workout. [33]Note that the duration of exercise does not include the warm-up or cool-down. [34]In general, research has shown that 20 to 30 minutes per exercise session is the least amount of time needed to improve physical fitness.

[35]The cool-down is a 5- to 15-minute period of low-intensity exercise that immediately follows the primary workout. [36]For instance, a period of slow walking might be used as a cool-down after a running workout. [37]A cool-down accomplishes several goals. [38]First, the cool-down allows blood to be returned from the muscles back toward the heart. [39]During exercise, large amounts of blood are pumped to the working muscles. [40]Once exercise ends, blood tends to remain in large blood vessels located around the muscles that were worked. [41]This is known as pooling. [42]Failure to redistribute pooled blood after exercise could result in you feeling lightheaded or even fainting. [43]Finally, some experts argue that post-exercise soreness may be reduced as a result of a cool-down.

—From *Total Fitness and Wellness Student Textbook Component,* 3rd ed., pp. 65–69 by Scott K. Powers and Stephen L. Dodd. Copyright © 2003 by Pearson Education, Inc. Printed and Electronically reproduced by permission of Pearson Education, Inc., Upper Saddle River, NJ.

Before Reading

Vocabulary in Context

_____a_____ **1.** The word **adherence** in sentence 12 means
    a. obedience.   c. time.
    b. esteem.

_____c_____ **2.** The word **component** in sentence 31 means
    a. benefit.   c. factor.
    b. goal.

Concept Maps

Finish the concept map with information from the passage.

Components of the Exercise Prescription

After Reading

Central Idea and Main Idea

___b___ **5.** Which sentence best states the main idea of the passage?
  a. sentence 3   c. sentence 6
  b. sentence 5

Supporting Details

___b___ **6.** Sentence 28 is a
  a. major supporting detail.
  b. minor supporting detail.

Transitions

___c___ **7.** What thought pattern describes the relationship between sentences 35 and 36?
  a. cause and effect   c. definition and example
  b. time order

Thought Patterns

___c___ **8.** The thought pattern used in the fifth paragraph (sentences 23–30) is
  a. cause and effect.   c. definition and example.
  b. time order.

Tone and Purpose

___a___ **9.** The author's tone and purpose in the passage are
  a. to inform with objective details.
  b. to entertain with subjective details.
  c. to persuade with discouraging details.

Inferences

10. Write **V** for valid by the inference that is most firmly based on the information in the passage.

___V___ A performance goal that is set too high can become a block to motivation.

_____ Sudden and intense exercise helps increase muscle mass more than a slower build up.

_____ In order to experience a complete workout, each exercise period should be at least two hours.

WHAT DO YOU THINK?

Why is exercise so important for a healthy lifestyle? Why is frequency, intensity, and the duration of exercise so important? What are some of the barriers that keep people from committing to an exercise program? Assume you are a personal trainer and create a personal exercise prescription for one or both of the following two potential clients: (1) Shantel, age 45, no known medical problems or limitations, has a desk job, and is 30 pounds overweight; (2) Richard, age 17, no known medical problems or limitations, trying out for a position on his high school track team, is at a good weight, but is out of shape.

REVIEW TEST 4   Score (number correct) _____ × 10 = _____ %

Making Inferences

Textbook
Skills

Before Reading: Survey the following passage adapted from the college textbook *Essentials of Sociology*. Skim the passage, noting the words in **bold** print. Answer the Before Reading questions that follow the passage. Then, read the passage. Next, answer the After Reading questions. Use the discussion and writing topics as activities to do after reading.

11.2 GE/455 words

Lara Croft, Tomb Raider: Changing Images
of Women in the Mass Media

[1]The mass media reflect women's changing role in society. [2]Portrayals of women as passive, as subordinate, or as mere background objects remain, but a new image has broken through. [3]Although this new image

exaggerates changes, it also illustrates a **fundamental** change in gender relations. [4]Lara Croft is an outstanding example of this change.

[5]Like books and magazines, video games are made available to a mass audience. [6]And with digital advances, they have crossed the line from what is traditionally thought of as games to something that more closely resembles interactive movies. [7]Costing an average of $10 million to produce and another $10 million to market, video games now have **intricate** subplots and use celebrity voices for the characters (Nussenbaum 2004). [8]Sociologically, what is significant is that the content of video games **socializes** their users. [9]As they play, gamers are exposed not only to action but also to ideas and images. [10]The gender images of video games communicate powerful messages, just as they do in other forms of the mass media.

[11]Lara Croft, an adventure-seeking archeologist and star of *Tomb Raider* and its many sequels, is the **essence** of the new gender image. [12]Lara is smart, strong, and able to utterly **vanquish** foes. [13]With both guns blazing, she is the cowboy of the twenty-first century, the term *cowboy* being purposefully chosen, as Lara breaks stereotypical gender roles and dominates what previously was the domain of men.

[14]She was the first female **protagonist** in a field of muscle-rippling, gun-toting **macho-caricatures** (Taylor 1999). [15]Yet the old remains powerfully **encapsulated** in the new. [16]As the photos on [the next] page make evident, Lara is a fantasy girl for young men of the digital generation.

[17]No matter her foe, no matter her **predicament**, Lara oozes sex. [18]Her form-fitting outfits, which flatter her **voluptuous** physique, reflect the mental images of the men who fashioned this digital character.

[19]Lara has caught young men's fancy to such an extent that they have bombarded corporate headquarters with questions about her personal life. [20]Lara is the star of two movies and a comic book. [21]There is even a Lara Croft candy bar.

[22]A sociologist who reviewed this text said, "It seems that for women to be defined as equal, we have to become symbolic males—warriors with breasts." [23]Why is gender change mostly one-way—females adopting traditional male characteristics? [24]To see why men get to keep their gender roles, these two questions should help:

[25]Who is moving into the traditional territory of the other? [26]Do people prefer to imitate power or powerlessness? [27]Finally, consider just

how far stereotypes have actually been left behind. [28]The ultimate goal of the video game, after foes are vanquished, is to see Lara in a nightie.

—From *Essentials of Sociology: A Down-to-Earth Approach*, 7th ed., p. 72. by James M. Henslin. Copyright © 2007 by Pearson Education, Inc. Reproduced by permission of Pearson Education, Inc., Boston, MA.

▲ The mass media not only reflect gender stereotypes but also they play a role in changing them. Sometimes they do both simultaneously. The images of Lara Croft not only reflect women's changing role in society, but also, by exaggerating the change, they mold new stereotypes.

Before Reading

Vocabulary in Context

1–2. Study the following chart of word parts. Then, read the passage for context clues to help you define the meaning of the word. Next, use your own words to define the terms. Finally, identify the context you used to determine the word's meaning.

Root	Meaning	Suffix	Meaning
macho	male	-*ure*	act, function
caricare	to load	-*s*	plural

1. In sentence 14, **macho-caricatures** are <u>exaggerations of male</u> <u>characteristics</u>.

2. What is the context clue used to determine the meaning of **macho-caricatures** in sentence 14? <u>general sense of the passage and examples such as</u> <u>muscle-rippling</u>

After Reading

Implied Central Idea

___b___ **3.** Which sentence best states the main idea of the passage?
   a. The mass media reflect women's changing role in society.
   b. Lara Croft encapsulates the changing roles of women in society.
   c. Lara Croft is a stereotype of feminine sexuality.
   d. Lara Croft appeals mostly to men.

Supporting Details

___b___ **4.** Sentence 7 is a
   a. major supporting detail.   b. minor supporting detail.

Transitions

___c___ **5.** The relationship within sentence 5 is
   a. cause and effect.   c. comparison.
   b. listing.   d. definition and example.

Thought Patterns

___d___ **6.** The main thought pattern for the second paragraph (sentences 5–10) is
   a. listing.   c. cause and effect.
   b. space order.   d. generalization and example.

Tone and Purpose

___c___ **7.** The author's tone and purpose in the passage are
   a. to inform the reader with objective details.
   b. to entertain with subjective observations.
   c. to persuade with graphic details.

Inferences

8–10. Write **V** for valid by the three inferences that are most firmly based on the information in the passage and the images of Lara Croft.

___V___ Lara Croft has developed a strong following among male consumers of entertainment.

_____ Lara Croft does not appeal to women consumers of entertainment.

__V__ Lara Croft video games and movies contain violence and sexuality.

_____ Lara Croft breaks completely free of female stereotypes.

__V__ Lara Croft is an aggressive action figure and main character in a series of video games, movies, and a comic book.

WHAT DO YOU THINK?

Do you think females are seen as less powerful than men? Why or why not? Have perceptions about men and women changed in recent years? Do you think video games send powerful messages about power or gender? Why or why not? Assume you are a concerned parent and you have decided to write an article about the messages contained in movies and video games to post on the community blog sponsored by your local newspaper. Consider using one of the following topics for your article: (1) Discuss what one may learn about our culture by playing video games, or a particular video game; (2) Write a review of a movie or video game based on the message it may send about violence or gender. Take a stand in support of or in opposition to the movie or video game.

 ## After Reading About Inferences

Before you move on to the Mastery Tests on inferences, take time to reflect on your learning and performance by answering the following questions. Write your answers in your notebook.

- How has my knowledge base or prior knowledge about inferences changed?
- Based on my studies, how do I think I will perform on the Mastery Test(s)? Why do I think my scores will be above average, average, or below average?
- Would I recommend this chapter to other students who want to learn more inferences? Why or why not?

Test your understanding of what you have learned about inferences by completing the Chapter 11 Review Card in the insert near the end of your text.

CONNECT TO myreadinglab

To check your progress in meeting Chapter 11's learning outcomes, log in to **www.myreadinglab.com** and try the following exercises.

- The "Inference" section of MyReadingLab gives additional information about inferences. The section provides an overview, model, practices, and tests. To access this resource, click on the "Study Plan" tab. Then click on "Inference." Then click on the following links as needed: "Overview," "Model," "Practice," and "Test."

- To measure your mastery of this chapter, complete the tests in the "Inference" section and click on Gradebook to find your results.

Read the following passage, adapted from a college biology textbook. Then, write **V** for valid by the five inferences most soundly based on the information.

Textbook
Skills

12.3 GE/426 words

Matters of the Heart

[1]Cardiovascular disease, which impairs the heart and blood vessels, is the leading cause of death in the United States, killing nearly 1 million Americans annually. [2]And no wonder. [3]Your heart must contract vigorously more than 2.5 billion times during your lifetime without once stopping to rest, forcing blood through vessels whose total length would encircle the globe twice. [4]Because these vessels may become constricted, weakened, or clogged, the cardiovascular system is a prime candidate for malfunction.

Atherosclerosis Obstructs Blood Vessels

[5]*Atherosclerosis* causes the walls of the large arteries to thicken and lose their elasticity. [6]This change is caused by deposits called *plaques,* which are composed of cholesterol and other fatty substances as well as calcium and fibrin. [7]Plaques are deposited within the wall of the artery between the smooth muscle and the tissue that lines the artery. [8]A plaque may rupture through the lining into the interior of the vessel, stimulating platelets to adhere to the vessel wall and initiate blood clots. [9]These clots further obstruct the artery and may completely block it. [10]Or a clot may break loose and clog a narrower artery "downstream." [11]Arterial clots are responsible for the most serious consequences of atherosclerosis: heart attacks and strokes.

[12]A *heart attack* occurs when one of the coronary arteries is blocked. [13](Coronary arteries supply the heart muscle itself.) [14]Deprived of nutrients and oxygen, a heart muscle whose blood supply is curtailed by a blocked artery dies rapidly and painfully. [15]Heart attacks are the major cause of death from atherosclerosis.

[16]About 1.1 million Americans suffer heart attacks each year, and about half a million people die from them. [17]But atherosclerosis also causes plaques and clots to form in arteries throughout the body. [18]If a clot or plaque obstructs an artery that supplies the brain, it can cause a stroke, in which brain function is lost in the area deprived of blood and its vital oxygen and nutrients.

Treatment of Atherosclerosis

[19]The exact cause of atherosclerosis is unclear, but it is promoted by high blood pressure, cigarette smoking, genetic predisposition, obesity, diabetes, lack of exercise, and high blood levels of a certain type of cholesterol bound to a carrier molecule called low-density lipoprotein (LDL). [20]If LDL-bound cholesterol levels are too high, cholesterol may be deposited in arterial walls. [21]In contrast, cholesterol bound to high-density lipoprotein (HDL) is metabolized or excreted and hence is often called "good" cholesterol. [22]Treatment of atherosclerosis includes the use of drugs or changes in diet and lifestyle to lower blood pressure and blood cholesterol levels.

—Text and Figure E20-1 (p. 382) below from *Life on Earth*, 5th ed., p. 382 by Teresa Audesirk, Gerald Audesirk, and Bruce E. Byers. Copyright © 2009 by Pearson Education, Inc. Printed and Electronically reproduced by permission of Pearson Education, Inc., Upper Saddle River, NJ.

___V___ A synonym for coronary artery is blood vessel.

___V___ Plaque is a sticky substance that hardens in the arteries.

___V___ Cardiovascular diseases include heart attacks and strokes.

_____ Most heart attacks come on suddenly.

_____ Cholesterol promotes a healthy heart.

___V___ The tendency to develop heart problems can be inherited.

___V___ Lifestyle choices have a significant effect on the health of the heart.

_____ Most people are too busy to exercise.

VISUAL VOCABULARY

Fill in the blanks with words from the passage that best complete the caption.

___Plaque___ clogs arteries: When the fibrous cap ruptures, a blood clot forms, obstructing the ___artery___ .

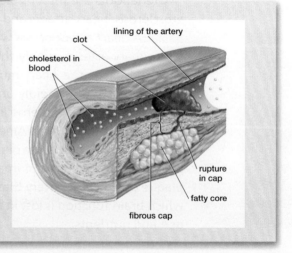

▶ **Figure E20-1**

Read the poem, and then answer the questions that follow.

Mr. Flood's Party

by Edwin Arlington Robinson

Old Eben Flood, climbing along one night
Over the hill between the town below
And the forsaken upland *hermitage   a dwelling where one lives alone
That held as much as he should ever know
On earth again of home, paused *warily.   cautiously
The road was his with not a native near;
And Eben, having leisure, said aloud,
For no man else in Tilbury Town to hear:

"Well, Mr. Flood, we have the harvest moon
Again, and we may not have many more;
The bird is on the wing, the poet says,
And you and I have said it here before.
Drink to the bird." He raised up to the light
The jug that he had gone so far to fill,
And answered huskily: "Well, Mr. Flood,
Since you propose it, I believe I will."

Alone, as if enduring to the end
A valiant armor of scarred hopes outworn,
He stood there in the middle of the road
Like Roland's ghost winding a silent horn.
Below him, in the town among the trees,
Where friends of other days had honored him,
A phantom salutation of the dead
Rang thinly till old Eben's eyes were dim.

Then, as a mother lays her sleeping child
Down tenderly, fearing it may awake,
He set the jug down slowly at his feet
With trembling care, knowing that most things break;
And only when assured that on firm earth
It stood, as the uncertain lives of men
Assuredly did not, he paced away,

And with his hand extended paused again:
"Well, Mr. Flood, we have not met like this
In a long time; and many a change has come
To both of us, I fear, since last it was
We had a drop together. Welcome home!"
*Convivially returning with himself,   sociably
Again he raised the jug up to the light;
And with an acquiescent quaver said:
"Well, Mr. Flood, if you insist, I might.

"Only a very little, Mr. Flood—
For auld lang syne. No more, sir; that will do."
So, for the time, apparently it did,
And Eben evidently thought so too;
For soon amid the silver loneliness
Of night he lifted up his voice and sang,
Secure, with only two moons listening,
Until the whole harmonious landscape rang—

"For auld lang syne." The weary throat gave out,
The last word wavered; and the song being done,
He raised again the jug regretfully
And shook his head, and was again alone.
There was not much that was ahead of him,
And there was nothing in the town below—
Where strangers would have shut the many doors
That many friends had opened long ago.

—From E. A. Robinson, Collected Poems. New York, The Macmillan Company, 1921.

_____b_____ **1.** The poem suggests that the narrator is
      a. young and distrustful.   c. middle-aged and frightened.
      b. old and lonely.

_____c_____ **2.** In the second and fifth stanzas, Eben Flood is talking to
      a. a friend.   c. himself.
      b. God.

_____a_____ **3.** In the second stanza, the narrator implies that Eben
      a. went to town to buy liquor.   c. loves poetry and birds.
      b. lives in town.

_____b_____ **4.** Overall, the poet suggests that Eben Flood is
      a. well known and well respected by the townspeople.
      b. lonely because he has outlived those who knew him.
      c. fearful of death.

Read the following passage taken from the novel *Forever Island* by Patrick Smith. Using inference skills, mark each of the statements that follow:

T for true

F for false

UK for unknown based on the information given

13 GE/524 words

From *Forever Island*

[1]Charlie had heard his father and his grandfather speak of the time when the Seminole lived on the land far to the north, the rich rolling hills with fertile soil that grew corn and squash and pumpkin in abundance, and the game was plentiful and the streams as clear as an open sky, and then the white man came and took the land, and there was fighting and blood and death and hunger; then the Seminole moved south, giving way to the white man, settling on the land north of the big lake, but the white man came again and wanted the land, more fighting and more running and more hunger, and they moved south again. [2]Then the white man said they could have this land and be bothered no more; but he came again and the blood ran red, and the white man brought in dogs to track the Seminole like an animal. [3]Then they placed a bounty on the Seminole, fifty dollars for a man, twenty-five dollars for a woman, fifteen dollars for a child, bands of white hunters surrounding the chickees at night, capturing the men and women and children, binding their hands and feet with rope, throwing them into wagons like sacks of feed and hauling them to the fort in the north where they collected the bounty and returned to the swamp for another hunt; then the fighting and the running until the Seminole disappeared into the heart of the swamp and into the Sea of Grass and did not come out again until it was safe to do so, and some had not come out yet.

[4]Charlie himself had seen the white man come into this land and slaughter the egret for its feathers, shooting them only when nesting on the rookery, killing them by the hundreds of thousands and leaving the young either to die in the nest and be eaten by vultures or fall out of the nest and drown, and the water around the mangroves turning red with blood; and he had seen the white man come into this land and slaughter the alligator, shipping out their hides fifty thousand at a time to be made into wallets and shoes, and he had once seen a thousand alligators killed

in one pond in one day, but this time not for the hides, for the white men pulled out the alligator's teeth to be sold as watch fobs and left the bodies with their hides to rot in the blistering sun; and he had seen the white man come with his mules and his curses and his saws and his puffing trains and strip the land of the giant bald cypress, cutting them down like fields of sugar cane; and he had seen the white man wipe out the tree snails so that their shells could be sold as trinkets; and he had seen the white man dig the canals and drain the land and come closer and closer until he was now here again, once more telling the Seminole that he could not live on this land because the white man wanted it.

___T___ **1.** Charlie and his family are Seminoles.

___UK___ **2.** Charlie and his family live in the Everglades in Florida.

___F___ **3.** At first the white man tried to live in peace with the Seminole.

___T___ **4.** The white man destroyed the natural environment because he was greedy.

___F___ **5.** The conflict between the white man and the Seminoles was over long ago.

Read the following passage from a college history textbook. Mark each of the statements that follow as **T** for **true**, **F** for **false**, or **UK** for **unknown** based on the information given.

13.0 GE/399 words

Textbook
Skills

Cuba

¹Cuba's modern history has been dominated by its revolution of 1959. ²Before the revolution, Cuba had been controlled by a former army sergeant, Fulgencio Batista, who had ruled on his own or through civilian presidents since 1934. ³Cuba's economy largely depended on sugar exports and American investment. ⁴And Cuba's capital, Havana, was a haven for American tourists (and gangsters), lured by the tropical climate and gambling casinos.

⁵Cuba's revolutionary movement was led by Fidel Castro (b. 1926). ⁶The son of a well-to-do sugarcane farmer, Castro was introduced to revolutionary politics as a law student at the University of Havana. ⁷In July 1953, he organized a disastrous attack on a garrison at Santiago. ⁸After serving a short prison term, he fled to Mexico and plotted a return. ⁹He and his rebel band of 80 sailed on the Granma in late 1956, but they were nearly all killed when they landed in Oriente province. ¹⁰Castro and a small band of rebels escaped to the Sierra Maestra Mountains in southeast Cuba, from which they waged a guerrilla war. ¹¹With popular support for Castro's movement growing and Batista's National Guard collapsing, Batista abruptly fled after his annual party on New Year's Eve, 1958. ¹²Castro's rebels marched unopposed into Havana.

¹³Although he billed himself as a nationalist reformer when he took power, Castro moved sharply to the left in 1960 and proclaimed the revolution socialist the following year. ¹⁴His rhetoric became stridently anti-American. ¹⁵Shortly after John F. Kennedy became the U.S. president in 1961, the United States supported an ill-fated invasion by Cuban exiles at the Bay of Pigs off the southern coast of Cuba. ¹⁶By then, the Cuban government was forging close ties with the socialist bloc, especially the Soviet Union.

—From *Civilizations Past and Present, Combined Volume*, 12th ed., p. 1041 by Robert R. Edgar, Neil J. Hackett, George F. Jewsbury, Barbara S. Molony, Matthew Gordon. Copyright © 2008 by Pearson Education, Inc. Reprinted by permission of Pearson Education, Inc., Upper Saddle River, NJ.

[17]Castro's policies were dogmatically socialist. [18]He built up the Communist party and jailed thousands of opponents, including former comrades. [19]His government created a command economy in which the government controlled most sectors of the economy. [20]It seized American property and nationalized businesses. [21]It also addressed social problems and launched successful campaigns to eradicate illiteracy and to provide basic health care to the lower classes. [22]Educational and health standards rose appreciably, as did living conditions among the peasants, who constituted the great majority of the population. [23]The professional and middle classes, however, suffered losses in both living standards and personal liberties, and many hundreds of thousands fled to the United States.

___UK___ **1.** Most people in Cuba think of Fidel Castro as a hero who liberated Cuba.

___T___ **2.** During the 1960s, Cuba and Russia became allies.

___T___ **3.** Communism is a type of socialism.

___F___ **4.** All social classes from the poor to the wealthy benefitted from the changes Castro brought to Cuba.

VISUAL VOCABULARY

Before Castro's revolution, Havana, Cuba, was a haven for American tourists. The best synonym for haven is

_b_____.

   a. trap.
   b. retreat.

The Basics of Argument

12

LEARNING OUTCOMES

After studying this chapter you should be able to do the following:

1. Define the terms *argument, claim,* and *evidence.* [Knowledge]
2. Identify the author's claim and evidence. [Comprehension]
3. Determine whether or not the evidence is relevant. [Analysis]
4. Determine whether or not the evidence is adequate. [Analysis]
5. Analyze the argument for bias. [Analysis]
6. Apply inference skills to evaluate arguments for validity. [Application, Evaluation]
7. Evaluate the importance of the basics of argument. [Evaluation]

Before Reading About the Basics of Argument

Many of the same skills you learned to make valid inferences will help you master the basics of argument. Take a moment to review the five steps in the VALID approach to making sound inferences. Fill in the following blanks with each of the steps.

Step 1: **V**erify and value the facts.

Step 2: **A**ssess prior knowledge.

Step 3: **L**earn from the text.

Step 4: **I**nvestigate for bias.

Step 5: **D**etect contradictions.

Use your prior knowledge about valid inferences, other reading skills, and the learning outcomes to create at least three questions that you can answer as you study: Answers may vary.

1. How will verifying and valuing the facts help me decide if supports in an

   argument are relevant   ?

2. How will learning from the text help me decide if supports in an argument

   are adequate   ?

3. How does an argument use bias

   _____   ?

Compare the questions you created based on your prior knowledge and the chapter learning outcomes with the following questions. Then, write the ones that seem the most helpful in your notebook, leaving enough space between questions to record your answers as you read and study the chapter.

How will verifying and valuing the facts help me decide if supports in an argument are relevant? How will learning from the text help me decide if supports in an argument are adequate? How does an argument use bias? What is the relationship between main ideas and the author's claim? How does opinion affect an argument? What is the connection between tone, purpose, and the basics of argument?

 ## What Is an Argument?

Have you noticed how many of us enjoy debating ideas and winning arguments? Many television shows such as the talk show *The View* and political programs such as *The Daily Show with Jon Stewart* or *Glenn Beck* thrive on conflict and debate. Likewise, talk radio devotes hours of air time to debating cultural and political issues on shows like *Rush Limbaugh* and *The Bill Press Show*. In everyday life, a couple may argue about spending priorities. Colleagues may argue how best to resolve a workplace dispute. One politician may argue in favor of corporate tax cuts while another politician argues against any kind of tax cut. Certain topics stir debate and argument. For many, sports contests can cause heated debate, and topics such as religion and evolution often evoke powerful debates.

Some people are so committed to their ideas that they become emotional, even angry. However, effective **argument** is reasoned: it is a process during which a claim is made and logical details are offered to support that claim.

An **argument** is made up of two types of statements:
1. The author's claim—the main point of the argument
2. The supports—the evidence or reasons that support the author's claim

The purpose of an argument is to persuade the reader that the claim is valid, that is, sound or reasonable. To decide if a claim is valid, you must analyze the argument in four basic steps.

1. Identify the author's claim and supports.

2. Decide whether the supports are relevant.

3. Decide whether the supports are adequate.

4. Check the argument for bias.

 ## Step 1: Identify the Author's Claim and Supports

Read the following claim:

> Competitive sports provide several benefits to participants and should be funded by public funds.

The claim certainly states the speaker's point clearly, but it probably wouldn't inspire most of us to support or become involved in competitive sports. Instead, our first response to the claim is likely to be, "What are the benefits to participants of competitive sports?" We need reasons before we can decide whether or not we think the claim is valid.

Read the following statements:

1. Competitive sports teach participants physical, social, emotional, and psychological skills.

2. Competitive sports set standards against which participants can measure growth and ability.

3. Competitive sports allow participants to experience the connection between effort and success.

These three sentences offer the supports for the author's claim. We are now able to understand the basis of the argument, and we now have details about which we can agree or disagree.

Writers frequently make claims that they want us to accept as valid. To assess whether the claim is valid, a master reader first identifies the claim and the supports.

EXAMPLES

A. Read each of the following groups of ideas. Mark each statement **C** if it is an author's claim or **S** if it provides support for the claim.

1. __C__ a. Staph is a particularly dangerous type of bacteria.

   __S__ b. Staph may cause skin infections that look like pimples or boils, which may be red, swollen, painful, or have pus or other drainage.

   __S__ c. Some strains of staph have developed antibiotic resistance, making a staph infection sometimes difficult to treat.

2. __S__ a. Aerobic training such as walking, biking, and swimming strengthens the heart and lungs.

   __C__ b. A comprehensive fitness program must combine aerobic and anaerobic training.

   __S__ c. Anaerobic training, using free weights, weight machines, and resistance bands, builds muscles and bones.

3. __S__ a. All Siamese cats are domesticated cats.

   __S__ b. All domesticated cats are excellent pets.

   __C__ c. Therefore, all Siamese cats are excellent pets.

B. Political cartoons offer arguments through the use of humor. The cartoonist has a claim to make and uses the situation, actions, and words in the cartoon as supporting details. Study the cartoon reprinted here. Then, write a claim based on the supports in the cartoon.

© 2010 Jeff Parker, Florida Today, and PoliticalCartoons.com <http://PoliticalCartoons.com/>

Answers may vary. See explanation.

_____

_____

_____

_____

_____

_____

EXPLANATIONS

A. Compare your answers to these.

1. In this example the opinion is phrased *particularly dangerous* and then supported with the evidence. Thus (a) is the claim and (b) and (c) are the supports.

2. The use of the word *must* identifies (b) as the claim; the other sentences provide support.

3. The word *therefore* signals the conclusion or claim.

B. Several claims may be suggested by the details in the cartoon. One possible claim is "Gang life leads to death or prison."

PRACTICE 1

A. Read the following groups of ideas. Mark each statement **C** if it is an author's claim or **S** if it provides support for the claim.

1. ___S___ a. As many as 9 million Americans have their identities stolen each year.

___C___ b. Identity theft is a serious crime that affects millions of people each year.

2. ___C___ a. Exposure to media violence causes increases in aggression and violence.

___S___ b. By the time a typical child finishes elementary school, he or she will have seen around 8,000 murders and more than 100,000 other acts of violence on TV.

3. ___S___ a. The use of cell phones while driving contributes to 25% of all traffic crashes.

___C___ b. A federal law should be passed to ban talking on a cell phone while driving.

4. __C__ a. Concealed handguns are not an effective form of self-defense.

__S__ b. A recent study found that someone carrying a gun for self-defense was 4.5 times more likely to be shot during an assault than a victim without a gun.

B. Study the following editorial cartoon. Write a claim based on the details of the cartoon.

CAGLECARTOONS.COM

© 2010 Mike Keefe, The Denver Post, and PoliticalCartoons.com <http://PoliticalCartoons.com/>

Answers may vary. Teacher merit pay is unfair to teachers.

 ## Step 2: Decide Whether the Supports Are Relevant

In Step 1, you learned to identify the author's claim and supports. The next step is to decide whether the supports are relevant to the claim. Remember, a claim, like any main idea, is made up of a topic and a controlling point. Irrelevant supports change the topic or ignore the controlling point. Relevant supports will answer the reporter's questions (*Who? What? When? Where? Why?* and *How?*). Use these questions to decide whether the supports for a claim are relevant.

For example, read the following argument a student makes about her grades. Identify the support that is irrelevant to her claim.

> [1]I deserve a higher grade than the one I received. [2]Even though I have missed some classes, I made sure to get all the lecture notes from classmates. [3]I turned in all my assignments on time, and my test scores average at the A-level. [4]It's not my fault I missed so many classes. [5]My mother became seriously ill, and she is the one who watches my children for me so I can come to school. [6]I also had car problems.

By turning this student's claim into a question, she and her teacher can test her ability to offer valid reasons: "How have I shown I have mastery of the course material?" Sentences 2 and 3 offer relevant examples of her mastery of the course material. However, sentences 4, 5, and 6 state irrelevant supports that shift the focus away from her grade. The argument is about her grade based on an appeal to pity or emotions.

When evaluating an argument, it is important to test each piece of supporting evidence to determine whether it is relevant.

EXAMPLES

A. Read the following lists of claims and supports. Mark each support **R** if it is relevant to the claim or **N** if it is not relevant to the claim.

1. Claim: All police should be equipped with Taser guns.
   Supports:

   _N_ a. Taser guns were developed by two brothers who wanted their mother to own a weapon for self-defense with which she could feel comfortable.

   _R_ b. The Taser gun is a *nonlethal* stun gun that disables suspects for five seconds by shooting them with 50,000 volts of electricity.

   _N_ c. Human rights activists warn that Taser guns can be abused as instruments of torture, especially since they leave no significant or enduring mark on the skin.

   _R_ d. Police officers in Miami, Florida, and Seattle, Washington, have had no incidents or sharply lower incidents of fatal police shootings since they began using Taser guns.

   _R_ e. The electrical shock caused by Taser guns has no long-term negative effect.

B. Argument is also used in advertisements. It is important for you to be able to understand the points and supports of ads. Many times advertisers appeal to emotions, make false claims, or give supports that are not relevant because their main aim is to persuade you to buy their product. Study the following mock advertisement for Cabre, a fictitious brand of red wine. Mark each of the statements **R** if it is relevant to the claim or **N** if it is not relevant to the claim.

◄ Cabre! To a happy and long life.
Recent research suggests that one glass of red wine daily may do more than reduce the risk of high levels of cholesterol. The grape skin and seeds appear to hold a natural cancer-fighting chemical.*

*Research conducted on animals only.

  2. Claim: Moderate consumption of red wine may have some health benefits.
     Supports:

      __N__   a. A beautiful woman drinks red wine.

      __R__   b. Red wine may reduce the risk of high levels of cholesterol.

      __R__   c. The grape skin and seeds appear to hold a natural cancer-fighting chemical.

      __N__   d. The woman is happy.

      __N__   e. Research conducted on animals only.

EXPLANATIONS

A.   **1.** Items *b*, *d*, and *e* are relevant to the claim. Items *a* and *c* are not relevant. The reason the Taser guns were created is not important to their use by police officers; and a warning about the possibility of Taser guns being used as instruments of torture is not the issue.

B.   **2.** Items *a*, *d*, and *e* are not relevant to the claim that moderate consumption of red wine may have some health benefits. Advertisers often use beautiful models who appear to be pleased with the product, but neither beauty nor personal preference of the model is relevant to health issues. Items *b* and *c* are relevant to the claim. However, interestingly, the smallest line of print in this mock advertisement discloses that the research only involved animals. Thus the "research" is not relevant to the claim. In fact, the disclaimer could lead a reasonable reader to discard all of the supports as not relevant.

PRACTICE 2

A. Read the following lists of claims and supports. Mark each support **R** if it is relevant to the claim or **N** if it is not relevant to the claim.

1. Claim: The need for organ and tissue donors is critical.
   Supports:

   ___R___   a. According to the Organ Procurement and Transplantation Network (OPTN), as of November 13, 2007, over 92,000 people were on a waiting list for an organ transplant.

   ___R___   b. According to the OPTN, only 19,249 transplants took place between January and August of 2007.

   ___R___   c. Each day 19 people on the waiting list die.

   ___R___   d. The organs needed for transplant include heart, kidneys, pancreas, lungs, liver, and intestines; the tissues needed are cornea, skin, bone marrow, heart valves, and connective tissue.

   ___N___   e. To become an organ donor, fill out and carry a donor card, indicate your intent to donate on your driver's license, and tell your family about your decision.

   —Adapted from "Organ Donation," *FirstGov*. 13 Nov. 2007
   http://www.organdonor.gov

2. Claim: Binge drinking is dangerous and irresponsible.
   Supports:

   ___R___   a. Binge drinking is commonly defined as drinking large quantities of alcohol in a short period of time: 5 drinks in a row for men; 4 drinks in a row for women.

_____N_____ b. Many young people do not think it is important to have alcohol at a party.

_____N_____ c. Eating a large meal before drinking slows down the effect of the alcohol.

_____R_____ d. The intent and purpose of binge drinking is to become intoxicated and to lose control.

_____R_____ e. Binge drinking is linked to vandalism, confrontations with police, injuries, alcohol poisoning, and death.

3. Claim: If expressions of religion are allowed in national government institutions, then prayer should be allowed in public schools.

Supports:

_____N_____ a. Banning prayer in public schools leads to moral decline.

_____R_____ b. Congress prays at the opening of each session.

_____R_____ c. Federal officials, including the President of the United States, take their oaths of office upon a Bible.

_____R_____ d. Moses and the Ten Commandments are prominently displayed in the Supreme Court building.

_____N_____ e. A majority of Americans favor prayer in schools.

4. Claim: Volunteers perform many selfless acts.

Supports:

_____R_____ a. Volunteers promote worthwhile causes and improve the lives of others.

_____N_____ b. Volunteers boost their own sense of self-worth and well-being.

_____R_____ c. Volunteers conserve funds for charities, nonprofits, and other community organizations by contributing their time.

_____R_____ d. They share their skills and expertise.

_____N_____ e. Volunteers improve their reputations and promote their careers.

B. Study the public service poster sponsored by the White House Office of National Drug Control Policy on the following page. Read the claim, and then mark each support **R** if it is relevant to the claim or **N** if it is not relevant to the claim.

Claim: Steer Clear of Pot.

Supports:

___N___ a. Stoners laugh a lot, eat junk food, and don't bug anyone.

___R___ b. It's dangerous to drive stoned.

___R___ c. An estimated 38,000 high school seniors in the United States reported in 2001 that they had crashed while driving under the influence of marijuana.

___N___ d. Everyone smokes pot.

___R___ e. Research shows that smoking weed affects a driver's perception, coordination, and reaction time.

—United States Executive Office of the President. "Steer Clear of Pot." The White House Office of National Drug Control Policy. Free Resources. 13 Nov. 2007. http://www.freevibe.com/Drug_Facts/free-resources.asp

Now that you have practiced identifying relevant supports in a list format, you are ready to isolate relevant supports in reading passages. In a passage, the thesis statement states the author's claim. Each of the supporting details must be evaluated as relevant or irrelevant supports for the thesis statement.

EXAMPLE Read the following passage.

Shell Eggs from Farm to Table

[1]Eggs are among the most nutritious foods on earth and can be part of a healthy diet; however, they are perishable just like raw meat, poultry, and fish. [2]Unbroken, clean, fresh shell eggs may contain *Salmonella enteritidis* (SE) bacteria that can cause foodborne illness. [3]While the number of eggs affected is quite small, several cases of foodborne illness have surfaced in the last few years. [4]To be safe, eggs must be properly handled and cooked.

[5]Bacteria can be present on the exterior of a shell egg because the egg exits the hen's body through the same passageway as feces is excreted; thus, eggs are washed and sanitized at the processing plant. [6]Bacteria can be present inside an uncracked, whole egg. [7]This interior contamination may be due to bacteria within the hen's ovary or oviduct before the shell forms around the yolk and white. [8]*Salmonella enteritidis* doesn't make the hen sick. [9]It is also possible for eggs to become infected by *Salmonella enteritidis* fecal contamination through the pores of the shells after they have been laid.

[10]Researchers say that, if present, the *Salmonella enteritidis* is usually in the yolk or yellow; however, experts cannot rule out the bacteria's presence in egg whites. [11]As a result, everyone is advised against ingesting raw or undercooked egg yolks and whites or products containing raw or undercooked eggs.

—Adapted from "Egg Products Preparation," Food Safety
and Inspection Service, U.S. Department of Agriculture,
7 March 2007. 4 May 2008. http://www.fsis.usda.gov/
Fact_sheets/Focus_on_shell_Eggs/index.asp

1. Underline the thesis statement (the sentence that states the author's claim).

_____d_____ **2.** Which sentence is *not* relevant to the author's point?
   a. sentence 2   c. sentence 3
   b. sentence 6   d. sentence 8

EXPLANATION

1. Sentence 4 is the central idea and states the author's claim.

2. The sentence that is *not* relevant to the author's point is *d*, sentence 8. The author's claim focuses on the health risks associated with eggs, not with the health of the hens laying the eggs.

PRACTICE 3

Read the following passages, and respond to the two questions following each of them.

The Street Outreach Program

[1]Today, in communities across the country, some young people are living on the streets, running from or being asked to leave homes characterized by abuse, neglect, or parental drug or alcohol abuse. [2]Once on the streets, such youth are at risk of being sexually exploited or abused by adults for pleasure or profit.

[3]To prevent the sexual abuse or exploitation of these young people by providing them with services that help them leave the streets, Congress established the Education and Prevention Services to Reduce Sexual Abuse of Runaway, Homeless, and Street Youth Program, through the Violence Against Women Act of the Violent Crime Control and Law Enforcement Act of 1994. [4]That program created Grants for the Prevention of Sexual Abuse and Exploitation (also known as the Street Outreach Program). [5]Naturally, not all at-risk youth can be reached through this program.

[6]The Street Outreach Program offers many services including the following: street-based education and outreach, access to emergency shelter, survival aid, individual assessments, treatment and counseling, prevention and education activities, information and referrals, crisis intervention, and follow-up support.

[7]The Education and Prevention Services to Reduce Sexual Abuse of Runaway, Homeless, and Street Youth Program should be supported with increased funding.

—Excerpted from "Family and Youth Services Bureau Street Outreach Program," Administration for Children and Families, 13 Nov. 2007 http://www.acf.hhs.gov/programs/fysb/streetout.htm

1. Underline the thesis statement (the sentence that states the author's claim).

<u>c</u> 2. Which sentence is *not* relevant to the author's point?

a. sentence 3	c. sentence 5
b. sentence 4	d. sentence 6

Preventing Identity Theft Is Your Responsibility!

[1]As with any crime, you can't guarantee that you will never be a victim, but you can take responsibility to minimize your risk. [2]To protect yourself against identity theft, you should take the following steps.

[3]First, don't give out personal information on the phone, through the mail, or over the Internet unless you've initiated the contact or are sure you know whom you're dealing with. [4]Identity thieves may pose as representatives of banks, Internet service providers (ISPs) and even government agencies to get you to reveal your SSN, mother's maiden name, account numbers, and other identifying information.

[5]Second, secure personal information in your home, especially if you have roommates, employ outside help, or are having service work done in your home. [6]Don't carry your SSN card; leave it in a secure place.

[7]Third, guard your mail and trash from theft. [8]Deposit outgoing mail in post office collection boxes or at your local post office rather than in an unsecured mailbox. [9]Promptly remove mail from your mailbox. [10]If you're planning to be away from home and can't pick up your mail, call the U.S. Postal Service to request a vacation hold. [11]You can have the amount of junk mail delivered to your home reduced by contacting Mail Preference Service, PO Box 643, Carmel, NY 10512.

[12]Finally, to thwart an identity thief who may pick through your trash or recycling bins to capture your personal information, tear or shred your charge receipts, copies of credit applications, insurance forms, physician statements, checks and bank statements, expired charge cards that you're discarding, and credit offers you get in the mail.

> —Adapted from "Protecting Against Identity Theft," Federal
> Trade Commission, 2003. 13 Nov. 2007 http://www
> .consumer.gov/idtheft/protect_againstidt.html#5

3. Underline the thesis statement (the sentence that states the author's claim).

_____d_____ **4.** Which sentence is *not* relevant to the author's point?

a. sentence 8   c. sentence 10

b. sentence 9   d. sentence 11

Step 3: Decide Whether the Supports Are Adequate

In Step 1 you learned to identify the author's claim and supports. In Step 2 you learned to make sure the supports are relevant. In Step 3 you must decide whether the supports are adequate. A valid argument is based not only on a claim and relevant support but also on the amount and quality of the support given. That is, supports must give enough evidence for the author's claim to be convincing. Just as you used the reporter's questions to decide whether supports are relevant, you can use them to test whether supports are adequate. Supporting details fully explain the author's controlling point about a topic. Remember, those questions are *Who? What? When? Where? Why?* and *How?*

For example, you may argue, "A low-carbohydrate diet is a more healthful diet. I feel much better since I stopped eating so much bread and pasta." However, the reporter's question "Why?" reveals that the support is inadequate. The answer to "Why is a low-carbohydrate diet a more healthful diet?" should include expert opinions and facts, not just personal opinion. Often in the quest to support a claim, people oversimplify their reasons. Thus, they do not offer enough information to prove the claim. Instead of logical details, they may offer false causes, false comparisons, forced choices, or leave out facts that hurt the claim. You will learn more about inadequate argument in Chapter 13.

In Chapter 11, you studied how to avoid invalid conclusions and make valid inferences (see pages 462–463). The same thinking steps you use to make valid inferences help you identify valid claims: consider the facts, don't infer anything that is not there, and make sure nothing contradicts your conclusion.

EXAMPLE Read the list of supports.

- Increasing levels of greenhouse gases like carbon dioxide (CO_2) in the atmosphere since pre-industrial times are well documented and understood.

- The atmospheric buildup of CO_2 and other greenhouse gases is largely the result of human activities such as the burning of fossil fuels.

- An "unequivocal" warming trend of about 1.0 to 1.7°F occurred from 1906–2005. Warming occurred in both the Northern and Southern Hemispheres, and over the oceans.

- The major greenhouse gases emitted by human activities remain in the atmosphere for periods ranging from decades to centuries. It is therefore virtually certain that atmospheric concentrations of greenhouse gases will continue to rise over the next few decades.

- Increasing greenhouse gas concentrations tend to warm the planet.

—U.S. Environmental Protection Agency. "Climate Change: Science: State of Knowledge." 28 Sept. 2009. http://epa.gov/ climatechange/science/stateofknowledge.html

Write **V** for valid by the claim that is adequately supported by the evidence.

_____ a. The earth's surface temperature is going to rise at least 1 degree Fahrenheit in the next century.

___V___ b. Human activities have changed the global climate and may lead to wide-ranging negative effects on humans, animals, and ecosystems.

_____ c. Coastal regions will be covered with water because of global warming and melting polar regions.

_____ d. Big oil companies such as Amoco, Marathon Oil, and Phillips Petroleum are responsible for global warming.

EXPLANATION Choices (a) and (c) jump to conclusions about the future effects of global warming, and choice (d) uses the evidence to jump to conclusions about the role of big oil companies in the cause of global warming. More evidence is needed to support any one of those claims. The only logical conclusion based on the evidence is (b).

PRACTICE 4

A. Read the list of supports taken from an article about using corn as an alternative energy. Then, write **V** next to the claim that is adequately supported by the evidence.

- Dwindling foreign oil, rising prices at the gas pump, and hype from politically well-connected U.S. agribusiness have combined to create a frenzied rush to convert food grains into ethanol fuel.

- Using corn or any other biomass for ethanol requires huge regions of fertile land, plus massive amounts of water and sunlight to maximize crop production.

- If the entire national corn crop were used to make ethanol, it would replace a mere 7% of U.S. oil consumption—far from making the U.S. independent of foreign oil.

- The environmental impacts of corn ethanol production include severe soil erosion of valuable food cropland; the heavy use of nitrogen fertilizers and pesticides that pollute rivers; and the required use of fossil fuels, releasing large quantities of carbon dioxide into the atmosphere, adding to global warming.

- More than 40 percent of the energy contained in one gallon of corn ethanol is expended to produce it, and that expended energy to make ethanol comes mostly from highly valuable oil and natural gas.

- Growing crops for fuel squanders land, water, and energy vital for human food production.

> —Pimentel, David. "Corn Can't Save Us: Debunking the Biofuel Myth." *Kennebec Journal.* 28 March 2008. http://www.kjonline.com/archive/corn-can_t-save-us-debunking-the-biofuel-myth.html?searchterm=biofuel+myt.

_____ a. Ethanol made from corn and other biomasses is an acceptable alternative energy form.

_____ b. The United States is too dependent on foreign oil.

_____ c. Fuels made from biomasses can reduce the United States's dependency on foreign oil.

___V___ d. The use of corn and other biofuels to solve our energy problem is an ethically, economically, and environmentally unworkable sham.

B. Study the following graph. Then, write **V** by the claim that is adequately supported by the evidence in the graph.

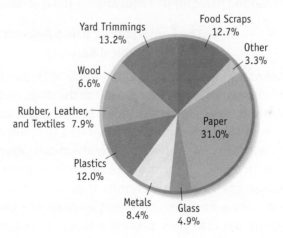

Total MSW Generation (by material), 2008
250 Million Tons (before recycling)

Food Scraps 12.7%
Yard Trimmings 13.2%
Other 3.3%
Wood 6.6%
Rubber, Leather, and Textiles 7.9%
Paper 31.0%
Plastics 12.0%
Metals 8.4%
Glass 4.9%

> —U. S. Environmental Protection Agency. *Municipal Solid Waste Generation, Recycling, and Disposal in the United States: Facts and Figures for 2008.* http://www.epa.gov/osw/nonhaz/municipal/pubs/msw2008rpt.pdf

_____ a. The United States government has ineffective policies for recycling.

_____ b. The people of the United States generate too much trash.

_____ c. The United States needs more landfills.

___V___ d. Recycling organic material will make the largest impact on waste management.

Step 4: Check the Argument for Bias

In Step 1, you learned to identify the author's claim and supports. In Step 2, you learned to make sure the supports are relevant to the claim. In Step 3, you learned to avoid false inferences and identify valid claims based on adequate supports. Again, the skills you use to make sound inferences help you determine whether an argument is valid. In Step 4, you must also check for the author's bias for or against the topic. Authors may use emotionally slanted language or biased words to present either a favorable or negative view of the topic under debate. In addition, authors may include only the details that favor the stances they have taken. A valid argument relies on objective, factual details. As you evaluate the argument for the author's bias, ask the following questions:

- Does the author provide mostly positive or negative supports?
- Does the author provide mostly factual details or rely on biased language?
- Does the writer include or omit opposing views?

EXAMPLE Read the paragraph. Then, answer the questions.

The Immorality of Using Animals in Medical Research

[1]Animals should not be used in medical research. [2]The lives of hundreds of thousands of mice, rabbits, birds, dogs, cats, horses, and pigs, among others, have been sacrificed in the quest to save human lives. [3]Hundreds of thousands more have suffered the pain and distress of being infected with diseases, blinded with chemicals, electrically shocked, or injected with drugs, all for the sake of improving the longevity and quality of human life. [4]The basic premise that humans are superior life forms falls short when one considers that animals are used in these horrific experiments because they possess enough physiological similarities to humans to make the research findings worthwhile for humans. [5]For example, much of what is known about the human immune system came from studies with mice, and understandings about the human cardiovascular system came from studies with dogs. [6]Even if humans believe themselves more worthy because they are self-aware creatures capable of reasoning, able to establish complex social orders, and gifted with written language, humans prove themselves to be mere animals when they inflict pain upon defenseless fellow creatures for personal gain, in an instinctive grapple

for "survival of the fittest." [7]Non-human animals are sentient beings, capable of intense suffering. [8]This fact alone makes the cost they pay too high—and human morals too low.

_a_ **1.** Overall, the passage relies on
    a. factual details.   b. emotionally slanted language.

_b_ **2.** Which of the following sentences includes an opposing view?
    a. sentence 5   c. sentence 7
    b. sentence 6   d. sentence 8

_c_ **3.** In this passage, the author expressed a biased attitude
    a. in favor of using animals in medical research.
    b. in favor of finding alternatives to using animals in medical research.
    c. against the belief that humans are a superior life form.
    d. against the belief that animals are capable of suffering.

EXPLANATION

1. Although the author uses emotionally slanted words occasionally, overall, the passage relies on (a) factual details that can be verified through research. Some of the biased words are *should not, sacrificed, horrific, mere, defenseless,* and *grapple.*

2. (b) Sentence 6 refers to the opposing view that humans are superior to other animals and thus their lives are more worthy of saving. The sentence even lists a few of the reasons the opposition holds this belief.

3. In this passage, the author expresses a bias (c) against the belief that humans are a superior life form by emphasizing the human willingness to inflict pain and suffering on other creatures.

PRACTICE 5

Read the paragraph. Then, answer the questions.

School Uniforms Benefit Students

[1]School uniforms should be mandatory in all public schools. [2]Uniforms promote school spirit and school values by establishing a group identity and making students feel as if they are part of a team. [3]School uniforms promote modesty and eliminate the distraction of sexually provocative

clothing. [4]They contribute to the sense that school is a place of order and work, as well as foster a respect for authority. [5]In such an environment, students are likely to approach learning more seriously. [6]School uniforms also minimize cliques based on socioeconomic differences; they increase attendance and reduce dropout rates. [7]In addition, school uniforms increase student safety in several ways. [8]Gang- and drug-related activity decline; students are less likely to bring weapons to school undetected; and teachers and administrators are more able to distinguish their students from outsiders. [9]For those who cannot afford uniforms or oppose uniforms on the basis of legitimate religious or philosophical beliefs, an "opt-out" policy should be in place so that students with the support of their families can apply for exemptions.

_____a_____ **1.** Overall, the passage offers supports that are
   a. mainly positive.
   b. mainly negative.

_____d_____ **2.** Which of the following sentences refers to an opposing view?
   a. sentence 6   c. sentence 8
   b. sentence 7   d. sentence 9

_____d_____ **3.** In this passage, the author expressed a biased attitude
   a. in favor of individual competition.
   b. in favor of freedom of expression.
   c. against the "opt-out" policy.
   d. against cliques based on socioeconomic differences.

Reading a Textbook: The Logic of Argument

Textbook Skills

Most of the subjects you will study in college rely on research by experts, and these experts may have differing views on the same topic. Often textbooks spell out these arguments. Sometimes textbook authors will present several experts' views. But occasionally, only one view will be given. In this case, be aware that there may be other sides to the story.

Textbook arguments are usually well developed with supports that are relevant and adequate. These supports may be studies, surveys, expert opinions, experiments, theories, examples, or reasons. Textbooks may also offer graphs, charts, and photos as supports. A master reader tests passages in textbooks for the logic of the arguments they present. The exercise that follows is designed to give you practice evaluating the logic of arguments in textbooks.

PRACTICE 6

Read the following passage from a college communications textbook and study the *Cathy* cartoon that accompanies it. Mark each statement in the passage **C** if it is an author's claim or **S** if it provides support for a claim. Then, write a sentence that states a logical conclusion that can be drawn from the *Cathy* cartoon about interpersonal communication.

Textbook Skills

Interpersonal Communication Involves Content and Relationship Messages

1Many conflicts arise because people misunderstand relationship messages and cannot clarify them. **2**Other problems arise when people fail to see the difference between content messages and relationship messages. **3**A good example occurred when my mother came to stay for a week at a summer place I had. **4**On the first day she swept the kitchen floor six times. **5**I had repeatedly told her that it did not need sweeping, that I would be tracking in dirt and mud from the outside. **6**She persisted in sweeping, however, saying that the floor was dirty. **7**On the content level, we were talking about the value of sweeping the kitchen floor. **8**On the relationship level, however, we were talking about something quite different. **9**We were each saying, "This is my house." **10**When I realized this, I stopped complaining about the relative usefulness of sweeping a floor that did not need sweeping. **11**Not surprisingly, she stopped sweeping.

Ignoring Relationship Considerations

12Examine the following interchange and note how relationship considerations are ignored:

Messages	*Comments*
13PAUL: I'm going bowling tomorrow. The guys at the plant are starting a team.	**14**He focuses on the content and ignores any relationship implications of the message.
15JUDY: Why can't we ever do anything together?	**16**She responds primarily on a relationship level and ignores the content implications of the message, and expresses her displeasure at being ignored in his decision.
17PAUL: We can do something together any time; tomorrow's the day they're organizing the team.	**18**Again, he focuses almost exclusively on the content.

[19]This example reflects research findings that show that men focus more on content messages; women focus more on relationship messages. [20]Once you recognize this gender difference, you can increase your sensitivity to the opposite sex.

—Text and cartoon from *Messages: Building Interpersonal Communication Skills*, 4th ed., p. 21. by Joseph A. DeVito. Copyright © 1999 by Pearson Education, Inc. Reproduced by permission of Pearson Education, Inc., Boston, MA.

—Cathy © 1992 Cathy Guisewite. Reprinted with permission of Universal Press Syndicate. All rights reserved.

____C____ **1.** sentence 1   ____C____ **8.** sentence 8   ____S____ **15.** sentence 15

____C____ **2.** sentence 2   ____C____ **9.** sentence 9   ____C____ **16.** sentence 16

____S____ **3.** sentence 3   ____S____ **10.** sentence 10   ____S____ **17.** sentence 17

____S____ **4.** sentence 4   ____S____ **11.** sentence 11   ____C____ **18.** sentence 18

____S____ **5.** sentence 5   ____S____ **12.** sentence 12   ____C____ **19.** sentence 19

____S____ **6.** sentence 6   ____S____ **13.** sentence 13   ____C____ **20.** sentence 20

____C____ **7.** sentence 7   ____C____ **14.** sentence 14

Men focus on content messages; women focus on relationship messages.

Note: Sentences 13, 15, and 17 are examples of interpersonal communication; sentences 14, 16, and 18 are the textbook author's claims about the meanings (the interpretations) of each example.

APPLICATIONS

Application 1: Argument—Author's Claim and Supports

A. Read the following groups of ideas. Mark each statement as **C** if it's an author's claim or **S** if it provides support for the claim.

_S_ a. Zoo staffers design activities that will occupy and challenge animals such as placing their food in stumps and forcing the animal to work to gain food.

_S_ b. Animals housed in large zoos also receive high-quality veterinary care.

_C_ c. Large American zoos today are concerned with the welfare of the animals in their exhibits.

_S_ d. Today, animals are housed in large, spacious natural settings that try to recreate the animal's habitat of origin.

_S_ e. In addition, zoo staffers work to provide opportunities for animals to fulfill natural functions, such as roaming and foraging.

B. Study the cartoon by Mike Lester from the *Rome News Tribune*. Then, write a sentence that states a claim or conclusion that can be asserted based on the details in the cartoon. Answers may vary.

© 2010 Mike Lester/Cagle Cartoons

Claim: _Trans fats have become forbidden, yet people still_

want food with trans fat.

Application 2: Argument: Relevant Supports and Author's Bias

Read the following editorial by Pamela G. Bailey, president and CEO of the Grocery Manufacturers Association, published in *USA Today*. Then, answer the questions.

Opposing View: Don't Blame Us

[1]As a mother of five, I know how hard it is to ensure kids are leading a healthy lifestyle. [2]Working parents have less time to prepare meals. [3]Schools are reducing PE. [4]The Internet and other distractions limit active playtime. [5]More spread out communities mean more driving and less walking and biking.

[6]All this contributes to the childhood obesity epidemic. [7]It will take robust solutions to address the crisis. [8]That's why it's so encouraging that first lady Michelle Obama's Let's Move initiative focuses on positive steps we all can take, rather than assigning blame.

[9]We recognize our role in fighting obesity. [10]In the past few years, we've changed more than 10,000 recipes to reduce calories, fat, sugar and salt and increase whole grains, fiber and other nutrients. [11]In recent weeks, we've seen announcements of sweeping reductions in salt and sugar and other healthy improvements.

[12]These measures will make a difference because they give parents choices that fit their lives—foods that are healthy, as well as convenient, tasty and affordable. [13]These recipe changes aren't the result of a government mandate. [14]They are the result of hundreds of millions of dollars in R&D and market research. [15]It is about businesses responding to consumers' changing preferences.

[16]A similar responsiveness is leading to marketing changes. [17]Today, the majority of advertising during children's programming showcases active lifestyles and healthy choices such as 100% fruit juices. [18]Labels are improving to provide consumers with clear and useful nutrition information. [19]And we are working with Congress and the White House to strengthen a law that would set science-based nutrition standards for foods in schools.

[20]America's food companies will keep making our products healthier, our marketing more responsible and our labeling more informative. [21]And in partnership with government and with consumers, we are committed to winning the battle over the childhood obesity crisis in our lifetimes.

—"Opposing View: Don't Blame Us" by Pamela G. Bailey from USA TODAY, March 31, 2010. Reprinted by permission of USA Today.

1. Underline the thesis statement that states the author's claim.

_____a_____ **2.** Which sentence is not relevant to the author's point?
   a. sentence 1   c. sentence 8
   b. sentence 3   d. sentence 15

_____c_____ **3.** In this article, the author expresses a biased attitude in favor of
   a. physical education classes in public schools.
   b. government mandates to monitor the grocery business.
   c. the efforts of the grocery business to address childhood obesity.
   d. assigning blame for childhood obesity.

Application 3: Argument: Adequate Supports

Study the graphic, which was published in *USA Today*. Then, choose the conclusion that is **not** adequately supported by evidence. (Indicate your choice with a check (✓) in the blank.)

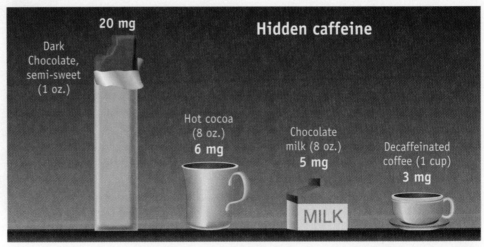

—"Hidden Caffeine" by Ying Lou and Gia Kereselidze from USA TODAY,
March 3, 2004. Reprinted by permission of USA Today.

_____ a. Caffeine is found in coffee, chocolate, and cocoa.

_____ b. Among the sources of caffeine that are compared, dark chocolate and semi-sweet chocolate contain the highest levels of caffeine per ounce.

✔ c. The public prefers candy bars over cocoa, chocolate milk, or decaffeinated coffee.

_____ d. Decaffeinated coffee contains some caffeine.

REVIEW TEST 1

Score (number correct) _____ × 10 = _____ %

Argument

A. Study the following mock advertisement. Then, study the claim and supports based on it. Mark each support **R** if it is relevant to the claim or **N** if it is not relevant to the claim. Then, answer the questions.

JUST SAY, "NO THANKS!"

- In 1999, 61% of adults in the United States were overweight or obese.

- Approximately 300,000 deaths each year in the United States may be attributable to obesity.

- Overweight and obesity are associated with heart disease, certain types of cancer, type 2 diabetes, stroke, arthritis, breathing problems, and psychological disorders, such as depression.

- Choose a diet that is low in saturated fat and cholesterol and moderate in total fat.

- Exercise three times a week for 30 minutes.

—Data from "Fact Sheet: What You Can Do," Overweight and Obesity. United States Office of the Surgeon General, 11 Jan. 07. 4 May 08. http://www.surgeongeneral.gov/topics/obesity/calltoaction/fact_whatcanyoudo.htm

Claim: The health risks associated with obesity can be reduced by diet choices.
Supports:

N **1.** In 1999, 61% of adults in the United States were overweight or obese.

R **2.** A meal consisting of a cheeseburger, French fries, and soda is high in saturated fat, total fat, and cholesterol.

_____R_____ **3.** Overweight and obesity are associated with heart disease, certain types of cancer, type 2 diabetes, stroke, arthritis, breathing problems, and psychological disorders, such as depression.

_____N_____ **4.** Exercise helps reduce obesity.

_____a_____ **5.** Overall, the relevant supports are
   a. statements of factual details.
   b. statements using biased language.

B. Read the following group of ideas from a government website. Mark each statement **C** if it is an author's claim or **S** if it provides support for the claim.

_____S_____ **6.** One small chocolate chip cookie (50 calories) is equivalent to walking briskly for 10 minutes.

_____S_____ **7.** The difference between a large gourmet chocolate chip cookie and a small chocolate chip cookie could be about 40 minutes of raking leaves (200 calories).

_____S_____ **8.** One hour of walking at a moderate pace (20 min/mile) uses about the same amount of energy that is in one jelly-filled doughnut (300 calories).

_____S_____ **9.** A fast-food "meal" containing a double-patty cheeseburger, extra-large fries, and a 24 oz. soft drink is equal to running $2^1/_2$ hours at a 10 min/mile pace (1,500 calories).

_____C_____ **10.** Food intake should be balanced with activity.

"Overweight and Obesity: What You Can Do," United States Office of the Surgeon General, 11 Jan. 07. 3 May 2008 http://www.surgeongeneral.gov/topics/obesity/calltoaction/fact_whatcanyoudo.htm

REVIEW TEST 2

Score (number correct) _____ × 20 = _____ %

Argument

Read the following passage, and then, answer the questions.

12.8 GE/286 words **Study Examines Spanking Among Minnesota Parents**

[1]Parents can effectively replace physical punishment with different methods of discipline. [2]When parents use nurturing and teaching methods

instead of spanking, their children become less aggressive and violent. [3]Those are the findings of an 8-year study led by the University of Minnesota's Extension Service in Goodhue County. [4]Researchers followed 1,000 parents of children younger than 13 to learn about their attitudes toward spanking.

[5]"If you hit your children, it will be very difficult to teach them not to hit others because they have experienced it from the most important person in their lives," said retired sociologist Ron Pitzer, who led the study. [6]During the study, a public awareness and educational campaign called "Kids: Handle with Care" sent the message to Goodhue County residents that it is never okay to spank a child. [7]The message was circulated through newspaper articles, radio programs, restaurant table tent cards, grocery bags and carts, church programs, parade floats, and a county fair exhibit.

[8]The following results were reported among Goodhue County parents at the conclusion of the study:

- [9]The use of physical punishment dropped from 36 percent to 12 percent.
- [10]Parents who spanked their children reported a sizeable increase in their children's aggressiveness.
- [11]Parents who reduced physical punishment reported their children were less aggressive.
- [12]Parents who attended classes were better at setting limits and enforcing consequences, and they were more calm and nurturing. [13]Their children were more obedient, communicated more openly, had a better attitude, and were calmer.
- [14]Fathers matched or exceeded mothers in alternative, more positive discipline methods.

[15]The findings indicate that the county-wide educational effort was successful in helping make the decision to eliminate spanking, resulting in happier parents and happier children.

> —Adapted from "Study Examines Spanking Among Minnesota Parents," Children's Bureau Express, U.S. Department of Human and Health Services, Apr. 2002. 3 May 2008 http://cbexpress.acf.hhs.gov/printer_friendly.cfm?issue_id=2002-04&prt_iss=1

_____a____ **1.** Which sentence states the author's claim?

    a. sentence 1   c. sentence 4

    b. sentence 3   d. sentence 5

Mark each of the following sentences (**2–5**) **C** if it is a claim or **S** if it provides support for the claim.

___C___ **2.** sentence 5

___S___ **3.** sentence 6

___S___ **4.** sentence 7

___b___ **5.** In this passage, the author expresses a biased attitude
   a. in favor of spanking children as a form of punishment.
   b. against the use of physical punishment as a form of discipline.

VISUAL VOCABULARY

An antonym for the word

nurturing is ___a_____.

   a. disengaged.
   b. involved.
   c. needed.

▶ A father who is nurturing has a positive impact on his child's development.

REVIEW TEST 3

Score (number correct) _____ × 10 = _____ %

Argument

Before Reading: Skim the following editorial published by *USA Today*. Answer the Before Reading questions that follow the passage. Then, read the passage. Next, answer the After Reading questions. Use the discussion and writing topics as activities to do after reading.

10.8 GE/535 words   **Our View on Obesity: Hooked on Junk Food**

¹"Betcha can't eat just one" may be a Frito-Lay marketing slogan for potato chips, but, as any dieter can tell you, most junk food creates addict-like behavior—and not just in adults.

²Nearly a third of children are overweight or obese, triggering a backlash—most recently Michelle Obama's Let's Move initiative to make kids eat better and exercise.

Vocabulary Preview

deter (19): discourage, prevent

akin (21): similar, related

applicably (22): relevant, connected, affecting

enticing (29): tempting, inviting

[3]But it's unlikely that Obama's effort—or any child-specific approach—will succeed by itself. [4]The food industry has just gotten too good at doing what businesses are supposed to do: give customers what they want. [5]Years of research and sales results have taught it that layering fat, sugar and salt into foods will give consumers the ultimate taste sensation. [6]All three trigger such a pleasurable response in the brain that people will keep eating even after they're stuffed. [7]Better yet for sales, the brain then remembers that enjoyable sensation, launching a pattern of craving and overeating that becomes an **entrenched**—and health-toxic—habit.

[8]This cycle, and the way it evolved, was documented a year ago by David Kessler, a former commissioner of the Food and Drug Administration and former dean of Yale's medical school, in his ground-breaking book *The End of Overeating*.

[9]While Kessler avoids using the word "addiction," a new study, published in *Nature Neuroscience*, demonstrates it's exactly the kind of behavior that continual access to junk food causes. [10]While rats that had occasional access to junk food could resist eating if electroshocks were administered, rats that had constant access kept eating even while being electrocuted. [11]Does that sound like anyone you know?

[12]If there's anything American culture offers, it's continuous access to junk food. [13]The latest entry: Wendy's Baconator Triple burger, weighing in at a whopping 1330 calories. [14]Add supersized portions and supermarkets crammed with fatty, processed foods lacking nutritional value, and you have a problem. [15]Eating never stops. [16]The average child consumes nearly three snacks a day.

[17]The first lady's proposals can help at the edges. [18]Increased activity burns off calories, while healthier school lunches could reduce calories consumed. [19]More prominent calorie labeling might **deter** some people. [20]But those messages will still be competing with more potent signals from the brain.

[21]Kessler's solution, like Obama's, is to induce a broad-based shift in social attitudes, **akin** to the one that has cut smoking in half. [22]That evolution has had many drivers: warning labels, taxes (which had a particular impact on teens), public education and, less **applicably**, lawsuits and bans. [23]But everyone agrees when the tide turned. [24]As evidence of smoking's health effects became undeniable, the first surgeon general's warning was ordered onto cigarette packs in 1965. [25]Odd as it may seem now, the move set off an uproar.

²⁶The push for healthier food has not attained the same critical mass, but the trend is strikingly similar to the early '60s. ²⁷Evidence linking obesity to illnesses is mounting, and an industry's attempt to induce addictive behavior is being dragged into public view. ²⁸Now Obama's move has brought the White House into the picture. ²⁹Given all the **enticing** bait that's so scientifically laid before us, the tide had better shift toward healthier food soon. ³⁰In a sense, we're all lab rats—only the shock treatment is missing.

—"Our View on Obesity: Hooked on Junk Food." from USA TODAY, March 31, 2010. Reprinted by permission of USA Today.

Before Reading

Vocabulary in Context

_____c_____ **1.** Based on the context of the passage, what is the best meaning of the word **entrenched** (sentence 7)?
  a. flexible
  b. positive
  c. fixed
  d. negative

Tone and Purpose

_____b_____ **2.** The overall tone of the passage is
  a. objective.
  b. biased.

_____c_____ **3.** The primary purpose of the passage is to
  a. inform.
  b. entertain.
  c. persuade.

After Reading

Central Idea and Main Idea

_____d_____ **4.** Which sentence best states the implied central idea of the passage?
  a. Childhood obesity cannot be overcome.
  b. Americans are hooked on junk food.
  c. The food industry, like the tobacco industry did with cigarettes, has made money by getting consumers addicted to junk food.
  d. The continuous access to junk food has caused an addiction to junk food that will require a broad-based shift in social attitudes to overcome childhood obesity.

Supporting Details

___a___ **5.** In the sixth paragraph (sentences 12–16), sentence 15 states a
a. main idea.
b. major supporting detail.
c. minor supporting detail.

Transitions

___c___ **6.** The relationship within sentence 21 is
a. time order.
b. listing.
c. comparison.
d. cause and effect.

Thought Patterns

___d___ **7.** The overall thought pattern of the passage is
a. time order.   c. comparison.
b. listing.   d. cause and effect.

Fact and Opinion

___b___ **8.** Sentence 3 is a statement of
a. fact.   c. fact and opinion.
b. opinion.

Inferences

___a___ **9.** Based on the information in the passage, the reader can infer that
a. many Americans are addicted to junk food.
b. people choose to be obese.
c. electroshock treatment may be a useful tool to fight childhood obesity.
d. Michelle Obama's Let's Move initiative will have a profound impact on reducing childhood obesity.

Argument

___d___ **10.** Which sentence is not relevant to the author's claim?
a. sentence 1   c. sentence 24
b. sentence 8   d. sentence 30

WHAT DO YOU THINK?

Do you agree with the editorial's view that the food industry has attempted to "induce addictive behavior" for a profit? Why or why not? Do you agree with the author's comparison of the food industry to the tobacco industry? Should the government use warning labels, taxes, and bans to fight childhood obesity? Why or why not? If so, what foods should be banned or taxed? What kind of labels should be on foods? Assume you are taking a college health class and your professor has asked you to write about a health issue of current importance. Take a stand for or against a new law to fight obesity that includes banning and taxing certain foods. In your article, identify the foods that might be taxed or banned.

REVIEW TEST 4   Score (number correct) _____ × 10 = _____ %

Argument

Textbook
Skills

Skim the following passage adapted from a college textbook about world civilizations. Answer the Before Reading questions that follow the passage. Then, read the passage. Next, answer the After Reading questions.

13.3 GE/565 words   **The Great Exchange**

Vocabulary Preview

migratory (4):
moving, traveling

ecological (6):
natural, environmental

imperialism (6):
government or
authority of an empire

immunities (7):
protections

[1]The arrival of the Spaniards and the Portuguese in the Americas began one of the most extensive and profound changes in the history of humankind. [2]The New World, which had existed in isolation since the end of the last ice age, was now brought into continual contact with the Old World. [3]The peoples and cultures of Europe and Africa came to the Americas through voluntary or forced immigration. [4]Between 1500 and 1850, perhaps 10 to 15 million Africans and 5 million Europeans crossed the Atlantic and settled in the Americas as part of the great **migratory** movement. [5]Contact also initiated a broader biological and ecological exchange that changed the face of both the Old World and the New World—the way people lived, what they ate, and how they died, indeed how many people there were in different regions—as the animals, plants, and diseases of the two hemispheres were transferred.

[6]It was historian Alfred Crosby who first called this process the *Columbian exchange*, and he has pointed out its profound effects as the

first stage of the **"ecological imperialism"** that accompanied the expansion of the West. [7]Long separated from the populations of the Old World and lacking **immunities** to diseases such as measles and smallpox, populations throughout the Americas suffered disastrous losses after initial contact. [8]Throughout North America, contact with Europeans and Africans resulted in epidemics that devastated the **indigenous** populations.

[9]Disease may have also moved in the other direction. [10]Some authorities believe that syphilis had an American origin and was brought to Europe only after 1492. [11]In general, however, forms of life in the Old World—diseases, plants, and animals—were more complex than those in the Americas and thus displaced the New World varieties in open competition. [12]The diseases of Eurasia and Africa had a greater impact on America than American diseases had on the Old World.

[13]With animals also, the major exchange was from the Old World to the New World. [14]Native Americans had domesticated dogs, guinea pigs, some fowl, and llamas, but in general domesticated animals were far less important in the Americas than in the Old World. [15]In the first years of settlement in the Caribbean, the Spanish introduced horses, cattle, sheep, chickens, and domestic goats and pigs, all of which were considered essential for civilized life as the Iberians understood it. [16]Some of these animals thrived in the New World. [17]For example, a hundred head of cattle abandoned by the Spanish in the Rio de la Plata area in 1587 had become 100,000 head 20 years later.

[18]In the exchange of foods, the contribution of America probably outweighed that of Europe, however. [19]New World plants such as tomatoes, squash, sweet potatoes, types of beans, and peppers, became essential foods in Europe. [20]Tobacco and cacao, or chocolate, both American in origin, became widely distributed throughout the world.

[21]Even more important were the basic crops such as potato, maize, and manioc, all of which yielded more calories per acre than all the Old World grains, except rice. [22]The high yield of calories per acre of maize and potatoes had supported the high population densities of the American civilizations. [23]After the Columbian voyages, these foods began to produce similar effects in the rest of the world. [24]After 1750, the world population experienced a dramatic rise. [25]The reasons were many, but the contribution of the American foodstuff was a central one.

Before Reading

Vocabulary in Context

Use context clues to state in your own words the definition of the following term. Indicate the context clue you used.

1. In sentence 8, what does the word **indigenous** mean?

native

2. Identify the context clue used for the word **indigenous** in sentence 8.

the synonym "native" in "Native Americans" and general sense of the passage

Tone and Purpose

___a___ **3.** What is the overall tone and purpose of the passage?
a. to inform the reader about the impact of the Columbian exchange
b. to persuade the reader that the Columbian exchange benefited America more than Europe
c. to engage the reader with little known facts about early American history

After Reading

Central Idea

4. Use your own words to state the central idea of the passage: Wording may vary.

The Columbian exchange had a profound impact that altered the environments

and lifestyles of people from both America and Europe.

Main Idea and Supporting Details

___c___ **5.** Sentence 17 states a
a. main idea.
b. major supporting detail.
c. minor supporting detail.

Transitions

___b___ **6.** The relationship between sentences 8 and 9 is
a. cause and effect.
b. addition.
c. time order.
d. contrast.

Thought Patterns

_____b_____   **7.** The overall thought pattern of the passage is
      a. cause and effect.   c. time order.
      b. listing.   d. contrast.

Fact and Opinion

_____c_____   **8.** Sentence 1 is a statement of
      a. fact.   c. fact and opinion.
      b. opinion.

Inferences

_____c_____   **9.** Based on the context of the information in the second paragraph (sentences 6–8), the term "ecological imperialism" in sentence 6 implies that
      a. natural resources exchanged between America and Europe dramatically changed the natural environments of both regions.
      b. Europe damaged the natural resources of America.
      c. the immigration of Europeans brought diseases and caused epidemics that weakened the resistance of native peoples to European control.

Argument

_____c_____   **10.** The following list of statements contains one claim and several supports from the third paragraph (sentences 9–12). Identify the support that is **not** relevant to the claim.
      a. Disease may have also moved in the other direction (from America to the Old World).
      b. Some authorities believe that syphilis had an American origin and was brought to Europe only after 1492.
      c. The diseases of Eurasia and Africa had a greater impact on America than American diseases had on the Old World.

WHAT DO YOU THINK?

What is the significance of the Columbian exchange? Which region benefitted the most from the Columbian exchange? How might life in the United States be different today if the Columbian exchange had not occurred? Assume you are taking a college course in world civilizations. Your professor has assigned a writing assignment as a chapter test. Choose one of the following prompts and write a three-paragraph essay: (1) Define the Columbian exchange and discuss key examples of its effect on America and Western Europe; (2) Take a stand in support of or in opposition to the following claim by the Office of the United States Trade Representative: "American families benefit from trade and open markets every day. Trade delivers a greater choice of goods—everything from food and furniture to computers and cars—at lower prices." Offer examples to support your stance.

 ## After Reading About the Basics of Argument

Before you move on to the Mastery Tests on the basics of argument, take time to reflect on your learning and performance by answering the following questions. Write your answers in your notebook.

- How has my knowledge base or prior knowledge about the basics of argument changed?
- Based on my studies, how do I think I will perform on the Mastery Test(s)? Why do I think my scores will be above average, average, or below average?
- Would I recommend this chapter to other students who want to learn more about the basics of argument? Why or why not?

Test your understanding of what you have learned about the basics of argument by completing the Chapter 12 Review Card in the insert near the end of your text.

CONNECT TO **myreadinglab**

To check your progress in meeting Chapter 12's learning outcomes, log in to **www.myreadinglab.com** and try the following exercises.

- The "Critical Thinking" section of MyReadingLab gives additional information about the basics of argument. The section provides an overview, model, practices, and tests. To access this resource, click on the "Study Plan" tab. Then click on "Critical Thinking." Then click on the following links as needed: "Overview," "Model," "Critical Thinking: Facts and Opinions (Flash Animation)," "Practice," and "Test."

- The "Study Skills Website" section of MyReadingLab also gives additional information about the basics of argument. To access these resources, go to the "Other Sources" box on the home page of MyReadingLab. Click on "Study Skills Website." Then scroll down the page to the heading "Life Skills" and click on "Critical Thinking." Explore each of the links on the bar on the left side of the page.

- To measure your mastery of this chapter, complete the tests in the "Critical Thinking" section and click on Gradebook to find your results.

Read the following passage and examine the graphic in this excerpt from a college sociology textbook. Then, answer the questions.

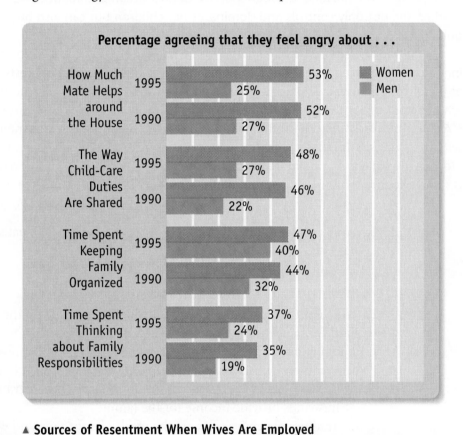

Percentage agreeing that they feel angry about . . .

▲ **Sources of Resentment When Wives Are Employed**

—Figure adapted from the 1995 Virginia Slims Opinion Research Poll conducted by Roper Starch Worldwide, 1996, p. 82; text and adapted figure from *Marriages and Families: Changes, Choices, and Constraints,* 4th ed., pp. 91–92, Figure 4.3 (p. 91). by Nijole V. Benokraitis. Copyright © 2002 by Pearson Education, Inc. Reproduced by permission of Pearson Education, Inc., Boston, MA.

Textbook Skills

10.6 GE/285 words

Gender Roles

[1]Traditional gender roles promote stability, continuity, and predictability. [2]Because each person knows what is expected of him or her, rights and responsibilities are clear. [3]Men and women do not have to argue over who does what: if the house is clean, she is a "good wife"; if the bills are paid, he is a "good provider." [4]If the costs and benefits of the relationship are fairly balanced and each partner is relatively happy, traditional gender roles can work well. [5]As long as both partners live up

to their role expectations, they are safe in assuming that they will take care of each other financially, emotionally, and sexually.

[6]Some women stay in traditional relationships because as long as they live up to the idealized role, they don't have to make autonomous decisions or assume responsibility when things go wrong. [7]An accommodating wife or mother can enjoy both power and prestige through her husband's accomplishments. [8]As a good mother, she not only controls and dominates her children but can also be proud of guiding and enriching their lives.

[9]But traditional roles are changing. [10]Many men have lost their jobs to downsizing and more women are working to pursue their own professional interests as well as to help out financially. [11]Black fathers, especially, are losing well-paying, low-skilled manufacturing jobs that are eliminated by automation and global job restructuring. [12]As a result, black and other ethnic fathers are now sharing the breadwinning role with their wives. [13]This has created more strain at home. [14]Although husbands of employed wives may be doing more of the household tasks than their fathers did, there is some evidence that men's resentment about the division of labor may be growing.

—Benoknaitis, *Marriages and Families*, 4th ed., 2002, pp. 91–92.

_____a_____ **1.** Which of the following sentences is a claim that is adequately supported by the details?

    a. sentence 1   c. sentence 7

    b. sentence 6   d. sentence 8

_____c_____ **2.** Which of the following is a logical conclusion based on the details in the passage?

    a. Traditional wives are completely dependent upon their husbands.

    b. Traditional husbands often help out with household chores.

    c. Traditional wives take care of the home and children; traditional husbands provide income for the family.

    d. Traditional gender roles are the ideal roles for men and women.

3–5. Based on the information in the graphic, place a check (✔) by the three statements that assert logical conclusions.

_____✔_____ Women are much more likely than men to feel angry about how much their mate helps around the house.

_____ More men lost their jobs as women entered the workforce.

_____✔_____ Men's resentment rose between 1990 and 1995, even though women say they do the bulk of the household chores and child care.

_____ Divorce rates increased from 1990 to 1995.

_____✔_____ Both wives and their mates were more dissatisfied overall with their share of family responsibilities in 1995 than in 1990.

Read the following passage from a college history textbook, and then answer the questions.

Textbook
Skills

11.7 GE/271 words

Is There a Right to Privacy?

[1]Nowhere does the Bill of Rights say that Americans have a right to privacy. [2]Clearly, however, the First Congress had the concept of privacy in mind when it created the first 10 amendments. [3]For example, freedom of religion implies the right to exercise private beliefs, and protections against "unreasonable searches and seizures" make persons secure in their homes. [4]In addition, private property cannot be seized without "due process of law." [5]In 1928, Justice Brandeis hailed privacy as "the right to be left alone—the most comprehensive of the rights and the most valued by civilized men."

[6]The idea that the Constitution guarantees a right to privacy was first expressed in a 1965 case involving the conviction of a doctor and family planning specialist for disseminating birth control devices in violation of a little-used Connecticut law. [7]The state reluctantly brought them to court. [8]They were convicted. [9]After wrestling with the privacy issue in *Griswold* v. *Connecticut*, seven Supreme Court justices finally decided that various portions of the Bill of Rights cast "penumbras" (or shadows), unstated liberties implied by the stated rights. [10]These protected a right to privacy, including a right to family planning between husband and wife. [11]Supporters of privacy rights argued that this ruling was a reasonable interpretation of the Fourth Amendment. [12]There were many critics of the ruling. [13]They claimed that the Supreme Court was inventing protections not specified by the Constitution.

[14]The most important application of the privacy rights, however, came not in the area of birth control but in the area of abortion. [15]The Supreme Court unleashed a constitutional firestorm in 1973 that has not yet abated.

—From *Government in America: People, Politics, and Policy*, 5th ed., p. 103 by George C. Edwards III, Martin P. Wattenberg and Robert L. Lineberry. Copyright © 2000 by Pearson Education, Inc. Reprinted by permission of Pearson Education, Inc., Glenview, IL.

_____ b **1.** The claim of the entire passage is stated in

    a. sentence 1.   c. sentence 3.

    b. sentence 2.   d. sentence 15.

_____a_____ **2.** The claim of the second paragraph is stated in

    a. sentence 6.   c. sentence 9.

    b. sentence 11.   d. sentence 13.

_____a_____ **3.** In the first paragraph, sentence 4 states

    a. a detail that is relevant.

    b. a detail that is not relevant.

_____b_____ **4.** In the second paragraph, sentence 7 states

    a. a detail that is relevant.

    b. a detail that is not relevant.

_____b_____ **5.** In the second paragraph, sentence 12 states

    a. a detail that is relevant.

    b. a detail that is not relevant.

VISUAL VOCABULARY

Which is the best synonym for
disseminated?

_____c_____

a. blown
b. gathered
c. spread

► Upon maturation, the dandelion turns into the well-known puffball containing
seeds that are disseminated by the wind.

Read the following passage from a college sociology textbook. Then, answer the questions.

Textbook
Skills

14.2 GE/302 words

The Impact of the Consumer Culture on the Growth of Suburbia

[1]Following World War II, a combination of factors had brought in a consumer culture, which has since come to dominate American culture. [2]The essence of the consumer culture is a focus on acquisition of material objects made possible by affluence, mobility, and leisure. [3]For instance, the automobile, mass produced and, thus, cheap enough to be available to a majority of people, led to the growth of the highway system on which the automobile could move freely and rapidly. [4]In turn, highways were especially responsible for the spread of suburbanization to the extent that it became a pervasive national phenomenon. [5]At the same time, other facets of social change became apparent and were reinforced by suburbanization.

[6]As the cities had done before them, the suburbs spawned their own lifestyle, revolving around the absence of the father for long portions of the day, the necessity for a private vehicle, and the chauffeuring of children to various activities. [7]In addition, trips to the shopping center or suburban mall had become the focus of recreation for suburbanites. [8]The booming economy permitted one family member—usually the husband and father—to be the sole breadwinner, leaving the wife and mother to do the chauffeuring and shopping chores.

[9]Originally, the suburbs attracted young married couples who were planning fairly large families—the baby boom parents of the years following World War II. [10]The postwar economy increased individual incomes and made mortgage money available, so that for the first time home ownership became a dream almost all could fulfill. [11]Most of the early suburbanites were between 25 and 45 years old, with children ranging in age from infancy to the teens. [12]They were predominantly white, middle-income, high school graduates, politically conservative, and morally "proper." [13]From these beginnings there developed the stereotype of the suburbs as "bedroom" communities of almost identical homes.

—John & Perry, *Contemporary Society: An Introduction to Social Science*, 10th ed., pp. 264–265.

___a___   **1.** Sentence 1 is a statement that is
   a. a claim.
   b. a support for a claim.

___b___   **2.** Sentence 3 is a statement that is
   a. a claim.
   b. a support for a claim.

___a___   **3.** Sentence 5 is a statement that is
   a. a claim.
   b. a support for a claim.

___b___   **4.** Sentence 6 is a statement that is
   a. a claim.
   b. a support for a claim.

___b___   **5.** Sentence 11 is a statement that is
   a. a claim.
   b. a support for a claim.

Read the following passage from a college biology textbook. Then, answer the questions.

13.8 GE/514 words **Natural Selection Tends to Preserve Genes That Help an Organism Survive and Reproduce**

[1]On average, organisms that best meet the challenges of their environment will leave the most offspring; these offspring will inherit the genes that made their parents successful. [2]Thus, natural selection preserves genes that help organisms flourish in their environment. [3]To create a hypothetical example, a mutated gene that caused ancestral beavers to grow larger teeth allowed those with this mutation to chew down trees more efficiently, build bigger dams and lodges, and eat more bark than "ordinary" beavers could. [4]Because these big-toothed beavers obtained more food and better shelter, they were able to raise more offspring who inherited their parents' genes for larger teeth. [5]Over time, less-successful, smaller-toothed beavers became increasingly scarce; after many generations, all beavers had large teeth.

[6]Structures, physiological processes, or behaviors that aid in survival and reproduction in a particular environment are called adaptations. [7]Most of the features that we admire so much in our fellow life-forms, such as the long limbs of deer, the wings of eagles, and the mighty trunks of redwood trees, are adaptations molded by millions of years of natural selection acting on random mutations.

[8]Over millennia, the interplay of environment, genetic variation, and natural selection inevitably results in evolution: a change in the genetic makeup of species. [9]This change has been documented innumerable times both in laboratory settings and in the wild. [10]For example, antibiotics have acted as agents of natural selection on bacterial populations, causing the evolution of antibiotic-resistant forms. [11]Lawn mowers have caused changes in the genetic makeup of populations of dandelions, favoring those that produce flowers on very short stems. [12]Scientists have documented the spontaneous emergence of entirely new species of plants due to mutations that alter their chromosome number.

[13]What helps an organism survive today can become a liability tomorrow. [14]If environments change—for example, as global warming occurs—the genetic makeup that best adapts organisms to their environment will also change over time. [15]When random new mutations increase the fitness of an organism in the altered environment, these mutations will spread throughout the population. [16]Populations within a species that live in different environments will be subjected to different types of natural selection. [17]If the differences are

great enough and continue for long enough, they may eventually cause the populations to become sufficiently different from one another to prevent interbreeding—a new species will have evolved.

[18]If, however, favorable mutations do not occur, a changing environment may doom a species to extinction. [19]Dinosaurs are extinct not because they were failures—after all, they flourished for 100 million years—but because they could not adapt rapidly enough to changing conditions.

[20]Within particular habitats, diverse organisms have evolved complex interrelationships with one another and with their nonliving surroundings. [21]The diversity of species and the interactions that sustain them are encompassed by the term biodiversity. [22]In recent decades, the rate of environmental change has been drastically accelerated by human activities. [23]Many wild species are unable to adapt to this rapid change. [24]In habitats most affected by humans, many species are being driven to extinction.

—From *Biology: Life on Earth*, 8th ed., p. 10 by Teresa Audesirk, Gerald Audesirk, and Bruce E. Byers. Copyright © 2008 by Pearson Education, Inc. Printed and Electronically reproduced by permission of Pearson Education, Inc., Upper Saddle River, NJ.

_____b_____ **1.** Sentence 1 states a
    a. claim.   b. support.

_____a_____ **2.** Sentence 2 states a
    a. claim.   b. support.

_____b_____ **3.** Sentence 6 states a
    a. claim.   b. support.

_____a_____ **4.** Sentence 7 states a
    a. claim.   b. support.

_____a_____ **5.** Sentence 8 states a
    a. claim.   b. support.

_____b_____ **6.** Sentence 9 states a
    a. claim.   b. support.

_____a_____ **7.** Sentence 13 states a
    a. claim.   b. support.

_____a_____ **8.** Sentence 17 states a
    a. claim.   b. support.

_____a_____ **9.** Sentence 18 states a
    a. claim.   b. support.

_____b_____ **10.** Sentence 19 states a
    a. claim.   b. support.

Advanced Argument: Persuasive Techniques

13

LEARNING OUTCOMES

After studying this chapter you should be able to do the following:

① Define the terms *fallacy, propaganda, personal attack, straw man, begging the question, name-calling, testimonial, bandwagon, plain folks, either-or, false comparison, false cause, card stacking, transfer,* and *glittering generalities.* [Knowledge]

② Detect fallacies based on irrelevant arguments: *personal attack, straw man,* and *begging the question.* [Comprehension, Analysis]

③ Detect propaganda techniques based on irrelevant arguments; *name-calling, testimonials, bandwagon,* and *plain folks.* [Comprehension, Analysis]

④ Detect fallacies based on inadequate arguments: *either-or, false comparison,* and *false cause.* [Comprehension, Analysis]

⑤ Detect propaganda techniques based on inadequate arguments: *card stacking, transfer,* and *glittering generalities.* [Comprehension, Analysis]

⑥ Evaluate the importance of advanced arguments: persuasive techniques. [Evaluation]

Before Reading About Advanced Argument

In this chapter, you will build on the concepts you studied in Chapter 12 about the basics of argument. Take a moment to review the four steps in analyzing an argument. Fill in the following blanks with each of the steps.

Step 1. Identify the author's claim and supports.

Step 2. Decide whether the supports are relevant.

Step 3. Decide whether the supports are adequate.

Step 4. Check the argument for bias.

To help you master the material in the chapter, create a three-column chart in your notebook. In the left column copy the headings as in the example that follows. Leave enough room between each heading to fill in definitions and examples as you work through the chapter.

General definition: A fallacy is

Fallacy	Definition	Example
Personal attack		
Straw man		

General definition: Propaganda is

Propaganda technique	Definition	Example
Name-calling		
Testimonials		

 ## Biased Arguments

Much of the information that we come in contact with on a daily basis is designed to influence our thoughts and behaviors. Advertisements, editorials, and political campaigns offer one-sided, biased information to sway public opinion.

This biased information is based on two types of reasoning: the use of **fallacies** in logical thought and the use of **propaganda**. A master reader identifies and understands the use of these persuasion techniques in biased arguments.

What Is a Fallacy in Logical Thought?

You have already studied logical thought in Chapter 12. Logical thought or argument is a process that includes an author's claim, relevant support, and a valid conclusion. A **fallacy** is an error in the process of logical thought. A fallacy leads to an invalid conclusion. You have also studied two general types of fallacies: irrelevant details and inadequate details. By its nature, a fallacy is not persuasive because it weakens an argument. However, fallacies are often used to convince readers to accept an author's claim. In fact, the word *fallacy* comes from a Latin word that means "to deceive" or "trick." You will learn more about irrelevant and inadequate arguments in the next sections of this chapter.

Fallacies are not to be confused with false facts. A fact, true or false, is stated without bias, and facts can be proven true or false by objective evidence. In contrast, a fallacy is an invalid inference or biased opinion about a fact or set of facts. Sometimes the word *fallacy* is used to refer to a false belief or the reasons for a false belief.

A **fallacy** is an error in logical thought.

EXAMPLE   Read the following sets of ideas. Mark each statement as follows:

> **UB** for unbiased statements
> **B** for biased arguments

__UB__   **1.** Henry Ford invented the automobile.

__B__   **2.** Jamal had been wearing his lucky shirt during every game in which he scored a winning point, and when he didn't wear his lucky shirt, he did not score. Now he wears his lucky shirt every game without fail.

__B__   **3.** Joanne lies all the time because she is incapable of telling the truth.

__UB__   **4.** Based on eyewitness accounts and the statement of Marji Thompson, the police report stated that Thompson had thought the car was in drive when it was actually in reverse. When she stepped on the gas, she backed into the car parked behind her, damaging her back bumper and the front bumper and hood of the other car.

__UB__   **5.** Four-time winner of NASCAR's Nextel Cup Championship, Jeff Gordon set new standards in the sport during the 2007 season with 6 victories, 21 top-five finishes, a record-breaking 30 top-ten finishes, and a 7.3 average finishing position with one DNF (Did Not Finish). Even though he came in second place behind Jimmie Johnson for the title during the season's Chase, Gordon has more career wins than almost all other drivers; only Richard Petty with seven wins has more victories.

EXPLANATION

1. This statement is unbiased (UB), but it is not true. The automobile was not invented by Henry Ford. The automobile evolved from inventors' efforts worldwide; the modern automobile is the result of over 100,000 patents. Ford did invent an improved assembly line.

2. This is a biased argument (B) based on a fallacy in logical thought. By not considering other reasons for his success, Jamal has identified a false cause and made an invalid inference. You will learn more about the fallacy of false cause later in this chapter.

3. This is a biased argument (B) based on a fallacy in logical thought. The statement about Joanne uses circular thinking; the statement restates the claim as its own proof. The phrase "lies all the time" is the claim, which is restated by the phrase "incapable of telling the truth." No factual evidence is given.

4. This is an unbiased statement (UB). Every detail can be verified through the police report and eyewitness accounts of the incident.

5. This is an unbiased statement (UB). This statement is factual and can be proven with eyewitness accounts and newspaper reports.

PRACTICE 1

Read the following sets of ideas. Mark each statement as follows:

> **UB** for unbiased statements
> **B** for biased arguments

___UB___ 1. The flea is the smallest insect.

___B___ 2. Watching violent programs causes youth to become violent criminals.

___B___ 3. Convicted felons should not have the right to vote because they have broken the law.

___UB___ 4. Cars that run on hydrogen are not dependent upon imported oil.

What Is Propaganda?

Propaganda is a means by which an idea is widely spread. The word *propaganda* comes from a Latin term that means to "propagate" or "spread." **Propaganda** is a biased argument that advances or damages a cause. Propaganda is often used in politics and advertising.

Read the following two descriptions of a mock sandwich called The Two-Fisted Bacon Burger. The first description is an advertisement for the sandwich. The second is the nutritional information for a meal that would include the sandwich and a small order of fries.

Advertisement: You're gonna love The Two-Fisted Bacon Burger! Two juicy 1/2 lb. patties fully loaded with crisp smokehouse bacon, mayo, ketchup, and thick-sliced cheddar cheese inside a fresh, soft bun. Nothing compares! Two handfuls of lip-smacking, mouth-watering pleasure. Get the combo! The Two-Fisted Bacon Burger with small fries is umm, umm, *delicious*!

Nutritional Facts:

	Calories	Calories from fat	Total fat (g)	Saturated fat (g)	Trans fat (g)	Cholesterol (mg)	Sodium (mg)	Carbs (g)	Fiber (g)	Sugar (g)	Protein (g)
The Two-Fisted Bacon Burger	1601	944	78.48	31.06	0	389	1398	18.8	.6	2	118.82
Small French Fries	271	130	14.5	3.4	3.7	0	165	31.9	3.4	0	4

The advertisement uses tone words that appeal to the senses of hunger—smell, taste, and vision—such as *two-fisted, juicy, crisp, smokehouse, thick-sliced, fresh, soft, lip-smacking, mouth-watering,* and *um, um, delicious.* These words are meant to tempt the customer into purchasing the sandwich. (For more about tone, see Chapter 10, "Tone and Purpose.") In contrast, the nutritional facts reveal objective data. These facts might keep someone who is concerned about a healthful diet from buying and eating this meal.

This advertisement is an example of **propaganda**. Propaganda uses fallacies to spread biased information.

> **Propaganda** is an act of persuasion that systematically spreads biased information that is designed to support or oppose a person, product, cause, or organization.

Propaganda uses a variety of techniques that are based on **emotional appeal**. If you are not aware of these techniques, you may be misled by the way information is presented and come to invalid conclusions. Understanding propaganda techniques will enable you to separate factual information from emotional appeals so that you can come to valid conclusions.

> **Emotional appeal** is the arousal of emotion to give meaning or power to an idea.

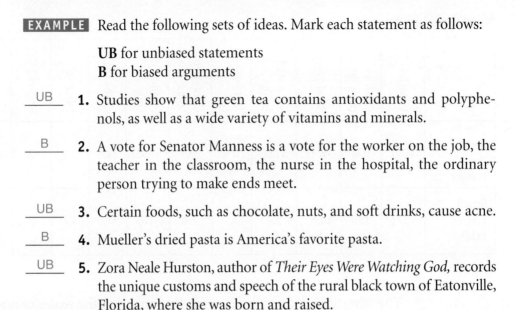

EXAMPLE   Read the following sets of ideas. Mark each statement as follows:

> **UB** for unbiased statements
> **B** for biased arguments

___UB___   **1.** Studies show that green tea contains antioxidants and polyphe-
nols, as well as a wide variety of vitamins and minerals.

___B___   **2.** A vote for Senator Manness is a vote for the worker on the job, the
teacher in the classroom, the nurse in the hospital, the ordinary
person trying to make ends meet.

___UB___   **3.** Certain foods, such as chocolate, nuts, and soft drinks, cause acne.

___B___   **4.** Mueller's dried pasta is America's favorite pasta.

___UB___   **5.** Zora Neale Hurston, author of *Their Eyes Were Watching God*, records
the unique customs and speech of the rural black town of Eatonville,
Florida, where she was born and raised.

EXPLANATION

1. This is an unbiased statement (UB). It is factual and can be proven with
objective evidence and expert opinions.

2. This is a biased argument (B) using the emotional appeal of propaganda.
The statement uses the "plain folks" appeal. Senator Manness is identified
as an everyday person with the same values as everyday people. You will
learn more about this propaganda technique later in this chapter.

3. This is an unbiased statement (UB); however, it is a false fact. Current
research does not support this claim.

4. This is a biased argument (B) using the emotional appeal of the propaganda techniques of "transfer" and "bandwagon." You will learn more
about these propaganda techniques later in this chapter.

5. This is an unbiased statement (UB). This statement offers factual information that can be verified by reading the novel and researching African
American customs and speech.

PRACTICE 2

Read the following sets of ideas. Mark each statement as follows:

> **UB** for unbiased statements
> **B** for biased arguments

_____B_____ **1.** Look like Sandra Bullock, Heidi Klum, or Jennifer Lopez—use Love Your Hair for silky, shimmering hair.

_____B_____ **2.** Be a true patriot; buy Liberty Bonds to support our troops.

_____UB_____ **3.** People with apple-shaped figures are at greater risk for heart disease, stroke, diabetes, and some types of cancer.

_____UB_____ **4.** Research exists both for and against milk consumption; while many experts agree that milk contains important vitamins and minerals for healthy bones, such as Vitamin D and calcium, other experts say milk contributes to heart disease and obesity.

Irrelevant Arguments: Fallacies

Writing based in logical thought offers an author's claim and relevant supporting details, and it arrives at a valid conclusion. Fallacies and propaganda offer irrelevant arguments based on irrelevant details. Irrelevant details draw attention away from logical thought by ignoring the issue or changing the subject.

Personal Attack

Personal attack is the use of abusive remarks in place of evidence for a point or argument. Also known as an *ad hominem* attack, a personal attack attempts to discredit the point by discrediting the person making the point.

For example, Maurice Long, a recovering alcoholic, decides to run for mayor. His opponent focuses attention on Maurice's history of alcohol abuse and ignores his ideas about how to make the community stronger with statements like "Don't vote for a Long record of poor decisions," or "Don't give the keys to the city to the town drunk." However, Maurice's past struggle with alcoholism has nothing to do with his current ability to work as a public servant; making this argument a personal attack.

EXAMPLE Read this discussion between a husband and wife, and then underline two uses of the logical fallacy of *personal attack*.

Budget Woes

[1]"Glenn, I am more than concerned about the amount of money you are spending," Jean says in a concerned but polite voice.

[2]"Oh, really?" Glenn replies with surprise.

³"How can you be surprised? ⁴We worked out this budget together, so you must know that you are spending more than we can afford," Jean retorts with exasperation.

⁵"I seem surprised because I have worked hard to stay within the budget, but the cost of gas at the pump has skyrocketed and is much more expensive than what we figured, and . . . " Glenn says defensively.

⁶Jean interrupts, "Stop! ⁷The price of gas is not the issue; you are eating out every day at lunch while the pantry is full of groceries you purchased, with my credit card, by the way, so you could save money by taking your lunch. ⁸You are playing golf twice a week, while you promised to cut back to playing only once a week."

⁹"Well, I only agreed to that budget because you are such a control freak and have to have everything your way," Glenn shouts, then continues in a controlled, measured voice. ¹⁰"The budget is unreasonable; we make enough money to live comfortably. ¹¹I wish you wouldn't worry so much."

¹²"What! ¹³Well, maybe I wouldn't get so 'freaked out' if you weren't such a manipulator." ¹⁴Jean's voice trembles with emotion as she continues. ¹⁵"You shouldn't have agreed to the budget if you didn't think it was realistic. ¹⁶It's not fair to agree with me knowing you are going to do as you please; we have to be honest with each other."

¹⁷"Okay, okay, so let's sit down together later tonight and create a budget that we can both live with," Glenn says as he embraces his wife.

EXPLANATION   Although much of this conversation is emotional, most of it is based on facts. However, sentences 9 and 13 sink into an exchange of personal attacks. Glenn accuses his wife of being a *control freak*, and she responds by calling him a *manipulator*.

Straw Man

A **straw man** is a weak argument substituted for a stronger one to make the argument easier to challenge. A straw man fallacy distorts, misrepresents, or falsifies an opponent's position. The name of the fallacy comes from the idea that it is easier to knock down a straw man than a real man who will fight back. The purpose of this kind of attack is to shift attention away from a strong argument to a weaker one that can be more easily overcome. Study the following example.

Governor Goodfeeling is campaigning against a movement by the populace to limit the size of public school classes to 15 students per teacher. His opponents run political advertisements that state the following:

"Governor Goodfeeling would rather invest in special interest tax breaks than our children's future. Governor Goodfeeling uses taxpayer money to fund her campaign against class-size reductions."

This passage doesn't mention Governor Goodfeeling's reason for opposing the limit on class size: the state does not have the additional $2.3 billion needed to implement such a major reform without a drastic tax increase. Her opponents used straw man fallacies to put forth views that do not address the governor's line of reasoning and are easier to attack than is her valid stand against smaller class sizes.

EXAMPLE Read the following paragraph, and then underline the logical fallacy of *straw man*.

[1]For the past five years, Senator Richy and his political party have consistently blocked action on the Patient's Bill of Rights while Americans have suffered mercilessly from HMO abuse and neglect. [2]For every day that Congress delays, medical treatment for tens of thousands of Americans is effectively denied or delayed by insurance companies. [3]Those, like Senator Richy, who stand against the Patients' Bill of Rights stand against the spirit of the original Bill of Rights and other fundamental freedoms, such as the freedom of speech, religion, and the freedom from unreasonable searches and seizures.

EXPLANATION The third sentence sets up a straw man, a misleading notion that those who oppose the Patients' Bill of Rights oppose basic constitutional rights. This approach effectively draws attention away from the actual reasons Senator Richy opposed this bill and denies the public an honest discussion of the facts involved in the issue.

Begging the Question

Begging the question restates the point of an argument as the support and conclusion. Also known as *circular reasoning*, begging the question assumes that an unproven or unsupported point is true. For example, the argument "Exercise is tiring because it is strenuous" begs the question. The point "Exercise is tiring" is assumed to be true because it is restated in the term *strenuous* without specific supports that give logical reasons or explanations. Compare the same idea stated without begging the question: "I find exercise such as weightlifting tiring because I have little endurance and strength."

EXAMPLE   Read the following paragraph. Underline the irrelevant argument of *begging the question*.

It's the Law for a Reason

[1]Current laws that mandate the use of bicycle helmets must not be repealed. [2]Properly fitted helmets protect the brain against debilitating injuries. [3]According to the Centers for Disease Control and Prevention, more than 500,000 people in the United States are treated in emergency rooms, and more than 700 people die as a result of bicycle-related injuries annually. [4]<u>In addition, if bicycle helmet laws are repealed, then these laws would cease to exist.</u>

EXPLANATION   Sentence 4 is a statement of begging the question. To say *these laws would cease to exist* is a restatement of the word *repeal*, which means "cancel." As a master reader, you want to know the reasons that explain how helmet laws have reduced the risks or incidents of injuries.

PRACTICE 3

Identify the fallacy in each of the following items. Write **A** if it begs the question, **B** if it constitutes a personal attack, or **C** if it is a straw man.

___A___   **1.** Health care is a universal right because everyone deserves adequate health care.

___B___   **2.** Sarah Clinton is a fatal cancer to the Republican party.

___B___   **3.** Opponents of health reform are afraid of the facts themselves. Their attempt to drown out opposing views is simply un-American.

___C___   **4.** "Nothing is not an option. You didn't send me to Washington to do nothing," President Obama, in defense of his $800 billion economic stimulus package in 2009.

 ## Irrelevant Arguments: Propaganda Techniques

Name-Calling

Name-calling uses negative labels for a product, idea, or cause. The labels are made up of emotionally loaded words and suggest false or irrelevant details that cannot be verified. Name-calling is an expression of personal opinion. For example, a bill for censorship of obscene speech on television and radio may be labeled "anti-American" to generate opposition to the bill. The "anti-American" label suggests that any restriction placed on the right of public speech is *against basic American values,* for which the Revolutionary War was fought.

EXAMPLE Read the following paragraph. Underline the irrelevant details that use *name-calling.*

1State Attorney John Q. Private's appointment to the U.S. Court of Appeals for the Sixth Circuit should not be confirmed. **2**Private is an ideological zealot with a long history of undermining legal and constitutional protections for ordinary Americans. **3**He has diligently opposed reproductive rights, environmental protections, and the separation of church and state. **4**In addition, he has consistently showed favoritism for big tobacco and the gun lobby. **5**It is clear that Private is a right-wing conservative, a partisan who values corporate interests more than the interests of the people.

EXPLANATION The paragraph offers little factual evidence to support the assertion that John Q. Private should not be confirmed to the U.S. Court of Appeals. Phrases such as *undermining legal and constitutional protections* and *diligently opposed reproductive rights, environmental protections, and the separation of church and state* are emotionally laden accusations that remain unsupported with evidence. The author couples these biased generalizations with name-calling. Sentences 2 and 5 label John Q. Private an *ideological zealot,* a *right-wing conservative,* and a *partisan.*

Testimonials

Testimonials use irrelevant personal opinions to support a product, idea, or cause. Most often the testimonial is provided by a celebrity whose only qualification as a spokesperson is fame. For example, a famous actor promotes a certain brand of potato chips as his favorite, or a radio talk show host endorses a certain type of mattress.

EXAMPLE Read the following paragraph. Underline the irrelevant details that use a *testimonial.*

The Brilliance of a Smile

1SmileBrite offers the fastest and best whitening results of all the leading paint-on and strip whiteners. **2**SmileBrite's secret is in its method of application and its secret combination of ingredients, which include peroxide. ³Film star Julia Famous loves SmileBrite: "SmileBrite is safe and effective; I trust my smile to SmileBrite." ⁴This special formula is gentle and will not damage the tooth's enamel, yet delivers tremendous results in just a few applications.

EXPLANATION   Sentences 1, 2, and 4 offer details about SmileBrite that can be verified. However, sentence 3 uses the testimonial of a famous actress. Being a famous actress doesn't make the spokesperson an expert on the safety or effectiveness of a product. A dentist, dental hygienist, or scientific researcher could offer a relevant expert opinion.

PRACTICE 4

Identify the propaganda technique used in each of the following items. Write **A** if the sentence is an example of name-calling or **B** if it is a testimonial.

___A___   **1.** Senator Fleming is a big-government socialist who works against the American way.

___B___   **2.** "I'm winning at losing weight. Winning at losing on Weight Watchers. Weight Watchers—because it works!" Jennifer Hudson.

___B___   **3.** "When my husband lost his job, we lost our health insurance. Then, my five year old was diagnosed with a brain tumor. When my husband finally got a new job several months later, the company's health insurance denied payment to treat our daughter, saying she had a pre-existing condition. We need health reform!" — Jennifer Cortez

___A___   **4.** Jay Leno is a thief who stole *The Tonight Show* from David Letterman and Conan O'Brian.

Bandwagon

The **bandwagon** appeal uses or suggests the irrelevant detail that "everyone is doing it." This message plays on the natural desire of most individuals to conform to group norms for acceptance. The term *bandwagon* comes from the 19th-century use of a horse-drawn wagon that carried a musical band to lead circus parades and political rallies. To *jump on the bandwagon* meant to follow the crowd, usually out of excitement and emotion stirred up by the event rather than out of thoughtful reason or deep conviction.

EXAMPLE Read the following paragraph. Underline the irrelevant details that use the *bandwagon* appeal.

A Matter of Honor

[1]Tyrell hated to write. [2]He often struggled with finding a topic, and once he found a topic, he then struggled with finding the words to express his ideas. [3]He knew he was in danger of failing his composition course, and the stress made it even harder for him to think of an idea for his major research project. [4]While he was searching the Internet for ideas, he came across a Web site that sold research essays. [5]As he paid for an essay, downloaded, and printed it out, he thought to himself, "No big deal, everybody cheats at least once in their college career."

EXPLANATION In sentence 5, Tyrell uses the bandwagon fallacy to justify his cheating. Finding permission in "everybody cheats" is not valid reasoning. The emotional appeal is the relief that you are one of "everybody," not an individual who has decided to engage in dishonest and unethical behavior.

Plain Folks

The **plain folks** appeal uses irrelevant details to build trust based on commonly shared values. Many people distrust the wealthy and powerful, such as politicians and the heads of large corporations. Many assume that the wealthy and powerful cannot relate to the everyday concerns of plain people. Therefore, the person or organization in power puts forth an image to which everyday people can more easily relate. For example, a candidate may dress in simple clothes, pose for pictures doing everyday chores like shopping for groceries, or talk about his or her own humble beginnings to make a connection with "plain folks." These details strongly suggest that "you can trust me because I am just like you." The appeal is to the simple, everyday experience, and often the emphasis is on a practical or no-nonsense approach to life.

EXAMPLE Read the following paragraph. Underline the irrelevant details that appeal to *plain folks.*

For the Good of the Children

[1]Helen McCormick, a well-known multimillionaire, is running for the school board. [2]Every day she dresses in sensible shoes and a conservative business suit and goes door to door in neighborhoods populated with young families with school-age children. [3]As she visits with them, she

reminds them of her success and attributes it to <u>hard work and a good education</u>, even though she inherited her fortune and has never held a job. **4**Her newspaper ads run the slogan "I am committed to public education. **5**My own children attend public school; help me help our children." **6**On the day of the election, Helen stands on the corner of the busiest intersection holding a sign that reads, "Helen cares about our children."

EXPLANATION Candidate Helen is described as wearing clothes that many "plain folks" also wear: *sensible shoes and a conservative business suit.* In sentence 3, the candidate asserts ideals valued by many people: *hard work and a good education.* She emphasizes her common bond with voters by stating *My own children attend public school; help me help our children.* Helen sets a friendly tone with the use of her first name. In addition, Helen's willingness to go door to door and stand on the street corner indicates she is humble and working hard for every vote. All of these details suggest that this multimillionaire, Helen, is just one of the "plain folks."

PRACTICE 5

Label each of the following items according to the propaganda techniques they employ:

A. plain folks	C. testimonial
B. bandwagon	D. name-calling

  A   **1.** An owner of a local car dealership stars in a commercial for his business dressed in jeans and a flannel shirt with his sleeves rolled up.

  B   **2.** Nine out of ten customers express deep satisfaction with Relora, the natural way to ease tension and lose weight.

  D   **3.** Don't be a butt head; stop smoking today!

  C   **4.** "Proactive keeps your skin acne free. Proactive means clear skin," says Jessica Simpson.

 # Inadequate Arguments: Fallacies

In addition to offering relevant supporting details, logical thought relies on adequate supporting details. A valid conclusion must be based on sufficient support. Fallacies and propaganda offer inadequate arguments that lack details.

Inadequate arguments oversimplify the issue and do not give a person enough information to draw a proper conclusion.

Either-Or

Either-or assumes that only two sides of an issue exist. Also known as the *black-and-white fallacy*, either-or offers a false dilemma because more than two options are usually available. For example, the statement "If you don't vote for social security reform, you don't care about the elderly" uses the either-or fallacy. The statement assumes only one reason for not voting for social security reform—not caring about the elderly. Yet it may be that a person doesn't approve of the particular reform being considered, prefers another solution, or, perhaps, believes the current social security program is strong and serves the elderly as well as could be expected. Either-or leaves no room for the middle ground or other options.

EXAMPLE Read the following paragraph taken from President Bush's Address to the Joint Session of Congress and the American people on September 20, 2001. Then, underline the logical fallacy of *either-or*.

> [1]Our response involves far more than instant retaliation and isolated strikes. [2]Americans should not expect one battle, but a lengthy campaign, unlike any other we have ever seen. [3]It may include dramatic strikes, visible on TV, and covert operations, secret even in success. [4]We will starve terrorists of funding, turn them one against another, drive them from place to place, until there is no refuge or no rest. [5]And we will pursue nations that provide aid or safe haven to terrorism. [6]Every nation, in every region, now has a decision to make. [7]Either you are with us, or you are with the terrorists. [8]From this day forward, any nation that continues to harbor or support terrorism will be regarded by the United States as a hostile regime.
>
> —George W. Bush, *The White House*, 20 Sept. 2001. 10 Apr. 2004.
> http:// www.whitehouse.gov/news/releases/2001/09/20010920-8.html

EXPLANATION President Bush's address is in direct response to the September 11, 2001, terrorist attacks on the United States. No one would dispute that the shocking, horrific loss that resulted from that attack demanded a strong response. However, Bush's use of the either-or fallacy in sentence 7 is undeniable. A reader may choose to assume that Bush is speaking only of terrorists and those who actively support their acts of terror. However, his use of this either-or statement allows his critics to infer that he equates those who may disagree with America's response to the situation with terrorists. In addition, his statement leaves no room for a country to take a neutral stance. This issue is difficult and emotional, which places an even greater responsibility on writers, speakers, listeners, and readers to analyze such statements and ideas for logical soundness.

False Comparison

False comparison assumes that two things are similar when they are not. This fallacy is also known as a *false analogy*. An analogy is a point-by-point comparison that is used to explain an unfamiliar concept by comparing it to a more familiar one.

For example, some people have compared the human heart to a plumbing system. The heart is thought of as a pump that sends blood throughout the body to vital organs, and the arteries and veins are compared to pipes that carry this nutrient-enriched fluid to its destination and take away waste material. However, the analogy breaks down when one considers all the differences between a mechanical plumbing system and the human anatomy. First, the heart is not totally responsible for transporting the blood throughout the body. For instance, arteries dilate and contract and move in a wavelike manner to regulate and move blood through the body. Also, the relationship between the pressure, volume, and rate of the heartbeat is very different from the workings of a mechanical pump. A false comparison occurs when the differences outweigh the similarities.

EXAMPLE Read the following paragraph. Underline the logical fallacy of *false comparison*.

> [1]Here at Great Foods we are in business to win. [2]We want to win customers and profits. [3]We do what it takes to make our products the best and to satisfy our customers. [4]We only hire the most talented and competitive workers, and we give them rigorous training in sales and service. [5]Just like a football team, we at Great Foods are a committed team, playing hard to beat the competition and build a loyal following.

EXPLANATION This paragraph draws a false comparison between a business and a football team. While a business may compete against other businesses for customers, the analogy breaks down upon closer examination. For example, in football, one team always wins and the other clearly loses; in contrast, two similar businesses can thrive in close proximity to each other. Furthermore, for a business to make a profit, the customer may lose a bargain. In football, each player is assigned a distinct role; oftentimes in a business, an employee may fulfill a variety of roles. In football, the rules of the game are fixed and known to all who play. However, in business, the "rules" may vary based on who is in charge and the type of business, and customers may not always understand the rules ("the fine print") until after a purchase is made. This false comparison relies on superficial similarities and oversimplifies the complexities of running a successful business.

False Cause

False cause, also known as **Post Hoc,** assumes that because events occurred around the same time, they have a cause-and-effect relationship. For example, a black cat crossing your path, walking under a ladder, and breaking a mirror are said to cause bad luck. What are the other possible causes? The Post Hoc fallacy is the false assumption that because event B *follows* event A, event B *was caused by* event A. A master reader does not assume a cause without thinking about other possible causes.

EXAMPLE Read the following paragraph. Underline the logical fallacy of *false cause.*

> [1]Leanne, a single mother of two children, decided to continue her education and become a registered nurse. [2]The long hours of study required a drastic change in her lifestyle. [3]Before enrolling in college, her lifestyle had been moderately active, and, as a conscientious mother, she had prepared well-balanced, healthy meals. [4]However, once she began her college career, her lifestyle became much more sedentary due to the long hours of attending class and studying at home. [5]In addition, she found that she was eating on the go (although she usually ordered healthful meals such as salad and grilled chicken sandwiches). [6]Over the course of her four-year college career, she gained forty pounds. [7]Leanne thought she probably had a thyroid problem, since her mother had had one. [8]When she went to the doctor, she discovered she did not. [9]Her weight gain was caused by her lack of exercise and poor diet. [10]Leanne started exercising regularly and eating better. [11]Within six months, she had lost the extra weight.

EXPLANATION Leanne jumped to a false conclusion about the cause of her weight gain. She had attributed her weight gain to a medical condition, when the real cause was changes in her lifestyle.

PRACTICE 6

Identify the fallacy in each of the following items. Write **A** if the sentence states a false cause, **B** if it makes a false comparison, or **C** if it employs the either-or fallacy.

_____B_____ **1.** Gossip is just like murder; it destroys a life.

_____A_____ **2.** Every time I made spaghetti for dinner, my husband and I fought, so I don't fix spaghetti any more.

_____A_____ **3.** I failed the test because the teacher doesn't like me.

_____C_____ **4.** A father said to his son, "I will only pay for your education if you decide to become a doctor."

_____C_____ **5.** Either you give me a raise, or I am going to quit immediately.

_____B_____ **6.** Which logical fallacy does the World War II poster reprinted here use?

—© Courtesy of National Archives, photo NWDNS-188-pp. 42.

Inadequate Arguments: Propaganda Techniques

Card Stacking

Card stacking omits factual details in order to misrepresent a product, idea, or cause. Card stacking intentionally gives only part of the truth. For example, a commercial for a snack food labels the snack "low in fat," which suggests that it is healthier and lower in calories than a product that is not low in fat. However, the commercial does not mention that the snack is loaded with sugar and calories.

EXAMPLE Read the following list of details about the product Carblaster. Place a check beside the detail(s) that would be omitted by *card stacking*.

_____ **1.** Carblaster guarantees weight loss by blocking as much as 45 grams of carbohydrates from entering the body.

_____ **2.** Carblaster contains the miracle ingredient phaselous vulgaris, an extract from the northern white kidney bean.

_____ **3.** The extract hinders an enzyme in the body that breaks down carbohydrates into glucose.

___✓___ **4.** Side effects can include severe gastrointestinal distress, heartburn, excessive gas, and diarrhea.

EXPLANATION The detail that would be left out by a writer or speaker using the method of card-stacking is the last detail in the list: *Side effects can include severe gastrointestinal distress, heartburn, excessive gas, and diarrhea.* Consumers might choose to avoid the risk of such side effects and not buy the product.

Transfer

Transfer creates an association between a product, idea, or cause with a symbol or image that has positive or negative values. This technique carries the strong feelings we may have for one thing over to another thing.

Symbols stir strong emotions, opinions, or loyalties. For example, a cross represents the Christian faith; a flag represents a nation; and a beautiful woman or a handsome man represents acceptance, success, or sex appeal. Politicians and advertisers use symbols like these to win our support. For example, a political candidate may end a speech with a prayer or the phrase "God bless America," to suggest that God approves of the speech. Another example of transfer is the television spokesperson who wears a white lab coat and quotes studies about the health product she is advertising.

Transfers can also be negative. For example, skull and crossbones together serve as a symbol for death. Therefore, placing a skull and crossbones on a bottle transfers the dangers of death to the contents of the bottle.

EXAMPLE Read the following paragraph. Underline the irrelevant details that use *transfer*.

Senator Edith Public

[1]Senator Edith Public is running for reelection to represent California in the Senate and is the guest of honor at a lavish Hollywood-sponsored fundraising party, which is being covered by CNN. [2]She is introduced by Ron Massey, a highly popular film actor. [3]And as she speaks, she is surrounded by some of the best known, successful producers, directors, and actors in Hollywood. [4]Senator Public says, "Thank you, Ron, for the warm and enthusiastic support. [5]I know that all of you in this room are concerned about education, the environment, and national health care. [6]As you know, the polls indicate that millions of hardworking Americans across this country are also concerned about these very issues. [7]I promise to work hard to encourage funding for research for alternative sources of energy, to increase national funding for public education, and to pass a Patients' Bill of Rights.

EXPLANATION Senator Edith Public is hoping that the public's affection and respect for these individuals will transfer to her and motivate the fans to vote for her. Interestingly, in her speech, the senator uses the plain folks appeal in the phrase *hardworking Americans* and the bandwagon appeal in her allusion to the polls that show these issues to be popular with the public.

Glittering Generalities

Glittering generalities offer general positive statements that cannot be verified. A glittering generality is the opposite of name-calling. Often words of virtue and high ideals are used, and the details are inadequate to support the claim. For example, words like *truth*, *freedom*, *peace*, and *honor* suggest shining ideals and appeal to feelings of love, courage, and goodness.

EXAMPLE Read the following paragraph. Underline the irrelevant details that use *glittering generalities*.

People for Democracy

[1]People for Democracy is a nonprofit organization dedicated to actively preserving the rights of democracy, which are under dire attack by the

conservative fanatics who are currently in control of the government. ²People for Democracy dedicate our time, energies, and talents to fight tirelessly and courageously for the rights and freedoms that make the United States a vibrant and diverse democracy. ³We are pro-life, fighting for a woman's right to choose. ⁴We advocate civil rights, fighting, like Lincoln, for the equal rights of all. ⁵We defend constitutional liberties, ensuring separation of church and state. ⁶We will not rest as long as radical demigods threaten our way of life. ⁷Our fight is the fight for freedom and justice.

EXPLANATION Most of the glittering generalities used to describe this fictitious organization call to mind American virtues; even the name of the organization is chosen to communicate democratic ideals. The paragraph offers no substantive details but relies on glittering generalities, which include the following: sentence 1 uses *preserving the rights of democracy;* sentence 2 uses *fight tirelessly and courageously, rights and freedoms,* and *vibrant and diverse democracy;* sentence 4 uses *equal rights of all;* sentence 6 uses *our way of life;* and sentence 7 states *Our fight is the fight for freedom and justice.* Sentence 1 and 6 also use name-calling with the labels *conservative fanatics* and *radical demigods,* and sentence 4 uses the technique of transfer by mentioning President Lincoln, a revered martyr for all these values.

PRACTICE 7

Label each of the following items according to the propaganda techniques they employ:

    A. transfer   C. card stacking
    B. glittering generality

_B_   **1.** A vote for Joan Willis is a vote for honesty, dedication, and fairness.

_A_   **2.** Hayden Panettiere, a star of the popular television series *Heroes,* poses in a "Got Milk" advertisement with a white milk mustache and says, "You don't have to be a hero to feel invincible. That's why I drink milk."

_B_   **3.** Dewdrop deodorant will increase your confidence and poise with its light and refreshing scent.

_A_   **4.** An individual dressed in a white medical coat holds a box of pain reliever and says, "Need immediate relief? Take Pain-away. Guaranteed to relieve headache pain in minutes."

_C_   **5.** Use Curl Right to turn frizzy hair into luscious, long-lasting curls. Curl Right's alcohol-free and vitamin-enriched formula restores your hair's natural moisture and vitality. Curl Right gives that hard-to-handle hair lasting volume and styling control.

Reading a Textbook: Examining Biased Arguments

Textbook
Skills

Textbooks strive to present information in a factual, objective manner with relevant and adequate support, in keeping with their purpose to inform. However, textbook authors may choose to present biased arguments for your examination. As a master reader, you are expected to evaluate the nature of the biased argument and the author's purpose for including the biased argument.

EXAMPLE The following passage appears in a college mass communications textbook. As you read the passage, underline biased information. After you read, answer the questions.

Trash TV

¹Television programs fell still lower in quality during the late 1980s and the 1990s with the popularity of "trash TV." ²Network programs and syndication shows alike tried to shock audiences with bloody reconstructions of lurid crimes, emphasis on sexual deviations, and confrontations on racial, sexual, and family problems.

³Many of these programs were presented in news and feature formats that emphasized such "news" as exposés of sexual misconduct by doctors, detailed depictions of grisly murders, and friendly interviews with prostitutes. ⁴News directors expressed anger, contending that the format debased their own legitimate work.

⁵The prime example of sensationalized TV was Geraldo Rivera, who hit perhaps his lowest level with a show on Satanism on NBC in which dismembered corpses and ritualistic child abuse were displayed.

⁶To the dismay of many television officials and critics, this program was the highest-rated two-hour documentary ever shown on network television. ⁷Indeed, putting this show in the same category with such true documentary classics as CBS's "The Selling of the Pentagon" was a gross misnomer.

⁸In the 1990s, some signs emerged that the orgy of sleaze was diminishing as advertisers began to shun the more extreme programs under pressure from viewers' groups and Congressional inquiries. ⁹Sleaze persisted, however, in such shows as "Cops" and its spin-off series including "Top Cops" and "Real-Life Cops" as well as "Studs," "The Love Connection," "Married . . . with Children," "X-Files," and "Tales from the Crypt."

¹⁰Violence predominated in many other shows not considered among the sleaze genre. ¹¹The National Coalition on Television Violence attacked two extremely violent series, "Freddy's Nightmare" and "Friday the 13th." ¹²The former featured intense torture, rape, the meathouse slaughter of women, cannibalism, and the killing of parents. ¹³Equally violent themes, including the serial killing of prostitutes, slow-motion murders, and satanic human sacrifice, characterized the "Friday the 13th" series. ¹⁴Late-evening horror movies replaced the two series in the mid-1990s.

—Agee, Ault, & Emery. *Introduction to Mass Communications*, 12th ed., pp. 83–84.

b   **1.** Overall, the tone of the passage is
    a. positive about "trash TV."
    b. negative about "trash TV."
    c. neutral toward "trash TV."

b   **2.** The primary purpose of the passage is
    a. to encourage readers to condemn "trash TV."
    b. to inform the reader about the nature of "trash TV."
    c. to persuade readers to boycott "trash TV."

a   **3.** In sentence 3, the word "*news*" illustrates the propaganda technique
    a. glittering generalities.   c. bandwagon.
    b. testimonial.   d. false cause.

c   **4.** The words *deviations, sleaze,* and *orgy* are examples of
    a. begging the question.   c. transfer.
    b. personal attacks.   d. straw man.

b   **5.** Sentence 6 illustrates the effect of the propaganda technique
    a. card stacking.   c. plain folks.
    b. bandwagon.   d. testimonial.

EXPLANATION The biased information includes the following words: *Trash, shock, bloody, lurid, deviations, confrontations, misconduct, grisly murders, anger, debased, legitimate, sensationalized, lowest level, Satanism, abuse, dismay, gross misnomer, orgy of sleaze, shun, extreme, sleaze, extremely violent, torture, rape, meathouse slaughter, cannibalism, killing, murders, satanic, sacrifice, horror.*

1. This list of biased words indicates the negative tone (b) toward "trash TV."

2. The primary purpose of the passage is (b) to inform the reader about the nature of "trash TV."

3. In sentence 3, the word "*news*" illustrates (a) glittering generalities. News is thought of as being objective and factual. Calling the content described as trash TV "news" gives a positive or glittering spin to this kind of programming, which is news only in the most general sense of the word.

4. The words *deviations, sleaze,* and *orgy* are examples of the use of transfer. These traits transfer a negative value to "trash TV."

5. Sentence 6 illustrates the effect of the (b) bandwagon technique. High ratings means millions of people jumped on the bandwagon and made trash TV popular.

PRACTICE 8

The following passage appears in a college history textbook. As you read the passage, underline biased words. After you read, answer the questions.

Textbook
Skills

Demon Rum

[1]Reformers must interfere with the affairs of others. [2]Thus there is often something of the busy-body and arrogant meddler about them. [3]How they are regarded usually turns on the observer's own attitude toward their objectives. [4]What is to some an unjustified infringement on a person's private affairs is to others a necessary intervention for that person's own good and for the good of society. [5]Consider the temperance movement, the most widely supported and successful reform of the Age of Reform. [6]Americans in the 1820s consumed huge amounts of alcohol, more than ever before or since. [7]Not that the colonists had been teetotalers. [8]Liquor, mostly in the form of rum or hard apple cider, was cheap and everywhere available. [9]Taverns were an integral part of colonial society. [10]There were alcoholics in colonial America, but because neither political nor religious leaders considered drinking dangerous, there was no alcohol "problem." [11]Most doctors recommended the regular consumption of alcohol as healthy. [12]John Adams, certainly the soul of propriety, drank a tankard of hard cider every day for breakfast. [13]Dr. Benjamin Rush's *Inquiry into the Effects of Ardent Spirits* (1784), which questioned the medicinal benefits of alcohol, fell on deaf ears.

[14]However, alcohol consumption increased markedly in the early years of the new republic, thanks primarily to the availability of cheap corn and rye whiskey distilled in the new states of Kentucky and Tennessee. [15]In the 1820s the per capita consumption of hard liquor reached 5 gallons, well over twice what it is today. [16]Since small children and many grown

people did not drink that much, others obviously drank a great deal more. [17]Many women drank, if mostly at home. [18]Reports of carousing among 14-year-old college freshmen show that youngsters did too. [19]But the bulk of the heavy drinking occurred when men got together, at taverns or grogshops and at work. [20]Many prominent politicians, including Clay and Webster, were heavy consumers. [21]Webster is said to have kept several thousand bottles of wine, whiskey, and other alcoholic beverages in his cellar.

[22]Artisans and common laborers regarded their twice-daily "dram" of whiskey as part of their wages. [23]In workshops, masters were expected to halt production periodically to drink with their apprentices and journeymen. [24]Trips to the neighborhood grogshop also figured into the workaday routine. [25]In 1829 Secretary of War John Eaton estimated that three-quarters of the nation's laborers drank at least 4 ounces of distilled spirits a day.

[26]The foundation of the American Temperance Union in 1826 signaled the start of a national crusade against drunkenness. [27]Employing lectures, pamphlets, rallies, essay contests, and other techniques, the union set out to persuade people to "sign the pledge" not to drink liquor. [28]Primitive sociological studies of the effects of drunkenness added to the effectiveness of the campaign. [29]Reformers were able to show a high statistical correlation between alcohol consumption and crime.

[30]In 1840 an organization of reformed drunkards, the Washingtonians, set out to reclaim alcoholics. [31]One of the most effective Washingtonians was John B. Gough, rescued by the organization after seven years in the gutter. [32]"Crawl from the slimy ooze, ye drowned drunkards," Gough would shout, "and with suffocation's blue and livid lips speak out against the drink!"

[33]Revivalist ministers like Charles Grandison Finney argued that alcohol was one of the great barriers to conversion, which helps explain why Utica, a town of fewer than 13,000 residents in 1840, supported four separate temperance societies in that year. [34]Employers all over the country also signed on, declaring their businesses henceforward to be "cold-water" enterprises. [35]Soon the temperance movement claimed a million members.

—From *The American Nation: A History of the United States to 1877, Volume I*, 10th ed., pp. 287–288 by John A. Garraty and Mark A. Carnes. Copyright © 2000 by Pearson Education, Inc. Printed and Electronically reproduced by permission of Pearson Education, Inc., Upper Saddle River, NJ.

<u> c </u>   **1.** Overall the tone of the passage
  a. is positive about alcohol consumption (drinking).
  b. is negative about alcohol consumption (drinking).
  c. remains neutral toward alcohol consumption (drinking).

_____b_____   **2.** The author's purpose is
      a. to argue against alcohol consumption.
      b. to inform the reader about the reason for the temperance movement.
      c. to amuse the reader by sharing the history of alcohol consumption in the United States.

_____d_____   **3.** Sentence 2 is an example of the propaganda technique
      a. bandwagon.   c. transfer.
      b. testimonials.   d. name-calling.

_____a_____   **4.** Sentences 34–35 are an example of
      a. bandwagon.   c. transfer.
      b. testimonials.   d. name-calling.

APPLICATIONS

Application 1

Read the following mock advertisement. Label each sentence using one of the following letters (some answers may be used more than once):

a. unbiased statement
b. bandwagon
c. plain folks
d. false cause

e. transfer
f. testimonial
g. glittering generality
h. false comparison

Be Free with NicoFree

¹Are you one of the 46 million smokers struggling to kick the habit? ²Are you tired of seeing your hard-earned dollars and good health go up in smoke? ³Take heart—NicoFree chewing gum guarantees instant relief from nicotine addiction. ⁴Just like former Dallas Cowboys' quarterback Troy Aikman, you too can give up smoking for good. ⁵NicoFree allows nicotine to be absorbed through the mucus membranes in the mouth when the gum is chewed. ⁶First, chew one piece of NicoFree until you feel its refreshing, tingling sensation. ⁷Then place the piece between your cheek and your gums or under your tongue. ⁸NicoFree turns the switch to your addiction off. ⁹NicoFree unplugs your cravings. ¹⁰Rap star Under Dawg says, "Like Me, Be Free with NicoFree!"

<u>b</u>	**1.**	<u>g</u>	**6.**
<u>c</u>	**2.**	<u>a</u>	**7.**
<u>d</u>	**3.**	<u>h</u>	**8.**
<u>e</u>	**4.**	<u>h</u>	**9.**
<u>a</u>	**5.**	<u>f</u>	**10.**

Application 2

Study the following photograph used in an anti-litter campaign.

<u>b</u>   **1.** Which of the following propaganda techniques is used in the advertisement?
  a. testimonial
  b. plain folks
  c. transfer

2. Write a caption for the photograph that uses a propaganda technique.

Answers may vary. Sample answer: Be a hero—make America beautiful.

REVIEW TEST 1   Score (number correct) _____ × 20 = _____ %

Biased Arguments

Read the following sets of ideas. Write **UB** if the statement is unbiased, or **B** if the idea is a biased argument.

_UB_ **1.** Many experts believe that human activities are causing temperatures around the world to increase.

_B_ **2.** Rising temperatures, without doubt, will lead to rising sea levels, catastrophic natural disasters, agricultural loss, and widespread disease.

_UB_ **3.** The Kyoto Protocol, established by the United Nations, is an international agreement that aims to reduce carbon dioxide emissions and the presence of greenhouse gases caused by human activities.

_B_ **4.** The effort to stop global warming by liberals like Al Gore and other rich celebrities are misguided and will damage the global economy.

_B_ **5.** Action must be taken to halt global warming.

REVIEW TEST 2   Score (number correct) _____ × 5 = _____ %

Biased Arguments: Fallacies in Logical Thought and Propaganda

A. Write the letter of the fallacy next to its definition.

a. begging the question   d. false cause

b. personal attack   e. false comparison

c. straw man   f. either-or

_c_ **1.** In this fallacy, the original argument is replaced with a weaker version that is easier to challenge than the original argument.

_e_ **2.** This fallacy assumes two things are similar when they are not.

_d_ **3.** This fallacy assumes that because events occurred around or near the same time, they have a cause-and-effect relationship.

___f___ **4.** This fallacy assumes that only two sides of an issue exist.

___a___ **5.** This fallacy restates the point of an argument as the support and conclusion.

___b___ **6.** This fallacy uses abusive remarks in place of evidence for a point or argument.

B. Write the letter of the propaganda technique next to its definition.

a. plain folks   e. name-calling

b. bandwagon   f. glittering generality

c. testimonial   g. card stacking

d. transfer

___c___ **7.** This technique uses irrelevant personal opinions to support a product, idea, or cause.

___b___ **8.** This technique uses or suggests the irrelevant detail that "everyone is doing it."

___g___ **9.** This technique omits factual details in order to misrepresent a product, idea, or cause.

___a___ **10.** This technique uses irrelevant details to build trust based on commonly shared values.

___d___ **11.** This technique creates an association between a product, idea, or cause with a symbol or image that has positive or negative values.

___e___ **12.** This technique uses negative labels for a product, idea, or cause.

___f___ **13.** This technique offers general positive statements that cannot be verified.

C. Write the letter of the fallacy used in each of the following items.

___b___ **14.** If you don't like the rules of the house, get out and live on your own.
   a. begging the question   c. personal attack
   b. either-or   d. straw man

___d___ **15.** The teacher doesn't care if you pass or fail—he still gets paid.
   a. false cause   c. begging the question
   b. either-or   d. personal attack

___a___ **16.** Studying for final exams is like running in a marathon.
   a. false comparison   c. begging the question
   b. straw man   d. false cause

___c___ **17.** Every time you get into serious trouble, Sam and Maurice are nearby. You are not allowed to see either one of them again.
   a. straw man   c. false cause
   b. either-or   d. personal attack

D. Write the letter of the propaganda technique used in each of the following items.

___b___ **18.** A vote for Social Security Reform is a vote for peace of mind.
   a. bandwagon   c. plain folks
   b. glittering generalities   d. transfer

___d___ **19.** A decorated war hero and proven military leader, General Smithenhouser says, "I fought shoulder to shoulder with Senator Treat in the trenches of Viet Nam and in the mountains of Afghanistan. I tell you, you will find no greater man for President of the United States. I pledge my full support to his candidacy."
   a. bandwagon   c. plain folks
   b. glittering generalities   d. transfer

___c___ **20.** If you long for fluffy, light biscuits just like the ones fresh from your grandmother's oven, then buy Country Biscuits.
   a. bandwagon
   b. glittering generalities
   c. plain folks
   d. transfer

REVIEW TEST 3   Score (number correct) _____ × 10 = _____ %

Advanced Argument

Before Reading: Survey the following editorial from *Washington Post*. Skim the passage, noting the words in **bold** print and answer the Before Reading questions. Then, answer the After Reading questions and respond to the writing prompt.

Vocabulary Preview

statutory rape (9):
sexual relations with a
minor, someone who
has not reached the
legal age of consent

consensual (14):
involving the
agreement of all

assaultive (17):
extremely aggressive or
disposed to attack

prevailing (20):
current, usual, popular

sentiment (20):
feeling, response,
opinion

Should We Be Criminalizing Bullies?

10.0 GE/710 words   *by Ruth Marcus*

[1]My heart aches for the parents of Phoebe Prince, the 15-year-old Massachusetts high school student who committed suicide in January after being relentlessly bullied at school and online.

[2]My heart aches for her younger sister, who found Phoebe hanging in the stairwell of the family's home. [3]A scarf the sister had bought her as a Christmas gift was knotted around Phoebe's neck.

[4]My heart aches for Phoebe, who arrived from Ireland last fall only to endure months of abuse from classmates at South Hadley High School, the apparent result of Phoebe's brief fling with a popular football player.

[5]My heart aches, but I also question the wisdom of filing criminal charges against nine of Phoebe's former classmates, as happened last week. [6]Bullying should be taken seriously—by teachers, administrators, parents and, yes, fellow students. [7]I'm doubtful, though, that criminal prosecution is the best way to punish or prevent it.

[8]Nine students were charged, including three girls not named because they are juveniles. [9]Two boys, 17 and 18, were accused of **statutory rape**; the age of consent in Massachusetts is 16.

[10]One of the juveniles is charged with "assault by means of a dangerous weapon, to wit: a bottle, can or similar beverage container"—apparently throwing a soda can at Phoebe as she walked home from school the day she died. [11]The other charges include stalking, harassment, violation of civil rights and, my favorite, disturbance of a school assembly.

[12]If this sounds derisive, it's not because I doubt the seriousness of the conduct but because the specific counts underscore how clumsy a tool criminal law is to deal with such behavior. [13]Charging nine students is casting an awfully wide net.

[14]The statutory rape charges are especially troubling, assuming the sex was **consensual**. [15]Teenage boys engage in this conduct with teenage girls every day without being prosecuted. [16]That activity, however unwise, does not suddenly acquire criminal overtones because the girl involved killed herself.

[17]In announcing the charges, District Attorney Elizabeth Scheibel described "a nearly three-month campaign of verbally abusive, **assaultive**

behavior and threats of physical harm . . . relentless activity directed toward Phoebe, designed to humiliate her and to make it impossible for her to remain at school." [18]The bullying, Scheibel said, "far exceeded the limits of normal teenage relationship-related quarrels."

[19]How does she know—and do we routinely want prosecutors making these calls? [20]*Slate*'s Emily Bazelon reported that among South Hadley students, "the **prevailing sentiment** was that, yes, Phoebe had been mistreated but not in some **unprecedented** way. [21]'A lot of it was normal girl drama,' one girl told me. [22]'If you want to label it bullying, then I've bullied girls and girls have bullied me. . . . [23]It was one of the worst things I've heard of some girls doing to another girl. [24]But it wouldn't have hurt most people that much.' "

[25]The criminalization of bullying risks a slippery slope down the age range. [26]In Waltham, Mass., in January an 11-year-old was charged with two counts of assault and battery with a dangerous weapon—using her foot and a locker door—and one count of assault with a dangerous weapon using scissors.

[27]The kids who bullied Phoebe Prince should be punished—suspended, expelled, required to attend counseling. [28]Still, to be a teenager is to do stupid things. [29]The teenage brain is a work in progress. [30]The prefrontal cortex, the part linked to impulse control, judgment and decision-making, is still maturing. [31]This is why all teenagers need adult supervision, from parents and teachers.

[32]And it is why not enough responsibility has been placed on those whose brains were fully developed: the school staff who apparently knew of the harassment and did not do enough to stop it. [33]As Scheibel reported, "The investigation has revealed that certain faculty, staff and administrators of the high school also were alerted to the harassment of Phoebe Prince before her death."

[34]The school says it did what it could when it knew. [35]To its credit, it had brought in an expert on bullying even before Phoebe's problems came to light. [36]Still, the consultant told *USA Today* that when she returned to the school after Phoebe's death, "I was told there was no visible sign these kids had faced consequences for what they'd done."

[37]As a legal matter, this is not a crime. [38]In a broader sense, it is nothing short of criminal.

Before Reading

Vocabulary

_____c_____ **1.** What is the best meaning of the word **unprecedented** in sentence 20?
a. normal
c. extraordinary
b. predictable
d. brutal

Tone and Purpose

_____c_____ **2.** The author's tone and purpose is
a. to entertain readers with shocking details about bullying.
b. to inform readers with objective details about the consequences of bullying.
c. to persuade readers with facts and opinions against prosecuting bullies.

After Reading

Central Idea

_____b_____ **3.** Which sentence best states the author's central idea?
a. sentence 1
c. sentence 6
b. sentence 7
d. sentence 38

Supporting Details

_____d_____ **4.** According to the passage, how long had Phoebe Prince been bullied?
a. a few weeks
c. 11 months
b. 15 months
d. 3 months

Thought Patterns

_____a_____ **5.** The thought pattern of paragraph 12 (sentences 27–31) is
a. cause and effect.
c. time order.
b. contrast.
d. classification.

Fact and Opinion

_____b_____ **6.** Sentences 37 and 38 are statements of
a. fact.
b. opinion.
c. fact and opinion.

Inferences

___d___ **7.** Based on the details of the passage, which of the following is a valid inference?
a. Phoebe was not bullied, but only experienced normal teenage relationship-related quarrels.
b. The bullies should not face serious consequences because a teenager does stupid things.
c. Bullying is unavoidable and cannot be stopped by parents or educators.
d. School administrators, faculty, and staff have a duty to report and stop bullying at school.

Argument

___a___ **8.** Bullying is a form of
a. personal attack.
b. testimonial.
c. straw man.
d. false comparison.

___b___ **9.** In sentence 28, the author uses the fallacy of
a. false comparison.
b. personal attack.
c. bandwagon.
d. begging the question.

___d___ **10.** In sentences 37 and 38, the author uses the fallacy of
a. false cause.
b. personal attack.
c. bandwagon.
d. begging the question.

WHAT DO YOU THINK?

Have you or anyone you know been involved in bullying? Do you think bullying is a widespread problem or are the cases mentioned in the article isolated events? Do you agree with the author's claim that bullying is not a crime? Why or why not? Assume you are taking a college course in sociology, and your professor has assigned weekly writing assignments on current events. Write an essay in which you agree with or disagree with the claim that teenagers should not be legally prosecuted for bullying other teenagers. In your essay, discuss the social climate in which bullying occurs. Discuss both the causes and effects of bullying.

Textbook
Skills

REVIEW TEST 4

Score (number correct) _____ × 10 = _____ %

Advanced Argument

Before Reading: Survey the following passage adapted from a college sociology textbook. Skim the passage, noting the words in **bold** print. Answer the Before Reading questions that follow the passage. Then, read the passage. Next, answer the After Reading questions. Use the discussion and writing topics as activities to do after reading.

Vocabulary Preview

rampant (3): uncontrolled

nomadic (5): wandering

ethnocentric (7): belief in the superiority of one's own ethnic group

immunity (15): resistance

accommodated (21): adjusted to

intervene (29): interfere

pacification (31): soothing, subduing

10.0 GE/673 words   **Native Americans**

¹"I don't go so far as to think that the only good Indians are dead Indians, but I believe nine out of ten are—and I shouldn't inquire too closely in the case of the tenth. ²The most vicious cowboy has more moral principle than the average Indian."

—Teddy Roosevelt, 1886 President of the United States, 1901–1909

³This quote from Teddy Roosevelt provides insight into the **rampant** racism of earlier generations. ⁴Yet, even today, thanks to countless grade B Westerns, some Americans view the original inhabitants of what became the United States as wild, uncivilized savages, a single group of people subdivided into separate tribes. ⁵The European immigrants to the colonies, however, encountered diverse groups of people with a variety of cultures— from **nomadic** hunters and gatherers to people who lived in wooden houses in settled agricultural communities. ⁶Altogether, they spoke over 700 languages. ⁷Each group had its own norms and values—and the usual **ethnocentric** pride in its own culture. ⁸Consider what happened in 1744, when the colonists of Virginia offered college scholarships for "savage" lads. ⁹The Iroquois replied:

¹⁰"Several of our young people were formerly brought up at the colleges of Northern Provinces. ¹¹They were instructed in all your sciences. ¹²But when they came back to us, they were bad runners, ignorant of every means of living in the woods, unable to bear either cold or hunger, knew neither how to build a cabin, take a deer, or kill an enemy . . . ¹³They were totally good for nothing."

¹⁴They added, "If the English gentlemen would send a dozen or two of their children to Onondaga, the great Council would take

care of their education, bring them up in really what was the best manner and make men of them." (Nash 1974; in McLemore 1994)

[15]Native Americans, who numbered about 10 million, had no **immunity** to the diseases the Europeans brought with them. [16]With deaths due to disease—and warfare, a much lesser cause—their number was reduced to about one-twentieth its original size. [17]A hundred years ago, the Native American population reached a low point of a half million. [18]Native Americans, who now number about 2 million, speak 150 different languages. [19]Like Latinos and Asian Americans, they do not think of themselves as a single people who fit neatly within a single label.

[20]At first, relations between the European settlers and the Native Americans were by and large peaceful. [21]The Native Americans **accommodated** the strangers, as there was plenty of land for both the newcomers and themselves. [22]As Native Americans were pushed aside and wave after wave of settlers continued to arrive, however, Pontiac, an Ottawa chief, saw the future—and didn't like it. [23]He convinced several tribes to unite in an effort to push the Europeans into the sea. [24]He almost succeeded, but failed when the English were reinforced by fresh troops.

[25]A pattern of deception developed. [26]The U.S. government would make treaties to buy some of a tribe's land, with the promise to honor forever the tribe's right to what it had not sold. [27]European immigrants, who continued to pour into the United States, would disregard these boundaries. [28]The tribes would resist, with death tolls on both sides. [29]The U.S. government would then **intervene**—not to enforce the treaty but to force the tribe off its lands. [30]In its relentless drive westward, the U.S. government embarked on a policy of **genocide**. [31]It assigned the U.S. cavalry the task of "**pacification**," which translated into slaughtering Native Americans who "stood in the way" of this territorial expansion.

—From *Essentials of Sociology: A Down-to-Earth Approach*, 7th ed., pp. 247–248. by James M. Henslin. Copyright © 2007 by Pearson Education, Inc. Reproduced by permission of Pearson Education, Inc., Boston, MA.

Before Reading

Vocabulary in Context

Use context clues to state in your own words the definition of the following term. Indicate the context clue you used.

1. In sentence 30, what does the word **genocide** mean? <u>extermination</u>
<u>of a group of people</u>

2. Identify the context clue used for the word **genocide** in sentence 30.
<u>the synonym "slaughter" and general sense of the passage</u>

Tone and Purpose

<u>b</u>   **3.** What is the overall tone and purpose of the passage?
     a. to inform the reader about the historical relationship between Native Americans, European settlers, and the U.S. government
     b. to persuade the reader that Native Americans have endured a pattern of racism that continues today
     c. to entertain the reader with surprising details about Native American history

After Reading

Central Idea

4. Use your own words to state the central idea of the passage: <u>Wording may</u>
<u>vary. Native Americans, a diverse and proud people, endured disease, racism,</u>
<u>and mistreatment from European settlers and the U.S. government.</u>

Main Idea and Supporting Details

<u>a</u>   **5.** Sentence 15 states a
     a. main idea.   c. minor supporting detail.
     b. major supporting detail.

Transitions

<u>d</u>   **6.** The relationship between sentences 4 and 5 is
     a. cause and effect.   c. time order.
     b. addition.   d. contrast.

Thought Patterns

<u>c</u>   **7.** The overall thought pattern of the passage is
     a. cause and effect.   c. time order.
     b. listing.   d. contrast.

Fact and Opinion

____b____ **8.** Sentences 1 and 2 are statements of
  a. fact.   c. fact and opinion.
  b. opinion.

Inferences

____b____ **9.** Based on the information in sentence 31, the U.S. government's use of "pacification" implies that
  a. the U.S. government tried to coexist peacefully with Native Americans.
  b. the U.S. government used a glittering generality as a propaganda technique to describe its violent actions against Native Americans.
  c. the Native Americans initiated violence and caused the actions taken against them by the U.S. government.

Argument

____b____ **10.** Sentences 1 and 2 are examples of the logical fallacy
  a. begging the question.   c. false comparison.
  b. straw man.   d. personal attack.

WHAT DO YOU THINK?

How did the values of the Iroquois differ from those of the colonists? Based on this passage, which group seems more "savage" and why? How would you define ethnocentric pride? What examples of ethnocentric pride have you observed or learned about? Assume your community is going to celebrate the various ethnic groups that live in your area during the traditional Fourth of July celebration. You have been asked to represent your ethnic group by giving a short speech that explains your heritage. Write a draft of your speech that is at least three paragraphs long. In your speech, define your ethnic group, the core values of your culture, and a key tradition that reflects those values.

 ## After Reading About Advanced Argument

Before you move on to the Mastery Tests on advanced argument, take time to reflect on your learning and performance by answering the following questions. Write your answers in your notebook.

- How has my knowledge base or prior knowledge about advanced argument, persuasive techniques changed?

- Based on my studies, how do I think I will perform on the Mastery Test(s)? Why do I think my scores will be above average, average, or below average?

- Would I recommend this chapter to other students who want to learn more about advanced argument: persuasive techniques? Why or why not?

Test your understanding of what you have learned about advanced argument: persuasive techniques by completing the Chapter 13 Review Card in the insert near the end of your text.

CONNECT TO myreadinglab

To check your progress in meeting Chapter 13's learning outcomes, log in to **www.myreadinglab.com** and try the following exercises.

- The "Critical Thinking" section of MyReadingLab gives additional information about advanced argument, persuasive techniques. The section provides an overview, model, practices, and tests. To access this resource, click on the "Study Plan" tab. Then click on "Critical Thinking." Then click on the following links as needed: "Overview," "Model," "Critical Thinking: Facts and Opinions (Flash Animation)," "Practice," and "Test."

- The "Study Skills Website" section of MyReadingLab also gives additional information about advanced argument, persuasive techniques. To access these resources, go to the "Other Sources" box on the home page of MyReadingLab. Click on "Study Skills Website." Then scroll down the page to the heading "Life Skills" and click on "Critical Thinking." Explore each of the links on the bar on the left side of the page.

- To measure your mastery of this chapter, complete the tests in the "Critical Thinking" section and click on Gradebook to find your results.

Chapter Review

Summary of Key Concepts of a Reading System for Master Readers

LEARNING OUTCOME

Assess your comprehension of prior knowledge and the reading process.

- Comprehension is <u>an understanding of what has been read</u>.
- Prior knowledge is <u>the large body of information that is learned throughout a lifetime of experience</u>.
- Use prior knowledge to <u>increase comprehension</u>.

  - Activate <u>prior knowledge</u> by asking <u>"What do I already know about this topic?"</u>
  - Check <u>new information</u> against prior knowledge by asking, <u>"Does this make sense based on what I know?"</u>
  - Check for <u>growth or change in your knowledge base</u> by asking, <u>"What did I learn?"</u>

- The reading process has three phases: <u>Before Reading, During Reading, and After Reading.</u>

- SQ3R, an acronym for a reading process, stands for <u>Survey, Question, Read, Recite, and Review</u>. SQ3R activates prior knowledge and offers strategies for each phase of the reading process:

  - Before Reading, <u>Survey</u>: Skim <u>titles, introductions, headings, bold and italic type, pictures, and graphs</u>. <u>Question</u>: Ask <u>"What is my purpose for reading? What do I already know? What do I need to know?"</u>
  - During Reading: <u>Read</u>. <u>Annotate</u> key words and ideas. Repair confusion. Reread.

- After Reading: <u>Recite</u>: Answer questions such as <u>"What did I learn? What is the most important idea? How have my views changed?"</u>

  <u>Review</u>: Recall <u>key ideas and terms</u>. Summarize.

- Textbook features help readers understand and learn the vast amount of information in a textbook. A few examples are as follows:

  - Table of Contents: <u>a list of chapters in order of appearance</u>
  - Index: <u>an alphabetical list of all the specific topics in a textbook</u>
  - Glossary: <u>an alphabetical list of specialized words and their meanings</u>
  - Preface: <u>a type of introduction that discusses the textbook's purpose, format and features</u>
  - Appendices: <u>sections of additional material</u>
  - Typographical features: <u>bold and italic type to draw attention to important ideas and terms</u>
  - Graphics: <u>graphs, tables, diagrams maps, photographs, etc. to support information</u>

Test Your Comprehension of A Reading System for Master Readers

Respond to the following question and prompt. Answers may vary.

LEARNING OUTCOME ① ② ③ ④ ⑤ ⑥ ⑦ ⑧

Describe your reading process. How did you read before your studied this chapter? Will you change your reading process? If so, how? If not, why not? _____

2 Chapter Review

Summary of Key Concepts of Vocabulary Skills

**LEARNING
OUTCOME
❶ ❹** Assess your comprehension of vocabulary skills.

- **Vocabulary** is all the words used or understood by a person .
- The acronym SAGE identifies four of the most common types of context clues: The four context clues and their definitions are as follows:

Context Clue	Definition
■ Synonym	a word that has the same or nearly the same meaning as another word
■ Antonym	a word that has the opposite meaning of another word
■ General context	the entire sentence or surrounding text that helps you to determine the meaning of a new or unfamiliar word
■ Example	clues often introduced with the signal words consisting of, for example, for instance, including, like, and such as

- The three basic word parts and their definitions are as follows:

Word Part	Definition
■ Root	the main part of the word
■ Prefix	the group of letters with a specific meaning added to the beginning of a word to make a new word
■ Suffix	the group of letters with a specific meaning added to the end of a word to make a new word

- Each subject matter has its own <u>specialized vocabulary</u>.
- A glossary is <u>an alphabetical listing of all the specialized vocabulary used</u> <u>throughout a textbook</u>, often provided as an extra section in the back of the book <u>the back of the book</u>.

Test Your Comprehension of Vocabulary Skills

Respond to the following prompts. Answers may vary.

LEARNING OUTCOME
2 **3** **4** **6**
8

Demonstrate your use of context clues. Use the headings below and create a chart based on the four types of context clues. Then, complete the chart with new words you have come across recently.

Type of Clue	New Word	Meaning of Word	Source Sentence of Word

LEARNING OUTCOME
3 **5** **6** **7**
8

Demonstrate your ability to decode the meaning of words using word parts. Use the blank word web below to create your own web of words linked by word parts. Use a family of words you have come across recently.

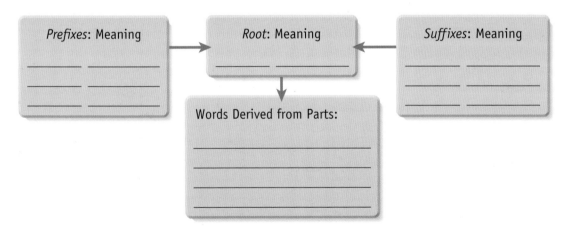

LEARNING OUTCOME
3 **5** **6** **7**
8

Create a glossary of terms for a subject you are currently studying; use the headings below to create your glossary. Then, complete the chart with new words you have come across recently.

Word	Definition	Source Sentence of Word

3 Chapter Review

Summary of Key Concepts of Stated Main Ideas

LEARNING OUTCOME ❶ ❸ ❺ Assess your comprehension of stated main ideas. Complete the following two-column notes with information from the chapter.

Reading Concept	Definition
Topic Sentence	The main idea of a paragraph stated in one sentence
Central Idea	The main idea of a passage made up of two or more paragraphs
Thesis Statement	A sentence that states the central point of a longer passage
Various Locations of the Stated Main Idea	In the beginning, in the middle, at the end, or in the beginning and the end
Deductive Thinking	The flow of ideas from general to specific
Inductive Thinking	The flow of ideas from specific to general

Test Your Comprehension of Stated Main Ideas

Respond to the following questions and prompts. Answers may vary.

LEARNING
OUTCOME
2 5

In your own words, what is the difference between deductive and inductive thinking? Deductive thinking states the main idea first followed by specific details of support. In contrast, inductive thinking begins with the details and leads up to the main idea, which is stated at the end of the passage.

LEARNING
OUTCOME
1 3

In your own words, what is the difference between a topic sentence and a thesis statement? A topic sentence is the stated main idea of a paragraph. In contrast, a thesis statement is the stated main idea of the central point of two or more paragraphs.

LEARNING
OUTCOME
2 4 5

Draw and label four graphs that show the possible locations of stated main ideas.

LEARNING
OUTCOME
5 6

Identify and discuss the two most important ideas in this chapter that will help you improve your reading comprehension. _____

Summary of Key Concepts of Implied Main Ideas

LEARNING OUTCOME ❶ Assess your comprehension of implied main ideas. Complete the following two-column notes, set up as question-answers, with information from the chapter.

Implied Main Ideas	
What is an implied main idea?	An implied main idea is a main idea that is not stated directly but is strongly suggested by the supporting details in a passage.
What three questions can help determine an implied main idea?	What is the topic of the passage? What are the types of supporting details in the passage? What is the controlling point of the passage?
What should be annotated in a passage to help determine a main idea?	Mark the topic; the words that reveal the author's bias; and thought patterns or types of details used in the passage.
What is the implied central idea?	An implied central idea is an unstated main idea of several paragraphs suggested by the details in the passage.

Test Your Comprehension of Implied Main Ideas

Respond to the following questions and prompts. Answers may vary.

LEARNING
OUTCOME
❷ ❸

How can the skills you use to identify the stated main idea help you determine the implied main idea? A stated main idea is a topic sentence, and a topic sentence states the topic and the author's controlling point about a topic. A passage that implies a main idea also has a topic and a controlling point. So I can use the topic and the supporting details to create a topic sentence that states the implied main idea.

LEARNING
OUTCOME
❼

Describe how you will use what you have learned about implied main ideas in your reading process to comprehend textbook material.

_____

_____

_____

_____

LEARNING
OUTCOME
❸ ❹ ❻

Study the following concept map. Then, write the implied main idea suggested by the details in the map.

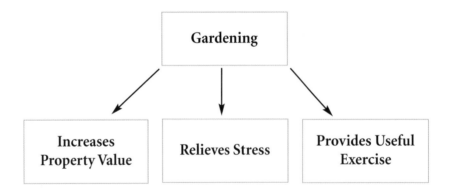

Implied main idea: Gardening has several benefits, such as increasing property value, relieving stress, and providing exercise.

LEARNING
OUTCOME
❺ ❼

Identify and discuss the two most important ideas in this chapter that will help you improve your reading comprehension. _____

_____

_____

_____

5 Chapter Review

Summary of Key Concepts of Supporting Details

LEARNING OUTCOME ❶ ❸ Assess your comprehension of supporting details. Fill in the blanks with information from the chapter.

- To locate supporting details in a passage, a master reader turns the _stated main idea_ into a _question_.

- A major supporting detail _directly explains, develops, or illustrates the main idea_.

- A minor supporting detail _explains, develops, or illustrates a major supporting detail_.

- A _summary_ is a _brief, clear restatement of the most important points of a paragraph or longer passage_.

- Often you will want to _paraphrase_, or restate, ideas in your own words.

- _Annotating_ or marking your text _during_ reading will help you create a _summary_ after you read.

- To create a summary for a passage with a stated main idea, _ask and answer questions based on the main idea_.

- To create a summary for a passage with an implied main idea, _ask and answer questions based on the title and the major supporting details_.

Test Your Comprehension of Supporting Details

Respond to the following questions and prompts. Answers may vary.

LEARNING OUTCOME ❶ ❸ In your own words, how do major and minor supporting details differ? _A major detail directly supports or explains the main idea of a passage. In contrast, a minor detail supports or explains a major detail. By_

5-1

giving information about a major detail, a minor detail indirectly supports the main idea. So major details are more important to the main idea than are minor details.

LEARNING OUTCOME ❷❹❺　In the space below, outline the steps for creating a summary for stated and implied main ideas. See pages 201–204.

Topic: Creating a Summary

Main Idea: A master reader can use headings, main ideas, and major supporting details to create a summary of a textbook passage.

A. **Major Supporting Details: Stated Main Ideas**

1. Determine the main idea.

2. Use the main idea to create a question.

3. Write this question in the margin of the textbook.

4. During reading, assign a number or letter to each major detail that answers the question based on the main idea.

5. After reading, briefly restate in your own words the ideas you marked in the text.

B. **Major Supporting Details: Implied Main Ideas**

1. Identify the topic of the passage.

2. Locate and label each heading or major supporting detail in the passage.

3. For each marked detail, ask the question "What controlling point or opinion about the topic does this detail reveal?"

4. Write a brief answer in the margin next to the detail you marked.

5. After reading, create a topic sentence or thesis statement for the passage.

6. Use only a few brief sentences to create the entire summary that combines the main idea and the major supporting details.

LEARNING OUTCOME ❺❻❼　Summarize the two most important ideas in this chapter that will help you improve your reading comprehension. _____
_____

_____

6 Chapter Review

Summary of Key Concepts of Outlines and Concept Maps

LEARNING OUTCOME ① Assess your comprehension of outlines and concept maps. Complete the chart with information from the chapter.

Outlines and Concept Maps: Question-Answer Two-Column Notes	
What is the purpose of an outline?	An outline shows the relationships among the main idea, major supporting details, and minor supporting details.
Which signal words may an author use to introduce a main idea?	An author may use the following signal words to introduce a main idea: a few causes, a number of reasons, several steps, or several kinds of.
Which signal words may an author use to introduce a supporting detail?	An author may use the following signal words to introduce a supporting detail: first, second, furthermore, moreover, next, or finally
How does a formal outline use Roman numerals and numbers?	A formal outline uses Roman numerals to indicate the main idea, capital letters to indicate the major details, and Arabic numbers to indicate the minor details.
What is a concept map?	A concept map is a diagram that shows the flow of ideas from the main idea to the supporting details.

Test Your Comprehension of Outlines and Concept Maps

Respond to the following questions and prompts. Answers may vary.

LEARNING OUTCOME ② ③ In the space below, create an outline and a concept map for the following terms from a college anatomy and physiology textbook.

Skeletal Muscle; Smooth Muscle; Muscle Types; Cardiac Muscle; Producing Movement; Maintaining Posture; Muscle Functions; Stabilizing Joints

Outline: _____   Muscles _____

    I. Muscle Types _____

        A. Skeletal Muscle _____

        B. Smooth Muscle _____

        C. Cardiac Muscle _____

    II. Muscle Functions _____

        A. Producing Movement _____

        B. Maintaining Posture _____

        C. Stabilizing Joints _____

Concept Map: _____

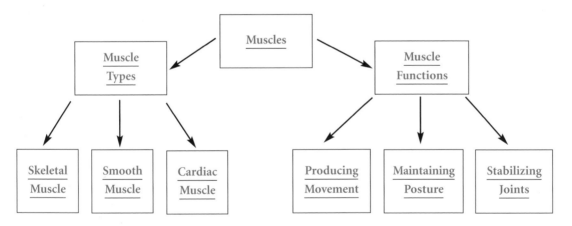

LEARNING OUTCOME ④ Summarize the two most important ideas in this chapter that will help you improve your reading comprehension. _____

_____

_____

7 Chapter Review

Summary of Key Concepts of Transitions and Thought Patterns

LEARNING OUTCOME ① ④ Assess your comprehension of transitions and thought patterns. Complete the following two-column notes of terms and definitions with information from the chapter.

Term	Definition/Examples
Transitions	are words and phrases that signal thought patterns by showing the logical relationship within sentences and between sentences
Thought pattern	shows the logical relationship among ideas in a paragraph or passage established by transitions
Time order: Narration Time order: Process	shows a chain of events shows steps, stages, or directions that can be repeated at any time with similar results
Listing pattern	presents an orderly series of reasons, details, or points
Examples of signal words for listing	and, also, and furthermore
Classification pattern	sorts ideas into smaller groups and describes the traits of each group
Examples of classification signal words	first type, second type, or another group
Space order pattern	describes a person, place, or thing based on its location or the way it is arranged in space
Examples of words used to establish space order pattern	adjacent, below, and underneath

Test Your Comprehension of Transitions and Thought Patterns

Respond to the following questions and prompts. Answers may vary.

LEARNING OUTCOME ① In your own words, what is a transition? A transition is a word that states the relationship of one idea to another or to a group of ideas. A transition signals the author's thought pattern.

LEARNING OUTCOME ① In your own words, what is a thought pattern? A thought pattern is the order of ideas an author uses to get a point across to a reader.

LEARNING OUTCOME ② ③ ⑤ In the space below, illustrate the thought pattern of the following ideas from a college human anatomy textbook by creating an outline or concept map.

Burns are classified according to their severity (depth) as first-, second-, or third-degree burns. In first-degree burns, only the epidermis is damaged. The area becomes red and swollen. First-degree burns are not usually serious and generally heal in two to three days without any special attention. Sunburn is usually a first-degree burn. Second-degree burns involve injury to the epidermis and the upper region of the dermis. The skin is red and painful, and *blisters* appear. Because sufficient numbers of epithelial cells are still present, regrowth can occur. First- and second-degree burns are referred to as partial-thickness burns. Third-degree burns destroy the entire thickness of the skin, so these burns are also called full-thickness burns. In third-degree burns, regeneration is not possible, and skin grafting must be done to cover the underlying exposed tissues.

—Adapted from Lutgens & Tarbuck. *Foundations of Earth Science*, 5th ed., pp. 4–6.

Burns are classified according to their severity (depth)

   A. In first-degree burns, only the epidermis is damaged.

   B. Second-degree burns involve injury to the epidermis and the upper region of the dermis.

   C. Third-degree burns destroy the entire thickness of the skin.

LEARNING OUTCOME ⑥ Summarize the two most important ideas in this chapter that will help you improve your reading comprehension.

8 Chapter Review

Summary of Key Concepts of More Thought Patterns

LEARNING OUTCOME ❶ Assess your comprehension of thought patterns. Complete the following two-column notes of terms and definitions with information from the chapter.

Term	Definition/Examples
Comparison	points out the ways two or more ideas are alike
Words and phrases of comparison	like, similarly, and likewise
Contrast	points out the ways two or more ideas are different
Words and phrases of contrast	but, despite, however, yet
Cause	states why something happens
Effect	states a result or outcome
Words and phrases of cause and effect	as a result, leads to, and therefore
Generalization and example	makes a general statement and offers an example or a series of examples to clarify the generalization
Definition and example	explains the meaning of new, difficult, or special terms. Examples show how the word is used or applied.
Words and phrases of example	an illustration, for example, for instance

Test Your Comprehension of More Thought Patterns

Respond to the following questions and prompts. Answers may vary.

LEARNING OUTCOME ❶
In your own words, what is the difference between comparison and contrast? Comparison explains how ideas or objects are similar to each other. Contrast explains how ideas or objects are different from each other.

LEARNING OUTCOME ❶
In your own words, what is the difference between a cause and an effect? A cause states the reason something happens. In contrast, an effect states a result. A cause leads to an effect.

LEARNING OUTCOME ❶
In your own words, what are the similarities and differences between these two thought patterns: *generalization and example and definition and example?* The generalization-and-example thought pattern is used when an author makes any kind of a broad or general statement. Then the author gives an example to make the general point clear, In contrast, the definition-and-example thought pattern is used to give the meaning of a specific word. Then the author gives an example to make the meaning of the word more clear. In both cases, the author uses examples as supporting details.

LEARNING OUTCOME ❷❸❹
In the space below, create a concept map based on the information in the paragraph.

According to research, meditation can have positive emotional and physical effects. Regular meditation leads to increased control over one's emotions. Regular meditation also contributes to lower blood pressure and cholesterol levels.

Emotional effect: increased control of emotions

Meditation⟶Positive effects

Physical effect: lowered blood pressure and cholesterol levels

LEARNING OUTCOME ❺
Summarize the two most important ideas in this chapter that will help you improve your reading comprehension.

9 Chapter Review

Summary of Key Concepts of Fact and Opinion

Copyright © 2011 Pearson Education, Inc.

LEARNING OUTCOME ❶ Assess your comprehension of fact and opinion. Complete the following two-column notes of terms and definitions with information from the chapter.

Term	Definition
A fact	a specific detail that is true based on objective proof
An opinion	an interpretation, value judgment, or belief that cannot be proved or disproved
Objective proof	physical evidence, an eyewitness account, or the result of an accepted scientific method
An informed opinion	develops by gathering and analyzing evidence
An expert opinion	develops through much training and knowledge in the field
A fact	states reality and uses unbiased words
An opinion	interprets reality and uses biased words
Biased words	express opinions, value judgments, and interpretations
A qualifier	may express an absolute, unwavering opinion using words like always or never

Test Your Comprehension of Fact and Opinion

Respond to the following questions and prompts. Answers may vary.

LEARNING OUTCOME 1 5

In your own words, what is the difference between a fact and an opinion? A fact can be proven or verified. An opinion is someone's value judgment, interpretation, or belief.

LEARNING OUTCOME 2 3 4

In your own words, what is the difference between an informed opinion and an expert opinion? The main difference between an informed opinion and an expert opinion is based on a person's education and experience in relationship to a particular topic. For example, a student can form an informed opinion by writing a research paper on a topic. In contrast, a professor has formed an expert opinion on a particular topic by earning an advanced degree, teaching others, and writing articles or books on the subject.

LEARNING OUTCOME 1 2 3 5

In your own words, describe how to distinguish between fact and opinion. To distinguish between a fact and an opinioin, a reader can ask the following questions: Can the statement be proved or disproved? Can the statement be observed in practice? Can the statement be verified by witnesses, manuscripts, or documents? Does the author use biased words or qualifiers? In addition, a reader can evaluate the context of the author, and the context of the source.

LEARNING OUTCOME 7

Identify the following two statements as fact or opinion. Then explain the importance of knowing the difference between fact and opinion.

___F___ Most fast food is high in calories and fat and low in nutrition.

___O___ Fast food tastes great.

It is important to know the difference between facts and opinions because it is important to know what has been proven and what is believed to be true. A fact is proven. An opinion is given. An opinion is quite often someone's judgment or viewpoint about a fact.

LEARNING OUTCOME 6

Summarize the two most important ideas in this chapter that will help you improve your reading comprehension. _____

10 Chapter Review

Summary of Key Concepts of Tone and Purpose

LEARNING OUTCOME ❶ ❸

Assess your comprehension of tone and purpose. Complete the following two-column notes of terms and definitions with information from the chapter.

Term	Definition
Tone	the author's attitude toward a topic
Objective tone words	usually present facts and reasonable explanations
Subjective tone words	describe feelings, judgments, or opinions
The author's purpose	is his or her reason for writing about a topic
The primary purpose	is the main reason the author writes the passage
The Purpose: To Inform	uses facts to teach or explain a main idea
The Purpose: To Entertain	amuses or interests the audience
The Purpose: To Persuade	combines facts with emotional appeals to sway readers to a particular point of view
Verbal irony	occurs when the author's words state one thing but imply the opposite
Situational irony	occurs when the events of a situation differ from what is expected

Test Your Comprehension of Tone and Purpose

Respond to the following questions and prompts. Answers may vary.

LEARNING
OUTCOME
2 **4** **5**

In your own words, what is the relationship between tone and purpose?
Tone reveals an author's purpose. For example, to inform, an author usually
uses unbiased, neutral words. To entertain, an author may use vivid,
exaggerated, or surprising details and descriptions. To persuade, an
author takes a strong stand with words like "should" and "must."

LEARNING
OUTCOME
2

In your own words, what is the difference between verbal and situational irony? Verbal irony is based on words—what someone says.
Situational irony is based on an event or series of events—what occurs.

LEARNING
OUTCOME
6 **7**

Use a checklist to help you determine the tone and purpose of passages. Select a passage to analyze; then complete the following checklist with information from the passage.

Title of Passage:			
Subjective Tone	**Yes**	**No**	**Examples (words or phrases)/Explanations**
Objective Tone			
Irony			
Verbal Irony			
Situational Irony			
Primary Purpose			
To Inform			
To Persuade			
To Entertain			

LEARNING
OUTCOME
7

Summarize the two most important ideas in this chapter that will
help you improve your reading comprehension. _____
_____
_____

Summary of Key Concepts about Inferences

LEARNING OUTCOME ❶❸❺ Assess your comprehension of inferences. Complete the following two-column notes of terms and definitions with information from the chapter.

Term	Definition
Inference	an unstated idea that is suggested by the facts or details in a passage
Valid inference	a logical conclusion based on evidence
Invalid conclusion	a false inference that is not based on the details, facts in the text, or on reasonable thinking
The 5-step VALID Thinking Process	Step 1: Verify and value the facts. Step 2: Assess prior knowledge. Step 3: Learn from the text. Step 4: Investigate for bias. Step 5: Detect contradictions.

 ## Test Your Comprehension of Inferences

Respond to the following questions and prompts. Answers may vary.

LEARNING OUTCOME ❶❷ In your own words, what is the difference between a valid and an invalid inference? A valid inference is based on the facts or evidence stated in the passage. An invalid inference cannot be supported by the details in the passage. Often, an invalid inference is based on the reader's opinion about the topic instead of the evidence given about the topic.

LEARNING
OUTCOME
4 5 6

Complete the following three-column notes about creative expression. Use your own examples.

Creative Expression: Literary Devices

Literary Device	Meaning	Example
Connotations of words	The emotional meaning of words	_____ _____ _____
Metaphor	A direct comparison	_____ _____
Personification	Giving human traits to things that are not human	_____ _____
Simile	An indirect comparison	_____
Symbol	Something that stands for something else	_____ _____

LEARNING
OUTCOME
7

Describe how you will use what you have learned about inferences in your reading process to comprehend textbook material. _____

_____

_____

_____

LEARNING
OUTCOME
7

Summarize the two most important ideas in this chapter that will help you improve your reading comprehension. _____

_____

_____

Summary of Key Concepts about the Basics of Argument

LEARNING OUTCOME ❶
Assess your comprehension of the basics of argument. Complete the question-answer study notes with information from the chapter.

What is an effective argument?	a reasonable process during which a claim is made and logical details are offered to support that claim
What two types of statements make up an argument?	(a) The author's claim (b) The evidence or reasons that support the author's claim
What is an invalid conclusion?	a false inference that is not based on the details, facts, or reasonable thinking
What are the four steps to analyze an argument?	(1) Identify the author's claim and supports. (2) Decide whether the supports are relevant. (3) Decide whether the supports are adequate. (4) Check the argument for bias.
What is a claim made without providing adequate support for the claim?	an invalid conclusion

 ## Test Your Comprehension of The Basics of Argument

Respond to the following questions and prompts. Answers may vary.

LEARNING OUTCOME ❶
In your own words, explain the relationship between making an inference and analyzing an argument. A valid inference is based on the facts or evidence stated in the passage. An invalid inference cannot be

supported by the details in the passage. Likewise, a valid argument is based on adequate and relevant details. And an invalid conclusion lacks adequate support for its claim. The same skills needed to make a valid inference are also needed to analyze an argument for its effectiveness.

LEARNING OUTCOME **②③④⑤⑥**

Create a valid argument. Assume you are going to create and distribute a brochure about distracted driving. You have found the following photograph to use in your brochure. Using details from the photo, write a claim and two supports that clearly support the claim.

Claim: Driver distractions come in many forms.

Support 1: Talking on the phone and texting are very dangerous while driving.

Support 2: Eating also takes a driver's attention away from the road.

LEARNING OUTCOME **⑦**

Describe how you will use what you have learned about the basics of argument in your reading process to comprehend written material in various sources such as textbooks or web sites. _____

_____

_____

LEARNING OUTCOME **⑥**

Summarize the two most important ideas in this chapter that will help you improve your reading comprehension. _____

_____

_____

13 Chapter Review

Summary of Key Concepts about Advanced Argument: Persuasive Techniques

LEARNING OUTCOME
① ② ③ ④
⑤

Assess your comprehension of advanced arguments and persuasive techniques. Complete the two-column notes with information from the chapter.

Fallacy	an error in logical thought
Irrelevant details	details that draw attention away from logical thought by ignoring the issue
Inadequate details	details that oversimplify the issue and do not give enough information to draw a proper conclusion
Propaganda	an act of persuasion that systematically spreads biased information that is designed to support or oppose a person, product, cause, or organization
Emotional appeal	the arousal of emotions to give meaning or power to an idea
Personal Attack	abusive remarks in place of evidence for a point or argument
Straw Man	a weak argument substituted for a stronger one to challenge an argument
Begging the question	restates the point of an argument as a support or conclusion of the argument
Name-calling	negative labels for a product, idea, cause, or person
Testimonials	irrelevant personal opinions to support a product, idea, cause, or person
Bandwagon	the irrelevant detail that "everyone is doing it"

Plain Folks	irrelevant details to build trust on shared values
Either-or	assumes only two sides of the issue exist; also known as black-and-white fallacy
False comparison	assumes two or more things are similar when they are not; also known as false analogy
False cause	assumes that because events occurred around the same time, they have a cause-effect relationship; also known as post-hoc
Card stacking	omits factual details in order to misrepresent a product, cause, idea, or person
Transfer	creates an association between a product, idea, or cause with a symbol or image that has positive or negative values
Glittering generalities	offers general positive statements that cannot be verified

Test Your Comprehension of Advanced Argument: Persuasive Techniques

Respond to the following questions and prompts. Answers may vary.

LEARNING OUTCOME ❶ In your own words, explain the relationship among the following terms: *fallacy, irrelevant details, emotional appeal, inadequate details,* and *propaganda.* Propaganda is used to convince people to support or oppose a person or cause. Propaganda often uses fallacies, or errors in logical thought, and emotional appeals to sway people's opinions. Two broad types of fallacies are irrelevant details and inadequate details. So a piece of propaganda might use an irrelevant detail or inadequate details to stir up emotions to win an argument.

LEARNING OUTCOME ❻ Summarize the two most important ideas in this chapter that will help you improve your reading comprehension. _____

Write the letter of the fallacy used in each statement.

_____b_____ **1.** If you cannot perform the duties listed on your job description, you'll have to find another job.
a. begging the question   c. personal attack
b. either-or   d. straw man

_____d_____ **2.** The government doesn't care about you. You are just a student who doesn't pay taxes.
a. false cause   c. begging the question
b. either-or   d. personal attack

_____a_____ **3.** Falling in love is like jumping off the high diving board.
a. false comparison   c. begging the question
b. straw man   d. false cause

_____c_____ **4.** Whenever you eat ice cream, you get irritable. We're not having dessert anymore.
a. straw man   c. false cause
b. either-or   d. personal attack

_____a_____ **5.** Most politicians are like alcoholics—drunk on power, in denial, and unwilling to stop their addiction to lying.
a. false comparison   c. straw man
b. begging the question   d. false cause

_____c_____ **6.** *Parent to teenager:* "You can't be trusted because you have proven you are untrustworthy."
a. straw man   c. begging the question
b. personal attack   d. either-or

_____a_____ **7.** My grandmother says that to cure a wart you should cut a potato in half, rub the wart with the cut potato, and then bury the potato at night during a full moon. The wart will go away within a week.
a. false cause   c. either-or
b. straw man   d. personal attack

_____d_____ **8.** *Speaker 1:* I propose a solution that will address the concerns of both developers and environmentalists. In every new neighborhood, developers will set aside green areas that can be used as parks or environmental havens. Funds to offset the cost of these green areas could be raised by a nominal county tax and donations from the Green-Friendly Organization.

Speaker 2: My opponent's solution to everything is to raise taxes.

a. begging the question   c. false comparison
b. personal attack   d. straw man

____c____ **9.** My Lexus is my favorite car of all those that I have ever owned because I like it so much.

a. straw man   c. begging the question
b. personal attack   d. either-or

____a____ **10.** City commissioner Jerome Little is a political bully who is determined to protect the wealthy at the expense of the middle class.

a. personal attack   c. false cause
b. straw man   d. either-or

A. Identify the propaganda technique used in each statement. Some techniques are used more than once.

a. plain folks   c. testimonial

b. bandwagon   d. name-calling

___a___ **1.** The founder of our company is just like you; she understands the pressures of everyday life, so she made sure that we offer affordable goods in the most efficient way possible to save you money and time.

___b___ **2.** Don't delay! Buy a lot in this gated community before they are all gone. Lots are moving quickly! Don't miss out on this opportunity to live in one of the most sought-after neighborhoods.

___d___ **3.** Of course Gerald Homey would vote for an increase in minimum wage; he is the puppet of labor unions.

B. Read each fictitious advertisement. Then, identify the detail from the list that was omitted from the ad for the purpose of card stacking.

___c___ **4.** For Sale: This two-year-old female Yorkie terrier has been neutered, house-trained, and has had all the required vaccinations. She is bright, energetic, and loving. She weighs three pounds and has silver coloring.
   a. The family is moving to a condominium where no pets are allowed.
   b. The terrier is a thoroughbred with registered papers.
   c. The terrier has a feisty personality with a history of biting.

___b___ **5.** Ageless Solutions is a miracle supplement that turns back the aging process. With a secret blend of natural ingredients, including vitamin D, the recommended daily dosage helps the body rebuild bone, protecting you from osteoporosis and other bone diseases.
   a. Ageless Solutions contains a complete daily dose of several necessary vitamins, including vitamin A, vitamin C, riboflavin, niacin, and folic acid.

    b. Certain batches of Ageless Solutions have been recalled due to labeling errors that led to excessive dosages of vitamin D. Taking excessive amounts of this vitamin can cause weakness, fatigue, headaches, nausea, vomiting, diarrhea, mental status changes, and even coma in severe cases.

    c. Ageless Solutions has been clinically tested with proven results.

Propaganda Techniques

A. Identify the propaganda technique used in each statement. A technique may be selected more than once or not at all.

a. plain folks   d. transfer

b. bandwagon   e. name-calling

c. testimonial   f. glittering generality

_____a_____ **1.** Sandra's Fruitcake is just like the one your mother made every Christmas. For the same fresh-baked, homemade taste, buy Sandra's Fruitcake.

_____d_____ **2.** A candidate says, "If you like what George Washington, Abraham Lincoln, and Martin Luther King, Jr. stood for, then you will cast your vote for me."

_____e_____ **3.** I would never recommend Professor Higgins; he is anti-American and subversive.

_____b_____ **4.** Please, Mother, I have to have a pair of low-riding jeans and a midriff shirt; it's what everybody is wearing.

_____c_____ **5.** Actress Heather McCoy says, "True Blond leaves my hair silky, shiny, and much more manageable."

_____a_____ **6.** The owner of a national fast-food chain dressed in a cotton short-sleeved shirt, sits at a table in one of his restaurants, surrounded by working-class people who are happily eating hamburgers and French fries. He says, "My wife and I started this business 30 years ago, and we are still here for you. Drop on in. We'll be glad to see you."

_____c_____ **7.** Famous race car driver Rick Ellington states, "I only use ValvoClean on the race track and on the road."

_____b_____ **8.** Supplies Limited. Only a few special edition Bag Babies are left. No more shipments expected before Christmas. Hurry before they are all gone.

_____f_____ **9.**

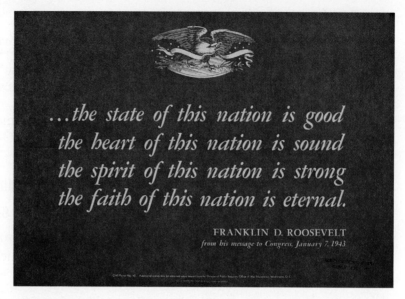

—From World War II Poster Collection, Northwestern University Library, 29 Oct. 2002. "The state of this nation is good," Franklin Roosevelt, message to Congress, 1943, U.S. Office of War Information. © Courtesy Northwestern University Library (www.library.northwestern.edu/govpub/collections/)

B. Read this fictitious advertisement. Then, identify the detail that was omitted for the purpose of card stacking.

_____c_____ **10.** Fun Water will turn your backyard into a water park for your children and their friends. Simply hook your water hose to Fun Water and watch the fun begin. Fun Water throws a sheet of water down a brightly colored slide that gently slopes into a shallow pool. Your children will slip and slide their way to fun all summer long.

    a. Fun Water is a highly popular, fast-selling product.

    b. Fun Water doesn't waste water because it recycles and reuses water.

    c. Several children have experienced minor injuries using Fun Water.

Textbook
Skills

Read the following passage from a college history textbook. Answer the questions that follow.

13.0 GE/507 words   **Moving Westward: Society and Politics
in the "Age of the Common Man"**

¹Campaigning for political office in Tennessee in the 1820s was not an activity for the faint of heart. ²Candidates competed against each other in squirrel hunts, the loser footing the bill for the barbecue that followed. ³A round of speechmaking often was capped by several rounds of whiskey drinking enjoyed by candidates and supporters alike. ⁴Into this boisterous arena stepped a man unrivaled as a campaigner. ⁵David Crockett ran successfully for several offices, including local justice of the peace in 1818, state legislator in 1821 and 1823, and member of the U.S. House of Representatives in 1827, 1829, and 1833. ⁶The plainspoken Crockett knew how to play to a crowd and rattle a rival. ⁷He bragged about his skill as a bear hunter and ridiculed the fancy dress of his opponents.

⁸He condemned closed-door political caucuses (small groups of party insiders who hand-picked candidates) and praised grassroots democracy. ⁹Crockett claimed he could out-shoot, out-drink, and out-debate anyone who opposed him. ¹⁰If his opponent lied about him, why, then, he would lie about himself: "Yes fellow citizens, I can run faster, walk longer, leap higher, speak better, and tell more and bigger lies than my competitor, and all his friends, any day of his life." ¹¹Crockett's blend of political theater and folksy backwoods banter earned him the allegiance of voters like him—people who, though having little formal education, understood the challenges of carving a homestead out of the dense thickets of western Tennessee.

¹²Crockett's raucous brand of campaigning appealed to Westerners: European Americans living just west of the Appalachian Mountains. ¹³His social betters might sniff that he was a rough, ignorant man—in the words of one Tennessee political insider, "more in his proper place, when hunting a Bear in the cane Brake, than he will be in the Capital." ¹⁴But newspaper reporters and defeated opponents alike grew to respect his ability to champion ordinary farmers. ¹⁵As a politician, Crockett spoke for debtors, squatters, and militia veterans of the Revolutionary War. ¹⁶He scorned the well born in favor of those who could shoot down and skin a wolf.

[17]During the 1820s, European American settlers in the trans-Appalachian West transformed the style and substance of American politics. [18]Beginning with Kentucky in 1792, western states began to relax or abolish property requirements for adult male voters. [19]Even the English that Americans spoke changed. [20]New words introduced into the political vocabulary reflected the rough-hewn, woodsman quality of western electioneering: candidates hit the campaign trail, giving stump speeches along the way. [21]They supported their party's platform with its planks (positions on the issues). [22]As legislators, they voted for pork-barrel projects that would benefit their constituents at home. [23]Emphasizing his modest origins, David Crockett became widely known as Davy Crockett. [24](It is hard to imagine anyone calling the Sage of Monticello Tommy Jefferson.)

[25]These developments reflected the movement of European Americans westward. [26]In 1790, 100,000 Americans (not including Indians) lived west of the Appalachian Mountains; half a century later that number had increased to 7 million, or about four out of ten Americans.

—From *Created Equal: A Social and Political History of the United States*, Combined Volume,
2nd ed., pp. 355–356 by Jacqueline Jones, Peter H. Wood, Thomas Borstelmann,
Elaine Tyler May, Vicki L. Ruiz. Copyright © 2006 by Pearson Education, Inc.
Printed and Electronically reproduced by permission of
Pearson Education, Inc., Upper Saddle River, NJ.

___a___ **1.** In sentence 4, the description of Davy Crockett uses
    a. glittering generalities.   c. personal attacks.
    b. false comparisons.   d. testimonials.

___c___ **2.** Overall, Davy Crockett's political appeal was based on
    a. personal attacks.   c. plain folks.
    b. transfer.   d. card stacking.

___c___ **3.** In sentence 7, Davy Crockett's boast in his skill as a bear hunter is an example of
    a. false comparison.   c. straw man.
    b. bandwagon.   d. testimonial.

___d___ **4.** In sentence 13, the opponents of Davy Crockett used a _____ against him.
    a. false comparison   c. testimonial
    b. bandwagon   d. personal attack

___b___ **5.** Sentence 22 is an example of the political use of
    a. false comparison.   c. straw man.
    b. bandwagon.   d. personal attack.

Additional Readings

Textbook
Skills

Textbook
Skills

The Connection Between Reading and Writing

The link between reading and writing is vital and natural. Written language allows an exchange of ideas between a writer and a reader. Thus, writing and reading are two equal parts of the communication process. In fact, reading is a form of listening or receiving information. And writing is like speaking—the sending of information. So a master reader makes every effort to understand and respond to the ideas of the writer. Likewise, a master writer makes every effort to make ideas clear so the reader can understand and respond to those ideas. Most writers find that reading improves their writing. Reading builds prior knowledge and fuels ideas for writing.

Because of this close relationship between reading and writing, both share similar thinking steps in their processes. In Chapter 1, you learned that the reading process has three phases: Before Reading, During Reading, and After Reading. The writing process also has three phases that occur before, during, and after writing: Prewriting, Drafting, and Proofing. By coordinating these two sets of process, you can improve both your reading and your writing. For example, the following statements sum up one way to connect reading and writing:

Reading is a prewriting activity. Drafting is an after reading activity.

Once you think of reading as a prewriting activity, you become a responsive or active reader during the reading process. In fact, you can begin using your writing skills as you read by annotating the text.

Annotating a Text

The word *annotate* suggests that you "take notes" in your book. Writing notes in the margin of a page as you read keeps you focused and improves your comprehension. You can quickly note questions where they occur, move on in your reading, and later return to clarify answers. In addition, after reading, your annotations help you review and respond to the material. The following suggestions offer one way to annotate a text:

How to Annotate a Text

- Circle important terms.
- Underline definitions and meanings.
- Note key ideas with a star or a check.
- Place question marks above words that are unknown or confusing.
- Number the steps in a process or items in a list.
- Write summaries at the end of long sections.
- Write recall questions in the margin near their answers.
- Write key words and meanings in the margin.

EXAMPLE The passage from a college communications textbook on page 596 is marked up as an example of an annotated text. Read the passage. Study the annotations. Then work with a peer or in a small group and create a summary of the text based on the annotations. See below to review how to write a summary.

Writing a Summary

Writing a summary is an effective step in the reading and studying process.

> A **summary** is a brief, clear restatement of a longer passage.

A summary includes only the passage's most important points. Often a summary is made up of the main idea and major supporting details. The length of a summary should reflect your study needs and the kind of passage you are trying to understand. For example, a paragraph might be summarized in a sentence or two, an article might be summarized in a paragraph, and a textbook chapter might be summarized in a page or two.

You can discover how well you understand a passage by writing a summary of it as an after reading activity. Use the annotations you make during reading to create your summary.

For example, read the following summary of "Recognize Culture Shock" from a college communications textbook. Underline the words and phrases that were annotated in the longer section on page 596:

[1]Culture shock is the "psychological reaction you experience when you're in a culture very different from your own." [2]When you are in culture shock, you can't communicate effectively and don't know even simple customs. [3]For example, you don't know how to ask for a favor, how to order a meal, or how to dress. [4]Anthropologist Kalervo Oberg coined the term "culture shock" and identifies its four stages. [5]Stage one, "the honeymoon," is filled with excitement and adventure. [6]Stage two, "the crisis," brings confusion and frustration due to unfamiliar customs and surroundings. [7]Stage three, "the recovery," is the process of learning how to function. [8]And stage four, "the adjustment," brings independence and enjoyment. [9]As the process indicates, culture shock can be overcome.

This summary includes the author's main idea and the major supporting details. However, this summary also brings in a few minor supporting details. For example, sentence 3 gives examples of customs that a person would not know. Including these details makes the summary longer than may be necessary. The version on page 601 includes only the main idea and the major supporting details.

Chapter 2 ■ **Culture in Interpersonal Communication**

Recognize Culture Shock Culture shock refers to the psychological reaction you experience when you're in a culture very different from your own (Furnham & Bochner, 1986). Culture shock is normal; most people experience it when entering a new and different culture. Nevertheless, it can be unpleasant and frustrating. Part of this results from feelings of alienation, conspicuousness, and difference from everyone else. When you lack knowledge of the rules and customs of the new society, you cannot communicate effectively. You're apt to blunder frequently and seriously. In your culture shock you may not know basic things:

(1) ■ how to ask someone for a favor or pay someone a compliment
(2) ■ how to extend or accept an invitation for dinner
(3) ■ how early or how late to arrive for an appointment
(4) ■ how long you should stay when visiting someone
(5) ■ how to distinguish seriousness from playfulness and politeness from indifference
(6) ■ how to dress for an informal, formal, or business function
(7) ■ how to order a meal in a restaurant or how to summon a waiter

7 basic communication tasks & simple customs you may not know

Anthropologist Kalervo Oberg (1960), who first used the term culture shock, notes that it occurs in stages. These stages are useful for examining many encounters with the new and the different. Going away to college, moving in together, or joining the military, for example, can also result in culture shock. In explaining culture shock, we use the example of moving away from home into your own apartment to illustrate its four stages.

Who first used the term "culture shock"?

(1) **Stage One:** The Honeymoon At first you experience fascination, even enchantment, with the new culture and its people. You finally have your own apartment. You're your own boss. Finally, on your own! When in groups of people who are culturally different, this stage is characterized by cordiality and friendship in these early and superficial relationships. Many tourists remain at this stage because their stay in foreign countries is so brief.

How many stages are there?

(2) **Stage Two:** The Crisis Here, the differences between your own culture and the new one create problems. No longer do you find dinner ready for you unless you do it yourself. Your clothes are not washed or ironed unless you do them yourself. Feelings of frustration and inadequacy come to the fore. This is the stage at which you experience the actual shock of the new culture. One study of foreign students coming from over 100 different countries studying in 11 different countries found that 25 percent of the students experienced depression (Klineberg & Hull, 1979).

What are the labels for each stage?

(3) **Stage Three:** The Recovery During this period you gain the skills necessary to function effectively. You learn how to shop, cook, and plan a meal. You find a local laundry and figure you'll learn how to iron later. You learn the language and ways of the new culture. Your feelings of inadequacy subside.

(4) **Stage Four:** The Adjustment At this final stage, you adjust to and come to enjoy the new culture and the new experiences. You may still experience periodic difficulties and strains, but on a whole, the experience is pleasant. Actually, you're now a pretty decent cook. You're even coming to enjoy it. You're making a good salary so why learn to iron?

Culture shock can be overcome!

[1]Culture shock is the "psychological reaction you experience when you're in a culture very different from your own." [2]When you are in culture shock, you can't communicate effectively and don't know even simple customs. [3]Anthropologist Kalervo Oberg coined the term "culture shock" and identifies its four stages: stage one is "the honeymoon"; stage two is "the crisis"; stage three is "the recovery"; and stage four is "the adjustment." [4]Culture shock can be overcome.

Remember, the length of the summary depends on your study needs as well as the length of the passage you are summarizing.

A Reading-Writing Plan of Action

Can you see how annotating a text lays the ground upon which you can build a written response? The steps you take during reading feed into the process of writing a response after reading.

Remember, reading and writing is a conversation between the writer and the reader. One writes; the other reads. But the conversation often doesn't end there. A reader's response to a piece of writing keeps the dialogue going. When you write a summary, your response is to restate the author's ideas. It's like saying to the author, "If I understood you, you said . . ." When you offer your own views about the author's ideas, you are answering the author's implied question, "What do you think?" In your reading and writing classes, your teacher often steps into the conversation. He or she stands in for the author and becomes the reader of your written response. In this case, your teacher evaluates both your reading and writing abilities. Your teacher checks your response for accuracy in comprehension of the author's message and development of your ability to write. The following chart illustrates this exchange of ideas.

The Conversation among Writers and Readers

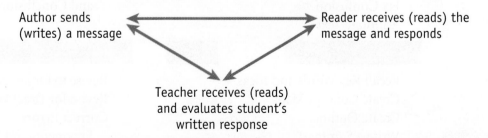

Author sends (writes) a message

Reader receives (reads) the message and responds

Teacher receives (reads) and evaluates student's written response

In each skill chapter of this textbook, the question "What Do You Think?" is posed after Review Tests 3 and 4. This question also appears after each reading selection in this section. The "What Do You Think?" writing assignments prompt you to respond to what you have read. This activity creates a writing situation and gives you a purpose for your written response. Just like a vocabulary word makes more sense in context than in a list, a writing assignment in context is more meaningful than an isolated topic or set of disconnected questions. The goal of "What Do You Think?" is to strengthen your connection between reading and writing. Because reading and writing are two distinct processes, it is helpful to have a guide that shows how to efficiently coordinate them. The following chart lays out a reading-writing plan of action. Note that the chart breaks the reading-writing process into a series of 6 steps. Keep in mind that any step can be repeated as needed. Also, you can move back and forth between steps as needed.

Study the 6-Step Reading-Writing Action Plan. Then work with a peer or small group of classmates and discuss the relationship between reading and writing, and how you will put this plan to use.

A 6-Step Reading-Writing Action Plan

Read		Write
1. Survey and Question	**BEFORE**	**4. Prewrite**
Call on Prior Knowledge		Build Prior Knowledge*
Identify Topic		Gather Information*
Identify Key or New Words		Read and Annotate*
Identify Patterns of Organization		Brainstorm Ideas
Note Visual Aids		Choose Your Topic
Skim Introductions and		Generate Your Details
Conclusions		Create a Concept Map
		Outline Ideas
2. Read	**DURING**	**5. Draft**
Monitor Comprehension		Write Introduction, Body,
Fix Confusion		and Conclusion
Annotate Text		
3. Review and Recite	**AFTER**	**6. Revise and Proofread**
Recall Key Words and Ideas		Revise to Organize
Create Concept Maps		Revise for Exact Wording
Create Outlines		Correct Errors
Write a Summary		Fragments and Run-ons
Write a Response		Spelling
		Punctuation

* Prewriting steps accomplished during reading

Sex, Lies and Conversation: Why Is It So Hard for Men and Women to Talk to Each Other? 9.8 GE/2367 words

by Deborah Tannen

Deborah Tannen is University Professor of Linguistics in the Department of Linguistics at Georgetown University in Washington, D.C. Tannen, the author of nineteen published books and nearly a hundred articles and the recipient of five honorary doctorates, is an expert on the nature of human language. She lectures worldwide and is also a frequent guest on television and radio news and information shows. Tannen is perhaps best known to the general public, however, as the author of *You Just Don't Understand: Women and Men in Conversation.* This groundbreaking book about gender-based communication was on the *New York Times* best-seller list for nearly four years, including eight months as the number one best-selling book. It was also a best-seller in Brazil, Canada, England, Germany, Holland, and Hong Kong. *You Just Don't Understand* offers helpful insights about gender differences in communication style. This article, adapted from *You Just Don't Understand: Women and Men in Conversation,* appeared in *The Washington Post.*

Vocabulary Preview

anecdotes (paragraph 1): illustrations, stories
concurred (paragraph 1): agreed
crystallizes (paragraph 2): becomes well defined
havoc (paragraph 2): chaos, disorder
tangible (paragraph 4): concrete, real, touchable
inequities (paragraph 4): injustices
socialization (paragraph 8): training to gain skills necessary to function successfully in society
attuned (paragraph 12): adjusted, in tune with
analogous (paragraph 13): similar, comparable
alienated (paragraph 14): separated
requisite (paragraph 19): necessary, essential
paradox (paragraph 22): contradiction
ethnic (paragraph 26): cultural

1   I was addressing a small gathering in a suburban Virginia living room—a women's group that had invited men to join them. Throughout the evening, one man had been particularly talkative, frequently offering ideas and **anecdotes**, while his wife sat silently beside him on the couch. Toward the end of the evening, I commented that women frequently complain that their husbands don't talk to them. This man quickly **concurred**. He gestured toward his wife and said, "She's the talker in our family." The room burst into laughter; the man looked puzzled and hurt. "It's true," he explained. "When I come home from work I have nothing to say. If she didn't keep the conversation going, we'd spend the whole evening in silence."

2   This episode **crystallizes** the irony that although American men tend to talk more than women in public situations, they often talk less at home. And this pattern is wreaking **havoc** with marriage.

3   The pattern was observed by political scientist Andrew Hacker in the late '70s. Sociologist Catherine Kohler Riessman reports in her new book "Divorce Talk" that most of the women she interviewed—but only a few of the men—gave lack of communication as the reason for their divorces. Given the current divorce rate of nearly 50 percent, that amounts to millions of cases in the United States every year—a virtual epidemic of failed conversation.

4   In my own research, complaints from women about their husbands most often focused not on **tangible inequities** such as having given up the chance for a career to accompany a husband to his, or doing far more than their share of daily life-support work like cleaning, cooking, social arrangements and errands. Instead, they focused on communication: "He doesn't listen to me," "He doesn't talk to me." I found, as Hacker observed years before, that most wives want their husbands to be, first and foremost, conversational partners, but few husbands share this expectation of their wives.

5   In short, the image that best represents the current crisis is the stereotypical cartoon scene of a man sitting at the breakfast table with a newspaper held up in front of his face, while a woman glares at the back of it, wanting to talk.

Linguistic Battle of the Sexes

6   How can women and men have such different impressions of communication in marriage? Why the widespread imbalance in their interests and expectations?

7   In the April issue of *American Psychologist*, Stanford University's Eleanor Maccoby reports the results of her own and others' research showing that children's development is most influenced by the social structure of peer interactions. Boys and girls tend to play with children of their own gender, and their sex-separate groups have different organizational structures and interactive norms.

8   I believe these systematic differences in childhood **socialization** make talk between women and men like cross-cultural communication, heir to all the attraction and pitfalls of that enticing but difficult enterprise. My research on men's and women's conversations uncovered patterns similar to those described for children's groups.

9   For women, as for girls, intimacy is the fabric of relationships, and talk is the

thread from which it is woven. Little girls create and maintain friendships by exchanging secrets; similarly, women regard conversation as the cornerstone of friendship. So a woman expects her husband to be a new and improved version of a best friend. What is important is not the individual subjects that are discussed but the sense of closeness, of a life shared, that emerges when people tell their thoughts, feelings, and impressions.

10 Bonds between boys can be as intense as girls', but they are based less on talking, more on doing things together. Since they don't assume talk is the cement that binds a relationship, men don't know what kind of talk women want, and they don't miss it when it isn't there.

11 Boys' groups are larger, more inclusive, and more **hierarchical**, so boys must struggle to avoid the subordinate position in the group. This may play a role in women's complaints that men don't listen to them. Some men really don't like to listen, because being the listener makes them feel one-down, like a child listening to adults or an employee to a boss.

12 But often when women tell men, "You aren't listening," and the men protest, "I am," the men are right. The impression of not listening results from misalignments in the mechanics of conversation. The misalignment begins as soon as a man and a woman take physical positions. This became clear when I studied videotapes made by psychologist Bruce Dorval of children and adults talking to their same-sex best friends. I found that at every age, the girls and women faced each other directly, their eyes anchored on each other's faces. At every age, the boys and men sat at angles to each other and

looked elsewhere in the room, periodically glancing at each other. They were obviously **attuned** to each other, often mirroring each other's movements. But the tendency of men to face away can give women the impression they aren't listening even when they are. A young woman in college was frustrated: Whenever she told her boyfriend she wanted to talk to him, he would lie down on the floor, close his eyes, and put his arm over his face. This signaled to her, "He's taking a nap." But he insisted he was listening extra hard. Normally, he looks around the room, so he is easily distracted. Lying down and covering his eyes helped him concentrate on what she was saying.

13 **Analogous** to the physical alignment that women and men take in conversation is their topical alignment. The girls in my study tended to talk at length about one topic, but the boys tended to jump from topic to topic. The second-grade girls exchanged stories about people they knew. The second-grade boys teased, told jokes, noticed things in the room and talked about finding games to play. The sixth-grade girls talked about problems with a mutual friend. The sixth-grade boys talked about 55 different topics, none of which extended over more than a few turns.

Listening to Body Language

14 Switching topics is another habit that gives women the impression men aren't listening, especially if they switch to a topic about themselves. But the evidence of the 10th-grade boys in my study indicates otherwise. The 10th-grade boys sprawled across their chairs with bodies parallel and eyes straight ahead, rarely

looking at each other. They looked as if they were riding in a car, staring out the windshield. But they were talking about their feelings. One boy was upset because a girl had told him he had a drinking problem, and the other was feeling **alienated** from all his friends.

15   Now, when a girl told a friend about a problem, the friend responded by asking probing questions and expressing agreement and understanding. But the boys dismissed each other's problems. Todd assured Richard that his drinking was "no big problem" because "sometimes you're funny when you're off your butt." And when Todd said he felt left out, Richard responded, "Why should you? You know more people than me."

16   Women perceive such responses as belittling and unsupportive. But the boys seemed satisfied with them. Whereas women reassure each other by implying, "You shouldn't feel bad because I've had similar experiences," men do so by implying, "You shouldn't feel bad because your problems aren't so bad."

17   There are even simpler reasons for women's impression that men don't listen. Linguist Lynette Hirschman found that women make more listener-noise, such as "mhm," "uhuh," and "yeah," to show "I'm with you." Men, she found, more often give silent attention. Women who expect a stream of listener noise interpret silent attention as no attention at all.

18   Women's conversational habits are as frustrating to men as men's are to women. Men who expect silent attention interpret a stream of listener noise as overreaction or impatience. Also, when women talk to each other in a close, comfortable setting, they often overlap, finish each other's sentences and anticipate what the other is about to say. This practice, which I call "participatory listenership," is often perceived by men as interruption, intrusion and lack of attention.

19   A parallel difference caused a man to complain about his wife, "She just wants to talk about her own point of view. If I show her another view, she gets mad at me." When most women talk to each other, they assume a conversationalist's job is to express agreement and support. But many men see their conversational duty as pointing out the other side of an argument. This is heard as disloyalty by women, and refusal to offer the **requisite** support. It is not that women don't want to see other points of view, but that they prefer them phrased as suggestions and inquiries rather than as direct challenges.

20   In his book "Fighting for Life," Walter Ong points out that men use "agonistic" or warlike, oppositional formats to do almost anything; thus discussion becomes debate, and conversation a competitive sport. In contrast, women see conversation as a ritual means of establishing rapport. If Jane tells a problem and June says she has a similar one, they walk away feeling closer to each other. But this attempt at establishing rapport can backfire when used with men. Men take too literally women's ritual "troubles talk," just as women mistake men's ritual challenges for real attack.

The Sounds of Silence

21   These differences begin to clarify why women and men have such different

expectations about communication in marriage. For women, talk creates intimacy. Marriage is an orgy of closeness: you can tell your feelings and thoughts, and still be loved. Their greatest fear is being pushed away. But men live in a hierarchical world, where talk maintains independence and status. They are on guard to protect themselves from being put down and pushed around.

22   This explains the **paradox** of the talkative man who said of his silent wife, "She's the talker." In the public setting of a guest lecture, he felt challenged to show his intelligence and display his understanding of the lecture. But at home, where he has nothing to prove and no one to defend against, he is free to remain silent. For his wife, being home means she is free from the worry that something she says might offend someone, or spark disagreement, or appear to be showing off; at home she is free to talk.

23   The communication problems that endanger marriage can't be fixed by mechanical engineering. They require a new conceptual framework about the role of talk in human relationships. Many of the psychological explanations that have become second nature may not be helpful, because they tend to blame either women (for not being assertive enough) or men (for not being in touch with their feelings). A sociolinguistic approach by which male-female conversation is seen as cross-cultural communication allows us to understand the problem and forge solutions without blaming either party.

24   Once the problem is understood, improvement comes naturally, as it did to the young woman and her boyfriend who seemed to go to sleep when she wanted to talk. Previously, she had accused him of not listening, and he had refused to change his behavior, since that would be admitting fault. But then she learned about and explained to him the differences in women's and men's habitual ways of aligning themselves in conversation. The next time she told him she wanted to talk, he began, as usual, by lying down and covering his eyes. When the familiar negative reaction bubbled up, she reassured herself that he really was listening. But then he sat up and looked at her. Thrilled, she asked why. He said, "You like me to look at you when we talk, so I'll try to do it." Once he saw their differences as cross-cultural rather than right and wrong, he independently altered his behavior.

Women who feel abandoned and de-   25 prived when their husbands won't listen to or report daily news may be happy to discover their husbands trying to adapt once they understand the place of small talk in women's relationships. But if their husbands don't adapt, the women may still be comforted that for men, this is not a failure of intimacy. Accepting the difference, the wives may look to their friends or family for that kind of talk. And husbands who can't provide it shouldn't feel their wives have made unreasonable demands. Some couples will still decide to divorce, but at least their decisions will be based on realistic expectations.

In these times of resurgent **ethnic**   26 conflicts, the world desperately needs cross-cultural understanding. Like charity, successful cross-cultural communication should begin at home.

a _____ Which phrase best expresses the meaning of *rapport* in the caption?

   a. a bond
   b. an idea
   c. a commitment

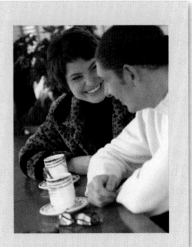

▶ Women see conversation as a way to establish rapport.

Choose the best meaning of each word in **bold** type. Use context clues to make your choice.

Vocabulary in Context   _b_   **1.** The word **Linguistic** in the heading "Linguistic Battle of the Sexes" (above paragraph 6) relates to
   a. gender.   c. relationship.
   b. language.   d. education.

Vocabulary in Context   _a_   **2.** "Boys' groups are larger, more inclusive, and more **hierarchical**, so boys must struggle to avoid the subordinate position in the group." (paragraph 11)
   a. ranked   c. logical
   b. brutal   d. submissive

Central Idea and Main Ideas   _c_   **3.** Which sentence is the best statement of the central idea of the passage?
   a. "Given the current divorce rate of nearly 50 percent, that amounts to millions of cases in the United States every year—a virtual epidemic of failed conversation." (paragraph 3)
   b. "My research on men's and women's conversations uncovered patterns similar to those described for children's groups." (paragraph 8)
   c. "A sociolinguistic approach by which male-female conversation is seen as cross-cultural communication allows us to understand the problem and forge solutions without blaming either party." (paragraph 23)
   d. "Like charity, successful cross-cultural communication should begin at home." (paragraph 26)

Central Idea and Main Ideas ___c___ **4.** Which sentence is the best statement of the implied main idea of paragraphs 14 through 20?

a. Men and women have different views of communication in marriage.

b. Men switch topics more often than women do during a conversation.

c. Women and men differ in their use of body language during the communication process.

d. Women are more effective listeners than men.

Supporting Details ___d___ **5.** According to Catherine Kohler Riessman, which of the following reasons did most women give for their divorces?

a. giving up the chance for a career to follow a husband

b. doing far more than their share of daily life-support work like cleaning

c. sexual infidelity

d. lack of communication

Supporting Details ___c___ **6.** Men reassure each other by

a. making direct eye contact when they communicate.

b. making listener-noise such as "mhm," "uhuh," and "yeah" to show "I'm with you."

c. implying "you shouldn't feel bad because your problems aren't so bad."

d. practicing "participatory listenership."

Transitions ___b___ **7.** "Little girls create and maintain friendships by exchanging secrets; similarly, women regard conversation as the cornerstone of friendship. So a woman expects her husband to be a new and improved version of a best friend." (paragraph 9)

The relationship of ideas between these two sentences is

a. time order.   c. comparison and contrast.

b. cause and effect.

Transitions ___a___ **8.** "The misalignment begins as soon as a man and a woman take physical positions." (paragraph 12)

The relationship of ideas within this sentence is

a. time order.   c. comparison and contrast.

b. cause and effect.

Thought Patterns ___a___ **9.** The overall thought pattern used in this passage is

a. a discussion of the differences in the ways men and women communicate.

   b. an argument against the various ways men use communication.

   c. a narrative that illustrates the different problems men and women face as they attempt to communicate.

   d. a step-by-step description of how to effectively communicate with the opposite sex.

Thought Patterns ___c___ **10.** The main thought pattern used in paragraph 24 is

   a. comparison.   c. time order.

   b. definition and example.

Fact and Opinion ___c___ **11.** Overall, the ideas in this passage are mainly based on

   a. the opinions and experiences of ordinary men and women.

   b. fictitious or hypothetical details.

   c. the research and observation of the author and other experts in the field of linguistics and communication.

Fact and Opinion ___b___ **12.** "Like charity, successful cross-cultural communication should begin at home." (paragraph 26)

   This sentence is a statement of

   a. fact.   c. fact and opinion.

   b. opinion.

Tone and Purpose ___c___ **13.** Which word best expresses the overall tone of the passage?

   a. biased   c. balanced

   b. condescending   d. emotional

Tone and Purpose ___b___ **14.** The overall tone of paragraph 1 is

   a. dismayed.   c. scornful.

   b. humorous.   d. neutral.

Tone and Purpose ___d___ **15.** The tone of paragraph 26 is

   a. mocking.   c. hopeful.

   b. objective.   d. persuasive.

Tone and Purpose ___c___ **16.** The author's main purpose is

   a. to persuade men and women to change their communication styles.

   b. to entertain readers with amusing incidents of miscommunication between men and women.

   c. to inform the reader about the differences in communication styles between men and women so that they can better understand one another.

Inferences   <u>b</u>   **17.** Based on the information in the article, generally men
  a. do not listen as well as women.
  b. are more competitive than women.
  c. prefer intimacy over independence, unlike women.

Inferences   <u>b</u>   **18.** The author implies that generally women
  a. are more comfortable and better at giving advice than are men.
  b. are more interested in establishing networks of support than are men.
  c. are more skilled at effective communication than are men.

Inferences   <u>b</u>   **19.** The details in paragraphs 21–26 imply that
  a. men are just as emotional as women.
  b. the hurt and tension between men and women are often based on misunderstanding the communication purpose of the other.
  c. women need to communicate more than men.

Argument   <u>c</u>   **20.** Men live in a hierarchical world, where talk maintains independence and status.

   Which statement does *not* support this claim?
  a. Men are on guard to protect themselves from being put down and pushed around.
  b. Men use "agnostic" or warlike, oppositional formats to do almost anything.
  c. He said, "You like me to look at you when we talk, so I'll try to do it."

Mapping

Complete the chart with information from the passage. Wording may vary.

Communication Approach of Men	Communication Approach of Women
Establish bonds based on <u>sharing activities</u>	Establish bonds based on talking
Jump from topic to topic	Talk at length about one topic
Expect silent attention	Practice "participatory listenership"
"Agnostic" or warlike, oppositional formats	Ritual means of establishing rapport
Discussion becomes debate	Talk creates <u>intimacy</u>

WHAT DO YOU THINK?

Do you think men and women differ in the way they communicate? Explain why or why not with examples you have observed. Given that men and women do differ in their approach to communication, how do these differences affect communication at work or school? Assume a friend of yours is having difficulty communicating with a boss or friend of the opposite sex. Write a letter to your friend in which you give advice based on what you learned from this article to help him or her communicate more effectively. Begin your letter with a summary of the author's main idea and major supporting details.

MASTER READER Scorecard

"Sex, Lies and Conversation"			
Skill	**Number Correct**	**Points**	**Total**
Vocabulary			
Vocabulary in Context (2 items)	_____ ×	4	= _____
Comprehension			
Central Idea and Main Ideas (2 items)	_____ ×	4	= _____
Supporting Details (2 items)	_____ ×	4	= _____
Transitions (2 items)	_____ ×	4	= _____
Thought Patterns (2 items)	_____ ×	4	= _____
Fact and Opinion (2 items)	_____ ×	4	= _____
Tone and Purpose (4 items)	_____ ×	4	= _____
Inferences (3 items)	_____ ×	4	= _____
Argument (1 item)	_____ ×	4	= _____
Mapping (2 items)	_____ ×	10	= _____
	Comprehension Score		_____

Teens, Nude Photos and the Law

by Dahlia Lithwick   11.8 GE/867 words

Dahlia Lithwick is a contributing editor at *Newsweek* and senior editor at *Slate*, where she has written for the *Supreme Court Dispatches* and *Jurisprudence* columns since 1999. Her writing has also appeared in *The New Republic*, the *Washington Post*, and the *New York Times*, and she has also been a frequent guest on the NPR program *Day-to-Day*. Ms. Lithwick was awarded the Online News Association's award for online commentary in 2001. In the following article for *Newsweek* magazine, Lithwick questions whether the "police should be involved when tipsy teen girls e-mail their boyfriends naughty Valentine's Day pictures."

Vocabulary Preview

confiscated (paragraph 1): took away

iteration (paragraph 1): repetition, instance

narcissism (paragraph 1): self-admiration, egotism, conceit

venue (paragraph 3): setting, scene

purveyors (paragraph 5): suppliers, sellers, sources

paternalism (paragraph 5): telling people what is best, a style of governing or managing in which the desire to assist and protect reduces personal choice and responsibility

perpetuates (paragraph 6): spreads, carries on, brings about

1   Say you're a middle-school principal who **confiscated** a cell phone from a 14-year-old boy, only to discover it contains a nude photo of his 13-year-old girlfriend. Do you (a) call the boy's parents in despair; (b) call the girl's parents in despair; or (c) call the police? More and more, the answer is (d) all of the above. Which could result in criminal charges for both of your students, and their eventual designation as sex offenders. "Sexting" is the clever new name for the act of sending, receiving or forwarding naked photos via your cell phone, and I wasn't fully convinced that America was facing a sexting epidemic, as opposed to a journalists-writing-about-sexting epidemic, until I saw a new survey done by the National Campaign to Prevent Teen and Unplanned Pregnancy. One teenager in five reported having sent or posted naked photos of themselves. Whether all this reflects a new child-porn epidemic, or just a new **iteration** of the old teen **narcissism** epidemic, remains unclear.

2   Last month, three girls (ages 14 or 15) in Greensburg, Pa., were charged with **disseminating** child pornography for sexting

their boyfriends. The boys who received the images were charged with possession. A teenager in Indiana faces felony obscenity charges for sending a picture of his genitals to female classmates. A 15-year-old girl in Ohio and a 14-year-old girl in Michigan were charged with felonies for sending nude images of themselves to classmates. Some of these teens have pleaded guilty to lesser charges. Others have not. If convicted, these young people may have to register as sex offenders, in some cases for a decade or two. Similar charges have been brought in cases reported in Alabama, Connecticut, Florida, New Jersey, New York, Pennsylvania, Texas, Utah and Wisconsin.

3   One quick clue that the criminal-justice system is probably not the best **venue** for addressing sexting? A survey of the charges brought in the cases reflects that—depending on the jurisdiction—prosecutors have charged the senders of smutty photos, the recipients of smutty photos, those who save the smutty photos and the hapless forwarders of smutty photos with the same crime: child pornography. Who is the victim here? Everybody and nobody.

4   There may be an argument for police intervention in cases that involve a genuine threat or cyberbullying, such as a recent Massachusetts incident in which the picture of a naked 14-year-old girl was allegedly sent to more than 100 cell phones, or a New York case involving a group of boys who turned a nude photo of a 15-year-old girl into crude animations and PowerPoint presentations. But ask yourself whether those cases are the same as the cases in which tipsy teen girls send their boyfriends naughty Valentine's Day pictures.

The argument for hammering every 5 such case seems to be that sending naked pictures might have serious consequences, so let's charge these kids with felonies, which will surely have serious consequences. In the Pennsylvania case a police captain explained that the charges were brought because "it's very dangerous. Once it's on a cell phone, that cell phone can be put on the Internet where everyone in the world can get access to that juvenile picture." The argument that we must prosecute kids as the producers and **purveyors** of kiddie porn because they are too dumb to understand that their seemingly innocent acts can harm them goes beyond **paternalism**. Child-pornography laws intended to protect children should not be used to prosecute and then label children as sex offenders. We seem to forget that kids can be as tech-savvy as Bill Gates but as **gullible** as Bambi. Even in the age of the Internet, young people fail to appreciate that naked pictures want to roam free.

The real problem with criminalizing 6 teen sexting as a form of child pornography is that the great majority of these kids are not predators. They think they're being brash and sexy. And while some of the reaction to sexting reflects legitimate concerns about children as sex objects, some **perpetuates** legal stereotypes and fallacies. A recent *New York Times* article quotes the Family Violence Prevention Fund, a nonprofit domestic-violence-awareness group, saying that the sending of nude pictures, even if done voluntarily, constitutes "digital dating violence." But do we truly believe that one in five teens is participating in an act of violence? Experts insist the sexting trend hurts teen girls more than boys, fretting that they feel "pressured" to take and send naked photos. Paradoxically, the girls in the Pennsylvania case were charged with "manufacturing, disseminating or possessing child pornography" while the boys were merely charged with possession. If the girls are the real victims, why are we treating them more harshly than the boys?

7   Judging from the sexting prosecutions in Pennsylvania, Ohio and Indiana this year, it's clear that the criminal-justice system is too blunt an instrument to resolve a problem that reflects more about the volatile combination of teens and technology than about some national cybercrime spree. Parents need to remind their teens that a dumb moment can last a lifetime in cyberspace. But judges and prosecutors need to understand that a lifetime of cyberhumiliation shouldn't be grounds for a lifelong real criminal record.

—"Teens, Nude Photos and the Law: Ask Yourself: Should the Police Be Involved When Tipsy Teen Girls E-mail Their Boyfriends Naughty Valentine's Day Pictures?" by Dahlia Lithwick from *Newsweek*, February 14 Copyright © 2009 Newsweek, Inc. All rights reserved. Used by permission and protected by the Copyright Laws of the United States. The printing, copying, redistribution, or retransmission of the Material without express written permission is prohibited. www.newsweek.com.

Choose the best meaning of each word in **bold.** Use context clues to make your choice.

Vocabulary in Context   __b__   **1.** "Last month, three girls (ages 14 or 15) in Greensburg, Pa., were charged with **disseminating** child pornography for sexting their boyfriends." (paragraph 2)
  a. creating   c. concealing
  b. distributing   d. enjoying

Vocabulary in Context   __c__   **2.** "We seem to forget that kids can be as tech-savvy as Bill Gates but as **gullible** as Bambi." (paragraph 5)
  a. dumb   c. naive
  b. clever   d. playful

Central Idea   __b__   **3.** Which of the following sentences states the central idea of the passage?
  a. "One teenager in five reported having sent or posted naked photos of themselves." (paragraph 1)
  b. "Child-pornography laws intended to protect children should not be used to prosecute and then label children as sex offenders." (paragraph 5)
  c. "The real problem with criminalizing teen sexting as a form of child pornography is that the great majority of these kids are not predators." (paragraph 6)

d. "Parents need to remind their teens that a dumb moment can last a lifetime in cyberspace." (paragraph 7)

Supporting Details ___a___ 4. According to the passage, teens caught sexting risk being charged with
   a. child pornography.   c. prostitution.
   b. sexting.   d. dating violence.

Supporting Details ___d___ 5. A recent *New York Times* article quotes the Family Violence Prevention Fund, a nonprofit domestic-violence-awareness group, saying that the sending of nude pictures, even if done voluntarily, constitutes
   a. cybercrime.   c. prostitution.
   b. cyberbulling.   d. digital dating violence.

Transitions ___a___ 6. "Do you (a) call the boy's parents in despair; (b) call the girl's parents in despair; or (c) call the police?" (paragraph 1)

   The relationship of ideas within this sentence is
   a. listing.   c. comparison and contrast.
   b. classification.   d. generalization and example.

Transitions ___c___ 7. "Experts insist the sexting trend hurts teen girls more than boys, fretting that they feel 'pressured' to take and send naked photos. Paradoxically, the girls in the Pennsylvania case were charged with 'manufacturing, disseminating or possessing child pornography' while the boys were merely charged with possession." (paragraph 6)

   The relationship of ideas between these sentences is
   a. cause and effect.   c. comparison and contrast.
   b. classification.   d. generalization and example.

Thought Patterns ___c___ 8. The thought pattern used in paragraph 4 is
   a. definition.   c. comparison and contrast.
   b. classification.   d. space order.

Thought Patterns ___a___ 9. The thought pattern for paragraph 5 is
   a. cause and effect.   c. comparison and contrast.
   b. classification.   d. generalization and example.

Fact and Opinion ___a___ 10. "One teenager in five reported having sent or posted naked photos of themselves." (paragraph 1)

   This sentence is a statement of
   a. fact.   c. fact and opinion.
   b. opinion.

Fact and
Opinion

_____b_____ **11.** "Child-pornography laws intended to protect children should not be used to prosecute and then label children as sex offenders." (paragraph 5)

This sentence is a statement of

a. fact.   c. fact and opinion.
b. opinion.

Fact and
Opinion

_____c_____ **12.** "A survey of the charges brought in the cases reflects that—depending on the jurisdiction—prosecutors have charged the senders of smutty photos, the recipients of smutty photos, those who save the smutty photos and the hapless forwarders of smutty photos with the same crime: child pornography." (paragraph 3)

This sentence is a statement of

a. fact.   c. fact and opinion.
b. opinion.

Tone

_____d_____ **13.** The overall tone of the author is

a. objective.   c. optimistic.
b. bitter.   d. skeptical.

Purpose

_____c_____ **14.** The overall purpose of the author is

a. to inform the public about the teen trend of sexting and its consequences.
b. to entertain the public with graphic details of teen sexting.
c. to persuade the public to decriminalize teen sexting.

Inferences

_____d_____ **15.** Based on the details in paragraph 1, we can infer that

a. most teens are involved in sexting.
b. sexting among teens is not a serious social problem.
c. only teens are involved in sexting.
d. most teens are not involved in sexting.

Inferences

_____a_____ **16.** Based on the details in paragraph 2, we can infer that

a. teens who are convicted of sexting could spend time in jail.
b. teens are not facing serious consequences when they are caught sexting.
c. teens who participate in sexting are sex offenders.
d. teen sexting is limited and occurs in only a few places.

Inferences

_____b_____ **17.** Based on the details in the passage, we can infer that

a. poor parenting is the cause of teen involvement in sexting.
b. teenagers are too immature to understand the consequences of sexting.

    c. teen sexting should be punished as a serious crime.

    d. teen sexting is a harmless rite of passage into adulthood.

Argument   __c__ **18.** Identify the persuasive technique used in the following sentence:

"The argument for hammering every such case seems to be that sending naked pictures might have serious consequences, so let's charge these kids with felonies, which will surely have serious consequences." (paragraph 5)

    a. false cause   c. begging the question

    b. personal attack   d. transfer

Argument   __b__ **19.** Identify the persuasive technique used in the following sentence:

"The argument that we must prosecute kids as the producers and purveyors of kiddie porn because they are too dumb to understand that their seemingly innocent acts can harm them goes beyond paternalism." (paragraph 5)

    a. false analogy   c. begging the question

    b. personal attack   d. transfer

Argument   __a__ **20.** Identify the persuasive technique used in the following sentence:

"We seem to forget that kids can be as tech-savvy as Bill Gates but as gullible as Bambi." (paragraph 5)

    a. false analogy   c. begging the question

    b. personal attack   d. transfer

Mapping

Complete the following pro-con chart for argumentation with information from the passage. Wording may vary.

Felony Charges for Teen Sexting	
Pro (for)	**Con (against)**
Teen sexting publishes **(1)** nude photos.	Kids are not **(4)** predators.
It disseminates **(2)** pornography.	Punishment is too harsh: Conviction of
It raises concerns about children as sex objects.	a felony and **(5)** registered as sex offender for decade(s).
It constitutes **(3)** "digital dating violence."	

WHAT DO YOU THINK?

Do you think teen sexting is a serious social problem? Why or why not? Why do you think one in five teens participate in sexting? How should society respond to teen sexting? Assume you are volunteer teen counselor at your local Boys and Girls Club, and it has come to your attention that several teens with whom you work are involved in sexting. In response, the Club has asked you to give a five-minute talk to the youth about the seriousness of teen sexting. Write a three-paragraph draft of a speech in which you warn teens about the dangers of sexting.

MASTER READER Scorecard

"Teens, Nude Photos and the Law"

Skill	Number Correct	Points	Total
Vocabulary			
Vocabulary in Context (2 items)	_____ ×	4 =	_____
Comprehension			
Central Idea (1 item)	_____ ×	4 =	_____
Supporting Details (2 items)	_____ ×	4 =	_____
Transitions (2 items)	_____ ×	4 =	_____
Thought Patterns (2 items)	_____ ×	4 =	_____
Fact and Opinion (3 items)	_____ ×	4 =	_____
Tone and Purpose (2 items)	_____ ×	4 =	_____
Inferences (3 items)	_____ ×	4 =	_____
Argument (3 items)	_____ ×	4 =	_____
Mapping (5 items)	_____ ×	4 =	_____
	Comprehension Score		_____

READING 3

Binge Drinking, A Campus Killer

by Sabrina Rubin Erdely   9.8 GE/2104 words

Sabrina Rubin Erdely, an investigative journalist, graduated from the University of Pennsylvania in 1994. Currently a senior staff writer at *Philadelphia* magazine and a contributing writer for *Cosmopolitan*, Erdely's work has earned her a number of awards, including nomination for the National Magazine Award in public interest writing. In the article reprinted here, Erdely explores the nationwide chronic problem of binge drinking on college and university campuses.

Vocabulary Preview

indulgences (paragraph 1): pleasures, excesses
surmise (paragraph 11): conclude, speculate
gratification (paragraph 11): satisfaction, pleasure
concoctions (paragraph 15): mixture, blend, brew
defibrillation (paragraph 18): an electrical shock applied to restore the heart's rhythm
equivalent (paragraph 19): equal, corresponding
illicit (paragraph 38): illegal, illegitimate, banned

---

1   Pregame tailgating parties, post-exam celebrations and Friday happy hours—not to mention fraternity and sorority mixers—have long been a cornerstone of the collegiate experience. But on campuses across America, these **indulgences** have a more alarming side. For some of today's college students, binge drinking has become the norm.

2   This past February I headed to the University of Wisconsin-Madison, rated the No. 2 party school in the nation by the college guide *Princeton Review,* to see the party scene for myself. On Thursday night the weekend was already getting started. At a **raucous** off-campus gathering, 20-year-old Tracey Middler struggled to down her beer as fist-pumping onlookers yelled, "Chug! Chug! Chug!"

3   In the kitchen, sophomore Jeremy Budda drained his tenth beer. "I get real wasted on weekends," he explained. Nearby, a 19-year-old estimated, "I'll end up having 17, 18 beers."

4   Swept up in the revelry, these partiers aren't thinking about the alcohol-related tragedies that have been in the news. All they're thinking about now is the next party. The keg is just about empty.

5   As the 19-year-old announces loudly, these college students have just one objective: "to get drunk!"

6 The challenge to drink to the very limits of one's endurance has become a celebrated staple of college life. In one of the most extensive reports on college drinking thus far, a 1997 Harvard School of Public Health study found that 43 percent of college students admitted binge drinking in the preceding two weeks. (Defined as four drinks in a sitting for a woman and five for a man, a drinking binge is when one drinks enough to risk health and well-being.)

7   "That's about five million students," says Henry Wechsler, who co-authored the study. "And it's certainly a cause for concern. Most of these students don't realize they're engaging in risky behavior." University of Kansas Chancellor Robert Hemenway adds, "Every year we see students harmed because of their involvement with alcohol."

8   Indeed, when binge drinking came to the forefront last year with a rash of alcohol-related college deaths, the nation was stunned by the loss. There was Scott Krueger, the 18-year-old fraternity pledge at the Massachusetts Institute of Technology, who died of alcohol poisoning after downing the equivalent of 15 shots in an hour. There was Leslie Baltz, a University of Virginia senior, who died after she drank too much and fell down a flight of stairs. Lorraine Hanna, a freshman at Indiana University of Pennsylvania, was left alone to sleep off her night of New Year's Eve partying. Later that day her twin sister found her dead—with a blood-alcohol content (BAC) of 0.429 percent. (Driving with a BAC of 0.1 percent and above is illegal in all states.)

Experts estimate that excessive drink- 9 ing is involved in thousands of student deaths a year. And the Harvard researchers found that there has been a dramatic change in why students drink: 39 percent drank "to get drunk" in 1993, but 52 percent had the same objective in 1997.

"What has changed is the across-the- 10 board *acceptability* of intoxication," says Felix Savino, a psychologist at UW-Madison. "Many college students today see not just drinking but being *drunk* as their primary way of socializing."

The reasons for the shift are complex 11 and not fully understood. But researchers **surmise** that it may have something to do with today's instant-**gratification** lifestyle—and young people tend to take it to the extreme.

In total, it is estimated that America's 12 12 million undergraduates drink the equivalent of six million gallons of beer a week. When that's combined with teenagers' need to drink secretly, it's no wonder many have a dangerous relationship with alcohol.

The biggest predictor of bingeing is 13 fraternity or sorority membership. Sixty-five percent of members qualified as binge drinkers, according to the Harvard study.

August 25, 1997, was meant to be a night 14 the new Sigma Alpha Epsilon pledges at Louisiana State University in Baton Rouge would never forget, and by 8 P.M. it was certainly shaping up that way. The revelry had begun earlier with a keg party. Then they went to a bar near campus, where pledges consumed massive quantities of alcohol.

Among the pledges were Donald 15 Hunt, Jr., a 21-year-old freshman and Army veteran, and his roommate, Benjamin

Wynne, a 20-year-old sophomore. Friends since high school, the two gamely drank the alcoholic **concoctions** offered to them and everyone else.

16   Before long, many in the group began vomiting into trash cans. (Donald Hunt would later allege in a lawsuit that these "vomiting stations" were set up for that very purpose, something the defendants adamantly deny.) About 9:30, **incapacitated** pledges were taken back to sleep it off at the frat house.

17   The 911 call came around midnight. Paramedics were stunned at what they found: more than a dozen young men sprawled on the floor, on chairs, on couches, reeking of alcohol. The paramedics burst into action, shaking the pledges and shouting, "Hey! Can you hear me?" Four couldn't be roused, and of those, one had no vital signs: Benjamin Wynne was in cardiac arrest.

18   Checking to see that nothing was blocking Wynne's airway, the paramedics began CPR. Within minutes they'd inserted an oxygen tube into his lungs, hooked up an I.V., attached a cardiac monitor and begun shocking him with **defibrillation** paddles, trying to restart his heart.

19   Still not responding, Wynne was rushed by ambulance to Baton Rouge General Hospital. Lab work revealed that his blood-alcohol content was an astonishing 0.588 percent, nearly six times the legal driving limit for adults—the **equivalent** of taking about 21 shots in an hour.

20   Meanwhile, three other fraternity pledges were undergoing similar revival efforts. One was Donald Hunt. He would suffer severe alcohol poisoning and nearly die.

21   After working furiously on Wynne, the hospital team admitted defeat. He was pronounced dead of acute alcohol poisoning.

22   One simple fact people tend to lose sight of is that alcohol is a poison—often pleasurable, but a toxin nonetheless. And for a person with little experience processing this toxin, it can come as something of a physical shock.

23   In general, a bottle of beer has about the same alcohol content as a glass of wine or shot of liquor. And the body can remove only the equivalent of less than one drink hourly from the bloodstream.

24   Many students are not just experimenting once or twice. In the Harvard study, half of binge drinkers were "frequent binge drinkers," meaning they had binged three or more times in the previous two weeks.

25   It also is assumed by some that bingeing is a "guy thing," an activity that, like cigar smoking and watching televised sports, belongs in the realm of male bonding. Statistics, however, show that the number of heavy-drinking young women is significant. Henry Wechsler's Harvard study found that a hefty 48 percent of college men were binge drinkers, and women were right behind them at 39 percent.

26   Howard Somers had always been afraid of heights. Perhaps his fear was some sort of an omen. On an August day in 1997 he helped his 18-year-old daughter, Mindy, move into her dorm at Virginia Tech. As they unloaded her things in the eighth-floor room, Somers noted with unease the position of the window. It opened inward like an oven door, its lip about level with her bed. He mentioned it, but Mindy dismissed his concern with a smile.

27   "I have gone through more guilt than you can imagine," Somers says now quietly. "Things I wish I had said or done. But I never thought this would happen. Who would?"

28   Mindy Somers knew the dangers of alcohol and tried to stay aware of her limits. She'd planned not to overdo it that Friday night, since her mother was coming in that weekend to celebrate Mindy's 19th birthday on Sunday. But it was Halloween, the campus was alive with activity, and Mindy decided to stop in at several off-campus parties.

29   When she returned to her room at 3 A.M., she was wiped out enough to fall into bed fully clothed. Mindy's bed was pushed lengthwise against the long, low window. Her roommate and two other girls, who were on the floor, all slept too soundly to notice that sometime after 4 A.M. Mindy's bed was empty.

30   When the paperboy found her face-down on the grass at 6:45 A.M., he at first thought it was a Halloween prank. Police and EMTs swarmed to the scene in minutes. Somers was pronounced dead of massive chest and abdominal injuries. She had a blood-alcohol content of 0.21 percent, equal to her having drunk about five beers in one hour.

31   Police surmised that Mindy had tried to get out of bed during the night but, disoriented, had slipped out the window, falling 75 feet to her death. "It was a strange, tragic accident," Virginia Tech Police Chief Michael Jones says.

32   A terrible irony was that the week prior to Mindy's death had been Virginia Tech's annual Alcohol Awareness Week.

33 While binge drinking isn't always lethal, it does have other, wide-ranging effects.

Academics is one realm where it takes a heavy toll.

34   During my trip to Wisconsin most students told me they didn't plan on attending classes the following day. "Nah, I almost never go to class on Friday. It's no big deal," answered Greg, a sophomore. According to a survey of university administrators, 38 percent of academic problems are alcohol-related, as are 29 percent of dropouts.

35   Perhaps because alcohol increases aggression and impairs judgment, it is also related to 25 percent of violent crimes and roughly 60 percent of vandalism on campus. According to one survey, 79 percent of students who had experienced unwanted sexual intercourse in the previous year said that they were under the influence of alcohol or other drugs at the time. "Some people believe that alcohol can provide an excuse for inappropriate behavior, including sexual aggression," says Jeanette Norris, a University of Washington researcher. Later on, those people can claim, "It wasn't me—it was the booze."

36   Faced with the many potential dangers, college campuses are scrambling for ways to reduce binge drinking. Many offer seminars on alcohol during freshman orientation. Over 50 schools provide alcohol-free living environments. At the University of Michigan's main campus in Ann Arbor, for instance, nearly 30 percent of undergrads living in university housing now choose to live in alcohol-free rooms. Nationwide several fraternities have announced that by the year 2000 their chapter houses will be alcohol-free.

37   After the University of Rhode Island topped the *Princeton Review* party list two

years in a row, administrators banned alcohol at all student events on campus; this year URI didn't even crack the top ten. Some campuses respond even more severely, unleashing campus raids and encouraging police busts.

38   Researchers debate, however, if such "zero-tolerance" policies are helpful or if they might actually result in more secret, off-campus drinking. Other academics wonder if dropping the drinking age to 18 would take away the **illicit** thrill of alcohol and lower the number of kids drinking wildly. Others feel this would just create more drinking-related fatalities.

39   Whatever it takes, changing student behavior won't be easy. "What you've got here are people who think they are having fun," Harvard's Henry Wechsler explains. "You can't change their behavior by preaching at them or by telling them they'll get hurt."

Around 2 A.M. at UW-Madison a hundred 40 kids congregate at a downtown intersection in a nightly ritual. One girl is trying to pull her roommate up off the ground. "I'm not that drunk," the one on the ground insists. "I just can't stand up."

Two fights break out. A police car 41 cruises by and the crowd thins, some heading to after-hours parties. Then maybe at 3 or 4 A.M. they'll go home to get some sleep, so they will be rested for when they start to drink again. Tomorrow night.

Choose the best meaning of each word in **bold** type. Use context clues to make your choice.

Vocabulary in Context ___d___ **1.** "At a **raucous** off-campus gathering, 20-year-old Tracey Middler struggled to down her beer as fist-pumping onlookers yelled, 'Chug! Chug! Chug!'" (paragraph 2)
    a. fun   c. illegal
    b. dangerous   d. wild

Vocabulary in Context ___b___ **2.** "About 9:30, **incapacitated** pledges were taken back to sleep it off at the frat house." (paragraph 16)
    a. mindless   c. dangerous
    b. disabled   d. young

Central Idea and Main Ideas ___d___ **3.** Which sentence is the best statement of the implied central idea of the article?
    a. Binge drinking is a normal and widespread trend in American college life.
    b. Parents, educators, and researchers are unable to stop the dangerous trend of college binge drinking.
    c. College students indulge in binge drinking to have fun and assert adultlike independence.

d. The national problem of binge drinking among college students is an alarming and escalating threat to their physical and academic well-being that has college campuses scrambling for solutions.

Central Idea ___a___
and Main Ideas

4. Which sentence states the main idea of paragraph 6?
   a. "The challenge to drink to the very limits of one's endurance has become a celebrated staple of college life."
   b. "In one of the most extensive reports on college drinking thus far, a 1997 Harvard School of Public Health study found that 43 percent of college students admitted to drinking in the preceding two weeks."
   c. "Defined as four drinks in a sitting for a woman and five for a man, a drinking binge is when one drinks enough to risk health and well-being."

Supporting ___c___
Details

5. Which university—"rated as the No. 2 party school in the nation"— did the author visit to research her article?
   a. Harvard
   b. Princeton
   c. University of Wisconsin-Madison
   d. University of Pennsylvania

Supporting ___b___
Details

6. For a man, binge drinking is defined by downing how many drinks in one sitting?
   a. 4   c. 8
   b. 5   d. 12

Transitions ___a___

7. "On Thursday night the weekend was already getting started. At a raucous off-campus gathering, 20-year-old Tracey Middler struggled to down her beer as fist-pumping onlookers yelled, 'Chug! Chug! Chug!'" (paragraph 2)

What is the relationship of ideas between these two sentences?
   a. time order   c. example
   b. contrast

Transitions ___c___

8. "In general, a bottle of beer has about the same alcohol content as a glass of wine or shot of liquor." (paragraph 23)

Which term best describes the relationship of ideas within this sentence?
   a. time order   c. comparison
   b. example

Thought Patterns   <u>a</u>   **9.** The overall thought pattern used by the author to organize her article is
    a. examples of binge drinking and its consequences.
    b. an argument to eliminate alcohol from college and university campuses.
    c. a discussion of the causes of binge drinking.
    d. a narrative about binge drinking.

Thought Patterns   <u>b</u>   **10.** The thought pattern in paragraph 11 is
    a. example.   c. time order.
    b. cause and effect.

Fact and Opinion   <u>b</u>   **11.** Overall, the ideas in this passage
    a. are based on research and statistics.
    b. are based on research and the personal observations of the author.
    c. objectively present the views of college students.
    d. angrily describe the causes and effects of binge drinking.

Fact and Opinion   <u>b</u>   **12.** "Many college students today see not just drinking but being *drunk* as their primary way of socializing." (paragraph 10)

This sentence is a statement of
    a. fact.   c. fact and opinion.
    b. opinion.

Tone and Purpose   <u>c</u>   **13.** The overall tone of the passage is
    a. sympathetic.   c. objective.
    b. humorous.   d. outraged.

Tone and Purpose   <u>c</u>   **14.** The tone of paragraph 8 is
    a. harsh.   c. matter-of-fact.
    b. regretful.   d. disgusted.

Tone and Purpose   <u>d</u>   **15.** The tone of paragraph 27 is
    a. angry.   c. humble.
    b. puzzled.   d. remorseful.

Tone and Purpose   <u>c</u>   **16.** The author's main purpose is
    a. to persuade parents, educators, and students to take action against binge drinking.
    b. to shock readers with alarming details about binge drinking.
    c. to inform readers about the depth and scope of the alarming national trend of binge drinking among college students.

Inferences ____c____ **17.** From paragraphs 8 and 9, we can conclude that
  a. deaths from binge drinking are inevitable.
  b. universities and colleges are responsible for the thousands of student deaths that occur each year.
  c. thousands of lives could be saved each year if binge drinking could be controlled.
  d. college students understand the risks associated with binge drinking.

Inferences ____b____ **18.** Based on the details about Mindy Somers (paragraphs 28–32), we can conclude that
  a. Mindy engaged in binge drinking frequently.
  b. Virginia Tech's annual Alcohol Awareness Week did not effectively educate Mindy about the dangers of binge drinking.
  c. Mindy's father should have known about the risks related to her drinking habits.
  d. binge drinking is always lethal.

Inferences ____a____ **19.** The details in paragraphs 2, 3, and 34 imply that
  a. the weekend binge drinking cycle probably begins on Thursday.
  b. most college students do not "get wasted" during the week.
  c. most college students are more interested in partying than in studying.
  d. males are more likely to binge and miss classes than are females.

Argument ____d____ **20.** The following list of ideas from paragraphs 9–11 contains a claim and supports for that claim. In the space, write the letter of the claim for the argument.
  a. "The Harvard researchers found that there has been a dramatic change in why students drink: 39 percent drank 'to get drunk' in 1993, but 52 percent had the same objective in 1997."
  b. "What has changed is the across-the-board *acceptability* of intoxication," says Felix Savino, a psychologist at UW-Madison.
  c. "Researchers surmise that it may have something to do with today's instant-gratification life-style—and young people tend to take it to the extreme."
  d. "Many college students today see not just drinking but being *drunk* as their primary way of socializing."

Mapping

Complete the concept map below. Fill in the blanks with the central idea and the missing supporting details from "Binge Drinking, A Campus Killer."

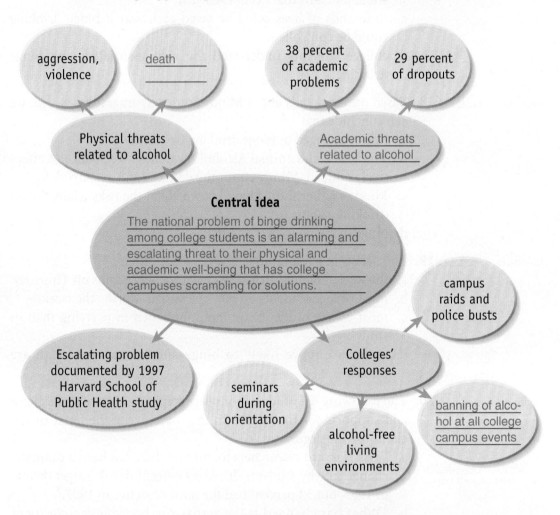

WHAT DO YOU THINK?

Do you think binge drinking is a problem at your college or university? What do you think is the best solution to binge drinking on college campuses? Assume you are a member of your Student Government Association (SGA). SGA has decided to raise awareness about this issue, so you have been asked to write an article for publication in the college and local newspapers. In your editorial, advise college students about the danger of binge drinking and suggest ways to avoid the dangers based on what you have learned from reading this article. Begin your editorial with a summary of the author's main ideas and major supporting details. Also identify and discuss some obvious and underlying reasons for student binge drinking.

MASTER READER Scorecard

"Binge Drinking, A Campus Killer"			
Skill	Number Correct	Points	Total
Vocabulary			
Vocabulary in Context (2 items)	_____ ×	4	= _____
Comprehension			
Central Idea and Main Ideas (2 items)	_____ ×	4	= _____
Supporting Details (2 items)	_____ ×	4	= _____
Transitions (2 items)	_____ ×	4	= _____
Thought Patterns (2 items)	_____ ×	4	= _____
Fact and Opinion (2 items)	_____ ×	4	= _____
Tone and Purpose (4 items)	_____ ×	4	= _____
Inferences (3 items)	_____ ×	4	= _____
Argument (1 item)	_____ ×	4	= _____
Mapping (4 items)	_____ ×	5	= _____
	Comprehension Score		_____

Is Substance Abuse a Social Problem?

by John D. Carl   11.4 GE/1751 words

Textbook
Skills

John D. Carl holds a Ph.D. in Sociology from the University of Oklahoma. His work history includes not only colleges but hospitals, schools, churches, and prisons. This passage is taken from his textbook *Think: Social Problems*. Carl's passion for sociology is evident as he expresses his goal for writing: "the goal of this book is rather simple: To teach students to view social problems critically and to use sociological thinking to help them do that." How would you evaluate the use of drugs in America?

Vocabulary Preview

plethora (paragraph 1): large or excessive amount or number
inebriation (paragraph 1): intoxicated, drunk
gratification (paragraph 9): satisfaction, fulfillment
socialization (paragraph 10): training or developing skills needed to function
   successfully in society

BASICS OF DRUG USE IN AMERICA

1   As you can imagine, drug use and abuse creates a **plethora** of social problems for society. These problems are not only because of the extra costs associated with trying to help people "kick the habit" but also due to the lost productivity, destroyed relationships, and personal injury that such abuse can cause. Of all the drugs available in the United States, tobacco and alcohol are the two most commonly used. Recent surveys have shown that 20.6 percent of Americans over 18 are current smokers. In addition, 23 percent of adults drink alcohol at a dangerous level, and even among youth, 91 percent of drinkers 12 to 14 years old

admit to binge drinking. College students in particular fall into the binge-drinking scene, as many students view **inebriation** as a rite of passage. This attitude has created a serious issue for schools, as alcohol-related hospitalizations and deaths are regular occurrences on many college campuses. In fact, numerous colleges are now making it illegal for anyone to consume alcohol on campus, regardless of their age.

CHARACTERISTICS OF DRUG USERS

Age

2   If you think teenagers and college students make up the majority of "users," you're mistaken. It's true that almost 20 percent of

18- to 25-year olds frequently use illegal drugs, compared to 5.8 percent of those 26 and older. However, a 2007 survey on drug use showed that 42 percent of Americans over 26 have used marijuana, while only about 16 percent of young adults have tried this drug. Researchers attribute this pattern to the aging baby boomer population who grew up in a culture of drug use.

3   Even if the researchers are correct in saying that anti-drug ads have been counter-productive, teen drug use has been steadily decreasing since the turn of the millennium. In 1999, it was estimated that more than half of high school seniors used illicit drugs, mostly marijuana. Even pre-teen drug use was high, as one fourth of eighth graders admitted to having been drunk at least once, and 44 percent reported that they smoked cigarettes. Compare those numbers to the current ones that estimate 44 percent of all high school seniors admit to alcohol use, and 18 percent admit to marijuana use.

Race

4   Although drug abuse occurs among all races in the United States, it is more prevalent in some races than others. Asians currently show the lowest rate of drug use among persons 12 and older (3.6 percent); Native Americans and Alaska Natives have the highest percentage of drug use in the United States (13.7 percent).

Socioeconomic Status

5   How does drug use effect socioeco-nomic status? Certainly, there are many studies that show the connection between illegal drug use and dropping out of school, lower educational attainment, unemploy-ment, and low rates of advancement in one's career. However, in terms of earnings, research suggests that lower incomes for drug users takes time to **manifest** itself. In other words, the effect of drug use has little impact on the individual when he or she is younger, but increases over time. This is in part due to the fact that early in their work lives, drug users tend to take jobs with little potential for growth. Over time, that choice keeps them from advancing, unlike their non-user peers.

PRESCRIPTION DRUG USE

6   As government and private organiza-tions work to thwart current forms of drug use, Americans are finding new ways to get high. The most current trend in drug abuse is the misuse of prescription drugs. Accord-ing to the Centers for Disease Control and Prevention, more than 1.8 billion prescrip-tion drugs were ordered or provided in 2006, the most frequently prescribed drugs being analgesics, or painkillers. Although these drugs are created and prescribed with the intention of healing or providing relief, they are sometimes abused rather than used appropriately.

7   The three types of prescription drugs that are most commonly abused are opiates (medically prescribed to treat pain), central nervous system depressants (prescribed to treat anxiety and sleep disorders), and stim-ulants (prescribed to treat disorders such as narcolepsy and attention deficit disorder). Although the use of these types of drugs can help an individual, abuse of these drugs can be extremely harmful to a user's body.

8   Amphetamines, such as Adderall or Ritalin, are some of the most widely abused

prescription drugs, especially among teens. Ritalin, a drug prescribed to individuals with attention deficit disorder, has been used without a prescription by as many as 1 in 10 teenagers. As you may already know, some of the most frequent abuse of amphetamines occurs on college campuses. Whereas some students might drink a can of Red Bull to stay alert for a long night of studying, others might turn to amphetamines. One student even admitted to me that he took Adderall to stay awake when he needed to pull all-nighters.

WHY DO WE USE DRUGS?

9   Our bodies have natural defenses against infection and disease; when we're in pain, our brains produce chemicals that dull the ache and make us feel happy. So, why do we need drugs? Some suggest that this is the wrong question. People have always used drugs and will likely continue to use them. Most of society's legal efforts to control drug use fail; the issue becomes how to control use while avoiding the harmful aspects of drug abuse. The causes of drug abuse are difficult to determine and often involve claims that abusers cannot delay **gratification** and have low self-control. However, many people do not agree that addiction is a sign of moral or psychological weakness. Treating addiction as a medical condition—as opposed to a moral failure—arose in the 20th century and resulted in a number of treatment programs and models. In general, these models hold two common beliefs: (1) Individuals have biological predispositions to addiction, and (2) these predispositions can be overcome through treatment.

SOCIALIZATION

10   Sociological theory and medical research are aware that determining why people use drugs is a complex issue. Researcher Denise Kandel suggests that there is an interaction between how a person is socialized and with whom they interact. Recall that we are socialized by a variety of individuals. Parents provide long-term values, and their use of drugs has the potential to influence their children. However, one's peers provide even more powerful **socialization**. Teens who get involved in drugs and/or alcohol generally have peers who are users. The selection of one's peer group provides the foundation for the likelihood of use by adolescents. This happens in part because they bond to users and learn to share their values and behaviors. Of course, we choose our friends not merely based on who we live near, but also by who interests us. In this way, people who get into drug-using groups in a sense choose their path, although, at the same time, they are being steered toward this path by their group. This is a dynamic process that usually starts with minor alcohol use, such as beer or wine, moves to cigarettes and hard alcohol, then to marijuana, and possibly to harder drugs. To put it simply, people can drift into drugs through a process of being socialized into their use.

11   Another part of drug socialization stems from the fact that the United States is increasingly becoming a medicalized society. Medicalization is the process by which we expand the use of medical terms and solutions to non-medical problems. Medical personnel often claim that certain social

components are diseases in need of treatment. Such an attitude expands the power of the medical community, but also increases the public's desire for medical solutions. This leads us to seek a pill to solve our problems. In 2006 alone, more than 1.8 billion prescription drugs were ordered or provided. Does that necessarily make things better? It's clear that what it does do is help socialize us into a mind-set whereby drug use is common.

12   At what point do we change from a culture of drug users to a culture of drug abusers? When so many people seem motivated to abuse substances and modify their behavior with drugs, it's easy to see how this problem can spread to the greater society. A student of mine who had an alcoholic husband put it this way: "Living with an addict is like living with an elephant in your house. It stinks up the place, makes lots of messes, and it's too big to simply act like it's not there because doing that will destroy your family, your children, and your sense of reality." The social problems of substance abuse are not just individual issues.

GO GLOBAL: THE MEXICAN DRUG WAR

13   The real Mexican-American War ended in 1848, but lately a new, covert war has begun. Like any other war, this conflict has resulted in casualties: 6,300 bodies in 2008 alone. This time, however, the Mexican and U.S. governments are working together, battling the rampant drug trafficking that goes on at the border.

14   It's not just drugs that officials are worried about. According to the Federal Bureau of Alcohol, Tobacco, Firearms and Explosives, roughly 90 percent of guns seized in raids of Mexican dealers are traced back to the United States. Drug traffickers cross the border on three-day shopping visas, purchase large quantities of assault weapons and ammunition from local merchants, then return home. It's estimated that nearly 2,000 firearms cross the border into Mexico daily.

15   Americans aren't just providing drug cartels with guns; they're also providing them with money. The majority of drugs cultivated in Mexico are sold to Americans, and Mexican drug dealers generate profits of $15 billion to $25 billion a year solely from the United States.

16   Mexico's drug war isn't only an issue south of the border. The U.S. Justice Department has stated that Mexican drug trafficking organizations represent the greatest organized crime threat to the United States. President Obama has been working with Mexican President Felipe Calderon to build a more aggressive offense against drug lords. "We are absolutely committed to working in partnership with Mexico to make sure that we are dealing with this **scourge** on both sides of the border," Obama said after meeting with Calderon. "You can't fight this war with just one hand. You can't have Mexico making an effort and the United States not making an effort."

17   So far, the President has sent Congress a war-spending request for $350 million to increase security along the United States-Mexico border. More efforts from the U.S. government are expected to be initiated as violence from the Mexican drug war continues to spread.

—Adapted from *Think Social Problems,* pp. 144–147 by John D. Carl. Copyright © 2011 by Pearson Education, Inc. Reproduced by permission of Pearson Education, Inc., Boston, MA.

Choose the best meaning of each word in **bold**. Use context clues to make your choice.

Vocabulary in Context _b_ **1.** "However, in terms of earnings, research suggests that lower incomes for drug users takes time to **manifest** itself." (paragraph 5)
   a. list
   b. reveal
   c. clear
   d. hide

Vocabulary in Context _c_ **2.** "'We are absolutely committed to working in partnership with Mexico to make sure that we are dealing with this **scourge** on both sides of the border,' Obama said . . ." (paragraph 16)
   a. whip
   b. law
   c. misery
   d. issue

Central Ideas and Main Ideas _a_ **3.** Which of the following sentences from paragraph 1 states the central idea of the passage?
   a. "As you can imagine, drug use and abuse creates a plethora of social problems for society."
   b. "These problems are not only because of the extra costs associated with trying to help people 'kick the habit' but also due to the lost productivity, destroyed relationships, and personal injury that such abuse can cause."
   c. "Of all the drugs available in the United States, tobacco and alcohol are the two most commonly used."
   d. "Recent surveys have shown that 20.6 percent of Americans over 18 are current smokers."

Central Ideas and Main Ideas _b_ **4.** Which of the following sentences states the central idea of paragraphs 6 through 8?
   a. "As government and private organizations work to thwart current forms of drug use, Americans are finding new ways to get high." (paragraph 6)
   b. "The most current trend in drug abuse is the misuse of prescription drugs." (paragraph 6)
   c. "The three types of prescription drugs that are most commonly abused are opiates (medically prescribed to treat pain), central nervous system depressants (prescribed to treat anxiety and sleep disorders), and stimulants (prescribed to treat disorders such as narcolepsy and attention deficit disorder)." (paragraph 7)
   d. "Amphetamines, such as Adderall or Ritalin, are some of the most widely abused prescription drugs, especially among teens." (paragraph 8)

Supporting Details ___c___ **5.** According to the passage, which of the following has the greatest influence an individual's drug use?
a. parents   c. peers
b. doctors   d. one's self

Supporting Details ___d___ **6.** According to the passage, how much money has President Obama requested from Congress to increase security along the United States-Mexican border?
a. $15 billion   c. $1.8 billion
b. $25 billion   d. $350 million

Transitions ___c___ **7.** "Although the use of these types of drugs can help an individual, abuse of these drugs can be extremely harmful to a user's body." (paragraph 7)

The relationship of ideas within this sentence is
a. addition.   c. comparison and contrast.
b. cause and effect.   d. generalization and example.

Transitions ___b___ **8.** "Recent surveys have shown that 20.6 percent of Americans over 18 are current smokers. In addition, 23 percent of adults drink alcohol at a dangerous level, and even among youth, 91 percent of drinkers 12 to 14 years old admit to binge drinking." (paragraph 1)

The relationship of ideas between these sentences is
a. cause and effect.   c. comparison and contrast.
b. addition.   d. generalization and example.

Thought Patterns ___b___ **9.** The overall thought pattern for paragraphs 2 through 5 is
a. cause and effect.   c. comparison and contrast.
b. classification.   d. definition and example.

Thought Patterns ___d___ **10.** The thought pattern for paragraph 4 is
a. cause and effect.   c. comparison and contrast.
b. classification.   d. generalization and example.

Thought Patterns ___a___ **11.** The thought pattern for paragraph 5 is
a. cause and effect.   c. comparison and contrast.
b. classification.   d. generalization and example.

Fact and Opinion ___a___ **12.** "Recent surveys have shown that 20.6 percent of Americans over 18 are current smokers." (paragraph 1)

This sentence is a statement of
a. fact.   c. fact and opinion.
b. opinion.

Fact and
Opinion

___b___ **13.** "Living with an addict is like living with an elephant in your house." (paragraph 12)

This sentence is a statement of
a. fact.   c. fact and opinion.
b. opinion.

Fact and
Opinion

___b___ **14.** "This leads us to seek a pill to solve our problems." (paragraph 11)

This sentence is a statement of
a. fact.   c. fact and opinion.
b. opinion.

Fact and
Opinion

___c___ **15.** "This time, however, the Mexican and U. S. governments are working together, battling the rampant drug trafficking that goes on at the border." (paragraph 13)

This sentence is a statement of
a. fact.   c. fact and opinion.
b. opinion.

Tone

___a___ **16.** The overall tone of the passage is
a. informal.   b. formal.

Tone

___d___ **17.** The overall tone of the author is
a. light-hearted.   c. dismayed.
b. belittling.   d. balanced.

Purpose

___a___ **18.** The author's purpose is to
a. inform the student about the sociological perspective of drug use in America.
b. entertain the student with interesting facts about drug use in America.
c. persuade the student to take a stand against drug abuse in America.

Inferences

___c___ **19.** Based on the details in paragraphs 7 and 8, we can infer that Adderall and Ritalin are
a. opiates.   c. stimulants.
b. depressants.   d. analgesics.

Argument _____a_____   **20.** Identify the persuasive technique used in the following statements:

"Living with an addict is like living with an elephant in your house. It stinks up the place, makes lots of messes, and it's too big to simply act like it's not there because doing that will destroy your family, your children, and your sense of reality." (paragraph 12)

a. false analogy
b. personal attack
c. begging the question
d. transfer

Outlining

Complete the following formal outline with information from the passage.

Central Idea: As you can imagine, drug use and abuse creates a plethora of social problems for society.

   I. Basics of Drug Use in America

  II. Characteristics of Drug Users

     A. Age

     B. Race

     C. Socioeconomic Status

  III. Prescription Drug Use

  IV. Why Do We Use Drugs?

   V. Socialization

  VI. Go Global: The Mexican Drug War

WHAT DO YOU THINK?

Did you learn any new information from this passage? If so, what did you learn? If you already knew all of the information in the passage, which parts of the passage are the most important and why? Do you think America is largely responsible for the drug trafficking between Mexico and the United States? Why or why not? Assume you are taking a college course in sociology, and your professor has handed out study topics for a unit review worth 25% of your final grade. When you and your study group divided the topics up among yourselves to answer and share with the group, you drew the following two topics: (1) Write a short essay that discusses and illustrates how a person is socialized into using drugs; (2) Give several reasons to support or oppose President Obama's request for money to increase security along the United States-Mexico border.

MASTER READER Scorecard

"Is Substance Abuse a Social Problem?"			
Skill	**Number Correct**	**Points**	**Total**
Vocabulary			
Vocabulary in Context (2 items)	_____	× 4 =	_____
Comprehension			
Central Idea and Main Ideas (2 items)	_____	× 4 =	_____
Supporting Details (2 items)	_____	× 4 =	_____
Transitions (2 items)	_____	× 4 =	_____
Thought Patterns (3 items)	_____	× 4 =	_____
Fact and Opinion (4 items)	_____	× 4 =	_____
Tone and Purpose (3 items)	_____	× 4 =	_____
Inferences (1 item)	_____	× 4 =	_____
Argument (1 item)	_____	× 4 =	_____
Outlining (5 items)	_____	× 4 =	_____
	Comprehension Score		_____

Think You're Operating on Free Will? Think Again

by Eben Harrell   12.5 GE/972 words

Do you believe in free will? Do you believe that you can control all the choices that you make? Do you believe that your choices determine your future? Why or why not? If not, what controls our decisions? Our genes, our society, supernatural powers? The following article by Eben Harrell, a reporter for *Time* magazine, points us to some interesting findings in recent scientific studies about our "will" to choose. Prior to joining the London bureau in 2007, Harrell worked at the *Aspen Times* in Colorado and the *Scotsman* in Edinburgh.

Vocabulary Preview

rational (paragraph 2): logical, reasonable, sound

subliminally (paragraph 4): without awareness

constructive (paragraph 5): positive, helpful

automaticity (paragraph 6): done unconsciously or from force of habit

skepticism (paragraph 6): disbelief, doubt

exceptionalism (paragraph 10): being different from the norm

undermines (paragraph 10): weakens, undercuts

id (paragraph 10): according to Sigmund Freud, the unconscious part of the mind, the source of inborn impulses and drives

voyagers (paragraph 11): travelers, explorers

1   Studies have found that upon entering an office, people behave more competitively when they see a sharp leather briefcase on the desk, they talk more softly when there is a picture of a library on the wall, and they keep their desk tidier when there is a vague scent of cleaning agent in the air. But none of them are consciously aware of the influence of their environment.

2   There may be few things more fundamental to human identity than the belief that people are **rational** individuals whose behavior is determined by conscious choices. But recently psychologists have compiled an impressive body of research that shows how

deeply our decisions and behavior are influenced by unconscious thought, and how greatly those thoughts are swayed by stimuli beyond our immediate comprehension.

3   In an intriguing review in the July 2 edition of the journal *Science*, published online Thursday, Ruud Custers and Henk Aarts of Utrecht University in the Netherlands lay out the mounting evidence of the power of what they term the "unconscious will." "People often act in order to realize desired outcomes, and they assume that consciousness drives that behavior. But the field now challenges the idea that there is only a **conscious** will. Our actions are very often initiated even though we are unaware of what we are seeking or why," Custers says.

4   It is not only that people's actions can be influenced by unconscious stimuli; our desires can be too. In one study cited by Custers and Aarts, students were presented with words on a screen related to puzzles—*crosswords*, *jigsaw piece*, etc. For some students, the screen also flashed an additional set of words so briefly that they could only be detected **subliminally**. The words were ones with positive associations, such as *beach*, *friend* or *home*. When the students were given a puzzle to complete, the students exposed unconsciously to positive words worked harder, for longer, and reported greater motivation to do puzzles than the control group.

5   The same priming technique has also been used to prompt people to drink more fluids after being subliminally exposed to drinking-related words, and to offer **constructive** feedback to other people after sitting in front of a screen that subliminally flashes the names of their loved ones or occupations associated with caring like *nurse*. In other words, we are often not even consciously aware of why we want what we want.

6   John Bargh of Yale University, who 10 years ago predicted many of the findings discussed by Custers and Aarts in a paper entitled "The Unbearable **Automaticity** of Being," called the *Science* paper a "landmark—nothing like this has been in *Science* before. It's a large step toward overcoming the **skepticism** surrounding this research." But Bargh says the field has actually moved beyond the use of subliminal techniques, and studies show that unconscious processes can even be influenced by stimuli within the realms of consciousness, often in unexpected ways. For instance, his own work has shown that people sitting in hard chairs are more likely to be more rigid in negotiating the sales price of a new car, they tend to judge others as more generous and caring after they hold a warm cup of coffee rather than a cold drink, and they evaluate job candidates as more serious when they review their résumés on a heavy clipboard rather than a light one.

7   "These are **stimuli** that people are conscious of—you can feel the hard chair, the hot coffee—but were unaware that it influenced them. Our unconscious is active in many more ways than this review suggests," he says.

8   Custers says his work demonstrates that subliminal-advertising techniques—which some countries have outlawed—can

be effective. But he says people concerned about being unconsciously manipulated "should be much more scared of commercials they can see, rather than those they can't see." Many soda commercials, he says by way of example, show the drink with positive-reward cues such as friends or beaches. "If you are exposed to these advertisements over and over again, it does create an association in your mind, and your unconscious is more likely to suddenly decide you want a Coke," he says.

9   But he also says that, at least when it comes to unhealthy food, policymakers are beginning to understand that "personal choice" may be a weak counter to heavy advertising. "We are starting to talk about 'toxic environments' with food and to understand how easy it is to mindlessly reach for a bag of potato chips. Removing such stimuli from the environment can be very effective," he says.

10   Both Custers and Bargh acknowledge that their research undermines a fundamental principle used to promote human exceptionalism—indeed, Bargh has in the past argued that his work **undermines** the existence of free will. But Custers also points out that his conclusions are not new: people have long sensed that they are influenced by forces beyond their immediate recognition—be it Greek gods or Freud's unruly **id**. What's more, the unconscious will is vital for daily functioning and probably evolved before consciousness as a handy survival mechanism—Bargh calls it "the evolutionary foundation upon which the scaffolding of consciousness is built." Life requires so many decisions, Bargh says, "that we would be swiftly overwhelmed if we did not have the automatic processes to deal with them."

11   For his part, Custers says that it is true that our conscious selves are sometimes **voyagers** on a vessel of which they have little control, but he does not see this as a cause for helplessness. "We have to trust that our unconscious sense of what we want and what is good for us is strong, and will lead us largely in the right direction."

—"Think You're Operating on Free Will? Think Again." by Eben Harrell from *Time Magazine,* July 2, 2010. Copyright Time Inc. Reprinted by permission. TIME is a registered trademark of Time Inc. All rights reserved.

Choose the best meaning of each word in **bold**. Use context clues to make your choice.

Vocabulary in Context   b

1. "But the field now challenges the idea that there is only a **conscious** will. Our actions are very often initiated even though we are unaware of what we are seeking or why," Custers says. (paragraph 3)

   a. uncontrolled   c. innocent
   b. deliberate   d. strong

Vocabulary
in Context ___d___ **2.** "These are **stimuli** that people are conscious of—you can feel the hard chair, the hot coffee—but were unaware that it influenced them." (paragraph 7)

    a. responses   c. effects

    b. supports   d. causes

Central Idea ___d___ **3.** Which of the following sentences from the first two paragraphs states the central idea of the passage?

    a. "Studies have found that upon entering an office, people behave more competitively when they see a sharp leather briefcase on the desk, they talk more softly when there is a picture of a library on the wall, and they keep their desk tidier when there is a vague scent of cleaning agent in the air."

    b. "But none of them are consciously aware of the influence of their environment."

    c. "There may be few things more fundamental to human identity than the belief that people are **rational** individuals whose behavior is determined by conscious choices."

    d. "But recently psychologists have compiled an impressive body of research that shows how deeply our decisions and behavior are influenced by unconscious thought, and how greatly those thoughts are swayed by stimuli beyond our immediate comprehension."

Main Idea ___a___ **4.** Which of the following sentences states the main idea of paragraph 4?

    a. "It is not only that people's actions can be influenced by unconscious stimuli; our desires can be too."

    b. "In one study cited by Custers and Aarts, students were presented with words on a screen related to puzzles—*crosswords, jigsaw piece*, etc."

    c. "For some students, the screen also flashed an additional set of words so briefly that they could only be detected subliminally."

    d. "When the students were given a puzzle to complete, the students exposed unconsciously to positive words worked harder, for longer, and reported greater motivation to do puzzles than the control group."

Main Idea ___b___ **5.** Which of the following sentences states the main idea of paragraph 8?

    a. "Custers says his work demonstrates that subliminal-advertising techniques—which some countries have outlawed—can be effective."

b. "But he says people concerned about being unconsciously ma-nipulated 'should be much more scared of commercials they can see, rather than those they can't see.'"

c. "Many soda commercials, he says by way of example, show the drink with positive-reward cues such as friends or beaches."

d. "'If you are exposed to these advertisements over and over again, it does create an association in your mind, and your un-conscious is more likely to suddenly decide you want a Coke,' he says."

Supporting Details   _c_   **6.** According to the passage, words such as *beach*, *friend*, or *home* were used subliminally

a. to prompt people to drink more fluids.

b. by John Bargh in the paper he wrote "The Unbearable Automaticity of Being."

c. in a scientific study involving students.

d. to prove the existence of free will.

Supporting Details   _b_   **7.** According to the passage, after holding a warm cup of coffee, people are more likely to

a. be rigid in negotiating the sales price of a new car.

b. judge others as more generous and caring.

c. evaluate job candidates as more serious.

d. be motivated to solve puzzles.

Transitions   _b_   **8.** "But recently psychologists have compiled an impressive body of research that shows how deeply our decisions and behavior are in-fluenced by unconscious thought, and how greatly those thoughts are swayed by stimuli beyond our immediate comprehension." (paragraph 2)

The relationship of ideas within this sentence is

a. classification.   c. comparison and contrast.

b. cause and effect.   d. time order.

Transitions   _c_   **9.** "Our actions are very often initiated even though we are unaware of what we are seeking or why." (paragraph 3)

The relationship of ideas within this sentence is

a. classification.   c. comparison and contrast.

b. cause and effect.   d. time order.

Transitions   c   **10.** "'People often act in order to realize desired outcomes, and they assume that consciousness drives that behavior. But the field now challenges the idea that there is only a conscious will. Our actions are very often initiated even though we are unaware of what we are seeking or why,' Custers says." (paragraph 3)

The relationship of ideas between these sentences is
a. cause and effect.   c. comparison and contrast.
b. classification.   d. generalization and example.

Thought   b   **11.** The thought pattern for paragraph 8 is
Patterns
a. classification.   c. comparison and contrast.
b. cause and effect.   d. time order.

Thought   a   **12.** The overall thought pattern for the passage is
Patterns
a. cause and effect.   c. comparison and contrast.
b. classification.   d. generalization and example

Fact and   b   **13.** "There may be few things more fundamental to human identity
Opinion
than the belief that people are rational individuals whose behavior is determined by conscious choices." (paragraph 2)

This sentence is a statement of
a. fact.   c. fact and opinion.
b. opinion.

Fact and   c   **14.** "In an intriguing review in the July 2 edition of the journal *Science*,
Opinion
published online Thursday, Ruud Custers and Henk Aarts of Utrecht University in the Netherlands lay out the mounting evidence of the power of what they term the 'unconscious will.'" (paragraph 3)

This sentence is a statement of
a. fact.   c. fact and opinion.
b. opinion.

Fact and   a   **15.** "In one study cited by Custers and Aarts, students were presented
Opinion
with words on a screen related to puzzles—*crosswords, jigsaw piece,* etc." (paragraph 4)

This sentence is a statement of
a. fact.   c. fact and opinion.
b. opinion.

Tone _____d_____ **16.** The overall tone of the passage is
   a. doubtful.   c. ironic.
   b. neutral.   d. persuasive.

Purpose _____a_____ **17.** The primary purpose of the passage is
   a. to inform.   c. to persuade.
   b. to entertain.

Inferences _____c_____ **18.** Based on the details in the passage, we can infer that
   a. people do not have the power to make a free choice in any situation, decision, or action.
   b. people are not responsible for the decisions they make or the actions they take.
   c. we are deeply influenced by our surroundings.
   d. humans are puppets controlled by unseen forces.

Argument _____a_____ **19.** Read the claim and supports taken from the passage. Then identify the detail that does not support the claim.

   Claim: "It is not only that people's actions can be influenced by unconscious stimuli; our desires can be too." (paragraph 3)
   a. "There may be few things more fundamental to human identity than the belief that people are rational individuals whose behavior is determined by conscious choices." (paragraph 2)
   b. "But recently psychologists have compiled an impressive body of research that shows how deeply our decisions and behavior are influenced by unconscious thought, and how greatly those thoughts are swayed by stimuli beyond our immediate comprehension." (paragraph 2)
   c. "'Our unconscious is active in many more ways than this review suggests,' he says." (paragraph 7)
   d. "We are starting to talk about 'toxic environments' with food and to understand how easy it is to mindlessly reach for a bag of potato chips." (paragraph 9)

Argument _____d_____ **20.** Identify the persuasive technique used by "subliminal-advertising techniques" as described in paragraph 8.
   a. false analogy   c. begging the question
   b. personal attack   d. transfer

Summarizing

Complete the following summary of the article "Think You're Operating on Free Will? Think Again" by Eben Harrell. Fill in the blanks with information from the article.

Recent research confronts the long-held belief in the <u>free will</u> of human beings. Studies now offer strong evidence that our decisions and behaviors are affected by <u>stimuli</u> beyond our awareness. According to researchers <u>Ruud Custers and Henk Aarts</u>, of Utrecht University in the Netherlands, our <u>"unconscious will"</u> sways our actions and our desires. Their findings agree with the earlier research of John Bargh of Yale University. Bargh also says that the unconscious will likely evolved before the <u>conscious</u> will as a tool for survival. The unconscious will helps us handle the endless number of decisions we face each day.

WHAT DO YOU THINK?

The article states that some countries have banned subliminal-advertising techniques. Do you think the United States should as well? What about banning the use of propaganda techniques such as transfer, the use of images like the beach or a group of friends, to sell products? Do you think that "'personal choice' may be a weak counter to heavy advertising"? Or do you think consumers are wise enough to resist the power of advertisements? Assume that a senator from your state is pushing a law that strictly controls the kind of advertisements that can be made in the United States. Write a letter to the senator that supports or opposes the ban. Use specific examples to support your stand.

MASTER READER Scorecard

"Think You're Operating on Free Will? Think Again"

Skill	Number Correct	Points	Total
Vocabulary			
Vocabulary in Context (2 items)	_____ ×	4 =	_____
Comprehension			
Central Idea and Main Ideas (3 items)	_____ ×	4 =	_____
Supporting Details (2 items)	_____ ×	4 =	_____
Transitions (3 items)	_____ ×	4 =	_____
Thought Patterns (2 items)	_____ ×	4 =	_____
Fact and Opinion (3 items)	_____ ×	4 =	_____
Tone and Purpose (2 items)	_____ ×	4 =	_____
Inferences (1 item)	_____ ×	4 =	_____
Argument (2 items)	_____ ×	4 =	_____
Summarizing (5 items)	_____ ×	4 =	_____
	Comprehension Score		_____

The Day Language Came into My Life

by Helen Keller   7.0 GE/1059 words

Helen Keller (1880–1968) was born a hearing child whose bout with disease left her both blind and deaf at the age of 19 months. With the dedicated and loving help of her gifted teacher Anne Sullivan, Helen Keller overcame these barriers to lead an extraordinary life. She graduated with honors from Radcliffe, devoted her life to good works, and was awarded the Presidential Medal of Freedom by Lyndon Johnson in 1964. Her autobiography, *The Story of My Life* (1902), was the basis of a play and two movies. The following passage, an excerpt from her autobiography, takes the reader through the miraculous events that taught her the meaning of words.

Vocabulary Preview

immeasurable (paragraph 1): vast
dumb (paragraph 2): silent
languor (paragraph 2): weariness
succeeded (paragraph 2): followed
plummet (paragraph 3): ball of lead
sounding-line (paragraph 3): a line or wire weighted, usually with a plummet, to measure the depth of water
quiver (paragraph 8): tremble, shiver

1   The most important day I remember in all my life is the one on which my teacher, Anne Mansfield Sullivan, came to me. I am filled with wonder when I consider the **immeasurable** contrast between the two lives which it connects. It was the third of March 1887, three months before I was seven years old.

2   On the afternoon of that eventful day, I stood on the porch, **dumb,** expectant. I guessed vaguely from my mother's signs and from the hurrying to and fro in the house that something unusual was about to happen, so I went to the door and waited on the steps. The afternoon sun penetrated the mass of honeysuckle that covered the porch and fell on my upturned face. My fingers lingered almost unconsciously on the familiar leaves and blossoms which had just come forth to greet the sweet southern spring. I did not know what the future held of marvel or surprise for me. Anger and bitterness had preyed upon me continually for weeks and a deep **languor** had **succeeded** this passionate struggle.

3   Have you ever been at sea in a dense fog, when it seemed as if a tangible white

darkness shut you in, and the great ship, tense and anxious, groped her way toward the shore with **plummet** and **sounding-line**, and you waited with beating heart for something to happen? I was like that ship before my education began, only I was without compass or sounding-line and had no way of knowing how near the harbor was. "Light! Give me light!" was the wordless cry of my soul, and the light of love shone on me in that very hour.

4   I felt approaching footsteps. I stretched out my hand as I supposed to my mother. Someone took it, and I was caught up and held close in the arms of her who had come to reveal all things to me, and, more than all things else, to love me.

5   The morning after my teacher came she led me into her room and gave me a doll. The little blind children at the Perkins Institution had sent it and Laura Bridgman had dressed it; but I did not know this until afterward. When I had played with it a little while, Miss Sullivan slowly spelled into my hand the word "d-o-l-l." I was at once interested in this finger play and tried to imitate it. When I finally succeeded in making the letters correctly I was flushed with childish pleasure and pride. Running downstairs to my mother I held up my hand and made the letters for doll. I did not know that I was spelling a word or even that words existed; I was simply making my fingers go in monkeylike imitation. In the days that followed I learned to spell in this uncomprehending way a great many words, among them *pin*, *hat*, *cup* and a few verbs like *sit*, *stand* and *walk*. But my teacher had been with me several weeks before I understood that everything has a name.

One day, while I was playing with my 6 new doll, Miss Sullivan put my big rag doll into my lap also, spelled "d-o-l-l" and tried to make me understand that "d-o-l-l" applied to both. Earlier in the day we had had a tussle over the words "m-u-g" and "w-a-t-e-r." Miss Sullivan had tried to impress it upon me that "m-u-g" is mug and that "w-a-t-e-r" is water, but I persisted in **confounding** the two. In despair she had dropped the subject for the time, only to renew it at the first opportunity. I became impatient at her repeated attempts and, seizing the new doll, I dashed it upon the floor. I was keenly delighted when I felt the fragments of the broken doll at my feet. Neither sorrow nor regret followed my passionate outburst. I had not loved the doll. In the still, dark world in which I lived there was no strong sentiment or tenderness. I felt my teacher sweep the fragments to one side of the hearth, and I had a sense of satisfaction that the cause of my discomfort was removed. She brought me my hat, and I knew I was going out into the warm sunshine. This thought, if a wordless sensation may be called a thought, made me hop and skip with pleasure.

We walked down the path to the well- 7 house, attracted by the fragrance of the honeysuckle with which it was covered. Someone was drawing water and my teacher placed my hand under the spout. As the cool stream gushed over one hand she spelled into the other the word *water*, first slowly, then rapidly. I stood still, my whole attention fixed upon the motions of her fingers. Suddenly I felt a misty consciousness as of something forgotten—a thrill of returning thought; and somehow the mystery of language was revealed to me. I knew then that "w-a-t-e-r" meant the wonderful cool something that was flowing over my hand. The living word awakened my soul, gave it light, hope, joy, set it free! There were barriers still, it is true, but barriers that could in time be swept away.

8   I left the well-house eager to learn. Everything had a name, and each name gave birth to a new thought. As we returned to the house every object which I touched seemed to **quiver** with life. That was because I saw everything with the strange, new sight that had come to me. On entering the door I remembered the doll I had broken. I felt my way to the hearth and picked up the pieces. I tried vainly to put them together. Then my eyes filled with tears; for I realized what I had done, and for the first time I felt **repentance** and sorrow.

I learned a great many new words that 9 day. I do not remember what they all were; but I do know that *mother, father, sister, teacher* were among them—words that were to make the world blossom for me, "like Aaron's rod, with flowers."* It would have been difficult to find a happier child than I was as I lay in my crib at the close of that eventful day and lived over the joys it had brought me, and for the first time longed for a new day to come.

---

* Aaron's rod is an allusion to a miracle recorded in the Old Testament wherein God caused a dead stick to sprout with flowers.

Choose the best meaning of each word in **bold**. Use context clues to make your choice.

Vocabulary in Context ___a___ **1.** "Miss Sullivan had tried to impress it upon me that 'm-u-g' is mug and that 'w-a-t-e-r' is water, but I persisted in **confounding** the two." (paragraph 6)

    a. confusing   c. hating
    b. repeating   d. remembering

Vocabulary in Context ___c___ **2.** "Then my eyes filled up with tears; for I realized what I had done and for the first time I felt **repentance** and sorrow." (paragraph 8)

    a. hurt   c. remorse
    b. resentment   d. relief

Central Idea and Main Ideas ___a___ **3.** Which sentence best states the central idea of the passage?

    a. "The most important day I remember in all my life is the one on which my teacher, Anne Mansfield Sullivan, came to me."
    b. "I am filled with wonder when I consider the immeasurable contrast between the two lives which it connects."

c. "I was like that ship before my education began, only I was without compass or sounding-line and had no way of knowing how near the harbor was."

d. "It would have been difficult to find a happier child than I was as I lay in my crib at the close of that eventful day and lived over the joys it had brought me, and for the first time longed for a new day to come."

Central Idea and Main Ideas   c   **4.** Which sentence is the best statement of the implied main idea of paragraph 3?

a. Helen Keller was afraid of the sea.
b. Helen Keller felt unloved.
c. Helen Keller couldn't wait to begin learning.
d. Helen Keller understood the sea.

Supporting Details   c   **5.** The morning after Miss Sullivan arrived, she gave Helen

a. a hug.
b. a cup of water.
c. a doll from the little blind children at the Perkins Institution.
d. a dose of discipline.

Supporting Details   c   **6.** Helen broke her doll because

a. she didn't care for it.
b. she was jealous of it.
c. she was angry at having to work with spelling words.
d. she was spoiled and mean.

Thought Patterns   a   **7.** The main thought pattern for the overall passage is

a. time order.   c. definition.
b. cause and effect.   d. classification.

Thought Patterns   c   **8.** The thought pattern for paragraph 3 is

a. cause and effect   c. comparison and contrast.
b. classification.

Transitions   a   **9.** "I stood still, my whole attention fixed upon the motions of her fingers. Suddenly I felt a misty consciousness as of something forgotten—a thrill of returning thought; and somehow the mystery of language was revealed to me." (paragraph 7)

The relationship of ideas between these two sentences is

a. time order.   c. example.
b. contrast.

Transitions ___c___ **10.** "I felt my teacher sweep the fragments to one side of the hearth, and I had a sense of satisfaction that the cause of my discomfort was removed." (paragraph 6)

The relationship of ideas within this sentence is
a. time order.
c. addition.
b. example.

Fact and Opinion ___c___ **11.** "I learned a great many new words that day."

This sentence from paragraph 9 is a statement of
a. fact.
c. fact and opinion.
b. opinion.

Fact and Opinion ___c___ **12.** "I do not remember what they all were; but I do know that *mother, father, sister, teacher* were among them—words that were to make the world blossom for me, 'like Aaron's rod, with flowers.'"

This sentence from paragraph 9 is a statement of
a. fact.
c. fact and opinion.
b. opinion.

Tone and Purpose ___a___ **13.** The overall tone of the passage is
a. reflective and joyful.
c. matter of fact.
b. angry and bitter.
d. calm and soothing.

Tone and Purpose ___c___ **14.** "Then my eyes filled up with tears; for I realized what I had done, and for the first time I felt repentance and sorrow."

The tone of this statement from paragraph 8 is
a. harsh.
c. regretful.
b. hopeful.
d. admiring.

Tone and Purpose ___a___ **15.** "As the cool stream gushed over one hand she spelled into the other the word *water*, first slowly, then rapidly. I stood still, my whole attention fixed upon the motions of her fingers. Suddenly I felt a misty consciousness as of something forgotten—a thrill of returning thought; and somehow the mystery of language was revealed to me."

The tone of these sentences from paragraph 7 is
a. excited.
c. pained.
b. confused.
d. humorous.

Tone and Purpose   _c_   **16.** The author's main purpose in "The Day Language Came into My Life" is
a. to persuade others about the joy of teaching the blind and deaf.
b. to entertain readers with a lighthearted story that has a happy ending.
c. to inform the reader about the significance of Anne Sullivan's impact on Helen Keller's life.

Inferences   _a_   **17.** From the passage, we can conclude that
a. the author was an intelligent and quick learner.
b. the author did not want to learn.
c. Helen Keller would never have learned to communicate without Anne Sullivan.
d. the author's family was ashamed of Helen's disabilities.

Inferences   _a_   **18.** Based on the details in paragraphs 5–7, we can conclude that
a. an important step in the learning of language is practicing skills.
b. Helen's stubbornness slowed down her learning process.
c. Anne Sullivan was a strict teacher.
d. Helen loved her doll.

Argument   _a_   **19.** "On entering the door I remembered the doll I had broken. I felt my way to the hearth and picked up the pieces. I tried vainly to put them together. Then my eyes filled with tears; for I realized what I had done, and for the first time I felt repentance and sorrow."

These details from paragraph 8 imply that
a. the doll meant more to Helen once she understood it had a name.
b. the doll can be fixed.
c. the doll was cheaply made and easily broken.
d. Helen had never had a doll before.

Argument   _a_   **20.** The following list of ideas contains a claim and the supports for that claim. In the given space, write the letter of the claim.
a. Anne Sullivan was a loving and patient teacher to Helen Keller.
b. Helen says that Sullivan "had come to reveal all things to me, and, more than all things else, to love me."
c. When Helen did not make progress with the words *mug* and *water*, Sullivan dropped the subject for a time, only to renew it at the next opportunity.
d. When Helen broke the doll, Sullivan swept the fragments out of the way and continued the lesson at the well-house.

Mapping

Complete the following time line with details for the passage.

1880–1887

Helen is grow-
ing up "lost in
the fog" of
blindness and
deafness.

March <u>1887</u>

<u>Anne Sullivan</u>
comes to teach
Helen.

First day,
Sullivan gives
Helen a doll
and begins
teaching her.

Helen breaks
the doll and
feels
<u>satisfaction</u>.

Sullivan takes
Helen to well,
pumps water in
her hand, and
spells "water."

The living <u>word</u>
awakens Helen's
soul, and she
learns how to
communicate.

Helen feels
<u>sorrow</u> for
breaking the
doll.

WHAT DO YOU THINK?

Like Helen Keller, many of us have overcome some obstacle in order to achieve
an education. Assume you are writing a letter to a younger member of your
family who is struggling academically. This person is seeking your advice about
why it is important to attend school. Think back to a defining time in your
education. What do you value most about your education, and who has helped
you to pursue this goal?

MASTER READER Scorecard

> **"The Day Language Came into My Life"**
>
> | Skill | Number Correct | Points | Total |
> |---|---|---|---|
> | *Vocabulary* | | | |
> | Vocabulary in Context (2 items) | _____ | × 4 = | _____ |
> | *Comprehension* | | | |
> | Central Idea and Main Ideas (2 items) | _____ | × 4 = | _____ |
> | Supporting Details (2 items) | _____ | × 4 = | _____ |
> | Thought Patterns (2 items) | _____ | × 4 = | _____ |
> | Transitions (2 items) | _____ | × 4 = | _____ |
> | Fact and Opinion (2 items) | _____ | × 4 = | _____ |
> | Tone and Purpose (4 items) | _____ | × 4 = | _____ |
> | Inferences (2 items) | _____ | × 4 = | _____ |
> | Argument (2 items) | _____ | × 4 = | _____ |
> | **Mapping** (5 items) | _____ | × 4 = | _____ |
> | | Comprehension Score | | _____ |

Fannie Lou Hamer

by Maya Angelou   10.0 GE/711 words

Poet, writer, performer, teacher, and director, Maya Angelou was raised in Stamps, Arkansas, then moved to San Francisco. In addition to her best-selling autobiographies, beginning with *I Know Why the Caged Bird Sings*, she has also written a cookbook, *Hallelujah! The Welcome Table*, and five poetry collections, including *I Shall Not Be Moved* and *Shaker, Why Don't You Sing?* The following passage appears in *Letter to My Daughter*, Angelou's first original collection in 10 years. In this collection of essays, she shares lessons based on the distilled knowledge of a lifetime well-lived. If you could choose a public figure to honor, whom would you choose? What lessons could be learned from this person's life?

Vocabulary Preview

imperative (paragraph 2): of vital importance, urgent
sequestered (paragraph 3): placed in isolation
laud (paragraph 5): praise
avert (paragraph 5): turn away
embolden (paragraph 11): encourage

---

1 "All of this on account we want to register, to become first-class citizens, and if the Freedom Democratic Party is not seated now, I question America, is this America, the land of the free and the home of the brave, where we have to sleep with our telephones off the hooks because our lives be threatened daily because we want to live as decent human beings, in America? Thank you."

—FANNIE LOU HAMER

2 It is important that we know that those words come from the lips of an African American woman. It is **imperative** that we know those words come from the heart of an American.

3 I believe that there lives a burning desire in the most **sequestered** private heart of every American, a desire to belong to a great country. I believe that every citizen wants to stand on the world stage and represent a noble country where the mighty do not always crush the weak and the dream of a democracy is not the sole possession of the strong.

4 We must hear the questions raised by Fannie Lou Hamer forty years ago. Every

American everywhere asks herself, himself, these questions Hamer asked:

5   What do I think of my country? What is there, which elevates my shoulders and stirs my blood when I hear the words, the United States of America: Do I praise my country enough? Do I **laud** my fellow citizens enough? What is there about my country that makes me hang my head and **avert** my eyes when I hear the words the United States of America, and what am I doing about it? Am I relating my disappointment to my leaders and to my fellow citizens, or am I like someone not involved, sitting high and looking low? As Americans, we should not be afraid to respond.

6   We have asked questions down a pyramid of years and given answers, which our children memorize, and which have become an integral part of the spoken American history. Patrick Henry remarked, "I know not what course others may take, but as for me, give me liberty or give me death."

7   George Moses Horton, the nineteenth century poet, born a slave, said, "Alas, and was I born for this, to wear this brutish chain? I must slash the handcuffs from my wrists and live a man again."

8   "The thought of only being a creature of the present and the past was troubling. I longed for a future too, with hope in it. The desire to be free, awakened my determination to act, to think, and to speak."

    —FREDERICK DOUGLASS

9   The love of democracy motivated Harriet Tubman to seek and find not only her own freedom, but to make **innumerable** trips to the slave South to gain the liberty of many slaves and instill the idea into the hearts of thousands that freedom is possible.

10   Fannie Lou Hamer and the Mississippi Democratic Freedom Party were standing on the shoulders of history when they acted to unseat evil from its presumed safe perch on the backs of the American people. It is fitting to honor the memory of Fannie Lou Hamer and surviving members of the Mississippi Democratic Freedom Party. For their gifts to us, we say thank you.

11   The human heart is so delicate and sensitive that it always needs some **tangible** encouragement to prevent it from faltering in its labor. The human heart is so robust, so tough, that once encouraged it beats its rhythm with a loud unswerving insistency. One thing that encourages the heart is music. Throughout the ages we have created songs to grow on and to live by. We Americans have created music to **embolden** the hearts and inspire the spirit of people all over the world.

12   Fannie Lou Hamer knew that she was one woman and only one woman. However, she knew she was an American, and as an American she had a light to shine on the darkness of racism. It was a little light, but she aimed it directly at the gloom of ignorance.

13   Fannie Lou Hamer's favorite was a simple song that we all know. We Americans have sung it since childhood . . .

14   "This little light of mine, I'm going to let it shine, Let it shine,

15   Let it shine,

16   Let it shine.

—"Fannie Lou Hamer" from *Letter to My Daughter* by Maya Angelou, pp. 83–85. Copyright © 2008 by Maya Angelou. Used by permission of Random House, Inc.

Choose the best meaning of each word in **bold**. Use context clues to make your choice.

Vocabulary in Context   _d_   **1.** "The love of democracy motivated Harriet Tubman to seek and find not only her own freedom, but to make **innumerable** trips to the slave South to gain the liberty of many slaves and instill the idea into the hearts of thousands that freedom is possible." (paragraph 9)

a. few   c. immense
b. specific   d. countless

Vocabulary in Context   _a_   **2.** "The human heart is so delicate and sensitive that it always needs some **tangible** encouragement to prevent it from faltering in its labor." (paragraph 11)

a. obvious   c. subtle
b. important   d. indescribable

Central Idea   _c_   **3.** Which of the following sentences states the central idea of the passage?

a. "It is important to know that those words come from the lips of an African American woman." (paragraph 2)
b. "We must hear the questions raised by Fannie Lou Hamer forty years ago." (paragraph 4)
c. "It is fitting to honor the memory of Fannie Lou Hamer and surviving members of the Mississippi Democratic Freedom Party." (paragraph 10)
d. "However, she knew she was an American, and as an American she had a light to shine on the darkness of racism." (paragraph 12)

Main Idea   _c_   **4.** Which of the following sentences states the main idea of paragraph 11?

a. "The human heart is so delicate and sensitive that it always needs some tangible encouragement to prevent it from faltering in its labor."
b. "The human heart is so robust, so tough, that once encouraged it beats its rhythm with a loud unswerving insistency."
c. "One thing that encourages the heart is music."
d. "Throughout the ages we have created songs to grow on and to live by."

Supporting Details   _b_   **5.** According to the passage, who said "I must slash the handcuffs from my wrists . . ."?

a. Patrick Henry   c. Fannie Lou Hamer
b. George Moses Horton   d. Frederick Douglass

Supporting Details ___c___ **6.** According to the passage, Harriet Tubman was motivated by
a. fear of slavery.
b. the shoulders of history.
c. love of democracy.
d. the work of Fannie Lou Hamer.

Transitions ___c___ **7.** "It was a little light, but she aimed it directly at the gloom of ignorance." (paragraph 12)

The relationship of ideas within this sentence is
a. cause and effect.
b. listing.
c. comparison and contrast.
d. generalization and example.

Transitions ___c___ **8.** "Fannie Lou Hamer knew that she was one woman and only one woman. However, she knew she was an American, and as an American she had a light to shine on the darkness of racism." (paragraph 12)

The relationship of ideas between these sentences is
a. cause and effect.   c. comparison and contrast.
b. listing.   d. generalization and example.

Thought Patterns ___c___ **9.** "The human heart is so delicate and sensitive that it always needs some tangible encouragement to prevent it from faltering in its labor. The human heart is so robust, so tough, that once encouraged it beats its rhythm with a loud unswerving insistency." (paragraph 11)

The thought pattern established by these two sentences is
a. cause and effect.   c. comparison and contrast.
b. listing.   d. definition and example.

Thought Patterns ___b___ **10.** The overall thought pattern for paragraph 5 is
a. cause and effect.   c. comparison and contrast.
b. listing.   d. definition and example.

Fact and Opinion ___c___ **11.** "It is imperative that we know those words come from the heart of an American." (paragraph 2)

This sentence is a statement of
a. fact.   c. fact and opinion.
b. opinion.

Fact and
Opinion

___b___ **12.** "I believe that there lives a burning desire in the most sequestered private heart of every American, a desire to belong to a great country." (paragraph 3)

This sentence is a statement of
a. fact.   c. fact and opinion.
b. opinion.

Fact and
Opinion

___c___ **13.** "We must hear the questions raised by Fannie Lou Hamer forty years ago." (paragraph 4)

This sentence is a statement of
a. fact.   c. fact and opinion.
b. opinion.

Tone

___d___ **14.** The overall tone of the author is
a. complaining.   c. bitter.
b. balanced.   d. inspirational.

Tone

___a___ **15.** The tone of the words of Fannie Lou Hamer in the first paragraph is
a. challenging.   c. frightened.
b. accepting.   d. respectful.

Purpose

___a___ **16.** The purpose of the author is
a. to inform the reader about the racism faced by African Americans such as Fannie Lou Hamer.
b. to entertain the reader with the words and deeds of highly regarded civil rights leaders.
c. to persuade the reader to appreciate and be inspired by Fannie Lou Hamer and the history she represents.

Inferences

___b___ **17.** Based on the details in the passage, we can infer that Fannie Lou Hamer was working to
a. gain freedom for slaves.
b. be officially represented in the political process.
c. be seated in a restaurant.
d. produce music to further the civil rights movement.

Inferences

___b___ **18.** Based on the details in the passage, we can infer that
a. there will always be injustice and oppression.
b. determined individuals can significantly impact society for the good.
c. freedom always comes through violence and loss of life.
d. citizens should love their country unconditionally.

Argument   _____c_____ **19.** Identify the persuasive technique used in the following sentence:

"I believe that every citizen wants to stand on the world stage and represent a noble country where the mighty do not always crush the weak and the dream of a democracy is not the sole possession of the strong." (paragraph 3)
a. false cause
b. personal attack
c. glittering generality
d. black and white fallacy

Argument   _____d_____ **20.** Read the claim and supports taken from the passage. Then identify the detail that does not support the claim.

". . . give me liberty or give me death." (paragraph 6)
a. false cause
b. personal attack
c. glittering generality
d. black and white fallacy

Summarizing

Complete the following summary of the passage:

(1) <u>Fannie Lou Hamer</u> and surviving members of the Mississippi Democratic Freedom Party should be honored because they stood on the historical shoulders of **(2)** <u>Patrick Henry</u>, **(3)** <u>George Moses Horton</u>, **(4)** <u>Frederick Douglass</u>, and **(5)** <u>Harriet Tubman</u> to shine a light on the gloom of ignorance and the darkness of racism.

WHAT DO YOU THINK?

Do you think it is important to pay tribute to people who have impacted our lives? Why or why not? Whom would you choose to honor for his or her impact on society? Assume you are taking a college course in sociology. Your professor sponsors a course webpage on which he posts samples of student essays about social issues. The current topic is as follows: After reading Maya Angelou's essay "Fannie Lou Hamer," write your own tribute (400–750 words) to a person who has had a significant impact on society. In your essay, identify the social problem and describe how this person made a difference.

MASTER READER Scorecard

"Fannie Lou Hamer"

Skill	Number Correct	Points	Total
Vocabulary			
Vocabulary in Context (2 items)	_____ ×	4 =	_____
Comprehension			
Central Idea and Main Ideas (2 items)	_____ ×	4 =	_____
Supporting Details (2 items)	_____ ×	4 =	_____
Transitions (2 items)	_____ ×	4 =	_____
Thought Patterns (2 items)	_____ ×	4 =	_____
Fact and Opinion (3 items)	_____ ×	4 =	_____
Tone and Purpose (3 items)	_____ ×	4 =	_____
Inferences (2 items)	_____ ×	4 =	_____
Argument (2 items)	_____ ×	4 =	_____
Outlining (5 items)	_____ ×	4 =	_____
	Comprehension Score		_____

The Truman Library Speech

by Kofi Annan   10.8 GE/1063 words

Kofi Annan delivered his final speech as United Nations Secretary General at the Truman Presidential Museum and Library in Independence, Missouri, in 2006. Throughout his speech, he discusses five lessons he learned as a world leader; the following excerpt is the final portion of his speech. What do you know about the United Nations? Does the world need an international organization to ensure peace and prosperity for all?

Vocabulary Preview

constrained (paragraph 3): controlled, limited
philanthropic (paragraph 4): charitable
Compact (paragraph 6): agreement
multilateral (paragraph 8): many-sided, involving many parties
bequeathed (paragraph 8): bestowed, handed down

1   My fourth lesson—closely related to the last one—is that governments must be accountable for their actions in the international arena, as well as in the domestic one.

2   Today the actions of one state can often have a decisive effect on the lives of people in other states. So does it not owe some account to those other states and their citizens, as well as to its own? I believe it does.

3   As things stand, accountability between states is highly skewed. Poor and weak states are easily held to account, because they need foreign assistance. But large and powerful states, whose actions have the greatest impact on others, can be **constrained** only by their own people, working through their domestic institutions.

4   That gives the people and institutions of such powerful states a special responsibility to take account of global views and interests, as well as national ones. And today they need to take into account also the views of what, in UN jargon, we call "non-state actors." I mean commercial corporations, charities and pressure groups, labor unions, **philanthropic** foundations, universities and think tanks—all the **myriad** forms in which people come together voluntarily to think about, or try to change, the world.

5   None of these should be allowed to substitute itself for the state, or for the democratic process by which citizens choose their governments and decide policy. But they all have the capacity to influence political

processes, on the international as well as the national level. States that try to ignore this are hiding their heads in the sand.

6   The fact is that states can no longer—if they ever could—confront global challenges alone. Increasingly, we need to enlist the help of these other actors, both in working out global strategies and in putting those strategies into action once agreed. It has been one of my guiding principles as Secretary General to get them to help achieve UN aims—for instance through the Global **Compact** with international business, which I initiated in 1999, or in the worldwide fight against polio, which I hope is now in its final chapter, thanks to a wonderful partnership between the UN family, the US Centers for Disease Control and—crucially—Rotary International.

7   So that is four lessons. Let me briefly remind you of them: First, we are all responsible for each other's security. Second, we can and must give everyone the chance to benefit from global prosperity. Third, both security and prosperity depend on human rights and the rule of law. Fourth, states must be accountable to each other, and to a broad range of non-state actors, in their international conduct.

8   My fifth and final lesson derives inescapably from those other four. We can only do all these things by working together through a **multilateral** system, and by making the best possible use of the unique instrument **bequeathed** to us by Harry Truman and his contemporaries, namely the United Nations.

9   In fact, it is only through multilateral institutions that states can hold each other to account. And that makes it very important to organize those institutions in a fair and democratic way, giving the poor and the weak some influence over the actions of the rich and the strong.

10   That applies particularly to the international financial institutions, such as the World Bank and the International Monetary Fund. Developing countries should have a stronger voice in these bodies, whose decisions can have almost a life-or-death impact on their fate. And it also applies to the UN Security Council, whose membership still reflects the reality of 1945, not of today's world.

11   That is why I have continued to press for Security Council reform. But reform involves two separate issues. One is that new members should be added, on a permanent or long-term basis, to give greater representation to parts of the world, which have limited voice today. The other, perhaps even more important, is that all Council members, and especially the major powers who are permanent members, must accept the special responsibility that comes with their privilege. The Security Council is not just another stage on which to act out national interests. It is the management committee, if you will, of our **fledgling** collective security system.

12   As President Truman said, "The responsibility of the great states is to serve and not dominate the peoples of the world." He showed what can be achieved when the US assumes that responsibility. And still today, none of our global institutions can accomplish much when the US remains aloof. But when it is fully engaged, the sky is the limit.

13   These five lessons can be summed up as five principles, which I believe are essential

for the future conduct of international relations: collective responsibility, global solidarity, the rule of law, mutual accountability, and multilateralism. Let me leave them with you, in solemn trust, as I hand over to a new Secretary General in three weeks' time.

14 My friends, we have achieved much since 1945, when the United Nations was established. But much remains to be done to put those five principles into practice.

15 Standing here, I am reminded of Winston Churchill's last visit to the White House, just before Truman left office in 1953. Churchill recalled their only previous meeting, at the Potsdam conference in 1945. "I must confess, sir," he said boldly, "I held you in very low regard then. I loathed your taking the place of Franklin Roosevelt." Then he paused for a moment, and continued: "I misjudged you badly. Since that time, you more than any other man, have saved Western civilization."

16 My friends, our challenge today is not to save Western civilization—or Eastern, for that matter. All civilization is at stake, and we can save it only if all peoples join together in the task.

17 You Americans did so much, in the last century, to build an effective multilateral system, with the United Nations at its heart. Do you need it less today, and does it need you less, than 60 years ago?

18 Surely not. More than ever today Americans, like the rest of humanity, need a functioning global system through which the world's peoples can face global challenges together. And in order to function, the system still cries out for far-sighted American leadership, in the Truman tradition.

19 I hope and pray that the American leaders of today, and tomorrow, will provide it.

—From "The Truman Library Speech" by Kofi Annan, December 11, 2006, http://www.un.org/News/ossg/sg/stories/statments_full.asp?statID=40. Reprinted by permission of the United Nations.

VISUAL VOCABULARY

The c _____ efforts of the United States supply donated food in Addis Abba, Ethiopia.

a. constrained
b. bequeathed
c. philanthropic

Choose the best meaning of each word in **bold**. Use context clues to make your choice.

Vocabulary in Context ___d___ **1.** "I mean commercial corporations, charities and pressure groups, labor unions, philanthropic foundations, universities and think tanks—all the **myriad** forms in which people come together voluntarily to think about, or try to change, the world." (paragraph 4)

a. real
b. little
c. limited
d. countless

Vocabulary in Context ___a___ **2.** "It is the management committee, if you will, of our **fledgling** collective security system." (paragraph 11)

a. developing
b. expert
c. weakening
d. soaring

Central Idea ___a___ **3.** Which of the following sentences states the central idea of paragraphs 1 through 6?

a. "My fourth lesson—closely related to the last one—is that governments must be accountable for their actions in the international arena, as well as in the domestic one." (paragraph 1)
b. "As things stand, accountability between states is highly skewed." (paragraph 3)
c. "But large and powerful states, whose actions have the greatest impact on others, can be constrained only by their own people, working through their domestic institutions." (paragraph 3)
d. "The fact is that states can no longer—if they ever could—confront global challenges alone." (paragraph 6)

Central Idea ___b___ **4.** Which of the following sentences states the central idea of paragraphs 8 through 12?

a. "My fifth and final lesson derives inescapably from those other four." (paragraph 8)
b. "We can only do all these things by working together through a multilateral system, and by making the best possible use of the unique instrument bequeathed to us by Harry Truman and his contemporaries, namely the United Nations." (paragraph 8)
c. "Developing countries should have a stronger voice in these bodies, whose decisions can have almost a life-or-death impact on their fate." (paragraph 10)
d. "And still today, none of our global institutions can accomplish much when the US remains aloof." (paragraph 12)

Supporting Details ___c___ **5.** According to the passage Rotary International partnered with the UN to
   a. engage in worldwide commerce.
   b. address worldwide poverty.
   c. fight polio worldwide.
   d. create multilateral institutions.

Supporting Details ___a___ **6.** According to passage, the United Nations was established
   a. in 1945.   c. in 1999.
   b. in 1953.   d. 60 years ago.

Transitions ___d___ **7.** "These five lessons can be summed up as five principles, which I believe are essential for the future conduct of international relations: collective responsibility, global solidarity, the rule of law, mutual accountability, and multilateralism." (paragraph 13)

   The relationship of ideas within this sentence is
   a. cause and effect.   c. comparison and contrast.
   b. time order.   d. listing.

Transitions ___d___ **8.** "None of these should be allowed to substitute itself for the state, or for the democratic process by which citizens choose their governments and decide policy. But they all have the capacity to influence political processes, on the international as well as the national level." (paragraph 5)

   The relationship of ideas between these sentences is
   a. cause and effect.   c. comparison and contrast.
   b. classification.   d. generalization and example.

Thought Patterns ___b___ **9.** The thought pattern for paragraph 7 is
   a. cause and effect.   c. time order.
   b. listing.   d. comparison and contrast.

Thought Patterns ___d___ **10.** The thought pattern for paragraph 11 is
   a. cause and effect.   c. time order.
   b. listing.   d. comparison and contrast.

Fact and Opinion ___b___ **11.** "In fact, it is only through multilateral institutions that states can hold each other to account." (paragraph 9)

   This sentence is a statement of
   a. fact.   c. fact and opinion.
   b. opinion.

Fact and
Opinion
_c_ **12.** "My friends, we have achieved much since 1945, when the United Nations was established." (paragraph 14)

This sentence is a statement of
a. fact.   c. fact and opinion.
b. opinion.

Fact and
Opinion
_c_ **13.** "You Americans did so much, in the last century, to build an effective multilateral system, with the United Nations at its heart." (paragraph 17)

This sentence is a statement of
a. fact.   c. fact and opinion.
b. opinion.

Tone
_a_ **14.** The overall tone of the author is
a. optimistic.   c. neutral.
b. pessimistic.

Tone
_d_ **15.** The tone of paragraph 3 is
a. balanced.   c. emotional.
b. timid.   d. frank.

Purpose
_c_ **16.** The primary purpose of the author is
a. to inform the audience about the purpose of the United Nations.
b. to entertain the audience with personal experiences and opinions about the United Nations.
c. to inspire American support of the United Nations with lessons learned by serving as leader of the UN.

Inferences
_a_ **17.** Based on the details in the passage, we can infer that the United States is
a. a superpower state with worldwide influence.
b. not well respected by the international community.
c. unfair in its treatment of other nations.
d. opposed to the United Nations.

Inferences
_c_ **18.** Based on the details in the passage, we can infer that Kofi Annan calls for
a. one government, the United Nations, to rule the world.
b. the United Nations to grow in military strength.
c. a balance of worldwide power and responsibility through the United Nations.
d. financial aid for the United Nations.

Argument   ___d___   **19.** Identify the persuasive technique used in the following sentence:

"All civilization is at stake, and we can save it only if all peoples join together in the task." (paragraph 16)

a. false analogy   c. personal attack.

b. either-or   d. transfer

Argument   ___d___   **20.** Identify the persuasive technique used in the following sentence:

"And in order to function, the system still cries out for far-sighted American leadership, in the Truman tradition." (paragraph 18)

a. false analogy   c. personal attack

b. either-or   d. transfer

Mapping

Complete the following concept map with information from the passage.

Kofi Annan's Lessons and Principles: The United Nations

Five Lessons	Five Principles
First, we are all responsible for each other's security.	Collective responsibility
Second, we can and must give everyone the chance to benefit from global prosperity.	Global solidarity
Third, both security and prosperity depend on human rights and the rule of law.	The rule of law
Fourth, states must be accountable to each other, and to a broad range of non-state actors, in their international conduct.	Mutual accountability
Fifth, we can only do all these things by working together through a multilateral system—The United Nations.	Multilateralism

WHAT DO YOU THINK?

Do you think powerful countries like the United States have a responsibility to other countries (such as Haiti, Cuba, Mexico, Israel, Iraq, Afghanistan, Great Britain to name a few)? Why or why not? Do you agree with Kofi Annan's opinions in this speech? Why or why not? Assume you eventually want to work with the United Nations, and have been surfing the Internet for information. Through your research, you learn about The World Bank's Essay Competition. The prizes range from $3,000 to $1,000 plus a trip to Sweden for the awards ceremony. The topic is *How can you tackle youth drug abuse through youth-led solutions?* Please answer all questions: (1) How does youth drug abuse affect you, your country, town, or local community? (2) What can you do, working together with your peers, to find a sustainable solution for youth drug abuse? (3) What national or international groups or organizations would you seek help from to reduce youth drug abuse?

MASTER READER Scorecard

From "The Truman Library Speech"

Skill	Number Correct	Points	Total
Vocabulary			
Vocabulary in Context (2 items)	_____ ×	4 =	_____
Comprehension			
Central Idea (2 items)	_____ ×	4 =	_____
Supporting Details (2 items)	_____ ×	4 =	_____
Transitions (2 items)	_____ ×	4 =	_____
Thought Patterns (2 items)	_____ ×	4 =	_____
Fact and Opinion (3 items)	_____ ×	4 =	_____
Tone and Purpose (3 items)	_____ ×	4 =	_____
Inferences (2 items)	_____ ×	4 =	_____
Argument (2 items)	_____ ×	4 =	_____
Mapping (5 items)	_____ ×	4 =	_____
	Comprehension Score		_____

The Price of Greatness

by Winston S. Churchill   10.4 GE/1298 words

Winston S. Churchill (1874–1965) was the acclaimed Prime Minister of the United Kingdom. At the outbreak of the Second World War, he was appointed First Lord of the Admiralty—a post he had held earlier from 1911 to 1915. In May, 1940, he became Prime Minister and Minister of Defence and remained in office until 1945. Known for his magnificent oratory, Churchill also won the Nobel Prize for Literature in 1953, and Queen Elizabeth II conferred upon him the dignity of Knighthood. In 1963, President Kennedy conferred on him the honorary citizenship of the United States. The following passage is an excerpt from the speech he gave in 1943 when he received an honorary degree at Harvard. Do you think the United States has a responsibility to the world?

Vocabulary Preview

remorselessly (paragraph 2): showing no pity or compassion; continuing without lessening in strength or intensity

indisputable (paragraph 4): beyond doubt, undeniable

prodigious (paragraph 5): extraordinary, impressive

Parliamentarians (paragraph 5): members of a parliament, a type of governing body

anarchy (paragraph 6): disorder, chaos, rebellion

conceptions (paragraph 8): broad understandings, ideas, theories

vigilant (paragraph 10): watchful, on guard

munitions (paragraph 11): weapons, arms

plenary (paragraph 12): comprehensive, complete, fully represented

Bismarck (paragraph 16): Prime Minister, of Prussia from 1862–1890, he oversaw the unification of Germany and designed the German Empire in 1871

amenity (paragraph 18): pleasantness, courtesy, advantage

1   Twice in my lifetime the long arm of destiny has reached across the oceans and involved the entire life and manhood of the United States in a deadly struggle.

2   There was no use in saying "We don't want it; we won't have it; our forebears left Europe to avoid these quarrels; we have founded a new world which has no contact

with the old." There was no use in that. The long arm reaches out **remorselessly**, and every one's existence, environment, and outlook undergo a swift and irresistible change. What is the explanation, Mr. President, of these strange facts, and what are the deep laws to which they respond? I will offer you one explanation—there are others, but one will suffice.

3   The price of greatness is responsibility. If the people of the United States had continued in a **mediocre** station, struggling with the wilderness, absorbed in their own affairs, and a factor of no consequence in the movement of the world, they might have remained forgotten and undisturbed beyond their protecting oceans: but one cannot rise to be in many ways the leading community in the civilized world without being involved in its problems, without being convulsed by its agonies and inspired by its causes.

4   If this has been proved in the past, as it has been, it will become **indisputable** in the future. The people of the United States cannot escape world responsibility. Although we live in a period so tumultuous that little can be predicted, we may be quite sure that this process will be intensified with every forward step the United States makes in wealth and in power. Not only are the responsibilities of this great Republic growing, but the world over which they range is itself contracting in relation to our powers of locomotion at a positively alarming rate.

5   We have learned to fly. What **prodigious** changes are involved in that new accomplishment! Man has parted company with his trusty friend the horse and has sailed into the azure with the eagles, eagles being

represented by the infernal (loud laughter)—I mean internal—combustion engine. Where, then, are those broad oceans, those vast staring deserts? They are shrinking beneath our very eyes. Even elderly **Parliamentarians** like myself are forced to acquire a high degree of mobility.

6   But to the youth of America, as to the youth of all the Britains, I say "You cannot stop." There is no halting-place at this point. We have now reached a stage in the journey where there can be no pause. We must go on. It must be world **anarchy** or world order.

7   Throughout all this ordeal and struggle which is characteristic of our age, you will find in the British Commonwealth and Empire good **comrades** to whom you are united by other ties besides those of State policy and public need. To a large extent, they are the ties of blood and history. Naturally I, a child of both worlds, am conscious of these.

8   Law, language, literature—these are considerable factors. Common **conceptions** of what is right and decent, a marked regard for fair play, especially to the weak and poor, a stern sentiment of impartial justice, and above all the love of personal freedom, or as Kipling put it:

9   "Leave to live by no man's leave, underneath the law"—these are common conceptions on both sides of the ocean among the English-speaking peoples. We hold to these conceptions as strongly as you do.

10   We do not war primarily with races as such. Tyranny is our foe, whatever trappings or disguise it wears, whatever language it speaks, be it external or internal, we must forever be on our guard, ever mobilized, ever **vigilant,** always ready to spring

at its throat. In all this, we march together. Not only do we march and strive shoulder to shoulder at this moment under the fire of the enemy on the fields of war or in the air, but also in those realms of thought which are consecrated to the rights and the dignity of man.

11   At the present time we have in continual vigorous action the British and United States Combined Chiefs of Staff Committee, which works immediately under the President and myself as representative of the British War Cabinet. This committee, with its elaborate organization of Staff officers of every grade, disposes of all our resources and, in practice, uses British and American troops, ships, aircraft, and **munitions** just as if they were the resources of a single State or nation.

12   I would not say there are never divergences of view among these high professional authorities. It would be unnatural if there were not. That is why it is necessary to have a **plenary** meeting of principals every two or three months. All these men now know each other. They trust each other. They like each other, and most of them have been at work together for a long time. When they meet they thrash things out with great candor and plain, blunt speech, but after a few days the President and I find ourselves furnished with sincere and united advice.

13   This is a wonderful system. There was nothing like it in the last war. There never has been anything like it between two allies. It is reproduced in an even more tightly-knit form at General Eisenhower's headquarters in the Mediterranean, where everything is completely intermingled and soldiers are ordered into battle by the Supreme Commander or his deputy, General Alexander, without the slightest regard to whether they are British, American, or Canadian, but simply in accordance with the fighting need.

14   Now in my opinion it would be a most foolish and **improvident** act on the part of our two Governments, or either of them, to break up this smooth-running and immensely powerful machinery the moment the war is over. For our own safety, as well as for the security of the rest of the world, we are bound to keep it working and in running order after the war—probably for a good many years, not only until we have set up some world arrangement to keep the peace, but until we know that it is an arrangement which will really give us that protection we must have from danger and aggression, a protection we have already had to seek across two vast world wars.

15   I am not qualified, of course, to judge whether or not this would become a party question in the United States, and I would not presume to discuss that point. I am sure, however, that it will not be a party question in Great Britain. We must not let go of the securities we have found necessary to preserve our lives and liberties until we are quite sure we have something else to put in their place, which will give us an equally solid guarantee.

16   The great **Bismarck**—for there were once great men in Germany—is said to have observed towards the close of his life that the most potent factor in human society at the end of the nineteenth century was the fact that the British and American peoples spoke the same language.

17   That was a pregnant saying. Certainly it has enabled us to wage war together with

an intimacy and harmony never before achieved among allies.

18   This gift of a common tongue is a priceless inheritance, and it may well someday become the foundation of a common citizenship. I like to think of British and Americans moving about freely over each other's wide estates with hardly a sense of being foreigners to one another. But I do not see why we should not try to spread our common language even more widely throughout the globe and, without seeking selfish advantage over any, possess ourselves of this invaluable **amenity** and birthright.

—From "The Price of Greatness" by Winston Churchill. Copyright © Winston S. Churchill. Reproduced with permission of Curtis Brown Ltd, London on behalf of the Estate of Sir Winston Churchill.

Choose the best meaning of each word in **bold**. Use context clues to make your choice.

Vocabulary in Context   __b__   **1.** "The price of greatness is responsibility. If the people of the United States had continued in a **mediocre** station, struggling with the wilderness, absorbed in their own affairs, and a factor of no consequence in the movement of the world . . ." (paragraph 3)
   a. unusual   c. special
   b. commonplace   d. extreme

Vocabulary in Context   __c__   **2.** "Throughout all this ordeal and struggle which is characteristic of our age, you will find in the British Commonwealth and Empire good **comrades** to whom you are united by other ties besides those of State policy and public need." (paragraph 7)
   a. enemies   c. friends
   b. soldiers   d. ideas.

Central Idea   __b__   **3.** Which of the following sentences states the central idea of the passage?
   a. "Twice in my lifetime the long arm of destiny has reached across the oceans and involved the entire life and manhood of the United States in a deadly struggle." (paragraph 1)
   b. "The price of greatness is responsibility." (paragraph 3)
   c. "It must be world anarchy or world order." (paragraph 6)
   d. "This gift of a common tongue is a priceless inheritance, and it may well someday become the foundation of a common citizenship." (paragraph 18)

Supporting Details   <u>c</u>   **4.** According to the passage prodigious changes in the world have occurred because of
   a. world wars.
   b. law.
   c. high mobility.
   d. the establishment of the United States.

Supporting Details   <u>d</u>   **5.** According to Bismarck, what was the most potent fact in human society at the end of the nineteenth century?
   a. free movement
   b. the great men of Germany
   c. the common values of Britain and the U. S.
   d. the common tongue of Britain and the U. S.

Transitions   <u>c</u>   **6.** "We hold to these conceptions as strongly as you do." (paragraph 9)

   The relationship of ideas within this sentence is
   a. cause and effect.
   b. time order.
   c. comparison and contrast.
   d. generalization and example.

Transitions   <u>d</u>   **7.** "There is no halting-place at this point. We have now reached a stage in the journey where there can be no pause." (paragraph 6)

   The relationship of ideas between these sentences is
   a. cause and effect.
   b. time order.
   c. comparison and contrast.
   d. generalization and example.

Thought Patterns   <u>a</u>   **8.** The thought pattern for paragraph 3 is
   a. cause and effect.
   b. time order.
   c. comparison and contrast.
   d. definition and example.

Thought Patterns   <u>c</u>   **9.** The thought pattern for paragraph 4 is
   a. cause and effect.
   b. time order.
   c. comparison and contrast.
   d. definition and example.

Fact and Opinion   <u>c</u>   **10.** "Certainly it has enabled us to wage war together with an intimacy and harmony never before achieved among allies." (paragraph 17)

   This sentence is a statement of
   a. fact.
   b. opinion.
   c. fact and opinion.

Fact and Opinion   <u>c</u>   **11.** "At the present time we have in continual vigorous action the British and United States Combined Chiefs of Staff Committee, which works immediately under the President and myself as representative of the British War Cabinet." (paragraph 11)

This sentence is a statement of
a. fact.   c. fact and opinion.
b. opinion.

Fact and   ___b___ **12.** "Now in my opinion it would be a most foolish and improvident
Opinion   act on the part of our two Governments, or either of them, to
                        break up this smooth-running and immensely powerful machinery the moment the war is over." (paragraph 14)

This sentence is a statement of
a. fact.   c. fact and opinion.
b. opinion.

Tone   ___d___ **13.** The overall tone of the author is
                        a. neutral.   c. arrogant.
                        b. critical.   d. approving.

Tone   ___c___ **14.** The tone of the author in paragraph 15 is
                        a. humiliated.   c. confident.
                        b. arrogant.   d. timid.

Purpose   ___b___ **15.** The primary purpose of the author is
                        a. to inform the audience of the accomplishments of Great Britain
                           and the United States during the war.
                        b. to celebrate the shared values, accomplishments, and responsibilities of Great Britain and the United States during and after
                           the war.
                        c. to persuade the audience to support the war efforts of Great
                           Britain and the United States.

Inferences   ___d___ **16.** Based on the details in paragraph 14, we can infer that **improvident**
                        means
                        a. wise.   c. important.
                        b. fateful.   d. careless.

Inferences   ___b___ **17.** Based on the details in the passage, we can conclude that Churchill
                        believes that the United States is responsible for
                        a. World War II.
                        b. the security of the rest of the world after the war.
                        c. our powers of locomotion.
                        d. the gift of a common language.

Argument   __c__ **18.** Identify the persuasive technique used in the following sentence:

"Man has parted company with his trusty friend the horse and has sailed into the azure with the eagles." (paragraph 5)
a. plain folks
b. either-or
c. glittering generality
d. false cause

Argument   __b__ **19.** Identify the persuasive technique used in the following sentence:

"It must be world anarchy or world order." (paragraph 6)
a. false comparison
b. either-or
c. plain folks
d. transfer

Argument   __a__ **20.** Identify the persuasive technique used in the following sentence:

"Not only do we march and strive shoulder to shoulder at this moment under the fire of the enemy on the fields of war or in the air, but also in those realms of thought which are consecrated to the rights and the dignity of man." (paragraph 10)
a. glittering generality
b. either-or
c. false cause
d. false comparison

Summarizing

Complete the following summary with information from the passage.

According to Winston Churchill in his speech given when he received an honorary degree at Harvard, the people of the United States cannot escape world responsibility . The responsibilities of the United States grow as its wealth and power increases, and the changes brought by locomotion shrinks the range of the world. The shared values and the common tongue of Great Britain and the United States built a smooth-running and immensely powerful machinery of war that should continue until some world arrangement to keep the peace is established .

WHAT DO YOU THINK?

Do you agree with Churchill's claim that a "gift of a common tongue" [the English language] is a priceless inheritance, and it may well someday become the foundation of a common citizenship? Why or why not? Why would a common language help secure world peace and prosperity? Do you think the United States should create a law that makes English its official language? Or do you think the United States should encourage its citizens to learn more than one language? If so, which language should be learned? Assume that your local Board of Education is considering adding a foreign language as a requirement for graduation from high school. Write a letter to the board in favor of or in opposition to this proposal. If you support the proposal, identify the language you believe should be taught and why. If you oppose the proposal, explain why students should learn only English.

MASTER READER Scorecard

From "The Price of Greatness"

Skill	Number Correct	Points	Total
Vocabulary			
Vocabulary in Context (2 items)	_____ ×	4 =	_____
Comprehension			
Central Idea (1 item)	_____ ×	4 =	_____
Supporting Details (2 items)	_____ ×	4 =	_____
Transitions (2 items)	_____ ×	4 =	_____
Thought Patterns (2 items)	_____ ×	4 =	_____
Fact and Opinion (3 items)	_____ ×	4 =	_____
Tone and Purpose (3 items)	_____ ×	4 =	_____
Inferences (2 items)	_____ ×	4 =	_____
Argument (3 items)	_____ ×	4 =	_____
Summarizing (5 items)	_____ ×	4 =	_____
	Comprehension Score		_____

Real People in the "Age of the Common Man"

11.7 GE/3657 words

Textbook Skills

by Jacqueline Jones, Peter H. Wood, Thomas Borstelmann, Elaine Tyler May, and Vicki L. Ruiz

In the preface of the *Created Equal* textbook from which this passage comes, the authors state, "*Created Equal* tells the dramatic, evolving story of America in all its complexity—a story of a diverse people 'created equal' yet struggling to achieve equality." The following excerpt addresses the American ideal of equality and the concept of the "common man." What do you think the term "common man" meant during the 1800s? How would you define the "common man" in America today?

Vocabulary Preview

hierarchy (paragraph 1): formally ranked group, chain of command
suffrage (paragraph 1): right to vote, act of voting
egalitarian (paragraph 1): democratic, equal, free
denigrate (paragraph 3): belittle, scorn, degrade
assimilate (paragraph 8): integrate, blend in, conform
interlopers (paragraph 9): intruders, trespassers
deference (paragraph 17): respect, submission
subversive (paragraph 19): rebellious, defiant
atole (paragraph 25): hot sweet drink made from corn dough
vanguard (paragraph 30): front line, forerunner
advocate (paragraph 35): supporter, activist

1   In the early 1830s, a wealthy Frenchman named Alexis de Tocqueville visited the United States and wrote about the contradictions he saw. In his book *Democracy in America* (published in 1835), Tocqueville noted that the United States lacked the rigid **hierarchy** of class privilege that characterized European nations. With universal white manhood **suffrage**, white men could vote and run for office regardless of their class or religion. However, Tocqueville also noted some sore spots in American democratic values and practices. He commented on the plight of groups deprived of the right to vote; their lack of freedom stood out starkly in the otherwise **egalitarian** society of the

United States. He sympathized with the southeastern Indians uprooted from their homelands. He raised the possibility that conflicts between blacks and whites might eventually lead to bloodshed. He even contrasted the situation of young unmarried white women, who seemed so free-spirited, with that of wives, who appeared cautious and dull. He concluded, "In America a woman loses her independence forever in the bonds of matrimony." In other words, Tocqueville saw America for what it was: a blend of freedom and slavery, of independence and dependence.

Wards, Workers, and Warriors: Native Americans

2   Population growth in the United States—and on the borderlands between the United States and Mexican territory—put pressure on Indian societies. Yet different cultural groups responded in different ways to this pressure. Some, like the Cherokee, conformed to European American ways and became sedentary farmers. Others were forced to work for whites. Still others either waged war on white settlements and military forces or retreated farther and farther from European American settlements in the hope of avoiding clashes with the intruders.

3   Nevertheless, prominent whites continued to **denigrate** the humanity of all Indians. In the 1820s Henry Clay claimed that Indians were "essentially inferior to the Anglo-Saxon race . . . and their disappearance from the human family will be no great loss to the world." In 1828 the House of Representatives Committee on Indian Affairs surveyed the Indians of the South and concluded that "an Indian cannot work" and that

all Indians were lazy and notable for their "thirst for spirituous liquours." According to the committee, when European American settlers depleted reserves of wildlife, Indians as a group would cease to exist.

4   Members of the Cherokee Nation bitterly denounced these assertions. "The Cherokees do not live upon the chase [for game]," they pointed out. Neither did the Creek, Choctaw, Chickasaw, and Seminole—the other members of the Five Civilized Tribes, so called for their varying degrees of conformity to white people's ways.

5   Charting a middle course between the Indian and European American worlds was Sequoyah, the son of a white Virginia trader-soldier and a Cherokee woman. A veteran of Andrew Jackson's campaign against the Creek in 1813–1814, Sequoyah moved to Arkansas in 1818, part of an early Cherokee migration west. In 1821 he finished a Cherokee syllabary (a written language consisting of syllables and letters, in contrast to pictures, or pictographs). The product of a dozen years' work, the syllabary consisted of 86 characters. In 1828 the Cherokee Phoenix, a newspaper based on the new writing system, began publication in New Echota, Georgia.

6   Sequoyah's written language enabled the increasingly dispersed Cherokee to remain in touch with each other on their own terms. At the same time, numerous Indian cultural groups lost their struggle to retain even modest control over their destinies. In some areas of the continent, smallpox continued to ravage native populations. In other regions, Indians became wards of, or dependent on, whites, living with and working for white families. Other groups, living close to whites, adopted their trading practices. In

Spanish California, the Muquelmne Miwok in the San Joaquin delta made a living by stealing and then selling the horses of Mexican settlers.

7   In other parts of California, Spanish missionaries conquered Indian groups, converted them to Christianity, and then forced them to work in the missions. In missions up and down the California coast, Indians worked as weavers, tanners, shoemakers, bricklayers, carpenters, blacksmiths, and other artisans. Some herded cattle and raised horses. Indian women cooked for the mission, cleaned, and spun wool. They wove cloth and sewed garments.

8   Nevertheless, even Indians living in or near missions resisted the cultural change imposed by the intruders. Catholic missionaries complained that Indian women such as those of the Chumash refused to learn Spanish. The refusal among some Indians to **assimilate** completely signaled persistent, deep-seated conflicts between native groups and incoming settlers. In 1824 a revolt among hundreds of newly converted Indians at the mission La Purisima Concepción north of Santa Barbara revealed a rising militancy among native peoples.

9   After the War of 1812, the U.S. government had rewarded some military veterans with land grants in the Old Northwest. Federal agents tried to clear the way for these new settlers by ousting Indians from the area. Overwhelmed by the number of whites, some Indian groups such as the Peoria and Kaskaskia gave up their lands to the **interlopers**. Others took a stand against the white intrusion. In 1826 and 1827 the Winnebago attacked white families and boat pilots living near Prairie du Chien, Wisconsin. Two years later, the Sauk chief Black Hawk (known to Indians as Maka-tai-me-she-kia-kiak) assembled a coalition of Fox, Winnebago, Kickapoo, and Potawatomi. Emboldened by the prospect of aid from British Canada, they clashed with federal troops and raided farmers' homesteads and miners' camps.

10   In August 1832 a force of 1,300 U.S. soldiers and volunteers struck back, killing 300 Indian men, women, and children encamped on the Bad Axe River in western Wisconsin. The massacre, the decisive point of what came to be called the Black Hawk War, marked the end of armed Indian resistance north of the Ohio River and east of the Mississippi.

Slaves and Free People of Color

11   In the 1820s the small proportion of free blacks within the southern population declined further. Southern whites perceived free blacks as an unwelcome and dangerous presence, especially given the possibility that they would conspire with slaves to spark a rebellion. For these reasons some states began to outlaw private manumissions (the practice of individual owners freeing their slaves) and to force free blacks to leave the state altogether.

12   One free black who inspired such fears was Denmark Vesey. Born on the Danish-controlled island of Saint Thomas in 1767, Vesey was a literate carpenter as well as a religious leader. In 1799 he won $1,500 in a Charleston, South Carolina, lottery and used some of the money to buy his freedom. In the summer of 1822, a Charleston court claimed to have unearthed evidence of a "diabolical plot" hatched by Vesey together with plantation slaves from the surrounding area.

13   Yet the historical record strongly suggests that no plot ever existed. Black "witnesses" who feared for their own lives provided inconsistent and contradictory testimony to a panel of judges. Authorities never located any material evidence of a plan, such as stockpiles of weapons. Under fire from other Charleston elites for rushing to judgment, the judges redoubled their efforts to **embellish** vague rumors of black discontent into a tale of a well-orchestrated uprising and to implicate growing numbers of black people. As a result of the testimony of several slaves, 35 black men were hanged and another 18 exiled outside the United States. Of those executed, Vesey and 23 other men said nothing to support even the vaguest charges of the court.

14   In the North, some blacks were granted the right to vote after emancipation in the late eighteenth century; however, many of those voting rights were lost in the early nineteenth century. New Jersey (in 1807), Connecticut (1818), New York (1821), and Pennsylvania (1838) all revoked the legislation that had let black men cast ballots. Free northern blacks continued to suffer under a number of legal restrictions. Most were not citizens and therefore perceived themselves as oppressed like the slaves in the South.

15   A new group of black leaders in the urban North began to link their fate to that of their enslaved brothers and sisters in the South. In Boston, North Carolina-born David Walker published his fiery *Walker's Appeal* to the Coloured Citizens of the World in 1829. Walker called for all blacks to integrate fully into American society, shunning racial segregation whether initiated by whites or by blacks themselves. Reminding his listeners of the horrors of the slave trade, he declared that black people were ready to die for freedom: "I give it as a fact, let twelve black men get well armed for battle, and they will kill and put to flight fifty whites."

16   Northern black leaders disagreed among themselves on the issues of integration and black separatism—for example, whether blacks should create their own schools or press for inclusion in the public educational system. A few leaders favored leaving the country altogether, believing that black people would never find peace and freedom in the United States. Founded by whites in New Jersey in 1817, the American Colonization Society (ACS) paid for black Americans to settle Monrovia (later named Liberia) on the west coast of Africa. The ACS drew support from a variety of groups: whites in the upper South who wanted to free their slaves but believed that black and white people could not live in the same country, and some slaves and free people of color convinced that colonization would give them a fresh start. A small number of American-born blacks settled in Liberia. However, most black activists rejected colonization. They had been born on American soil, and their forebears had been buried there. Maria Stewart, an African American religious leader in Boston, declared, "But before I go [to Africa] the bayonet shall pierce me through."

17   Northern whites sought to control black people and their movements. Outspoken black men and women such as Walker and Stewart alarmed northern whites who feared that if blacks could claim decent jobs,

white people would lose their own jobs. African Americans who worked outdoors as wagon drivers, peddlers, and street sweepers were taunted and in some cases attacked by whites who demanded **deference** from blacks in public. In October 1824 a white mob invaded a black neighborhood in Providence, Rhode Island. They terrorized its residents, destroyed buildings, and left the place "almost entirely in ruins." The catalyst for the riot had come the previous day, when a group of blacks had refused to yield the inside of the sidewalk—a cleaner place to walk—to white passersby.

18   The South's silence was broken in 1831 when white Southerners took steps to reinforce the institution of slavery, using both violent and legal means. That year Nat Turner, an enslaved preacher and mystic, led a slave revolt in Southampton, Virginia. In the 1820s the young Turner had looked skyward and had seen visions of "white spirits and black spirits engaged in battle . . . and blood flowed in streams." Turner believed that he had received divine instructions to lead other slaves to freedom, to "arise and prepare myself, and slay my enemies with their own weapons." In August he and a group of followers that eventually numbered 80 moved through the countryside, killing whites wherever they could find them. Ultimately, nearly 60 whites died at the hands of Turner's rebels. Turner himself managed to evade capture for more than two months. After he was captured, he was tried, convicted, and sentenced to death. A white man named Thomas Gray interviewed Turner in his jail cell and recorded his "confessions" before he was hanged.

Published in 1832 by Gray, *The Confessions of Nat Turner* reached a large, horrified audience in the white South. According to Gray, Turner said that he had exhibited "uncommon intelligence" when he was a child. As a young man, he had received inspiration from the Bible, especially the passage "Seek ye the kingdom of Heaven and all things shall be added unto you." Perhaps most disturbing of all, Turner reported that, since 1830, he had been a slave of "Mr. Joseph Travis, who was to me a kind master, and placed the greatest confidence in me; in fact, I had no cause to complain of his treatment to me." Turner's "confessions" suggested the **subversive** potential of slaves who were literate and Christian and those who were treated kindly by their masters and mistresses. 19

After the Turner revolt, a wave of white hysteria swept the South. In Virginia near where the killings had occurred, whites assaulted blacks with unbridled fury. The Virginia legislature seized the occasion to defeat various antislavery proposals. Thereafter, all the slave states moved to strengthen the institution of slavery. For all practical purposes, public debate over slavery ceased throughout the American South. 20

Legal and Economic Dependence: The Status of Women

In the political and economic realms, the egalitarian impulse rarely affected the status of women in a legal or practical sense. Regardless of where they lived, enslaved women and Indian women had almost no rights under either U.S. or Spanish law. Still, legal systems in the United States and the Spanish borderlands differed 21 in their treatment of women. In the United States, most of the constraints that white married women had experienced in the colonial period still applied in the 1820s. A husband controlled the property that his wife brought to the marriage, and he had legal authority over their children. Indeed, the wife was considered her husband's possession. She had no right to make a contract, keep money she earned, vote, run for office, or serve on a jury. In contrast, in the Spanish Southwest, married women could own land and conduct business on their own. At the same time, however, husbands, fathers, and local priests continued to exert much influence over the lives of these women.

22   European American women's economic subordination served as a rationale for their political inferiority. The "common man" concept rested on the assumption that only men could ensure American economic growth and well-being. According to this view, men had the largest stake in society because only they owned property. That stake made them responsible citizens.

23   Yet women contributed to the economy in myriad ways. Although few women earned cash wages in the 1820s, almost all adult women worked. In the colonial period, society had highly valued women's labor in the fields, the garden, and the kitchen. However, in the early nineteenth century, work was becoming increasingly identified as labor that earned cash wages. This attitude proved particularly common in the Northeast, where increasing numbers of workers labored under the supervision of a boss. As this belief took root, men began valuing women's contributions to the household economy less and less. If women did not earn money, many men asked, did they really work at all?

24   In these years, well-off women in the northeastern and mid-Atlantic states began to think of themselves as consumers and not producers of goods. They relied more and more on store-bought cloth and household supplies. Some could also afford to hire servants to perform housework for them. Privileged women gradually stopped thinking of their responsibilities as making goods or processing and preparing food. Rather, their main tasks were to manage servants and create a comfortable home for their husbands and children. They saw their labor as necessary to the well-being of their families, even if their compensation came in the form of emotional satisfaction rather than cash.

25   In contrast, women in other parts of the country continued to engage in the same forms of household industry that had characterized the colonial period. In Spanish settlements, women played a central role in household production. They made all of their family's clothes by carding, spinning, and weaving the wool from sheep. They tanned cowhides and ground blue corn to make tortillas, or **atole**. They produced their own candles and soap, and they plastered the walls of the home.

26   Like women's work in general, the labor of wives and mothers in Spanish-speaking regions had great cultural significance. In the Mexican territory of California, women engaged in backbreaking efforts so that members of their families could wear snow-white linen clothing. One community member recalled that "certainly to do so was one of

the chief anxieties" of well-to-do households: "There was sometimes a great deal of linen to be washed for it was the pride of every Spanish family to own much linen, and the mothers and daughters almost always wore white." Women used homemade soap to scrub the clothes on the rocks of a nearby spring. Then they spread out the wet garments to dry on the tops of bushes that grew on the mountainside.

27   In the Spanish mission of San Gabriel, California, the widow Eulalia Perez cooked, sewed, ministered to the ill, and instructed children in reading and writing. As housekeeper, Perez kept the keys to the mission storehouse. She also distributed supplies to the Indians and the vaqueros (cowboys) who lived in the mission. She supervised Indian servants as well as soap makers, wine pressers, and olive oil producers.

28   At Mission San Diego, Apolonaria Lorenzana worked as a healer and cared for the church sacristy and priestly vestments. From the time she arrived in Monterey at age 7 (in 1800) until her death in the late nineteenth century, Lorenzana devoted her life to such labors. Although the priests tried to restrict her to administering the mission hospital, she took pride in her nursing abilities, "even though Father Sanchez had told me not to do it myself, but to have it done, and only to be present so that the servant girls would do it well."

29   Indian women also engaged in a variety of essential tasks. Sioux and Mandan women, though of a social rank inferior to men, performed a great deal of manual labor in their own villages. They dressed buffalo skins that the men later sold to traders. They collected water and wood, cooked, dried meat

and fruit, and cultivated maize (corn), pumpkins, and squash with hoes made from the shoulder blades of elk. These women worked collectively within a network of households rather than individually within nuclear families.

Many women, regardless of ethnicity, 30 were paid for their work with food and shelter but not money. Nevertheless, some women did work for cash wages during this era. New England women and children, for example, were the **vanguard** of factory wage-earners in the early manufacturing system. In Massachusetts in 1820, women and children constituted almost a third of all manufacturing workers. In the largest textile factories, they made up fully 80 percent of the workforce.

The business of textile manufacturing 31 took the tasks of spinning thread and weaving cloth out of the home, where such tasks often were performed by unpaid, unmarried daughters, and relocated those tasks in factories, where the same workers received wages. The famous "Lowell mill girls" are an apt example. Young, unmarried white women from New Hampshire, Vermont, and Massachusetts, these workers moved to the new company town of Lowell, Massachusetts, to take jobs as textile machine operatives. In New England, thousands of young men had migrated west, tipping the sex ratio in favor of women and creating a reserve of female laborers. But to attract young women to factory work, mill owners had to reassure them (and their parents) that they would be safe and well cared for away from home. To that end, they established boarding houses where employees could live together under the supervision of a matron—an older woman who served as their mother-away-from-home.

32   Company towns set rules shaping employees' living conditions as well as their working conditions. In the early 1830s, a posted list of "Rules and Regulations" covered many aspects of the lives of the young women living at the Poignaud and Plant boardinghouse at Lancaster, Massachusetts. The list told the women how to enter the building (quietly, and then hang up "their bonnet, shawl, coat, etc. etc. in the entry") and where to sit at the dinner table (the two workers with greatest seniority were to take their places at the head of the table). Despite these rules, many young women valued the friendships they made with their coworkers and the money they made in the mills. Some of these women sent their wages back home so that their fathers could pay off the mortgage or their brothers could attend school.

33   But not all women wage-earners labored in large mills. In New York City, single women, wives, and widows toiled as needle workers in their homes. Impoverished, sewing in tiny attics by the dim light of candles, these women were at the mercy of jobbers—merchants who parceled out cuffs, collars, and shirt fronts that the women finished. Other urban women worked as street vendors, selling produce, or as cooks, nurse-maids, or laundresses.

34   The new **delineation** between men's and women's work and workplaces intensified the drive for women's education begun after the Revolution. If well-to-do women were to assume domestic responsibilities while their husbands worked outside the home, then women must receive their own unique form of schooling, or so the reasoning went. Most ordinary women received little in the way of formal education. Yet elite young women had expanded educational opportunities, beginning in the early nineteenth century. Emma Willard founded a female academy in Troy, New York, in 1821, and Catharine Beecher established the Hartford Female Seminary two years later in Connecticut. For the most part, these schools catered to the daughters of wealthy families, young women who would never have to work in a factory to survive. Hailed as a means to prepare young women to serve as wives and mothers, the schools taught geography, foreign languages, mathematics, science, and philosophy, as well as the "female" pursuits of embroidery and music.

35   Out of this curriculum designed especially for women emerged women's rights activists, women who keenly felt both the potential of their own intelligence and the degrading nature of their social situation. Elizabeth Cady, an 1832 graduate of the Troy Female Seminary, later went on to marry Henry B. Stanton and bear seven children, but by the 1840s she strode onto the national stage as a tireless **advocate** of women's political and economic rights.

VISUAL VOCABULARY

a_____ is hard won in many places across the world.

a. suffrage
b. assimilation
c. subversion

Choose the best meaning of each word in **bold**. Use context clues to make your choice.

Vocabulary in Context ___b___ **1.** "Under fire from other Charleston elites for rushing to judgment, the judges redoubled their efforts to **embellish** vague rumors of black discontent into a tale of a well-orchestrated uprising and to implicate growing numbers of black people." (paragraph 13)

    a. decorate   c. adorn
    b. exaggerate   d. simplify

Vocabulary in Context ___c___ **2.** "The new **delineation** between men's and women's work and workplaces intensified the drive for women's education begun after the Revolution." (paragraph 34)

    a. description   c. discrimination
    b. unity   d. phase

Central Idea ___d___ **3.** Which of the following sentences from the first paragraph states the central idea of the passage?

    a. "In the early 1830s, a wealthy Frenchman named Alexis de Tocqueville visited the United States and wrote about the contradictions he saw."

    b. "With universal white manhood suffrage, white men could vote and run for office regardless of their class or religion."

    c. "However, Tocqueville also noted some sore spots in American "democratic values and practices."

    d. "In other words, Tocqueville saw America for what it was: a blend of freedom and slavery, of independence and dependence."

Central Idea ___a___

4. Which of the following sentences states the central idea of paragraphs 2 through 10?

a. "Population growth in the United States—and on the borderlands between the United States and Mexican territory—put pressure on Indian societies." (paragraph 2)

b. "Charting a middle course between the Indian and European American worlds was Sequoyah, the son of a white Virginia trader-soldier and a Cherokee woman." (paragraph 5)

c. "Overwhelmed by the number of whites, some Indian groups such as the Peoria and Kaskaskia gave up their lands to the interlopers." (paragraph 9)

d. "The massacre, the decisive point of what came to be called the Black Hawk War, marked the end of armed Indian resistance north of the Ohio River and east of the Mississippi." (paragraph 10)

Implied ___a___
Central Idea

5. Which of the following sentences states the implied central idea of paragraphs 11 through 20?

a. Southern states enacted laws to support slavery and force free blacks to leave the region.

b. Northern states granted blacks the right to vote in the late eighteenth century only to revoke voting rights for blacks in the nineteenth century.

c. Black leaders disagreed about the issues of integration and black separation.

d. The United States enacted laws in the eighteenth and nineteenth century that enslaved blacks and limited the rights of free blacks.

Central Idea ___a___

6. Which of the following sentences states the central idea of paragraphs 21 through 35?

a. "In the political and economic realms, the egalitarian impulse rarely affected the status of women in a legal or practical sense." (paragraph 21)

b. "Yet women contributed to the economy in myriad ways." (paragraph 23)

c. "In these years, well-off women in the northeastern and mid-Atlantic states began to think of themselves as consumers and not producers of goods." (paragraph 24)

d. "The new delineation between men's and women's work and workplaces intensified the drive for women's education begun after the Revolution." (paragraph 34)

Supporting _____c_____ **7.** According to the passage, Nat Turner led a slave revolt because he
Details
    a. was beaten as a slave.
    b. was a literate Christian.
    c. believed he had divine instructions to act.
    d. had been sentenced to death.

Transitions _____b_____ **8.** "Most were not citizens and therefore perceived themselves as oppressed like the slaves in the South." (paragraph 14)

The relationship of ideas within this sentence is
    a. classification.   c. comparison and contrast.
    b. cause and effect.   d. time order.

Transitions _____c_____ **9.** "With universal white manhood suffrage, white men could vote and run for office regardless of their class or religion. However, Tocqueville also noted some sore spots in American democratic values and practices." (paragraph 1)

The relationship of ideas between these sentences is
    a. cause and effect.   c. comparison and contrast.
    b. classification.   d. generalization and example.

Thought _____b_____ **10.** The overall thought pattern for the passage is
Patterns
    a. cause and effect.   c. comparison and contrast.
    b. classification.   d. generalization and example

Thought _____a_____ **11.** The thought pattern for paragraph 11 is
Patterns
    a. cause and effect.   c. comparison and contrast.
    b. classification.   d. definition and example.

Fact and _____a_____ **12.** "In the early 1830s, a wealthy Frenchman named Alexis de
Opinion
Tocqueville visited the United States and wrote about the contradictions he saw." (paragraph 1)

This sentence is a statement of
    a. fact.   c. fact and opinion.
    b. opinion.

Fact and _____c_____ **13.** "Charting a middle course between the Indian and European
Opinion
American worlds was Sequoyah, the son of a white Virginia trader-soldier and a Cherokee woman." (paragraph 5)

This sentence is a statement of
    a. fact.   c. fact and opinion.
    b. opinion.

Fact and
Opinion

___a___ **14.** "In Massachusetts in 1820, women and children constituted almost a third of all manufacturing workers." (paragraph 30)

This sentence is a statement of
a. fact.   c. fact and opinion.
b. opinion.

Tone

___b___ **15.** The overall tone of the passage is
a. angry.   c. sympathetic.
b. neutral.   d. cold.

Purpose

___a___ **16.** The primary purpose of the passage is
a. to inform.   c. to persuade.
b. to entertain.

Inferences

___b___ **17.** Based on the details in the passage, we can infer that
a. discrimination against minorities occurred mostly in the South during the Age of the Common Man.
b. the Age of the Common Man favored white males.
c. women had more rights than other minority groups during the Age of the Common Man.
d. all the various groups of people attained freedom during the Age of the Common Man.

Argument

___d___ **18.** Read the claim and supports taken from the passage. Then identify the detail that does not support the claim.

Claim: "In America a woman loses her independence forever in the bonds of matrimony." (paragraph 1)
a. "A husband controlled the property that his wife brought to the marriage, and he had legal authority over their children." (paragraph 21)
b. "Indeed, the wife was considered her husband's property." (paragraph 21)
c. "She had no right to make a contract, keep money she earned, vote, run for office, or serve on a jury." (paragraph 21)
d. "Elizabeth Cady, an 1832 graduate of the Troy Female Seminary, later went on to marry Henry B. Stanton and bear seven children, but by the 1840s she strode on the national stage as a tireless advocate of women's political and economic rights." (paragraph 35)

Argument   **19.** Identify the persuasive technique used in the following sentence:

"In 1828 the House of Representatives Committee on Indian Affairs surveyed the Indians of the South and concluded that 'an Indian cannot work' and that all Indians were lazy and notable for their 'thirst for spirituous liquours.'" (paragraph 3)

a. false analogy   c. begging the question

b. personal attack   d. transfer

Argument   _c_   **20.** Identify the persuasive technique used in the following sentence:

"European American women's economic subordination served as a rationale for their political inferiority." (paragraph 22)

a. false analogy   c. begging the question

b. personal attack   d. transfer

Mapping

Complete the following concept map with information from the passage.

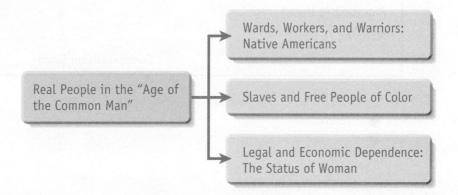

WHAT DO YOU THINK?

Now that you have read the passage, how would you define the Common Man in America during the first half of the 1800s? Do you think the idea of a Common Man still exists in America today? If so, how would you define the term today? Assume you are taking a college history course and you have been assigned an essay that connects what you are learning about history to current life. Choose one of the groups of people discussed in the passage and compare the status of that group during the Age of the Common Man to their current status today.

MASTER READER Scorecard

> **"Real People in the 'Age of the Common Man'"**
>
> | Skill | Number Correct | Points | | Total |
> |---|---|---|---|---|
> | *Vocabulary* | | | | |
> | Vocabulary in Context (2 items) | _____ | × | 4 = | _____ |
> | *Comprehension* | | | | |
> | Central Idea and Implied Central Idea (4 items) | _____ | × | 4 = | _____ |
> | Supporting Details (1 item) | _____ | × | 4 = | _____ |
> | Transitions (2 items) | _____ | × | 4 = | _____ |
> | Thought Patterns (2 items) | _____ | × | 4 = | _____ |
> | Fact and Opinion (3 items) | _____ | × | 4 = | _____ |
> | Tone and Purpose (2 items) | _____ | × | 4 = | _____ |
> | Inferences (1 item) | _____ | × | 4 = | _____ |
> | Argument (3 items) | _____ | × | 4 = | _____ |
> | **Mapping** (4 items) | _____ | × | 5 = | _____ |
> | | | Comprehension Score | | _____ |

Combined-Skills Tests

Part Three contains 10 tests. The purpose of these tests is twofold: to track your growth as a reader and to prepare you for the formal tests you will face as you take college courses. Each test presents a reading passage and questions that cover some or all of the following skills: vocabulary in context, central ideas, supporting details, thought patterns, fact and opinion, tone and purpose, inferences, and argument.

TEST 1

Read the following passage, and then, answer the questions.

An Account of Alfred C. Cooley's Plight in the Face of Hurricane Katrina

10.1 GE/1377 words

by Sandra Offiah-Hawkins

[1]I am **aghast** by the sudden series of events. [2]There is no time to figure out the next day, for there is no time to visualize where we are going to all sleep this night—new, used, and old cars line up along Interstate 10 and Highway 1 as we all travel 10 miles an hour and wait in five-mile long lines in hopes of getting gas before the stations run out. [3]There are thirty-five of us traveling in a caravan: a Dodge Caravan, a Ford Taurus, a 2000 Grand Prix, and a Toyota CRV just to name a few. [4]All the relatives we can contact in New Orleans on this day August 27, 2005, are with us; we have been asked to leave our homes immediately, for the strong winds, the deluging rain, the terrible wrath of Hurricane Katrina is headed straight to New Orleans—our home.

[5]All of us leave our worldly possessions that day, bringing with us essentials for two days: I never think for a minute this is the end of what I have called home in the Ninth Ward for more than 50 years; all of us feel this is going to be a "James Brown turnaround." [6]I never think the wife and children I have been blessed with over the past 30 years would never again know life as they had known it in New Orleans.

***

[7]Throughout my life, I have known suffering: I suffer from Sickle Cell Anemia; my parents were told that I would not live past age 16, but here I am! [8]Within the last eight years, I have had two hip replacements as well as operations on my shoulder and on my left eye. [9]I have been placed in a situation of sometimes raising my four daughters as a single parent, and for many years, I have cared for my aging parents. [10]Now this—the unanticipated fury of Katrina.

***

[11]Once the storm hits, the power, as expected, is off for days in New Orleans, so it is Tuesday evening or Wednesday before we find out the Levee has broken. [12]Since we left home on Saturday, we have been traveling—first to Alexandria, Louisiana, where we sleep wherever there is a space on the floor at Dora Ann's house, my sister's former daughter-in-law's

home. ¹³The next day, we plan our next move: my parents, sisters, and one brother stay there, but the remaining sixteen of us head East on I-10 towards Memphis, Tennessee, to the home of Stanley Trotter, my ex-wife's cousin, where there were now 20 people sharing a house.

¹⁴As the sixteen of us from New Orleans sit and watch television, we see the water begin to cover the roof of the familiar Circle Food Store, on North Clayborne Avenue and St. Bernard Avenue near the home we just abandoned; we realize now, we will not be returning home.

¹⁵It is extremely difficult for anyone watching the news, but it has to be most difficult for those of us witnessing everything we have worked for being destroyed right before our eyes; we have no idea what we should do or where we should go from here; we begin to mourn for friends and neighbors gone from our lives forever. ¹⁶We continue watching as the Super Dome and Convention Center prove to be inadequate for the more than three thousand people seeking shelter and assistance; we listen to the reports of water leaks and criminals raping people in the Dome; we watch the people standing along the bridge in the smoldering heat with no sanitation, no food, no water; we see dead people floating in the water; we see another person dead in a wheelchair—not even covered. ¹⁷"Why is help so slow to arrive?" we cry out at the television.

***

¹⁸My heart is truly heavy, and I can barely watch or believe what I am witnessing on television. ¹⁹During this time, I think of my brother and his adult son, Robert Jr., both of whom remained in New Orleans when we left: I pray to God they survive—not knowing until days later that they have located a car and driven to Alexandria to be with my parents and other siblings; I pray to God they survive—not knowing that they have returned to help the people and the clean-up efforts in the areas hit hardest by Katrina and the tornadoes that followed.

***

²⁰My mind drifts in time back to my uncles' and aunts' homes in Picayune, Mississippi, less than an hour's drive from New Orleans, and I think about all of my relatives living there: my cousins, my grandmothers, and paternal grandfather—I contemplate memories of Pilgrim Bound Baptist Church and other churches as the neighborhood readies for the 5th Sunday Singing. ²¹Every fifth Sunday, all the churches in the area gather as members from the various congregations hope for an opportunity to be placed on the program to sing two selections each. ²²Reverend Woods, the announcer, is always filled with the Holy Spirit as he listens to the lyrics of songs and hymns both old and new: "What a Friend We Have

in Jesus," "Amazing Grace," "Do Lord Remember Me," and "Jesus Paid It All." [23]My father, brothers, and I would often travel to participate in the program as an all-male guest quartet from New Orleans, LA.

[24]Oh, I will never forget those days—they remain an inspiring part of my life because I had an opportunity to meet many people; some I had forgotten until now: Mrs. Jewel had a candy store next door to where my grandmother, aunt, and uncle lived; only a few blocks away, Bossie Boys, a place where teenagers would meet and dance on the weekends, was located just a few feet from my Uncle Bishop's barber shop.

***

[25]In the wake of Katrina, we move to Atoka, Tennessee, and it does not take long for people to hear about the sixteen people who fled New Orleans. [26]I shall never forget—Mrs. Snead of St. Mark Baptist Church and Pastor McGee alert church members, the fire department, and other social agencies about our **plight**; church members help us get food and clothing and raise money so that we can begin reestablishing ourselves; through the Red Cross, we are able to obtain proper documentation for identification. [27]No, I shall never forget—all the blessings that flowed from throughout the community to my family during these darkest hours.

[28]Finally people are allowed to return briefly to New Orleans to check out their property and help others during the aftermath of Katrina—I am anxious. [29]My son-in-law Javelle and I rent a van to go back and salvage what we can. [30]On the way, a police cruiser clocks my speed on the highway at 89 mph in a 70 mph zone; I tell the officer who I am, where I am going and why I am going there; he makes me prove that I have lived in New Orleans all of my life; then, he voids my ticket with a warning to slow down. [31]How ironic—I have to prove that I am a "real" life-long New Orleans "native."

[32]Getting off of Highway 610 at Franklin Avenue, we can see the marks of high water levels, and so much trash—garbage and debris strewn everywhere—we see the damage, the loss, and oh so much more—we see a holocaust: we see wind damage; we see cars flipped on their sides; we see homes with nothing more than a frame of what once was; we see X's marked on still-standing homes, with a number 1, 2, 3, or more to indicate the dead inside.

[33]When you have a near death experience, it is said, your life flashes before you. [34]That is exactly my experience during Katrina. [35]Burdens are heavy, I cannot sleep, and I worry about my family; days pass, and I know the end of my life is near: I now realize that it is the end of my life as I have known it—as I walk in what was once my parent's home on Clouet

Street. ³⁶I see just how high the water had come, and there, I raise my hands to lift several pictures off the wall.

Vocabulary _____c_____ **1.** The best meaning of the word **aghast** as used in sentence 1 is
a. excited.   c. horrified.
b. puzzled.   d. unaffected.

Vocabulary _____b_____ **2.** The best meaning of the word **plight** as used in sentence 26 is
a. promise.   c. situation.
b. troubles.   d. hope.

Implied _____b_____ **3.** Which sentence best states the author's implied central idea?
Central Idea
a. Hurricane Katrina destroyed Alfred C. Cooley's home in New Orleans.
b. Hurricane Katrina dramatically and unexpectedly changed the lives of Alfred C. Cooley, his family, and other victims of the storm.
c. Alfred C. Cooley and his family suffered more than most who lived through Hurricane Katrina.
d. The people of New Orleans did not receive adequate help during Hurricane Katrina.

Main Idea, _____c_____ **4.** Sentence 3 states a
Supporting Details
a. main idea.   c. minor supporting detail.
b. major supporting detail.

Thought _____d_____ **5.** What is the overall thought pattern of the passage?
Patterns
a. cause and effect   c. generalization and example
b. classification   d. time order

Transitions _____c_____ **6.** What is the primary relationship of ideas within sentence 7?
a. cause and effect   c. generalization and example
b. classification   d. time order

Purpose _____b_____ **7.** The overall purpose of the passage is
a. to entertain the reader with a personal story about living through Hurricane Katrina.
b. to inform the reader about the suffering caused by Hurricane Katrina.
c. to persuade the reader to give aid to the survivors of Hurricane Katrina.

Tone _____a_____ **8.** The tone of sentence 31 is
         a. sarcastic.   c. angry.
         b. amused.   d. neutral.

Fact and _____c_____ **9.** Overall, the passage uses
Opinion   a. fact.   c. fact and opinion.
         b. opinion.

Argument _____a_____ **10.** Sentence 34 states a
         a. claim.   b. support for a claim.

TEST 2

A Look at Man through The Vapid Eyes
of His Captives

10.1 GE/773 words   ***by Pierre Tristam***

[1]Disturbingly recent exceptions aside, civilized nations now agree that burning fellow human beings at the stake, torturing them or enslaving them is inhuman. [2]The day will come when civilized nations will agree that imprisoning wild animals in zoos, whipping them about in circus acts from city to city or forcing them to do tricks for our amusement in such places as SeaWorld, Marineland and Epcot is as cruel to the animals as it is lewd of the people watching them.

[3]That day is far off, no doubt.[4] Pulling profits and emoting power over weaker creatures, vicariously enjoyed by those audiences that delight in the safe splashing of a killer whale or the harmlessness of a caged animal, are strong impulses. [5]Too strong to be outdone by notions of rights for beasts that don't speak English or pay taxes.

[6]Until then, handlers of animals forced into unnatural situations will continue to die, as SeaWorld's Dawn Brancheau did in February when a killer whale dragged her underwater after turning the tables and making her its plaything. [7]I keep reading references to Brancheau's death as "tragic." [8]What lazy news writers mean is that her death was sad, unfortunate, avoidable and, from the spectators' (but not the whale's) perspective, **lurid**, as it was for SeaWorld's PR.

[9]Brancheau's death was foretold. [10]Besides practicing drills by coaching their prisoners to follow a script, trainers like her practice not getting killed for a reason. [11]They presume at every moment to outwit a predator's instincts. [12]They can't outwit the law of averages. [13]For a brief moment, the whale that killed Brancheau went off script. [14]It acted in character. [15]Mauling her might have been the most natural thing the whale had done in years. [16]If it's an education spectators wanted, they finally got an authentic one.

[17]I don't mind the work with animals of people like the late Steve Irwin, the Australian of "Crocodile Hunter" fame killed by a stingray in 2006. [18]Irwin had his moments of cruelty when he wanted to prove that he could best a beast bigger, bitier or faster than him. [19]But mostly he worked on the animals' turf, on their terms. [20]He did not rearrange their nature for our amusement. [21]He risked his life to show us how wild these animals are, and how freely noble and untamable they should remain.

[22]This isn't to argue against domestication or even the slaughtering of animals. [23]We are animals and predators. [24]But domesticating an animal for help or companionship and certainly killing an animal for sustenance will always be more morally defensible than taming one for entertainment or "education." ([25]The less defensible gobs of cruelty in the chicken farms and the feedlots of the West, where cattle are turned into walking mummies of drugs and fat, have more to do with a nation's gluttony than sustenance. [26]But that's another story.)

[27]Places like SeaWorld love to claim that their shows give people a close-up of something unique that fosters an appreciation for nature and conservation. [28]Florida residents give the lie to that invention. [29]They've been converging on SeaWorld from subdivisions that have plowed under entire ecosystems and obliterated the habitats of 111 plants and animals (at last count). [30]That's not about to change.

[31]"The sensational Shamu show" itself plows under the killer whales' natural instincts to make them fit human **conceits**. [32]It doesn't honor the killer whales or their place in nature, since that place is nowhere at SeaWorld, so much as it pumps up man's capacity to synchronize dives, sentimental music and greeting-card philosophy with 5-ton creatures.

[33]The show, called "Believe," is motivational splashing. [34]And in an age when entire cable channels and other media by the ant pile are devoted to natural science, there's no justification anymore for amusement-park animal exploitation. [35]A minute's worth of a nature show like "Planet Earth," even on a television screen—which takes the viewer to untold places with an intimacy and humility that really does put humans'

insignificance in perspective—does more to inspire reverence for nature as it really is than any Shamu schmoozing that mostly warms up your gift shop's cockles.

[36]As for zoos, I've visited some of the great ones in the country. [37]I've also walked the wards of several jails and prisons, including death row in Nashville, Tenn. [38]In both places I saw the identical shuffling lethargy and vapid look of captivity. [39]Criminals are presumably imprisoned as a result of their own misdeeds. [40]Animals aren't. [41]The crime of their captivity, reflected in their eyes, is ours every time we visit a zoo or clap like dopes at a mud-wrestling show whenever Shamu flips. [42]Forget Willie. [43]Free them all.

> —"A Look at Man Through The Vapid Eyes of His Captives" by Pierre Tristam from *The Daytona Beach News-Journal*, March 7, 2010, p. 10A. Reprinted by permission of Copyright Clearance Center.

VISUAL VOCABULARY

The natural ecosystem has been obliterated in preparation for development.

The best meaning of **obliterated** is ___c___.

a. overlooked.
b. restored.
c. destroyed.

Vocabulary ___a___ **1.** The best meaning of the word **lurid** as used in sentence 8 is
    a. shocking.   c. exciting.
    b. colorful.   d. expected.

Vocabulary ___a___ **2.** The best meaning of the word **conceits** as used in sentence 31 is
    a. prideful ideas.   c. instincts.
    b. humility.   d. sense of adventure.

Central Idea ___b___ **3.** Which sentence best states the author's central idea?
    a. sentence 1   c. sentence 5
    b. sentence 2   d. sentence 33

Supporting _____c_____ **4.** Sentence 18 states a
Details
       a. main idea.   c. minor supporting detail.
       b. major supporting detail.

Thought _____d_____ **5.** What is the overall thought pattern of the passage?
Patterns
       a. time order   c. cause and effect
       b. classification   d. generalization and example

Purpose _____c_____ **6.** The overall purpose of the passage is
       a. to entertain the reader with details about human treatment of captive animals.
       b. to inform the reader about the problems associated with keeping wild animals captive for entertainment or educational purposes.
       c. to argue against keeping wild animals captive for human entertainment or educational purposes.

Tone _____b_____ **7.** The overall tone of the passage is
       a. neutral.   c. sad.
       b. biting.   d. reasonable.

Fact and _____b_____ **8.** Sentences 3 and 4 (paragraph 2) are statements of
Opinion
       a. fact.   c. fact and opinion.
       b. opinion.

Argument _____d_____ **9.** In sentence 8, the author uses the propaganda technique of
       a. false cause.   c. false analogy.
       b. straw man.   d. personal attack.

Argument _____c_____ **10.** In paragraph 10 (sentences 36–43), the author uses the propaganda technique of
       a. false cause.   c. false analogy.
       b. straw man.   d. personal attack.

TEST 3

Read the following passage, and then, answer the questions.

11.5 GE/251 words   **What Risks Are Involved in Tattooing?**

    [1]Despite the obvious popularity of body art, several complications can result from tattooing.

²Tattooing can cause infections. ³Unsterile tattooing equipment and needles can transmit infectious diseases, such as hepatitis; thus the American Association of Blood Banks requires a one-year wait between getting a tattoo and donating blood. ⁴Even if the needles are sterilized or never have been used, the equipment that holds the needles may not be sterilized reliably due to its design. ⁵In addition, a tattoo must be cared for properly during the first week or so after the **pigments** are injected.

⁶Tattooing involves removal problems. ⁷Despite advances in laser technology, removing a tattoo is a painstaking process, usually involving several treatments and considerable expense. ⁸Complete removal without scarring may be impossible.

⁹Although allergic reactions to tattoo pigments are rare, when they happen they may be particularly troublesome because the pigments can be hard to remove. ¹⁰Occasionally, people may develop an allergic reaction to tattoos they have had for years.

¹¹Tattoos may also result in granulomas and keloids. ¹²Granulomas are nodules that may form around material that the body perceives as foreign, such as particles of tattoo pigment. ¹³If you are prone to developing keloids—scars that grow beyond normal boundaries—you are at risk of keloid formation from a tattoo. ¹⁴Keloids may form any time you injure or traumatize your skin. ¹⁵According to experts, tattooing or micropigmentation is a form of trauma, and keloids occur more frequently as a consequence of tattoo removal.

—Adapted from "Tattoos and Permanent Makeup." U.S. Food and Drug Administration Center for Food Safety and Applied Nutrition Office of Cosmetics and Colors Fact Sheet. 29 November 2000; Updated 14 July 2006. Online 8 July 2004. http://www.cfsan.fda.gov/~dms/cos-204.html

Vocabulary _____c_____ **1.** The best meaning of the word **pigments** as used in sentence 5 is
a. infections.   c. dyes.
b. protections.   d. skin.

Central Idea _____a_____ **2.** The sentence that best states the central idea of the passage is
a. sentence 1.   c. sentence 5.
b. sentence 2.   d. sentence 12.

Transitions _____a_____ **3.** The relationship between sentences 11 and 12 is one of
a. definition.   c. time order.
b. cause and effect.   d. addition.

Transitions _____b_____ **4.** The relationship of the ideas within sentence 3 is
a. definition.   c. time order.
b. cause and effect.   d. comparison and contrast.

Thought
Patterns _____ b _____

5. What is the overall thought pattern of the passage?
  a. comparison and contrast   c. time order
  b. cause and effect   d. definition

Supporting
Details _____ a _____

6. Sentence 6 is a
  a. main idea.
  b. major supporting detail.
  c. minor supporting detail.

Purpose _____ a _____

7. The author's main purpose in the passage is
  a. to inform.
  b. to entertain.
  c. to persuade.

Tone _____ c _____

8. The tone of the passage is
  a. graphic.   c. objective.
  b. judgmental.   d. pessimistic.

9–10. Complete the outline below with information from the passage.

Central idea: Several complications can result from tattooing.

  I. Tattooing can cause infections.

  II. Tattooing involves removal problems.

  III. Tattooing may cause allergic reactions.

  IV. Tattooing may result in granulomas and keloids.

TEST 4

Read the passage from a history textbook, and then, answer the questions.

12.4 GE/217 words

**Textbook
Skills**

The Stewardship of Natural Resources History:
Mapping Puget Sound and Western Washington

¹Nestled between two dramatic mountain ranges, the Olympics and the Cascades, the lush and mild Puget Sound region provided abundant natural resources for fishing, timbering, and farming for Native Americans for thousands of years before the arrival of British Captain George Vancouver and Lieutenant Peter Puget in 1792. ²Seattle grew in the twentieth century as

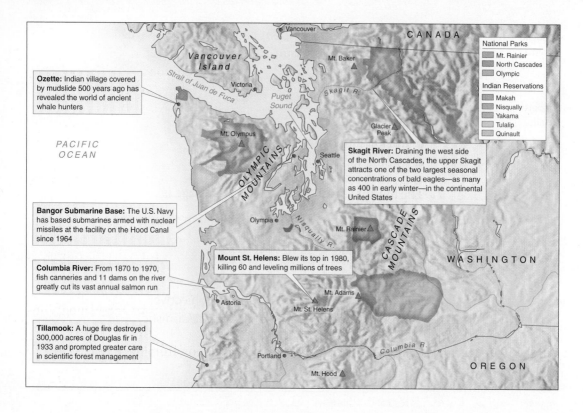

Map labels and callouts:

National Parks
- Mt. Rainier
- North Cascades
- Olympic

Indian Reservations
- Makah
- Nisqually
- Yakama
- Tulalip
- Quinault

Ozette: Indian village covered by mudslide 500 years ago has revealed the world of ancient whale hunters

Skagit River: Draining the west side of the North Cascades, the upper Skagit attracts one of the two largest seasonal concentrations of bald eagles—as many as 400 in early winter—in the continental United States

Bangor Submarine Base: The U.S. Navy has based submarines armed with nuclear missiles at the facility on the Hood Canal since 1964

Columbia River: From 1870 to 1970, fish canneries and 11 dams on the river greatly cut its vast annual salmon run

Mount St. Helens: Blew its top in 1980, killing 60 and leveling millions of trees

Tillamook: A huge fire destroyed 300,000 acres of Douglas fir in 1933 and prompted greater care in scientific forest management

CANADA — Vancouver — Vancouver Island — Mt. Baker — Strait of Juan de Fuca — Victoria — Puget Sound — Skagit R. — Glacier Peak — PACIFIC OCEAN — Mt. Olympus — OLYMPIC MOUNTAINS — Seattle — Olympia — Nisqually R. — Mt. Rainier — CASCADE MOUNTAINS — WASHINGTON — Astoria — Mt. Adams — Mt. St. Helens — Columbia R. — Portland — Mt. Hood — OREGON

a trading port, particularly with east Asian markets, and as the original aircraft manufacturing site of Boeing Corporation. [3]With the permanently snow-capped volcanic peaks of the Cascade range visible on clear days, Seattle continued to attract new residents and tourists alike. [4]The population of the former frontier state of Washington nearly doubled from 1970 to 2003, topping 6 million.

[5]Seattle was also the departure point for most Americans traveling north to Alaska. [6]Passenger ferries crisscrossed Puget Sound, providing an alternative method of commuting to work in Seattle for residents of other area communities. [7]In the 1980s the city became associated with the extraordinary business success of computer software giant Microsoft and coffee retailer Starbucks. [8]Recreation Equipment Incorporated (REI) began in Seattle as a consumer **cooperative** for buying products for outdoor activities such as rock-climbing and backpacking. [9]By 2000 REI had built stores across the United States.

—From *Created Equal: A Social and Political History of the United States, Volume II (from 1865)*, 2nd ed., p. 1019 by Jacqueline Jones, Peter H. Wood, Thomas Borstelmann, Elaine Tyler May, Vicki L. Ruiz. Copyright ©2006 by Pearson Education, Inc. Printed and Electronically reproduced by permission of Pearson Education, Inc., Upper Saddle River, NJ.

Vocabulary ___c___ **1.** The best meaning of the word **stewardship** in the title is
   a. duty.   c. management.
   b. need.   d. benefit.

Vocabulary ___c___ **2.** The best meaning of the word **cooperative** as used in sentence 8 is
   a. helper.   c. company.
   b. companion.   d. product.

Implied ___d___ **3.** Based on the title and the details, which sentence best states the
Main Idea   implied main idea of the passage?
   a. The Puget Sound region is a beautiful area that needs no stewardship.
   b. Stewardship is needed because commerce and development are harming the Puget Sound region.
   c. Under the stewardship of Native Americans, the Puget Sound region provided abundant natural resources for fishing, timbering, and farming.
   d. The natural environment of the Seattle area has greatly influenced the economic development of the area.

Thought ___a___ **4.** The main thought pattern of the passage is
Patterns   a. time order.   c. classification.
   b. cause and effect.   d. listing.

Tone ___b___ **5.** The tone of the passage is
   a. admiring.   c. critical.
   b. neutral.   d. persuasive.

Answer the following questions based on information in the map.

Supporting ___d___ **6.** Based on the map, where does the vast salmon run occur?
Details   a. Skagit River   c. Tillamook
   b. Puget Sound   d. Columbia River

Supporting ___c___ **7.** Based on the map, how many Indian reservations are in the region?
Details   a. two   c. five
   b. three   d. six

Purpose ___a___ **8.** The purpose of the map is
   a. to inform the reader about various historical resources, facts, and traits of the region.

     b. to persuade the reader that, historically, human activity has harmed the natural resources of the region.

     c. to entertain the reader with little known historical facts about the region.

Inference   __b__ **9.** Based on the information in the map, we can infer that

     a. the salmon run is more vast than it once was.

     b. Mount St. Helens is an active volcano.

     c. the fire at Tillamook was started by human activity.

     d. the Bangor Submarine Base has a nuclear power plant.

Argument   __d__ **10.** *Claim*: The Puget Sound region is rich in natural resources.

     Which of the following statements is not relevant to the claim?

     a. An Indian village covered by mudslide 500 years ago has revealed the world of ancient whale hunters.

     b. The U.S. Navy has based submarines with nuclear missiles at the facility on the Hood Canal since 1964.

     c. The upper Skagit attracts one of the two largest seasonal concentrations of bald eagles—as many as 400 in early winter—in the continental United States.

     d. Native Americans live on reservations that are smaller in size than the three national parks in the region.

TEST 5

Read the following passage, and then, answer the questions.

10.2 GE/360 words   **Medgar Evers**

    1Medgar Evers was one of the first martyrs of the civil-rights movement. **2**He was born in 1925 in Decatur, Mississippi, to James and Jessie Evers. **3**After a short stint in the army, he enrolled in Alcorn A&M College, graduating in 1952. **4**His first job out of college was traveling around rural Mississippi selling insurance. **5**He soon grew enraged at the **despicable** conditions of poor black families in his state, and joined the NAACP. **6**In 1954, he was appointed Mississippi's first field secretary.

    7Evers was outspoken, and his demands were radical for his rigidly segregated state. **8**He fought for the enforcement of the 1954 court decision of *Brown* v. *Board of Education of Topeka,* which outlawed school segregation;

he fought for the right to vote, and he advocated boycotting merchants who discriminated. [9]He worked unceasingly despite the threats of violence that his speeches **engendered**. [10]He gave much of himself to this struggle, and in 1963, he gave his life. [11]On June 13, 1963, he drove home from a meeting, stepped out of his car, and was shot in the back.

[12]Immediately after Evers's death, the shotgun that was used to kill him was found in bushes nearby, with the owner's fingerprints still fresh. [13]Byron de la Beckwith, a vocal member of a local white-supremacist group, was arrested. [14]Despite the evidence against him, which included an earlier statement that he wanted to kill Evers, two trials with all-white juries ended in deadlock decisions, and Beckwith walked free. [15]Twenty years later, in 1989, information surfaced that suggested the jury in both trials had been tampered with. [16]The assistant District Attorney, with the help of Evers's widow, began putting together a new case. [17]On February 5, 1994, a multiracial jury re-tried Beckwith and found him guilty of the crime.

[18]The loss of Evers changed the tenor of the civil-rights struggle. [19]Anger replaced fear in the South, as hundreds of demonstrators marched in protest. [20]His death prompted President John Kennedy to ask Congress for a comprehensive civil-rights bill, which President Lyndon Johnson signed into law the following year. [21]Evers's death, as his life had, contributed much to the struggle for equality.

—"Medgar Evers" from *African American Almanac*, 7th ed. by Carney Smith and Chuck Stone. Belmont: Gale, a part of Cengage Learning, Inc., 1996.

Vocabulary ___a___ **1.** The synonym of the word **despicable** in sentence 5 is
    a. contemptible.   c. mean-spirited.
    b. obvious.   d. civilized.

Vocabulary ___c___ **2.** The best meaning of the word **engendered** as used in sentence 9 is
    a. performed.   c. provoked.
    b. gratified.   d. halted.

Main Idea, ___b___ **3.** Sentence 11 is
Details
    a. a main idea.   c. a minor supporting detail.
    b. a major supporting detail.

Central Idea ___a___ **4.** The central idea of the passage is best stated in sentence
    a. 1.   c. 5.
    b. 2.   d. 20.

Supporting Details   c   **5.** When did Medgar Evers become a martyr of the civil rights movement?

   a. 1952   c. 1963

   b. 1954   d. 1994

Transitions   a   **6.** What is the relationship of ideas between sentences 18 and 19?

   a. cause and effect   c. classification

   b. comparison and contrast   d. time order

Transitions   b   **7.** What is the relationship of ideas within sentence 14?

   a. cause   c. definition

   b. contrast   d. classification

Purpose   a   **8.** The author's main purpose is

   a. to inform the reader about the contributions Medgar Evers made to the civil rights movement.

   b. to inspire the reader with the story of a civil rights leader.

   c. to persuade the reader that Medgar Evers is a martyr.

Tone   b   **9.** The tone of the passage is

   a. detached.   c. cynical.

   b. admiring.   d. unbiased.

Fact and Opinion   c   **10.** Sentence 7 states

   a. a fact.   c. fact and opinion.

   b. an opinion.

TEST 6

Read the following passage from the college textbook *Psychology and Life*, and then, answer the questions.

Textbook Skills

11.6 GE/289 words   **Mnemonics**

¹One memory-enhancing option is to draw on special mental strategies called *mnemonics* (from the Greek word meaning "to remember"). ²**Mnemonics** are devices that **encode** a long series of facts by associating them with familiar and previously encoded information. ³Many mnemonics work by giving you ready-made retrieval cues that help organize otherwise **arbitrary** information.

⁴Consider the *method of loci*, first practiced by ancient Greek orators. ⁵The singular of *loci* is *locus*, and it means "place." ⁶The method of loci is a means of remembering the order of a list of names or objects—or, for the orators, the individual sections of a long speech—by associating them with some sequence of places with which you are familiar. ⁷To remember a grocery list, you might mentally put each item sequentially along the route you take to get from home to school and find the item associated with each spot.

⁸The *peg-word method* is similar to the method of loci, except that you associate the items on a list with a series of cues rather than with familiar locations. ⁹Typically, the cues for the peg-word method are a series of rhymes that associate numbers with words. ¹⁰For example, you might memorize "one is a *bun*," "two is a *shoe*," "three is a *tree*," and so on. ¹¹Then you would associate each item on your list interacting with the appropriate cue. ¹²For your grocery list, you might have the bread nestled among several buns, a shoe filled up with orange juice, a tree with ice cream cones rather than leaves, and so on. ¹³You can see that the key to learning arbitrary information is to encode the information in such a fashion that you provide yourself with efficient retrieval cues.

—From *Psychology and Life*, 16th ed., pp. 236–237 by Richard J. Gerrig and Philip G. Zimbardo. Copyright © 2002 by Pearson Education, Inc. Reproduced by permission of Pearson Education, Inc., Boston, MA.

Vocabulary ___d___ **1.** The best meaning of the term **encode** as used in sentence 2 is
a. approve.   c. unlock.
b. understand.   d. program.

Vocabulary ___c___ **2.** The best meaning of the word **arbitrary** as used in sentence 3 is
a. logical.   c. random.
b. long-term.   d. frivolous.

Main Idea, Details ___b___ **3.** Sentence 9 is
a. a main idea.   c. a minor supporting detail.
b. a major supporting detail.

Central Idea ___b___ **4.** Which sentence best states the central idea of the passage?
a. sentence 1   c. sentence 3
b. sentence 2   d. sentence 4

Transitions ___a___ **5.** What is the relationship of ideas within sentence 8?
a. comparison and contrast   c. cause and effect
b. addition   d. classification

Transitions   _a_   **6.** What is the relationship of ideas between sentences 6 and 7?
- a. definition and example
- c. cause and effect
- b. comparison and contrast
- d. time order

Purpose   _a_   **7.** The author's main purpose is
- a. to inform the reader about two mnemonic techniques.
- b. to entertain the reader with ways to remember information.
- c. to persuade the reader to improve memory skills.

Tone   _d_   **8.** The tone of the passage is
- a. bored.
- c. subjective.
- b. challenging.
- d. objective.

Fact and Opinion   _a_   **9.** Overall, the details of this passage are
- a. fact.
- c. fact and opinion.
- b. opinion.

10. Complete the summary with information from the passage.

Mnemonics are mental strategies that encode facts by associating them with familiar and previously encoded information, such as the

method of loci and peg-word method.

TEST 7

Read the following excerpt from the speech President Bush delivered to honor novelist Harper Lee with the nation's highest award. Answer the questions.

10.1 GE/397 words

Harper Lee and the Presidential Medal of Freedom

[1]"Harper Lee has made an outstanding contribution to America's literary tradition. [2]At a critical moment in our history, her beautiful book, *To Kill a Mockingbird*, helped focus the Nation on the turbulent struggle for equality."

—The text of Harper Lee's citation for the Presidential Medal of Freedom presented by President Bush on November 5, 2007.

President Bush: [3]"The story of an old order, and the glimmers of humanity that would one day overtake it, was unforgettably told in a book by Miss Harper Lee. [4]Soon after its publication a reviewer said this: 'A hundred pounds of sermons on tolerance, or an equal measure of **invective** deploring the lack of it, will weigh far less in the scale of enlightenment than a mere 18 ounces of a new fiction bearing the title *To Kill a Mockingbird*.'

⁵"Given her legendary **stature** as a novelist, you may be surprised to learn that Harper Lee, early in her career, was an airline reservation clerk. ⁶Fortunately for all of us, she didn't stick to writing itineraries. ⁷Her beautiful book, with its grateful prose and memorable characters, became one of the biggest-selling novels of the 20th century.

⁸"Forty-six years after winning the Pulitzer Prize, *To Kill a Mockingbird* still touches and inspires every reader. ⁹We're moved by the story of a man falsely accused—with old prejudice massed against him, and an old sense of honor that rises to his defense. ¹⁰We learn that courage can be a solitary business. ¹¹As the lawyer Atticus Finch tells his daughter, 'before I can live with other folks I've got to live with myself. ¹²The one thing that doesn't abide by majority rule is a person's conscience.'

¹³"One reason *To Kill a Mockingbird* succeeded is the wise and kind heart of the author, which comes through on every page. ¹⁴This daughter of Monroeville, Alabama had something to say about honor, and tolerance, and, most of all, love—and it still resonates. ¹⁵Last year Harper Lee received an honorary doctorate at Notre Dame. ¹⁶As the degree was presented, the graduating class rose as one, held up copies of her book, and cheered for the author they love.

¹⁷"*To Kill a Mockingbird* has influenced the character of our country for the better. ¹⁸It's been a gift to the entire world. ¹⁹As a model of good writing and humane sensibility, this book will be read and studied forever. ²⁰And so all of us are filled with admiration for a great American and a lovely lady named Harper Lee."

"President Bush Honors Medal of Freedom Recipients."
Office of the Press Secretary. 5 Nov. 2007.
http://www.whitehouse.gov/news/releases/2007/11/20071105-1.html.

Vocabulary _____a_____ **1.** The best meaning of the word **invective** in sentence 4 is
a. criticism.   c. wisdom.
b. support.   d. emotion.

Vocabulary _____b_____ **2.** The best meaning of the word **stature** as used in sentence 5 is
a. height.   c. weight.
b. status.   d. acceptance.

Central Idea _____a_____ **3.** Which sentence best states the central idea of the passage?
a. sentence 1   c. sentence 8
b. sentence 3   d. sentence 20

Thought Patterns   <u>d</u>   **4.** The overall thought pattern used in the passage is

       a. time.
       c. cause and effect.

       b. listing.
       d. generalization and example.

Transitions   <u>d</u>   **5.** The relationship of ideas between sentence 10 and sentence 11 is

       a. time.
       c. cause and effect.

       b. listing.
       d. generalization and example.

Fact and Opinion   <u>c</u>   **6.** Sentence 2 is a statement of

       a. fact.
       c. fact and opinion.

       b. opinion.

Purpose   <u>a</u>   **7.** The main purpose of the passage is

       a. to inspire the reader to learn more about Harper Lee and read her novel *To Kill a Mockingbird*.

       b. to entertain the audience by honoring the popular novelist, Harper Lee.

       c. to inform the audience about and praise Harper Lee for her literary contribution: *To Kill a Mockingbird*.

8–10. Complete the summary based on information from the passage.

On November 5, 2007, President Bush awarded novelist Harper Lee the Presidential Medal of Freedom for her (8) "<u>beautiful</u> book" *To Kill a Mockingbird*. The Pulitzer Prize-winning novel is "about a man falsely accused—with old (9) <u>prejudice</u> massed against him, and an old sense of (10) <u>honor</u> that rises to his defense."

TEST 8

Read the following passage from the college textbook *Educational Psychology*, and then, answer the questions.

Textbook Skills

11.6 GE/241 words   **Sources of Misunderstandings**

¹Some children are simply better than others at reading the classroom situation because the participation structures of the school match the structures they have learned at home. ²The communication rules for

most school situations are similar to those in middle-class homes, so children from these homes often appear to be more **competent** communicators. ³They know the unwritten rules. ⁴Students from different cultural backgrounds may have learned participation structures that conflict with the behaviors expected in school. ⁵For example, one study found that the home conversation style of Hawaiian children is to chime in with contributions to a story. ⁶In school, however, this overlapping style is seen as "interrupting." ⁷When the teachers in one school learned about these differences and made their reading groups more like their students' home conversation groups, the young Hawaiian children in their classes improved in reading.

⁸The source of misunderstanding can be a subtle sociolinguistic difference, such as how long the teacher waits to react to a student's response. ⁹Researchers White and Tharp (1988) found that when Navajo students in one class paused in giving a response, their Anglo teacher seemed to think that they were finished speaking. ¹⁰As a result, the teacher often unintentionally interrupted students. ¹¹In another study, researchers found that Pueblo Indian students participated twice as much in classes where teachers waited longer to react. ¹²Waiting longer also helps girls to participate more freely in math and science classes.

—From *Educational Psychology*, 8th ed., p. 188 by Anita E. Woolfolk.
Copyright © 2001 by Pearson Education, Inc. Reproduced by
permission of Pearson Education, Inc., Boston, MA.

Vocabulary ___b___ **1.** The best meaning of the word **competent** in sentence 2 is
    a. inept.   c. thoughtful.
    b. proficient.   d. confident.

Thought Patterns ___b___ **2.** The thought pattern suggested by the organization of sentences 8 through 12 is
    a. time.   c. comparison and contrast.
    b. cause and effect.   d. definition.

Supporting Details ___b___ **3.** Sentence 12 is
    a. a major supporting detail.   b. a minor supporting detail.

Central Idea ___a___ **4.** The central idea of the passage is best stated in sentence
    a. Sentence 1.   c. Sentence 4.
    b. Sentence 2.   d. Sentence 8.

Transitions ___a___ **5.** The relationship of ideas within sentence 2 is one of
a. cause and effect.   c. time order.
b. comparison and contrast.

Purpose ___a___ **6.** The author's main purpose is
a. to inform.   c. to entertain.
b. to persuade.

Fact and ___c___ **7.** Sentence 1 is a statement of
Opinion
a. fact.   c. fact and opinion.
b. opinion.

8–10. Complete the summary with ideas from the passage.

Communication ___rules___ learned at home impact the student's ability to effectively ___communicate___ in the classroom. Rules for participating in schools are similar to the communication rules in middle-class homes; thus students from different ___cultural___ backgrounds may be misunderstood. For example, rules about contributing to the discussion and the length of pauses in response differ among cultures and can be misunderstood in a classroom situation.

TEST 9

Read the following passage from the college textbook *Life on Earth,* and then, answer the questions.

Textbook
Skills

11.3 GE/378 words   **How Is Life on Land Distributed?**

¹On land, the crucial limiting factors are temperature and liquid water. ²A **biome** comprises regions that have similar climates and vegetation owing to the interaction of temperature and rainfall or the availability of water. ³Tropical forest biomes, located near the equator, vary in the amount of rainfall they receive. ⁴Tropical deciduous forests occur in drier climates and contain deciduous trees that lose their leaves seasonally, typically in the driest months. ⁵Tropical rain forests occur where rainfall is

plentiful and are dominated by huge broadleaf evergreen trees. ⁶In rain forests, most nutrients are tied up in vegetation, and most animal life is arboreal. ⁷Rain forests, home to at least 50% of all species, are rapidly being cut for agriculture, although the soil is extremely poor. ⁸The African savanna, a grassland studded with scattered trees, has pronounced wet and dry seasons. ⁹It is home to the world's most diverse and extensive herds of large mammals.

¹⁰Most deserts are located between 20° and 30° north and south latitude or in the rain shadows of mountain ranges. ¹¹In deserts, plants are often widely spaced and have adaptations to conserve water. ¹²Most animals are small and nocturnal. ¹³Chaparral exists in desert-like conditions that are moderated by proximity to a coastline, allowing small trees and bushes to thrive. ¹⁴Grasslands, concentrated in the centers of continents, have a continuous grass cover without trees. ¹⁵They have the world's richest soils and have largely been converted to agriculture. ¹⁶Temperate deciduous forests, whose broadleaf trees drop their leaves in winter to conserve moisture, dominate the eastern half of the United States and are also found in Western Europe and East Asia. ¹⁷Precipitation is higher than in grasslands. ¹⁸The wet temperate rain forests, dominated by evergreens, are on the northern Pacific Coast of the United States. ¹⁹The taiga, or northern coniferous forest, covers much of the northern United States, southern Canada, and northern Eurasia. ²⁰It is dominated by conifers whose small, waxy needles are adapted for water conservation and year-round photosynthesis. ²¹The tundra is a frozen desert where permafrost prevents the growth of trees, and bushes remain stunted. ²²Nonetheless, diverse arrays of animal life and perennial plants flourish in this fragile biome, which is found on mountain peaks and in the Arctic.

—From *Life on Earth*, 5th ed., pp. 621–622 by Teresa Audesirk, Gerald Audesirk, and Bruce E. Byers. Copyright © 2009 by Pearson Education, Inc. Printed and Electronically reproduced by permission of Pearson Education, Inc., Upper Saddle River, NJ.

Vocabulary   b   **1.** The best meaning of the word **biome** in the passage is
- a. living organism.
- b. environment.
- c. temperature.
- d. vegetation.

Transitions   d   **2.** The relationship of ideas within sentence 10 is one of
- a. time order.
- b. comparison and contrast.
- c. cause and effect.
- d. space order.

Supporting Details   a   **3.** Sentence 4 is
- a. a major supporting detail.
- b. a minor supporting detail.

Supporting Details   <u>a</u>   **4.** Sentence 8 is

         a. a major supporting detail.   b. a minor supporting detail.

Central Idea   <u>b</u>   **5.** The best statement of the central idea is

         a. sentence 1.   c. sentence 3.

         b. sentence 2.   d. sentence 4.

6–10. Complete the outline with ideas from the passage.

Types of Biomes on Land

A. <u>Tropical Forests</u>

B. African <u>Savanna</u>

C. Deserts

D. <u>Chaparral</u>

E. Grasslands

F. <u>Temperate Deciduous Forests</u>

G. Taiga, Northern Coniferous Forest

H. <u>Tundra</u>

TEST 10

Read the following passage from the college textbook *Politics in America,* and then, answer the questions.

Textbook Skills

7.4 GE/98 words

[1]The United States is a nation of immigrants, from the first "boat people" (Pilgrims) to the latest Haitian refugees and Cuban *balseros* ("rafters"). [2]Historically, most of the people who came to settle in this country did so because they believed their lives would be better here, and American political culture today has been greatly affected by the beliefs and values they brought with them. [3]Americans are proud of their immigrant heritage and the freedom and opportunity the nation has extended to generations of "huddled masses yearning to be free"—words **emblazoned** on the Statue of Liberty in New York's harbor. [4]Today about 8 percent of the U.S. population is foreign-born.

⁵Immigration policy is a responsibility of the national government. ⁶It was not until 1882 that Congress passed the first legislation restricting entry into the United States of persons alleged to be "undesirable" and virtually all Asians. ⁷After World War I, Congress passed the comprehensive Immigration Act of 1921, which established maximum numbers of new immigrants each year and set a **quota** for immigrants for each foreign country at 3 percent of the number of that nation's foreign-born who were living in the United States in 1910, later reduced to 2 percent of the number living here in 1890. ⁸These restrictions reflected anti-immigration feelings that were generally directed at the large wave of Southern and Eastern European Catholic and Jewish immigrants (from Poland, Russia, Hungary, Italy, and Greece) entering the United States prior to World War I. ⁹It was not until the Immigration and Naturalization Act of 1965 that national origin quotas were abolished, replaced by preference categories for close relatives of U.S. citizens, professionals, and skilled workers.

—Dye, *Politics in America*, 5th ed., pp. 40–42.

Vocabulary ___b___ **1.** The best meaning of the word **emblazoned** in sentence 3 is
  a. shouted.
  b. inscribed.
  c. required.
  d. maintained.

Vocabulary ___b___ **2.** The best meaning of the word **quota** in sentence 7 is
  a. statement.
  b. allowance.
  c. price.
  d. expectation.

Thought Patterns ___b___ **3.** The overall thought pattern for the passage is
  a. the effects of immigration on the United States.
  b. the history of immigration in the United States.
  c. the differences between United States natural-born citizens and immigrants.
  d. the traits of an immigrant to the United States.

Supporting Details ___d___ **4.** Sentence 7 is a supporting detail that gives information about
  a. why people immigrate into the United States.
  b. the reasons for limiting immigration into the United States.
  c. an effect of immigration on the United States.
  d. the origin of an immigration law.

Central Idea ___a___   **5.** The best statement of the central idea of this passage is
        a. sentence 1.   c. sentence 5
        b. sentence 3.   d. sentence 8.

Transitions ___c___   **6.** The relationship of ideas between sentences 7 and 8 is one of
        a. listing.   c. cause and effect.
        b. comparison and contrast.   d. time order.

Purpose ___a___   **7.** The author's main purpose is
        a. to inform the reader about the nature and history of immigration into the United States.
        b. to amuse the reader with little known details about immigration into the United States.
        c. to defend the immigration policies of the United States.

Tone ___d___   **8.** The tone of the first paragraph is
        a. quarrelsome.   c. assertive.
        b. ironic.   d. positive.

Fact and Opinion ___c___   **9.** Sentence 3 is a statement of
        a. fact.   c. fact and opinion.
        b. opinion.

Inference ___b___   **10.** The best title for the passage is
        a. Restricting Immigration.
        b. A Nation of Immigrants.
        c. Quotas and Restrictions.
        d. The Lure of Freedom and Democracy.

Text Credits

Aaron, Jane E. *The Little, Brown Compact Handbook,* 4th ed. Copyright © 2001 by Pearson Education, Inc. Reprinted by permission of Pearson Education, Inc., Glenview, IL.

Agee, Warren K., Philip H. Ault, and Edwin Emery. "Types of Media" and "Trash TV" from *Introduction to Mass Communications,* 12th ed. Boston: Allyn and Bacon, 1997.

Angelou, Maya. "Fannie Lou Hamer" from *Letter to My Daughter.* Copyright © 2008 by Maya Angelou. Used by permission of Random House, Inc.

Annan, Kofi. "The Truman Library Speech," December 11, 2006, http://www.un.org/News/ossg/sg/stories/statments_full.asp?statID=40. Reprinted by permission of the United Nations.

Audesirk, Teresa, Gerald Audesirk, and Bruce E. Byers. *Biology: Life on Earth,* 8th ed. Copyright © 2008 by Pearson Education, Inc. Printed and Electronically reproduced by permission of Pearson Education, Inc., Upper Saddle River, NJ.

Audesirk, Teresa, Gerald Audesirk, and Bruce E. Byers. *Life on Earth,* 5th ed. Copyright © 2009 by Pearson Education, Inc. Printed and Electronically reproduced by permission of Pearson Education, Inc., Upper Saddle River, NJ.

Barker, Larry L., and Deborah Gaut. "Initiating" from *Communication,* 8th ed. Boston: Allyn & Bacon, 2002.

Baron, Robert A., and Donn Byrne. *Social Psychology with Research Navigator,* 10th ed. Copyright © 2004 by Allyn & Bacon, Inc. Reproduced by permission of Pearson Education, Inc., Boston, MA.

Benokraitis, Nijole V. *Marriages and Families: Changes, Choices, and Constraints,* 4th ed. Copyright © 2002 by Pearson Education, Inc. Reproduced by permission of Pearson Education, Inc., Boston, MA.

Bergman, Edward, and William H. Renwick. *Introduction to Geography: People, Places, and Environment,* 4th ed. Copyright © 2008 by Pearson Education, Inc. Printed and Electronically reproduced by permission of Pearson Education, Inc., Upper Saddle River, NJ.

Bittinger, Marvin L., and Judith A. Beecher. *Introductory and Intermediate Algebra: A Combined Approach,* 2nd ed. Copyright © 2003 by Pearson Education, Inc. Reproduced by permission of Pearson Education, Inc., Boston, MA.

Blake, Joan Salge. *Nutrition and You,* 1st ed. Copyright © 2008 by Pearson Education, Inc. Printed and Electronically reproduced by permission of Pearson Education, Inc., Upper Saddle River, NJ.

Bradley, John P., Leo F. Daniels, and Thomas C. Jones. *The International Dictionary of Thoughts: An Encyclopedia of Quotations from Every Age for Every Occasion.* Chicago: J. G. Ferguson Pub. Co., 1969.

Brownell, Judi. *Listening: Attitudes, Principles, and Skills,* 2nd ed. Copyright © 2002 by Pearson Education, Inc. Reproduced by permission of Pearson Education, Inc., Boston, MA.

Carl, John D. *Think Social Problems.* Copyright © 2011 by Pearson Education, Inc. Reproduced by permission of Pearson Education, Inc., Boston, MA.

Carlson, Neil R., and William Buskist. *Psychology: The Science of Behavior,* 5th ed. Boston: Allyn & Bacon, 1997.

Carson, Clayborne, Emma J. Lapsansky-Werner, and Gary B. Nash. "The Jazz Age" from *The Struggle for Freedom: A History of African-Americans, Volume II.* White Plains: Longman, 2007.

Churchill, Winston S. "The Price of Greatness." Copyright © Winston S. Churchill. Reproduced with permission of Curtis Brown Ltd, London on behalf of the Estate of Sir Winston Churchill.

"Coacoochee" from *The Ormond Beach Historical Trust.* Ormond Beach: The Ormond Beach Historical Trust, 1999.

Cook, Roy A., Laura J. Yale and Joseph J. Marqua. *Tourism: The Business of Travel,* 4th ed. Copyright © 2010 by Pearson Education, Inc. Printed and Electronically reproduced by permission of Pearson Education, Inc., Upper Saddle River, NJ.

Danny Yee's Book Reviews, August 1992, http://dannyreviews.com/h/Animal_Farm.html. Reprinted by permission of Danny Yee.

Danny Yee's Book Reviews, June 1998, http://dannyreviews.com/h/Beyond_Boundary.html. Reprinted by permission of Danny Yee.

DeVito, Joseph A. *Essentials of Human Communication,* 4th ed. Copyright © 2002 by Pearson Education, Inc. Reproduced by permission of Pearson Education, Inc., Boston, MA.

DeVito, Joseph A. *The Interpersonal Communication Book,* 10th ed. Copyright © 2004 by Pearson Education, Inc. Reproduced by permission of Pearson Education, Inc., Boston, MA.

DeVito, Joseph A. *The Interpersonal Communication Book,* 11th ed. Copyright © 2007 by Pearson Education, Inc. Reproduced by permission of Pearson Education, Inc., Boston, MA.

DeVito, Joseph A. *Messages: Building Interpersonal Communication Skills.* Copyright © 1999 by Pearson Education, Inc. Reproduced by permission of Pearson Education, Inc., Boston, MA.

DeVito, Joseph A. *Messages: Building Interpersonal Communication Skills,* 6th ed. Boston: Allyn & Bacon, 2005.

Divine, Robert A., George M. Fredrickson, R. Hal Williams, and T. H. Breen. *The American Story,* 1st ed. Copyright © 2002 by Pearson Education, Inc. Reprinted by permission of Pearson Education, Inc., Upper Saddle River, NJ.

Donatelle, Rebecca J., and Lorraine G. Davis. *Access to Health,* 7th ed. Copyright © 2002 by Pearson Education, Inc. Printed and Electronically reproduced by permission of Pearson Education, Inc., Upper Saddle River, NJ.

Donatelle, Rebecca. "Do Restaurants and Food Marketers Encourage Overeating?" from *Access to Health*, 11th ed., Green Edition. Copyright © 2010 by Pearson Education, Inc. Printed and Electronically reproduced by permission of Pearson Education, Inc., Upper Saddle River, NJ.

Donatelle, Rebecca J. "Eating Disorders" from *Health: The Basics*, 7th ed. Copyright © 2007 by Pearson Education, Inc. Printed and Electronically reproduced by permission of Pearson Education, Inc., Upper Saddle River, NJ.

Donatelle, Rebecca J. "Reinforcement" and "Caffeine Addiction" from *Health: The Basics*, 5th ed. Copyright © 2003 by Pearson Education, Inc. Printed and Electronically reproduced by permission of Pearson Education, Inc. Upper Saddle River, NJ.

Dye, Thomas R. *Politics in America, National Version*, 5th ed. Copyright © 2003 by Pearson Education, Inc. Reprinted by permission of Pearson Education, Inc., Glenview, IL.

Dye, Thomas R. *Politics in America*, 7th ed. Copyright © 2007 by Pearson Education, Inc. Reprinted by permission of Pearson Education, Inc., Glenview, IL.

Edgar, Robert R., Neil J. Hackett, George F. Jewsbury, Barbara S. Molony, and Matthew Gordon. "Cuba" and "The Iroquois of the Northeast Woodlands" from *Civilizations Past & Present, Combined Volume*, 12th ed. Copyright © 2008 by Pearson Education, Inc. Reprinted by permission of Pearson Education, Inc., Upper Saddle River, NJ.

Edwards, George C. III, Martin P. Wattenberg and Robert L. Lineberry. *Government in America: People, Politics, and Policy*, 5th ed., Brief Version. Copyright © 2000 by Pearson Education, Inc. Reprinted by permission of Pearson Education, Inc., Glenview, IL.

Eldin, Peter. *Jokes & Quotes for Speeches*. London: Ward Lock, Ltd., 1989.

Erdely, Sabrina Rubin. "Binge Drinking, A Campus Killer," *Reader's Digest*, November 1998. Reprinted by permission of author.

Faigley, Lester. *The Penguin Handbook*. White Plains: Longman, 2003.

Fernandez-Armesto, Felipe. *The World: A History, Combined Volume*, 2nd ed. Copyright © 2010 by Pearson Education, Inc. Reprinted by permission of Pearson Education, Inc., Upper Saddle River, NJ.

Folger, Joseph P., Marshall Scott Poole, and Richard K. Stutman. *Working through Conflict: Strategies for Relationships, Groups, and Organizations*, 4th ed. Boston: Allyn & Bacon, 2001.

Folkerts, Jean, and Stephen Lacy. *The Media in Your Life: An Introduction to Mass Communication*, 2nd ed. Boston: Allyn & Bacon, 2001.

Fowler, H. Ramsey, and Jane E. Aaron. *The Little, Brown Handbook*, 9th ed. Copyright © 2004 by Pearson Education, Inc. Reprinted by permission of Pearson Education, Inc., Glenview, IL.

Garraty, John A., and Mark A. Carnes. *The American Nation: A History of the United States to 1877, Volume I*, 10th ed. Copyright © 2000 by Pearson Education, Inc. Printed and Electronically reproduced by permission of Pearson Education, Inc., Upper Saddle River, NJ.

Gerrig, Richard J., and Phillip G. Zimbardo. *Psychology and Life*, 16th ed. Copyright © 2002 by Pearson Education, Inc. Reproduced by permission of Pearson Education, Inc., Boston, MA.

Gerrig, Richard J., and Philip G. Zimbardo. *Psychology and Life*, 19th ed. Copyright © 2010 by Pearson Education, Inc. Reproduced by permission of Pearson Education, Inc., Boston, MA.

Girdano, Daniel A., George S. Everly, Jr. and Dorothy E. Dusek. "Physical Effects of Modern Life" from *Controlling Stress and Tension*, 6th ed. Boston: Allyn & Bacon, 2001.

Griffin, Ricky W., and Ronald J. Ebert. *Business*, 8th ed. Copyright © 2006 by Pearson Education, Inc. Printed and Electronically reproduced by permission of Pearson Education, Inc., Upper Saddle River, NJ.

Harrell, Eben. "Think You're Operating on Free Will? Think Again" from *Time Magazine*, July 2, 2010. Copyright TIME INC. Reprinted by permission. TIME is a registered trademark of Time Inc. All rights reserved.

Harris, Marvin, and Oma Johnson. *Cultural Anthropology*, 7th ed. Copyright © 2007 by Pearson Education, Inc. Printed and Electronically reproduced by permission of Pearson Education, Inc., Upper Saddle River, NJ.

Henslin, James M. *Essentials of Sociology: A Down-to-Earth Approach*, 7th ed. Copyright © 2007 by Pearson Education, Inc. Reproduced by permission of Pearson Education, Inc., Boston, MA.

Henslin, James M. *Sociology: A Down-to-Earth Approach*, 9th ed. Copyright © 2008 by James Henslin. Reproduced by permission of Pearson Education, Inc., Boston, MA.

"Hidden Caffeine" by Ying Lou and Gia Kereselidze from USA TODAY, March 3, 2004. Reprinted by permission of USA Today.

Hughes, Langston. "I, Too" from *The Collected Poems of Langston Hughes* by Langston Hughes, edited by Arnold Rampersad with David Roessel, Associate Editor. Copyright © 1994 by the Estate of Langston Hughes. Used by permission of Alfred A. Knopf, a division of Random House, Inc.

"Introduction" from *The Cubist Paintings of Diego Maria Rivera*. http://www.nga.gov/exhibitions/2004/rivera/intro.shtm. Reproduced by permission of National Gallery of Art, Washington, D.C.

Jaffe, Michael L. *Understanding Parenting*, 2nd ed. Boston: Allyn & Bacon, 1997.

Jones, Jacqueline, Peter H. Wood, Thomas Borstelmann, Elaine Tyler May, and Vicki L. Ruiz. *Created Equal: A Social and Political History of the United States, Combined Volume*, 2nd ed. Copyright © 2006 by Pearson Education, Inc. Printed and Electronically reproduced by permission of Pearson Education, Inc., Upper Saddle River, NJ.

Jones, Jacqueline, C Peter H. Wood, Thomas Borstelmann, Elaine Tyler May, and Vicki L. Ruiz. *Created Equal: A Social and Political History of the United States, Volume II (From 1865)*, 2nd ed. Copyright © 2006 by Pearson Education, Inc. Printed and Electronically reproduced by permission of Pearson Education, Inc., Upper Saddle River, NJ.

Joyce, James. "On the Beach at Fontana" from *Oxford Book of Modern Verse* by W. B. Yeats. New York: Oxford University Press, 1936.

Karren, Keith J., *Mind/Body Health: The Effects of Attitudes, Emotions, and Relationships*, 2nd ed. Copyright © 2002 by Pearson Education, Inc. Reprinted by permission of Pearson Education, Inc., Upper Saddle River, NJ.

Kennedy, X. J., and Dana Gioia. *Literature: An Introduction to Fiction, Poetry, and Drama*, 8th ed. Copyright © 2002 by Pearson Education, Inc. Reprinted by permission of Pearson Education, Inc., Glenview, IL.

Kennedy, X. J., and Dana Gioia. "Blues" from *Literature: An Introduction to Fiction, Poetry, and Drama*, 3rd Compact ed.. Copyright © 2003 by Pearson Education, Inc. Reprinted by permission of Pearson Education, Inc., Glenview, IL.

Kennedy, X. J., and Dana Gioia. *Literature: An Introduction to Fiction, Poetry, and Drama*, 4th ed. Copyright © 2005 by Pearson Education, Inc. Reprinted by permission of Pearson Education, Inc., Glenview, IL.

Kishlansky, Mark, Patrick Geary, and Patricia O'Brien. "God Kings" from *Civilization in the West*, 4th ed. White Plains: Longman, 2001.

Kosslyn, Stephen M., and Robin S. Rosenberg. "Semantic versus Episodic Memory" from *Fundamentals of Psychology: The Brain, the Person, the World*. Boston: Allyn & Bacon, 2002.

Kosslyn, Stephen M., and Robin S. Rosenberg. *Psychology: The Brain, the Person, the World*. Boston: Allyn & Bacon, 2002.

Kunz, Jennifer. "Characteristics of Successful Stepfamilies" from *Think Marriages & Families*. Copyright © 2011 by Pearson Education, Inc. Reproduced by permission of Pearson Education, Inc., Boston, MA.

Lee, Sharon, and Barry Edmonston. "New Marriages, New Families: U.S. Racial and Hispanic Intermarriage" from *Population Bulletin*, June 2005, Volume 60, Number 2. Washington, DC: Population Reference Bureau, 2005.

Lefton, Lester A., and Linda Brannon. *Psychology*, 8th ed. Boston: Allyn & Bacon, 2003.

Levack, Brian, Edward Muir, Meredith Veldman and Michael Maas. *The West: Encounters & Transformations, Atlas Edition, Combined Edition*, 2nd ed. Copyright © 2008 by Pearson Education, Inc. Printed and Electronically reproduced by permission of Pearson Education, Inc., Upper Saddle River, NJ.

Levinthal, Charles F. "Drugs in Our Lives" and "Differences in the Effects of Drugs" from *Drugs, Behavior, and Modern Society*, 3rd ed. Boston: Allyn and Bacon, 2002.

Lithwick, Dahlia. "Teens, Nude Photos and the Law: Ask Yourself: Should the Police Be Involved When Tipsy Teen Girls E-mail Their Boyfriends Naughty Valentine's Day Pictures?" from *Newsweek*, February 14 Copyright © 2009 Newsweek, Inc. All rights reserved. Used by permission and protected by the Copyright Laws of the United States. The printing, copying, redistribution, or retransmission of the Material without express written permission is prohibited.

Lutgens, Frederick K., Edward J. Tarbuck, and Dennis Tasa. *Foundations of Earth Science*, 5th ed. Copyright © 2008 by Pearson Education, Inc. Printed and Electronically reproduced

by permission of Pearson Education, Inc., Upper Saddle River, NJ.

MacDougall, Alice Foote. *The Autobiography of a Business Woman*. Boston: Little, Brown and Company, 1928.

Madura, Jeff. *Personal Finance*, 2nd ed. Copyright © 2004 by Pearson Education, Inc. Reproduced by permission of Pearson Education, Inc., Boston, MA.

Madura, Jeff. *Personal Finance*, 3rd ed. Copyright © 2007 by Pearson Education, Inc. Reproduced by permission of Pearson Education, Inc., Boston, MA.

Maier, Richard. *Comparative Animal Behavior: An Evolutionary and Ecological Approach*. Boston: Allyn and Bacon, 1998.

Marieb, Elaine N. *Essentials of Human Anatomy and Physiology*, 9th ed. Copyright © 2009 by Pearson Education, Inc. Reprinted by permission of Pearson Education, Inc., Glenview, IL.

Martin, James Kirby, Randy J. Roberts, Steven Mintz, Linda O. McMurry and James H. Jones. *America and Its Peoples, Volume I: A Mosaic in the Making*, 3rd ed. Copyright © 1997 by Pearson Education, Inc. Printed and Electronically reproduced by permission of Pearson Education, Inc., Upper Saddle River, NJ.

Martin, James Kirby, Randy J. Roberts, Steven Mintz, Linda O. McMurry and James H. Jones. *America and Its Peoples: Volume II: A Mosaic in the Making*, 3rd ed. Copyright © 1997 by Pearson Education, Inc. Printed and Electronically reproduced by permission of Pearson Education, Inc., Upper Saddle River, NJ.

Maugham, W. Somerset. "An Appointment in Samarra" from *Sheppey* by W. Somerset Maugham. Copyright © 1933 by W. Somerset Maugham. Used by permission of Doubleday, a division of Random House, Inc. and A.P. Watt Ltd.

Mayer, Richard E. "Types of Learners Table" and "Three Facets of the Visualizer-Verbalizer Dimension" from *Journal of Educational Psychology*, 2003. Copyright © 2003 by the American Psychological Association. Adapted and Reprinted by permission of author and American Psychological Association, Washington, D.C.

McGuigan, F. J. *Encyclopedia of Stress*, 1st ed. Copyright © 1999 by Pearson Education, Inc. Printed and Electronically reproduced by permission of Pearson Education, Inc., Upper Saddle River, NJ.

Miller, Barbara. *Cultural Anthropology*, 4th ed. Copyright © 2007 by Pearson Education, Inc. Printed and Electronically reproduced by permission of Pearson Education, Inc., Upper Saddle River, NJ.

O'Connor, Karen J., and Larry J. Sabato. "Native Americans" from *American Government*, 2008 edition, 9th ed. Copyright © 2008 by Pearson Education, Inc. Reprinted by permission of Pearson Education, Inc., Glenview, IL.

Offiah-Hawkins, Sandra. "An Account of Alfred C. Cooley's Plight in the Face of Hurricane Katrina." Reprinted by permission of author.

"Opposing View: Don't Blame Us" by Pamela G. Bailey from USA TODAY, March 31, 2010. Reprinted by permission of USA Today.

"Our View on Obesity: Hooked on Junk Food" from USA TODAY, March 31, 2010. Reprinted by permission of USA Today.

"People," PBS: Sahara, PBS.org, December 29, 2003. Reproduced by permission of Telenova Productions.

Perry, John A., and Erna K. Perry. "The Impact of the Consumer Culture on the Growth of Suburbia" from *Contemporary Society: An Introduction to Social Science*, 10th ed. Boston: Allyn & Bacon, 2003.

Phillips, John C. *Sociology of Sport*. Copyright © 1993 by Allyn & Bacon. Reproduced by permission of Pearson Education, Inc., Boston, MA.

Pimentel, David. "Corn Can't Save Us: Debunking the Biofuel Myth" from *Kennebec Journal*, March 28, 2008. Reprinted by permission of Kennebec Journal.

Powers, Scott K., and Stephen L. Dodd. "Life Style Assessment" from *Behavior Change Log Book*, 3rd ed. Upper Saddle River: Pearson Education, Inc., 2003.

Powers, Scott K., and Stephen L. Dodd. *Total Fitness and Wellness Student Textbook Component*, 3rd ed. Copyright © 2003 by Pearson Education, Inc. Printed and Electronically reproduced by permission of Pearson Education, Inc., Upper Saddle River, NJ.

Powers, Scott K., Stephen L. Dodd and Virginia J. Noland. *Total Fitness and Wellness*, 4th ed. Copyright © 2006 by Pearson Education, Inc. Printed and Electronically reproduced by permission of Pearson Education, Inc., Upper Saddle River, NJ.

Pruitt, B. E., and Jane J. Stein. *Healthstyles: Decisions for Living Well*, 2nd ed. Copyright © 1999 by Pearson Education, Inc. Printed and Electronically reproduced by permission of Pearson Education, Inc., Upper Saddle River, NJ.

Queen Latifah and Karen Hunter. *Ladies First: Revelations of a Strong Woman*. New York: HarperCollins Publishers, 1999.

Ruggiero, Vincent R. *The Art of Thinking: A Guide to Critical and Creative Thought*, 7th ed. Copyright © 2004 by Pearson Education, Inc. Reprinted by permission of Pearson Education, Inc., Glenview, IL.

Schmalleger, Frank J. *Criminal Justice Today: An Introductory Text for the 21st Century*, 10th ed. Copyright © 2009 by Pearson Education, Inc. Printed and Electronically reproduced by permission of Pearson Education, Inc., Upper Saddle River, NJ.

"Seasonal Affective Disorder," Mental Health America, Copyright 2010 Mental Health America, http://www.mentalhealthamerica.net/go/sad.

Shiraev, Eric B., and David A. Levy. "Adolescence" from *Cross-Cultural Psychology: Critical Thinking and Contemporary Applications*, 3rd ed. Boston: Allyn and Bacon, 2007.

"Should We Be Criminalizing Bullies?" from *The Washington Post*, Copyright © April 7, 2010 The Washington Post. All rights reserved. Used by permission and protected by the Copyright Laws of the United States. The printing, copying, redistribution, or retransmission of the Material without express written permission is prohibited.

Simon, Todd F. "Levels of Protected Communication." Reprinted by permission of the author.

Smith, Carney, and Chuck Stone. "Medgar Evers" from *African American Almanac*, 7th ed. Belmont: Gale, a part of Cengage Learning, Inc., 1996.

Smith, Patrick D. *Forever Island*. Copyright © 1973 by W. W. Norton & Company, Inc. Used by permission of W. W. Norton & Company, Inc.

Smith, Thomas M., and Robert Leo Smith. *Elements of Ecology*, 4th ed. Copyright © 2000 by Pearson Education, Inc. Reprinted by permission of Pearson Education, Inc., Glenview, IL.

Smith, Thomas M., and Robert Leo Smith. *Elements of Ecology*, 6th ed. Copyright © 2006 by Pearson Education, Inc. Reprinted by permission of Pearson Education, Inc., Glenview, IL.

Sporre, Dennis J. *The Creative Impulse; An Introduction to the Arts*, 8th ed. Copyright © 2009 by Pearson Education, Inc. Reprinted by permission of Pearson Education, Inc., Upper Saddle River, NJ.

Stearns, Peter N., Michael B. Adas, Stuart B. Schwartz, and Marc Jason Gilbert. *World Civilizations: The Global Experience, Combined Volume, Atlas Edition*, 5th ed. Copyright © 2008 by Pearson Education, Inc. Printed and Electronically reproduced by permission of Pearson Education, Inc., Upper Saddle River, NJ.

Steinbeck, John. *East of Eden*. New York: Penguin Group (USA) Inc., 1952, 1980.

Sting. "The Mystery and Religion of Music." Boston: Berklee College of Music, 1994.

Tannahill, Neal R. "Taking Sides: Constitutional Principles" from *Think American Government*, 2nd ed. Copyright © 2011 by Pearson Education, Inc. Reprinted by permission of Pearson Education, Inc., Glenview, IL.

Tannen, Deborah. "Sex, Lies, Conversation" from *The Washington Post*, June 24, 1990, p. C3. Copyright © by Deborah Tannen. Reprinted by permission of author. This article is adapted from *You Just Don't Understand: Women and Men in Conversation*. New York: Ballantine, 1990. New paperback edition: New York: Quill, 2001.

"Tattoos: The Ancient and Mysterious History" by Cate Lineberry from Smithsonian.com, January 1, 2007. Copyright © 2010 by Smithsonian Institution. Reprinted by permission of Smithsonian Magazine. All rights reserved. Reproduction in any medium is strictly prohibited without permission from Smithsonian Institution. Such permission may be requested from Smithsonian Magazine.

Tristam, Pierre. "A Look at Man Through The Vapid Eyes of His Captives" from *The Daytona Beach News-Journal*, March 7, 2010, pp 10A. Reprinted by permission of Copyright Clearance Center.

Walvin, James. *Atlas of Slavery*. Copyright © 2006 by Pearson Education Limited. Reprinted by permission of Pearson Education Limited.

Wilen, William, Margaret Ishler, Janice Hutchison, and Richard Kindsvatter. *Dynamics of Effective Teaching*, 4th ed. White Plains: Longman, 2000.

Withgott, Jay H., and Scott R. Brennan. *Essential Environment: The Science Behind the Stories,* 3rd ed. Copyright © 2009 by Pearson Education, Inc. Reprinted by permission of Pearson Education, Inc., Upper Saddle River, NJ.

Wood, Samuel E., Ellen Green Wood, and Denise Boyd. *Mastering the World of Psychology*, 3rd ed. Copyright © 2008 by Pearson Education, Inc. Reproduced by permission of Pearson Education, Inc., Boston, MA.

Woolfolk, Anita E. *Educational Psychology,* 8th ed. Copyright © 2001 by Pearson Education, Inc. Reproduced by permission of Pearson Education, Inc., Boston, MA.

Woolfolk, Anita E. *Educational Psychology,* 10th ed. Copyright © 2007 by Pearson Education, Inc. Reproduced by permission of Pearson Education, Inc., Boston, MA.

Young, Billie Jean. "Fear Not the Fall" from *Fear Not the Fall: Poems and a Two-Act Drama.* Reprinted by permission of NewSouth Books, Montgomery, AL.

Photo Credits

Index